Jonathan Edwards's Vision of Reality

Princeton Theological Monograph Series

K. C. Hanson, Charles M. Collier, D. Christopher Spinks,
and Robin Parry, Series Editors

Recent volumes in the series:

Nathan Montover
*Luther's Revolution: The Political Dimensions
of Martin Luther's Universal Priesthood*

Eric G. Flett
*Persons, Powers, and Pluralities:
Toward a Trinitarian Theology of Culture*

Christian T. Collins Winn
The Pietist Impulse in Christianity

Mitzi J. Smith
*The Literary Construction of the Other in the Acts of the Apostles:
Charismatics, the Jews, and Women*

Myk Habets
Trinitarian Theology after Barth

Michael S. Whiting
*Luther in English: The Influence of His Theology of Law
and Gospel on Early English Evangelicals (1525–35)*

Samuel K. Elolia
*Religion, Conflict, and Democracy in Modern Africa:
The Role of Civil Society in Political Engagement*

Matthew D. Kirkpatrick
*Attacks on Christendom in a World Come of Age:
Kierkegaard, Bonhoeffer, and the Question of "Religionless Christianity"*

Jonathan Edwards's Vision of Reality

The Relationship of God to the World, Redemption History, and the Reprobate

John J. Bombaro

◆PICKWICK *Publications* • Eugene, Oregon

JONATHAN EDWARDS'S VISION OF REALITY
The Relationship of God to the World, Redemption History, and the Reprobate

Princeton Theological Monograph Series 172

Copyright © 2012 John J. Bombaro. All rights reserved. Except for brief quotations in critical publications or reviews, no part of this book may be reproduced in any manner without prior written permission from the publisher. Write: Permissions, Wipf and Stock Publishers, 199 W. 8th Ave., Suite 3, Eugene, OR 97401.

Pickwick Publications
An Imprint of Wipf and Stock Publishers
199 W. 8th Ave., Suite 3
Eugene, OR 97401

www.wipfandstock.com

ISBN 13: 978-1-61097-456-1

Cataloging-in-Publication data:

Bombaro, John J.

Jonathan Edwards's vision of reality : the relationship of God to the world, redemption history, and the reprobate / John J. Bombaro.

Princeton Theological Monograph Series 172

xviii + 328 p. ; 23 cm. Includes bibliographical references and indexes.

ISBN 13: 978-1-61097-456-1

1. Edwards, Jonathan, 1703–1758. 2. I. Title. II. Series.

BX7260.E3 B52 2012

Manufactured in the U.S.A.

To Melinda.
One life, one love.

CHRISTIAN RELIGION . . . God has communication with or influence upon all other creatures according to their nature, upon bodies according to the nature and capacity of body; and how unreasonable is it to suppose that He holds no communication with [intelligent perceiving] spirits according to their *nature* and *capacity*!

—Jonathan Edwards, *"Miscellanies,"* no. 204

Contents

Preface / ix

Acknowledgments / xi

Abbreviations / xii

Introduction / 1

Jonathan Edwards's Spiritual Vision of Reality / 25

A *Personal Narrative* of the Vision of God / 37

Comprehensive Theocentricity / 53

The Formulation of Jonathan Edwards's Theocentric Metaphysics (Part I) / 71

Divine Comprehensiveness and Edwardsean Panentheism: The Formulation of Jonathan Edwards's Theocentric Metaphysics (Part II) / 79

The Becomingness of God: The Formulation of Jonathan Edwards's Theocentric Metaphysics (Part III) / 94

The Application of Jonathan Edwards's Dispositional Concepts / 106

The Beauty of Being: An Aesthetic Ontology of Human Being / 127

Re-conceiving Human Being / 146

God Glorified in Man's Existence / 185

The First Sin / 207

Jonathan Edwards's Vision of Salvation / 233

Dispositional Peculiarity, History, and Edwards's Evangelistic Appeal to Self-Love / 254

Conclusion / 289

Appendix A: Panentheistic, but not Process Philosophy / 297

Appendix B: Sufficient and Efficacious Grace / 300

Contents

Bibliography / 305

Name Index / 319

Subject Index / 325

Preface

SINCE THE PUBLICATION OF SANG HYUN LEE'S INFLUENTIAL BOOK, *THE PHILOSOPHICAL Theology of Jonathan Edwards* (1988), a number of scholars have given considerable attention to the possibilities of understanding various aspects as well as the whole of Jonathan Edwards's (1703–1758) thought in terms of dispositional laws, forces, and habits. To be sure, Lee's work has made an important and, what promises to be, lasting contribution toward understanding—in a more systematic way—the micro and macro levels of Edwards's philosophical-theology.

However, some scholars reject the notion of a dispositional ontology in Edwards, while others have taken the concept of disposition in Edwards's thought well beyond the usage the Northampton minister ever indicated or would have intended. Indeed, Anri Morimoto, Gerald McDermott, and even Lee, at different times and in different ways, present concepts of disposition and conclusions drawn from them that hardly would have been recognized, let alone owned, by Edwards.

Meanwhile, the surging interest in Edwards studies by many scholars attracted to his enduring contributions to divinity, philosophy, and ethics, but who are rather unsympathetic to his particularistic Calvinist theology, has resulted in either revisionist work on his views of unregenerate humanity or a partial or total repudiation of his theological appraisement of the "reprobate." Thus, on the one hand, there are those who see Edwards's doctrine of the reprobate as barbaric, archaic, unsophisticated, and unaccommodating: there being no useful or constructive element in his thought concerning those he referred to as "devils," "fuel for [hell-]fire," "adamant stones," and "wholly useless, except in their damnation." (The reprobate includes all persons from non-evangelical Protestant religions who die "outside of Christ.") While on the other hand, there are those who, in their overstated applications of Edwards's dispositional ontology, claim that Edwards was moving toward a soteriological perspective that was inclusivistic. They say that, in the last two decades of his life, Edwards was developing a moralistic view of salvation for not only non-evangelical Christian sects, but also non-Christian religions and even non-religious moral persons.

My work here bridges the polarity of the aforementioned positions within the context of Edwards's overarching principle for interpreting reality, namely, relating all things to God's purpose of self-glorification. I argue that Edwards indeed employed disposition(s) in his philosophy, but that his theocentrism, theological tradition, and Calvinist particularism established its boundaries. Moreover, I contend that, while his theological assessment of the reprobate was for the most part denunciatory, yet the logic of dispositions in his aesthetic ontology and its consequent epistemology, prescribed inherent value and a positive functional role for all intelligent beings—*including the reprobate*—in God's program of self-glorification within the spatiotemporal realm and, in accord with his particularistic theological persuasion, eternal life hereafter.

A note on the composition: The Jonathan Edwards Center at Yale University has set forth conventions for citing the Yale University Press print and the Jonathan Edwards Center's online editions of the *Works of Jonathan Edwards*. I have done my best to adopt their citation guidelines here. The access dates for all *WJE Online* citations are 21–26 March 2011 unless otherwise indicated. I have taken the necessary liberty to edit some of Edwards's unpublished sermons for purposes of readability.

Acknowledgments

Kenneth P. Minkema, Executive Editor of the Yale Edwards Project, deserves recognition for his accessibility and invitation to engage the Edwards MSS. Wilson H. Kimnach's contributions came in the form of expert comments concerning Edwards's sermons. Peter Thuesen and Doug Sweeney quickly responded to every trans-Atlantic inquiry I raised, saving me time, money, and headaches.

Special thanks to: Dusty Gulleson, not so much for tracking down obscure and out-of-print Edwards resources, but for the example of Christian perseverance; Eric Gregory for help with materials concerning Edwards, Augustine, and self-love; Michael J. McClymond, Catherine A. Brekus, and John Kearney for sharing unpublished papers; and, of course, Oliver Crisp, for edifying and challenging conversations at the Strand concerning our respective projects on "JE."

The staff of the Beinecke Rare Book and Manuscripts Library, Yale University, has my sincere appreciation for accommodating every request with patience and consideration. Their professional efforts made working at the Beinecke (as any Edwards commentator would agree) a pleasure and joy. So, too, the staff at the Speer Library of Princeton Theological Seminary and Cambridge University Library must be acknowledged for their charitable efforts to meet my requests.

Without the help of Sang Hyun Lee of Princeton Theological Seminary, whose work sparked my own, this project would not have materialized. The hours Professor Lee took out of his demanding schedule (*and* sabbatical) to regularly meet with me to discuss the various problems, applications, and possibilities of the logic of disposition in Edwards's thought, have been greatly appreciated.

The insightful comments and criticisms of Steven R. Holmes, Reginald Quirk, Myron Penner, and Jeff Leininger, all of whom read either portions or the whole of this book in draft form, contributed to make it presentable. Joanne Helms and Gretchen Jordan assisted with compiling the indices. Any remaining conceptual or grammatical infelicities are entirely my own property.

I express my gratitude to the editors of the *Westminster Theological Journal* and *The Clarion Review* for permission to reproduce the contents of chapters 6–8, 12, and 13.

Robin Parry, an editor for the Princeton Theological Monograph Series, made the transition from proposal to publication painless.

Finally, Professor Paul Helm, thank you for intellectual mentorship while at King's College London; and most importantly, Melinda, who more than anyone supported this work with devotion and untold personal sacrifice—thank you for giving me this opportunity and welcoming the likes of Jonathan Edwards and Martin Luther into our family.

John J. Bombaro
Eastertide

Abbreviations

Primary Literature

Jonathan Edwards

Banner-Works	*The Works of Jonathan Edwards.* With a Memoir by Sereno E. Dwight. Revised by Edward Hickman. 2 vols. Edinburgh: Banner of Truth, 1974.
Dwight-Works	*The Works of President Edwards with a Memoir of His Life.* 10 vols. New York, Converse, 1829–30.
Sermon Outlines	*Jonathan Edwards' Sermon Outlines.* Edited by Sheldon B. Quincer. London: Pickering & Inglis, 1958.
Select Sermons	*Selected Sermons of Jonathan Edwards.* Edited by Norman Gardiner. New York: McMillan, 1904.
Treatise	Helm, Paul, ed. *Treatise on Grace and other Posthumously Published Writings.* Cambridge: Clark, 1971.
PJE	Townsend, Harvey G. *The Philosophy of Jonathan Edwards from His Private Notebooks.* Eugene, OR: University of Oregon Press, 1955.
JE Collection	"General MSS 151" catalog, Beinecke Library, Yale University.
WJE 1	*Freedom of the Will. The Works of Jonathan Edwards*, vol. 1. Edited by Paul Ramsey. New Haven: Yale University Press, 1957.
WJE 2	*Religious Affections. The Works of Jonathan Edwards*, vol. 2. Edited by John E. Smith. New Haven: Yale University Press, 1959.
WJE 3	*Original Sin. The Works of Jonathan Edwards*, vol. 3. Edited by Clyde A. Holbrook. New Haven: Yale University Press, 1970.
WJE 4	*The Great Awakening. The Works of Jonathan Edwards*, vol. 4. Edited by C. C. Goen. New Haven: Yale University Press, 1972.
WJE 5	*Apocalyptic Writings. The Works of Jonathan Edwards*, vol. 5. Edited by Stephen J. Stein. New Haven: Yale University Press, 1977.

WJE 6	*Scientific and Philosophical Writings. The Works of Jonathan Edwards*, vol. 6. Edited by Wallace E. Anderson. New Haven: Yale University Press, 1980.
WJE 7	*The Life of David Brainerd. The Works of Jonathan Edwards*, vol. 7. Edited by Norman Pettit. New Haven: Yale University Press, 1985.
WJE 8	*Ethical Writings. The Works of Jonathan Edwards*, vol. 8. Edited by Paul Ramsey. New Haven: Yale University Press, 1989.
WJE 9	*A History of the Work of Redemption. The Works of Jonathan Edwards*, vol. 9. Edited by John F. Wilson. New Haven: Yale University Press, 1989.
WJE 10	*Sermons and Discourses, 1720–1723. The Works of Jonathan Edwards*, vol. 10. Edited by Wilson H. Kimnach. New Haven: Yale University Press, 1992.
WJE 11	*Typological Writings. The Works of Jonathan Edwards*, vol. 11. Edited by Wallace E. Anderson, Mason I. Lowance, and David H. Watters. New Haven: Yale University Press, 1993.
WJE 12	*Ecclesiastical Writings. The Works of Jonathan Edwards*, vol. 12. Edited by David D. Hall. New Haven: Yale University Press, 1994.
WJE 13	*The "Miscellanies" (Entry Nos. a–z, aa–zz, 1–500). The Works of Jonathan Edwards*, vol. 13. Edited by Thomas A. Schafer. New Haven: Yale University Press, 1994.
WJE 14	*Sermons and Discourses, 1723–1729. The Works of Jonathan Edwards*, vol. 14. Edited by Kenneth P. Minkema. New Haven: Yale University Press, 1997.
WJE 15	*Notes on Scripture. The Works of Jonathan Edwards*, vol. 15. Edited by Stephen J. Stein. New Haven: Yale University Press, 1998.
WJE 16	*Letters and Personal Writings. The Works of Jonathan Edwards*, vol. 16. Edited by George S. Claghorn. New Haven: Yale University Press, 1998.
WJE 17	*Sermons and Discourses, 1730–1733. The Works of Jonathan Edwards*, vol. 17. Edited by Mark Valeri. New Haven: Yale University Press, 1999.
WJE 18	*The "Miscellanies" (Entry Nos. 501–832). The Works of Jonathan Edwards*, vol. 18. Edited by Ava Chamberlain. New Haven: Yale University Press, 2000.

Abbreviations

WJE 19	*Sermons and Discourses, 1734–1738. The Works of Jonathan Edwards*, vol. 19. Edited by M. X. Lesser. New Haven: Yale University Press, 2001.
WJE 20	*The "Miscellanies" (Entry Nos. 833–1152). The Words of Jonathan Edwards*, vol. 20. Edited by Amy Plantinga Pauw. New Haven: Yale University Press, 2002.
WJE 21	*Writings on the Trinity, Grace, and Faith. The Works of Jonathan Edwards*, vol. 21. Edited by Sang Hyun Lee. New Haven: Yale University Press, 2003.
WJE 22	*Sermons and Discourses, 1739–1742. The Works of Jonathan Edwards*, vol. 22. Edited by Harry S. Stout and Nathan O. Hatch, with Kyle P. Farely. New Haven: Yale University Press, 2003.
WJE 23	*The "Miscellanies" Nos. 1153–1360. The Works of Jonathan Edwards*, vol. 23. Edited by Douglas A. Sweeney. New Haven: Yale University Press, 2004.
WJE 24	*The Blank Bible. The Works of Jonathan Edwards*, vol. 24. Edited by Stephen J. Stein. New Haven: Yale University Press, 2006.
WJE 25	*Sermons and Discourses, 1743–1758. The Works of Jonathan Edwards*, vol. 25. New Haven: Yale University Press, 2006.
WJE 26	*Catalogues of Books. The Works of Jonathan Edwards*, vol. 26. Edited by Peter J. Theusen. New Haven: Yale University Press, 2008.
WJE Online 27	*The Works of Jonathan Edwards Online*, vol. 27, "Controversies" *Notebooks*. Jonathan Edwards Center, Yale University, 2008.
WJE Online 28	*The Works of Jonathan Edwards Online*, vol. 28, *Minor Controversial Writings*. Jonathan Edwards Center, Yale University, 2008.
WJE Online 29	*The Works of Jonathan Edwards Online*, vol. 29, *Harmony of the Scriptures*. Jonathan Edwards Center, Yale University, 2008.
WJE Online 31	*The Works of Jonathan Edwards Online*, vol. 31, "History of Redemption" *Notebooks*. Jonathan Edwards Center, Yale University, 2008.
WJE Online 34	*The Works of Jonathan Edwards Online*, vol. 34, "Original Sin" *Notebook*. Jonathan Edwards Center, Yale University, 2008.
WJE Online 42	*The Works of Jonathan Edwards Online*, vol. 42, *Sermons, Series II, 1723–1727*. Jonathan Edwards Center, Yale University, 2008.

WJE Online 43	*The Works of Jonathan Edwards Online*, vol. 43, *Sermons, Series II, 1728–1729*. Jonathan Edwards Center, Yale University, 2008.
WJE Online 44	*The Works of Jonathan Edwards Online*, vol. 44, *Sermons, Series II, 1729*. Jonathan Edwards Center, Yale University, 2008.
WJE Online 45	*The Works of Jonathan Edwards Online*, vol. 45, *Sermons, Series II, 1729–1731*. Jonathan Edwards Center, Yale University, 2008.
WJE Online 46	*The Works of Jonathan Edwards Online*, vol. 46, *Sermons, Series II, 1731–1732*. Jonathan Edwards Center, Yale University, 2008.
WJE Online 47	*The Works of Jonathan Edwards Online*, vol. 47, *Sermons, Series II, 1731–1732*. Jonathan Edwards Center, Yale University, 2008.
WJE Online 48	*The Works of Jonathan Edwards Online*, vol. 48, *Sermons, Series II, 1733*. Jonathan Edwards Center, Yale University, 2008.
WJE Online 49	*The Works of Jonathan Edwards Online*, vol. 49, *Sermons, Series II, 1734*. Jonathan Edwards Center, Yale University, 2008.
WJE Online 50	*The Works of Jonathan Edwards Online*, vol. 50, *Sermons, Series II, 1735*. Jonathan Edwards Center, Yale University, 2008.
WJE Online 51	*The Works of Jonathan Edwards Online*, vol. 51, *Sermons, Series II, 1736*. Jonathan Edwards Center, Yale University, 2008.
WJE Online 52	*The Works of Jonathan Edwards Online*, vol. 52, *Sermons, Series II, 1737*. Jonathan Edwards Center, Yale University, 2008.
WJE Online 53	*The Works of Jonathan Edwards Online*, vol. 53, *Sermons, Series II, 1738, and Undated, 1734–1738*. Jonathan Edwards Center, Yale University, 2008.
WJE Online 54	*The Works of Jonathan Edwards Online*, vol. 54, *Sermons, Series II, 1739*. Jonathan Edwards Center, Yale University, 2008.
WJE Online 55	*The Works of Jonathan Edwards Online*, vol. 55, *Sermons, Series II, January–June 1740*. Jonathan Edwards Center, Yale University, 2008.
WJE Online 56	*The Works of Jonathan Edwards Online*, vol. 56, *Sermons, Series II, July–December 1740*. Jonathan Edwards Center, Yale University, 2008.
WJE Online 57	*The Works of Jonathan Edwards Online*, vol. 57, *Sermons, Series II, January–June 1741*. Jonathan Edwards Center, Yale University, 2008.

Abbreviations

WJE Online 58	*The Works of Jonathan Edwards Online*, vol. 58, *Sermons, Series II, July–December 1741*. Jonathan Edwards Center, Yale University, 2008.
WJE Online 59	*The Works of Jonathan Edwards Online*, vol. 59, *Sermons, Series II, January–June 1742*. Jonathan Edwards Center, Yale University, 2008.
WJE Online 60	*The Works of Jonathan Edwards Online*, vol. 60, *Sermons, Series II, January–June 1742, and Undated, 1739–1742*. Jonathan Edwards Center, Yale University, 2008.
WJE Online 61	*The Works of Jonathan Edwards Online*, vol. 61, *Sermons, Series II, 1743*. Jonathan Edwards Center, Yale University, 2008.
WJE Online 62	*The Works of Jonathan Edwards Online*, vol. 62, *Sermons, Series II, 1744*. Jonathan Edwards Center, Yale University, 2008.
WJE Online 63	*The Works of Jonathan Edwards Online*, vol. 63, *Sermons, Series II, 1745*. Jonathan Edwards Center, Yale University, 2008.
WJE Online 64	*The Works of Jonathan Edwards Online*, vol. 64, *Sermons, Series II, 1746*. Jonathan Edwards Center, Yale University, 2008.
WJE Online 65	*The Works of Jonathan Edwards Online*, vol. 65, *Sermons, Series II, 1747*. Jonathan Edwards Center, Yale University, 2008.
WJE Online 66	*The Works of Jonathan Edwards Online*, vol. 66, *Sermons, Series II, 1748*. Jonathan Edwards Center, Yale University, 2008.
WJE Online 67	*The Works of Jonathan Edwards Online*, vol. 67, *Sermons, Series II, 1749*. Jonathan Edwards Center, Yale University, 2008.
WJE Online 68	*The Works of Jonathan Edwards Online*, vol. 68, *Sermons, Series II, 1750*. Jonathan Edwards Center, Yale University, 2008.
WJE Online 69	*The Works of Jonathan Edwards Online*, vol. 69, *Sermons, Series II, 1751*. Jonathan Edwards Center, Yale University, 2008.
WJE Online 71	*The Works of Jonathan Edwards Online*, vol. 71, *Sermons, Series II, 1753*. Jonathan Edwards Center, Yale University, 2008.
WJE Online 72	*The Works of Jonathan Edwards Online*, vol. 72, *Sermons, Series II, 1754–1755*. Jonathan Edwards Center, Yale University, 2008.
WJE Online 73	*The Works of Jonathan Edwards Online*, vol. 73, *Sermons, Series II, 1756–1758, Undated, and Fragments*. Jonathan Edwards Center, Yale University, 2008.

Worcester-Works	*The Works of President Edwards*. 8 vols. Edited by Samuel Austin. Worcester, MA: Thomas, 1808–9.
WJE Online	*Works of Jonathan Edwards Online*, vols 27–73. Jonathan Edwards Center at Yale University, 2008.

Other Primary Texts

An Inquiry	Hutcheson, Francis. *An Inquiry into the Original of Our Ideas of Virtue*. London: Darby, 1725.
Institutes	Calvin, John. *Institutes of the Christian Religion*. The Library of Christian Classics XX–XXI. Edited by John T. McNeill, London, SCM, 1961.
Institutes	Turretin, François. *Institutes of Elenctic Theology* [*Institutio Theologiae Elencticae*, 1679–85]. ET George M. Giger, edited by James T. Dennison Jr. 3 vols. Phillipsburg, NJ, Presbyterian and Reformed, 1992–97.
Meditations	Descartes, René. *Meditations on First Philosophy* (1641). In *The Philosophical Works of Descartes*. ET Elizabeth S. Haldane and G. R. T. Ross. Cambridge: Cambridge University Press, 1911.
Treatise Concerning	Stoddard, Solomon. *A Treatise Concerning Conversion: Conversion Shewing the Nature of Saving Conversion To God, and the Way wherein it is wrought; Together with an Exhortation to Labour after it*. Boston, 1719.
Theoretico-Practica	Van Mastricht, Petrus. *Theoretico-Practica Theologia qua per Singula Capita Theologia, pars Exegetica, Dogmatica, Elenchtica et Practica, Perpetua Successione Conjugantur*. Thomæ Appels. Rhenum, 1699.
WA	*D. Martin Luthers Werke. Kritische Gesamtausgabe* (*WA*), 58 vols. Weimar: Bohlau, 1833–1993.
Workes Perkins	Perkins, William. *The VVorkes of that Famovs and VVorthy Minister of Christ in the Vniversitie of Cambridge, M. William Perkins* . . . 3 vols. London, 1612, 1613, 1631 respectively.

Introduction

THE PASSING OF THE TERCENTENNIAL ANNIVERSARY OF THE BIRTH OF JONATHAN Edwards (1703–58) coincided with a profusion of articles, books, and dissertations on the Colonial American Congregational preacher and theologian. This extraordinary interest in Edwards, initiated by Perry Miller's 1949 intellectual biography and which has produced over five thousands secondary sources, has made this Puritan minister, once banished from his own church in Northampton to serve as a missionary to Indians on the Massachusetts Frontier, a twentieth- and now twenty-first-century intellectual and religious phenomenon.[1]

Aside from the early efforts of Perry Miller, H. Richard Niebuhr, and Sydney Ahlstrom, scholarly interest in Edwards continues through the celebrated Yale University Press edition of *The Works of Jonathan Edwards* (26 vols. 1957–2008). Although older editions of Edwards's works continue to circulate, the Yale letterpress edition is distinguished by its incorporation of previously unpublished original manuscripts, and a critical introductory essay in each volume. In addition to providing a more complete and holistic understanding of his thought and influence, another value of these influential essays is their contribution to correcting the hagiographical bias and defective caricaturing of Edwards, which at times has been endemic to Edwardsean scholarship and literature.[2]

Yet despite these and other notable and balanced scholarly efforts, dark clouds still shroud Edwards's intellectual legacy. This is due in no small part to his uncompromising retention of the more ominous doctrines of Calvinism: total depravity, inherent corrup-

---

1. Though Miller's *Jonathan Edwards* retains its importance as a modern intellectual biography of Edwards, Marsden's *Jonathan Edwards* provides an eloquent and much needed revision as a compliment to the Yale edition of *The Works of Jonathan Edwards*. Lesser's *Jonathan Edwards* estimates that at the present there are over five thousand secondary sources concerned with Edwards. Cf. Manspeaker, *Jonathan Edwards*. By "religious phenomenon," I mean the interest which large numbers of ministers, laypersons, churches, and religious organizations have in Jonathan Edwards as a figure of authority in matters of doctrine and religious practices (especially revivals), evidenced by the profusion of literature produced and consumed on Jonathan Edwards, as well as the number of conferences and websites dedicated to the promotion and discussion of his thought and works.

2. Partisan accounts have characterize Jonathan Edwards as a promoter and defender of charismatic revival and gifts of charismata (Chevreau, *Catch the Fire*), as the quintessential Calvinist theologian (Lloyd-Jones, "Jonathan Edwards and the Crucial Importance of Revival"), as proto-Barthian (Cherry, *Reappraisal*), and as a Reformed "classical" apologist *par excellence* (Gerstner, *Rational Biblical*), among other things. He also has been misrepresented as a prodigy child of unprecedented genius (Rogers, "Essay on His Genius and Writings" in *The Works of Jonathan Edwards, A.M.* [Hickman edition] 1:xii; and Davidson, *Jonathan Edwards*), as a nearly faultless example of Puritan piety and Christian devotion (Murray, *New Biography*), and as the minatorial sermonizer frightening children and relishing in thoughts of an unbelieving child's damnation (Greven, *Spare the Child*, 57; and Crooker, "Jonathan Edwards: A Psychological Study").

tion, limited atonement/particular redemption, irresistible grace, and eternal perdition.³ For many, the first two doctrines translate into a sinister and pessimistic biblical anthropology, the next two bespeak of antiquated religious particularism (i.e., spiritual "salvation" is found in Jesus Christ alone) and a fatalistic violation of freedom, while the last term captures the frightful predestinated consequences of the non-elect by a narcissistic, if not hateful, deity, namely, endless and irremediable torment in hell.⁴

The theological worldview framed by these doctrines asserts that, outside of the elect portion of the human race, the rest of humanity (i.e., "natural-men"⁵ or "reprobates," who were, according to Edwards, "ruined by the fall") are left to "perish, and burn in hell forever."⁶ These were cardinal doctrines of Edwards's particularist soteriological and eschatological perspective—a perspective that he vigorously promoted as truth from God.

Edwards claims that from the time of his conversion (1721), his first opinion of these "truths" completely changed. Describing his view of predestinarian theology prior to his conversion experience he said, "From my childhood up, my mind had been wont to be full of objections against the doctrine of God's sovereignty, in choosing whom he would to eternal life, and rejecting whom he pleased; leaving them eternally to perish and be everlastingly tormented in hell. It used to appear like a horrible doctrine to me."⁷

But upon his conversion there occurred "a wonderful alteration in my mind." He came not only to have a "delightful conviction" about God's sovereignty in double particular election, but "a new kind of apprehensions and ideas of Christ, and the work of redemption, and the glorious way of salvation." Edwards saw God not only in the gospel of Jesus Christ, but *in everything*: "the appearance of everything was altered . . . God's excel-

---

3. I am not here referring to the so-called "five points" of Calvinism formulated at the Synod of Dordrecht.

4. It should be noted that in the "Preface" to his treatise *Freedom of the Will*, Jonathan Edwards distinguishes himself as something other than a disciple of John Calvin by saying, "I utterly disclaim a dependence on Calvin, or believing the doctrines which I hold, because he believed and taught them" (*WJE* 1:131): Jonathan Edwards believing that his theology emerged from careful study of the Bible, not the *Institutes*. To be sure, on occasion the differences between Calvin and Jonathan Edwards are considerable and numerous. Yet, despite this caveat in his "Preface," Jonathan Edwards had no problem subscribing to the Westminster Confession and the Savoy Declaration.

5. Because "natural man" can mean humanity as originally created, human beings in their natural state, or the unregenerate posterity of Adam, the latter will be designated "natural-man" (understood to be a gender inclusive term within historic Calvinism) to avoid confusion and retain Jonathan Edwards's meaning in "Miscellanies," no. 683, where he says, "unregenerate men are called natural because they have nothing but nature" (*WJE* 18:246). Prior to regeneration, the elect are "natural-men." Theologically, reprobates are those persons on the negative side of predestination. The doctrine of reprobation or preterition teaches that God, according to His sovereign will, "passes over" some sinners in the bestowment of regenerating (special) grace, thereby leaving them in their sinful disqualification and, at last, God condemns them for their moral corruption. Jonathan Edwards's doctrine of reprobation is notably stronger than this. Of the three general categories of predestination (single particular election, double particular election, and general election) he holds to "double particular election," which asserts that God has a positive elective purpose to damn certain individuals. See 729. MS Sermon on Rev 14:15 (Jan 1744), Jonathan Edwards Collection.

6. *Sermon One*, *WJE* 9:124; *Justice of God in the Damnation of Sinners* (1736), *Banner Works* 1:672.

7. "Personal Narrative" in *WJE* 16:791.

lency, his wisdom, his purity and love, seemed to appear in everything; in the sun, moon and stars . . . and all nature."[8]

He attributed this aesthetic and theocentric vision of reality to a "new spiritual sense." Not simply an intellectual apprehension of divine things or just an emotional sensitivity to religious discourse or phenomena, the "new spiritual sense" is a mystical yet coherent conjunction of the cognitive and affectional faculties that perceives communicated spiritual/moral ideas from God about reality. The sense, however, is neither fleeting nor occasional. Instead, it is a disposition infused at regeneration that facilitates a progressive reorientation of one's thoughts, affections, and perspective on reality in the light of "true religion."[9] And "true religion," as Edwards testified in his "Personal Narrative," is about sensing God and His glory and beauty "in everything." Through the spiritual sense one "sees" God's self-glorifying designs and purposes present at the center of "everything": salvation, history, and even nature.

This radical change in perspective meant that not even salvation is primarily about human beings; it is mostly about God. Indeed, *all* of God's dealings with humanity revolve around the "end of creation," which is God's self-glorification through self-communication. This idea lies at the heart of Edwards's theocentric worldview. Thus, for him, the history of the world is the narrative of divine glorification,[10] where God "disposes with His creatures as He sees fit." And if God determines to save a *particular* remnant and burn the rest in hell (who deserve it anyway), then blessed be God, for "His will and pleasure are of infinitely more importance than the will of creatures."[11] For Edwards, these principles are not only the testimony of revelation, but "most reasonable" and therefore "exceedingly pleasant."[12]

Such a perspective on humanity, indeed, on world history, was precisely what Enlightenment religion did *not* represent. As Gerald R. McDermott explains, "John Toland, Matthew Tindal, and other deists focused on the problem of particularity,[13] which in their case meant the realization that only one-sixth of the world had heard the gospel . . . and that according to Calvinism the other five-sixths were damned. This threatened traditional notions of God's goodness and justice and led deists to reshape God and religion in ways that undermined both Catholic and Protestant understandings of revelation."[14] Thus, instead of special revelation (the Bible) only being given to a *particular* group for their salvation (viz., "the covenant people of God"—Jews and Christians), God's goodness and justice were in his giving sufficient natural endowments and revelation to all. All human beings were understood to have a fair share in revelation, and were accountable only

---

8. Ibid., 791–94.
9. "Miscellanies," no. l, *WJE* 13:168–69.
10. *WJE* 8:419–35.
11. *The Sole Consideration, that God is God, Sufficient to Still All Objections to His Sovereignty* (1735), *Banner-Works* 2:108.
12. *All God's Methods Are Most Reasonable* (1727), *WJE* 14:165–97.
13. "Particularity" refers to soteriological restrictivism as opposed to universalism or inclusivism.
14. McDermott, *Confronts the Gods*, 5.

to live according to its light and natural reason—which any and all religious and moral persons naturally did anyway.[15]

Hence, Enlightenment religion (contra Calvinistic particularism) was hallmarked by a particularly *positive* view of human beings qua reason—redeemed or unredeemed, Christian or heathen. The history of the world was the drama of human progress and enlightenment. Talk of predestination, particularism, or perdition was decidedly unenlightened.

A hundred years later, Oliver Wendell Holmes, as one who continued in the spirit of Enlightenment religion, could not but see Edwards's worldview (especially his thoughts concerning human beings) as "polluted" with Calvinist "barbarism." Catherine A. Brekus retells the story of Holmes painting a vivid portrait of a stern, grim-faced Edwards telling his son that God despised him. Holmes was repulsed that "hardhearted Edwards" would promulgate a doctrine which esteemed even his own three-year-old child "a viper, and worse than a viper." Holmes could only hope that "almost celestial Mrs. Jonathan Edwards would never allow such 'hateful' doctrines to demoralize her children." In order to complete his repudiation of Edwards's thought, he denounced the Puritan's theocentric principles as "not only false, not only absurd, but also . . . *disorganizing forces* in the midst of the thinking apparatus. Edwards's system seems, in the light of today, to the last degree barbaric, mechanical, materialistic, pessimistic."[16]

Likewise, novelist and critic Harriet Beecher Stowe (1811–1896) and Unitarian theologian William Ellery Channing (1780–1842) lamented that Edwards had wasted his intellectual abilities defending and promoting Calvinism's "false theology."[17] For Holmes, Stowe, and Channing, the "natural-man" is a person living according to the light of reason and nature and, therefore, ought to be considered a neutral if not positive contributor to spatiotemporal existence. Moreover, they would argue, each and every person has inherent value as a human being, simply because they *are* human beings, religion notwithstanding.

Much of the non-evangelical, late nineteenth- and early twentieth-century criticism of Edwards's particularism was even more scathing: Edwards came to embody his "demented" theology. Reproaching the man sometimes became the same thing as condemning his theological perspectives. So Edwards sometimes was depicted as mentally deranged, a giftless recluse, an anachronism in his own time, and even a "blight upon posterity."[18]

15. See, Kaakonssen, *Enlightenment and Religion*; Hunter, "Problem of 'Atheism' in Early Modern England"; Cragg, *From Puritanism to the Age of Reason* and *Church in the Age of Reason, 1648–1789*; and also McDermott's excellent overviews of Enlightenment religion and its relation to Jonathan Edwards in *Confronts the Gods*, 17–33, 34–51. For a contemporary account see Leland, *View of the Principal Deistical Writers*.

16. Brekus, "Remembering Jonathan Edwards's Ministry to Children," 40–41. See Holmes, *Over the Teacups*, 249–50.

17. See Channing, *"Remarks on National Literature"* and Stowe, *Minister's Wooing*.

18. Stephen, "Jonathan Edwards," 4:42–102; Parrington, "The Anachronism of Jonathan Edwards," 1:148–63; Parks, *Jonathan Edwards*, cited in McClymond, *Encounters*, 114 n. 7. Evangelical intellectual assessments of Jonathan Edwards's life and worldview continued to be charitable, if not complimentary, yet not entirely uncritical or recommending, particularly at Princeton and upstart Westminster Theological Seminary where Jonathan Edwards's theology continued to have influence. See Nelson, "Rise of the Princeton Theology"; and, Noll, "Jonathan Edwards and Nineteenth-Century Theology," 260–87.

Introduction

Even Edwards's own theological tradition distanced itself from his severe particularism, which included child depravity and infant damnation.[19] Few nineteenth- and twentieth-century Confessional Calvinists, tempered by a humanitarian climate, wanted to preserve Edwards's uncompromising and pessimistic views concerning infant reprobation and damnation. Their sentimentalist views of childhood and Edwards's vision of God's total sovereignty to "dispense with his creatures as he pleases" were simply incompatible.[20]

Recently, however, scholars have begun once again to give analytical attention to Edwards's worldview. And while *ad hominem* criticism has been exchanged for constructive scholarship, little or nothing positive is said about his assessment of human beings in their relation to God's self-glorifying purposes in creation and history.[21] The problem continues to be Edwards's particularism and the negative anthropological assessment associated with it.

Modern-day Edwards scholar Michael J. McClymond finds his present disapproval of Edwards's assessment of human beings succinctly expressed in Alexander V. G. Allen's criticism of 1889: "The great wrong which Edwards did, which haunts us as an evil dream throughout his writings, was to assert God at the expense of humanity." McClymond adds, "it is hard to see how God's proportionate regard [where God regards beings according to their "excellency" and "worthiness"] includes a concern for mere mortals. Moreover, there is a moral as well as a metaphysical issue, since humans are not only finite but sinful. The morally depraved are not obvious objects for God's proportionate regard."[22] Consequently, critics conclude that Edwards's particularism despoils his God-centered

---

19. In "Miscellanies," no. *n*, "INFANT DAMNATION," Jonathan Edwards wrote, "[I]t is most just, exceedingly just, that God should take the soul of a new-born infant and cast it into eternal torments" (*WJE* 13:169).

20. Sereno Dwight, in his ten-volume edition of his great-grandfather's works, edited out many denunciatory passages in order to make Jonathan Edwards appear more serene, balanced, and (presumably) enlightened. So, too, Lyman Beecher and others tied to temper Jonathan Edwards's rhetoric and doctrinal statements. But the stigma of a hell-fire preacher of infant damnation was, at that time for Jonathan Edwards, an irrepressible caricature. Thus, when a wave of optimism regarding universal infant salvation swept through confessional Presbyterianism and Congregationalism, Jonathan Edwards's thoughts on the matter were denounced. Indeed, during the 1880s–1900s, his position became that which conservative Calvinism in the Presbyterian Church in the USA set itself over-against (see Shedd, *Calvinism*, 38–41, 57–68).

21. Notable exceptions are Lee (see "Edwards on God and Nature," 15–44); Morimoto, who in *Catholic Vision* argues that Jonathan Edwards's soteriology of ontological transformation is really "inclusivistic," not "restrictivistic"; and McDermott (*Confronts the Gods* and "A Possibility of Reconciliation," 173–202). In *Confronts the Gods,* McDermott presents Jonathan Edwards's high view of "reason" in both fallen and unfallen man. In the end, however, McDermott rightly observes that despite whatever natural abilities an unregenerate person may or may not have, and no matter how much natural revelation they understood, "without an infusion of grace, the heathen [i.e., unregenerates] were damned" (222). Of course, there will be a number among the traditionally Reformed who would find Jonathan Edwards's biblical assessment of "natural-man" agreeable.

22. Allen cited in McClymond, *Encounters*, 63; 50–64. McClymond's criticisms basically are the same as those expressed in the late eighteenth- through nineteenth-centuries (cf. Holbrook, *Ethics*, 113–33). Jonathan Edwards has also been the object of discussion by contemporary proponents of "open theism" (a theological movement endorsing the passibility of God, synergism, limited divine foreknowledge, and God's susceptibility to time, among other things). Jonathan Edwards's kind of Calvinist particularism/determinism has been a focus of open theism's critical repudiation of orthodox Reformed theology and soteriology. See for example, Pinnock, *A Wideness in God's Mercy*, 157–60; and Sanders, *No Other Name*, 42–43.

worldview, depreciates his moral philosophy, and remains without a viable theodicy. According to McClymond and others, Edwards's radically theocentric worldview not only does not but *cannot* allow for a positive contribution to spiritual, moral, and mental reality by the natural-man or reprobate: for according to Edwards's "scale of being," where excellency or substantiality of being is measured by nearness to God, they are "worthless" and "as little as nothing."[23] Obviously, regenerate persons possess relational (i.e., ontological) excellence through their union with Christ. The indwelling presence of the Holy Spirit "so united to their souls" substantiates their being. They are valuable to God because in and through them God replicates His inner-trinitarian perfections. But what "excellence" could the natural-man and reprobate possibly possess since they are outside of Christ and without the Holy Spirit?

St. Andrews University's Stephen R. Holmes furthers the complexity of this point when he considers Edwards's trinitarian doctrine of creation. Holmes asks, if, for Edwards, creation is a divine act of *ekstasis* (i.e., of the sending of the Son and Spirit by the Father, directed towards a sharing or enlargement of the triune life), then where does this logic of creation leave the non-elect? Holmes concludes that, since they are "Christless" and "Spiritless," then the non-elect are in "the perilous position of lacking true humanity, or indeed true being."[24]

Edwards's sermons on Daniel 5:25, Ezekiel 15:2–4, and Deuteronomy 32:35 (just to name a few), with doctrines such as "God's manner of dealing with wicked men that continue in sin first to finish their days and then to bring 'em into judgment and then to destroy 'em," "Mankind, if they bring forth no fruit to God are wholly useless unless it be in their destruction," and "There is nothing that keeps wicked men at each moment out of hell but the meer [sic] pleasure of God," seem only to lend credence to the opinion that he regards natural-men and especially reprobates as having absolutely no contributive value or significance in *this* realm other than as extras in God's historical drama of accomplishing and applying salvation to his elect, or perhaps in their amassing sins for their eternal destruction, so that God and His saints could delight in the exercising of His wrathful power.[25] Indeed, in light of the imprecatory content of not a few of his sermons,[26] one may

---

23. *God Makes Men Sensible of Their Misery Before He Reveals His Mercy and Love* (1730), WJE 17:143; "Miscellanies," no. 41, WJE 13:223.

24. Holmes, *God of Grace*, 241–43.

25. 650a. Sermon on Dan 5:25 (Jan. 1742), Jonathan Edwards Collection; *Wicked Men Useful in Their Destruction Only* (1734), *Sinners in the Hands of an Angry God* (1741), *When those that continue in sin shall have filled up the measure of their sin, then wrath will come upon them to the uttermost* (1735), Banner-Works 2:125ff, 7ff, 122ff. Holmes argues that the destruction of reprobates promotes God's glory by a "vision across the chasm," where saints rejoice over seeing sinners being justly punished and sinners suffer more from seeing saints in glory. Thus, God is glorified in the saints' happiness and the reprobates' misery (*God of Grace*, 213ff.).

26. Fiering suggests that "perhaps less than 2 percent" of Jonathan Edwards's surviving sermons were of the maledictorial type (*Moral Thought*, 204). However, by my estimates there are nearly seventy sermons (or about 10 percent) that contain for their "Doctrine" meditations on hell torments, future punishments, and God's wrath. Plus one must take into account that many of these sermons bear marks indicating that they were re-preached. This estimate excludes the hundreds of denunciatory expositions of varying lengths throughout his sermon corpus on "wicked men," "man's nature," "original sin," "inherent corruption," "man's Fall [from grace]," and other moral, theological, and anthropological themes.

be prompted to ask, "If, in Edwards, I am only 'fuel for the fire' after this life, then what function and value do I hold in spatiotemporality? Why did not God glorify Himself by creating me in hell?" The question could be rephrased to ask, "How can the existence of the natural-man and, particularly, the reprobate have contributive, cosmic significance in the world when, for Edwards, they are accounted as worthless?"

John E. Colwell summarizes the impasse in Edwards's theocentric thought when he writes: "Less easy to resolve is the disjunction between themes of beauty and harmony on the one hand, and on the other, the perception that God's glory demonstrated in the justice of hell and the mercy of heaven. For all the christocentric anticipations of Barth this disjunction favors of an unnecessary yet central incoherence."[27]

Is Edwards simply a misanthropist, a theologian of glory who, for the sake of God's glory, relegates reprobates into a sub-human category of fuel for hell-fire? Or is there some place within his theocentric thought where he ascribes real worth and substantiality to the existence of natural-men and reprobates?

For anyone familiar with only the most widely-circulated of Edwards's written works it is an undeniable fact that he vigorously denounced the Enlightenment's assessment of human nature as basically good (or even self-determining), that he wrote a lengthy defense of "The Great Christian Doctrine of Original Sin," that he believed "Christ is the *only* door by which men enter into a state of salvation," that he forcefully attacked annihilationism in support of the reality of everlasting hell, and that "absolute sovereignty" was what he loved to ascribe to God.[28] In short, there really is no avoiding the fact that he held to a thoroughly uncompromising form of Calvinistic particularism. Nevertheless, it cannot be said that he was a fatalist (a strong determinist, to be sure). Nor can it be said that his thoughts concerning the natural-man were exclusively negative. Instead of only denunciations about the natural-man, Edwards also held a surprisingly positive perspective on the existence and function of natural-man (though not character or nature), even ascribing a great deal of significance and value to the reprobate's life and purpose *in this world*. More than just fuel for the fire or a viper to be destroyed, reprobates were and are both active and vital agents in God's self-glorifying purposes within the created order.

Edwards, of course, had both theological and philosophical reasons to support his position. Theologically, natural-men are the subject of redemption. God's trinitarian redeeming work was accomplished for and is applied to depraved human beings. Of course, natural-men are redeemed *from* something, namely, inherent corruption, slavery to sin, bondage to the devil, and the wrathful judgment of God: common themes in Edwards's expository tradition. In short, the plight man brought upon himself as the consequence of the fall from grace. (Again, not a very flattering picture of human beings.) But still, natural-men play a very active and important role in the drama of redemption history. They are the recipients of both common and redeeming graces, both natural and special

---

27. Colwell, "Jonathan Edwards," 175.

28. *WJE* 1; *WJE* 3, title page; 939. Sermon on John 10:9 (Aug. 1749), *WJE Online* 67, access 12 April 2011; "Personal Narrative" in *WJE* 16:792. I say this conscious of the efforts of Morimoto and McDermott, whose opinions I contest in chaps 12–13.

revelation. But then again, if any grace avails unto salvation we are no longer speaking about natural-men but the elect of Edwards's Calvinistic particularism.

Theologically nothing positive is really being said about reprobates or natural-men per se, only about what God does *to* them in order to extract glory for Himself (e.g., redeem them, judge and destroy them, etc.), or has done among them (e.g., the Incarnation). The deist charge echoes again: What about the five-sixths of the heathenish world who not so much have even heard the gospel, let alone "gospel sinners," who have heard and yet continue in a natural or reprobate condition? What intrinsic value do they have, and what is their active role in glorifying God in the world?

Hence my contention that if we hope to find positive significance and worth for the natural-man and reprobate in Edwards's theocentric thought, then we cannot merely look to his theology. Looking only at his Reformed theology will yield only Calvinistic particularism, at least in this respect. Likewise, trying to understand his larger theocentric worldview in the light of the particulars of his Reformed theology is only to work in the opposite fashion to which Edwards thought. The "new spiritual sense" is an aesthetic vision not of the doctrine of double predestination, but of God's beauty. In light of *that* beauty we theoretically begin to appreciate and understand the beauties of God's special revelation, the Bible, through which He conveys the "reasonable" manner of His interaction with human beings and orchestration of history. All of which is to say, we must step back from a close examination of Edwards's Reformed theology and consider his assessment of natural-men/reprobates from the perspective of his philosophical-theology in order to understand in what capacity they serve God and how they possesses inherent value in time and space.

In effect, this is what a distinguished company of Edwards commentators (specifically, Anri Morimoto and Gerald R. McDermott) have done by adopting what may be deemed a "new perspective" on the Northampton sage's philosophical theology, a perspective that proposes a thoroughly modern foundation for his metaphysics. The *Ursprung* of the new genesis in Edwards studies may be traced to the pioneering work of Sang Hyun Lee on the subject of Edwards and dispositions. In *The Philosophical Theology of Jonathan Edwards: The Idea of Habit and Edwards' Dynamic Vision of Reality*, Lee offers a veritable "new perspective" on Edwards, which claims that "There is in Edwards' thought a shift of categories in terms of which the very nature of things is explicated. Edwards departed from the traditional Western metaphysics of substance and form and replaced it with a strikingly modern conception of reality as a dynamic network of dispositional forces and habits."[29] Not only is the ontology of human beings and all sentient and non-sentient existences included in this reinterpretation of reality, but also the very being of God is to be exclusively understood in terms of law-like dispositions and nexuses of dispositions.[30] In "The Mind" notebook, Edwards once wrote: "It is laws that constitute all permanent

---

29. Lee, *Philosophical Theology*, 4, 77. Lee is the Kyung-Chik Han Professor of Systematic Theology at Princeton Theological Seminary and a member of the Editorial Committee for *WJE*. He has written the "Editor's Introduction" to *WJE* 21, and is the editor of *The Princeton Companion to Jonathan Edwards*, along with several important articles on Jonathan Edwards's dispositional conception of reality.

30. Lee, *Philosophical Theology*, 175–85; "Jonathan Edwards on Nature," 40–42; "Editor's Introduction," *WJE* 21:8–9, 13–17, 57–58.

Introduction

being in created things, both corporeal and spiritual." A short while later he added the thought that "laws" are "stated methods fixed by God," on which "the very being of created things depend."[31] These laws operate with a kind of conditionality, according to Lee's understanding of "Miscellanies" no. 241, in which Edwards states, "all habits [are] a law that God has fixed, that such actions upon such occasions should be exerted."[32] Habits and dispositions are therefore understood as the laws according to which God causes actions and events. (Habits are but dispositions of sentient beings.) For Lee, Morimoto, and McDermott, these principles also constitute the axiom of Edwards's dispositional ontology. Concomitant with these principles are two contrasting claims that are, in the words of Morimoto, "integrated in a dynamic unity: the world's radical and total dependence upon God, and its relative permanence and integrity."[33]

Concerning the first claim, Lee argues that all things depend entirely on the intervention of God's causal power. As Morimoto puts it, "If being is essentially laws and habits . . . then all created entities tend inherently and unceasingly toward actual existence through the immediate exercise of divine power in them." He then cites Lee, who writes: "Reality is not something that is achieved once and for all but something that is achieved again and again."[34] This interpretation is then set forth to explain Edwards's doctrine of continuous-creation (i.e., the conservation of matter).

The second claim argues that laws and habits possess their own mode of reality apart from actual exercise. Thus, Edwards's etiology only *appears* occasionalistic and creationistic: "in Edwards [dispositions] are not just an indication of likelihood that similar events happen in similar circumstances; they are active and prescriptive laws that determine events and actions in specific detail. As conditional laws, habits and dispositions certainly become active when the specified occasions arise. Habits are an 'active tendency,' that is, always tending to actual existence. Once conditions are met, the exertion of habits is necessary and automatic . . ."[35] An unexercised disposition's abiding and permanent reality, therefore, lies in its "real possibility" or "virtuality," though it becomes fully actual when in actual exercise.

How Lee's relocation of the metaphysical foundation for Jonathan Edwards figure into a reassessment of the value of the natural-man comes out in Morimoto and McDermott's analogous interpretations the soteriology of Solomon Stoddard's successor. Where McClymond and Holmes encounter an impasse in Edwards's particularist system concerning the place of reprobates, and to a lesser degree, natural-men, Morimoto and McDermott find little difficulty. That is, because of Edwards's dispositional ontology, Morimoto and McDermott do not see him supporting a restrictivist position inclusive of a doctrine of reprobation. These commentators opine that in his *private* notebooks Edwards really was an inclusivist, or at least flirted with possibilities of inclusivism if not

---

31. "Subjects to be Handled in the Treatise on the Mind," nos. 36 and 50 in *WJE* 6:391, 392. Cf. "Miscellanies," no. 241, *WJE* 13:357–78.

32. *WJE* 13:358.

33. Morimoto, *Catholic Vision*, 55.

34. Ibid.; Lee, *Philosophical Theology*, 50.

35. Morimoto, *Catholic Vision*, 55; cf. Lee, *Philosophical Theology*, 40, 44.

hypothetical universalism (pace: Edwards the pseudo-Amyraldian). Quite the contrary: His public theology simply does not reflect the direction his theology had taken in the confidentiality of his Northampton study. In private, Morimoto and McDermott would argue, Edwards experimented with his dispositional ontology and the universal implications of Christ's redemptive work. The implications of Lee's metaphysical reassessment of Edwards are clear: metaphysics determines ontology; ontology drives soteriology.

Thus fueled by a Lee-inspired dispositional conception of reality in terms of law-like powers and forces, Morimoto and McDermott follow the logic of disposition wherever it may lead, be it a synthesis with Tridentine theology (per Morimoto) or a clandestine inclusivism, if not "Augustinian universalism"[36] (à la McDermott). For both Morimoto and McDermott soteriology and etiology are coordinate disciplines: a potentially saving disposition is not unlike Edwardsean dispositions in causality. In a prescribed connection, a law-like disposition (d), in specified circumstances (c), yields its manifestation (m) $(d + c \Rightarrow m)$.

According to Morimoto, initial salvation occurred at the cross: this work of Christ is universal in scope and application—all reap the saving benefit of an infused gracious disposition. The bare (i.e., unexercised) possession of it constitutes regeneration and, therefore, salvation. For Morimoto, Edwards's soteriology is primarily about ontological transformation, i.e., regeneration; justification is linked with conversion—an altogether secondary issue.

So, in addition to this kind of universalism, Edwards allegedly evinces a more prominent inclusivistic position, particularly when he publicly presses for a justified community. In Morimoto's reading, Edwards's evangelistic preaching was not about salvation from imminent damnation, but intended to "trigger" the gracious disposition to an exercise of faith, thereby "converting" the individual and allowing them the benefit of *affectionally* enjoying Christ's saving work. Since all are, for all intents and purposes, accounted believers because of the faith *virtually* contained within the disposition (hence, its law-like *tendency*), only those who exercise it attain this second salvation.[37] The disposition, Morimoto maintains, is not unlike Edwardsean dispositions in causality: in a prescribed connection, a law-like disposition yields its manifestation. In this case, it yields faith in connection with certain Christian means of grace.

McDermott advances Morimoto's revision as he considers Edwards's extensive interest in non-Christian religions. Taking his lead from Morimoto, McDermott argues that, in light of Edwards's dispositional philosophy, the combination of the powers of reasoning in the "heathen" and the plethora of natural revelation available to them allows for the possibility of those unreached by the gospel—the "five-sixths of the world"—to worship and even be "justified," i.e., converted, by the Christian God of special revelation, *without* having to trust in Jesus Christ for salvation.[38] Just as the disposition yields justifying faith in connection with Christian means and ordinances in Morimoto's *Catholic*

---

36. McDermott's thesis corresponds with Oliver Crisp's arguments for "Augustinian universalism." See Crisp, "Augustinian Universalism," 127–45.

37. Morimoto, *Catholic Vision*, chaps 3–4.

38. McClymond, *Confronts the Gods*, 3, 12–13.

Vision of Salvation, so too, according to McDermott, God has provided the heathen with non-Christian means and ordinances to educe an exercise of faith for their justification. Edwards, famed for sermons like "Sinners in the Hands of an Angry God," turns out to be not only is not an inclusivist but a hyper-inclusivist, if not crypto-universalist or at least out of his desire to be so he furtively opened a door of opportunity for others.[39]

Again, for these commentators, the superstructure of soteriology is supported by the infrastructure of ontology, which itself rests upon Edwards's metaphysic of dispositions, as expounded by Sang Hyun Lee.

While Lee's analysis of Edwards's philosophy of dispositions is a significant and, in many ways, bona fide contribution toward understanding in a more systematic way the micro and macro levels of Edwards's philosophical-theology, yet Morimoto and McDermott have cast their lines too far from their subject's expressed thought. As a result, their work fails to accurately represent the thought of Jonathan Edwards for three main reasons:

1. Their unqualified acceptance of Lee's reconfiguration of Edwardsean dispositions. Lee's work cannot be accepted in its entirety. There are, in fact, a number of contestable positions fundamental to Lee's overall project, not the least of which are his accounts of Edwards's causality (the cornerstone of his metaphysics) and so-called "complete departure" from the Aristotelian-Scholastic ontology of "substance."

2. Their refusal to read Edwards according to his admittedly (and one might add, manifestly) confessional theological position. Edwards is much more of an avowed Calvinist than either of the authors allow.

3. Perhaps most importantly, they fail to work with deference to the grand scale and organic nature of Edwards's theocentric and telic-oriented and theological metaphysical system.

At the fore of Edwards's thought—whether exegetical, theological, or philosophical—is a principle of theocentricity.[40] In nearly everything he wrote or preached, from the time of his conversion to the last great work he proposed, God is at center. At first, both his Reformed tradition, which stressed that the universe did not run "by chance" but "by God the sovereign disposer of all [things],"[41] and his theological or perhaps pietistic desire to remove the Enlightenment wedge of rationalism from its lodgings between a mechanistic

---

39. McDermott's principal monograph on this subject promises "A Strange, New Edwards" but the delivery is short. In later publications McDermott has softened and qualified his provocative thesis from *Confronts the Gods*. See, e.g., McDermott, "Response to Gilbert," 77–80; and "Missions and Native Americans," 258–73.

40. McClymond states that it is the "principle of theocentricity . . . where God is the measure of all things," which gives coherence to the various fundamental and distinctive motifs operating in Jonathan Edwards's complex thought, as well as his diverse and voluminous writings (*Encounters*, 28). The claim that theocentrism is the principal organizing concept in Jonathan Edwards's thought is not an overly reductionistic statement. For Jonathan Edwards, theocentrism is not a monodimensional doctrine; it is a genus with many species, which, having enveloped any number of disciplines, terminate in some God-centered idea. Scholars are beginning to form a consensus to this end, see for instance, Colwell, "Jonathan Edwards," 175; Holmes, *God of Grace*, 22–23, 244–45; McClymond, "God the Measure," 43–59; Elwood, *PTJE*, 10–12; Schafer, "Jonathan Edwards," 4:381–82, 381–82; Holbrook, *Ethics of Jonathan Edwards*, 2–7.

41. Calvin, *Institutes*, III.2.1. Cf. Westminster Confession of Faith, V, "Of Providence."

universe and Christian supernaturalism, contributed significantly to his pre-conversion theocentric impulses. He understood that to be a Calvinist was to be a theocentrist: it was just a matter of degrees as to how theocentric one really was. Early on, Edwards seems only to have parroted this trait characteristic of his theological tradition. He was more focused on Enlightenment thought than the promotion of God-at-the-center-of-everything.

However, following the events of spring 1721, the time when Edwards testifies that he began to "see" God's being, telic purposes, and cosmic design "in everything," his conditioned God-centered impulses became to him a permanent, pervasive, and axiomatic mental principle. No longer did he have to reason through the apparatus of logic to ascertain the connection between, say, a flower and God's purpose and presence with relation to that flower. Now he intuitively "sensed" the spiritual reality through which the flower possessed meaning and existence. That reality, he said, is the Divine Being: "God and real existence are the same."[42] And "existence" itself is fulfilling a purpose and moving toward an "ultimate end." Thus, as his *Concerning the End for Which God Created the World* makes unmistakably clear, Edwards pushed the theocentric trait characteristic of Calvinistic thought to its limit by making a *theocentrism of ends* the foremost regulative principle of his philosophical theology. Shooting straight to the point, a theocentric metaphysics of finality—not dispositions—comprises the bedrock of Edwards's vision of reality.

Subsequently, he no longer troubled himself with the need to reconcile his youthful doubts and disenchantment with the doctrine of God's self-glorifying, sovereign disposal of the created order. Indeed, it was no longer a question for him, but an assured worldview. Now the question was, How does one express the concept of the immanence of God and His telic purposes of self-glorification in time and space? That is, How does one reasonably explain the "vision" of God transcendent/God immanent with relation to the created order? His *philosophical* answer is presented in the technical idea of *divine comprehensiveness*.[43] For Edwards, the idea of God's comprehensiveness, the notion that God's very existence encompasses created reality itself, metaphysically explains both why and how God and His glory and purposes are "seen" in everything. Simply put, God's comprehension of reality is the both the *terminus a quo* and *terminus ad quem* of Edwards's metaphysics.

This idea not only corresponded with his post-conversion theocentric and aesthetic vision, but, according to Edwards, it was Scriptural, trinitarian in nature, and made sense of passages like, Acts 17:28, "In Him we live and move and have our being."[44] He also

---

42. "The Mind," no. 15 in *WJE* 6:345.

43. This idea receives further attention in chaps 1–4. Jonathan Edwards's theological answer to this question is found in his trinitarian account of creation discussed in chaps 3 and 8. Though it should be mentioned here that by "comprehensiveness" I mean the sense in which God's being includes, overlaps, and exists through the created order. Rupp and Lee both use the term "coextensive" and therewith indicate that God's being actually extends in the created order. As we shall see there is a sense in which Jonathan Edwards indicates that God extends Himself in the created order. But to use the terms "coextensive" or "coextend" creates a series of philosophical difficulties by giving God dimensional boundaries in time and space. In my use of "comprehensiveness" I seek to maintain Jonathan Edwards's differentiation between the being of God and the created order, as well as uphold the ontological priory he gives to God. Furthermore, unlike "coextend," "comprehensive" is a term and idea used by Jonathan Edwards himself in this connection. Rupp, "The 'Idealism' of Jonathan Edwards," 214; Lee, *Philosophical Theology*, 170f.

44. *Practical Atheism* (1730), *WJE* 17:51. Cf. Sermon on Ps 139:7–10, *God is everywhere present* (1729), Kistler, *Jonathan Edwards*, 207–22.

believed it was rational: it provided an accommodating explanation of providence and natural theology, as well as a "reasonable" (read: "rational") answer to why God created the world.

Additionally, it is within the context of his contemplative thoughts about God and God's relation to reality that, whatever dispositional concepts Edwards may have been introduced to during his time at Yale, then come to the fore.[45]

Tracing the logic of God's comprehensiveness backwards Edwards quickly came to the conclusion that there must be a perfecting disposition within God to supply the impulse by which He communicates the idea of His perfections *externally*. Such a disposition could not be any thing or power apart from God, and so he reasoned that God's essence must consist of a disposition or a set of dispositions saying, "the diffusive disposition that excited God to give creatures existence was rather a communicative disposition in general, or a disposition in the fullness of the divinity to flow out and diffuse itself."[46] Though not original to Edwards, he was now to conceive of God as a communicative, self-enlarging being, whose essence communicates its entire *ad intra* "fullness" *ad extra*.[47] The ideas of comprehensiveness and disposition, then, are crucial concepts for Edwards's post-conversion conception of God and His relation to temporal reality. These concepts are treated in chapters 3–9.

Despite his emergent dispositional philosophy, Edwards did not completely depart from the Aristotelian-Scholastic ontology of "substance," as Sang Lee argues.[48] Lee stands correct in certain respects, particularly with regard to matter, but not so of God's essential being. Lee over-extends his application of Edwards's employment of ontological dispositions to make God's irreducible essence a disposition. To be sure, Edwards's use of dispositions in ontology did begin with a consideration of what *in* God brought about His creative activities—a certain dynamic disposition. Moreover, Lee is correct to say (with Wallace E. Anderson) that Edwards's dispositional concepts facilitated his reconception of the ontological structure of the Trinity, and that both these notions had radical implications upon how the created order was conceived by him. But neither God nor man is to be thought of *only* in terms of disposition: Edwards retained "substance" concepts and terminology for both.

---

45. Many of my insights concerning disposition have arisen from either my conversations with Lee or my reading of his work on Jonathan Edwards. However, my work on "divine comprehension," the essence of God and man (in terms of substance), and the conclusions I draw from them, frequently differ from his interpretations.

46. *WJE* 8:434–35. Although expressed here in the mature reflection of "Concerning the End for which God Created the World" (c.1754, posthumously published 1765), Jonathan Edwards had been articulating this idea since 1723, if not before. See "Miscellanies," nos. 87, 92, and 107[b] in *WJE* 13.

47. E.g., the Cambridge Platonist John Smith spoke about the idea of God's communicating Himself *ad extra* in the creation. Smith also held that the creation was the externalizing of that which was prior within the Deity. Furthermore, God was moved to create, according to Smith, out of His "fullness." See Smith, "A Discourse Concerning the Existence and Nature of God" in *Select Discourses*. See also Kimnach's confirmation and brief analysis of the remarkable conceptual and rhetorical correlations between Smith and Jonathan Edwards in "General Introduction," *WJE* 10:6–9.

48. Lee, *Philosophical Theology*, 4, 77.

Edwards does express, however, that God's comprehension of reality is the dispositional result of the divine "fullness" or essence.[49] He also reasons that since God's relation to the created order is founded upon dispositional principles, then the created order must be conceived in like terms of dispositional forces and laws. For Edwards, this meant a reevaluation of all the created order—*including the ontological status and epistemic perspective of natural-men and reprobates*—in light of God's all-comprehensive reality and ontological structure. For us, the idea of God's comprehension of reality, along with the ontological arrangement of God's trinitarian self, facilitates new possibilities for understanding in Edwards's thought the existence and function of *all* intelligent perceiving beings, but with the following criteria: (1) that we allow Edwards to guide us concerning his intellectual positions as he connects them or they manifest their connection with certain events in his life; (2) we do not presume against the evidence, and even Edwards's oft repeated profession of confessional adherence, that he held contradictory public and private theologies; and (3) we keep in focus the controlling principle of telic-theocentrism and narrative of God's self-glorification through bilateral redemptive activities (i.e., in terms of electing a church and effecting salvation for them, and justly damning and punishing the reprobate portion of humankind) characteristic of his philosophical-theology.

By approaching Edwards's treatment of the existence and function of human beings from the perspective of his dispositional philosophical-theology in lieu of the aforementioned parameters, we may ascertain the positive significance and inherent value he intends, indeed, requires for natural-men and reprobates *as* natural-men and reprobates. Every human being possesses inherent value and functional significance in his theocentric metaphysics in at least two ways. First, Edwards ascribes inherent, ineradicable value to the being of natural-man by conceiving of natural-man's ontological structure in such a way that it, in and of itself, is an instance of beauty, imaging forth the beauty of God. It is to be remembered that Edwards was not obsessed by the wrath of God but by His beauty; a beauty that constitutes the matrix of existence, created and uncreated, unfallen or fallen. The very being of the natural-man, inasmuch as it is to be found within that matrix, itself is an instance of divine beauty. For Edwards, an intelligent perceiving being's[50] mental existence is the most complete form of the *imago Dei* in time and space (save for the Incarnation and the noetic restoration of the regenerate), and therefore the only substantial mental image of God outside the Trinity. Because Edwards primarily associates a human being's divine image with its ontological structure, I have not included it as a positive element of his theology, though there undoubtedly is considerable overlap.[51] The particular question of how the bare existence of the reprobate is directly related to creation as *ekstasis* will be discussed in due course.

49. "End of Creation" in *WJE* 8:433; "Miscellanies," no. 553, *WJE* 18:97.

50. I will use "intelligent perceiving minds" to designate a category of consciousnesses that, along with human beings, includes angelic beings.

51. E.g., according to Jonathan Edwards's reading of the Bible, natural-man possesses eradicable value because he is created in "the image of God," which, though marred by the fall, remains as that "which belongs to the nature of man" (*WJE* 3:381). As shown in succeeding chapters (5–8), by the "nature of man" Jonathan Edwards means the ontological mental structure and essential dispositions of man that constitute human being as such.

Introduction

Secondly, we find that in Edwards's philosophical idealism (which in large measure developed alongside his philosophy of dispositions) the natural-man/reprobate has a positive function in God's program of self-glorification in time and space. Edwards's idealism is based upon the axiom, "all [created] existence is perception," that is, the perception of ideas.[52] These "ideas" are God's communicated ideas-of-existence. According to Edwards, the perceiving of such ideas requires an intelligent perceiving something to receive (perceive) them. That something is "intelligent perceiving being" or human being. In order for the total idea of God's fullness to be "*ad extra*," there must be an intelligent perceiving consciousness *ad extra* to God in order to perceive the ideas associated with His fullness. Human beings, even fallen natural-men, are the world's consciousness and therefore have value to God in that regard.

This, of course, ties into the theocentric/telic reason of *why* God created, namely, to perfect the divine disposition to "externalize" His prior beauty and actuality ("fullness"); a process Edwards identifies as God's self-communication for glorification. First, however, the process is internal to God and thoroughly trinitarian: God the Father's "fullness" is His perfections, which only and summarily consist in the Son and the Spirit.[53] The Son is the Father's perfect image and knowledge of Himself, the Spirit His love and delight of Himself. Thus, God's essence consists of one innertrinitarian idea of Himself perfectly known and loved. Then the process turns external: God, Edwards explains, also delights to have His innertrinitarian perfections glorified by "existing *ad extra*."[54] But for God's perfections to exist *ad extra* according to their nature, they must be perceived in a manner that corresponds to those perfections. Minds created in His image are capable of intellectually and affectionally perceiving the idea of God's knowledge and love. Once that idea is emanated (communicated) and perceived in a fashion corresponding to His perfections (knowledge and love of Himself), those perfections are replicated and God is glorified: hence Edwards's conclusion that the telic function of created existences is to "remanate" the glory of God.[55] In Edwards's idealism intelligent perceiving beings not so much authenticate as facilitate God's program of self-enlargement. Which is to say, Edwards's idealism requires God to have intelligent minds *perceive* the divine communication of Himself *ad extra* in order for it to be real or concretely present to them and valuable to God.[56] Without perceiving minds (or "consciousnesses," as Edwards calls them) to perceive God's ideas, God cannot manifest Himself *ad extra*. The reason for this is obvious to Edwards: such communications and glorifying "had as good not be as be" without perceivers. Therefore, if the creation is to exist and God is going to communicate the idea of Himself in/through it, then the world "must be conscious of its own being." That is, the world must be conscious of its own reality and God's presence within the world for it "to be of any value."[57]

52. *WJE* 6:384.
53. Holmes, *God of Grace*, 69.
54. "End of Creation" in *WJE* 8:531.
55. For an analysis of Jonathan Edwards's dynamic conception of the glory of God, which employs the logic of disposition, see Jang, "The Logic of Glorification."
56. See chaps 4–7.
57. "Miscellanies," no. 1, *WJE* 13:197; "The Mind," no. 67 in *WJE* 6:384.

For Edwards, an intelligent perceiving being's ontological status is derivative of God's reality.[58] Furthermore, I propose that Edwards indicates that the ontological status of sentient beings determines the content of their epistemological perspectives (whether it is spiritual or not) and, consequently, what they "sensibly" know and perceive about reality (whether it corresponds with God's truth/reality or not). Thus, the calculated "degree" of "value" that Edwards attributes to the existence of an intelligent perceiving being, as well as their knowledge and states of consciousness, is determined by an ontological factor—nearness to God in terms of likeness or, stated theologically, union with Christ. This is to say, Edwards's philosophy for evaluating both the quality and purpose of existence of an intelligent perceiving being, inclusive of the reprobate, is based upon an ontological system of relations, not proximity. So far from embracing a representative Neo-Platonic conception of the universe, Edwards proposes an ontological conception of reality that makes use of philosophical idealism, modern dispositional concepts (which represent created existences as relational and progressive), *and* Scholastic notions of substance (where dispositions have or are designated a *locus*). And it is within this proposal that even the natural-man and reprobate contribute to the matrix of divine beauty by virtue of their relationally determined ontological value and the kind of knowledge they perceive and remanate.

Therefore, if we are to accurately represent Edwards's philosophical-theology concerning the functional existence of the natural-man/reprobate, then it must be in light of God's comprehension of reality. Simply stated, God will be our centerpiece for developing the discussion of Edwards's philosophy of the function of the reprobate, on account of the fact that God invades every aspect of his thought concerning existence and knowledge.

The sudden prominence of Edwards's "theocentrism of ends" in his writings from 1723 onwards also compels me to grant that a metaphysical reconception of reality was not at the fore of his intellectual agenda from the start; rather, it was, as he himself explains, more the product of his post-conversion perspective. His first metaphysical speculations, which probably coincided with his senior collegiate year and graduate studies at Yale (1719–1721), were relatively unimaginative, as he attempted to harmonize favorable points in Locke, Newton, More, Shaftesbury, and others, with his theological heritage. Again, it would appear that his post-conversion perspectives changed this. For immediately after that time, he began to show his originality as a thinker through his independently creative theology and, coinciding with its development, the modernity of his thought through his dispositional and relational ideas.[59] But what his emergent idealism

---

58. Rupp, "The 'Idealism' of Jonathan Edwards," 214. Indeed, the ontological status of any finite existence is determined by its nearness to God in terms of likeness of being.

59. Schafer points out that Sereno Dwight's assignment of "Of Being" in its entirety to Jonathan Edwards's early college years has encouraged many scholars to produce work showing Jonathan Edwards's dependence on Locke and Berkeley for these conclusions. "But," Schafer explains, "it seems clear that Edwards evolved his so-called 'idealism' without the benefit of Locke's [or Berkeley's] ideas, against the background of his own previous conclusions about matter and more directly his own single-minded contemplations of God and his works" ("Editor's Introduction," *WJE* 13:46–47). Schafer's position has now become the consensus among scholars.

and dispositional concepts revolved around, indeed, facilitated, and were subservient to, was a radically theocentric perspective of reality.

Thus, when Edwards embarked upon an idealistic reconception of reality, using dispositional concepts to explain its relevance to a Newtonian world, or when he contemplated the existence and ontological structure of human beings, such thoughts were intended to be consistent with his continuing idea of God. His idea of divine dispositions, for example, is the result of his doctrinally informed post-conversion perception of God. What is more, we can be sure that his biblical-theological presuppositions—such as God's immutability, eternity, and aseity—color, mold, and shape his metaphysical speculations. These uncompromiseable doctrines of Reformed Scholasticism—indeed, even of Augustine, Thomas Aquinas, and Calvin—establish a continuous identification between Edwards's philosophical-theology and his theological and soteriological heritage, while on the other hand they also particularly distinguish his dispositional concepts about God and reality from later process thought and (Gilbert) Rylean causal dispositions.

Yet it is also *because* Edwards frequently mirrored a medieval depiction of an immutable God and openly asserted his dependence upon the Bible, as well as rigorously defended fundamental doctrines of Calvinism, many scholars have neglected his philosophical innovations and simply cast him as an extraordinary *Puritan* thinker, or in the language of his day, as a "philosophizing divine." In other words, on account of his pervasive theocentricity, in which he clearly aligned himself with his theological tradition and pressed a theocentric worldview to an extreme, some interpreters of Edwards cannot see him other than as a hybrid Reformed Scholastic and fringe Enlightenment philosopher.[60] Certainly his view on God and the Bible are undeniable and pervasive aspects of his thought.[61] To be sure, Edwards's emphasis and reliance upon special revelation colors almost every aspect of his thought—from his most speculative theological excursions to the most foundational of his philosophical precepts.[62] So much so, that George Gordon once complained, "It is not edifying to see Edwards, in the full movement of speculation, suddenly pause, begin a new section of his essay, and lug into his argument proof texts from every corner of the Bible to cover the incompleteness of his rational procedure."[63] For this same reason, John Gerstner points out that Peter Gay denounced Edwards as con-

---

60. For example, Whittemore depicts Jonathan Edwards as far more medieval than modern in *The Transformation of New England Theology*. Chai portrays Jonathan Edwards as an aspiring, yet failing Enlightenment thinker in *Limits of Enlightenment*, while Gerstner presents Jonathan Edwards as the quintessential Reformed Scholastic theologian who anticipated Thomas Reid's common sense philosophy and mounted a "classical" apologetic defense against aberrant streams of Enlightenment thought in *Rational Biblical*, 1:1–139.

61. Smith writes: "Edwards accepted totally the tradition established by the Reformers with respect to the absolute primacy and authority of the Bible, and he could approach the biblical writings with that conviction of their inerrancy and literal truth" ("Jonathan Edwards as Philosophical Theologian," 306). Cf. Stephen, "The Spirit and the Word," 118–30.

62. For examples of his imaginative theological work see, MS sermon on Ps 8:4–5 (1744/45), Jonathan Edwards Collection, "Miscellanies," no. 591, *WJE* 18:24–25, and "Typological Writings" in *WJE* 11. For a distinctly Bible-based philosophical precept, see "Things to be Considered an[d] Written Fully About" no. 44 in *WJE* 6:238.

63. Cited Foster, *A Genetic History*, 51.

fined to a biblical "cage" and concluded that he was not a true Enlightenment thinker.[64] But neither Edwards's theocentrism nor his biblicism strictly marginalized his philosophical thought. Rather than denying him a standing among Enlightenment thinkers on account of his God-centeredness, it was his theocentrism of ends that gave rise to his conception of reality as composed of telic-oriented dispositions—a conception which establishes him as a modern "theocentric metaphysician."[65] To be sure, his conception of reality demonstrates a philosophical content that is, in many respects, identifiably modern and not purely medieval, though his connection with the Scholastic tradition (both Medieval and Reformed) is undeniable and pervasive.[66]

One of the features of this book shall be to evidence the claim that Edwards, on the whole, exemplifies a synthesis between the *via antiqua* and *via moderna*, moving from being to divine intentionality and back again as the primal metaphors for understanding God, shifting from metaphysics to metahistory and back again as a means of understanding God's relation to the created world, and shifting from the ontological to the logical and back again as a methodology for doing theology. In short, this study shall regard the idea that Edwards, as a somewhat independent and imaginative spirit, was a formal system builder of a philosophical-theology that exhibited an organic nature beyond the allegedly closed system of seventeenth-century Puritans and Reformed Scholastics.

Explicating the basic content of Edwards's dispositional concepts around God not only corresponds with his patent theocentrism, it also proves a suitable method for explaining their relation to matter, causality, and, of course, created intelligence. What amounts to a principle of telic-theocentricity is a regulating precept for all matters theological, historical, philosophical, and ethical. For Edwards, every created thing relates to God in some programmatic way (so that God gets His glory), and through and in God every thing gains meaning, purpose, and even existence. In other words, he goes beyond saying God's ways and purposes can be typologically discerned in things, to say God's being is really manifest in everything. Edwards's theocentrism is, then, the cohesive hermeneutical principle by which he reads, interprets, and understands reality.

His thoughts on natural-men and reprobates are therefore no exception to his theocentric parameters for speculation. He confidently set forth a metanarrative for all existences, to which all existences are subject. That metanarrative is God's program of self-glorification through self-communication/replication. Edwards insists God's being is "expansive" and the Divine Being created the world that He may replicate His *ad intra* perfections *ad extra*. That replication, he explains, obtains through the ontological and epistemological dimensions of human beings, even fallen ones, even those predestined for damnation. The ways and purposes of God are in this for His own glory.

What the reader should then expect within the pages that follow is a piece of scholarly exposition, clarification, and commentary almost entirely internal to the presuppositions, views, and logic of Jonathan Edwards: a thesis showing that Edwards's thinking is

---

64. Gay, *A Loss of Mastery*, 97. Cf. Opie, ed., *Edwards and the Enlightenment*, 101–5.

65. Fiering considers Jonathan Edwards's theocentric metaphysics comparable to Malebranche and Leibniz ("The Rationalist Foundations of Jonathan Edwards," 77).

66. This holds true even with respect to dispositional concepts vis-à-vis Thomas Aquinas.

consciously of a grand scale and systematic, driven by the single vision of God and His self-glorification. I intend to throw new light on how he philosophically understood the relationship of not just the natural-man, but specifically the reprobate, to God's grand scheme of self-glorification through self-replication and redemption. The assertion that his philosophical-theology not only accommodates an affirmative and contributive (functional) view of man but also requires such a view, builds on the premise that his theocentric vision solidified his idea of God's comprehensiveness and that this idea significantly contributed to his employment of dispositional concepts. In turn *Jonathan Edwards's Vision of Reality* argues that a consistently thorough application of dispositional concepts meant, for Edwards, the reconsideration of the cosmic design and telic purposes of intelligent perceiving beings, who, in light of his doctrine of divine comprehension, are constructive ontological and epistemological participants in the matrix of divine beauty, which is our spatiotemporal reality.

Throughout the following pages we shall find that, although Edwards in no way retreats from his theological tradition's assertion of total depravity, original sin, reprobation, and hell torments, yet he philosophically proposes that the ontological structure and epistemic content of unregenerate human beings positively contribute to the spatiotemporal beautification of God[67] and, theologically, the progress of redemption history. However, just as the concept of disposition accounts for the ontological and epistemological contribution of intelligent perceiving beings, so too it provides Edwards with a metaphysical rationale for the sinful nature of the unregenerate, as well as how and why God can be glorified in the temporal retributions and eternal destruction of the reprobate. Thus, Edwards's philosophy of dispositions provides both a comprehensive and internally coherent foundation for his positive philosophical and negative theological representations of the natural-man and, especially, the reprobate.

Therefore, *Jonathan Edwards's Vision of Reality: The Relationship of God to the World, Redemptive History, and the Reprobate* affirms Edwards's underlying principles for reprobation as a necessary and inescapable consequence of his vision of reality in God. Contrary to the assertions of certain revisionist commentators, the idea of reprobation for Edwards is neither the theological residuum of his early particularist convictions (supposedly abandoned for more inclusivist opinions), nor an incompatible element in his philosophical-theology. Rather, it is an integral part of his theocentric worldview, laden with metaphysical reasoning, and not at all inconsistent with his doctrines of God, creation, and salvation.[68]

---

67. "Miscellanies," no. 204, *WJE* 13:339. When Jonathan Edwards speaks of God communicating "with spirits according to their nature and capacity" he must be understood to be operating within the boundaries of his idealism and dispositional philosophy, where "nature" corresponds with his ontological intentions and "capacity" with his epistemological intentions. Hence this "Miscellanies" entry, like so many others, is not simply about the epistemological issue of revelation, but inasmuch as the communication of any idea—especially a divine idea—is both intellectually and inclinationally perceived, it is internally related to the perceiver, and therefore has ontological significance. That is, the ability to perceive divine ideas, Jonathan Edwards says, is only consequent upon an ontological relation (union) to the source of spiritual ideas, viz., God.

68. Fiering, writing with a view to Jonathan Edwards's moral theology, affirms the same: "In addition to [Jonathan Edwards's] major books on free will and original sin, his various writings on hell complete the story of man's reprobation, making the entire presentation exceedingly thorough" (*Moral Thought*, 205).

As the chapters progress, the ideas represented in them will reflect an eighteenth-century character who was strongly Calvinistic in his theology, a hard determinist in his etiology, consciously teleological in his worldview, unapologetic about his biblical anthropology and soteriological particularism, but also creative and serious about his evangelistic engagement with unregenerates.

The reader should not expect particulate, unrelated chapters, but a single discussion progressing in an attempt to exemplify Edwards's theocentrism of ends in which dispositions function as the regulative mechanism within his metaphysics of finality. Moreover, the reader should not expect a critique from other than Edwards's own perspective, except for my interaction with modern-day scholars and my own personal reflections found in the "Conclusion."

Edwards has several distinct approaches to conveying aspects of God's self-enlarging disposition and its implications for his theological anthropology: an apologetical approach, an exegetical or theological approach, and a philosophical approach. In some places more than others, and for didactic or polemical purposes, he at times emphasizes one of these approaches above the others to achieve a particular effect. However, no one approach is to be understood as unconnected and particulate, but for the most part form a highly integrated, interdependent method. In his writings he is not in one place a theologian, in another a Puritan minister, and in another a philosopher. He rarely if ever approaches any subject mono-dimensionally. Rather, he is a New England Puritan philosophical theologian. Paul Ramsey rightly warns that to abstract Edwards's "philosophy from its theological context tends to obscure Jonathan Edwards' extraordinary confidence that the truths of faith and of reason are *one*."[69] Thus, apart from certain papers (which were not theologically void, but frequently possess some religious content for the purpose of expounding or complementing a theocentric principle) he produced no purely philosophical works.[70] In the truest sense, Edwards was a Calvinist metaphysician who viewed and analyzed the world as a technometria.

In light of the intertwined nature of his philosophy and theology I have chosen to incorporate the use of Edwards's sermon corpus (in addition to his notebooks and treatises) as a means of exploring and evincing the function of the natural-man in God's self-glorifying scheme. Not only do his treatises teem with philosophical reflections, all of which were intended to clarify and define his theological positions, but his sermons do as well.

We may therefore expect the content of the following chapters to be philosophical, but necessarily theological. Yet, inasmuch as Jonathan Edwards is a historical figure working within identifiable theological, intellectual, and social settings, certain portions of this work may well be deemed historiographical, though it is not within the proposed purview of this study to trace the historical circumstances or intellectual influences that may or may not have caused Edwards to think the way he did on each and every occasion. This is not to say those studies are not helpful, they certainly are, and have substantially informed

---

69. Ramsey, "Editor's Introduction," *WJE* 8:6 n. 5.

70. The relevance of his philosophical contemplations also found their way into doctrinal matters via applications or "corollaries" affixed to the end of his more philosophical entries.

my work here.⁷¹ But unlike McDermott's book, *Jonathan Edwards Confronts the Gods*, which is a context and source study of how Edwards *apologetically* responded to the radical Enlightenment's challenge to Reformed orthodoxy, here we focus on the cosmological and teleological implications of Edwards's modern dispositional philosophy as it applies to reality in God and, in particular, the enigma of unregenerate human beings in his heritage of Calvinistic theology.

The question of exactly how "modern" he was itself remains to be definitively answered and would be the subject of another study.⁷² Accordingly, our efforts here will not feign to be conclusive concerning the placing of Edwards's modernity. This is to say, locating his philosophical thought in history is less a concern of this study, than the content of that thought.⁷³

In the first of two chapters we explore what prompted Edwards's philosophical endeavors in the direction of a metaphysical reconception of reality. I propose that there were three major contributing factors: (1) his theological heritage; (2) the progressive intellectual climate of the Enlightenment that, in his eyes, both permitted and required a rejoinder from Christian orthodoxy; and, (3) by his own admission, his perspective-altering conversion experience of 1721. The first two factors have been subjects of several recent studies that have enriched our understanding of not only the cultural-historical milieu in which Edwards lived and worked, but also the intellectual forces that motivated his work.⁷⁴ Therefore I will concentrate my efforts on the third and, by Edwards's own admission, the most decisive factor, his conversion, or (better) his post-conversion theological vision, which a growing number of scholars believe significantly influenced his philosophical experimentations in an effort to accommodate his "new spiritual" worldview.

---

71. For interesting and valuable studies tracing the Jonathan Edwards's intellectual inheritance and development see, Morris, *The Young Jonathan Edwards*; Fiering, *Moral Thought*; Warch, *School of the Prophets*; Morison, *Harvard College in the Seventeenth Century*; Miller, *The New England Mind*. Important resources on Jonathan Edwards's reading are Johnson, "Jonathan Edwards' background of reading," 193–222; and Thuesen, "Editor's Introduction," *WJE* 26:1–114.

72. The historiography of seventeenth- and eighteenth-century philosophy is in a period of revision at present, with results that are likely to lead to a more accurate conception of early American philosophy and therefore how we are to understand Jonathan Edwards. Fiering has rightly argued that such revisions will evidence Jonathan Edwards's thought to be far more nuance, complex, and original, than simply denominated Rationalist or Empiricist, Malebranchean or Lockean ("Rationalist Foundations of Jonathan Edwards," 73–101).

73. Whether Jonathan Edwards was modern in his thought really is no longer a point of dispute amongst scholars. Now the real questions are how modern was he, and in what way? Certainly Jonathan Edwards was engaged with characteristic eighteenth-century intellectual issues—for example, empiricism, British moral philosophy, and the deistic controversy, which brought him to respond polemically to a number of European thinkers. To designate Jonathan Edwards as a modern, however, is not to deny that he was influence by the Scholastics.

74. Such as the editors' introductions to *WJE*; Zakai, *Jonathan Edwards's Philosophy of History*; Moody, *Jonathan Edwards and the Enlightenment*; Copan, "Jonathan Edwards's Philosophical Influences", 107–24; McDermott, *One Holy and Happy Society*; Guelzo, *Edwards on the Will*; Hoopes, *Consciousness in New England*; De Prospo, *Theism in the Discourse of Jonathan Edwards*; Fiering, *Moral Philosophy at Seventeenth-Century Harvard*; Stevenson, "Ministerial and Theological Purposes of Jonathan Edwards's Thought"; Opie, ed., *Jonathan Edwards and the Enlightenment*; and Emily Watts, "Jonathan Edwards and the Cambridge Platonists."

Chapters 1 and 2 examine this aspect of Edwards's own account of his conversion experience. Chapter 3 explores how that event pressed a comprehensively God-centered vision of reality upon his mind, which ultimately brought about a transformation in the way he conceived of God and reality.

In chapters 4 through 7, we further reflect on those transformations and how Edwards employs them. His "spiritual vision" of God revealed that the Divine Being was present in reality in knowledge, essence, and power. The knowledge he received from this vision (confirmed by the contents of Scripture) showed that God's presence was all encompassing, intentional, and fixed for particular "ends" and even an "ultimate end." For Edwards, metaphysics would need to be orientated in a way that corresponded with God's telic and cosmologic relation to reality.

In these chapters I explain that Edwards managed and organized his telic and cosmologically affected metaphysics by subsuming the whole discussion under the rubrics of being and causation. By relegating all causal occurrences to God's power, Edwards ensures that the ends of creation—in every instance—will attain in full (that is, that they will be God-glorifying and contribute to the "ultimate" end of creation). Precisely *how* God does this is by creating all things to function in a law-like way. What ensures that such and such a thing always attains to God's desired end(s) is its dispositional composition. God fashions, as it were, a network of existence that is composed of law-like dispositional forces.

Yet God is also *in* those things in some way, namely, in "essence and power." Moreover, whatever existence there may be is provided by the "only real being"—God. It is God's being that constitutes the matrix of reality. God, therefore, comprehends all existence, for His being is the "sum of all being" and "the being of beings," according to Edwards.

Sang Lee has given a great deal of attention to explaining Edwards's reconception of metaphysical reality in terms of disposition, and provides detailed treatments of causality, material entities, and significantly, sentient beings. The work in these chapters attempts to further as well as correct some of Lee's findings, and present a number of key concepts important for the ensuing discussions of the remaining chapters.

Chapters 8 and 9 present Edwards's ontological conception of man, predicated upon his dispositional reconception of the ontological structure of the Trinity. This presentation shows, in response to the concerns of Michael McClymond and Stephen Holmes, how the ontological structure of every human being—including the unregenerate and reprobate—possess inherent God-glorifying principles.

The tenth and eleventh chapters build on the preceding chapters by first considering how the logic of ontological disposition accounts for the transition of man from a state of concreatedness to fallenness, and even sin. Central to the discussion are the issues raised by Holmes concerning Edwards's failure to provide a trinitarian account for the creation and existence of the reprobate.

The Fall brings with it both ontological and epistemological consequences for biblical Adam and his posterity. I argue in this chapter that the ontological status of sentient beings (determined by their relations) regulates how and what they can know. Focusing on the unregenerate natural-man, Edwards says that their fallen constitution (i.e., "carnal" state of mind) prohibits extensive relations with God, neighbor, and nature. Consequently,

Introduction

they are specifically unable to affectionally cognize or perceive "true" reality, which, according to Edwards, is pregnant with spiritual significance and purpose (i.e., God's program of glorification). Despite his theological indictment of natural-men/reprobates, who categorically can do nothing to enhance their ontological status, Edwards insists that they can and do glorify God through certain epistemic perceptions.

In the twelfth and thirteenth chapters, I offer a refutation of Morimoto and McDermott's revisionist accounts of Edwards's so-called soteriology of ontological transformation and understanding of redemption history. In addition, we shall consider Edwards's evangelistic engagement with the unregenerate, as well as the reprobates' role in the history of the divine work of redemption.

Edwards, of course, was not just a philosopher-theologian but also a Puritan minister. His whole professional career, save for two short months as the president of the College of New Jersey, was spent as a pastor or gospel missionary.[75] In that capacity he saw the dissemination of the word of God as the necessary and indispensable, yet insufficient means of supernatural redeeming grace. Through the promotion of the gospel of Jesus Christ God "ingathered" His elect from the world. Thus Edwards found it his duty to admonish the unregenerate to "seek" and "strive" for salvation in the hope that they may become non-meritorious recipients of mercy.

Despite his doctrine of double particular election, Edwards refined a strategy of sermon rhetoric, which, though sometimes minatorial, sometimes importunate, was in large part founded upon principles stemming from his dispositional ontology. His doctrine of preparation exemplifies this claim. It, like so many things, was affected by the way he attempted to convey the idea of God's direct interaction with the world. The idea he settled upon, and from which his theological method would emerge, was ultimately a linear historical approach.

In *A History of the Work of Redemption*, Edwards rehearses God's work of redemption "from the fall of man to the end of the world," and there we find that the natural-man and reprobate function, both at individual and collective levels, in a way that parallels repetitive stages in the work of redemption's constitutive history.[76] Just as the *historia salutis* develops along the lines of "preparation," "achievement," and "application," so too the individual life is a microcosm of this work. For example, in a MS sermon on Revelation 14:15 (1744) Edwards writes, "There are two kinds of persons that are here in this world in a preparatory state, elect and reprobates. Both are continued here in a state

---

75. The original College of New Jersey was renamed Princeton College and is not to be confused with the former Trenton State College, presently known as The College of New Jersey. Jonathan Edwards's first ministerial charge was to a Presbyterian church in New York City (10 August 1722—26 April 1723). This was followed by another short stint at a Congregational church in Bolton, Connecticut (July 1723—April 1724). After two years as a tutor at Yale College Jonathan Edwards was invited to Northampton, Massachusetts, to assist his ailing grandfather, Solomon Stoddard. He arrived there in September 1726, obtained settlement on 21 November, and was ordained 22 February, 1727. Following the death of Stoddard in 1729, Jonathan Edwards remained the sole minister of the Northampton Church until the congregation voted for his removal in 1750. From 1751–57 he served as a missionary-pastor in Stockbridge, Massachusetts to a few white settlers and the Housatonic and Mohawk Indians. He began his presidential duties at Princeton in January 1758. On 23 February, he was inoculated with an infected vaccine for smallpox and died 22 March 1758, age 54.

76. *Sermon One*, *WJE* 9:116.

of preparation for an eternal state. Elect are here to be prepared [for heaven]. Reprobates are preparing [for hell]. They are ripening. And there are none [who] stand still, neither saints or sinners."[77] "Achievement" for the elect is found in Christ, and for the reprobate in judgment. "Application" for the elect is salvation and ultimately glorification, and for the reprobate damnation. The final function of the reprobate in God's program of glorification is their destruction in hell, where they eternally replicate in their minds and resurrected bodies the power of God's wrath.

The "heathen" nations also take part collectively in the grand scheme of redemption history. Their knowledge of certain religious truths serves to prepare former reprobate nations for the application of saving grace. Conversely, their present rejection of the Messiah accounts for Edwards's negative theological assessment, as he holds the natural-man fully culpable for failing in his epistemic responsibilities, ontological structure notwithstanding. Their place in redemption history is therefore twofold: to further the work of redemption for future generations and to replicate the punitive aspects of God's inner actuality.

Hence in the final chapter we find the natural-man and reprobate playing important roles in the advancement of the drama of redemption both prior and subsequent to the first advent, and in eternity. We also find that the logic of Edwards's dispositional ontology provides a certain amount of consistency concerning both his philosophical and theological treatment of human beings. The natural-man and reprobate alike possess intrinsic worth and functional value in God's program of self-glorification, not only in this life but in eternal life as well.

Although Jonathan Edwards ascribes inherent value to the natural-man and reprobate, yet our closing image of his philosophical-theology is far from flattering. Plainly, God creates the reprobate to glorify Him in hell through the increased capacity of their minds: hence, the trinitarian nature of their eternal destruction. Justified talk of Edwards's potential soteriological inclusivism is simply fiction. Commentators will, therefore, have to take Edwards on his own restrictivist terms—however objectionable those terms may be. Internally, his theocentric philosophical-theology remains a coherent and cohesive piece: it (perhaps, uncomfortably) takes sin and punishment seriously, but also finds a place for them in God's beautiful and beautifying being which, in the end, is perhaps the most distressing proposition of this thinking. But such is the world according to Edwards.

---

77. 729. Jonathan Edwards Collection.

Jonathan Edwards's Spiritual Vision of Reality

> PREFACE: To shew how all arts and sciences, the more they are perfected, the more they issue in divinity, and coincide with it, and appear to be as parts of it. And to shew how absurd for Christians to write treatises of ethics distinctly from divinity as revealed in the Gospel.
>
> —Notes for "A Rational Account of the Main Doctrines of the Christian Religion Attempted"

LIKE MANY PHILOSOPHICAL THEOLOGIANS AND SYSTEMATICIANS THROUGHOUT CHURCH history, Jonathan Edwards strove for a holistic Christian worldview that could make sense of seemingly disparate concepts such as the eternal and temporal realms, the unchangeableness of God and his creativity, and the relation of body and soul. Edwards attempted to accomplish a coherent and balanced understanding of God, the world, and the Christian faith through an innovative metaphysical reconception of the nature of reality in terms of ideas, dispositions, and relationality. To be sure, he was a man of his time. The theological and ecclesiastical tradition in which he was nurtured, his eighteenth-century New England context, as well as his academic training at Yale, ensured that, whatever philosophical digressions he might take, God would be (at least in theory) providentially involved in causality, while special revelation in the form of the Bible would be the infallible repository of truth for matters soteriological and ethical. Nonetheless, in the spirit of the time, Edwards remained open to new ideas about how to articulate confessional divinity over-against the challenges of the Enlightenment.

But for him to do justice to his Puritan upbringing and theological tradition while engaging the ideas of the Enlightenment he had to overcome a number of difficulties. The intellectual climate in Europe had changed radically during the seventeenth century, and was beginning to influence the way New Englanders thought. In Europe, professed adherents to the church and its creeds (whether Catholic or Protestant) quickly learnt that philosophy could be done, indeed was being done, without God and His redeeming purposes in the foreground. Heliocentricity, radical advances in astronomy, the transmission of knowledge, the proliferation of the tools and reliable methods of science, advances in algebra and geometry by François Viète and René Descartes, the discovery of calculus by Leibniz and Newton, the harnessing and mechanization of everything from physics to biology, led men like Descartes and Spinoza in attempts to reduce metaphysics to mathematical form. The days of Thomas Aquinas and the Scholastics were over: God drifted into the background. Descartes and Locke, for example, found ways to work through (or develop) problems in philosophy that placed God in a secondary or derivative role. God became the guarantor of what were primary epistemological concerns. There was an intellectual paradigm shift: philosophers no longer were discussing the issues of divine and ecclesiastical authority or the particulars that constituted the doctrines of God and salvation. Reason was now final arbiter in matters of politics, morality, and religion, and the human knower took center-stage. The Divine examination in Job chapters 38–42 was reversed: man was scrutinizing God; revelation had to answer to reason.

Yale College, where Edwards was attending, knew all this well enough. The pervasive effects of the seventeenth-century rebirth of philosophy upon Christian thought brought far-reaching consequences—consequences that crept ashore in New England in the form of heterodoxical or heretical ideas, books, and pamphlets. Without rehearsing the story of this well documented epoch in modern history, suffice it to say that many churchmen in the British Isles gave themselves to the Enlightenment project and began to examine theology, ecclesiology, and Christian ethics under the rubric of rational investigation. Within New England, churchmen therefore watched with a close eye the transformations taking place within Anglicanism and liberal Presbyterianism, where certain ecclesiastics in England and Scotland abandoned creedal formulas and Reformation theology in favor of a naturalized, reasonable, and moral-theory laden religion. They feared that in some church circles theism had already given way to deism. And while the scientific discoveries of the Enlightenment could not be ignored in America, and were in fact hailed by the likes of Cotton Mather, yet the question of *how* a mechanical and calculable universe, characterized by efficient laws, could be sufficiently reconciled with Christianity's supernaturalism and its disputed epistemological source, revelation, as well as Calvinism's particularism, remained a perplexing difficulty. Simply asserting classical dogma was doing little in the way of persuasion: the communion of saints was shrinking and fragmenting, while skeptics, cynics, and deists multiplied.

Whatever the final answers might be for the dilemma and whatever forms it might take, one thing was certain: Edwards's theological tradition would insist upon the prominence of God in metaphysics and moral philosophy. It was the framework within which the philosophically minded young Edwards would have to work or risk jeopardizing his covenant faith and heritage—something his intellectual training and family nurturing fortified him against.

In the final year of his graduate studies (1722), the recently converted Edwards surveyed the Enlightenment's intellectual landscape with a "new spiritual sense." With or without this sense he would have encountered the skeptical and even hostile intellectual current of many Enlightenment thinkers toward traditional, supernatural Christianity. To Edwards, and many like him, the threat to Christian orthodoxy from Enlightenment philosophers and unorthodox clergy went beyond the skeptical rationalization of the miracles of supernaturalism. At stake was the truth of the immediacy of God's activity, that is, His immanence and relevance.[1]

---

1. McDermott states that the most celebrated debates of the Enlightenment were "contests between rival portraits of God." "The real disagreement," he says, "was not about whether God existed, or whether or not

But having read Newton's published treatises and even after finding "more Satisfaction and Pleasure in studying [Locke], than the most greedy Miser,"[2] Edwards nonetheless concluded that the God of orthodox subordinate standards, such as the Westminster Confession and the Savoy Declaration, did not need to be redefined (let alone denied) to accommodate the changing intellectual tides of man. Yet, at the same time, he maintained that neither should the many supernatural themes of the Bible cause the Christian believer to repudiate the newfound discovery of an apparently mechanistic natural realm. Nor should the believer dispense with faith when pitted against the common sense of reason. Edwards was convinced that both the natural and supernatural could be compatibly affirmed.[3]

In his mind, the requisite change lay neither in the science of God nor in the physical sciences but in the prevailing perception of reality held by the church: a philosophical conception which he was convinced languished under the assault of Enlightenment reason armed with the tools of science, and could no longer maintain reasonable value in the hostile marketplace of ideas. He thought a spiritually informed conception of reality, which respected the findings of science and stood in awe of the God of Israel, could compatibly unite the increasingly polarized realms of historic Christianity and Enlightenment reason. The reconception that Edwards proposed was above all the product of a "new vision" of God, in which all things were entirely dependent upon God and God was immanently present in all things.

According to Edwards's new aesthetic and theocentric vision and the ontic, telic, and cosmic conclusions he draws from it, all created existences derive their being from God's "comprehension" of reality: for all reality is directly related to, encompassed by, and derived from, God Himself. For Edwards, the Enlightenment antithesis between the natural and the supernatural is false: the transcendent God of Scripture is an immanently relevant and necessary fact of spatiotemporal reality.

Through this perception of reality, where the "fullness" of the Divine Being extends into and in fact constitutes the ontic matrix of the created order, Edwards mediates between inflexible permanent actuality and progressive reality. God, for him, is intensely personal and immediately present in human affairs, thoughts, and time. To Edwards this was not only reasonable and apparent in Scripture, but also epistemologically justifiable by a philosophy of spiritual perception. Whereas Enlightenment rationalists tended to sever God from created reality and Baruch Spinoza naturalized God through his pantheism, Edwards proposes a middle way with his theory of spiritually perceiving God's "comprehensiveness."

This chapter argues that the "vision" of "God as God is in Himself" that coincided with Edwards's conversion experience significantly advanced his consideration of God's

---

belief in his existence was essential to healthy polity (nearly all believed that it was), but about the nature of goodness and justice—and, consequently, the nature of God" (*Confronts the Gods*, 17–18).

2. Hopkins, *Life and Character*, 3.

3. See *WJE* 16:355–56 and Anderson, "Editor's Introduction," *WJE* 6:8–23, 42–43. Jonathan Edwards's work with and within the parameters of Newtonian science has been well documented. See Faust, "Jonathan Edwards as a Scientist," 393–404; Hornberger, "The Effect of the New Science," 196–207.

direct relation to everything. That is, that his philosophy of the "spiritual sense" resulted in a doctrine of divine comprehensiveness. For Edwards, God's comprehension of reality meant more than omniscience; it also meant that God immediately envelops all existence. Upon further reflection he discovers a "theocentricity of ends" or metaphysics of finality. This suggested to him that God's immanent presence was purposed to specific ends and that reality itself was designed to attain those ends in every moment. God's subordinate ends were manifold but culminated in one "ultimate end" of consummate divine self-glorification.

Unlike Calvin and Luther, whose discussions on the being of God were conditioned by a fundamental rejection of speculation about "God in Himself" (*Deus apud se*) in favor of God in His revelation toward us (*Deus ergo nos*),[4] Edwards asserts that God revealed in spiritual encounter does not differ from God in Himself, and neither does that revelatory encounter eclipse or usurp Scripture, but rather confirms and merges with it.

According to his autobiographical *Personal Narrative* it was upon his conversion—the point at which Edwards received the celebrated "new sense"—at which he began to view and therefore contemplate reality anew. To be sure, Edwards was trained to contemplate reality with God at its center, but the challenges of Enlightenment made it difficult for him to conceive of God's interaction with the world in merely a traditionally confessional way. "Spiritual perception," however, brought about a different perspective on reality and his confessional faith. God was really more dynamically present than his theological heritage had articulated. God was at the center of not only world history and, of course, soteriology, but literally everything was pregnant with some spiritual aspect of God's ontological presence, theological purpose, and self-glorifying design, in a word, being as "excellence"— if only one could *sense* it. God-at-the-center-of-reality was articulated by God's comprehensiveness which, in turn, was later elucidated by dispositional concepts.

Edwards articulates God's comprehensiveness in two ways: in metaphysical terms of "being" and "excellency," and theologically. In this chapter we concentrate on the former.

Theological Borders

Edwards's intellectual endeavors in the direction of a philosophical reconception of the nature of reality were conditioned by three things in particular: (1) his Reformed theological heritage, which heavily emphasized the sovereignty of God, (2) the progressive intellectual climate of the Enlightenment, and (3) his conversion experience. Concerning the first of these, Edwards's theological instruction helped to train his mind to theoretically perceive the sovereign work of God in all the affairs of mankind. This, of course, did not necessitate a philosophical reconception of the nature of reality, but it did provide an overarching narrative by which events of the world could be interpreted: the metanarrative of God's glorification. This too became an integral tenet of his theological learning.

After young Edwards arrived at Yale College he was introduced to a wide array of Enlightenment thought: religious, scientific, and philosophical. He would either scrutinize or accommodate this "new learning" with the heritage of his Calvinistic creed. While

---

4. Weber, *Foundations of Dogmatics*, 1:405.

certain aspects of the creedal Calvinism would require rethinking in light of the new learning, yet his traditional faith could not permit an alteration to the biblical metanarrative. If God and His self-glorification were not at center, then the foundation of classical Christianity (according to Reformed symbolics) would be jeopardized.

The combination of Edwards's elementary training in Calvinistic thought and a shifting intellectual climate in Europe, which had left a profound impact upon Christian thinking in England and was now encroaching upon New England, challenged him to rethink the philosophical moorings of his theological heritage, while at the same time preserving the non-negotiable aspects of the doctrine of God and Reformed theocentric worldview that he owned as orthodox. However, these two factors alone were not enough to commit Edwards to a philosophical reconception of the nature of reality. It was only subsequent to his conversion that his thinking became radically theocentric *and* aesthetic. Edwards testified that this experience resulted in a new perspective on reality, which in turn facilitated the possibility of understanding all things in relation to the reality of God's all-comprehensive being.

By employing a typology of the pre- vs. post-conversion perspectives of Edwards, I do not intend to suggest a drastic dichotomy in his conviction about Reformed theology.[5] True, Edwards did confess to some reservations about certain Calvinistic doctrines prior to his conversion (e.g., the divine decrees), yet to say that his theology was not Reformed prior to that event would be untenable. Instead, I intend to accentuate a particular theme already present in his Reformed thought—theocentricity—and show how the "vision" acquired at his conversion (1) broadened and spiritualized his perspective on reality so as to connect all things to God's self-glorifying immanent reality, (2) brought about a doctrine of divine comprehensiveness, and (3) a regulative principle of *telic*-theocentrism, within his system.[6]

From Timothy Edwards's Preparatory School to Yale College

Jonathan Edwards's theological training began in his childhood home. The household which the Reverend Timothy Edwards managed assured that his children—ten daughters and son Jonathan—were thoroughly versed in the Westminster Confession, and, in particular, it's Shorter Catechism. If their indoctrination into confessional Calvinism's monergistic soteriology did not ensure the enthronement of God and His self-glorifying purposes in their minds, they also were submersed into a culture of church-life in which God seemed to encroach upon every aspect of their social and personal worlds.[7]

Through the catechism and mentoring of his father, Edwards learned the sovereignty of God in all the affairs of mankind. This was agreeable to the teaching of Calvin, Perkins,

---

5. The few surviving papers that antedate his conversion give no indication that his theology was anything but Reformed: there is no pre-conversion, anti-Reformed Jonathan Edwards and a post-conversion, Calvinistic Jonathan Edwards.

6. Chapters 3–5 develop points (2) and (3). Zakai likewise states that Jonathan Edwards's conversion was determinant for the way he views and resolves certain issues ("The Conversion of Jonathan Edwards," 127–38).

7. Tarbox, "Timothy Edwards," 256–74; Minkema, "The Edwardses," *passim*.

and the Westminster divines. His catechism's VIth chapter, "Of Creation," stated that, "It pleased God the Father, Son, and Holy Ghost, for the manifestation of the glory of his eternal power, wisdom, and goodness, in the beginning, to create, out of the nothing, the world, and all things therein whether visible or invisible." The providences of God made that distant activity local and daily. God was immanent in the world through ordinary means, secondary causes, positive decrees, and, of course, the Holy Spirit. Through these channels God sovereignly implemented His will. Puritan theology strove to balance the Scholastic tendency to reify the God of Israel with doctrines that made the Divine proximate. Though the desired effect was not always achieved, particularly in the seventeenth century when Reformed Scholasticism rose to prominence and Calvinistic sacramental theology gravitated toward Platonic dualism, nonetheless, a concerted effort was made to forge a livable theology accessible and relevant to all, in all situations.[8]

The small revivals that broke out in his father's parish of East Windsor, Connecticut left the younger Edwards with empirical evidence for God's sovereign handling of the souls of men and providential ordering of the universe. If there ever was any difficulty in Edwards seeing God present in, say, "the wondrous and curious works of the spider," there certainly was none when it came to the "remarkable stirring and pouring out of the Spirit of God" during times of revival.[9] In these ways, young Edwards was intellectually conditioned to link his environment and circumstances to the sovereign activity of God.

After training in his father's preparatory school, twelve-year-old Edwards entered the Connecticut Collegiate School (Yale College) in 1716. In New Haven, as at Harvard, instruction in Christian doctrine was part of the weekly curriculum. Chief pedagogical figures were the Reformed theologian Johannes Wollebius and Puritan divine William Ames, former pupil of William Perkins, all of whom emphasized God's predestination of man and terrestrial events for His own glory.[10] Edwards also was required to recite his Shorter Catechism weekly. This exercise appears to have reinforced his earlier doctrinal convictions and secured their retention throughout his life.[11] In addition to these catechetical rehearsals there was Bible reading, the attending of divine services, the recitation of sermons, and personal examinations. As his "Diary" and "Resolutions" reveal, Bible study and self-examinations were to become central elements in his devotional life following his conversion.

---

8. See Andre Biéler, *Social Humanism of Calvin* and Niebuhr, *Kingdom of God in America*.

9. Letter to Judge Paul Dudley, October 31, 1723; Letter to Mary Edwards, December 12, 1721 in *WJE* 16:41; 29.

10. William Haller, *Rise of Puritanism*, 83. Cf. Wallace Jr., *Puritans and Predestination*. Wollebius's *Compendium theologiae Christanae*, when translated into English (1626), became a popular textbook in Scotland and New England. Ames's *Medulla SS. theological* and *Theses logicae* were required texts at Yale in Jonathan Edwards's day. Perkins's famous work on predestination was "A Golden Chaine" (*The Workes of . . . William Perkins*, 1:9–116). All are listed in Jonathan Edwards's reading "Catalogue" (see *WJE* 26:131, 341–42, 429, 456).

11. In a letter to John Erskine (July 5, 1750), Jonathan Edwards (then age forty-eight) wrote: "As to my subscribing to the Westminster Confession, there would be no difficulty" (*WJE* 16:355)—a conviction he reiterated on several occasions.

Calvinistic religious instruction and exercises, then, did not stop with the commencement of his collegiate career, but were a vital part of it. Thus, from his youth throughout his New Haven sojourn, Edwards was trained in the art of acknowledging the sovereign and providential presence of God; so that, when he looked upon the wonders of God's creation he saw the "wisdom" and "exuberant goodness of the Creator."[12]

Following the donation of the so-called "Dummer Library," a catalogue of five hundred volumes given to Yale College in January 1713, the sleepy New England port town of New Haven became an intellectual center for scrutinizing the ideas of Europe, particularly Britain. It was through this collection that Edwards encountered Locke's *Essay*, Newton's *Principia Mathematica* and *Optics*, the works of Bacon and Descartes, Nicolas Malebranche's *Search after Truth*, and several works of the Cambridge Platonists, most notably those of Henry More and John Smith, who were to have an early and lasting influence on Edwards's thought.[13]

Yale Rector Timothy Cutler and tutors Samuel Johnson and Elisha Williams skillfully introduced to their pupils these intellectual innovations of Europe in a manner that complemented their theological system. The collection was sifted; cautions and warnings were issued about authors x and y, ideas p and q; while the neutral or positive portion of the Dummer Catalogue was harmonized with "orthodox" Christian thought, disseminated, and celebrated. Edwards and his classmates were then taught that the nomic regularity of the universe was agreeable with the immutability of God, its geometric calculability with divine cosmology, and so on. The more adventuresome and advanced students would independently learn that Malebranche helped preserve the viability of miracles as well as divine agency in causation through the doctrine of occasionalism, and that Locke, through his monumental analysis of human knowledge, helped in the assessment of the noetic effects of sin upon the intellectual powers of man. At least this is how the Yale trustees hoped the new learning would be employed. Caveats and catechesis were not mere formalities of procedure at Yale: they established the boundaries of truth in an age of growing skepticism, deism and atheism.[14]

Students were also made aware of the fact that many ministers and theologians, since the grand rise of humanism, had succumbed to the temptation to understand the Christian faith in light of the dogmas of the Enlightenment, rather than the Enlightenment in the light of the dogmas of the Christian faith. Accordingly, the centerpieces of seventeenth-century Scholastic theology represented in the Dummer Catalogue by the works of Stephen Charnock, John Edwards, Edward Stillingfleet, and others, were commended as fine blends of the strength of reason in the power of faith.[15] If theology had to be done

---

12. *WJE* 6:155. I am indebted to Iain H. Murray (*Jonathan Edwards*, 31) for the details of devotional life at Yale College.

13. Thuesen, "Editor's Introduction," *WJE* 26:2–14. See Patterson and Bryant, "List of Books Sent From England" (423–92), for an inventory of the Dummer collection. Cf. Stokely. "The Books Sent From England," 7–44. Anderson provides biographical information and discussion about the writers whose works in this collection are relevant to Jonathan Edwards ("Editor's Introduction," *WJE* 6:7–27). Cf. Miller, *New England Mind*, 95–124.

14. Smyth, "'New Philosophy,'" 242–60; Ellis, *New England Mind*.

15. Leslie, *Short and Easy Method with the Deists*, 6–11.

in the midst of the new learning, college authorities admonished, then it should be done not only conscious of the potential benefits of Enlightenment ideas but also their dubious nature. Either way, theology was always to be done with eminent respect to their confessional tradition. No exceptions.

We have every reason to believe that Edwards took this counsel seriously: his provincial upbringing in the East Windsor parsonage, catechetical instruction, and collegiate tutelage were effective. He imbibed the Enlightenment's rationalistic method, garnered their ideas, and yet was repulsed by the use of reason against historic Christianity. Particularly abhorrent to Edwards were not so much the Charles Blount and John Toland types, "professed infidels" who assailed the faith from without, but those who were wreaking havoc from within the halls of faith.[16] To be sure, Edwards considered Blount, Toland, Hobbes, Anthony Collins, and others, as "deistical" enemies of the faith,[17] but his chief worry was how men from within the church—influenced by those outside the church—were naturalizing his tradition's historic and supernatural faith. Leaders within the church who had become engaged with Enlightenment ideologies regarding revealed religion, particularly Christianity, whether they were in ecclesiastical office or academic chair had one of two options according to Edwards: they could either apostatize or combat Enlightenment religion and thereby strengthen and purify the house of faith. Edwards, of course, chose the latter.[18]

He first encountered "apostate clerics" the same way he met Locke and More—through the Dummer Catalogue, which harbored some of the dreaded heresies that were "plaguing" the British Isles. Numbered among the distrusted books were Daniel Whitby's *Discourse on the Five Points* and John Tillotson's *Sermons*.[19] Edwards read these and was scandalized. Samuel Johnson's 1715 warning that "the new philosophy would bring a new divinity"[20] came a half century too late for England, but in New England there was still hope that aspiring ministers, such as Edwards, would use the new learning to the advantage of orthodoxy.

A Failing Attempt at Enlightenment Methodology

While critical of heretical or dissonant ideas, young Edwards nonetheless remained in favor of the intellectual methods employed by Enlightenment thinkers, especially Anthony Ashley Cooper, the Third Earl of Shaftesbury. Edwards considered Shaftesbury's style and

---

16. *WJE* 9:432.

17. *Banner-Works* 2:479, 485, 496. Sullivan (*John Toland and the Deist Controversy*, 212–15) and McDermott (*Confronts the Gods*, 19–21) point out the historiographical problem of categorizing these men as "deists." Yet, notwithstanding the denials of "deism" by Blount, Toland, and Collins, we may accept the label as a general designation for those who, based on reason, "common sense," and nature, repudiate special revelation and divine immanence in favor of a naturalized religion and/or morality.

18. Letter to the Rev. Thomas Gillespie, September 4, 1747 in *WJE* 16:224–35.

19. Whitby's *Discourse on the Five Points*, along with Chubb's *A Collection of Tracts*, were the focus of Jonathan Edwards's sustained attack on Arminianism and deism in *Freedom of the Will*. Jonathan Edwards refutes Tillotson in "The Eternity of Hell Torments" (1739), and calls him a "great figure among the new fashioned divines."

20. Schneider, *Samuel Johnson*, 1:4. This is the Samuel Johnson of Stratford, Connecticut.

power of reasoning worthy of imitation,[21] though Shaftesbury was no friend to Reformed theology. Whether friend or foe to his faith, Edwards gleaned ideas and methods from a host of English, Scottish, and Continental minds, while striving to the best of his ability to rationally present a Christian worldview in consonance with Newtonian science. After all, the brightest and most able Christian thinkers rationally defended and promoted the faith. Of such were William Ames and Alexander Richardson, Charles Leslie, Richard Bentley, and the Dutch Calvinist logicians Franco Burgersdicius and Adrian Heereboord.[22] Even in New England, Cotton Mather undertook to show that philosophy and natural science were not enemies, but "mighty and wondrous incentives to religion."[23]

Edwards found the Cambridge Platonists particularly exemplary. While Francis Bacon drew a sharp distinction between reason and faith, Benjamin Whichcote critically replied that "reason is the voice of God."[24] Both Ralph Cudworth and Henry More joined the attack on Bacon, but concentrated their efforts refuting Hobbes's materialism. More, above all, took seriously the findings of the new science, contended against the materialism and mechanical determinations of Hobbes and the mechanistic pretensions of the Cartesians and, in return, received Edwards's admiration and imitation through a short essay entitled "Of Atoms." Although the Cambridge Platonists for the most part resisted Calvinism as dogmatic, irrational, and therefore opposed to the true interests of both religion and morality, yet their strong "sense of divinity" seemed to Edwards the most immediate testimony of reason. In his untested eyes the blend of a sincere defense of Christianity through a life of devotion armed with a confidence in *reason* was the most commendable approach for confessional Calvinism's engagement with Enlightenment thought.[25]

Young Edwards then thought, perhaps sophomorically, to make rational that which the "Enlightened world" and even the Cambridge Platonists opposed in Calvinism, namely the relation between God, morality, and creedal soteriology. With regard to God's operating in an "arbitrary" manner, he later confessed in his *Personal Narrative* that he, too, questioned and doubted the doctrines of predestination and absolute sovereignty.[26] At this time, however, he more comfortably followed the lead of Whichcote and his Cambridge disciples, who strenuously argued that God was essentially rational—like

---

21. "Rule of Style" no. 15 (of 21), cover of MS "Notes on Natural Science" (1722), Jonathan Edwards Collection.

22. See Richardson, *Providence and Precept*; Bentley, *Folly of Atheism* and *Remarks upon a late Discourse of free-thinking*; Heereboord, Ερμηνεια Logica.

23. Mather, *Christian Philosopher*, cited in Anderson, "Editor's Introduction," *WJE* 6:38.

24. Whichcote, *Moral and Religious Aphorisms*, 76.

25. Simon Patrick and Cudworth were also members of the Royal Society with More. Peter Sterry and Nathanael Culverwel, despite the latitudinarian beliefs they shared with the other Cambridge Platonists, were professed Calvinists. To be sure, "true religion" for Whichcote, Smith, More, Cudworth, etc., did not mean the same thing as what Jonathan Edwards meant by "true religion." Still, Jonathan Edwards did share in their enthusiasm for defending the existence of God, immortality and value of the human soul, the existence of the spirit activating the natural world, and finally, their emphasis upon the correspondence between the rational and divine. Cf. Weyer's biographical references in Weyer, *Die Cambridge Platonists*, 167–81.

26. "Personal Narrative" in *WJE* 16:791–92. Cf. "Miscellanies," no. 654, *WJE* 18:196.

man.²⁷ Edwards found in the Cambridge Platonists a suitable compromise with the spirit of the Enlightenment: since it is unreasonable to suppose God an irrational being (which is to say, God is a perfectly rational being), then "All God's methods of dealing with men [must be] most reasonable."²⁸ Thus, Christianity itself, as he was convinced of it within his tradition, must be reasonable and therefore, in the words of Henry More, "the deepest and choicest piece of philosophy."²⁹

Early attempts at a rational presentation of a presumably informed Christian worldview are evident in Edwards's scant pre-conversion writings. For instance, in his earliest extant sermon (late 1720?), Edwards places a repeated emphasis upon man as a "reasonable being" characterized by rational capacity. Conspicuously missing in this almost academic lecture are the accent on affections, the aesthetic vision of divine things, and a candid depiction of Calvinistic anthropology that habitually hallmark his later theology. Instead, the premium rests on rationality: "God always deals with men as reasonable creatures, and every [word] in the Scriptures speaks to us as such."³⁰

The prominence of reason and the absence of affections continue in his next two extant sermons. Probably drafted for purposes of candidating, the doctrines of depravity and hell torments surface in these showcase sermons. However, in *The Value of Salvation* (1721), he juxtaposes the body and corporeal beauty with the soul and spiritual things, *not* in a way that reflects his later Hutchensonian distinction between secondary (material) and primary (spiritual) beauty, but as a dichotomy. Likewise, the sermon *Wicked Men's Slavery to Sin* (1720) shares with other pre-conversion homilies an essential optimism in linking innate reason and religion, and, as Wilson Kimnach points out, "his insistence that sin is somehow beneath man, or a kind of morbidity, clearly indicates his exalted conception of man's potential for real virtue."³¹

The deficiency of the aesthetic and affectional dimensions of his post-conversion theology is therefore significant. In his attraction to arguments of "reasonableness" and rational methodology, Edwards attempts to present creedal Calvinism according to the rules and even ideas of the Enlightenment itself. Interestingly, he unwittingly sets reason over-against an ontologically grounded revelation. That is, he permits the knowledge of Christian revelation to be pried from its source—God—in which there was a necessity intrinsic in revelation to the real (i.e., God) to be founded upon something ineffably arbitrary, namely, a rational metaphysics. In accord with Jesuit philosophical theologian Francisco Suárez (1548–1617), Edwards suggests that one could recognize the positive fact of revealed truth (a biblical proposition), before assenting to it. No longer did revelation disclose God in His divine nature; instead, it concerns pieces of information that God has decided to impart, which even the spiritually unaltered mind is capable of fully comprehending. Accordingly, in these early sermons Edwards sounds as uncompromisingly innatist as the Cambridge Platonists: human reason has inherited immutable intellectual,

27. Whichcote, *Aphorisms*, 76. See Cragg, *Cambridge Platonists*, 11.
28. *Christian Happiness* (1720); *WJE* 10:300; *WJE* 14:167.
29. More, *Divine Dialogue*, 5.
30. *Christian Happiness* (1720), *WJE* 10:296.
31. *WJE* 10:338.

moral, and religious notions "sufficient in our sense," which when fêted depreciates other epistemological sources. For example, Edwards maintains in these sermons that the doctrines of final judgment, depravity, hell, and the immortality of the soul, are evidenced and can be appreciated *as* divine truths by the human reasoning of natural law.[32]

These early writings display Edwards's confidence that even his confessional theology (with the role of predestination diminished) could be argued and presented "according to reason." In his naïveté, he hardly offers a convincing presentation of his choice of Christian doctrines, let alone critically engages the ideas of the Enlightenment: instead, he only mimics its methods.

Perhaps the best example of this is his attempt to refute metaphysical materialism with an atomistic approach borrowed directly from Henry More. More stated that bodies were "impenetrable," "a perfect solidity" of "resistance" from annihilation. In "Of Atoms," so did Edwards. It would appear that Edwards's innovation lay in the claim that *God* was the power that causes infinite resistance, but More said it first.[33] One might even say that the God-centeredness present in this essay is altogether subservient to his "rational" agenda. This again would show the influence of the Cambridge Platonists upon Edwards. Their "*Appeal to the Naturall faculties of the Minde of man, whether there be not a God*" and Edwards's proposed "A Rational Account of the Main Doctrines of the Christian Religion Attempted" hardly would appear distinguishable in terms of methodology and emphasis.[34] Not that Edwards distances himself from the parameters of his theological tradition (save for his private cavils over predestination) or aligns himself with Enlightenment religion, it is just that at this point he does not have a clear vision of God-at-the-center-of-reality other than soteriologically, and even that only with reservations. Hence, the total absence of the aesthetic language of "excellency," "sweetness," "beauty," as well as the distinguishing full theocentric indicators "glory," "fitness," and "arbitrary" which, after this period, are used to explain the divinity of not just the Christian religion but also morality, existence, and the natural order itself.

Although his studies in the arts at Yale would have made correlations to God's presence or design or beauty, yet, at this time, Edwards seems to indicate an inability to intuitively apprehend such realities without the tools of logic and rational induction. Later for him the arts, sciences, and philosophy ideally would have no separate status from theology: as they become more perfect, he would argue, they "issue in divinity, and coincide with it, and appear to be a part of it"[35] within the technometria of God's creation. At this time, however, save for "Of Atoms," his writings in the natural sciences, along with his philosophical composition "Of the Prejudices of Imagination," make no reference to God whatsoever. Even the original draft of the "Spider letter" (properly, "Of Insects") contains

---

32. *Importance of a Future State* (1722), WJE 10:360.

33. More, *Antidote Against Atheism*. To be fair, Jonathan Edwards did press the conclusion further than More by saying that God was therefore "*Ens Entium*."

34. Full title of More's *Antidote*; WJE 6:396.

35. WJE 6:397.

only two token corollaries in which God, almost as an afterthought, is tangentially acknowledged and prosaically referred to as "the Creator."[36]

Thus, while Edwards found the rational argumentation and methodological presentation agreeable, and Enlightenment religion "the opposition that Satan has made against the Reformation," yet his writings prior to the spring of 1721 and the testimony of his *Personal Narrative* reveal that he did not possess that all-encompassing theocentric and spiritual worldview "by which I was brought to those new dispositions, and that new sense of things, that I have since had." He admitted that his profession of Christianity prior to his conversion, while theologically informed, was only theoretical. Later he would pejoratively call this type of engagement with religion "notional" or "speculative," due to an inability to "spiritually perceive" the divinity and reality of the truths of Scripture and God's presence in the world.

∼

Prior to his conversion experience Edwards offers no new insights to any field, much less philosophy or theology. Although he desired to address the heterodoxical innovations entering the Christian religion by Enlightenment proposals and, perhaps, took an initial step toward that goal with the composition "Of Atoms," yet he could not think of any other way to do so while taking advantage of the "new learning" and remaining true to his theological heritage other than by arguing for the observable and innate reasonableness of Christianity.

Once he began to have "a new kind of apprehensions and ideas" of God and His glory, in which his "sense of divine things gradually increased," then he began to interpret reality in light of the presence of "divine glory" in "everything."[37] To be sure, God-at-the-center-of-reality was essential to his understanding the world, but a certain dynamic element about that reality hitherto failed to resonate with him, namely a sensible vision of it. And without that, the Christian religion was for him but cerebral.

For whatever other intangible reasons, Edwards explains that it was the pivotal event of his conversion that engendered a "new spiritual sense," which, in turn, harnessed his confessional theology and enthusiasm/abhorrence for Enlightenment reason/ideas and brought about a shift in perspective and theological emphasis. In turn, the alteration of his worldview affected a shift in philosophical categories that would have far-reaching implications upon his interpretation of reality over-against the unorthodox innovations of the Enlightenment.

---

36. As Anderson notes, the practice of making charitable inferences to the providential or creative involvement of God in natural phenomena by scientists and scientific writers was commonplace in Jonathan Edwards's day ("Editor's Introduction," *WJE* 6:48). It would not have been unusual for Jonathan Edwards to add such corollaries. My point is that Jonathan Edwards's earliest "religious" corollaries may have been out of respect to convention, rather than intentional theological or teleological improvements. The original composition of the "Spider Letter" occurred at Yale around 1719/1720, and was later drafted in Jonathan Edwards's "public" hand (1723) in hope of publication.

37. *Sermon Twenty-Four*, *WJE* 9:432; "Personal Narrative" in *WJE* 16:790.

A *Personal Narrative* of the Vision of God

> The first instance that I remember of that sort of inward, sweet delight in God and divine things that I have lived much in since, was on reading those words [1Tim 1:17] "Now into the King eternal, immortal, invisible, the only wise God, be honour and glory for ever and ever, Amen." As I read the words, there came into my soul, and was as it were diffused through it, a sense of the glory of the Divine Being; a new sense, quite different from any think I ever experienced before.
>
> —*Personal Narrative*

A Personal Narrative of the Vision of God

JONATHAN EDWARDS DATES HIS OWN CONVERSION TO "ABOUT A YEAR AND A HALF" before August 1722, which we can narrow to May or June 1721.[1] His *Personal Narrative* does not reveal the exact process of his conversion, not because he wrote it almost twenty years after from the event, but because he consciously intended to distance himself from the Puritan "step-model" conversion.[2] According to that "preparationist" model, he need only chart his progress from one standardized element of subjective phenomena to another (e.g., conviction by "legal fear," terrors leading to contrition, humiliation, etc.), in order to ascertain the moment the final step of preparation yielded in regeneration. Such steps, however, were conspicuously missing from his experience.[3]

To be sure, he remained part of a Calvinist tradition that had long occupied itself with analysis of the conversion experience, and had inherited the relatively conventional

---

1. None of Jonathan Edwards's personal letters prior to May/June 1721 indicate anything of this momentous personal event. His "Diary" began Dec. 18, 1722.

2. Claghorn describes the "Personal Narrative" as Jonathan Edwards's "extended historical account of his own spiritual journey [which] may have been written in response to a request from his future son-in-law Aaron Burr" in Dec. 1740 (*WJE* 16:747). The structured "Personal Narrative" is reflective of the genre of didactic Puritan autobiographies, and contrasts the pessimistic self-examinations indicative of his "Diary," again, characteristic of its literary genre. See Shea, "Art and Instruction of Jonathan Edwards's *Personal Narrative*," 299–311; and Johnson, "Jonathan Edwards's 'Sweet Conjunction,'" 270–81.

3. "Diary" in *WJE* 16:759. Kimnach adds, "Indeed, the extent of the 'Diary' suggests that Edwards may have actually begun his diary in order to deal with the problem [of his atypical conversion]" (*WJE* 10:269). This is not to deny that Jonathan Edwards had and maintained a doctrine of "preparation"; he certainly did. It was, however, subordinate to his thoughts concerning God's programmatic pattern of effecting redemption. See chapter 13, where I give this assertion further attention.

scheme of conversion by steps.⁴ But almost immediately after his atypical conversion Edwards became troubled by the determined parameters of the "step" or "phasing" model. His conversion was more of an *event*, or in his own words, "a *delightful* conviction" of the "sense of divinity" of the Christian religion, rather than a traceable transition from one typical stage to another. He attributed the alteration in his attitude toward the sovereignty of God and the reality of divine things not to a predicable passing from one phase to the next, but a sudden "sense of the glory of the divine being; a new sense, quite different from anything I ever experienced before."⁵

His experience eclipsed the merely emotional and fleeting subjective sensations of fear or joy; it converged on a conscious "new sense" of "the *supreme holy beauty* and comeliness of divine things, as they are in themselves, or in their own nature."⁶ Hence, for Edwards, conversion was more than the emotional outworkings of psychologized English and New England morphologies of conversion, it was also intellectually engaging—a dynamic, even mystical conjunction of the affections *and* the understanding.

As Edwards contemplated in his "Miscellanies" what he experienced on that spring day and what caused his "sense of divine things" to "gradually increase," he became assured of the instantaneousness of justification and regeneration.⁷ The Holy Spirit did not seep into the soul, but overtook it by laying hold of the mind and becoming intellectually and inclinationally its greatest apparent good.⁸ The step-model of conversion seemed to Edwards too banal, too insipid, and entirely too anthropocentric. Nor was it his experience of things. Still, he never abandoned the idea of preparation. As he once stated, "As to preparatory work before conversion, there is undoubtedly always, except in very extraordinary cases, such a thing."⁹ He did, however, make several important clarifications to his employment of the doctrine.¹⁰ But with regard to his own conversion, there was no doubt: it was a radical, definitive, and instantaneous renovation of the soul, wrought entirely by God Himself.

---

4. See Pettit, *Heart Prepared* and Stoever, "A Faire and Easie Way to Heaven." Both Timothy Edwards, Jonathan Edwards's maternal grandfather, Solomon Stoddard, were notable proponents of preparationism and its role in the step-model of conversion (see Timothy Edwards's MS sermon on Cant. 4:16 [Beinecke Library, Yale University], where he cites Stoddard's *Treatise Concerning Conversion*; and Stoddard, *Defects of Preachers Reproved*). Cf. Kimnach, "Preface to the New York Period," *WJE* 10:271–72. Minkema offers the most complete analysis of Timothy Edwards's pastorate and theory of conversion in "The Edwardses."

5. "Personal Narrative" in *WJE* 16:792. Jonathan Edwards treats the adjustment to the affections concerning "hard" doctrines in "Miscellanies," no. 866, *WJE* 20:107.

6. *True Grace Distinguished from the Experience of Devils* (1752), Banner-Works 2:48.

7. "Personal Narrative" in *WJE* 16:793. See "Miscellanies," no. *l*, *WJE* 13:168–69.

8. "Miscellanies," no. 284, *WJE* 12:380–81.

9. "Miscellanies," no. *r*, *WJE* 13:173. "Extraordinary cases," e.g., infant conversions.

10. See chapter 13, where I discuss the distinction he makes between autonomous preparation (the ability of a sinner to advance himself, in an unassisted manner, to the threshold of salvation—a possibility that Jonathan Edwards rejects) and heteronomous preparation (the idea of a sinner prepared by God for salvation) and a third kind taught by Jonathan Edwards, in which a sinner exposes himself to the "forum" of salvation.

"New Kind of Apprehensions"

Upon the event of his conversion, Edwards intuitively sensed that salvation was not so much about the self as it was about Christ's "excellencies" and the manifestation of divine glory: "From about that time, I began to have a new kind of apprehensions and ideas of Christ, and the work of redemption, and the glorious way of salvation by him. I had an inward sense of these things . . . and my soul was lead away in pleasant views and contemplations of them."[11]

His problem did not chiefly rest with the *manner* of preparatory exercises, though he would question some of them, but with the *structure* and *content* of conversion itself.[12] Rather than describe the initial and subsequent occurrences of faith in dated experimental predestinarian terms of movements of both the intellect and will, Edwards, in rejecting the subordination of one faculty to another, reintroduced the familiar Puritan language of "inward spiritual sense" or "sense of the heart."[13] For Edwards, the "sense of the heart" is a spiritual monocratic principle, inseparable yet distinguishable from the soulish faculties of man. It consists of an appreciative intellect, a willing disposition, and affectional movements of the soul toward God in Jesus Christ. Conversion, then, marks the initial transition from a theoretical, abstract, and conditional understanding of Christian theocentrism to an authentic, progressive, and lively "sense" that the propositional doctrines of soteriology are indeed an experientially agreeable, beautiful, and credible, reality.

The spiritual sense gained in conversion conveys to the soul of man "divine light." This spiritual illumination makes "divine things," such as the person and work of Christ, God's sovereignty in salvation, and the whole administration of redemption, "appear excellent, beautiful, glorious, which [it] did not when the soul was of another spirit."[14]

In Edwards, conversion affects all the distinguishable faculties of the soul through such coordination that there can be "no clear distinction between the two faculties of understanding and will, as acting distinctly and separately in this matter."[15] Thus, from his conversion onward, he tends to speak of the concerted "man" (mind). This corresponds with his trinitarian formulations and dichotomous anthropological arrangement. He agrees with both Calvin and Locke in regarding as altogether improper the tripartite distinction of the reason, will, and appetites in traditional psychology.[16] Hence, while using the fashionable language of distinct faculties of the mind, Edwards circumspectly denies the conception of their independence as distinct human powers. In this he again was not

---

11. "Personal Narrative" in *WJE* 16:793.

12. "Diary" and "Personal Narrative" in *WJE* 16:759, 791.

13. See Greenham, *Workes of Richard Greenham*, 77–123; Perkins, *Clovd of Faithfull Witnesses*, v.7 "Noah's faith." The language and idea of "divine light" and "sense of the heart" was prevalent among Pietists and the Cambridge Platonists. Jonathan Edwards would have encountered their usage in figures like Perkins, but also John Smith, whose *Select Discourses* in many places anticipate the terminology, phrasing, and concepts of Jonathan Edwards's *Religious Affections* (1746). *Select Discourses* was donated by Isaac Newton to the Dummer Collection and would have been available to Jonathan Edwards at Yale College.

14. "Miscellanies," no. 397, *WJE* 13:462–63.

15. *WJE* 2:272. Elsewhere he states, "How the Scriptures are ignorant of the philosophic distinction of the understanding and the will" ("The Mind," no. 14, *WJE* 6:389).

16. See Calvin's *Institutes*, I.5.9–14, III.2.7–8, and Locke's *Essay*, bk. I.

unlike Calvin or Locke, for all three oppose the assumption that faculties are distinct entities rather than different abilities or functions of a unitary mind. For Edwards, faculties are properties of the soul, and the soul is one.[17]

However, if a situation deemed it expedient, Edwards would explain that man is bipartite, not just in his biblically created state (body and soul), but also in the basic configuration of the soul. He would employ a traditional medieval distinction between the will and understanding, with no distinction between desire and will or the will and the affections.[18] Thus, when speaking of the particular exercises of the mind he is wont to adopt the dichotomy of soul characteristic of Calvinism—understanding and will; emotions are subsumed under the will. Such an arrangement of the faculties conveniently served his 1754 diatribe against the Arminians. The will could not be determined by the emotions, he argued, because they were different sides of the same coin. The determination of the will must be considered in light of its integrated relation to the understanding.[19]

Again, the distinctions between the faculties are not ultimate for Edwards; they are but useful conventions of pedagogy. For example, although he conceives of the powers or faculties of man as an "interpenetrating unity" (to use Conrad Cherry's terminology), yet in *The Freedom of the Will*, for example, he regularly retains a key distinction between understanding and will when underscoring the difference between a person's "merely notional understanding" or "speculative knowledge" and that person being "in some way inclined" or "sensible" either by attraction (agreeableness) or aversion (disagreeableness) to an object, option, or proposition. However, the distinction is not absolute. The difference between notional-understanding/speculative-knowledge and affectional-knowledge is not really between the faculties: the affections are inescapably active in abstract ratiocination. For example, one's mind could find the abstraction $4^3=64$ agreeable, pleasing. Likewise, the rational mind partakes in an evaluative judgment of that to which the will passionately inclines. Instead, the difference respects the type of knowledge one possesses of a given object, option, or proposition—whether accurate or not, and whether the affections included in that knowledge correspond to the reality conceived; that is, whether they correspond to *God's* conception of (spiritual) reality. This distinction is particularly important when discussing the noetic mind and conversion.

In conversion, the act of faith does not consist of distinctly isolated movements of intellect and will, consent, and volitional motion (as it did for Thomas Aquinas); for, as Cherry states, Edwards understood them as a pervaded whole.[20] The idea of "trusting" in

---

17. For a commendable assessment of Jonathan Edwards's holistic concept of the self, see Smith, "Editor's Introduction," *WJE* 2:11–15.

18. *WJE* 2:97. Jonathan Edwards adds that affections "are no other than the more vigorous and sensible exercises of the inclination and will of the soul" (96). Affections, then, are the intensifications of dispositions of "agreeableness" or "disagreeableness" in choosing. Smith rightly explains that Jonathan Edwards's usage of "affections" can be synonymous with "emotions" if only understood to mean a felt or "sensed" response to an "object, event, or situation that is called forth by an *understanding* of the nature of the object" (Smith, *Puritan, Preacher, Philosopher*, 1992, 33).

19. See *WJE* 1. Yet, this distinction did not tend to subordinate the understanding to feelings, as Miller and Aldridge contend (Miller, *Jonathan Edwards*, 184; Aldridge, *Jonathan Edwards*, 22).

20. Cherry, *Reappraisal*, 17.

the converting act of faith, then, includes in its very nature a judgment regarding the *reality* of its object, a forensic notion of "consent" to that object as "good, eligible or desirable," dependence, hope, and a posture of servitude on the basis of the object.[21] What is more, his Calvinian notion of trust also includes an affectional dimension that corresponds to an aesthetic factor, namely, the "beauty" or "excellence" of the object. The object, of course, is Jesus Christ, the Son of God.[22]

In no way, therefore, does Edwards limit his understanding of faith to merely a special kind of relation characterized by trust, commitment, obedience, etc. To do so would have categorized his notion of faith as merely existential. But something within and of faith must be understood; it must have a cognitive, intellectual dimension—the cognition of its object's *beautiful reality* or, which is to say the same thing, "beautiful being."[23] Affectional faith is, therefore, not abjectly mystical; rather, it possesses aesthetic philosophical objectivity. For this reason the explanatory distinctions between "faculties and powers" become obstructive and must be abandoned.[24]

The whole conversion process can also be explained in trinitarian theological terms: God the Father's perfect idea of His Self (viz., the Son crucified and resurrected) must be known and loved (corresponding to the Spirit) *ad extra* as He is *ad intra*; that is, in a fashion worthy and identifiable with Himself. In faith, then, the powers of intellect and will, of knowing and loving that beautiful reality—the Father through the Son in the Spirit—become one just as God is One: the various movements of the unified consciousness in the act of faith are not distinct acts but are different modes of the same act.[25] When a person possesses faith in God they know Him as beautiful in Jesus Christ and love that beauty in the Spirit. Thus, for Edwards, conversion is the moment when the mind perceives the gospel's object as irresistibly beautiful and lays hold of that object by responding in faith.

Significantly, then, "the spiritual sense" is an effect in and of a singular *mind*, not this or that faculty. Likewise, the result of conversion occurs not in terms of a domino effect, but a radical, pervasive, and instantaneous alteration of the collective soul.[26]

The Spiritual Sense as "New Simple Idea"

From the start Edwards struggles in his efforts to convey the idea of spiritual sensibilities. He admits on more than one occasion that it is not only a challenging idea conceptually, but even more difficult to encapsulate in language. His attempts to better explicate the nature of conversion and its end product—spiritual sensibilities—continued for decades. In this respect, his later works defending revival may be seen as a collective explanation of his views on these issues.

---

21. "Observations Concerning Faith" in Austin, *Works of President Edwards*, 2:621; "Miscellanies," no. 568, *WJE* 18:105.
22. "Miscellanies," no. 108, *WJE* 12:278–80. Cf. "The Mind," no.1, *WJE* 6:332–38.
23. See "Beauty of the World" and "The Mind," no. 45 in *WJE* 6:305–6; 362–65 respectively.
24. Cherry, *Reappraisal*, 16–18.
25. As discussed in Cherry, *Reappraisal*, 12–24.
26. "Miscellanies," no. 379, *WJE* 13:448–50.

In one early attempt, he resorts to ideas in Locke's *Essay*, particularly Locke's process of collating knowledge into simple and complex ideas. In the end Edwards retains the empiricist's terminology of ideas, but alters his usage of new simple ideas and largely discards the theory of complex ideas. Locke's view that experience produces ideas, which are the immediate objects of thought, led him to adopt a causal or representative view of human knowledge. In perception, said Locke, persons are not directly or immediately aware of physical objects. Instead, they are directly aware of the ideas that objects "cause" and which "represent" the objects in their understanding or consciousness. Further, once a person receives some "new simple idea," it becomes almost altogether incommunicable, a sort of "tacit" spiritual knowledge (to adapt a Polanyian concept). One certainly could not repeat (better, reproduce) it through language. Essentially, the experience and the content of a "new simple idea" are individualized. The Lockean doctrine of knowledge by means of *ideas* that are causally connected with but only representations of objects distinct from the mind intrigued Edwards with respect to explaining the "new spiritual sense."

Outside of "Miscellanies" no. 123, the "new simple idea" is not so concisely defined in Edwards. Neither has there been any degree of unanimity among scholars on his precise meaning and usage of the term. Nonetheless there is conformity that the notion of the "new simple idea" corresponds with his writings on the "sense of the heart." Perry Miller initiated the uniform recognition of the "new simple idea" with Edwards's teaching on the "new" or "spiritual sense," or "sense of the heart," and its importance in his thought, calling it "the heart of Edwards' metaphysics."[27]

There is a sense, however, in which Edwards's usage of the Lockean "new simple idea" is epistemologically misleading. For Locke, it is a straightforward increase of knowledge not previously added, but for Edwards it means a new input and interpretation of that knowledge *and*, in its larger context, a *re*interpretation of associated prior knowledge. We may use Locke's example of a pineapple to illustrate: both Locke and Edwards taste it and gain some "new" idea; but Edwards gets something more out of it: an inimitable input that intuitively places "pineapple" into the larger context of mental reality. Whether he has previous knowledge of "pineapple" or engages it for the first time, its taste possesses meaning for him that extends beyond the simple idea of "the taste of pineapple." Likewise, the input he gains from tasting pineapple is interpreted so as to include spiritual, mental, and moral dimensions of reality. The input of its taste, though empirically the same as Locke's, meets a different interpretation. The "new spiritual sense," therefore, also functions like a template—an interpretive framework by which the mind processes reality. So while agents A and B (B possessing the spiritual sense) have equal access to phenomena x, A perceives x as x and interprets it as x, yet B perceives x as $\{x\}$ and interprets it as such.[28] Edwards's analogy of the "sweetness of honey" attempts to demonstrate both the newness of input and interpretation:

---

27. Miller, "Jonathan Edwards on the Sense of the Heart," 124.

28. Gilbert Ryle approximated this in his attempt to express the distinction between knowing-*how* and knowing-*that* (*Concept of Mind*, 25–61).

> [I]n gracious exercises and affections which are wrought in the minds of the saints, through the saving influences of the Spirit of God, there is a new inward perception or sensation of their minds . . . and there is, as it were, a new spiritual sense that the mind has, or principle of new kind of perception or spiritual sensation, which is in its whole nature different from any former kind of sensation of the mind, as tasting is diverse from any of the others senses; and something is perceived by a true saint, in the exercises of this new sense of mind, in spiritual and divine things, as entirely diverse from anything that is perceived in them, by natural men, as the sweet taste of honey is diverse from the ideas men get of honey by only looking on it, and feeling it.[29]

While this illustration is helpful in explaining that the "new spiritual sense" facilitates new input and interpretation, yet it stands clear that the "new simple idea" itself is only an *analogy* of sorts for Edwards: hence the proviso "as it were" and the concept's ultimate failure to sufficiently represent the idea.

Understanding Edwards's "new simple idea" not as a definitive expression or designation of the "new spiritual sense" but analogous to the content and nature of the "sense of the heart" may not only account for the ambiguity of the concept but the failure of interpreters to agree on his meaning and usage.[30]

Perry Miller, among others, fails to appreciate the "sense of the heart" as a sort of analogy and, by closely associating Edwards's thought with Locke's "way of ideas" (in which all mental conceptions originate in sense experience), interprets the Edwardsean experience of divine grace—whether initially or subsequent to conversion—as a kind of sensation. He explains that, although for Edwards, "Conversion is a perception, a kind of apprehension derived exactly as Locke said mankind gets all simple ideas, out of natural sensory experience," yet in the new sense, "there is nothing transcendental; it is rather a sensuous appreciation of the total situation." The "sense of the heart," or conviction of salvation, or spiritual things is merely a succeeding epistemological stage that "depends on and presumes the first." According to Miller, "the supernatural effect thus becomes, in Edwards's vision of the cosmos, integrated 'naturally and immediately' in nature."[31]

Miller denies that there is something really *new* about the "input"; indeed, that there is a different input whatsoever. Instead, there is only a contrived, passional interpretation (affected by Edwards's "rhetoric of sensation") *about* conventional input.[32] Because Miller consciously analyzes Edwards in the shadow of Locke, he explains Edwards's "new simple

---

29. *WJE* 2:205–6.

30. The "new simple idea" as a kind of analogy is further evidenced by Jonathan Edwards's belief that all men have some idea of God, albeit in a vague, perverted and suppressed way. The ideas that come with spiritual regeneration cannot be, in the most absolute sense, unconditionally and perfectly "new."

31. Miller, *Jonathan Edwards*, 139; "Jonathan Edwards on the Sense of the Heart," 127–28.

32. Similarly, John Hick states that there is no new or substantially different input for the Christian, just a different interpretation about shared input ("Non-Absoluteness of Christianity," 23ff). On the "rhetoric of sensation": Miller presents the idea that due to Locke's nominalist separation of words from things themselves, Jonathan Edwards developed a "rhetoric of sensation" that linked words of judgment and feeling to ideas with the intent of establishing an inseparability of idea and emotion ("The Rhetoric of Sensation" in Miller, *Errand into the Wilderness*, 167–83). Thus, for Miller, Jonathan Edwards's "rhetoric of sensation" facilitates a more ready expression of tacit knowledge.

idea" merely as a sensationalized form of Locke's idea and therefore ignores the fact that Edwards found their basic conceptions analogous not homogeneous. It is no surprise, then, that Miller's perspective neglects Edwards's insistence on *God's* immediate presence to mind for conversion, let alone a dispositional *in-*generating of the Holy Spirit.

Through an encounter with God, the individual acquires *new* supernatural knowledge that was previously unattainable through the senses or any other means. Neither reason nor empirical sense experience can establish spiritual sensibilities: they are categorically different.[33] This is because spiritual illumination has a *supernatural* epistemic quality: it is *revelatory*. Michael J. McClymond explains that the revelatory nature of spiritual illumination "does not merely 'enlarge' natural reason but transcends it," conferring some new input which the human mind could never attain "by its own resources."[34] Man is unable to independently conceive or create a new spiritual sense. Such powers are "supernatural and reserved for God" alone.[35] So, when Edwards develops his "sense of the heart" and identifies it with Locke's simple idea, he claims by analogy that only God could impart such a "sense" in the soul.

The new sense is epistemic in nature: it conveys information about God. The kind of information it conveys is not, strictly speaking, mystical or charismatic, but aesthetic, cognitive, and informative. One should not, however, restrict its input to only incorporeal subject matter; for when empirical phenomena are *spiritually perceived* they undergo re-interpretation by a distinctly religious hermeneutic to be sensibly perceived *as* illuminant.

The Spiritual Sense as Epistemic Principle

Of the wide scope of material written on Edwards's "new spiritual sense," McClymond's current exposition emerges as the most useful analysis of its epistemological dimension. He clarifies our understanding of the spiritual sense by delineating its interrelated elements: content, mode, and sensibility.

First, the *content* of perception is divine or spiritual "excellency," (also designated "holiness," "beauty," or "amiability"). Spiritual perception of God must be "full," according to McClymond, and include God's majesty and mercy, glory and excellence, wrath and love, justice and forgiveness.[36] Subjectively, spiritual perception confers an immediate certainty, yet still possesses objectivity—the intellectual certitude of the believer's spiritual perception transcends any certitude contrived by human reasoning about God. As Edwards writes: "The gospel of the blessed God don't go abroad begging for its evidence . . . it has its highest and most proper evidence in itself." Thus, "The first objective ground of gracious affections," he claims, "is the transcendently excellent and amiable nature of divine things, *as they are in themselves*; and not any conceived relation they bear to self, or self-interest."[37] Despite his pervasive interest in the human affections, Edwards

---

33. *WJE* 2:206.
34. McClymond, *Encounters with God*, 16.
35. Ibid.
36. Ibid., 18. "Personal Narrative" in *WJE* 16:792–95.
37. *WJE* 2:240, 307. Italics added.

nonetheless insists that the spiritual sense is an appropriate human response to *God as God is in Himself*.[38] Edwards neither abandons nor neglects human religious sensitivity or divine objectivity when unfolding his theory of spiritual sense, but rather, as McClymond writes, "The subjective and objective aspects of religious experience come together in the notion of spiritual perception."[39]

Secondly, the *mode* of perception is the "divine and supernatural light," operating in and alongside the unified human consciousness. One of McClymond's insights states that the subjective correlate to the encounter or revelatory manifestation is *perception*. Since an encounter with God is a spiritual event, then the corresponding perception must be spiritual. Here Edwards's spiritual epistemology discloses its relation to his early idealism: if God's glory is to "exist in emanation," then it must be perceived within the realm of its manifestation in order for it to be "real" in *that* realm. In Edwards, "There is no glory without perception, and the perception God intended is surely as much *in* the person that is the subject of the work, as any."[40] In a converting encounter with God the mind becomes spiritually perceptive, while at the same time God manifests His glory through that perception.

And lastly, the *sensibility* of perception is the "spiritual sense" or "new sense," whose essence consists of "delight," "agreeableness," or, especially, "consent in God."[41]

These three aspects of the new sense are important to Edwards to distinguish the regenerate mind from the unregenerate. The difference between the notional appreciation of the unregenerate and the spiritual appreciation of the regenerate lies in the sensible perception of the divine "excellency" and "reality" of propositions specially revealed in Scripture.

Prior to a converting encounter the unregenerate may rationally know such propositions, but their affections will not correspond ("consent") to the beauty or reality of them. The unregenerate finds these objective spiritual truths "disagreeable" and fictitious. On the other hand, spiritual perception, when either initiated in the divine encounter or subsequently exercised, intuitively apprehends *with* consent (read: "love" according to "The Mind," nos. 1 and 45) the aesthetic dynamic and reality, both experientially and propositionally. This is to say, the direct object of spiritual perception is spiritual beauty; the which, when consentingly apprehended, is perceived to be *spiritual*. Meanwhile, the indirect objects in this equation are spiritual facts or truths simultaneously apprehended as the counterpart of spiritual beauty.[42]

∽

---

38. McClymond, *Encounters with God*, 16.
39. Ibid. Cf. Wainwright, *Reason and the Heart*, 26–30.
40. "Miscellanies," no. 354, *WJE* 13:428.
41. McClymond, *Encounters with God*, 17–22.
42. Wainwright, *Reason and the Heart*, 30. See "Miscellanies," no. 123, *WJE* 13:286–87.

The acquisition of spiritual perception through regeneration carries with it a sort of certainty of faith that is different from reason and yet such a belief may be altogether agreeable to reason and the "exactest rules" of philosophy, according to Edwards.

Spiritual perception or awareness is *experiential* in the way it contrasts merely discursive thinking about God. The spiritual sense that Edwards labors to describe, writes Schafer, "sees and feels in its object, in the experience itself, such marks of the divine as to produce an intuitive certainty that the object of faith and devotion is indeed the Deity."[43] As McClymond explains, in the revelatory encounter with God the unified consciousness intuitively takes it that God has been *presented*, or *given* to its unified consciousness. Edwards goes beyond simply transposing the meaning and terminology of Locke's "way of ideas" for the purpose of epistemologically defending and justifying his own religious experience.[44] Indeed, the "new spiritual sense" as "new simple idea" is the mental experience of a new kind of knowledge, a distinctly spiritual knowledge of "spiritual beauty" or "excellency" or, correspondingly, God as God is in Himself. In short, the acquisition of the spiritual sense functions for Edwards as the epistemological gateway to an authentic (spiritual) and perspectival theocentrism.

Joshua Moody comments that it is easy to see why Edwards was so confident in his Great Awakening sermons and treatises, that the "new sense" could be used as a sign of an operation of God's Spirit and a reliable mark of "true religion."[45] Apologetically, it was to offer a subtle, yet powerful epistemological line of reasoning for the validity of Christian revelation and the converting and reviving work of the Spirit, which, in turn, left "Old Light" opponents like Charles Chauncy confused but proponents of supernatural regeneration and spiritual revivals appreciative for centuries to follow.[46]

The Spiritual Sense: An Ontological Principle

Ultimately, however, the new spiritual sense is the consequence of a spiritual union, a real *ontological* union with Christ through the Third Person of the Trinity.[47] Thus, it is the Holy Spirit who effectively communicates the dynamic idea of spiritual reality to the consciousness of the believer. Edwards does not explain this idea as the addition of any new faculty or so-called "sixth sense," but in terms of a "new disposition."[48] This assertion rests, however, upon the metaphysical principles of his independently developed idealism.

---

43. Schafer, "Editor's Introduction," *WJE* 13:44.

44. In fact, Jonathan Edwards distances himself from Locke by changing Locke's original usage of "complex idea" (see especially "Miscellanies," no. *aa*, *WJE* 13:177) and conditioning the "new simple idea" according to the principles of his own independently developed idealism. Cf. Locke, *Essay* II, xii.

45. Moody, *Jonathan Edwards and the Enlightenment*, chap 2. Jonathan Edwards's "Diary" and "Personal Narrative" also served as outlets to explain and defend his view of conversion and sanctification. The treatises *Religious Affections* and *Distinguishing Marks* especially explain the significance of affectional religion for God's glorification.

46. See Goen, "Editor's Introduction," *WJE* 4:1–95.

47. "Miscellanies," nos. *bb* and *ff*, *WJE* 13:178, 183.

48. *WJE* 2:206. David Lyttle, James Hoopes, and Paul Helm entertain the idea that Jonathan Edwards's spiritual sense may be a "sixth sense." See Lyttle, "The Sixth Sense of Jonathan Edwards," 50–51; Hoopes, "Jonathan Edwards's Religious Psychology," 849–65; and Helm, "John Locke and Jonathan Edwards," 51–61.

In order to show how God may dwell in the mind of man as a new ontic disposition, we must give a brief account of the operating principles of Edwards's idealism.

At first, Edwards's idealism supplements his account of atoms and, consequently, has the objective of proposing an alternative immaterialistic metaphysic to materialism and the dichotomy of objects and qualities. He claims matter is a merely derivative phenomenon of consciousness through the proposal: all that exists "exists only mentally."[49] What we perceive are ideas within the mind, not material objects: the world is not independent of the mind.

Soon after this proposal and while contemplating the *purpose* of God's immanent presence in reality, Edwards again takes to writing about idealistic principles. In the first of these "Miscellanies" (no. *gg*), he reasons that the world "would be of no use if there was no intelligent being but God, for God could neither receive good himself nor communicate good." "Wherefore," he continues, "it necessarily follows that intelligent beings are the end of creation, that their end must be to behold and admire the doings of God, and magnify him for them, and to contemplate his glories in them." Which is to say, intelligent creatures are useless unless their end is "to behold [later, 'perceive'] and admire . . . God."

These ideas are refined through "Miscellanies," nos. *kk* and *ll*, and culminate in the idealism of *pp*, where he writes that there can be no being, neither angels, nor men, nor the world, without a consciousness of it. His argument in "Miscellanies," no. *pp*, supposes a time when God's consciousness as well as that of finite beings was intermitted, and concludes: "I say, the universe for that time would cease to be, of itself; and not only, as we speak, because the Almighty could not attend to uphold the world, but because God knew nothing of it." Following a further illustration in which he contemplates the removal of secondary qualities from matter, he announces: "It follows from hence, that those beings which have knowledge and consciousness are the only proper and real substantial beings, inasmuch as the being of other things is only these. From hence we may see the gross mistake of those who think material things the most substantial beings, and spirits more like a shadow; whereas spirits only are properly substance."[50]

This conclusion reiterates the idealism from his essay "Of Being," in which he states, "Nothing has any existence anywhere else but in consciousness . . . either in created or uncreated consciousness."[51] Such statements are not to be taken hypothetically, but as

---

49. "The Mind," no. 27, *WJE* 6:350. Commentators have taken Jonathan Edwards's statement that all exists only mentally or "only in the mind" a number of different ways. Anderson, for instance, asserts that Jonathan Edwards's leading metaphysical thesis states that "nothing can be without being known" (ibid., 76). He concludes that Jonathan Edwards is an idealistic phenomenologist with respect to the phenomena presented to the senses: an idea is an empirical object or sensation when determined to be a fixed mode in our mind after a series established by God. De Prospo's alternative explanation holds that idealism need not necessarily imply that the universe exists only subjectively in the mind: "[Jonathan Edwards] means not that nature is phenomenologically a projection of the mind, but that nature can be experienced by men only through the mind's ideal impression of nature's objective being" (*Theism in the Discourse of Jonathan Edwards*, 150). However, I am persuaded that Anderson and McClymond are correct: Jonathan Edwards's idealism is a product of his ontological conception of perception and knowing. The idea of the world is an idea communicated by God.

50. "Of Being" in *WJE* 6:204, 203–6. Here I am following Schafer's analysis in, "Editor's Introduction," *WJE* 13:47–48.

51. *WJE* 6:204, 206.

explanations of agents of consciousness and their existence and objects of consciousness and how they exist, as well as how existence itself is qualified on his "scale of existences." In religion, however, these speculative exercises propose an eminently mental/spiritual universe in which God is not only preeminently being but the causal progenitor of the perception of ideas and their *telos*: ideas are not the product of empirical sensations; they are created and communicated by something spiritual—God Himself.

We may conclude that Edwards holds at this stage at least three operating principles of idealism: (1) The mind is the ultimate metaphysical principle of reality; (2) only that which is perceptible to intelligent perceiving minds has status as "real" in time and space; and (3) that reality ultimately consists in the communication, shared conception and perception, of ideas by God to intelligent perceiving minds.

An important conclusion Edwards draws from the aforementioned principles, and one of immediate bearing on our present discussion, concerns the Divine Being's conscious idea of Himself constituting His essence. God's perfect consciousness of His own Being renders Him totally *ens a se*, and this places Him, as it were, at the head of the "great chain of being."[52]

The connection between the epistemic content of the "new spiritual sense" and ontological union with Christ becomes apparent in Edwards's statement: "So if all God's ideas are only the one idea of himself, as has been shown, then [God's idea of himself] must be his essence itself," which, when understood in light of the spiritual sense, means that the spiritual perception of God or (better) the *idea of spiritual reality* communicated to the believer by the Spirit, is in fact the idea of God Himself. However, the Spirit who communicates the idea of God is not a complex idea to the perceiver, but a "new simple idea"—a "new disposition":[53]

---

52. "God's intuition on himself, without doubt, is immediate . . . his idea [of himself] is his essence" ("Miscellanies," no. 94, *WJE* 13:258). Human beings who are fashioned after God's own existence as agents of consciousness, have a consciousness of their own self, that is, they are conscious of their own being, and therefore have as it were a self-sustaining mental existence independent from other *created* entities. They are, of course, "comprehended" by the Divine Being and thus depend on God to conceive of them *as* distinct existences. Human beings, then, as nearly independent self-actuating existences (in that they mentally reflect upon their own being), are *like* God, but yet depend on God's conception of them as distinct existences, which, while comprehended by God, are neither divine, nor autonomous existences. Further down the scale are non-sentient entities such as animals, which require intelligent perceiving minds to receive the communication of the idea of their existence from God. Their existence is a less rarified mental existence (and therefore less "real") due to their highly regulated and determined existence by laws. The existence of non-mental entities (objects of consciousness) is completely determined by laws, which places them at the bottom of the chain. See chapters 5 and 6 for an account of God's self-consciousness and, derivatively, human self-consciousness in chapters 8 and 9. Jonathan Edwards is peculiar in that he only understands self-aware/conscious beings to be sentient beings. All else, including animals, are designated non-sentient.

53. Helm, *Treatise on Grace*, 74–75. Cf. Lee, *Philosophical Theology*, 143; Lee, "Editor's Introduction," *WJE* 21:46–53. When Jonathan Edwards discusses "Being in general" (God) he usually uses the term "habit" as the equivalent of "disposition," but in soteriological matters he prefers the term "disposition." In other contexts he uses the following: "tendency," "propensity," and "principle" (*WJE* 2:206–7; 283–84; *WJE* 2:124f). Cf. McDermott, "A Possibility of Reconciliation" in *Edwards in Our Time*, 183–84. To simplify matters, I employ the term "disposition" in most places.

> The Spirit of God is given to the true saints to dwell in them ... to influence their hearts, as a principle of new nature, a holy disposition, or as a divine supernatural spring of life and action ... [H]e is represented as being there so united to the faculties of the soul, that he becomes there a principle or spring of new nature and life ... there he exerts and communicates himself, in this his sweet and divine nature, making the soul a partaker of God's beauty ... From hence it follows ... there is a new inward perception or sensation of their minds.[54]

Edwards, then, grounds his epistemology of spiritual perception and knowledge upon an ontological arrangement—union with Christ or the infused disposition of holiness, which is nothing other than the Holy Spirit. Hence, the epistemic content of the spiritual sense results from a *new ontic state of mind*. Since "God is excellent," then the subject's "perception of excellence" through the Holy Spirit consists of nothing other than the apprehension of God, or God's communication of the idea of His "excellent perfections" (the Son and Spirit—God as He is in Himself) *in* the unified consciousness of the believer.[55]

Knowledge for Edwards is the perception of the aesthetic "union or disunion of ideas, or the perceiving whether two or more ideas belong to one another." That is, the soul, as it were, naturally associates ideas that are similar because of mental dispositions that intuitively recognize the connections between things *or* because of the likeness of mind or disposition.[56] In the case of spiritual perception it is both. The idea of the "excellence" and reality of divine things—whether in propositional truths, experiential perceptions, or divine encounter—is an idea which, by virtue of its intrinsic excellency, "agrees" with the disposition of the regenerate *because* their disposition or "principle of holiness" consists of divine excellency itself, the Holy Spirit.[57] In other words, since Edwards's metaphysics constitutes the entire universe in consciousness (which, of course, leaves no possibility of unconscious mental phenomena), then his phenomenology of religious consciousness means that the conceptual, passionate, and "agreeable" perception of the idea of "God" is in fact God. "Hence we learn," Edwards explains, "what is done in conversion is nothing but conferring the Spirit of God, which dwells in the soul and becomes there a principle of life and action" ("Miscellanies," no. 397), which "consists in giving the sensible knowledge of the things of religion, with respect to their spiritual good or evil: which indeed does all originally consist in a sense of the spiritual excellency, beauty, or sweetness of divine things" ("Miscellanies," no. 782).[58]

Since, in Edwards, only Christ possesses full and acceptable knowledge of God and the Spirit right love of God, then any one who affectionally cognizes the beauty of God must participate in His essential love and knowledge of Himself, that is, they must have ontological union with God in Christ through the Spirit.

---

54. *WJE* 2:200–201, 205.
55. "Miscellanies," no. 117, *WJE* 13:284.
56. "The Mind," no. 71, *WJE* 6:329.
57. "Discourse on the Trinity" in *WJE* 21:122–31, 144, esp. 123. Cf. "Miscellanies," no. 471, *WJE* 13:514.
58. "Miscellanies," no. 397, *WJE* 13:462; "Miscellanies," no. 782, *WJE* 18:464.

Where Edwards appears ambiguous in his explanation of the "new spiritual sense" as analogous to "new simple ideas," he leaves no room for doubt in the sphere of ontology: The "new sense" is an ontic disposition, a "vital principle" ingenerated upon conversion, whereby the regenerate mind affectionally cognates God's beauty, presence, and purpose in the world.

I submit, therefore, that the degree to which previous interpretations of Edwards's "sense of the heart" have neglected the ontological relation of the subject to the object (based on his "correspondence of ideas" concept) as an ultimate extension of his idea of God, exhibits the degree to which his employment of empirical and psychological terminology with relation to the "spiritual sense" have been misconstrued and misrepresented. Clearly for Edwards that which is infused into the believer upon justification/regeneration is neither a new faculty for the rational apprehension of Christian doctrines, nor a "sixth sense," nor even an "ideal apprehension" in terms of natural, sense experience conjured up through what Miller calls a "rhetoric of sensation." Instead, it is a "new disposition," the Holy Spirit Himself, who communicates the idea of divine beauty and reality *in* the consciousness of the believer.[59]

A New Disposition

By "disposition" or "habit" Edwards means an active and ontologically real tendency, not merely a custom or regularity. However, to speak in such away about the Holy Spirit may seem to depersonalize the Spirit, making this member of the Trinity to sound more like a mechanistic power instead of a *person*. But Edwards by no means intends to reduce the Holy Spirit to some nebulous force or impersonal power. Rather, by saying the Spirit dwells as an active disposition in the believer, he means to say that this person of the Trinity only acts according to His immutable nature—in holiness and with divine arbitrariness. And since what the Spirit communicates in the unified consciousness of the believer are "the excellencies of Christ," "holiness," and "all things divine," He both personally and intensely communicates His Divine nature. However, the Spirit does not communicate these things with nomic regularity, but only in accord with His divine arbitrariness ("Miscellanies," no. 1263).[60] For Edwards, there is nothing higher than God's will, for it is not something different than God's mental nature. Consequently, there is a sense in which strong or complete arbitrariness (as opposed to weak or self-limited or restrictive arbitrariness) may be considered part of the divine nature. This is to say, though the Spirit may dwell "*as* a principle of life and a principle of action," yet He does it "*in His own proper nature*," that is, with some degree of arbitrariness.[61] I say, "some degree," because the Spirit confederates with the Father and the Son to accomplish specific "ends" in redemption, sanctification, and even history. In this respect, the Spirit retains, as it were, innertrinitarian covenantal obligations, what Edwards likes to refer to as the eternal confederation within the Godhead.

---

59. "Miscellanies," no. *l*, *WJE* 13:168–69. Cf. "Miscellanies," nos. *bb*, 27 and 77. See also Fiering, *Moral Thought*, 121, 126.

60. *WJE* 23:201–12. See Lee's analysis of this assertion in "Editor's Introduction," *WJE* 21:53–57.

61. *WJE* 14:384. Italics added.

Thus, the occasional exercises of the believer's "new principle of nature" are not the result of some created principle of grace, but only the Spirit acting according to His nature "*as*" or "*after the manner of*" a principle of nature:

> So that that holy, divine principle . . . is God, and in which the Godhead is eternally breathed forth and subsists in the third person of the blessed Trinity. So that true saving grace is no other than that very love of God; that is, God, in one of the persons of the Trinity, uniting himself to the soul of a creature, *as* a vital principle, dwelling there and exerting himself by the faculties of the soul of man, *in his own proper nature, after the manner of* a principle of nature.[62]

When this "vital principle" or holy disposition is infused into and "united to the soul of a creature," it brings entirely new and dynamic relations, thought patterns, and moral government of the soul: hence the "new spiritual sense," the necessity of sanctification, and the radically theocentric vision and interpretation of reality. The Holy Spirit, as that new, active, and availing disposition, gives the believer constitutive ontological integrity, assurance that persevering in holiness and righteousness will be effected, and, significantly, an epistemic perspective on "reality" heretofore unobtainable in an unregenerate condition. In short, the spiritual sense is a holy disposition—the Holy Spirit—which, when infused into the believer's consciousness at the moment of regeneration, both communicates and facilitates the perception/reception of spiritual ideas of divine "excellency" and reality. However, this does not extinguish the regenerate intelligent perceiving being's consciousness. Instead, it paradigmatically expands it, which accounts not only for new input and interpretation, but the reinterpretation of prior input, as the "Treatise on Grace," *Religious Affections*, and dozens of "Miscellanies," make patently evident.

Without the Holy Spirit unregenerate intelligent perceiving beings are devoid of an ontological disposition to have such ideas either appear in their minds or correspond to their mental states. What unregenerate minds do not perceive about God and reality (which also renders them culpable) are the relations or unions that exist between ideas and truth itself. For Edwards, all truth is an idea in the mind that has been divinely communicated to the mind, and which idea corresponds to God's idea. If God communicates a perfect or total idea p in a mind, then all of its relations (r) are perfectly conceived and truth and knowledge obtain in that mind concerning reality, i.e., there is an agreement or "mutual consent," as Edwards says, between the ideas of the perceiver and God. But if God communicates p only in part to an agent or the agent is only capable of apprehending certain unions between ideas, say, non-special revelatory items because the agent is not ontologically disposed to all the unions or relations of p (due to the noetic affects of sin, for example), then the agent's perception of the truth of p only corresponds to the degree with which there exists a consistency of the mind's idea of p with divine communications $p(r)$: partial truths or secondary beauty may be perceived. The unregenerate mind, then, makes inaccurate connections between ideas; that is, in its failure to perceive how or whether two or more ideas belong together in $p(r)$, it contrives other (false) relations that

---

62. "Treatise on Grace" (1753) in *WJE* 21:194. Emphasis added.

exclude God from the equation.[63] In Augustinian categories, this is the Romans 1:18–23 effect. Correspondingly, Edwards asserts their culpability before God in three things: (1) the failure of their ideas to agree with the ideas of God (about Himself and, therefore, reality); (2) inconsistent and insufficient supposition of relations (which is falsehood); and (3) the suppression of the perceived union of certain ideas that have obtained in order to construct or adopt a set of relations which resonate with one's fallen nature (perversion). For lack of a disposition the unregenerate mind remains incapable of perceiving holiness or the beauty of God *as* God's excellency, and consequently, reality's relation or union to God as such.

So while the regenerate and the unregenerate abide in the same temporal realm and have access to the same empirical phenomena and speculative understanding of God, yet only the regenerate, by virtue of an ontological union, have epistemological access to the spiritual reality of God and His excellency. What reality or, better, God's excellency looks like through the lens of a "new spiritual sense" is the subject of our next study.

---

63. See "The Mind," nos. 10, 15, and 71, *WJE* 6.

Comprehensive Theocentricity

> The appearance of everything was altered: there seemed to be, as it were, a calm, sweet cast, or appearance of divine glory, in almost everything. God's excellency, his wisdom, his purity and love, seemed to appear in everything.
>
> —*Personal Narrative*

All Things Anew

WITH A "NEW SPIRITUAL SENSE" EDWARDS'S PROJECT OF REASONED CHRISTIANITY SHIFTS epistemological foundations, from first principles of reason to an idiosyncratic combination of intuition and revelation. It was upon this latter base that he was to build a logical system of Christian theology and worldview. The order in which Edwards describes his theocentric vision in the *Personal Narrative* is, therefore, significant. It tells us precisely what he, by the illuminating operation of the Spirit, spiritually perceives and subsequently reconsiders about reality. Here Edwards reports back on the beginnings of his new methodological approach to divinity. For him, the vision of God coincides with conversion, and therefore naturally stands first in order of significance and priority.

The scope and depth of the aesthetic and theocentric "vision" or "sense" extends with maturation. Thus, Edwards's *Personal Narrative* continues by delineating the successive order of things affected by his new perspective. They are three in particular: Christ and redemption, the transcendence/immanence of God, and "everything": nature, causes, consciousnesses, etc.

> From about that time,[1] I began to have a new kind of apprehensions and ideas of Christ, and the work of redemption, and the glorious way of salvation by him ... Not long after I first began to experience these things ... I was walking there, and looked up on the sky and clouds; there came into my mind, a sweet sense of the glorious majesty and grace of God ... I seem to see them both in a sweet conjunction ... After this my sense of divine things gradually increased, and became more and more lively, and had more of that inward sweetness. The appearance of everything was altered: there seemed to be, as it were, a calm, sweet cast, or appearance of divine glory, in almost everything. God's excellency, his wisdom, his purity and love, seemed to appear in everything.[2]

---

1. I.e., following his "first" spiritual encounter with "God and divine things" (*WJE* 16:792).
2. *WJE* 16:792–94.

Christ and redemption are mentioned first because of their relation to special revelation and God's "end of creation" summarily being accomplished through the Son of God. In the Bible God said He would ultimately glorify Himself in the person and work of the Son of God, Jesus the Christ. Thus, God's "end of creation" is the glorification of Himself through the perfect idea or image of Himself, viz., the Son crucified and resurrected. A "new kind of apprehension of Christ," therefore, is not categorically different than apprehending God as God. The connection between content, mode, and sensibility of perception first converge on the spiritual sense as the facilitator of right thoughts and affections about God *through* Christ or, similarly, God as Savior. Here Edwards's epistemology and soteriology merge together. Thus, when he writes, "The first that I remember that ever I found anything of that sort of inward, sweet delight in God and divine things, that I have lived much in since, was on reading those words [from 1 Tim 1:17]," we find that these words are the climatic conclusion to a sixteen-verse celebratory discourse on the gospel of Christ. The "vision" of God as God is mediated by the Spirit as a "vision" of God through the Christ presented in the pages of the New Testament as the eternal Logos (Divine Word) incarnated. Edwards's theocentrism, we learn, is never without an element of logocentricity: the Word inscripturated serves as the means by which God converts the soul.[3]

Upon the initial instance of union with Christ (regeneration), the Spirit savingly initiates an exercise of faith.[4] Concomitant with the infusion of this disposition of faith and holiness is a diffusive apprehension of the "excellency" of Christ. For Edwards, a "sense" of the "excellency of Christ" is the minimum epistemological effect that regeneration has upon the mind. Consequently, in the moment of salvation it is not necessary for the spiritual sense to perceive the reality of God's transcendence/immanence or the divine glory in everything, only the "excellency of Christ." The former, Edwards would argue, pertains to the nature of sanctification, while the latter is of the essence of saving faith.[5] Curiously, neither have much to do with holy baptism.

The spiritual sense of "the glorious majesty and grace of God" is not unlike the vision of Christ, or God as God. Just as Christ is seen as both lamb and lion, human and divine, so the unincarnate Deity is perceived in His "transcendent excellency" and immanent "presence."[6] Significantly, this sense of the transcendence/immanence of God exists as the heart of Edwards's new theocentric vision. In this capacity, the "new spiritual sense" initiates his examination into how God could be "really present" in temporal reality and, consequently, gives rise to a holistic and comprehensively theocentric worldview. Seen this way Miller would be correct to regard "spiritual perception" the heart of Edwards's metaphysics. So while the perception of Christ takes priority in terms of salvation, the "vision" of the "sweet conjunction" of God-transcendent/God-immanent is the most important philosophically.

---

3. *WJE* 9:183, 459. See chapter 13, "The Mediator of Means."

4. "Miscellanies," no. 637, *WJE* 18:167.

5. See chapters 12–13, where Morimoto and McDermott's positions on this point are rehearsed and refuted.

6. "Types of the Messiah" in *WJE* 11:256–57. *Banner-Works* 2:619 §263.

The foundation of Edwards's theocentrism was laid in his youth. It was a principle that stayed with him throughout his college years and guided his reading of More, Locke, Newton, Smith, Norris, and others. But how it was to function as a regulative and overarching principle of his thinking apparatus seems only to have become clear to him following his "vision" of God "in everything." To be sure, the seminal ideas of locating God's immediate presence in the world and doctrine of omnipresence, as well as the "*Ens Entium*" conclusion he drew from More's atomism, were already present in Edwards's theology prior to his conversion experience. Yet, his spiritual perception thesis brings both the religious and metaphysical dimensions of reality together: the design, purpose, existence, and present beauty of the world are one in God. If nothing else, his encounter with God seems to have given him occasion to rethink the way he understood God and God's relation to everything.

The certainty and pervasiveness of Edwards's spiritual sense results from its being grounded in what, for him, is ultimately real—the Being of God, who is the infinite ontological reality behind finite phenomena. This gives the fragility, changeableness, and material fabric of this world a depth dimension that includes a spiritual/moral aspect, as well as eternal element. In short, God's beauty, glory, and design are understood as intrinsically present within Newton's physical universe and the world of intelligent existences. (What this means in light of Edwards's idealism shall be discussed below.) For Edwards, anything other than a radically theocentric depiction of reality, in which God dwells immanently present, is false; a deviation from Scriptural revelation, and in total conflict with the data received by spiritual perception: in short, the world of unbelief, materialism, and deism.

A Beautiful Matrix

The intellectual setting of the Enlightenment permitted Edwards to follow the prevailing tendency of the day, to reconsider the criterion of truth, to seek for some new principle of certitude amid the decay of antiquated systems of thought and unaccommodating alternative worldviews. But his *spiritual* perspective on reality confirmed for him that his criterion, the Bible, was truth, *the* repository for truth. There was no need then to seek or develop another criterion. Instead, the challenge for Edwards was to present his biblical worldview in a way that took account of the advances in sciences and conversations in philosophy. He believed that biblical truth about reality—corroborated by spiritual sensibilities—was was threefold: (1) There was a real distinction between affectional knowledge and mere intellectual knowledge that applied to the things of divinity;[7] (2) that that distinction emerged out of an ontological factor—a new disposition; and (3) that reality was saturated with divine presence, glory, beauty, design, and purpose—in a word, with God Himself.

For Edwards, then, the question was neither, as deistical religion pondered, "Is there a place for God in this world?" nor was it as the Christian rationalists mused: "How do we make a place for God in this world?" To the spiritually perceptive, "God's excellencies" were omnipresent throughout the created order, and for the unregenerate there was

---

7. Wainwright, *Reason and the Heart*, 9; Miller, "Sense of the Heart," 138.

enough natural theology and general revelation to render them "inexcusable," according to Edwards and his reading of Paul's Epistle to the Romans.[8] Nor, was there any longer a question in his mind about God's sovereignty in predestination: supernatural light had transformed God's arbitrariness into "an exceeding pleasant, bright and sweet doctrine." (From this point onward he would rationally defend "divine arbitrariness" as a critical concept in his philosophical worldview.)[9] Rather, Jonathan Edwards concerned himself at this time with finding a unifying principle that made sense of God's immanent presence with corporal and incorporeal existences; some synoptic view by which created and uncreated entities were bridged and contextualized.

In the months immediately ensuing June 1721, Edwards therefore set his mind to working out how God transcendent could concurrently be God immanent. Some of his considerations were theological, some philosophical. In the philosophical essay "Of Being," we find him setting forth an apodictic argument for the existence of God and concluding (again) with Henry More that "God is space."[10] This philosophical essay, like nearly all that were to follow, culminates in a rash of theocentric corollaries purposed to evince the etiological, teleological, cosmological, and ontological realities of God. "Of Being" adds to his understanding of the Divine Presence in the universe and furthers his effort to assert the priority of the spiritual, but it does not explain what it is about God that concretely establishes His transcendent being in the temporal realm. Nevertheless, Edwards persisted in his attempt to articulate the content of his aesthetic and theocentric "vision" of reality.

This effort can be seen in sermons drafted immediately after his conversion and throughout his New York pastorate; sermons that demonstrate a shift in focus away from his earlier optimism in man's rational abilities to "God's glorious grace" and "excellencies." For example, in perhaps the first of these sermons (Zech 4:7 *Glorious Grace*), where while enjoined in a sustained celebration of "the work of redemption" Edwards juxtaposes the "dreadful wickedness and the horrible ingratitude of man's heart" with the "glorious, amiable, beautiful" being of God.[11] This is soon followed by a sermon on Psalm 89:6 with

---

8. See 706. Two Sermons on Rom 1:20 with the doctrine: "The being and attributes of God are clearly to be seen by the works of creation" (June 1743; repreached Aug. 1756), *WJE Online* 61.

9. "Personal Narrative" in *WJE* 16:792. That is, instead of trying to establish the independent rationality of Calvinist particularism, Jonathan Edwards sets forth on a new agenda, viz. to present the arbitrariness and sovereignty of God as most "fitting" or "suitable" to reason. He uses the aesthetic terms "fitting" and "suitable" to soften the causal inferences indicative of Ramist logic or syllogistical reasoning. Particularism becomes subsumed beneath rubric of the sovereign exercises of God and sovereignty under divine arbitrariness. "Arbitrary," for Edwards, does not have the connotation of capricious, but rather is, in the words of McClymond, "a technical term ... which he uses ... in its Latin etymological meaning of 'a matter of the [arbiter's] will'" (*Encounters with God*, 20). Jonathan Edwards writes: "'Tis the glory of God that He is an arbitrary being, that originally he, in all things, acts as being limited and directed in nothing but His own wisdom, tied to no rules and laws but the directions of his own infinite understanding" ("Miscellanies," no. 1263, *WJE* 23:202–3).

10. *WJE* 6:202–3. More, *Collection of Several Philosophical Writings* (London, 1662), 165.

11. Schafer dates extant sermons nos. 6–24 between Nov. 1722 to Apr. 1723, coinciding with "Miscellanies," nos. *a-z* and *aa-zz* ("Table 2" in *WJE* 13:91–92), but nos. 3–5 between Aug.–Nov. 1722 to correspond with the New York pastorate, which began 10 Aug. 1722 (–26 Apr. 1723). I am convinced, however, that sermons 1–4 (and perhaps 5) were written prior to his conversion experience, that is, June 1721. Both Schafer and

the doctrine, "God is infinitely exalted in gloriousness and excellency above all created beings." In this sermon Edwards ambitiously declares that "God's excellencies" are the crux to the whole of Christianity. "God's excellencies," of course, is a direct referent to the aesthetic perception engendered by one's spiritual sense. Edwards seems to have consciously latched on to how the "spiritual perception" of God transcendent may be concurrent with God immanent by an analysis of the effects of the spiritual sense itself. Such an analysis appears to be what he attempted during his first opportunity for regular preaching. If we were to suppose that he drafted this undated batch of New York sermons with a sense of semblance or coherence, where one sermon was associated with another, it would not be difficult to see nearly the whole of his homiletical efforts in New York as a general and perhaps systematic explication of his emergent philosophy of spiritual perception. If this indeed were the case to which both internal and external evidence lend themselves then it would be no surprise to find a sermon on spiritual perception logically following *Glorious Grace* and *God's Excellencies*, which *Christ the Light of the World* may have done.[12]

Anticipating "Miscellanies," no. 782, and *A Divine and Supernatural Light* (1734), *Christ, the Light of the World* (1723) publicly introduces Edwards's version of the "new spiritual sense" by presenting the essence of his personal experience as the *sine qua non* of "true religion": "Christ enlightens the soul by his Holy Spirit . . . Jesus Christ, when he enlightens the mind, sends forth the Holy Spirit to dwell in the soul, to be as a continual internal light to manifest and make known spiritual things to the believer."[13] The "spiritual things" the illuminating activity of the Holy Spirit makes known are the infinite "excellency and beauty" of God in Christ along with the subtler issue of human reality.[14]

Kimnach affirm that this is a viable possibility due to the content and style of the compositions, and also because the orthography, water-marks, and ink used to ascertain undated materials permits such a supposition (Edwards did not regularly date his sermons until 1733). Upon this supposition I propose that no. 6 on Zech 4:7 (Nov. 1722), or perhaps no. 5, is the first of the extant sermons written after June 1721, and that if he wrote any sermons between Aug.–Nov. 1722 they are either lost or consist of nos. 5 and 6. My reasons are five: (1) the "foolscap" paper remains consistent for all of his extant MSS from Jan.1721—Dec.1722, and may be from as early as Sept. 1720, which permits the dating of sermons 3–5 prior to June 1721; (2) such sermons would have been necessary for candidating prior to the completion of his Yale graduate studies and call to New York; (3) Schafer's dating sermons 3–5 between Aug.–Nov. 1722 is conjectural; (4) it is likely that if Jonathan Edwards preached during the months of Aug.–Oct. he would have utilized sermons already drafted: this would be consistent with his practice in Bolton and Northampton; and (5) significantly, the content of the Zech 4:7 sermon marks a notable shift in content and emphasis from earlier sermons (and essays).

12. *WJE* 10:392–93; 416, 425. Indeed, the order of what I ascertain to be the nineteen (nos. 6–24) extant sermons from the New York period (excluding no. 5, "Fragment on Seeking"), save for Zech 4:7 (no. 6), is uncertain. However, one may speculate that it is likely Edwards took the opportunity of regular preaching to systematically explicate his developing body of divinity. This supposition not only corresponds with his future habit of purposeful and occasioned preaching, but also dispels any notion that Jonathan Edwards was without a method, merely preaching random and isolated topical sermons (cf. Kimnach, "General Introduction," *WJE* 10:130–79). Internally, we find themes or ideas present in one sermon continue (developmentally) in another. If the New York sermons were read by Jonathan Edwards as a broad-based series, then the order of the first sermons may have been nos. 6, 8, 16, 7, 11, 10, and 23.

13. Ibid., 543.

14. Cf. "Pure in Heart Blessed," *WJE* 17:64: "[T]o see God is this: it is to have an immediate and certain understanding of God's glorious excellency and love. (1) . . . I say direct and immediate to distinguish from a mere acknowledging that God is glorious and excellent by ratiocination, which is a more indirect and medi-

The beauty of God "in everything" simply means that the spectrum of human experience and existence is remarkably woven together with the reality of divine beauty. Divine beauty or "excellence," then, is the key to understanding the "sweet conjunction" of transcendence/immanence. Indeed, it is vital to understanding how the eternal and temporal realms are integrated.[15] For Edwards, if spiritual perception entails the idea of the excellency or beauty of God, then God Himself must be intrinsically excellent or beautiful (it is at this point the idealism mentioned above comes into play) because it is really the being of God that one perceives.[16] Not only does Scripture confirm the aesthetic dimension of God's reality for Edwards, but reason, a personal encounter, and the sensibility of spiritual perception are confirmatory also. It follows that, if God is an intrinsically excellent/beautiful being prior to the creation and that excellency/beauty is made spatiotemporally present then God must possess an antecedent disposition within Himself to communicate that excellence/beauty in time and space.[17] Pushing the thought further, Edwards concludes that such a disposition in God could not be anything entirely distinct from what belongs to the essence of God and that God's essence therefore must possess an excellent, beautifying disposition. But more on this last thought in the next chapter. Now we turn our attention to Edwards's concept of "excellency" to ascertain its ontological significance, bearing in mind that this moral-cum-spiritual or spiritual-cum-moral perception of being is difficult to encapsulate in words. Edwards is happy to speak in deontological categories then shift to ontological or aesthetic nomenclature without signaling a change in meaning. Consequently, I employ the use of the "/" symbol to link together categories that blend together in Edwards's aesthetic ontology.

"EXCELLENCY"

The "Miscellanies" begun during the New York period provide Edwards an outlet for working out the logic of divine beauty. Those entries, developing the theme of God's beauty as the central synoptic element of reality, plus the quasi-systematic sermonic treatment of the "spiritual sense," come to a climactic head in the philosophical essay "EXCELLENCY."[18] In it Edwards links God's beauty or excellence with the idea of divine comprehensiveness and, in turn, renders the whole of created existence a matrix of divine beauty. He arrives at this conclusion through an analysis of "excellency" as something far more than an aesthetic category—"excellency" is basic to being.

---

ate way of apprehending things than intuitive knowledge . . . (2) There is a certain understanding of his love; there is a certain apprehension of his presence."

15. "Beauty of the World" in *WJE* 6:305–6.

16. "Of Being" (second stratum) in *WJE* 6:206. In order for the spiritual idea of divine excellence to be real *ad extra* and *to the mind* of an intelligent perceiving being it must be both communicated in and perceived by the mind as *that* spiritual idea of God's excellence.

17. "Miscellanies," nos. 87 and 89, *WJE* 13:251–52, 253. Cf. Lee, *Philosophical Theology*, 173.

18. Originally drafted as "Miscellanies," no. 78, in the summer of 1723 "EXCELLENCY" was deleted and copied into a new and separate philosophical notebook, "The Mind." Such was its unique importance for Jonathan Edwards.

As early as "Miscellanies," no. 42 (July 1723), Edwards begins to attach philosophical meaning to "excellency" by characterizing it with spiritual designators. Soon after this, he explains that God, in particular, should be understood in terms of His "infinite greatness and excellency" ("Miscellanies," no. 44), and finally concludes that God and all that He does "is nothing but excellent" ("Miscellanies," no. 87). However, his philosophical intentions become clear in the essay, "EXCELLENCY," where he provides a systematic treatment of the subject. He at once assumes that "excellency" is the axiomatic principle of timology: it accounts for both moral and aesthetic value. This was no original idea. Edwards borrowed a definition of "excellency" directly from the Third Earl of Shaftesbury's *Characteristicks*.[19] Shaftesbury wrote that, "all excellency is harmony, symmetry or proportion." This definition suited Edwards's purposes well. Not that he had become a disciple of Shaftesbury or that he found the Earl authoritative (Edwards indirectly criticizes Shaftesbury in *The Nature of True Virtue* and "Book of Controversies"[20]). It is just that, in his openness to new ideas (something Yale did not forbid), he was happy to utilize constructive ideas no matter where he found them. Consequently, he does not challenge Shaftesbury's definition, but adopts it as a more fundamental metaphysical category than the Earl. "Excellency," Edwards ruminates, "therefore seems to consist in equality," otherwise, "there is no beauty . . . simple equality, without proportion, is the lowest kind of regularity and may be called simply beauty; all other beauties and excellencies may be resolved into it. Proportion is complex beauty."[21]

This may read like a rather pedestrian reflection on Baumgarten's *le beaux arts*, but it's actually the foundation for Jonathan Edwards's theory of being. His intentions for "excellency" begin with the last statement: "Proportion is complex beauty." The complexity of proportion arises from and depends upon an equality of ratios. This provides the hypothesis that "excellency" consists in equality. From this reflection comes the general theory: the more complex the composition, and the more its parts and their arrangements exhibit equalities of relation, the greater the "complex beauty." As Edwards ruminates further, we find that complex beauty is not merely a combination of simple beauties; indeed, complex objects often have some "simple beauties omitted for the sake of the harmony of the whole." Furthermore, irregularities may even enhance the overall beauty by intensifying the complexity of the beauty. At this point Wallace Anderson remarks, "That equalities and proportions extending through the whole of a complex have a priority over those that are confined to parts, will become an important element in the general ontological theory toward which Edwards is moving."[22] Indeed, all things—simple equalities, complex beauties, even deformities—exist together and are enveloped by a universal matrix of excellency, or, which is the same thing to him, the beautiful being of God.[23] "Excellency"

---

19. Shaftesbury, *Characteristicks*, 2:12.

20. "The Nature of True Virtue" is the second of "Two Dissertations" in *WJE* 8:537ff. The "Controversies" Notebooks are reproduced in *WJE* 21:291ff. See also, *Controversies Notebook, WJE Online* 27.

21. "The Mind," no. 1, *WJE* 6:332–33.

22. "Editor's Introduction," *WJE* 6:82.

23. See chapter 8.

JONATHAN EDWARDS'S VISION OF REALITY

is not a merely an aesthetic consideration. It is the starting point of Jonathan Edwards's metaphysical ontology.

The introduction of his general theory begins with the thought: "All beauty consists in similarness, and all identity between two consists in identity of relation." As a further clarification he says, "in identity of relation consists all likeness, and all identity between two consists in identity of relation."[24] Here Edwards strives to account for all sameness or "likeness" of qualities and quantities by a sameness of *relations*.[25] Anderson understands Edwards to speak of universals here and comments, "all universals, Edwards is plainly asserting—whatever can be common to different things—are relations . . . relations alone are universal, and two things can exemplify or partake of the same universal only by virtue of themselves or their constituent parts standing in the same relations."[26] Nonetheless, at this stage of his analysis the ontological weight of "relations" is not yet felt.

It is only when Edwards advances his discussion of existence beyond the Aristotelian distinction between different categories of accidents and the idea of substance itself and combines both concepts in a category of dispositional relatedness that we sense the importance of relations in his system. "For being," he explains, "if we examine narrowly, is nothing else but proportion."[27] Proportion, however, requires a plurality. This leads Edwards to his universal definition of "excellency": "The consent of being to being, or being's consent to entity." The logic of which is: "The more the *consent* is, and the more extensive, the greater the excellency."[28] But before we proceed further we must ascertain what Edwards means by "consent," and why the concept of "excellency" hinges upon it.

"Consent" finds explanation in "The Mind," no. 45, also titled "EXCELLENCE." There Edwards claims that there is no proper "consent" but that of minds, "even of their wills," which he says, "when it is of minds towards minds, it is love, and when of minds towards other things it is choice." He has in mind to explain "consent" not in terms of permission, or sympathy or complacency with regard to something, but in a highly specialized meta-

---

24. *WJE* 6:334.

25. Earlier we noted this principle manifesting itself in Jonathan Edwards's epistemology: the affectional perception of "truth" (and goodness) consists of a corresponding relation of the mind to a given idea. In his metaphysics this means that truth is the consistency and agreement of our ideas—"communicated immediately to us by God"—with the ideas of God ("The Mind," nos. 6 and 10, *WJE* 6:340, 341. Cf. Locke's definition of truth as "the joining or separating of signs, as the things signified by them do agree or disagree with one another," and of knowledge as, "the perception of the connection or agreement, or disagreement and repugnancy of any of our ideas" [*Essay* IV, v, 2; IV, i, 2]). Truth is not *our* association of simple ideas from sensation, but rather "the determination, and fixed mode, of God's exciting ideas in us," and exciting them "so that truth in these things is an agreement of our ideas with that series in God." Therefore, "Truth is the perception of the relations there are between ideas" (*WJE* 6:344–45, 398). So where there is a *relationship* by divine constitution in between *ideas*, that relationship *is* the truth. Truth, then, has "excellency" of its own which consists of mental relations with respect to ideas. In his coherence theory of truth, when a relation or sharing in an idea(s) holds, a proposition is true.

26. "Editor's Introduction," *WJE* 6:83.

27. *WJE* 6:336.

28. Ibid. See Delattre's insightful analysis of Jonathan Edwards's thoughts on beauty, in which he emphasizes the philosophical notion of beauty itself as opposed to Jonathan Edwards's well-known concept of the sensibility of beauty (*Beauty and Sensibility*; and "Beauty and Theology," 60–79, reprinted in Scheick, *Critical Essays on Jonathan Edwards*, 136–49).

physical sense that bespeaks of its Latin derivation: a mental coming together *with* feeling. Hence, for him, "consent" almost invariably means "love." In this qualified sense, it entails a *giving* of one's whole mind to an idea *p*, but also the *receiving* of the (other) mind that suggests/communicates *p*. That is, consent involves the unified consciousness of man; it is not merely a principle of the will,[29] but of the affections and understanding as well. Its ontological significance, therefore, lies in its being "a constitutive principle of intelligent perceiving being."[30] That is, in Edwards's system, human consent is the very principle that constitutes the being of a union; it possesses a union making capacity.

So when Edwards considers the "excellence" of "other things" (i.e., material entities) he borrows the meaning of both "excellence" and "consent" from spiritual or mental things, for both are really spiritual/mental/moral concepts. For example: When an intelligent perceiving being "consents" to an external or sensible thing, *x*, it finds *x* "agreeable" to its consciousness. The "agreeableness" of *x* to the mind lies in its equality, likeness, or proportion—that is, to its aesthetic presence. The mind "agrees" with such "secondary beauties," as Edwards calls them, because they concretely embody or represent the nature of "mental existence" as an agreement between minds.[31] The mind chooses *x* because *x* corresponds with that which the mind perceives to be most "agreeable" to its constitutional tendencies, namely "the consent to being" or existence. An intelligent perceiving being, then, inclines to *x* qua "being" or, in other words, God qua its own existence.[32] Strictly speaking, the consent between the mind and *x* is not mutual but mono-directional. It therefore cannot be designated "love" or "spiritual" in the proper sense. Nevertheless, because it is *like* the agreement between minds, Edwards borrows the word "consent" from spiritual things. So much for non-sentient entities.

With regard to sentient beings, however, the correspondence *is* between minds. "Agreeableness" may now be spoken of in terms of "love." Consent as love represents mental, that is to say, an intellectual and inclinational "congruity" between minds.[33] No longer does one indirectly consent to the mind (or idea) behind external or sensible beauties, now mind directly consents to mind. For Edwards, the congruity or consent between minds carries ontological, not merely forensic, weight. "Consent," in Edwards, is the *mutual* reception of one mind to another that they should actively join themselves to one another. It is the act of the unified mind's capitulation to the (beautiful) idea of shared existence—a union.[34] Consent not only establishes, as it were, the terms of "agreement" or love between minds, but it ontologically constitutes the union itself.[35] Not just ideas are shared, but

---

29. Thomas Aquinas makes consent the sixth movement of human action—the third of the will (*Summa*, I–II, Q15). Strictly speaking, for Thomas consent is an act of the will acquiescing in a judgment of mind, i.e., the will's determination to implement the verdict of the mind that something is worthwhile.

30. Delattre, *Beauty and Sensibility*, 208.

31. "The Mind," nos. 34 and 51, *WJE* 6:353–55; 368.

32. Here Jonathan Edwards shows a remarkable likeness not so much to Shaftesbury but Plotinus (see *Enneads* 1.6.2).

33. "Miscellanies," no. 729, *WJE* 18:356. Cf. Fiering, *Moral Thought*, 73–74.

34. "Miscellanies," no. 568, *WJE* 18:105. Cf. Ramsey, "The Ineluctable Impulse," 302–22.

35. *WJE* 6:362. Cf. "Miscellanies," no. 568, *WJE* 18:105.

the existence of the other mind. Mind *A* does not simply have "agreement" with mind *B*, but *B* becomes part of *A*, and *A* part of *B*, as they instantiate mental, spiritual, and moral excellence. The "excellency" of the relationship consists not in two distinct minds that love, but one with a plurality.[36] Therein lay its complexity, proportionality, and (relative to God) ontological superiority over mono-directional consent. More will be said of consent in succeeding chapters. For now, we note that consent involves the unified consciousness as an active exercise of the constitutive dispositions of intelligent perceiving being.[37]

Returning to our discussion, Edwards employs consent as a quantifying and qualifying factor in the determination of a being's existence. For him, the more "agreement" or consent between being (an existence) and beings (another created existence) and "being in general" (God plus all created existences), the more proportion or "excellency" being possesses—where proportion and excellence are the aesthetic quantifiers of spiritual existence: the more excellence, the more perfect or "substantial" the being. Substantiality constitutes the "realness" of existence measured by its mental/spiritual/moral likeness—*through a consenting relation* (its qualifier)—to God's being, which is pure arbitrary mind or spirit.[38] "One alone, without reference to any more, cannot be excellent," Edwards explains, "for in such a case there can be no manner of relation no way, and therefore no such thing as consent. Indeed, what we call one may be excellent, because of a consent of parts, or some consent of those in that being that are distinguished into a plurality some way or other. But in a being that is absolutely without any plurality there cannot be excellence, for there can be no such thing as consent or agreement."[39]

"Excellency" or being consists, therefore, *in relations*. Beauty is proportion; proportion is excellence; and excellency is relational plurality or existence itself. Thus, to be is to be in relation.[40] Excellency emerges, then, as the aesthetic expression of relations of consent—the principle components of ontological structures.[41]

In the above quote from "The Mind," no. 1, Edwards, of course, refers to the ontological Trinity: God's essential excellence consists of necessary relations.[42] Within His triune being God's excellency "consists in the love of Himself." God not only knows Himself

---

36. This is to say, over-against Lee's assertion that Jonathan Edwards "collapses" properties and substance itself into a single category of disposition, that there is no such "collapse." See Lee, *Philosophical Theology*, 11–14, 49–51, 77–78.

37. Delattre, *Beauty and Sensibility*, 208f.

38. "Miscellanies," no. 1263, *WJE* 23:202–3, 206, 212.

39. "The Mind," no. 1, *WJE* 6:337. Cf. "Miscellanies," no. 117, *WJE* 13:283–84.

40. Lee, *Philosophical Theology*, 77–80. See below for the connection of this idea with Jonathan Edwards's idealism.

41. Through his use of "proportionality" or the *analogia relationis*, Jonathan Edwards shows ontological similarities with Thomas. See Fiering, *Moral Thought*, 325ff.; and Jinkins's response in "'The Being of Beings,'" 175–77. Compare also Anthony J. Lisska's analysis of Aquinian *adequatio* and its relation to the aesthetic qualifier "proportion" with respect to ontology in *Aquinas' Theory of Natural Law*.

42. Anderson explains the significance of Jonathan Edwards's innovative conception of the Trinity, by saying: "it seems evident that his new concept of being, when applied to the divine perfections, stands in sharp contrast to the long tradition of philosophical theology into which he was born. God's goodness is not grounded in the absolute unity and simplicity of his being, but belongs to him only as he constitutes a plurality involving relations" ("Editor's Introduction," *WJE* 6:84; cf. Delattre, *Beauty and Sensibility*, 117–24).

perfectly (hence, the Son), but also perfectly loves that knowledge of Himself (the Spirit). Thus, the excellency between the Father and the Son is the Spirit. Such love is eternal and "of infinite proportions . . . the sum of all perfection."[43] Yet God has, as it were, *another* excellent relation, namely, to the creation.

Having reached this conclusion, Edwards now explains God's comprehensiveness in terms of excellence or beauty, agreeable to his aesthetic vision of God. He reasons in his notebooks in the following manner: "God is excellent" and "infinitely the most beautiful being," therefore His relations are perfectly excellent.[44] And if He is related to reality then that relation is excellent and beautiful (as the Bible and the spiritual sense evidenced). But since He is the one "seen" present and acting in that reality, then somehow He must be immediately present with it; for what appears is not the beauty of another, but God's own excellency and beauty.[45] And since God is one and His excellence is ontologically inseparable from His being (for it is His being), then the very beauty of God not only immediately extends into the created order, but the created order itself only exists in, with, and as, a matrix of divine beauty. God's beauty is, as it were, the beautiful landscape out of which the flower of creation emerges as an extension or instance of the landscape.[46]

Significantly, then, Edwards's thoughts on "excellency" are a major development in his movement toward a systematically theocentric and panentheistic conception of reality, particularly as "excellency" becomes an established concept in his metaphysical thought in conjunction with "being-in-relation" (i.e., "being as manifest," to use his oft repeated term). Indeed, the concept of "excellency" not only plays a prominent role in his understanding of God's cosmological and teleological relation to the world, but also marks the beginning of the evolutionary process by which Edwards would relate these concepts to the ontological nature of all things, which, in turn, determinatively affects the knowledge content and functional role of human being.

Ideal Existence

The mechanics of Edwards's concept of "excellency" and its role in his emergent doctrine of divine comprehensiveness hinge on his principles of perception, which are only properly understood in conjunction with his philosophical idealism. For instance, in "Miscellanies," no. 87, he writes: "It appears also from the nature of happiness, which is the perception of excellency; for intelligent beings are created to be the consciousness of the universe, that they may perceive what God is and does. This is nothing else but to perceive

---

43. "The Mind," no. 45, *WJE* 6:365, 363.

44. Jonathan Edwards makes a similar connection regarding God's holiness (Hopkins, *Life and Character*, 29–30). He further explains in *End of Creation* that, God's holiness is His excellency, which "chiefly consists in a regard to HIMSELF" (*WJE* 8:421–22). Concerning God, then, love and consent may be collapsed into holiness.

45. Recalling Jonathan Edwards's formula: All being is proportion and proportion is excellency or being. In No. 45 he goes on to say, "doubtless, in metaphysical strictness and propriety, He is, as there is none else. He is likewise infinitely excellent, and all excellence and beauty is from Him" (*WJE* 6:364).

46. See "Miscellanies," nos. 42, 46, 87, 93; "The Mind," nos. 1, 45, 62, 64; *WJE* 8:551.

the excellency of what he is and does. Yea, he is nothing but excellent; and all that he does, nothing but excellent."[47]

The perception of God's essential excellence and the perception of that excellence in what He does (e.g., create, sustain, and exhibit Himself in the universe) are synonymous: God active and manifest is none other than God transcendent. But it must be remembered that this "excellency" or beauty of God is spiritual, moral, and mental; for, in Edwards, mental or spiritual excellencies are the highest degree of being.[48] God, therefore, is pure spirit, a perfectly arbitrary mind, and absolutely moral.[49] The perception of divine excellency in, say, a tree, then, is a thoroughly spiritual/moral/mental vision, an apprehension of *primary beauty*.[50] The mere apprehension of the qualities that constitute the corporeal ("natural") *secondary beauty*[51] of the tree does not attain to the spiritual reality behind the bare sense perception of the tree. For the spiritually perceptive, however, the tree also exhibits a "primary" or "spiritual" beauty in addition to its "secondary" or "common" beauty. To be sure, the world's secondary beauty is derived from primary beauty, or God. Edwards writes in "The Mind," no. 45, "all excellence and beauty is derived from Him," but only as "a shadow of His [primary beauty]."[52] For this reason, he says that the whole of reality can be understood as a matrix of divine beauty, but with different levels or accesses of perception: natural perception corresponds with secondary beauty and the natural laws established to effect the regular perception of such equalities; while on the other hand, spiritual perception corresponds with primary beauty, and the arbitrary operation of the Spirit to resonate spiritual realities in the mind of the regenerate perceiver.[53]

McClymond's analysis notes that spiritual perception's *content* consists of "excellency." So, if God's excellency pertains to both His internal and external relations, and if the idea of relations are communicated to/in the mind by God, then those ideas become an excellent or ontological relation for the recipient. This is to say the idea of God that the Spirit

---

47. *WJE* 13:252.

48. "One of the highest excellencies is love. As nothing else has proper being but spirits, and as bodies are but shadow of being, therefore, the consent of bodies to one another, and the harmony that is among them, is but the shadow of excellency. The highest excellency, therefore, must be the consent of spirits one to another" ("The Mind," no. 1, *WJE* 6:337). Simply then, consent or love, is the highest spiritual/mental/moral excellence. Jonathan Edwards considers the "consent of being to being" to be existence itself.

49. "The Mind," no. 1, *WJE* 6:336; "Miscellanies," no. 64, *Works* 13:235; "Miscellanies," no. 1263, *WJE* 23:202–12.

50. "Subjects to be Handled in the Treatise on the Mind," nos. 15, 20, 26, 56, *WJE* 6:389, 390, 393; "The Mind," no. 1, *WJE* 6:338.

51. "The Mind," no. 1, *WJE* 6:333, 335. In *The Nature of True Virtue*, Jonathan Edwards articulates the ethical translation of these aesthetic-ontological concepts (*WJE* 8:539–44, 564–66, 573–74, *et passim*). Cf. Fiering, *Moral Thought*, 110–22.

52. *WJE* 6:364.

53. Again, the parallels with not Hutcheson or Shaftesbury, but Plotinus's thought are remarkable. In *Enneads* (1.6.2) Plotinus differentiates between "primary" and "sensible" beauty (agreeable to Jonathan Edwards's "secondary" beauty). Primary beauties are mental (2.9.17), while sensible beauties are "shadows and images" of intellect, which point beyond themselves to invisible beauties of "the One" (1.6.4). But when Plotinus says, "the things in this world are beautiful by participating in form," Jonathan Edwards avers that they are of God. Even with such striking similarities, Jonathan Edwards's philosophy stands markedly independent from Plotinus.

communicates to the minds of regenerates is itself the Divine Being. Again, the difference in perception between the regenerate and the unregenerate concerns the perceiver's ontic state of mind. To speak more accurately about "being" in Edwards's philosophical idealism, one must say that "to be is to be *perceived* and *to perceive* in relation." However, one's dispositional constitution or (better) one's ontic propensities toward certain relations (e.g., self, others, God or the sum of all existence) determine whether one has access to the affectional-intellectual perception facilitated through each respective "level" of relation. But this caveat does not vitiate Edwards's idealism since all respective "levels" of relation are actualized through other *regenerate* individuals, whereby their objects of perception gain phenomenological reality and theoretically persist through their necessary interrelatedness in the matrix. In the case of spiritual realities, access comes through union with the Spirit of Christ, who effectively communicates such ideas in the rectified consciousness of regenerates.

Such thinking constrains Edwards to reconsider his earlier approach to unregenerate humanity who, it must be said, also perceive "secondary" beauties. At first, Edwards shows confidence in man's ability to rationally apprehend and embrace confessional truths about God, salvation, and reality. Now, however, he recognizes that natural-man's rejecting and "suppressing the truth in unrighteousness" (Rom 1:18), particularly the truth of God's temporal presence, concerns not so much a problem with the reasonableness of Christian particularism or theology proper, but with natural-man's perception of reality itself.[54] So, for example, while the "spiritual" matter of the immortality of the soul might be believed according to Plato's reasoning in *Phaedrus*, yet the ideas "which be of the Spirit," namely, the beauty and excellency of the divine reality, can only be apprehended *as* spiritual upon an "alteration made in the soul."[55] Edwards would say that you must be born again. The differentiation between kinds of beauty concerns the perceiver primarily and the object secondarily.[56] Stated in biblical categories: unless you are born of the water and the Spirit you cannot see the kingdom of God.

The idea of God's objective excellency in reality—be it nature, events, etc.—must be an idea that resonates subjectively *in* the minds of perceivers for it to be real to them. In order for it to resonate the soul must be altered by "communicating and infusing grace and holiness," that is, the Holy Spirit. The Holy Spirit, then, operating in and through the unified consciousness of the regenerate person, communicates the reality of God in the created order in the same way that the Spirit illuminates the Scriptures. This is to say, the Spirit of God is the one who communicates the idea of God as God is in Himself to a regenerate mind. He is the one who authenticates that idea by conveying an epistemic notion of reality and certainty and He is the one who regulates the intensity and frequency of the perception of God temporally present. Just as one requires the Spirit to discern the

---

54. *Nakedness of Job* (1722), *WJE* 10:406.

55. "Miscellanies," no. 675, *WJE* 18:236.

56. I say "the object secondarily" because any given object, though manifesting secondary beauty, must have the *idea* of its primary beauty immediately communicated to a perceiving mind in order to make it "real" in time and space and to God *ad extra*.

spiritual sense of Scripture, so, too, one needs the Spirit to interpret the spiritual sense of reality or, better yet, reality as spiritual.[57]

Edwards anchors certain crucial concepts in his philosophical-theology by leaving the determination of how and which ideas will be perceived by created intelligent minds to God's purposeful resolve. Theologically, for Edwards, God's determination of which ideas man may perceive secures divine omnipotence, omniscience, and sovereignty. Soteriologically, it fixes firmly God's predestination of all creatures: man has no access to the converting idea of "Christ's excellencies" unless God determines to communicate it. Interestingly, however, Edwards's transformative private encounter with God divests holy baptism as an established "means of grace" to effectively yield the new sense. In a bit of irony, while firmly entrenching God in this world, it seems that the one place God is not present to regenerate is in the waters of baptism; the same sacrament the Church Fathers associated with "enlightening."

∼

In Jonathan Edwards, reality is a matrix of divine beauty; it is what he perceived about existence when he analyzed God's presence in the world. This matrix consists of both secondary beauties, which are merely indicators of the greater reality beyond them, and primary beauties. To perceive either is to experience something of the divine mind, but at different levels of sensibility—either naturally and indirectly or spiritually and directly.

God's relation to the created order, as Edwards envisions it, is simply the excellent relation the Divine Being has to Himself beyond His innertrinitarian perfections.

Correspondence with Scripture

The Bible also holds an important role in the spiritual perception of divine excellence within temporal reality. "The Book of Scripture," according to Edwards, provides the objective hermeneutic for reading the "book of nature," through which a host of primary beauties manifest themselves. The ability to spiritually perceive divine realities in the world of natural phenomena is not without boundaries: one simply cannot ascribe a subjective meaning to the objective reality perceived by the spiritual sense. Edwards claims that the Bible, in conjunction with the illuminating operation of the Holy Spirit, contextualizes and clarifies the significance of spiritual signifiers outside of the pages of Scripture "by declaring to us those spiritual mysteries that are indeed signified or typified in the constitution of the natural world; and secondly, in actually making application of the signs and types in the book of nature as representations of those spiritual mysteries in many circumstances."[58] Consequently, the contents of Scripture and reality's spiritual significations are not dissimilar: the spiritually perceptive mind "senses" in some given object, event, or idea not only the "sweet conjunction" of God-transcendent/God-immanent, but also some Scriptural truth(s) regarding redemption and the divine attributes associated with that work. This implies that the redemptive subject matter in Scripture possesses

---

57. "Miscellanies," no. 64, *WJE* 13:235; "Images" no. 166, *WJE* 11:112.
58. "Images," no. 156, *WJE* 11:106.

a correspondence someplace in nature. However, both subjective and objective factors regulate the connection between reality's extra-biblical data and the contents of Scripture. Subjectively, the illuminating effect of the Spirit resonates in the regenerate mind such and such an idea of divinity that agrees in some way to a divinely inspired idea in Scripture. The Spirit determines which idea or set of ideas in some extra-biblical source will correspond to the idea of a certain biblical truth(s).[59] Objectively, the nature of that connection is determined by something *in* Scripture itself—the hermeneutical principle of typology. Accordingly, typological associations (where the type is only the representation or shadow of a thing, but the antitype is the very substance, and the true thing) extend beyond the boundaries of Old Testament types fulfilled in christocentric New Testament antitypes, to include every facet of temporal existence; but with this crucial qualification: the whole range of typological associations in reality prevail only as extensions of the idea of redemption (and all that it entails) in the Bible.[60]

By limiting the extent of the interpretation of extra-biblical signifiers and types to the theological themes of the Bible, Edwards was clearly establishing Christian boundaries for his natural theology (*theologia naturalis*). Certainly an American Indian might claim an ecstatic vision of The Great Spirit, but if it did not correspond with the objective measure for authentic revelatory encounter—the Bible—then such an experience proves false.[61] The Spirit who illuminates the pages of Scripture is the same Spirit who facilitates spiritual perception and communicates the biblically oriented content of the same. The reason for their correspondence is plain: the ideas of Scripture and the spiritual truths of nature are one, that is, consistent;[62] they are of the same divine mind and communicated by the same Spirit to achieve a like effect, namely, a corresponding beauty, or an instance of excellency between minds: the divine mind in the idea of nature's spiritual type and the divine mind united to the regenerate soul that resonates that idea. The resulting "congruency" of the natural type to Scripture constitutes spiritual truth.

Nevertheless, Edwards maintains that unregenerate readers of God's word and observers of nature could derive some idea of God's person and power (as we shall see in chapters that follow), yet only the regenerate know of God's beauty or excellency; only they sense the "reality" that corresponds with Scripture. Likewise, the full meaning of

---

59. To be sure, Jonathan Edwards did not suggest that the Spirit associates ideas in and out of Scripture in a contingent, moment-to-moment fashion. Rather, the connection between some instance of divine excellence in nature and some idea in Scripture, though potentially differing from one point in time to another, are pre-established connections according to God's eternal and infinite wisdom. The differences between ideas $x(T^1)$ and $y(T^2)$, though they share identical circumstances, save for time, are accounted for by God's telic purpose for each specific time segment.

60. "Images," no. 70, *WJE* 11:74.

61. 1158. MS sermon on 1 John 3:10: Doctrine: "All mankind through the whole world are of one of these two sorts, either God's people or the devil's people," Preached to Stockbridge Indians (1756), Jonathan Edwards Collection.

62. "Wherever we are and whatever we are about, we may see divine things excellently represented and held forth, and it will abundantly tend to confirm the Scriptures, for there is an excellent agreement between these things and the Holy Scriptures" ("Images," no. 70, *WJE* 11:74).

types remains closed to the natural-man.[63] For Edwards, the "light" that the Spirit imparts in conversion enables the regenerate to comprehend more fully the harmony of creation, human experience, and redemption as conveyed in Scripture. Meanwhile, the beauty of the world for the natural-man remains a "shadow and image" of the spiritual or true reality of the world—a distant "secondary beauty."

As God's concrete and universally accessible parables concerning the Divine reality and the arrangement of the cosmic order, typological associations are Edwards's frame of reference for communicating the content and contextual elements of the spiritual sense. His appeal to the new sense through the mediation of concrete ideas and history prevents him not only from being labeled an audacious mystic, but gives him signs and signifiers, as well as a biblically regulated hermeneutic of typology and analogy to help articulate what is virtually inarticulable. In this scheme, all of God's creative activities and works of providence become, "a kind of voice or language of God, to instruct intelligent beings in things pertaining to himself."[64] Edwards cannot but recognize the mediating factors of reason, nature, society, and history; for Scripture, reason, and his spiritual perception only convey the reality of it. His is a realistic conception of immediacy in which God, through ideas, enters directly into our consciousness "in, with, and under" our total environment.[65] In one sense, he can say that God has been pleased to mediate (emanate) Himself through a matrix of divine beauty to accommodate the creature's inferiority to His infinite and Holy Being. But this "end," of course, is subordinate to another end: the glorification of God through the perception of His "manifest excellencies."

The natural-man can notionally learn something of this "language" and hear something of this "voice of God" but it will not seem *real* to him and neither will he appreciate it, nor find it "agreeable" to his unified faculties or being. An encounter with God is necessary for spiritual sight.

Concluding Remarks

Jonathan Edwards claims he came face-to-face, as it were, with ultimate and personal reality, not publicly at the church's baptismal font but privately in marshy swamp. He would not associate his regeneration to an external performative speech act of God (even though he was baptized in his infancy), but to an internal meditation on God's sovereignty. This event for him was a conversion experience that embodied the truth about reality—a reality that could only be adequately described through metaphors and analogies because of its spiritual basis and subjective receptivity.

From the time of his conversion when he claimed the ability of spiritual perception, Edwards began to connect all things, their existence and telic purposes, with the one theocentric vision of God's self-glorification. His theological "vision" of God-immanent moved him to consider how God could be so, and how the world stood with relation to God's being. In doing so, Edwards shows a remarkable aptitude for thinking through

---

63. That scriptural typology is reserved for the benefit of the regenerate see, *WJE* 11:192.
64. "Images," no. 77, *WJE* 11:79. Cf. Knight, "Learning the Language of God," 531–51.
65. Elwood, *PTJE*, 90–93.

and creatively expressing his confession-based beliefs, articulating them in a way that was integrated with its spirituality but was never simply an abstraction or intellectualization of an experience.

"Excellency" as relational existence harmonized all of reality for Edwards.[66] The world should not be thought of as completely outside and other than God, but as God projecting, emanating the idea of Himself *ad extra*. Thus, the general beauty of the universe or the whole of "universal proportion" may be considered a matrix of divine beauty—the temporal extension of God's beautiful Being. It appears that Edwards's interests in the connection between God and beauty were chiefly ontological and did not merely arise from an effort to fortify his epistemological system of spiritual perception. Indeed, in his system the epistemological rests upon an ontological foundation, God.

Though at times Edwards's rhetoric pushes him to the brink of pantheism, the content of his thought does not commit him: he is moving more toward a panentheistic expression of the existence of the world to God and God to the world. However, by doing so he simply means to underscore the ontological superiority, immensity, and distinction that God possesses when compared to His intelligent creatures and, to the best of his ability, to articulate the dynamic vision of the "new spiritual sense."

Edwards also underscores the priority of the spiritual. What is spiritual or mental is ultimately real. His idea of identifying God's excellence with the beauty of relational existence constitutes a further attempt to not only verbalize the epistemic content of his "new spiritual sense," but also a conscious effort to recover from the materialists and deists a Christianized ontology consonant with authentic, that is to say, confessional Christian doctrine. For Edwards and his theological tradition, authentic Christian doctrine fundamentally requires the immanent presence of God in the world. The "new spiritual sense" allows Edwards to take this fundamental doctrine one step further to make it personal, experiential, and apologetical, facilitating new opportunities for the articulation of biblical anthropology, a Christian worldview of history and nature, as well as soteriological and sacramental theologies. For the spiritually acute person, human experience in this world becomes an engageable index of reality, a reality that affirms God's presence and the verity of Scripture.[67]

Though Edwards evidences a penchant for new considerations and speculative theologizing, yet he no way intends to depart from the theological communiqués of his tradition, at least at this point. He merely sought to describe the world in a manner more in tune with the spiritual reality—God's reality—in which the world gained its existence and beauty.

So, in accord with the general spirit of the Westminster Confession, but keenly aware of the epistemological and ontological innovations emerging from Enlightenment thinkers, Edwards restates how God is at the center of existence and, even more so, how regenerate persons (such as himself) perceive reality. The creeds did not need to change, perspectives did; but so did the way his theological tradition philosophically envisioned

---

66. Cf. Morris, *Young Jonathan Edwards*, 574; Fiering, *Moral Thought*, 74.

67. Fiering, *Moral Thought*, 58–59.

reality. They needed to understand the world in closer agreement with the "new science" and, epistemologically, in germane terms that corresponded to *that* reality as perceived through the spiritual sense. Edwards shows his eagerness to supply both the concepts and terminology to achieve a systematic updating. In retrospect, his tradition never embraced the idea of doing nuanced theology in abstruse philosophical terms of the "new simple idea," "Being in general," "excellency" and "spiritual sensibilities," or even in the typological categories associated with his theology of nature.[68] Nevertheless, in light of the profound epistemic chasm between the regenerate mind and the unregenerate that the spiritual sense assured, Edwards's early efforts to represent the rationality of Christianity must be seen as an attempt to establish, in the midst of the intellectual climate in which he lived, the respectability and comparative viability of his religious tradition as a philosophy of life. Armed with not only a new perspective but also a new spiritual sense, Edwards set out on a program to reinterpret reality emphasizing God's all-encompassing presence over-against the Enlightenment's God-marginalizing worldview. It would be God's excellent Being, not rationality, that would harmonize the various dimensions of reality into a unified whole. It became clear to him, then, as to why clerics within the church could be so blind concerning the reality of God in the world vis-à-vis Enlightenment contrarians, notwithstanding their baptisms: they were never truly regenerated through an encounter with God like him and therefore never came into possession of the "new spiritual sense." If they had, then they would have been part of the vanguard against the new learning instead of its disciples.

---

68. Ibid., 111 n. 14.

The Formulation of Jonathan Edwards's Theocentric Metaphysics (Part I)

> END OF CREATION. GLORY OF GOD. When God is said (Prov. 16:4) to make "all things for himself," no more is necessarily understood by it, than that he made all things for his own designs and purposes, and to put them to his own use. 'Tis as much as to say that everything that is, that comes to pass, is altogether of God's ordering, and God has some design in it; 'tis for something that God aims at and will have obtained, that this or the other thing is or happens, whatever it be.
>
> —"Miscellanies," no. 581

THE PRECEDING QUOTE FROM A 1732 "MISCELLANIES" INDICATES THAT JONATHAN Edwards's theocentrism consciously entails goal-orientation. His spiritual vision of God "in everything" is not just about the immanence of God, but also God's "ends" in and for everything. Although the movement of all existences, or what he called "the great chain of being,"[1] is toward some "ultimate end,"[2] yet this did not diminish the fact that "God has some design" in each and every thing "that is, that comes to pass."[3] For Edwards, even the most mundane event or minute thing has a divine "end" to it.

Theologically the same point can be made at macro and micro levels. Here, Edwards's eschatology is not simply the culminative part of the *historia revelationis*, but a normative principle in his systematic approach to dogmatics. At the macro level, his eschatology is theological in its concern for the questions of how God is finally glorified through the created order, and how His will is fully achieved. Edwards's eschatology is also anthropological and christological: it moves to a satisfying answer to man's sin for each individual and collectively. Important to our study, Edwards's eschatology is cosmological. The study of the last things—whether at the micro level (sinners *A* and *B*) or the macro (the end of creation)—is inseparably bound up with God's design of those things and the *telic* nature woven into them. Eschatology, then, is really the study of future teleological achievements in Christ but also the Spirit.

In Edwards, teleology means that any and all existences act for an end. Telic propensity and orientation, however, are not the result of anything other than God's design. Even for human beings teleology does not result from human desires *per se*. Instead, it

---

1. "End of Creation" in *WJE* 8:546 and 546 n. 6.
2. Ibid., 413 *et passim*.
3. "Miscellanies," no. 581, *WJE* 18:117.

is ontologically determined by God fashioning human nature as a set of telic-oriented dispositions. For Edwards, God is no interventionist, but an orchestrationist.

Edwards is able to manage and organize his telic-cosmology by subsuming the whole discussion under the metaphysical rubrics of causation and being. By delegating all causal occurrences to God's power, he ensures that the ends of creation—in every instance—will attain in full (that is, that they will be God-glorifying and contribute to the "ultimate" end of creation). Precisely *how* God does this is by creating all things to function in a law-like way. What ensures that such and such a thing always attains to God's desired end(s) is its dispositional constitution. God fashions, as it were, a network of existences composed of law-like dispositional forces, which we know as the universe.

Yet God is also *in* those things in some way, namely in power. And if we, like Edwards, identify the "power" of law-like dispositions with God, then we can say with him that God Himself gives causal occurrence and existence to all things. God, then, designs His own causal efficacy into the very structure of existence: the power of God along with the beauty of God makes up the matrix of spatiotemporal reality. Edwards realizes that *seeing* God merely present in everything is not enough to *effect* the ends God designed for creation. God must be the causal force behind the universe. For him, nothing else could be properly theocentric, nor satisfy his desire to offer an "orthodox" Christian response to the materialists and deists.[4] This is how Edwards wound up using the "new learning" of John Smith, Shaftesbury, Locke, More, and others, numbered among the tomes of Yale's "Dummer Collection" to the advantage of confessional Protestantism.

So, for Edwards, law-like dispositions account for both the effect of creation and its movement toward a unified end. His whole conversation about divine pancausality is, in essence, another way for him to articulate God's all-encompassing being, to get at a "theory of everything" vis-à-vis nouveau Enlightenment religion and worldviewing.

Now that a spiritually perceptive Jonathan Edwards "saw" the divine presence in the world of physical phenomena and was willing to say, like Malebranche, that God is the only true causal agent, there were several things that required explanation: for example, the status of material bodies within the matrix of divine beauty. How would he explain God's inclusivity while conscious of the standard Newtonian conception of material bodies, which he learnt at Yale College?[5] What role would dispositions have in the realm of physics and etiology?

In the last chapter I suggested that Edwards's use of dispositional concepts was prompted by his analysis of the spiritual sense, which he understood to be an ontological alteration of the soul (the infusing of a "new disposition" that affected mental perceptions), along with his tracing the logic of God's transcendent/immanent presence backwards (that God Himself must possess an excellent, beautifying disposition). Edwards, in conceiving of essential and necessary telic-oriented dispositions in the being of God (in order to explain God's "comprehension" of reality), established the groundwork for how

---

4. Interestingly, however, Jonathan Edwards never comments on the nomic principle Malebranche uses in his theodicy, viz., that God always acts in the simplest way possible, that is, through law-like general volitions.

5. In *Principia Mathematica* (London, 1713), Isaac Newton explained that material bodies were masses composed of hard particles (480–86).

he was to think of causality, matter, minds, and God's triunity. Relations (the structural components of disposition) were to explain the phenomena of world of created existences just as they explained by what impulse God created the world. More than that, they were integral to his explanation of minds modeled after the triune Godhead.

In this chapter and the next, we shall endeavor to reflect further on how Edwards's "spiritual vision" of God reveals the Divine Being present "in everything" in terms of knowledge, essence, and power. The understanding he receives from this vision, confirmed by the content of Scripture and mature deliberation, reveals that God's presence is all-encompassing, intentional, and fixed toward particular "ends" and even an "ultimate end." The upshot of this understanding meant that Edwards's metaphysics would need to be orientated in a way that corresponded with God's telic and cosmologic relation to reality. First, however, we shall look at how he recapitulated his "vision" of God in his doctrine of God.

As we shall see, the outcome of his doctrine of God is an "all-comprehending Being." What Edwards means by "comprehension," however, is something far more nuance than the Divine Being's omniscience: it is something of a technical term that includes not just the knowledge of God, but His essence and power. Thus, for Edwards, God's comprehensiveness becomes the backdrop for metaphysical speculation, the "supposition" of metaphysics.[6]

The sections that follow the discussion on God provide a series of brief explications on how Edwards attempted to explain God's metaphysical presence with "everything." Sang Hyun Lee has given a great deal of attention to explaining Edwards's reconception of metaphysical reality in terms of disposition. Lee provides detailed treatments of causality, material entities, and significantly, sentient beings. My work here attempts to harmonize as well as correct some of Lee's findings on dispositions with Edwards's idealism and doctrine of "comprehensiveness." Harmonizing these concepts should, no doubt, prove contributory and corrective for future discussions surrounding Edwards's philosophical theology, soteriology, and remaining branches of systematics.

The movement of this chapter and the next several chapters is one that attempts to show how pervasive his spiritual and then "rational" principle of God-at-the-center affected the way he thought of "everything" from cosmology to causality, from matter to man.

God's Design in Everything

Because God is, for Edwards, "the head of the universal system of existence; the foundation and fountain of all being,"[7] as well as the center and first thing perceived by his spiritual sense, we start our discussion of how he was to formulate a theocentric metaphysics with a closer examination of his conception of God.

Edwards proposes that God may be perceived immanently present due to His actual presence in created reality. The world is not God and God is not "it," yet the world is an

---

6. "Miscellanies," no. 880, *WJE* 20:122.
7. "The Nature of True Virtue" in *WJE* 8:551.

extension of divine "excellency" or beauty and the result of His immediate power, established as an externalized matrix of God's trinitarian excellencies. Thus, "God is the sum of all being, and there is no being without his being; all things are in him and he in all."[8] And while this implies panentheism, the concern at present stresses the fact that metaphysical reality for Edwards *is* the reality of God, an ideal reality, which when communicated or "emanated" *in* other minds constitutes the idea of created existence, and when apprehended spiritually (and therefore affectionally) in a union of mutual consent manifests the beauty of divine excellence or, in other words, God *ad extra*.[9]

Necessary Being

How, then, does Edwards begin with God? His earliest and preferred form of discussion comes in slightly modified variations of the ontological argument for the existence of God.[10] Not unlike the arguments presented in Samuel Clarke's *Discourse* and Malebranche's *Search After Truth*, Edwards's apophatic argument appears early and frequently in his various notebooks.[11] It is important to remember that nearly all of his theological and philosophical notebooks were begun after his conversion and, as one of their purposes, served as repositories for some given project or projects. The "Miscellanies" and "The Mind" notebooks were first given to a proposed treatise entitled, "A Rational Account of the Principles and Main Doctrines of the Christian Religion."[12] He intended this treatise to offer not just a systematic theology but also a demonstration of the rationality or reasonableness of Christian doctrine, even the particularism of Calvinism. Though the "Rational Account" project was abandoned for another by 1740,[13] both notebooks retain his preparatory thoughts for such an undertaking. Consequently, we find in them "rational proofs" for the existence of God, usually argued from the position of classical apologetics.

But while the ontological arguments that Edwards laid to form the foundation of his aborted project of reasoned Christianity eventually failed to produce the enduring results he had initially intended, yet because these arguments were more dynamic than mere conventions of deductive apologetics they retained an enduring purpose and effect in his system. Important to Edwards in these early "Miscellanies" and "The Mind" entries was the rational establishment of a metanarrative for the Christian religion and all reality, which he found in God's spatiotemporal program of self-glorification. Furthermore, the refinement of this metanarrative helped him to determine which kind of theocentrism (whether a theocentrism of origins, of religion, of ends, etc.) would be the regulating factor in his philosophizing and theologizing.

The notebooks, then, were the place he harmonized the truths of the Bible, the spiritual vision of God, and those derived from scientific and philosophical discovery, whether

---

8. "Miscellanies," no. 880, *WJE* 20:122.
9. "The Mind," nos. 1 and 45, *WJE* 6:332–38, 362–66.
10. Schafer, "Concept of Being."
11. Ibid., 93.
12. For an outline of the "Rational Account" see *WJE* 6:396–97.
13. Chamberlain, "Editor's Introduction," *WJE* 18:29–31.

from Newton or Locke or whomever. In them we find that God's "arbitrariness" (not capriciousness, but *God unconstrained by laws*, where laws are a lower level of constructed reality, possessing less relational "excellency" or being) is no longer a difficulty for Edwards, as it was for the Cambridge Platonists. Following his conversion, the spiritually sensible Edwards appreciated its "fittingness."[14] A great number of entries are therefore given to explaining and unfolding the reasonable implications of this theocentric perspective. Thus, God is brought into time and space through His relation to created existences, causation, motion, the conservation of matter, intelligent beings, and especially redemption.

Indicative of Enlightenment concerns, the issue of causation stands prominent in many of his notebook entries. In them Edwards makes every existence an effect of God's necessary and eternal existence.[15] In addition to his "theocentrism of origins" (where all things originate with God), causation serves as another way to introduce divine immanence. In Edwards's etiology the effect of created existence has no power within itself to sustain a continued existence. Therefore God, or at least His power, must be immediately and continuously present if there is to be a universe: He is the eternal *sine qua non* of all existence—powerfully present throughout all reality, producing the effect of existence each and every moment.[16]

As a necessary and eternal being, which is *ens a se* and "the sum of all being," God possesses "absolute perfection."[17] According to Edwards, this means that God is entirely prior to the created order in completeness and perfection: "[I]t is evident, by both Scripture and reason, that God is infinitely, eternally, unchangeably, and independently glorious and happy; that he stands in no need of, cannot be profited by, or receive anything from the creature [or creation]; or be truly hurt, or be the subject of any sufferings or *impair* of his glory and felicity from any other being."[18]

Consequently, what some brusquely call the "full-bucket theory" of God is for Edwards nothing but the orthodox doctrine of divine self-sufficiency. Both the natural and moral attributes of God are eternally perfect, unchangeable, and necessary.[19] Accordingly, Edwards defines God's eternity in the familiar language of classic orthodox theology: "[T]he eternity of God's existence . . . is nothing else but his immediate, perfect and invariable possession of the whole of his unlimited life, together and at once; *vitae interminabilis, tota, simul et perfecta possessio*."[20] This, Edwards says, is "so generally allowed," that he "need not stand to demonstrate it." Theological meliorism, "open theism," and "new

14. In Jonathan Edwards, aesthetic referents such as "fittingness" have ontological as well as epistemological import. See, e.g., "The Mind," nos. 1 and 45, *WJE* 6:332–38, 362–66.

15. "Miscellanies," nos. *pp* and 124, *WJE* 13:188, 288. Cf. Jinkins, "'Being of Beings,'" 174–76.

16. "Things to be Considered an[d] Written fully about," no.47 and "The Mind," no.27, *WJE* 6:241–42, 350–51; "Miscellanies," no. 880, *WJE* 121–39.

17. "Miscellanies," no. 650, *WJE* 18:190–91. Cf. Anselm's idea of *aseitas* in *Monologion*.

18. *WJE* 8:420. Cf. 494. Two sermons on 1 Tim 6:15 (Nov. 1738): "DOC. God is a being possessed of the most absolutely perfect happiness," [L. 3r], *WJE Online* 53. "Happiness," as chapter 8 will show, holds not so much emotional as ontological significance. Jonathan Edwards quotes from Andrew Baxter to say that "God is . . . *vitae interminabilis*" (Baxter, *An Enquiry*, 2:409f).

19. 107. Sermon on Num 23:19 (1729), *WJE Online* 44.

20. *WJE* 1:385–86.

model" proposals of select contemporary theologians, which advance notions of the passibility and/or "openness" of God,[21] are utterly foreign to his understanding of a plausible, that is to say, biblical theological paradigm: "The notion of God's creating the world in order to receive anything properly from the creature [or creation] is not only contrary to the nature of God, but inconsistent with the notion of creation."[22]

Edwards reasons that a created order implies a being or entity receiving its existence, "and all that belongs to its being," *ex nihilo*, "and this implies the most perfect, absolute and universal derivation and dependence."[23] Therefore, "The being of the Creatures is not something added to that of the Creatour but all the being & Excellency that is in them is comprehended in his being & Excellency for they are but Communications from Him. Communications of being ben't additions of Being."[24] For in God there exists an infinite fullness, "a *fullness* of every perfection, of all excellency and beauty, and of happiness."[25] In Edwards's way of thinking, any investigation into the foundations of cosmology, teleology, etiology, or timology, ultimately terminate in ontological considerations of God. God's existence provides the unity and harmony of "being" upon which Edwards grounds his analogies and argues for evidences of harmony in nature.[26] Such is the scope of Edwards's theocentric reasoning.

God as "Being in General"

The idea of God's necessary existence and immanent power/presence gains philosophical sophistication when Edwards, like Malebranche, identifies God with the metaphysical referent, "Being in general."[27] God as "Being in general" emerges as a key metaphysical

---

21. Theological meliorism is the belief that God is omnibenevolent but not omnipotent. Humanity, in this case, must work together with the forces of God in creating a universe with less evil and more good. "New Model" theology (sometimes called "open-view theism," "openness theism," "presentism," and often "free-will theism") purports that God neither knows nor controls (i.e., eternally predestines, immutably decrees, or sovereignly influences) all things that happen or will happen. Rather, man dialectically or synergistically participates in a relational experience with God to bring the future into being (see Bassinger, *Case for Freewill Theism*; Sanders, *God Who Risks*; Boyd, *God of the Possible*; for an opposing views, Ware, *God's Lesser Glory*; and Wright, *No Place for Sovereignty*.

22. *WJE* 8:420. Cf. "Miscellanies," no. 679, *WJE* 18:237–39.

23. Ibid.

24. See 706. [L. 47r] Two Sermons on Rom 1:20 (June 1743; repreached Aug. 1756), *WJE Online* 61. Cf. "Miscellanies," no. 448, *WJE* 13:495–96.

25. *WJE* 8:432–33. "I shall often use the phrase 'God's FULLNESS,' as signifying and comprehending all the good which is in God natural and moral, either excellence or happiness" (434–35 n.7).

26. "Miscellanies," no. 1263, *WJE* 23:204–5.

27. Malebranche's and Jonathan Edwards's ontological arguments for the existence of God, inasmuch as they start with the conception of being itself, may be seen, therefore, to differ from Anselm's origin of the idea of God as the most perfect or greatest conceivable being. (Note also that Jonathan Edwards takes "being" itself as the most abstract of our ideas [cf. "The Mind," no.7, *WJE* 6:340].) "The Mind," nos. 1 and 45 make explicit the synonymous identification between "God" and "Being in general": "When we speak of being in general, we may be understood [to speak] of the divine Being, for he is an infinite being" (*WJE* 6:332–38, 362–64). By "being in general," Norman Fiering explains, Jonathan Edwards means "the transcendent God *plus* His ordered creation" (*Moral Thought*, 326). That is, when Jonathan Edwards intends "being" to have ontological significance "being in general" is its prime signification, equivalent to "being as such," being qua being. Cf.

concept through which the created order is understood with relation to God's extension. God is the immediate apprehension of being, as well as the power and essence of being. Generated existences are, then, an extension of participation in Being. In Edwards, participation in God and participation in being or existence come to the same thing.[28]

If "Being in general" is thus understood, it would be easy to conclude a diminution of existence and value the further created entities were from the "source" of being, just as Thomas Schafer indicates.[29] Indeed, Edwards seems to indicate this with his ostensibly Neo-Platonic system of "scales or series of created existences."[30] But the "great chain" or "scale" is only *descriptively* Neo-Platonic.[31] Substantiality (i.e., mental realnesss) and value of being are not measured in terms of proximity to the "source of being," but according to degrees of excellency and perfection. Even when Edwards employs his emanationistic phraseology (e.g., "emanate," "diffuse"), "Being in general" should not be construed as a kind of gray scale, for it has structure.[32] Without structure, in terms of a variety of distinguishable existences with qualitative and even quantitative differentiations, Edwards would, of course, run the risk of pantheism. But qualifiers are present. The design evident in the structure of being and the laws that govern it is nothing less than the *analogia entis* among all the orders of creation.[33]

However, the main thrust of Edwards's referent "Being in general" lies in another direction. It refers not merely to God plus the "sum" of particular beings at a given time, but also the *power* of being in "whatsoever may be said to exist" (Schafer). For this reason Edwards designates God "*Ens Entium*" ("the Being of beings") and concludes that God "is the sum of all being and there is no being without his being."[34] The theoretical alternative

---

Malebranche, *Recherche de la Vérité*, 3:2 §8. *Search after Truth* (*Recherche de la Vérité*) is entered as read on p. 3 of Jonathan Edwards's "Catalogue."

28. "Natural Philosophy," *WJE* 6:238.

29. Schafer, "The Concept of Being," 95f.

30. Elsewhere: "great chain." Elwood denies a "chain" or "scale of being" in Jonathan Edwards's thought (*PTJE*, 28). But see, "Miscellanies," nos. tt (*WJE* 13:189–91) and 1263 (*WJE* 23:203, 211–12), *Wicked Men Useful in their Destruction Only* (Worcester-Works, 4:300–12), and *WJE* 8:546 n.6, to the contrary.

31. Cf. Holbrook, "Editor's Introduction," *WJE* 3:42.

32. In "End of Creation" (*WJE* 8:433 n.5), Paul Ramsey raises the question of how Edwards's use of "emanation" or "diffusion" should be understood—whether as Neo-Platonic or not? He explains that Jonathan Edwards's usage of imagery, such as the sun or fountain (ibid., 433), is always employed in the context of communication. Furthermore, such images were intended to be *biblical* illustrations, not Neo-Platonic. Thus, Jonathan Edwards's meaning of communication governs the use and meaning of emanation and diffusion. Jonathan Edwards's unusually circumspect language in the employment of images typically employs verbal qualifiers, such as: "in effect" and "as it were." Ramsey's conclusion is supported by Claghorn's evaluation of Jonathan Edwards's use of "emanation" in "The Mind," no. 45 (see *WJE* 16:632). Likewise, Holmes's trinitarian account of Jonathan Edwards's doctrine of creation renders a Neo-Platonic reading of Jonathan Edwards implausible (*God of Grace*, 44–59).

33. Schafer, "Concept of Being," 96–97. "Miscellanies," no. 651, *WJE* 18:191–92.

34. Though in one place Jonathan Edwards says that God is "*Ens Entium*" with respect to bodies (*WJE* 6:238), yet his application of God's all-encompassing being extends to all existences. For instance, in "The Mind," he says "God and real existence are the same" (*WJE* 6:345).

to God as "real existence," says Edwards, is "absolute nothing," which he claims to have shown is "the essence of all contradictions."[35]

If "God is being" is a strict metaphysical identification, then God is the totality of all manifestations of existence, and all entities are encompassed by Him as aspects of a matrix (or as Schafer says, "parts to a whole"). The matrix itself may therefore be identified with the excellent being of God. "Being in general," then, possesses the capacity and efficacy of promoting "excellence," which when translated into ontological terms is "mental existence," or in relational terms, "love" or "consent to being."[36]

With the idea of "Being in general" Edwards ontologically links all existences to that one necessary and all-encompassing existence, God. He does so not only through the aesthetic and relational feature of excellency, but also power—the activity or promotion of being. Together excellency and power comprise the structure of existence, the matrix of perceived reality.

In short, sharing in the "excellency" or beauty of God is the same thing as sharing in existence itself—"Being in general." To put it differently, existence for created entities consists of existing as an instance of divine "excellency" or, as Edwards phrases it, "being-as-manifest." Thus, "Being in general" and the matrix of Divine beauty (or "being-as-manifest") are in essence the same thing. The power of Being that effects ontological instances of "excellency" is the power or Being of God.[37]

Edwards now possesses a conceptual, theocentric metaphysical foundation by which he may begin to explain God's "comprehensive" or panentheistic relation to everything.

---

35. "Miscellanies," no. 27a, *WJE* 13:213. Cf. "Natural Philosophy," no. 44, *WJE* 6:238.
36. "The Mind," nos. 34 and 51, 1 and 45, *WJE* 6:353-55, 368; 334–36, 362–66.
37. "The Mind," nos. 29 and 34, *WJE* 6:352, 353.

Divine Comprehensiveness and Edwardsean Panentheism
The Formulation of Jonathan Edwards's Theocentric Metaphysics (Part II)

JONATHAN EDWARDS EMPLOYS TO CONSIDERABLE PHILOSOPHICAL AND THEOLOGICAL affect the Malebrachean concept of "Being in general," by which the Calvinist metaphysician ontologically links all existences (sentient and non-sentient alike) to that one necessary and all-encompassing existence, God. Edwards does so not only through the aesthetic and relational feature of "excellency" but also an etiological attribute "power," by which, when speaking in ontological categories, Edwards means the activity or promotion of being. Together then "excellency" and "power," both of which are basic to God's *esse* as such, comprise the structure of existence, the matrix of perceived reality.

In Edwards's vision of reality, sharing in the "excellency" or beauty of God is the same thing as sharing in existence itself or participating in "Being in general." Stated differently, existence for created entities consists of existing as an instance of divine "excellency" or, as Edwards likes to say, "being-as-manifest." Thus, "Being in general" and "being-as-manifest" (or the matrix of divine beauty) essentially are the same thing. The power of being that effects ontological instances of "excellency" is the power or being of God.[1]

Through a developmental synthesis of (1) Malebranche's "Being in general," (2) inherited classical theistic propositions, and his (3) affectional "new spiritual sense" and its related aesthetic ontology Edwards arrives at theocentric metaphysical foundation by which he may begin to explain God's "comprehensive" relation to everything.

Panentheistic Implications

Articulating the created world's ontological connection with God's being has always been sticky business. Once the Apostle Paul aired his apologetical evangelism to the philosophers on Mars Hill a Pandora's Box was opened for ensuing Christian thinkers to explain just how in God "we live, and move, and have our being" (Acts 17:28). Resulting ruminations have left not a few expositors branded heterodox or worse. Saying less said more about your orthodoxy. Saying nothing kept the burden on Aquinas.

Edwards, however, says much. When he identifies being-as-manifest with Being in general Edwards extrapolates on the metaphysical content of Paul's sermon in the explicit. In doing so Northampton's minister invites critical analysis of his understanding of the

---

1. "The Mind," nos. 29 and 34, *WJE* 6:352, 353.

Creator/creation distinction. As Edwards moves closer to a full development of God's immanence and telic purposes of self-glorification in time and space through the concept of divine comprehensiveness (as expressed in *End of Creation* or the MS Sermon on Rom 1:20), he forces us to comment on whether he is pantheistic or panentheistic or simply employing a rhetoric that suggests pantheism or panentheism, but really intends to prioritize God's being and indicate distinction (a contingent inclusion) between the Creator and the creation.

Before we consider these options we shall deal with the misnomer that Edwards's comments on these topics within "The Mind" and "Miscellanies" notebooks were merely *private* speculations on difficult and mysterious matters. One might contend that, if such statements were confidential ruminations, then we must not scrutinize over these private documents, which receive later (and presumably more orthodox) refinements for publication. But two things militate against this. First, as Thomas Schafer and Ava Chamberlain have shown, the "Miscellanies" were *semi*-private notebooks that Edwards envisioned as publishable material.[2] He also used them in a tutorial capacity and allowed ministerial candidates under his tutelage, along with others, to freely engage them. Secondly, some of his published works, such as *Two Dissertations*, repeat verbatim the content under question. *End of Creation*, for example, records a statement from "The Mind" that, "[God] comprehends all entity, and all excellence is His own essence. The first Being, the eternal and infinite Being, is in effect, *Being in general*; and comprehends universal existence"; or, again, from the "Miscellanies": "God [is] seeking Himself in the creation of the world."[3]

Not only were such statements semi-private but they appear throughout his corpus. The consistency and permanence of his thought on God and His relation to created existences is evident in examples from 1723, where we find him writing, "God and real existence are the same"; and twenty years later in "Miscellanies" no. 880, "God is the sum of all being and there is not being without His being";[4] and just two years before his death, "God [is] in effect, universal, all-comprehending being."[5] Such statements, then, reflect his enduring thought on the matter.

Some commentators find these statements indicative of pantheism.[6] Another scholar, Arthur B. Crabtree, tells of two distinct streams of thought in Edwards, one that is "pure pantheism," the other an "Augustinian-Calvinistic concept of God."[7] According to Crabtree, each is a self-contained doctrine employed by Edwards at different times (but never together) for different purposes. Douglas Elwood, however, does not see Edwards expressing pantheistic statements but pan*en*theistic descriptions, such as: "All things are in Him and He in all" ("Miscellanies," no. 880). Despite Robert Whittemore's rejoinder,

---

2. See Schafer, "Editor's Introduction," *WJE* 13:7–10, 545–46; and, Chamberlain, "Editor's Introduction," *WJE* 18:8–10.

3. *WJE* 8:452, 461. "End of Creation" incorporates whole or parts of at least 15 "Miscellanies" entries.

4. *WJE* 20:122.

5. "The Mind," no. 15, *WJE* 6:345; Elwood, *PTJE*, 87; "End of Creation" in *WJE* 8:456.

6. E.g., Hornberger, "Effect of the New Science," 196–207, 198; and Edwards, *Return to Moral and Religious Philosophy*, 65.

7. Crabtree, *Jonathan Edwards' View of Man*, 17, 18.

Elwood's suggestion of Edwardsean panentheism stands correct based on manuscript evidence, though Edwards is not the proto-Hartsthornean process theologian that Elwood would have him to be.[8]

If pantheism, as a general rule, holds that God is *identical* with everything, and that, generally speaking, panentheism is the view that God is *in* all things, or all things are in God, then Edwards clearly belongs to the latter category. His idealist vision of reality as a matrix of divine beauty/excellency (= the ontological) and power (= the etiological) clearly evinces traits of panentheism. God is in all things, for it is His excellency that constitutes the being of any and all existence, and it is His power which instantiates and maintains all existence. Additionally, Edwards articulates an accompanying proposition: "all [things] are in God."[9]

However, when he makes *pan*theistic statements like, "To be is to be all, and it would be a contradiction to suppose two alls,"[10] he does not mean that God is identical or identified by all. Instead, he means that God panentheistically *comprehends* all. For Edwards this term "comprehend" and its forms are technically employed in his attempt to explain God's unique and necessary being. He understands God as a necessary being in three ways: in terms of necessary existence, necessary consciousness, and necessary power. These three, which embody the foundational suppositions of his ontology, idealism, and etiology, are conveniently encased in one term, "comprehension." Consider its usage in *Two Dissertations*:

> God . . . comprehends all entity, and all excellence in his own existence. The first Being, the eternal and infinite Being, is in effect, *Being in general*; and comprehends universal existence . . . God is not only infinitely greater and more excellent than all other being but he is the head of the universal system of existence; the foundation and fountain of all being and all beauty—*of whom*, and *through whom*, and *to whom* is all being and all perfection; and whose being and beauty is as it were the sum and comprehension of all existence and excellence.[11]

In these excerpts "comprehend" not only means God possesses infinite knowledge and understanding, but that His being actually encompasses all existence. So where some use the term to mean either (a) to grasp mentally or (b) to include, or embrace, Edwards means both and with ontological implications. God is not in a mode of acquisition concerning either (a) or (b), since His knowledge and being are prior and immutable aspects of His essence. Instead, God's infinite "knowledge and essence" are what constitute existence itself: hence the declaration, "God is the sum of all being and there is no being without his being. All things are in Him, and He in all."[12]

---

8. Elwood, *PTJE*, 22–29, 53; Whittemore, "Jonathan Edwards and the Theology of the Sixth Way," 60–75. For a brief discussion on the differences between Jonathan Edwards and process theology, see Appendix A; and Holmes, "Does Edwards Use a Dispositional Ontology?," in *Jonathan Edwards: Philosophical Theologian*, 107–10.

9. "Miscellanies," no. 91, 139, *WJE* 13:254–56, 295.

10. "Miscellanies," no. 697, *WJE* 18:281.

11. End of Creation" in *WJE* 8:461; "The Nature of True Virtue" in *WJE* 8:551.

12. "Miscellanies," no. 880, *WJE* 20:122.

His doctrine of omnipresence, then, is really more a doctrine of omniscience-cum-omnipotence. Edwards explains in his sermon on the biblical *locus classicus* for omnipresence, Psalm 139:7–10 (1728), that other things do not exclude God by being in the same place at the same time as His "essence"; rather, "God is there where other things are not only round about 'em but *in* 'em. We are in God ... and God is in us and in every part of us." He continues, however, by insisting that God does not have parts: "We must take heed that we han't too gross a notion of God's immensity and omnipresence. We must not conceive of it as if part of God were in no place and part in another; for God is not made up of parts, for He is a simple pure act ... It is not part of God that is in us but God is in us."[13]

His denial of divine "parts" is significant in that it separates his understanding from monistic pantheism or a numeric identification of God and the universe. Consequently, when Schafer concludes that all entities are related to God "as parts to a whole" or, as I say, "aspects of a matrix," we are not rendering void Edwards's claim to the *deus simplicitum* principle.[14] Edwards makes this clear as he explains how God should be conceived: not in terms of extended spatial immensity with x or ∞ number of parts, but in terms of comprehension of knowledge and power: "God is neither little nor great with that sort of greatness, even as the soul of man; it is not at all extended, *no more than an idea*, and is not present anywhere as bodies are present."[15] Greatness of being, he insists, lies in its comprehensiveness of *idea* and extendedness of operation: "So the infiniteness of God consists in His perfect comprehension of all things and the extendedness of his operations equally to all places." Hence, God's essence is conceived as perfect idea (the Son) and *actus purus* (the Spirit). God, then, is understood as a trinity of "omnipotence, perfect knowledge and perfect love;" and not extended any otherwise than panentheistically as power, knowledge, and love are extended, "and not as if it was a sort of unknown thing that we call substance, that is extended."[16]

The unity of the Godhead follows from God's being infinite in terms of comprehension.[17] Being itself, however, does not consist of parts, but rather divine proportion, power, and knowledge: hence, God's unity, infinity, and omnipresence. And while God comprehends the entity of all His creatures, yet their entity or existence does not add to His (as if they were not comprehended by it); for they are "but communications from Him ... Communications of being ben't additions of being."[18] God, therefore, is relationally immutable: The accent falling on "communications," for Edwards.

So far from making God identical with everything, Edwards in his rhetoric consciously intends to underscore the distinction between God and the world. McClymond

---

13. 44. [L. 3r] MS Sermon on Psalm 139:7–10 [1728], *WJE Online* 42. This rendition is my own.

14. Crisp challenges this claim in "Jonathan Edwards on Divine Simplicity," 23–41. See also Pauw, "One Alone Cannot be Excellent," in *Jonathan Edwards: Philosophical Theologian*, 115–25.

15. "Miscellanies," no. 194, *WJE* 13:334–35. Emphasis added.

16. Ibid., 335. The reference here is to material substances as such, as well as the unknown substance of Newton and Locke.

17. "Miscellanies," no. 697, *WJE* 18:281–82.

18. Ibid. This quote is copied verbatim in 706. Sermon on Romans 1:20; a sermon that elaborates on this subject considerably.

states it well: "Edwards' identification of God as 'Being in general' is designed chiefly to highlight the utter uniqueness and incommensurability of God. Precisely because of God's own infinite Being, God transcends creatures that exist only in partial and particular ways."[19] But his rhetoric also is intentionally panentheistic in that he makes the transcendent yet personal God of Christian theism encompass all existence and all existence abide in and as His excellence and power.[20] Though his language frequently tends to pantheism, yet the intent and full scope of his thought lead to a panentheistic scheme. God's perfections, whether conceived theologically or metaphysically, include the essential idea of those perfections communicated *ad extra*.

God and the "Scale of Being"

If "Being in general" includes "the scale of being," then "being-as-manifest" and the matrix of divine beauty come to the same thing, just as we concluded above. All the orders of creation—the "scale"—give the matrix a hierarchical connotation. This hierarchy is, as it were, the superstructure of the ontological matrix of divine beauty. The infrastructure consists of relations.

But none of this is devoid of purpose: In possession of a panentheistic explanation of the ontological relation between God and the world, Edwards gives considerable attention to *why* things are such. Theology merges with metaphysics as Edwards allows the biblical narrative of redemption and, in particular, its eschatological themes to transform an Aristotelian-Thomistic "metaphysics of finality" into a Christian theocentrism of ends. Consequently, in Edwards's thought, we find that the argument from telic causes is interwoven with that from design, for he cannot think of structure or design apart from its use concomitant to its ends.[21] So far from being static, the "great chain of being" is telic-oriented and thus progressing toward an ultimate integrated "end," namely, the consummate glorification of God's excellent being.

There are three general divisions to Edwards's scale of being: God, finite spirits, and the material world.[22] Each level of being is linked to the other through (1) an aestheti-

---

19. McClymond, *Encounters with God*, 31. Pantheism may be contrasted with Jonathan Edwards on this point: where pantheism either mutes or rejects the transcendence of God in favor of radical immanence, Edwards extols transcendence. He also brings God's transcendence into this realm through his spiritual vision of "God as God."

20. It is within the discussion in which he states, "Existence or entity is that into which all excellency is to be reduced," that Edwards says that the "Divine Being . . . is the infinite, universal and all comprehensive existence" ("The Mind," no. 62, *WJE* 6:381).

21. Schafer, "Concept of Being," 96. See to this end "Miscellanies," nos. 274, 651, and 880, *WJE* 13:375–76; 18:191–92; 20:121–39.

22. An important conclusion Jonathan Edwards draws from his idealism, and one bearing on our present discussion, concerns the Divine Being's conscious idea of Himself constituting His essence. God's perfect consciousness of His own being renders Him totally *ens a se*, and this places Him, as it were, at the head of the "great chain of being." As Edwards writes in "Miscellanies," no. 94: "God's intuition on himself, without doubt, is immediate: his idea [of himself] is his essence" (*WJE* 13:258). Human beings, who are fashioned after God's own existence as agents of consciousness, have a consciousness of their own self, that is, they are conscious of their own being, and therefore have as it were a self-sustaining mental existence independent from other *created* entities. They are, of course, "comprehended" by the Divine Being and thus depend on God to con-

cally determined factor—*relations*, and (2) divinely prescribed *telic-orientation*. The whole matrix of reality may then be thought of as a network of interconnected relations moving toward a determined telos. As such, Edwards metaphysically guarantees the consummate achievement of God's program since the matrix of reality is bound up with the Divine Being, who infallibly and programmatically obtains His "ends." Ontological and etiological determinism become united functions in Edwards's philosophical theology: the existence and movement of the world is understood as the manifest being and activity of God.

God is also the "greatest of all beings" and has the most rarefied and extensive relations—all as one, while non-sentient entities have the least. Edwards is always careful to treat God specially, so with reference to the "great chain" he considers God ontologically prior and supreme, for God internally possesses perfect innertrinitarian relations (the sum and substance of God's "excellency") and, externally, the most extensive (all as one) and substantial relations (which for Edwards is but one trinitarian relation) for the sole reason that all things are related to God as His own self-extension/replication.[23] God, therefore, may be considered relationally immutable because He is ever only related to Himself, even through the manifest extension or replication of Himself.[24] The ontological priority Edwards ascribes to God not only differentiates God from created existences, but also serves to explain the inclusiveness of God with respect to the creation.

∼

In the wake of his conversion well into his years of mature theological reflection Edwards presented in sometimes unoriginal material all of the classic incommunicable attributes of God with certain and necessary proximity to his fundamental arguments for God's being. The distant goal may have been to set forth a "Rational Account" of Christian doctrine, but at first there was the need to ground all existence in the being of God Himself in order to legitimize metaphysically the theocentric, spiritual vision of God's presence "in everything." In Edwards's mind, God as "Being in general" accomplished just that.

His "rational proofs" were not merely concerned with the *idea* of God but His *reality* and, in connection with God's purposes in redemption, His perfections and personality.

---

ceive of them *as* distinct existences. Human beings, then, as nearly independent self-actuating existences (in that they mentally reflect upon their own being), are *like* God in terms of their relative arbitrariness, but yet depend on God's conception of them as distinct existences, which, while comprehended by God, are neither divine, nor autonomous existences. Further down the scale are non-sentient entities such as animals, which require intelligent perceiving minds to receive the communication of the idea of their existence from God. Their existence is a less rarefied, non-arbitrary mental existence (and therefore less "real") due to their highly regulated and determined existence by laws (see "Miscellanies," no. 1263, WJE 23:201–12). The existence of non-mental entities (objects of consciousness) is completely determined by laws, which places them at the bottom of the chain (211–12). Jonathan Edwards is peculiar in that he only understands self-aware/conscious beings to be sentient beings. All else, including animals, are designated non-sentient.

23. Through his use of "proportionality" or the *analogia relationin*, Jonathan Edwards shows ontological similarities with Thomas Aquinas. See Lisska's analysis of Aquinian "*adequatio*" and its relation to the aesthetic qualifier "proportion," with respect to ontology in *Aquinas' Theory of Natural Law*.

24. *God Glorified in Man's Dependence*, WJE 17:207–10. See Holmes, "Does Edwards Use a Dispositional Ontology?," 108ff.

Considered solely as arguments for the existence of God, his material on design and disposal is frequently circular and ineffective, especially in light of Hume's devastating criticisms.[25] Still, the conception which emerges is of "a necessary being" and "Being in general"; God is one, infinitely full, omniscient, omnipotent, omnipresent, and filling aeviternity; He also is spirit and perfect mind. In a word, next to Edwards's "scale of existence according to excellence and perfection," God is "infinitely the greatest and most excellent being . . . the sum of all being, and all other positive existence is but a communication from him, hence it will follow that a proper regard to himself is the sum of his regard."[26] God's being transcends the scale and, yet, encompasses it.

Edwards's panentheistic expressions hint at other ontological peculiarities in God beyond the notion of all-comprehensiveness. For instance, he intimates that the created order is really the *temporal extension* of God, which implies divine potentiality—an idea that cuts across classical theistic statements of *actus purus* and *deus simplicitum*. Any question concerning potentiality or temporality and God's timeless eternity and immutability, however, find their answers in Edwards's larger questions concerning *why* God's being must be spatiotemporally present and what is it *in* God's being that could make it such? These were important questions for a man formulating a response to Enlightenment challenges to a pre-critical understanding of reality. It is to these questions that we now turn.

God's End in Creation

In order to ascertain the answers to these questions, we must know more precisely what God's program of self-glorification is according to Edwards. For what this program entails carries with it an explanation of God's telic purposes in creation and how those purposes are effected.

Although mentioned in the "Miscellanies" as early as 1723, Edwards's most complete synopsis of this topic finds expression in a treatise composed in 1756–57, entitled, *Concerning the End for which God Created the World* ("End of Creation"). Written as a complex response to New England's increasingly rationalistic/moralistic tendencies, as well as deism and the fashionable "sentimentalist" philosophical schools, *End of Creation* coupled with *The Nature of True Virtue* comprise the posthumously published *Two Dissertations* (1765). Published as a single tome these treatises argue, among other things,

---

25. Conscious of the inadequacy of his cosmological arguments (*WJE* 6:339–40), Jonathan Edwards was to learn that mere rational argumentation for the proof of the deity only treated God according to the criteria of Enlightenment rationalists; thus neglecting the immediate intuition of spiritual perception/sensibilities. Furthermore, the principle that the cause must be equal to the effect can, by itself, lead only to a linear infinite succession of contingent existences. Schafer argues that, whether Jonathan Edwards was conscious of this latter difficulty or not, he constantly tended to base his argument, in the last analysis, "upon the immediate leap from the contingent character of all beings to the necessity of being in general" ("Concept of Being," 135). His ontological work reflects this certainty of the ontological necessity of "Being in general," by moving from necessary being to the contingent creature, from the self-existent to derived being. Outside of his ruminations in idealism and teleology, Jonathan Edwards does little to fill in the gap between necessary and contingent existence. Consequently, we find him one moment speaking with panentheistic intentions and in the next moment explaining "being" in terms of a Neo-Platonic hierarchical "chain," which would agree better with a pantheistic scheme.

26. "Miscellanies," no. 1077, *WJE* 20:460.

that the love of God is the necessary context for all truly moral actions, and that morality finds its apposite and exclusive fulfillment in authentic religion (i.e., Spirit generated Christianity). Important to our discussion, it provides Edwards's most sustained treatment of God's creative activities.

Its opening chapter is suitably titled, "What Reason Teaches Concerning This Affair." The apologetical premise of this chapter assumes that both divine and human agencies are necessarily *telic* or goal-oriented beings. But what Edwards requires as a necessary and defining element of intelligent and voluntary beings, namely, a telic propensity, proves to be a dispositional element in his ontology. Upon a supposition of the logic of disposition he then forges a philosophical and apologetical argument for God's "ultimate end" in creation.

Significantly, his assumed telic-oriented dispositional principle establishes the distinction between "ultimate" and "subordinate" ends. In *End of Creation*, Edwards, as a self-appointed defender of Christian orthodoxy, must have a way of affirming that God's "ultimate end" (an end sought for its own sake as opposed to a "subordinate end," that is, one sought for the sake of another end) in creating *is* God's own self, without reverting to pure philosophical ratiocination which would have appeared less biblical (he leaves most of that for the second dissertation). Therefore he sets upon this task in the first section of chapter one by insisting that God creates the world out of an inherent "glorious" self-regard, that is, out of a "disposition in his fullness" to regard Himself "supremely above all things." When asked why? Edwards gives an aesthetic philosophical reason: because it seems "a thing in itself fit, proper and desirable" that God, in acting, has highest regard for what is most worthy ("valuable") and honorable, namely, His own being ("fullness" or "perfections"), attributes and nature.[27]

God's "fullness," however, "is capable of communication or emanation *ad extra*."[28] This is because it contains a "disposition to communicate himself or diffuse his own *fullness*," which Edwards insists "must be conceived of as being originally in God as a perfection of his nature."[29] It follows that God not only has a regard for His perfections, attributes, and nature (a nature or metadisposition that possesses or consists of essential dispositions toward certain exercises, like "*diffusing his own infinite fullness*") but also a "delight in their proper exercise and expression."[30]

Thus Edwards contends that it is not "fit" or reasonable that God's internal fullness should lack any external manifestation or exercise *and*, pressing the point, he suggests

---

27. Normative terms such as "fit," "proper," "amiable," serve as verbal signals that Jonathan Edwards is speaking from an aesthetic frame of reference. These indicators are often linked to providing a rational, or at least, cogent explanation of divine arbitrariness. See Delattre, *Beauty and Sensibility*, for a more in-depth analysis of this aspect of Jonathan Edwards's thought.

28. "End of Creation" in *WJE* 8:433.

29. Ibid., 433–34.

30. Ibid., 435. See Jonathan Edwards's statement: "*For the same reason that he esteems his own sufficiency wisely to contrive and dispose effects, he also will esteem the wise contrivance and disposition itself*" (430). God's "metadisposition" (my term, not Jonathan Edwards's) is toward Himself supremely. If we may speak thus, then there are, as it were, other dispositions within God subordinate to His "metadisposition." One such disposition is toward God exercising Himself "*ad extra*."

that each divine attribute be interpreted as "a sufficiency to certain acts and effects" or a capacity for producing "correspondent effects." God not only sees it a thing that is "fit" and "excellent" (thereby giving sufficient reason to the exercise of this disposition), but there is even a kind of ontological inevitability that He must exercise those dispositions necessary to His nature and essence *to* a particular corresponding effect.

What, then, is God's program of self-glorification? It is the inevitable exercising of the goal-oriented disposition(s) in God "capable of communication or emanation *ad extra*," to the end that "there might be a glorious and abundant emanation of his infinite fullness of good *ad extra* and the disposition to communicate himself or diffuse his own *fullness*, which we must conceive of as being originally in God as a perfection of his nature."[31]

This entails a program by which all the internal perfections of God, all His fullness, and the glorious relational aspects of the Trinity, could achieve optimum glorification and presentation in a dimension not *ad intra* to God, but *ad extra*. In God, Edwards explains, "there is an infinite fullness of all possible good . . . a fullness of every perfection, of all excellency and beauty, and of infinite happiness."[32] Happiness ultimately consists in mutual consenting relations. Such relations are considered "excellent" and therefore promotional of being. In Edwards's way of thinking, for God to be perfectly excellent, as well as *Ens Entium*, He must be perfectly related to Himself "outside" of Himself or (which is the same thing) to Himself through another excellent relation. That other excellent relation is the "fruit" of the exercise of the divine diffusive disposition:

> The excellency of God's nature appears in that, that he loves and seeks whatever is in itself excellent. One way that the excellency of God's nature appears is in loving himself, or loving his own excellency and infinite perfection; and as he loves his own perfection, so he loves the effulgence or shining forth of that perfection, or loves his own excellency in the expression and fruit of it. 'Tis an excellent thing that that which is excellent should be expressed in proper *act* and *fruit*.[33]

Quite simply the "*act*" is the exercising of that necessary and essential disposition in God to externalize His excellent fullness; the "*fruit*" is that fullness externally manifested.

However, it is not enough for the divine fullness to be manifested, that manifestation must be perceived, known, and appreciated by *other* consciousnesses.[34] Here again Edwards's idealism resurfaces to simplify matters through the maxim: whatever is not present to perceiving consciousness is as good as non-extant. So he says of God's self-communication, "if the expressions of his attributes ben't known, they are not; the very

---

31. Ibid., 433–34. Another way (other than by philosophical theology) that Jonathan Edwards approaches this matter of divine fullness is to explicate it through biblical exegesis. See, for example, "Notes on Scripture," no. 235, *WJE* 15:185. Additionally, chap 2 of "End of Creation" is devoted to "What is to be Learned from Holy Scriptures Concerning God's Last End in the Creation of the World." In it Jonathan Edwards essentially recasts the apologetical nature of chap 1 in biblical phraseology, supplying "proof" texts and extracting the doctrine from Paul's usage of πλερωμα ("fullness") (434 n. 7).

32. Ibid., 435.

33. "Miscellanies," no. 699, *WJE* 18:282. Italics added.

34. "End of Creation" in *WJE* 8:430–32.

being of the *expression* depends on the perception of created understandings."[35] Certainly God knows these expressions, but Edwards's burden lies in the point that *they are expressions*, just as earlier the accent fell on "communications" from God. For the fullness of God (that is, God's idea of Himself) to be an "*ad extra*" expression it must resonate *in* other intelligent consciousnesses; consciousnesses that are, of course, unified in terms of cognition and inclination, understanding and affections.[36] Hence the treatise on *Religious Affections*, the ethical dimension to his idealist position and the crux of his theory of virtue ethics: God must not only be known as a beautiful spiritual reality by perceiving being, but He must receive "consent," which results in "excellency" or being.[37] (Here Edwards's trinitarian framework stands out: knowledge of the idea = the Son; matching affections = the Spirit.)

The circuit is now complete. God's fullness is not only capable of communicating itself *ad extra*, but also capable of replicating an excellent relation (a mental likeness) to affectionally perceive His fullness as external. Such relations are consenting instances of excellency which, in turn, facilitate "being-as-manifest" or "Being in general" *ad extra*. The whole process may be seen as a kind of reflexive idealistic occasionalism. Reality, for Edwards, now has a metaphysical antecedent to justify discussions concerning God's activities in the world.

Redemption: The Means to God's "Ultimate End"

According to Edwards, God's mechanism for achieving total self-glorification through self-communication is the work of redemption. God's self-communication consists of replicating or externalizing the Divine Being's internal perfections, which, according to Stephen Holmes's insightful analysis, consist "only and precisely in the Son and the Spirit."[38] How then does the Father conceive of Himself? His perfect image of Himself consists of dialectical redemptive concepts of God crucified and God resurrected, God glorified in weakness and God vindicated in judgment: in a word, the Son; but affectionally so, therefore, the Son and the Spirit.[39] Thus, for Edwards, only through the work of redemption could those divine attributes (subsumed under the divine perfections, Son and Spirit) that pertain to the personal and relational dimensions of God's nature—love, mercy, justness, graciousness, generosity, willingness to forgive, even anger and wrath—be adequately communicated (expressed) and glorified.

Consequently all things—whether works of creation or providence—are subordinate to the work of redemption;[40] for this work (and program) is "but one work of God" with

---

35. "Miscellanies," no. 662, *WJE* 18:200. Emphasis added.

36. It would follow upon the logic of this reasoning that intelligent perceiving beings are themselves manifestations of the divine fullness and not just perceivers.

37. See "The Mind," no. 45, *WJE* 6:362–66.

38. Holmes, *God of Grace*, 69. See also Holmes's convincing account of Jonathan Edwards's theology of creation as trinitarian in *God of Grace*, chap 3.

39. See "Discourse on the Trinity" in *WJE* 21:113–44; Holmes, *God of Grace*, 70.

40. "[Verse 19] is here mentioned from respect to the reason why God 'created all things by Jesus,' viz. because the creation of all things was with an aim and subordination to that great work of Christ as mediator,

one supreme end. In Edwards's own words, "'Tis all one scheme, one contrivance; and one that is the scheme, contrivance and work of glorifying himself and his Son Jesus Christ."[41]

Redemption is not only intrinsic to the creation of this world; it seems it would have been the impetus for the creation or existence of any and all other possible worlds. Since for Edwards this one work of redemption is such that constitutes the sum total of the idea of God's program for self-glorification, and since even notions of creation and providence are subordinate to it, he concludes that redemption functions as the interpretive factor for all meaning and existence.[42] Everything—all existence, all occurrences, whatever may be said to have been, is, or will be—is connected to God's program to glorify Himself through the Son and Spirit in the work of redemption. Here we have the theological translation of Edwards's metaphysics of finality, viz., a theocentrism of ends—"ends" determined by God's choice, an ultimate (ontological) end that is God Himself, as He is in Himself.

But for Edwards the idea of other possible worlds is simply an exercise in sophistry. Questions about "best possible worlds" are red herrings that shift emphasis away from God to man, from the entire scheme of things to the individual. Certainly things *may* have included a greater degree of good or happiness for persons A and B. In other words, the world that exists does so by divine choice. Edwards says as much in a 1747 letter to Scottish divine, Thomas Gillespie: "God . . . is carrying on his own designs in everything; but he is not carrying on that which is not his design."[43] The point implies that the actualization of this world from among possible worlds (those which are *not* God's design) is based upon an act of the will in God. In Edwards, God's will is the final and ultimate arbiter (hence Edwards's understanding, definition and usage of divine "arbitrariness").[44] Consequently, as Paul Ramsey puts it, "there was no structure of possibilities above and beyond God's providence and superior to his sovereignty."[45] Deviating from a theocentric perspective on the world to investigate other "possibilities" only casts aspersions on, first, God's absolute sovereignty and, secondly, His omnisapience. Such posturing, Edwards believes, never contends with the two central issues of reality: (1) that "The Sole Consideration, that God

---

viz. the work of redemption. It was not only God's design in all the works of providence from the beginning of the world, as in the foregoing words, but also in the creation of the world itself. And therefore God 'created all things by Jesus Christ.' Christ was to be the great means of God's glory, and that by which chiefly he was to be so was the work of redemption, which he was to work out, and to which all other works, and even the creation of the world itself, were subordinate, which the following verse confirms. It was meet therefore that, seeing the principal work was to be wrought by Christ, that other works subordinate thereto should be so likewise. And therefore both the beginning of the world and the end of the world are by Christ, for both are subordinate to the great purposes of the work of redemption. He is therefore both the creator and the judge of the world" ("Blank Bible," note on Eph 3:9, *WJE* 24:1100–101).

41. "Miscellanies," no. 702, *WJE* 18:296.

42. *Sermon Twenty-Nine*, *WJE* 9:513.

43. Letter to the Reverend Thomas Gillespie, September 4, 1747, *WJE* 16:230. Consequently, this particular world is not absolutely necessary—another point which argues against the charge of pantheism in Jonathan Edwards.

44. For more on Jonathan Edwards's notion of divine arbitrariness see "Miscellanies," no. 1263 *WJE* 23:201–12.

45. "Editor's Introduction," *WJE* 1:117. Herein lies Jonathan Edwards's chief point of disagreement with Gottfried Wilhelm Leibniz' position with respect to "the best possible world."

is God," if honestly contemplated, is "Sufficient to Still All Objections to His Sovereignty"; and (2) that God has "sufficient reasons" for whatever He wills.[46] For Edwards, these assertions, especially the second of these, take precedence over all personal and sentimental concerns. Divine arbitrariness, omnipotence, and omnisapience are not doctrines for exploring hypotheticals; rather, they are the doctrines of God's power to exercise effortlessly Himself to all that He is judiciously disposed. Edwards does not aim to refute the potentiality of other worlds (a thing that is irrelevant to him), but to underscore the fact there *is* only one world, because the creation only exists for the sake of God's self-communicating/glorifying purposes through redemptive activities.[47]

This raises an interesting question: Could God have failed with regard to His redemptive and self-glorifying "ends" in this world? Edwards speculates on this to one degree or another in *Freedom of the Will* when he articulates an apology for Christ's impeccability, and answers that such a question begs for the impossible. Due to God's nature and character, there is no way His will could founder. Consequently, Edwards does not speculate on what God might have done in another possible world; for him, only this reality matters to God. In one respect, then, the metaphysics argued in *End of Creation* prove insufficient and ultimately fall back on a trinitarian foundation. For Edwards's reasoning goes beyond a contention of "fittingness" and the idealist argument: "Were there no creation, then God would express Himself in vain," to imply that, without a creation God would not will the expressions of His nature/perfections.

We now have the beginnings of an answer as to why God must be spatiotemporally present. It was not due to any temporality or potentiality in God *per se*, but because God's idea of a redemption scheme required time-orientation for the *ad extra* manifestation/communication of certain trinitarian attributes and, correspondingly, time-oriented beings to perceive the communication of those divine perfections and trinitarian attributes. "Miscellanies" nos. 553 and 662 state it best:

> There are many of the divine attributes that, if God had not created the world, never would have had any exercise: the power of God, the wisdom and prudence and contrivance of God, and the goodness and mercy and grace of God, and the justice of God.[48]

> It may be inquired why God would have the exercises of his perfections and expressions of his glory known and published abroad. *Ans.* It was meet that his attributes and perfections should be expressed. It was the will of God that they should be expressed and should shine forth. But if the expressions of his attributes ben't known, they are not; the very being of the expression depends on the perception of created

---

46. *Sole Consideration that God is God* (1735), *Banner-Works* 2:107; *WJE* 1:388–91. See Leibniz' remarks in *Leibniz-Clarke Correspondence*, 16.

47. Ramsey makes the connection between the aggregate good of the world and God's end in it: "While God need not bring to pass all the good that is possible for each individual, the good of the whole which he brings to pass suffers no limitation from any realm of in-compossibility external to his own rational will. A world over which God rules is no doubt a good world, even the best world; but it is not to be termed the best *of all possible worlds*, nor . . . the best that may have been chosen of all the possibilities. It is simply God's world in the whole of it" ("Editor's Introduction," *WJE* 1:117).

48. "Miscellanies," no. 553, *WJE* 18:97.

understandings. And so much the more as the expression is known [i.e., cognitively and affectionally], so much the more it is.[49]

But here too one may be tempted to say that there must have been a kind of inevitability to God exercising Himself toward this *epochal* "end," that there must have been some real temporality *in* God's disposition to exercise Himself temporally. Edwards, however, conscious of the philosophical difficulties that would arise if he allowed for temporality in God (especially in light of his theological tradition) speaks generically but cautiously by saying that it was "a communicative disposition *in general*, or a disposition in the fullness of the divinity to flow out and diffuse itself."[50] He recognizes that God's atemporality can only be upheld if and only if God is timeless intrinsically and extrinsically, internally and externally. The way he circumvents the problem of atemporalism is to say that God is timeless in His causal relation to the universe because that relation is "entirely mental." Prior actuality is all that there is for God.[51] The difference between God creating "in time" and the notion of time being created "in God's mind" or the idea of time communicated is a permanent fixture in Edwards's thinking apparatus: "Things as to God exist from all eternity alike. That is, the idea is always the same, and after the same mode."[52] God, therefore, does not create within the boundaries of time, but rather God invents and communicates the idea of time to intelligent minds, which, in turn, perceive some sequential rhythm of existence. But in God's mind, the series or sequence is but one changeless idea: His timelessness is both intrinsic and extrinsic. The idea of time in no way constrains God's omniscience or omnipotence, though it remains inevitable to the scheme of redemption and, therefore, God's program to manifest His fullness "*ad extra*."

All of this takes us to Edwards's final thesis in *End of Creation*, that it was a telic-oriented disposition in God to replicate externally His internal "fullness" that "excited" Him to create: "Therefore to speak more strictly according to truth . . . *a disposition in God, as an original property of his nature, to an emanation of his own infinite fullness, was what excited him to create the world; and so that the emanation itself was aimed at by him as a last end of the creation.*"[53]

It is this disposition in God that makes it possible for the Divine Being to "emanate" His fullness "*ad extra*." And it is this idea of an essential divine disposition that gives philosophical expression to Edwards's metaphysically-loaded vision of divine comprehensiveness.

Because Edwards believes that God's "disposition to communicate himself or diffuse his own *fullness*" is an original perfection of the divine nature, a disposition toward specific

---

49. "Miscellanies," no. 662, *WJE* 18:200.

50. "End of Creation" in *WJE* 8:434–35.

51. Thus it could be contended that Lee is wrong on this point: there is no before/after for God—even with respect to the exercising of His dispositions. See *WJE* 1:266–69; and Holmes, "Does Edwards Use a Dispositional Ontology?," 107–10.

52. "The Mind," no. 36, *WJE* 6:355. That there is no change in God's knowledge of reality, that is, no true element of temporality or sequential progression, see "Freedom of the Will," "Sec. 12. Foreknowledge Inconsistent with Contingency" in *WJE* 1:266–69.

53. "End of Creation" in *WJE* 8:435.

exercises which must have full expression, he therefore claims without qualification that God must have His fullness manifested externally. This is to say, God *must* create. Edwards does not say that God *needs* to create because of some insufficiency, but He must because of who and what He is. Is divine freedom constrained with regard to creation? Only in the sense that if there was a possibility for God to have created another world it would have been *like* this one, for the world is the particular "fruit" of a particular telic-oriented divine disposition.[54] Edwards seems to think that a totally different world would require a totally different telos and, consequently, compromise the centrality of God's redemptive scheme and triune excellency.

Thus we find Edwards wrestling with his Reformed tradition concerning divine freedom and creation. Not only *must* God create but He is in some non-absolute sense dependent upon intelligent perceiving minds in order for both that creation (and their existence) and His being to have an *ad extra* reality and value. The telos of redemption limits God's acts concerning creation by making it a relational process, not just amongst the economic Trinity, but also with *other* perceiving minds. Edwards denies that this is a limitation of divine omnipotence. Instead, it is *The Wisdom of God Displayed in the Way of Salvation* (1733),[55] and therefore a resolute expression of omnipotence. Either way, even a hint of God's dependence upon the creature for "*ad extra*" manifestation would have caused John Calvin and Theodore Beza not a little discomfort, particularly from one famed for sermons like *God Glorified in Man's Dependence* (1731).[56]

Edwards's "Miscellanies" entries on the "end of creation," which culminated in the dissertation on the topic, signal a second and final shift in the emphasis of his theocentricity. The first shift occurred shortly after his conversion when he moved from what could be called a generic "theocentrism of religion" (God at center of the Christian religion) to a something like a "theocentrism of origins" (God, the necessary being for existences, consciousnesses, and causes). The final shift was from this to one that became not only the distinct emphasis of his philosophical-theological career, but also a principle that operated as the cohesive and overarching theory in his thought: a "theocentrism of ends."

Thus far we have considered (1) how Edwards's spiritual sense facilitated for him a vision of God-at-the-center-of-reality, the foundation of his metaphysical thinking apparatus, (2) how he understood that reality to be a matrix of divine beauty or the reality of God's comprehensiveness, and (3) that God's all-comprehension includes and comprises

---

54. In distinction from the strongly necessitarian disposition of God toward Himself (God's metadisposition), the disposition which brings about creation may be considered weakly necessitarian. There is a necessity or inevitability to the emanationistic disposition—it must be exercised and, with respect to redemption, it must have certain features of a certain kind; for instance, every set of that kind must have a fall, a divine Redeemer, etc. This is not unique to Jonathan Edwards, Thomas Aquinas in *Contra Gentiles* said God had to create but not necessarily *this* world, though the world is the result of the fullness of God. See Scott C. MacDonald's discussion on Thomas Aquinas in *Being and Goodness*, chap 4.

55. *Banner-Works* 2:141–56.

56. *WJE* 17:200–16.

the "fruit" of a particular disposition essential to God's nature and essence: which is to say, Edwards's metaphysics of finality suggests that the "ends" appropriate to the divine nature are inseparable from the very nature or essence that determines the Divine Being. We may further add that, for Edwards, telic-orientation is not a "non-moral" propensity, but one intrinsically moral due to its relational nature. (Edwards at any time can turn the conversation into one of God's love or His self-expression as love, as he frequently does in his notebooks and sermons.)

As Edwards's spiritual worldview begins to take shape, it incorporates and develops fundamental theological concepts of God, the Trinity, the work of Christ and the Spirit, and the entire drama of redemption in time. It also incorporates and develops foundational metaphysical categories of being and causation. Reality was not only to be conceived and interpreted in light of God's all-encompassing presence, but also gains its teleology and idealistic value from the Divine Being's purposeful presence in every facet of existence.

6

The Becomingness of God

The Formulation of Jonathan Edwards's Theocentric Metaphysics (Part III)

IN THE PREVIOUS CHAPTER WE CONSIDERED (1) HOW EDWARDS'S SPIRITUAL SENSE FACILItated for him a vision of God-at-the-center-of-reality, (2) how he understood that reality to be a matrix of divine beauty or the reality of God's comprehensiveness, and (3) that God's all-comprehension includes and comprises the "fruit" of a particular disposition essential to God's nature and essence.

As Edwards's spiritual worldview begins to take shape, it incorporates and develops fundamental theological concepts of God, the Trinity, the work of Christ and the Spirit, and the entire drama of redemption in time. Reality was not only to be *re*conceived and *re*interpreted in light of God's all-encompassing presence, but also the purpose of the Divine Being's presence in every facet of existence.

Be that as it may, the conversation concerning Jonathan Edwards and divine dispositions has been dominated, in an almost entirely uncontested fashion, by Sang Hyun Lee's interpretations. Lee believes Edwards's concept of God is ontologically unique, and that its uniqueness lays in his conception of God "as essentially a disposition,"[1] where God's most irreducible essence *is* a disposition, replacing Aristotelian-Scholastic notions of substance with the idea of disposition or habit. Edwards's ontology for the Divine Being, according to Lee, has cosmological implications as well. For, as Lee argues, the exercise of the divine disposition of self-communication is truly expansive: it replicates *ad extra* the prior inner actualities of God. Consequently, in spatiotemporality, God expands. He is, as it were, more than before.

Here, however, certain of Lee's views on divine dispositions are shown to be more eisogetical than exegetical commentary on Edwards's theocentric metaphysics. Edwards does not abandon Thomistic "substance" language in favor of dispositional forces and habits, nor does he conceive of God's self-enlargement as an essential (ontological) expansion. So far from anticipating the categories and concepts of process theology, Edwards's concepts and nomenclature concerning the becomingness of God must be understood in light of his philosophical idealism. It is in intelligent perceiving minds that "enlarges" Himself in the cosmos. For Jonathan Edwards, God *ad extra* is the idea of God perceived by minds in another realm.

---

1. Lee, *Philosophical Theology*, 173.

The Immutable Mutable God

Like so many theological systematicians and philosophical theologians throughout the ages, Jonathan Edwards sought to maintain a coherent balance between the presentation of an immutable God and God's creative, communicative, and purposeful activity: the God that he spiritually envisioned as sublimely but beautifully present in *this* realm. So when his apologetical "*Ens Entium*" was philosophically depicted in "Miscellanies" no. 107[B] as the Being whose "essence is inclined to communicate himself," he was making a conscious attempt to assuage the tension between the God who "*enlarges* himself in a more excellent and divine manner" (*End of Creation*) and a totally changeless God, without any element of potentiality in Him (Westminster Confession of Faith, Art. II). In "Miscellanies" no. 107[B], Edwards addressed the same question with which every notable theologian from antiquity to Thomas Aquinas and Aquinas to himself wrestled: How could an immutable Being be capable of any creative and purposeful activity with the world?

This question is also one of value and meaning. If the life of God is unaffected by His relation to the world (the doctrine of impassibility), then how can God's involvement in the world have any genuine meaning to either Himself or the world? Held in tension by these questions are the issues of the being and becoming of God, and the impassibility and communicativeness of God; the implications of which encroach upon both sentient and non-sentient beings. For Edwards, then, the challenge was to coherently present God's immanence (contra emergent Enlightenment deism), while maintaining God's transcendent immutability (contra materialism).

Interpreters of Edwards have usually understood his idea of God's creativity not as static, but as an activity of divine self-communication.[2] Self-communication in this scheme is a mono-directional activity in which God, in His prior actuality and perfection, gives rather than receives. Since the Divine Being only gives out of His "fullness," God's completeness and actuality presumably are not compromised. God still is, so to speak, a "full bucket."[3]

Yet, even if the self-communicating God of Edwards is not just an inherently beautiful being, but an inherently *beautifying* being creating out of his "fullness" (à la Delattre),[4] such an idea, as Sang Lee points out, still does not explain the sense in which Edwards speaks of God's *self-enlargement* and *expansion* through divine activity in the time-space continuum. Additionally, explains Lee, the analysis of Edwards's idea as merely Neo-Platonic, emanationistic, hierarchical, proves inadequate upon recognition of the fact that he combines his emanationistic metaphorical language with a teleological vision in his discussion of God's self-communication.[5] As Edwards explains, God creates out of "a delight in his own infinite goodness; or the exercise of that glorious propensity of his

---

2. McClymond, *Encounters with God*, 56; Lee, *Philosophical Theology*, 172.

3. Cf. Delattre, *Beauty and Sensibility*, 168–84; and Smith, "Jonathan Edwards as Philosophical Theologian," 314–19.

4. *Beauty and Sensibility*, 169. Delattre does not collapse being in to beauty, but maintains being as a more basic metaphysical category: "Beauty," he says, "is ultimately to be resolved into being" (ibid., 25).

5. Lee, *Philosophical Theology*, 172.

nature to diffuse and communicate himself, and so gratifying this inclination of his own heart . . . to communicate of his own excellent fullness."[6]

There is a premium on intentionality here. God is not simply "diffusing" or "emanating" meaninglessly. Instead there is a very real, singular, and functional telos to God's willful creative activity. A merely Neo-Platonic or emanationistic analysis of Edwards's "scale of being"[7] does not answer the question why? To Edwards, God's "ultimate end" is "the glory of God."[8] Therefore, he asserts, the movement of world history has real meaning to God, while God gives meaning and ontology to world history. Thus far Thomas Aquinas and Reformed Scholasticism and Jonathan Edwards are on the same page. All would agree that God created in a certain way, namely in a telic fashion. Yet Edwards seems to intend more than mere self-communication as the divine telos. Lee is quick to point out that in *End of Creation* Edwards says God's emanating activities are "an *increase, repetition,* or *multiplication*" of the divine excellency or fullness.[9] On this evidence, it seems Edwards does not merely wish to say with his theological tradition that God solely intends to communicate His perfection for glorification, but that God somehow "enlarges" Himself by expanding into (perhaps *as*) temporality.

Κατα Lee

Sang Lee believes Edwards's concept of God is ontologically unique, and that its uniqueness lays in his conception of God "as essentially a disposition."[10] Lee does not merely say that God possesses dispositions but that His most irreducible essence *is* a disposition. "The philosophical renovation utilized in Edwards's theological reconstruction," Lee argues, "is the replacement of the age-old notion of substance with the idea of disposition or habit." This assertion does not simply apply to the created order but holds for God too. Edwards began to think about God's being, explains Lee, "in terms not of substance . . . but—utilizing a new language—in terms of dispositional forces."[11] Despite making "a new beginning in Christian theology," according to Lee, the mediating capacity of Edwards's new ontology enables him "to reaffirm in the strongest possible terms his theological tradition" within a "modern philosophical framework."[12] That is, Edwards remained faithful to his theological tradition because he conceived of God's dispositional essence as "perfect in actuality and also inherently disposed to further actualizations—that is, to repetitions of the prior actuality."[13]

The upshot of this thinking holds that what is "repeated" *ad extra* really is God in all His fullness, not merely in terms of communicated glory, but God exercising His "diffusive disposition" in such a way that His prior actuality remains intact. Yet if we consider this

---

6. "End of Creation" in *WJE* 8:445–46.
7. Ibid., 546 n. 6.
8. Ibid., 526.
9. Ibid., 433.
10. Lee, *Philosophical Theology*, 173.
11. Ibid., 4.
12. Ibid.
13. Lee, "Edwards on God and Nature" in *Edwards in Our Time*, 18, 17.

scenario sequentially it suggests "more" God after He exercises His diffusive disposition than before. Is Lee correct? Does Edwards posit a God that expands sequentially, proportionately, essentially, or otherwise?

There is no question that Lee is correct to assert Edwards's employment of dispositional concepts in his ontology. This is clear from "Miscellanies" no. 241 and a number of other places within Edwards's written corpus. Stoddard's successor even speaks of dispositions that are "necessary" to "the divine nature and essence itself" (MS sermon Deut 32:4).[14] Nevertheless, there are two things which must be addressed here: (1) how Edwards conceives of God's essence; and (2) what he really means and intends by "*ad extra*," which in turn affects the meaning of "an *increase*, *repetition*, or *multiplication*"; phrases upon with much depends for Lee's reading and that of his interpretative devotees.

Κατα Edwards

Concerning the first point, Lee has been too reductionistic in his analysis of Edwards and dispositions. Edwards never abandoned speaking of God's essence in terms of "substance." For instance, we find him writing a year after his conversion that, "there is no proper substance but God himself," and again in 1727 that, "there is no such distinction in God of substance and property." There is also a 1747 "The Mind" notebook entry entitled "SUBSTANCE," in which he speaks of God's "substance" composing the substratum of reality. In fact, in 1756, approximately a year before his death, he drafted a series of notes known as "Notes on Knowledge and Existence" that correspond in content to some of the philosophical arguments in his monumental treatise *Original Sin*. In them he writes, "God is as it were the only substance, or rather, the perfection and steadfastness of his knowledge, wisdom, power and will."[15]

Neither did Edwards conceive of God's essence *only* as a disposition (or even a set of dispositions). Instead, his usual manner of speaking of God's essence (while distinctly idealist) retains a Thomistic (i.e., Aristotelian-Scholastic) character. Consider, for example, "Miscellanies" no. 94:

> God's intuition on himself, without doubt, is immediate. But 'tis certain it cannot be, except his idea be his essence; for his idea is the immediate object of his intuition . . . And if so, and all God's ideas are only the one idea of himself, as has been shown, [then God's idea of himself] must be his essence itself. It must be a substantial idea, having all the perfections of the substance perfectly.[16]

And now Thomas Aquinas:

---

14. 42. [L. 2r] Sermon on Deuteronomy 32:4 (1728), *WJE Online* 42. Minkema's analysis suggests that this sermon was likely composed and preached in spring 1728 (*WJE* 14:544).

15. "Of Atoms" in *WJE* 6:215; cf. "Things to be Considered an[d] Written Fully About," no. 44, *WJE* 6:238; 42. Sermon on Deut 32:4 (1728), *WJE Online* 42; "The Mind," no. 61, *WJE* 6:376; *WJE* 6:398.

16. "Miscellanies," no. 94, *WJE* 13:258. Cf. "Observations Concerning the Trinity" in *Treatise on Grace*.

> The supreme and perfect grade of life is found in mind . . . the highest perfection of life is in God, where activity is not distinct from being, and where the concept is the divine essence, and where substance is not distinct from essence.[17]

Nor can Lee claim that the philosophical nomenclature that Edwards employed was new. Both Thomas Aquinas and Reformed Scholastics spoke of God's dispositions. Lee cannot even say that the meanings of "substance," "subsistence," and "property" have changed for Edwards to accommodate a dispositional conception of God. As the MS sermon on Deuteronomy 32:4 shows, substance and property are employed in fashion completely compatible with Scholastic use: "In our selves we distinguish between our souls and the disposition or inclination of our souls—the one in a substance, the other an accident or property of that substance. But there is no such distinction in God of substance and property. This is opposite to the simplicity of God's nature; but all that is in God is God."[18]

In contradistinction to the various levels of reality, Thomas Aquinas and the Scholastics asserted that God alone is incomposite and purely actual, that the essence of every substance except God is distinct from its existence. The difference between God and created existences lies in the fact that existence is not included in the notion of an essence or quiddity, that is, being or existence is not contained in the *definition* of their essence. God serves as the only exception, for He is, in short, subsistent being, in whom substance and properties are collapsed into *esse*. We cannot conceive of His essence as non-existent, for in Him essence and existence are identical in reality.[19] Edwards never abandons these ideas, but aligns himself with them.[20]

To be sure, Edwards does speak about dispositions that are necessary to the divine nature and essence, but such that have a *locus*—they are *of* the divine nature and essence, and they are *in* God. Moreover, it is God's *fullness* that is capable of communication or emanation *ad extra*. Excerpts from *End of Creation* make these assertions certain: "The disposition to communicate himself or diffuse his own *fullness*, which we must conceive

---

17. *IV Contra Gentiles*, II. Cf. Opusc. VII, *de Substantiis ad Pratrum Reginaldum socium carissimum*: "[T]he substance of God is his understanding of himself," (12). I refer to Thomas Aquinas only comparatively. He neither appears in Jonathan Edwards's "Catalogue" of books (read and desired) nor the "Dummer" Library Collection of Yale College nor Timothy Edwards's library, though Jonathan Edwards's maternal grandfather Solomon Stoddard did possess two volumes of Thomas's works and one of the later Thomist, Francisco Suárez (see Fiering, "Solomon Stoddard's Library at Harvard," 262–69). The Yale 1742 library (listed in 1743) does include "Aqinatis Summa" (ed. and number of vols. not specified). But it is by no means certain that this was in the Yale Library when Jonathan Edwards was a student and later tutor of the college; nor can we be certain that Jonathan Edwards read Stoddard's volumes. Surprisingly, there is not a single reference to Thomas Aquinas in Jonathan Edwards's entire written corpus.

18. 42. [L. 2r] Sermon on Deuteronomy 32:4 (1728), *WJE Online* 42. My rendition.

19. See Thomas Aquinas, *Being and Essence*, IV, §§6, 7.

20. Here Lee would claim that in Jonathan Edwards's dispositional conception of reality, "Habits and laws . . . *are* the abiding principles of reality" (*Philosophical Theology*, 48). Thus Lee attempts to equate being with dispositions. But, as Leon Chai argues, such an arrangement requires the equating of laws with powers, which cannot be maintained: "a law has to do with the manner in which a power is exercised, rather than the power itself" (*Limits of Enlightenment*, 143). Moreover, since Jonathan Edwards states that God's essence is "the one idea of Himself," Lee would have to equate disposition with ideas, which is precisely what he thesis does not say. For Lee, dispositions have "a distinguishable reality not only from human minds but also from God as well" ("Edwards on God and Nature" in *Edwards in Our Time*, 28).

of as being originally *in God* as a perfection of his nature . . . The diffusive disposition *in the nature of God*, that moved him to create the world . . . or a disposition *in the fullness* of the divinity to flow out and diffuse itself."²¹

According to Edwards, "all that is in God is God." This includes essential dispositions but it does not make God a disposition. As a matter of fact, so far is Edwards from abandoning Scholastic categories in this sense, he even says that, conceptually speaking, God's irreducible essence is an inexplicable "substance" ("the one idea of Himself") and the disposition to diffuse Himself may be thought of as a property: "[W]e may suppose *that a disposition in God, as an original property of his nature, to an emanation of his own infinite fullness, was what excited him to create the world.*"²²

In reality, however, there is "no such distinction in God between substance and property," for both God's *ens* and *esse* are one. Such concessions by Edwards in his articulation of a decidedly substance-property conception of God are altogether unaccommodating for Lee's hermeneutical schema.

In our second point (what Edwards means by "*ad extra*"), we find Lee takes Edwards too literally. When Edwards writes about God's "multiplication," "increase," and "repetition," in each case he prefaces these words with the rhetorical qualifiers, "in some sense," "as it were" or "in effect."²³ Because Lee does not take Edwards's language figuratively, he can assert that dispositions have an abiding ontological existence not in but outside of the mind of God, and that it is in this world of abiding ontological existences that God truly "multiplies" His reality in another reality, so that, sequentially and proportionately, one may say, God has increased or there is "more" God upon such dispositional exercises.

But Lee's analysis proves inadequate for a number of reasons. First, Edwards's language neither calls for nor lends itself to a literal interpretation. Second, Lee almost makes the exercise of God's disposition to communicate Himself a mechanistic impulse rather than understanding it in conjunction with Edwards's idealism. (This criticism ties into the first point about God's essence being "the idea He has of Himself" ["Miscellanies," no. 94]). Lastly (and in connection with the preceding point), the whole notion of self-communication/self-replication must be understood within the framework of Edwards's idealism. If, as Lee says, God's idea of Himself is prior and actual (agreeable to Edwards), then we must understand that what the divine impulse aims at is to have that *idea* (of the divine fullness) perceived. As this idea is perceived, or (better) communicated to intelligent perceiving minds by God, it becomes, "*as it were, ad extra*" in the sense that it is *in other minds*: God outside Himself is the idea of Himself (or His "fullness") *in* the minds of intelligent perceivers. *This* is how God replicates Himself, according to Edwards.

Even the idea of those minds is *not* to be thought of as perfectly outside of the mind of God; they too are ideas prior to God about how God might be *ad extra*. Thus when God conceives of Himself *ad extra* in/through those minds, He must also somehow conceive of Himself *as* those minds. Jonathan Edwards, sensitive to the need of having to account for the perceiving minds in/through which God "replicates" Himself, resorts to pantheistic

---

21. *WJE* 8:422, 432, 433, 434, 435. Emphasis mine.
22. Ibid., 435. Italics Jonathan Edwards.
23. Ibid., 433, 440. Cf. Suter, "A Note on Platonism," 283–84.

and panentheistic language and makes their existences instances of God's being: hence, God is "the sum of all being," "the only real being," "Being in general," etc.

Being in Perception is Edwardsean Becomingness

Strictly speaking, Edwards's idea of God *in* other minds attributes something of ontological peculiarity to God and therefore a diversion from his theological tradition. For instance, Reformed theology has typically made a distinction between God's essential and manifest glory. Usually it is the manifested glory that is intended when the question is asked, whether God does everything for His own glory; whether in His works His object is to reveal to intelligent beings the intrinsic and inherent glory of His being and nature. The essential glory of God typically means all that is glorious in God; in other words, His "fullness." Likewise for Edwards, "glory" is a general term to denote the sum-total of all the qualities that constitute God's excellence. The nature and attributes of God are the glory of God. They make Him a glorious being. Where it seems that Edwards incorporates innovations to this position is with his statement regarding God's "own glory *existing* in its emanation." His tradition would assert that the essential glory of God is a fixed quality. There can be neither increase nor diminution of it. The manifestation of the glory of God in the temporal realm is just that, a manifestation of glory. God is not present here in any quasi-substantial or essential sense, but in activity and will—the glory manifested in the work of creation. However, Edwards's language and intent must be distinguished from a mere "language of glory" or say, Thomas Aquinas's assertion that "the first cause, who is purely active and without possibility, does not work to acquire an end, but intends solely to communicate his perfection."[24] As Edwards contends, God's manifest glory is *not* something distinct from His substantial glory: for him, God's fullness, whether *ad intra* or *ad extra*, is God. "Ad extra" is really God present in, "as it were," another mode or sphere of existence, namely *in* created minds as Himself and the beautiful matrix of existences which, when narrowly considered, really is no different *kind* of existence to God, because all modes of God's existence are, as Edwards says, "always the same, and after the same mode."[25] Thus, there is no change as to how God conceives of Himself.

Edwards's ontological peculiarity, then, does not consist of God really expanding in the sense that Lee intimates. Rather, it consists of the *idea* of God's glory *in* created minds, which is nothing other than the immutable God in the mind by degrees.[26] This is Edwards's middle way where he articulates something orthodox and something innovative in the same thought; the innovations, however, being restrained by his Calvinistic confessional convictions. In one instance, he says all that is communicated is God's manifest glory (this is the end of creation to which his tradition would concede),[27] while in the same breath

---

24. *Summa Theologia*, I, Q44, A4.

25. "The Mind," no. 36, *WJE* 6:355.

26. Correspondingly, argues Jonathan Edwards, our conception of reality is understood by "degrees" ("Miscellanies," No. 662, *WJE* 18:200). The more God communicates ideas that resonate in our minds, the more of God (who communicates the "ideas of existence") we perceive, and therefore the more our perception of reality corresponds with the "truth," i.e., God's truth concerning reality.

27. Jonathan Edwards reinforces the point with the statement: "He [God] can't create the world to the end that he may have existence; or may have such attributes and perfections, and such an essence" (*WJE* 8:469).

he says that God is, *as it were*, expanded because what *is* present *is* God, not simply His manifest glory.[28]

Thus, if we understand expressions of "repetition" not in an unqualified literal sense, but in the sense that these are concepts which help to communicate the idea of God giving exercise to a disposition(s) to communicate Himself as existing in a different realm, then we are in a position to ascertain the inner logic of Edwards's notion of the self-communication of God.

What constitutes his doctrine concerning God as absolutely prior and patently self-"enlarging" in and through created minds may be found in *End of Creation*, where Edwards responds to a charge of inconsistency for holding both positions:

> Though it be true that God's glory and happiness are in and of himself, are infinite and can't be added to, unchangeable for the whole and every part of which he is perfectly independent of the creature; yet it don't hence follow, nor is it true, that God had no real and proper delight, pleasure or happiness, in any of his acts or communications relative to the creature; or effects however produces in them; or in anything he sees in the creature's qualifications, dispositions, actions, and state. God may have a real and proper pleasure or happiness in seeing the happy state of the creature: *yet this may not be different from his delight in himself*; being a delight in his own infinite goodness; or the exercise of that glorious propensity of his nature to diffuse and communicate himself, and so gratifying this inclination of his own heart . . . to communicate of his own excellent fullness.[29]

The act of creation—where we find the whole "scale of created existence"—is, then, the exercise of that propensity in God's nature to "diffuse" and "communicate" the fullness of Himself. Clarified further, Edwards believes that the diffusive disposition that moved God to give creatures and non-sentient entities existence was a communicative disposition "in general," precluding the hypothetical existence of any thing or being: "This disposition or desire in God must be prior to the existence of the creature, even in intention and foresight . . . For it is a disposition that is the original ground of the existence of the creature."[30]

After concluding that creation is the effect of an inherent telic-oriented disposition in God to "emanate," Edwards explains how God "manifests a supreme and ultimate regard to himself in all his works." He reasons that God's self-regard generates, "as it were," an external impulse toward self-communication because God is disposed to an "abundant communication, and glorious emanation of that infinite fullness of good which he possesses in himself."[31] This propensity in God to "diffuse" Himself may be considered as "a propensity to *himself diffused*" (Lee), or "to his own glory existing in its emanation"

---

28. "Miscellanies," no. 448, *WJE* 13:495.
29. "End of Creation" in *WJE* 8:445–46. Emphasis added.
30. Ibid., 438.
31. Ibid., 436, 438. Paul Ramsey comments that, "Insofar as this . . . Pauline concept [of πληρωμα] is used in the first chapter [of "End of Creation"] as a concept in philosophical theology referring to one of the metaphysical perfections of Deity, it displaces 'goodness' in Jonathan Edwards's lifelong attempts to express adequately his vision of God's end in *originally* giving creatures being. The same overriding importance must be ascribed to God's 'love' or 'benevolence' in its larger sense" (*WJE* 8:438 n. 4). In short, "fullness" replaces "goodness" in "End of Creation" as an explanation of that perfection *in* God that gives futurition to creatures.

(Edwards).³² What he means by this are three things. First, that there is a disposition within God to manifest His glory in another dimension, namely a temporal dimension; and that that manifestation of His glory cannot be separated from what it is that makes Him glorious, namely His beautiful being. Therefore, if God is to "externally" manifest His glory He must externally manifest Himself. This is accomplished by exercising His disposition toward that particular end. Second, this particular "end" of manifestation is inextricably bound up with the totality of God's attributes or the "fullness" of His being. And third, although God does not create out of need to fulfill a lack or deficiency, yet there is a kind of inevitability that God must create and that His presence in whatever world He creates must be perceived from within that realm in order for it to be a "manifested," "expressed" and "expanded" reality.

Thus we have what may be considered both the "beingness" and "becomingness" of God presented in the concept of an essentially diffusive disposition: "God looks on the communication of himself, and the emanation of the infinite glory and good [the becomingness of God] that are in himself [the beingness of God] to belong to the fullness and completeness of himself, as though he were not in his most complete and glorious state without it."³³ For Edwards, then, God *is* full and fully actual, but because of God's diffusive disposition it is requisite that that fullness be, as Edwards puts it, "*ad extra.*"

∼

God replicated in temporal reality does not mean that the Divine Being is "more" than before. Indeed, not even the incarnation added to God's glory. According to Edwards, in the incarnation God's glory simply "received an additional manifestation."³⁴ Instead, God's temporal replication facilitates an extra-dimensional manifestation.³⁵ In the *historia salutis*, the incarnation, crucifixion, and resurrection are that process at its apogee. Its culmination is the consummation of the age.

God's expansiveness (or comprehensiveness) therefore facilitates a mode of existence for God's fullness that is beyond temporality in the limiting, constraining sense that human beings experience, but which is not simply a negation of temporality altogether. It must be stressed, however, that what seems to be an allowance for potentiality in God with respect to time and change is really an eternal *mental* reality in the divine mind:

> 553 . . . 'Tis true that there was from eternity that act in God within himself and towards himself, that was the exercise of the same perfection of his nature. But it was

---

32. Ibid., 439.

33. Ibid.

34. "Miscellanies," no. 727, *WJE* 18:353.

35. Therefore, Keith Ward's well-known proposal of a God possessed of a "dynamic infinity," where there is an admission of temporality and potentiality in God, does not apply in Jonathan Edwards's case. Although Jonathan Edwards does offer several innovations concerning dispositions and ontological structure, and though he claims that there is a sense in which the universe is an inevitable expression or emanation of the reality God, yet his claims for divine self-sufficiency, immutability, and impassibility do not allow him to be categorized as one who espouses "inclusive infinity." See Ward, *Rational Theology and the Creativity of God*, 2–5.

not the same kind of exercise; it virtually contained it, but there was not explicitly the same exercise of his perfection. God, who delights in the exercise of his own perfection, delights in all the kinds of its exercise . . . But God, who delights in his own perfection, delights in seeing those exercises of his perfection explicitly in being, that are fundamentally implied.[36]

God's idea of Himself, therefore, includes an idea of Himself "virtually" manifested and, therefore, may be considered a perfect and unchanged idea, for to God "the idea is always the same, and after the same mode."[37] The point is that, although the disposition to be externally replicated was not actualized from a temporal perspective "until" created intelligences existed (presumably for Edwards there is no *temporal* "until" in this respect), nevertheless it possessed a mode of reality for which he can find no better term than "virtual" that, for all intents and purposes, could be accounted as a full exercise and prior actuality. But for there to be a reality *ad extra* it must move beyond theoretical virtuality to manifest reality with respect to the dimension God purposes to "expand" Himself, namely as being perceived in/through created intelligences.[38] This seeming potentiality is, then, the actuality of God's all-comprehension.

Divine Comprehensiveness

Henry B. Veatch suggests that the tendency to consider a universal as a changeless entity arose with Descartes and the rise of the new science.[39] The mathematical paradigm determined the Cartesian metaphilosophy. The Cartesian revolution in philosophy, Anthony Lisska argues, destroyed the concept of disposition as a significant ontological category: "Without this category Aquinian accounts of essence fall by the wayside."[40] By bringing essential dispositions into his discussion of God Edwards was inadvertently addressing Descartes' mathematical ontology while consciously contesting Hobbes's material ontology, wherein dispositions were excluded from the discussion because of the difficulty of ascribing numeric values or material properties (or substance-being) to them. For Edwards, divine dispositions allow for God to be free from the scrutiny of scientific measurement and the "atheism" of materialism,[41] yet their logic gives a strong degree of certainty concerning their exercises. His conception of dispositions in God, therefore, is not like Descartes' static *habitus*, but akin to Thomas Aquinas's dynamically expansive

---

36. "Miscellanies," no. 553, *WJE* 18:97.

37. "The Mind," no. 36, *WJE* 6:355.

38. This calls for a distinction in Jonathan Edwards's use of "real," "reality," "actual" and "actuality." On the one hand, there is God's reality about Himself, which is complete and full. While on the other hand, there is the creature's perspective that consists of God's communication of His reality as their temporal reality, which they only receive (perceive) in part, due to their finite capacities and God's selective (accommodating and purposeful) method of communication.

39. Veatch, "Telos and Teleology in Aristotle's Ethics," 279–86.

40. Lisska, *Aquinas's Theory of Natural Law*, 97.

41. Jonathan Edwards offers sustained critiques of atheism and its relation to what he calls "Hobbesical materialism" in 706. Two Sermons on Romans 1:20 (June 1743; repreached Aug. 1756), *WJE Online* 61; and *Practical Atheism* (1730) in *WJE* 17:47ff.

habitus in a God who must create because of that inherent propensity to create.[42] They are peculiar and fundamental to the Divine Being in that, while they necessarily and indissolubly belong to God's ontological essence, they also make up the relational structure of God's triunity.

What Edwards has been trying to account for through his explanation of a "diffusive" divine disposition are four things: (1) a philosophical explanation for how God could be temporally present; (2) an answer to the questions of how and why God could/would intentionally create anything at all, (3) and provide a means of accounting for the value of each and everything that is created; and (4) account for the difference between his understanding of teleology as the account of the temporal actualization of a divine disposition (which, by virtue of its very nature, tends toward a telos or "end") and the developmental teleology as evidenced in the writings of pantheists or deists. In short, his employment of disposition in this capacity offered a philosophical explanation of God's comprehensiveness.

Although Edwards's meaning of comprehension was explained earlier, yet one point requires emphasizing before we begin to examine in the final installment of this four-chapter examination into Jonathan Edwards's formulation of a theocentric metaphysic. As we move ahead we must hold in mind how, in light of this doctrine, he applied dispositional concepts in metaphysics. The point concerns the matrix of reality and its being "comprehended" by God's existence. This point is reiterated because it will be important for us to take into account that whether Edwards speaks of causal occurrences, material bodies, or minds, this world cannot in any way be thought of as existing or operating independent of God's immediate knowledge, essence, and power. The importance of this point as fundamental to his vision of reality will certainly come to bear on the ensuing chapters.

Concluding Remarks

Following his conversion Edwards saw God's excellence or beauty in every aspect of life. He concluded that for God's beauty to be so it must be inclusive of the create order. Since the beauty was the same, that is, it was all one beauty—the beauty of God's being, he concluded that God's beautiful being must be the matrix through which created reality exists, is known and experienced.[43] His metaphysical designation for this was "Being in general," under which both "the system of created being" and the Creator Himself were subsumed. "Being in general" is, in Edwards's words, "the great all-comprehending system," "comprehending the sum total of universal existence, both Creator and creature."[44] God's comprehensiveness is that "system" or, as contemporaries readers may prefer, "matrix." It is the manifestation or external replication of the divine fullness. It is how God's abiding immanent/transcendent presence may be understood; and it is the mode of God's

---

42. *Summa Theologia*, I, Q12, A5. Lee provides a detail history and noteworthy analysis of the ideas of "habit" or "disposition" in Jonathan Edwards's background (*Philosophical Theology*, 15–46).

43. "[God's] fullness . . . is the fountain, and so the sum and comprehension of everything that is excellent . . . [He] comprehends all entity, and all excellence in His own excellence" ("End of Creation" in *WJE* 8:460).

44. "End of Creation" in *WJE* 8 556, 423.

reality in the world that is the spiritual/mental/moral reality of the world, which comprehends all of the Divine Being's acts and power.[45] In a word, divine comprehensiveness is God's inclusiveness or His fullness replicated "*ad extra*." This corrective of Sang Hyun Lee's otherwise indispensable interpretation is the heart of Edwards's theocentric metaphysics internal to his own writings.

---

45. Ibid., 406.

7

The Application of Jonathan Edwards's Dispositional Concepts

> GLORY OF GOD. For God to glorify Himself is to discover Himself in His works or to communicate Himself in His works, which is all one.
>
> —"Miscellanies" no. 247

AS EDWARDS CONTINUED TO REFINE HIS EXPLANATIONS OF CONVERSION, THE "END OF creation," and God's activity and presence in both, he would turn to his scientific and philosophical notebooks from time to time and pen an entry on how the dispositional concepts connected with those ideas would/could be applied to "Natural Philosophy."[1] Some of the entries pertained to causality or atoms, some to minds, and others to phenomena like motion, light, or gravity. All, however, evidence his conviction that, "It is laws that constitute all permanent being in created things, both corporeal and spiritual."[2]

This conviction emerged from his analysis of (1) God's relation to the world, which he perceived to be so purposeful, ordered, and consistent as to be law-like; (2) his understanding of Newtonian physics in which the world's phenomena were understood to be mechanistic and law-like; and (3) his grasp of biblical anthropology and eschatological fulfillment. These ideas meet in telic-dispositions: the world is established as a network of, and God's relation to the world is conducted through, law-like principles. To be sure, the world in fact is an ideal one, but one that can be described and understood in terms of law-like dispositions.

In "Miscellanies" no. 1263, Edwards explains that there are two ways in which God operates, arbitrarily (which is an unmitigated and simple mental exercise) and naturally (operations that are "limited" by fixed laws, which God establishes by his arbitrary operation). The one is unsounded and impenetrable; the other is regular and established. Edwards's analysis of all created phenomena, mental or otherwise, rests upon the latter. Not only are all ideas "communicated to us, and to other minds, according to certain fixed and exact established methods and laws" by God, but even God's ideas about the world are "constant and regular," due to the "infinitely exact, precise and stable will [of God]." Consequently, Edwards writes that, "God is pleased to act by Rules which He fixes: thus

---

1. "Natural Philosophy" also is a collection of essays and scientific notes, which include a number of metaphysical and epistemological essays. For more on the content, composition, and significance of this series see Anderson's "Editor's Introduction," *WJE* 6:29–31, 173–91 and *Dwight-Works* 1:664–761.

2. *WJE* 6:391.

the Law of nature—the Laws which natural effects are produces."[3] Therefore, if, as Edwards says, "the very being of created things depends on laws, or stated methods fixed by God, of events following one another,"[4] then it would not be difficult to see how God may be *in*—as well as control—all things, by conceiving of them as telic-oriented principles, that is, as law-like dispositions, whereupon, "such actions upon such occasions should be exerted."[5] The same applies to the reception/perception of ideas: all things are composed and regulated by divinely established and empowered law-like dispositions.

In the present chapter we take a necessary excursion into Edwards's meaning of disposition and how, in his conception of God comprehending the created order, dispositions are used to explain God's relation to causality, material bodies, and created existences; or, in other words, how he applies his theocentric metaphysics to evidence God's comprehension of everything. This will lead us into a consideration of Edwards's innovative conception of God's triunity, upon which his ontology and calculus of value for human beings are based.

Edwards, a Platonic Realist?

To begin with, what made Edwards's use of these telic-oriented, dispositional concepts possible were several things. First, it was entirely permissible. Here I am not talking about the intellectual climate of the Enlightenment, but Edwards's own theological heritage, which traditionally employed dispositional concepts. As Sang Lee points out, Reformed theologians and Puritan divines like William Ames, John Owen, and Thomas Shepard, found it permissible to apply the nomenclature of disposition to theological subjects.[6] Secondly, he would have been familiar not only with the theological employments of "disposition," but also the accommodating definitions provided by the logicians he read at Yale.[7] Third, a "theocentrism of ends" did not conflict with the usage of dispositions, but rather complemented it. For example, in his way of thinking, a dispositional property, by definition, is a potentiality directed toward a specific development or "end"; hence its telic-orientation. A disposition, then, is a capacity to "do something" which an object possesses. Like most Aristotelian terms, there are analogical uses of disposition, but also for Edwards there are ontological dispositions that constitute the ontic structure of relational existence (more on this below). Fourth, dispositions could be defined and employed in such a way as to be theoretically compatible with the nomic regularity of Newtonian science, which had become the touchstone for any proposal discussing the phenomena of the universe. And lastly, there was Edwards's disappointment with John Locke's failing attempt to resolve being into a something, "which we know not what."[8] What Locke did not know

3. "Miscellanies," no. 1263, *WJE* 23: 202–3, 204.
4. "The Mind," nos. 27, 13, and "Subjects to be Handled" in *WJE* 6:351, 344, 391–92.
5. "Miscellanies," no. 241, *WJE* 13:358.
6. Lee, *Philosophical Theology*, 22–25. This statement, of course, could be extended to include Calvin (see, *Institutes*, I.14.17; III.3.7, 8). While at Yale, Jonathan Edwards would have encountered a variety of ideas concerned with "habit" and "disposition" in Dummer's philosophical and theological literature.
7. E.g., Heereboord.
8. Locke, *Essay* II, xxiii, 2.

about essence and substance, Edwards was ready to ascribe to God[9]—and he was ready to do so in terms that either combined the use of "substance" and relational dispositions or simply employed the latter (e.g., matter). He was also ready to blame the deficiencies of Locke's ontology on the empiricist's positivism and nominalism.[10] For Edwards, dispositional concepts offered a plausible and coherent alternative to understanding perceived reality because they deferred the origination, continuation, and termination of all existence and causality to God. This, of course, gelled nicely with his Calvinist view of divine sovereignty.

Dispositions, then, were not only essential for Edwards's characterization of the world they also served as an important feature in his metaphysical theory of being:[11] "[The soul's] essence consists in powers and habits."[12] Dispositions were no nominalistic device, they were real; their structural components—*relations*—were universals; and relational dispositions constituted the essential structure of reality.[13]

Lee additionally explains that it was Edwards's realist reconception of an original Aristotelian concept of *hexis* (and later, Thomas Aquinas's idea of *habitus*) that made his metaphysical reformulation of reality possible.[14] But this is not to say that Edwards was a metaphysical, direct, or representative realist. Where, on the one hand, metaphysical realism represents the view that there are "real" objects (usually spatiotemporal objects) that exist independently of our experience or our knowledge of them, and have properties and enter into relations independently of the concepts with which we understand them, Edwards, on the other hand, ardently holds to an anti-realist idealism in respect of the creation. That is, with respect to the real existence of abstract ideas Edwards is Platonic: there is, for example, real beauty without created perceiving minds. But with respect to the world, Edwards is a thoroughgoing idealist.

Yet, with that said, Lee points out that there is a sense in which dispositional laws have a mode of "reality" without being perceived by minds. He claims their reality is not by name but as ontologically real potentialities that are "a distinguishable reality not only

---

9. "The Mind," no. 61, *WJE* 6:380: "that 'something' is He by whom all things consist."

10. Locke, while continuing to speak of essences, distinguished between real and nominal essences. For him, the familiar objects of common sense are collections of copresent sensible ideas to which we attach a single name like "tree" or "man" or "flower." Identifying the ideas constitutive of the relevant collections gives us the nominal essence of a tree, man, or flower. He did not deny that real essences might underlie such collections, but he insisted that it is nominal rather than real essences to which we have epistemic access. Essence, therefore, does not equal subsistence in Locke. Jonathan Edwards's rejection of the Lockean account of spirit, mind, and matter, is indicated in "The Mind," no. 11 (1724) and "Miscellanies," no. 267 (1726), but becomes explicit in "The Mind" Nos. 70–72 (1748) in connection with personal identity. See Anderson's discussion on Edwards's various points of disagreement with Locke in "Editor's Introduction," *WJE* 6:101–2, 112–17, 128–31.

11. I say this mindful of Jonathan Edwards's provisos about God's being. Locke, it has been observed, had difficulties with the notion of habit, concluding that mental habits or dispositions were settled by "custom" (*Essay*, II, xxxiii, 5–9; cf. Lee, *Philosophical Theology*, 25–32). Thus, the scope of the epistemic function of habit (indeed, if there is one for Locke) is limited only to the aberrational connections among ideas, where habits possess no ontological status.

12. "Miscellanies," no. 241, *WJE* 13:358.

13. Anderson, "Editor's Introduction," *WJE* 6:83; cf. Fiering, *Moral Thought*, 78.

14. Lee, *Philosophical Theology*, 10–25.

from human minds but also from God as well."[15] He goes on to say that, while at first Edwards held that such a reality was in the divine consciousness, he quickly abandoned this idea to make a distinction not only between the "eternal existence" of things in God's consciousness and their temporal existence via human minds, but between dispositions existing as objects and ideas: "The created world abides as a system of the permanently fixed general laws or tendencies that God has established and according to which he causes actual existences (actual ideas) in time and space. The world, therefore, exists abidingly in the mode of *virtuality* or *real possibility* that is a midpoint between pure potentiality and full actuality."[16]

In asserting this, however, Lee has been incautious on three counts: by not strictly identifying such "actual existences" with ideas of divine power; by not explicitly stating that the source of such realism for Edwards lies in the disposition's peculiar mode of existence *in the divine mind*; and, by not strictly identifying the "midpoint" as the divine power, which moves a thing from a "before" existence to an "after" existence. In Edwards, dispositions' relation to God is understood in the following ways: (1) their applications are the "immediate" exercising of God's power (corresponding with Edwards's occasionalism); (2) inasmuch as God's power cannot be conceived of something foreign to His peculiar essence, then even those dispositions are, in some sense, of and in God Himself *as an idea* of how His power would be concerning the world; and, (3) the source of their abiding "reality" (prior to an actual manifestation/application) lies in their enduring in the divine mind.

In Edwards's system such dispositions themselves are ideas. Lee's proposal would have law-like "realities" maintaining an existence external to the divine mind without their being perceived by other minds corresponding to *that* external existence. This is to say, certain law-like dispositions possess a "reality" independent of the parameters of Edwards's idealism where things "can exist nowhere else but in the mind, either infinite or finite."[17]

Yet Lee is not entirely off the mark, for just as I have indicated, Edwards indeed holds that dispositions are abiding principles. As Anri Morimoto notes, Edwards makes an important modification to his earliest expression of idealism by qualifying the "reality" of certain ideas and laws as they pertain to *this* world. Things or objects (which Edwards equates with ideas) are in the *temporal realm* only when perceived by created minds or by their relational connection to other perceived ideas.[18] For Edwards, the idea of the existence of things in spatiotemporality is nothing other than an idea communicated from God to intelligent perceiving minds: "[The] truth as to external things, is the consistency of our ideas with those ideas, or that train and series of ideas, that are raised in our minds according to God's stated order and law."[19] For, "Man, or intelligent beings, are the con-

---

15. Lee, "Edwards on God and Nature" in *Edwards in Our Time*, 28.
16. Lee, *Philosophical Theology*, 63.
17. "Of Being" in *Works* 6:206. Dispositions do not determine God's idea of Himself, but vise versa.
18. See, e.g., "Miscellanies," nos. *pp*, 94, 238 and 239 in *WJE* 13.
19. "The Mind," no. 10, *WJE* 6:342.

sciousness of creation, whereby the universe is conscious of its own being, of what is done in it of the actions of the Creator and Governor with respect to it."[20]

The point toward which Edwards is moving holds that the *idea* of "external things" and the laws that govern them have a certain mode of reality before (even beyond) their existence in created minds. Ontologically speaking, the laws that govern the particulars of a given entity *x* have a particular mode of existence without the perception of an intelligent perceiving mind. However, this is not to say, as Morimoto does, that Edwards has left behind his idealist or immaterialist position. Rather, it has become *more* idealistic as his causality becomes more occasionalistic. Though divinely constituted laws are prior to perception, yet unless there is an intelligent perceiver *within* the realm in which those laws have their tendency, they will not have the occasion to be, as it were, in that domain. In God's determination of values they had "as good not be as be" without perceivers. The way that they become phenomenologically "real" or conceptually present is through God's communication of the idea of those laws or dispositions *in* some intelligent perceiving mind.[21] But the presence of some mind does not *cause* God's idea to be communicated or anything else for that matter. No relation or connection causes or stimulates occurrences. Instead, God Himself brings about particular results. The arrangements upon those occasions are simply a matter of some "fitness" determined by God's infinitely wise arbitration. Yet laws and rules that God determines govern the particular non-causal connections and their corresponding results. The divine power to effect results constitutes the midpoint between cause and effect—a law-like disposition or tendency toward some particular effect.

While Edwards understands that a disposition has a mode of ontological existence independent of intelligent perceiving minds, yet it is only as a certain *idea* of God's power. An abiding dispositional law (that is, one that has *not* been communicated to a created intelligence) does not have a quasi-independent metaphysical reality apart from the divine mind and neither does it consist of something other than God's power—a point which Lee himself admits. Rather, prior to the creation of angelic or human minds, they abide only as a certain determination in the divine mind and, even after the temporal presence of intelligent perceiving minds, they are entirely dependant upon God to continuously conceive of them as such, as well as communicate the idea of His power manifested in a particular way (as a thing or event).

Their "abiding" existence, then, lies in the notion that they continue as law-like ideas of how God's power will be exercised when those ideas—in the divine mind—are communicated to other minds. When the divine idea of any thing is communicated to an intelligent perceiving mind it becomes, as it were, concretely "real" to *that* mind; that is,

---

20. "Miscellanies," no. 1, *WJE* 13:197. Elsewhere, he uses the terms "perception" instead of consciousness to express the same point. The term "perception" may have been more favorable because it could stand for both having empirical contact with physical phenomena and having an idea of spiritual as well as physical things. Although in "Miscellanies," nos. 3, 87, and 354, for example, Edwards uses the designation "intelligent beings" (which could be interpreted as something broader than humanity, e.g., angels), "Miscellanies," nos. gg, 1, 104, 108, and 114, clearly show that humanity is intended by that designation to be "the consciousness or perception of the creation" ("Miscellanies," no. 104, *WJE* 13:272). The reason for this is discussed in chapters 8–9.

21. "The Mind," no. 69, *WJE* 6:385.

the idea of that thing gains a phenomenological or conceptual realness to/in that created mind and may be deemed an "*ad extra*" manifestation of divine power or beauty or being.[22] Thus, it is only in the sense that the source of such realism for Edwards lies in the dispositions' peculiar mode of existence (an idea) abiding in God's mind that he can be considered a so-called philosophical realist with regard to dispositions.

Divine Reality and Perceived Reality

There are two ways to talk about "reality" in Edwards. First, there is reality in the divine mind, where, "Things as to God exist from all eternity alike." So, if one wishes to speak about the unmanifested ontological reality of dispositions or the world, then one must understand their reality "established" as a complete "series" in the divine mind. Second, there is reality that pertains to perceiving finite minds. "Real," "reality," and "actual" in this latter sense refers to the created mind's perception (reception) of God's communicated idea of a thing's (i.e., the exercise of His power in a particular fashion to produce the effect of that thing) or the world's reality in His own mind (where it is real as an unchangeable idea). Consider Edwards's differentiation between these realities and his explanation of how they come together:

> Though we suppose that the existence of the whole material universe is absolutely dependent on idea, yet we may speak in the old way, and as properly and truly as ever: God in the beginning created such a certain number of atoms, of such a determinate bulk and figure, which they yet maintain and always will; and gave them such a motion of such a direction, and of such a degree of velocity; in a continued series. *Yet all this does not exist anywhere perfectly but in the divine mind.* But then, if it be inquired what exists in the divine mind, and how these things exist there, I answer: there is his determination, his care and his design that *ideas* shall be united forever, just so and in such a manner as is agreeable *to such a series*.[23]

He continues by giving instance to this contention, and closes by stating his conclusion:

> All the ideas that ever were or ever shall be to all eternity, in any created mind, are answerable to the existence of such a peculiar atom in the beginning of creation, of such a determinate figure and size, and have such a motion given it. That is, they are all such as infinite wisdom sees would follow, according to the series of nature, from such an atom so moved. That is, all ideal changes of creatures are just so, as if just such a particular atom had actually all along existed even in some finite mind, and never had been out of that mind, and had in that mind caused these effects which are exactly according to nature, that is, according to the nature of other matter that is actually perceived by the mind. God supposes its existence; that is, he causes all changes to arise as if all these things had actually existed in such a series in some created mind, and as if created minds had comprehended all things perfectly. And although created minds do not, yet the divine mind doth, and he orders all things according to his mind, and his ideas.[24]

---

22. *WJE* 6:215.
23. "The Mind," no. 34, *WJE* 6:353–54. Italics mine.
24. Ibid., 354.

The perception of "reality" or a thing perceived as conceptually or phenomenologically "real" or "actual" is a consequence of an intelligent perceiving mind's consciousness of the Divine Being's idea about reality or that thing; it is the "truth." The appearance of change or permanence lies in the presentation of the divine series in/to perceiving minds.[25] To the perceiver, that *communicated* series *is* their reality. To God, reality's mode and prescribed content never changes: it consists in a perfect idea of a communicated and remanated "series" of ideas.

In Edwards's theocentric metaphysics, the created mind's perception of thing—the idea of that thing in God's mind which He conceives of as communicated to that mind—is, in effect, the creature becoming conscious of "Being in general." Reverting to our previous discussion, Edwards's realism must be understood in terms of *degrees of coherence*: his is no correspondence theory of truth or reality, for the belief that instance *p* is true iff *p* cannot obtain verification without an ontological basis (God), which connects all instances *p* to an entire system that is consistent and harmonious—Being in general. Universals (e.g., relations), then, must be understood as patterns or blueprints that exist in the mind of God, where they are real and where dispositions have, as it were, a prior ontological reality. Their reality in the divine mind is perceived by created mind in degrees, either expanding or contracting their relationally determined perspective of a single system of reality, Being in general. This perceived reality (communicated by God, of course) is the reality of created minds, no matter what degree of it they perceive.

If we consider this in connection with Edwards's "scale of being" we get an idea of how "value" and "substantiality of being" are estimated: the greater the degree of a created mind's perception of ideas communicated from the divine mind, the more that created being is conscious of "Being in general," and therefore the more "consent" to being it has. The more consent to being, the more "excellency": the more "excellency" the more like God it becomes and, therefore, the more real or substantial. Conversely, the opposite holds for material entities.[26]

Dispositions, Causal Occurrences, and the Existence of the World

What distinguishes Edwards's theory of dispositions regarding causality from those of select contemporary physical and psychophysical theorists who employ dispositional concepts are two qualified things: (1) the ontological reality of dispositions apart from circumstantial manifestation; and (2) the reality of dispositions whether or not they are observed by created minds, as indicated in the above sections. As stated, Lee would have no difficulty with (1) and (2), for he asserts as much in his own writings.[27] However, important qualifiers must be added. Both (1) and (2) are qualified by Edwards's idealism and occasionalism in that they limit the "perceived reality" of unmanifested dispositions to a "virtual" status (a mid-point between cause and effect which Edwards denominates "power"), and ultimately resolve both the disposition and its manifestation to ideas of

---

25. "Miscellanies," no. 134, *WJE* 13:295.
26. "The Mind," nos. 1 and 45, *WJE* 6:335–36, 362–64.
27. Lee, *Philosophical Theology*, 42–48.

God's power and beauty—an arrangement determined and effected by God.[28] (Hence, the ultimate source of their reality lies in God's idea of Himself or, synonymously for Edwards, His essence.)

In a counterfactual argument, Edwards says dispositions permanently exist in a particular state, whether they are expressed or observed or not:

> In memory, in mental principles, habits, and inclinations, there is something really abiding in the mind when there are no acts or exercises of them, much in the same manner as there is a chair, in this room when none perceives it, we mean that the minds would perceive chairs here according to the law of nature in such circumstances. So when we say, a person has these and those things laid up in his memory, we mean they would actually be repeated in his mind upon certain occasions, according to the law of nature.[29]

By asserting that the "laws of nature" ("which God hath fixed") do not solely rest in the sphere of epistemology, but also ontology ("there is something really abiding"), Edwards underscores a critical facet of his account of dispositions. As he describes it, ontology is the foundation of epistemology, it sets epistemic limits: the science of knowledge is not separate from the question of existence.[30] Disposition is more than occurrent; it possesses a mode of reality independent of perceived events *as* a general law that governs the manner or character of actual existence, actions, and events, through which it gains external acknowledgement—and here is the critical part—*only when that idea in the divine mind is communicated*.[31]

So while Edwards rejects the epistemological theory that the attribution of dispositions is the consequence of such and such occasion, stimulus, or circumstance, due to his belief in the ontological basis of dispositions in the divine mind, he nevertheless maintains that such and such a disposition *certainly will* demonstrate its tendency upon given conditions: "All habits [are] only a law that God has fixed, that such actions upon such occasions should be exerted."[32] Significantly, however, the certainty of expression, inevitableness, or necessity of disposition's manifestation upon certain conditions lies in its being fashioned as an active tendency and connection within a *divinely determined series*.[33] The "power" in its activity is God's power. Strictly speaking, dispositions themselves are not causes; God exerting His power is the cause. God's power supplies the causal force within/of a disposition. A law-like disposition is, then, the way that power will be exerted. This forms the

---

28. "The Mind," no. 29, *WJE* 6:352. See "Miscellanies," nos. 553, 729 (*WJE* 18), 1337 (*WJE* 23), where Jonathan Edwards uses the words "virtual," "virtually," "actual," "potential," and "mere possibility" in this connection.

29. "The Mind," no. 69, *WJE* 6:385.

30. Elwood, *PTJE*, 12.

31. "The Mind," no. 40, *WJE* 6:357. Indeed, as Anderson confirms: "Nothing is more apparent in [Jonathan Edwards's] theory of supposed existence than that Edwards conceives of generals laws of nature to be ontologically prior to the objects of the world" ("Editor's Introduction," *WJE* 6:109).

32. "Miscellanies," no. 241, *WJE* 13:358.

33. It is not unlikely that Jonathan Edwards acquired this notion of "active principles" from Newton. Lee pursues this thought in *Philosophical Theology*, 31–34. It may be, however, that Jonathan Edwards simply deduced the notion of "active principles" from the telic orientation of created existences.

basis of Edwards's occasionalism and basically accounts for how occurrences take place. The status of Edwards's dispositions are certain through the grounding of occurrences in (1) the law-likeness of dispositions, where the laws are God's "natural operation" (as opposed to arbitrary, according to their differentiation in "Miscellanies" no. 1263); the causal force or power they govern is God's power; and (2) their "prior" existence as a "train or series of ideas . . . according to God's stated order or law." These dispositional laws ensure that occurrences will take place not only because they govern the way God's power is exercised toward resulting phenomena (mental or otherwise), but also because they are "real" ontological principles in the divine mind, and have their place within a completed series of exercises—"as to God."

As we noted in a preceding section, the idea of manifest reality in God's mind consists of a determined "series of ideas." When viewed as a whole, the series is the world, the matrix of reality, God "*ad extra*." When viewed characteristically, the series is a network of law-like dispositions regulating God's power toward specific exertions. The way the series achieves "*ad extra*" manifestation is through a divinely determined occasionalistic scheme.

Edwards's own unique brand of occasionalism is a two-fold doctrine, emphasized in one of two ways: idealistically or concerning the phenomena of causal occurrences. The first part of his two-fold doctrine pertains to his "idealistic occasionalism," to which I have referred earlier. Within this larger and overarching set, God utilizes perceiving minds to produce the effect of Himself communicated—the matrix of reality. The arrangement is one of God emanating and remanating ideas to/from perceiving minds. Subsumed within the first part, is the second, which assumes the idea of an initially manifested world and takes note of causal occurrences therein. To be sure, God is the causal power in both.

Within Edwards's idealistic occasionalism the ideas of why God created the world and how He effects its initial achievement come together. God's end is to glorify and replicate Himself "*ad extra*": perceiving minds provide the occasion, not out of absolute necessity, but because God determines it so: "[T]he creatures are made that God may in them have occasion to fulfill his pleasure in manifesting and communicating himself."[34] God in His own wisdom determines that without perceiving minds, the world would be valueless (Edwards's weak necessitarian view.) Therefore, God prescribes intelligent perceiving minds a role, not as causal agents, but as a condition in His scheme. Their "necessary" role in God's arrangement (why God "needs" them) concerns the world's value to God. They provide "minds" by which God may have His idea of Himself "*ad extra*" "remanated" back to Him.[35] The benefits intelligent perceiving beings receive in this arrangement and the love or pleasure God enjoys in such self-giving are altogether different matters, matters of theology, matters of soteriology.

How does Edwards know that dispositional laws pertaining to occasionalistic causality abide in the divine mind? He answers, "'Tis discover'd in the Constancy of the Laws of nature."[36] As a follow up question one might ask, "If general laws or dispositions are not

---

34. "Miscellanies," no. 448, *WJE* 13:495.

35. *WJE* 8:531.

36. 107. [L. 5v] Sermon on Numbers 23:19 (1743), *WJE Online* 44. Cf. *WJE* 3:126 and "Miscellanies," no. 241, *WJE* 13:358.

exercised, then what is their status of existence when in a state of inactivity?" Again, the answer is that they are a completed series in God's mind; they only are perceived in or as a temporal series by created minds. The "virtual" status of unmanifested dispositions pertains more to the created mind than to the divine mind.[37] Thus, when Edwards says that "God supposes [a thing's] existence," he is not saying that "virtual," "potential," and "mere possible" realities are real states of consciousness for God about things. Rather, God supposing the existence of a thing is His determination of the series of that thing's perceived reality *from* the perspective of a created mind. "Suppose" and "virtual" are temporal referents. For God, the movement from virtuosity to communicated reality is meaningless—the idea "is always the same and after the same mode." God knows "real" only one way: hence His timelessness and changelessness and perfection. The creature, however, remains subject to a linear or chronological progression of existence, where things become "real" or "actual" in their minds.

When Edwards discusses things from the perspective of the creature, he speaks from within the framework of a linear progression of temporal series (more on this later). Thus, in his causal theory a cause is that "after or upon the existence of which, or the exercise of it after such a manner, the existence of another thing follows."[38] What connects the idea of a prior existence to that "after" existence is "power": "The connection between these two existences [past and present], or between the cause and effect, is what we call power,"[39] writes Edwards in "The Mind" notebook.

Laws also explain how God resolves to communicate ideas of perceived reality to minds, and what the power of His laws tends toward. Which means that, the operation of God, or the exercise of His mind concerning creation, is law-like, so that "the immediate agency, will, and power of God," or the cause, is God, answerable to His law-like effect.

> [It] should be remembered, what nature is, in created things: and what the established course of nature is; that . . . it is nothing, separate from the agency of God . . . A father, according to the course of nature, begets a child; an oak [likewise] . . . produces an acorn, or a bud; so according to the law of nature, the former existence of the trunk of the tree is followed by its new or present existence. In the one case, and the other, the new effect is consequent on the former, only by the established laws, and settled course of nature; which is allowed to be nothing but the continued immediate efficiency of God, according to a constitution that he has been pleased to establish.[40]

It is through and in such laws that God exercises His power with regard to the created order: "God is pleased to act by Rules which he fixes, thus the Law of nature—the Laws by which natural effects are produced."[41] The immediacy of God's activity is not removed

---

37. See Anderson's discussion on whether ideas can exist without being perceived in which he examines Edwards's theory of "supposed" existences ordained by God, in "Editor's Introduction," *WJE* 6:107–8.

38. "The Mind," no. 26, *WJE* 6:350.

39. "The Mind," no. 29, *WJE* 6:352.

40. *WJE* 3:401. Cf. *WJE* 6:234.

41. 107. [L. 3r] Sermon on Numbers 23:19 (1743), *WJE Online* 44. Cf. "Miscellanies," no. 1263, *WJE* 23:202.

though laws are used. This, of course, is consistent with standard definitions of occasionalism, in which *ipso facto* laws cannot be causal, but they can be divine regularities at the creaturely level of observation. Thus, it is through laws, which govern *divine causal powers*, that God affects the result of created reality.[42]

~

Edwards's specific qualifications to occasionalism accommodate and do not extinguish the permanent nature of the laws constitutive of fully actualized spatiotemporal existences. The Edwardsean tendency that created entities are each moment the effect of God's immediate agency is upheld. For him, general laws *are* "the immediate exercise of divine power," not concurrent causes. If there is something that "permanently abides in the mind" even when there is no effect, then it is God's power. If it is manifest, that is, if it is communicated to perceiving minds, then it is His beauty and their reality. Thus, the objectivity of the world has a divine reference, not a physical or creaturely one, though its temporal reference becomes objectified when there is "the consistency and agreement of our ideas with the ideas of God."[43]

When Edwards refers in his etiology to dispositions or habits, he means active and real tendencies, not merely conventions or even a Humean "general regularities," because of their place within a series or a network, or, in other words, because of their *relation* to the whole series of ideas concerning the reality to be communicated to perceiving minds.[44] In this way, Edwards's occasionalism stands akin to the ontological status of Malebranche's ideas.[45]

Quoting again from "Miscellanies" no. 241, Edwards says, "All habits [are] a law that God has fixed, that such actions upon such occasions should be exerted." "Should" is not to be understood as "could" but really as "would," even "certainly would." For Edwards, an active tendency to a kind of phenomenological event will actually bring about such an event whenever a certain divinely prescribed set of conditions within the series is present.[46] Failure of occurrence simply is not possible due to any given disposition or thing's status within a "series." Dispositions then function with a kind of conditional necessity, in which God moves an event associated with a certain dispositional manifestation from its status within the divine series to "actual" occurrence or phenomenologically or mentally "real" with respect to created minds.

---

42. "Miscellanies," no. 629, *WJE* 18:157–58.
43. "The Mind" no. 10, *WJE* 6:341–42.
44. Ramsey, "Editor's Introduction," *WJE* 1:35, 118.
45. McCracken (*Malebranche and British Philosophy*) and Fiering ("The Rationalistic Foundations of Jonathan Edwards" in *American Experience*, 73–101) have shown several striking parallels between Edwards and Malebranche. For instance, both taught that God is "Being in general," the world is an ideal one, and God is the only and immediate cause. Cf. Cook, "Ontological Status of Malebranchean Ideas," 525–44; Nadler, *Malebranche and Ideas*.
46. Lee, *Philosophical Theology*, 35.

What actually triggers the actual application of a disposition is "a full, fixed, and certain connection."⁴⁷ "Philosophical necessity," Edwards says, "is really nothing else than a full and fixed connection." Necessity therefore lies in a particular *connection* with certain conditions.⁴⁸ It is the connection within the divine series itself that assures that necessity is "nothing different from certainty." The active tendency of disposition is necessitated by its connection with certain conditions, a *law of relation*, which God establishes. Dispositions or habits may be designated causes in this sense. Thus, dispositions function with a kind of necessity in bringing about a type of event or operation under a type of circumstances. These circumstances, which include the ideas of time, locale, and prescribed variable or variables, ascribe individuality, particularity, or identity to events and things.

Disposition, then, is an active, relationally connected causal power, triggered by God, to bring about events of a particular sort. The relational connection of a particular disposition links it with all other ideas in a single, comprehensive series in God's mind. Consequently, what are understood to be past, present, and future events or existences, are connected as a network/matrix. The series of created existences, as a whole, is one and abides in God's mind,⁴⁹ though it is made up of innumerable series of instances. The priority of God in Edwards's system means that it is God who constitutes how laws exist and in what manner they are communicated or fully realized as actual ideas to perceiving intelligent minds. Both metaphysics and physics emerge out of the "necessary being" and the "natural operations" of God.⁵⁰

The Activity of Resistance

In Edwards's first engagement with Enlightenment religion we find him countering the materialists' purge of the spiritual by nullifying the "substance" of matter. Shortly thereafter he adds to his reasoning that, if God was "*Ens Entium*" and present with the universe itself, then the possibility of there being competing substances (such that Newtonian physics proposed) with the "substance" of God was implausible. To him, even the least molecule outside of the immediate controlling power of God jeopardized divine sovereignty and compromised the doctrine of God's comprehensiveness. Therefore he countered with a critical analysis of solidity or "resistance," which was counted as a universal and essential property of matter, and concluded that this infinite power of resistance could not reside in an underlying substance, but rather must be a constant exercise of the infinite power

---

47. Miller (*Jonathan Edwards*, 121–22) and Alan Heimert (*Religion and the American Mind*, 73) have emphasized Jonathan Edwards's opposition to the notion of an efficient cause.

48. *WJE* 1:152, 156. For a discussion on Edwards's distinction between "moral and natural necessity," see Ramsey, "Editor's Introduction," *WJE* 1:34–37.

49. God's knowledge is an important topic in *Freedom of the Will* and several "Miscellanies." Jonathan Edwards never doubts the eternal completeness of God's perfect knowledge. It is upon this supposition that he strenuously argues against Arminian "contingency" theories. *WJE* 1:257–73; and "Miscellanies," no. 1154, *WJE* 23:59.

50. This statement might lead into a discussion of Jonathan Edwards's doctrine of providence, in which he distinguishes between God's "arbitrary" and "natural" operations, but I defer to Lee, *Philosophical Theology*, 68–75.

of God. Far from being undiscoverable by logical analysis, God alone is "substance" while matter is the immediate effect of the exercise of the infinite power of God.

"Resistance" itself came to rest on dispositional principles and came to play an important role in explaining Edwards's conception of reality. Indeed, the principles of the early composition "Of Atoms" were never abandoned; instead, they were brought into harmony with his developing idealism and philosophy of dispositions.

As we noted earlier, existing, for Edwards, occurs only in accord with general laws. The logic of which meant that laws not only constitute the abiding dimension of an entity as a disposition, but also determine the manner of its existence. Existence, as Lee explains, is in a particular manner—in the particular way a particular divinely established general law requires.[51] Laws, then, are the abiding principles of the structure and order of reality. "Therefore," Edwards says, "we may infallibly conclude that the very being, and the manner of being, and the whole of bodies depends immediately on the divine *power*" or Being, who causes "indefinite resistance in that place where it is" according to fixed laws.[52] Thus, material bodies themselves exist in a particular manner—*resisting*—according to the demand of a particular divinely established law, or the divine being exerting power in a law-like manner. For Edwards, the question of material bodies is not so much *what* exists but *how*.

The concept of "resistance," which appears in Edwards's explanatory corollaries to his propositions on the being of entities, is an essential part of his "idealistic phenomenalism"[53] response to the materialism of Hobbes, as well as the undiscoverable "substances" of Newton and Locke. In opposition to the materialism of Hobbes, his main point is that the very existence of bodies depends immediately upon the exercise of God's infinite power, and that bodies do not exist by themselves as substances. Instead, the material world "can exist nowhere else but in the mind, either infinite or finite," or again, "corporeal things exist no otherwise than mentally, either in created or uncreated consciousness."[54] According to Edwards, then, a material entity is not Locke's something, "which we know not what,"[55] or a subject to which solidity or the activity of resisting inheres, but rather a body is solidity—resistance from annihilation itself. For a body to be is for there to be resistance of a certain kind at a given time and place. Resistance or the extension and cohesion of bodies is the activity of God's infinite power, for only God can offer the power necessary to resist annihilation. Consequently, material bodies are not substances that exist independently,

---

51. Lee, *Philosophical Theology*, 40.

52. *WJE* 6:235, 215.

53. Anderson, "Editor's Introduction," *WJE* 6:53.

54. "Natural Philosophy" in *WJE* 6:186–87; "The Mind," no. 10, *WJE* 6:342. Despite Edwards's 1753 confession: "it happens I never read Mr. Hobbes" (*WJE* 1:374), "Natural Philosophy" indicates that he at least came across excerpts or summations of Hobbes's philosophy through secondary writers.

55. Jonathan Edwards picks up where Locke and Newton were unsure what the substance that supports the properties of bodies might be: "it follows that the opinion that philosophers used to have concerning a certain unknown substance, which they used to say it was impossible for a man to have an idea of, is nothing at all distinct from solidity itself; or, if they must needs apply that word to something else that does really and properly subsist by itself and support all properties, they must apply it to the Divine Being or power itself" (*WJE* 6:215).

but "the Deity acting in that particular manner in those parts of space where he thinks fit."[56] By removing the "material" substance from materialism, Edwards makes sense of his seemingly paradoxical statement, "No matter is, in the most proper sense, matter."[57] In general, however, his idealist-phenomenalistic view of the physical universe retained and emphasized its character as a Newtonian system of physics.

So, then, there are three important things to note here: First, in accord with preceding sections, the meaning of *material* substance has changed for Edwards from a medieval to a modern conception, as Sang Lee has rightly stated;[58] second, the activity of resistance itself *is* existence or being of bodies or bodies themselves; and third, the resistance activities caused by God are divinely established laws or, in other words, God's power exercised in a law-like fashion.

"Material substance" is reduced to the activity of resistance, or is dismissed altogether with reference to bodies. So that, if one were to speak of material substance as it appears in Edwards's scheme after mid-1722, one ought not to be speaking about the Aristotelian-Scholastic tradition of the ultimate underlying "stuff" or *concreta* which theoretically composed the "what-ness" of bodies. Edwards understands God's power to be the "substance" of bodies: "speaking most strictly, there is no proper substance but God" ("Of Atoms"). Edwards's conceptual approach to matter, as well as its conclusions, differs as widely as the predestined "end" of saints and reprobates.

Lawlike Dispositions and Created Existences

If, as we have concluded above, dispositions are laws understood as ontological principles with or without circumstantial manifestation, and material bodies themselves are essentially dispositions, then the question needs to be asked (in light of our redirection of Lee's analysis of Edwardsean dispositions with respect to the Divine Being) whether or not dispositions are the abiding principles of created existence. The logic of Edwards's conception of the material universe directs an affirmative conclusion. But does this logic of disposition apply to all intelligent being, the final subject of our study? In a note reminding himself to expand this very subject, Edwards indicates that indeed law-like dispositions constitute "all permanent being": "The manifest analogy between the nature of the human soul and the nature of other things; how laws of nature take place alike; how it is that laws constitute all permanent being in created things, both corporeal and spiritual. In how many respects the very being of created things depend on laws, or stated methods fixed by God, of events following one another."[59]

The comprehensiveness suggested by his proposal leads to the conclusion that laws do more than "constitute all permanent being in created things, both sentient and

---

56. Ibid., 214–15.
57. *WJE* 6:235. Cf. Wainwright, "Jonathan Edwards, Atoms, and Immaterialism," 79–89.
58. Lee, *Philosophical Theology*, 54.
59. *WJE* 6:391–92. Robert Jenson is correct to note that "'Spiritual' does not here have primarily the sense of *invisible*, but rather of *personal*, indeed *communal*" (*America's Theologian*, 17). Aside from stressing the importance of keeping this shift in emphasis in mind, I would make an amendment by changing "communal" to *relational*.

nonsentient," that they in fact *are* the principles of being for created existences, just as Sang Lee suggests. When referring to spiritual or perceiving beings, Edwards wrote in "Miscellanies" no. 241 that, "the [soul's] essence consists in powers and habits," meaning that "powers and habits" (dispositions) do not merely belong to entities as a type of component, but rather they are constitutive of their being.[60] Edwards expresses the same point at times by associating the Divine Being closely with the divine power.[61] The difference between the Divine Being and created existences lies in the fact that God is the One who "constitute[s] all permanent being" in "laws, or stated methods." While created existences can in some sense be reduced and said to be "dependent on" law-like dispositions, yet God cannot, though they are essential to His being. And in this respect, Sang Lee errs.

Insofar as powers and laws are associated with dispositions, bodies, beasts, and sentient entities do not merely have dispositions, but *are*, for all intents and purposes, law-like dispositions; and, as Lee explains, dispositions are the essence of things, albeit with certain caveats for intelligent perceiving beings (as we shall see in chapter 9). For instance, Edwards insists that such essential dispositions have a locus. To be sure, Edwards has abandoned the Aristotelian-Scholastic idea of the material world, but nevertheless maintains a concept of "substance" as a locus for the essential dispositions of "spirits" and sentient beings. By doing so, Edwards is proposing a dispositional conception of all created existences, of all perceived reality, in order to facilitate his vision of telic-theocentricity and which also remains in keeping with customary notions of *imago Dei* and the *analogia entis*.[62] In the end, the logic of God's "comprehension" of created reality not only posits necessary dispositions to God, but inasmuch as God's "expansive" disposition encompasses the temporal realm as a matrix of divine beauty, then all things are rendered compositions of dispositions.

A Trinitarian Model of Internal Relations

As we noted earlier, Edwards's discussions on "EXCELLENCY" began not only to play a prominent role in his understanding of God's cosmological and teleological relation to the world, but also the evolutionary process by which he related them to the ontological nature of all things. God, in particular, is "infinite greatness and excellency" ("Miscellanies," no. 44). In saying this, Edwards recalls his axiom concerning the ontological significance of "excellency," namely that being must consist in *relations* or else there can be "no such thing as consent."[63]

---

60. Lee, *Philosophical Theology*, 48.

61. "Miscellanies," nos. 94 and 259, *WJE* 13:262, 367. Holbrook alludes to this when he notes that Jonathan Edwards deposits at the onset both value and power in being itself. Value did not have to be imported from elsewhere into the realm of power, since both were inherent in being. Holbrook concludes by saying, "God does not create value, law or ethical essences which He then obeys. They are constitutive of being itself" (*Ethics of Jonathan Edwards*, 136). Cf. Delattre, *Beauty and Sensibility*, chap 3.

62. Bodies and sentient entities differ in that the latter's dispositions are designated a *locus*, which Edwards calls "substance." This is further explained in chapter 9 as an improvement upon Lee.

63. "The Mind," no. 1, *WJE* 6:337.

The corollary "Miscellanies" (no. 117) that demonstrates the validity of this principle focuses on the Godhead. In it he writes, "Again, we have shown that one alone cannot be excellent; inasmuch as, in such case, there can be no consent. Therefore, if God is excellent, there must be plurality in God; otherwise there can be no consent in him."[64] Wallace Anderson explains the significance of Edwards's innovative conception of the Trinity: "it seems evident that his new concept of being, when applied to the divine perfections, stands in sharp contrast to the long tradition of philosophical theology into which he was born. God's goodness is not grounded in the absolute unity and simplicity of his being, but belongs to him only as he constitutes a plurality involving relations."[65]

The important thing for us to note is that Edwards now explains the ontological structure of being in terms of internal relations. He uses God as his primary illustration for trying the plausibility of his aesthetic experiments in ontology because the Divine Being is for him the first and necessary being, "the head of the universal system of existence; the foundation and fountain of all being."[66] After using God as his test case or prototypical model, he then makes application to created existences on the "scale of being."

In Edwards, there are three relational principles that make God God. (1) Self-relation: the Godhead is an inner trinity of excellent relations. This is to say, who God is is inseparable from His relations to Himself. (2) The *quality* of God's relation to Himself determines the nature of his existence. Since God is an infinitely excellent or beautiful being, His being is of infinite "proportion." (3) The *extent* of God's consent to Himself and other entities communicates something about His being. For God to be "love" He must infinitely consent to His own innertrinitarian self and the idea of Himself replicated "*ad extra*."[67]

Edwards then applies these three relational principles to his "scale of being," by employing his philosophy of dispositions to depict their teleological significance. For inasmuch as God's emanationistic activities through the created order have one telic purpose, viz. the glory of God, created existences are included in that functional end. In this way, the external, expansive character of the divine beauty is explained through the "scale of being," where God's infinite being encompasses external existences. According to Edwards, all value and substantiality (realness) of being on the scale is understood in terms of nearness to God and other beings through "mutual consent." Thus, beauty or the relationality of "excellency" determines the ontological status and value of all being, including humans, even reprobates within a double predestination schema.

So, just as Edwards predicates the whole scale of created existences upon ontological arguments for a necessary being, so too his analysis of being in terms of excellency rests upon God; this time in terms of necessary beauty and plurality. In other words, Edwards gives philosophical depth to his philosophy of being by modeling the ontological structure of created existences upon his trinitarian formula and analysis of God's constitutive inner relations. What is more, God's relational excellence is not external to God but, inasmuch

---

64. *WJE* 13:284.
65. "Editor's Introduction," *WJE* 6:84; cf. Delattre, *Beauty and Sensibility*, 117–84.
66. "Nature of True Virtue" in *WJE* 8:551.
67. See Lee, *Philosophical Theology*, chap 7.

as God's relational excellence is His idea of Himself "*ad extra*" (replicated in other minds), it must be considered *internal*, according to Edwards, and therefore constitutive of the Divine Being's essential idea of Himself. It is the internal dynamics of God that provide Edwards's metaphysical rationale for divine comprehensiveness and the unity, interrelatedness, and connectedness of the matrix of existence, as well as his own penchant for panentheistic expressions of the these things.

In the outcome of Edwards's trinitarian formulation we find that the most important implication of his definition and use of excellency is that every real being must, as a condition of its existence, stand in some relation to other things, and ultimately to all other things.[68] This, of course, implies that the universe itself is necessarily pluralistic and bound to God's being in a matrix of relations. Consequently, the ontological status of perceiving beings in terms of substantiality or realness on the "scale of being" is defined by the extent and quality of their *relation*(s) to other beings.

Lee delineates the contents of Edwards's model for ontological structure, to show the plurality of the universe as well as its inner relational composition, by correctly presenting its three maxims. "First of all," says Lee, "*what an entity is, is inseparable from its relations*."[69] Just as the inner being of God is explained through dispositional and relational concepts, so too created entities, modeled after the defining inner plurality of the Godhead, are likewise presented with *relational necessity*. With God, however, there is a peculiar internal uniqueness which does not permit existences outside of the Godhead to be ontologically defined in a manner identical to God: "'Tis peculiar to God that he has beauty within himself, consisting in being's consenting with his own being, or the love of himself in his own Holy Spirit."[70] For all existences outside of the Godhead, being is determined by how an entity is related with *other* entities *and* to God. With God, however, existences are comprehended by His being. Either way, determinative relations are not external but internal to being.[71]

Lee identifies the second maxim of Edwards's relational conception of the structure of being as: "*relations determine the existence of an entity*." Since laws (dispositions) are the quality of resistance (existence) itself, laws must be exercised if there is to be existence. And, since the exercise of laws (the relation of relationships) can only mean a multiplication of relations of particular sorts, entities cannot actually exist without actual relations. In other words, the relationality of the created order does not admit that any one of its pluralities of entities is an ultimate substance or stark singularity in the sense that it can exist independently of all others, or that it can have any unity, autonomy, or self-identity apart from the relations in which it stands to others. There is no aseity outside of God. This is not to say that all individuality is extinguished in a particular entity because of its relational constitution. Bodies, we remember, exist in a *particular* point in time and space, and have a particular functional purpose (telic-orientation) in their divinely determined existence. Nevertheless, entities never enjoy pure individuality: "Since the law that gov-

68. Ibid., 77.
69. Ibid.
70. "The Mind," no. 45, *WJE* 6:365.
71. Lee, *Philosophical Theology*, 78.

erns the individual activities of resisting [existing] is a relation of relations, the acts of resisting can only be the acts of relating to other entities—that is, the acts of resisting in a particular sort of relationship with other entities."[72] The result is a nexus of laws of dispositions, a matrix of excellent relations or existences. Therefore, a being is not only defined or constituted through its relations, but it also exists only through its relations. The whole of reality is, as it were, a network or matrix of interrelated relationships.

The third element of Edwards's model for ontological structure has to do with the *extent* of the mutual relations of all entities. In his ontology, an entity's structure is defined as a law or a nexus of laws. And since laws are relations of relationships, the very existence and the essence of an entity is inseparable from its relations. The most fundamental logical ground for such a perspective is his contention that the universe is the external expression and repetition of God's internal being. Since God is a unified being (with internal plurality), then His *ad extra* existence must be a unified system.[73] In sum, what a thing is is also determined by its "*tendency to be related with other entities*" in a manner harmonious with the law of the whole, that is, with the beauty of God.[74]

The beauty or excellency of God, then, is the standard, point of reference, goal or "end" of creation, as well as the foundational and defining reality for all other beings. Being is not simply determined by being-in-relation, even to the whole of being (point number two), but being's quality and quantity of being-in-relation. Being-in-relation necessarily means being part of the network or matrix of relations and, to a degree, related to all relations. The operative word for Edwards however is "degree." The degree of being's "substantiality" is qualitatively and quantitatively determined, which, in turn, determines being's value on the "scale of being" and, therefore, worth to God.

The three relational concepts determinative of being are the same with created existences as they are within the Godhead. The three dimensions of relatedness are: (1) the relationship an entity has to itself, (2) to certain other entities, and (3) to the (law of the) whole (i.e., God).

A material body, then, is related to itself in its particularity—a resistance in a particular time and place. Secondly, a material body is related to other bodies through the laws which govern that particular type of body. And thirdly, a nonsentient being is related to the whole by virtue of its perceived place with the total matrix of reality. This is how the idea of its existence may be understood *as* a perceived existence. To Jonathan Edwards, of course, a material body is nothing more than an idea. Dispositions, relations, and a matrix of existences are simply real ideas in God's mind communicated to intelligent perceiving minds about the perceived reality of such ideas.

Of course, Edwards's most important application of these relational principles is to human beings. As with God, so too a human being's essential nexus of relations contains three elements, which we unpack from Edwards's dense formula: "[Existence], consists in

---

72. Ibid. Cf. "Miscellanies," no. 125[A], *WJE* 13:288.
73. Ibid., 80–82.
74. Ibid. 80.

the perception of these three things: of the consent of being to its own being; of its own consent to being; and of being's consent to being."[75]

1. Intelligent perceiving being's self-identity or the consent that exists between its constituent parts ("the consent of being to its own being");
2. Its relations with other entities (its "consent to being"); and
3. Its consent to the whole ("being's consent to being").

Likewise, the "happiness" of intelligent perceiving being consists in the knowledge and love of beauty.

What does this three-dimensional structure of being mean for the nature of human beings? It means that the essential structure of a human being, first of all, is conceived by Edwards as a nexus of laws that is a tendency to three relationships: to one's self (where we find Edwards's trinitarian formula applied to the psychological constitution of intelligent perceiving being[76]), to others, and to the whole ("Being in general"/"Being-as-manifest"). As we shall see in the next chapter, each relation corresponds to a relation within the Godhead. God's mind and ontological relations and human minds and ontological relations are parallels of sorts, differentiated by autonomy, necessity of being, and, significantly, by degrees.

There is, then, a three-dimensional structure in the essence of a human being, where the first two relational dimensions are governed by the third.

Concluding Remarks

Jonathan Edwards's conversion marked the beginning of not only a spiritual and theological journey, but a philosophical one as well. The "holy disposition" infused into his soul brought with it a capacity to "perceive" reality, as it truly was—an extension of God's "excellency." Convinced that the "vision" of God in reality was not his affected narrative but God's, he set himself to reconstruct the evidence of nature (and, later, history) accordingly. The content of his Spirit-regulated, spiritual sensibilities was, for him, an authentic Christian and spiritual view of the world, one which corresponded to Holy Scripture and, conveniently, concurred with his reading of Reformed confessions.

He discovered through his experience that one cannot satisfactorily understand God's reality in light of man and the world, as the rationalists attempted, but vice versa. Indeed, he learned that the world and all things associated with it were pregnant with cosmic significance through God's purposeful presence.

This was Edwards's post-conversion starting point, the mental state with which he engaged the Enlightenment and his colonial New England context. The vision of "God as God" took precedence over established theological positions, philosophical theories, and any and all competing worldviews, scientific or otherwise. For, according to Edwards, the

---

75. "The Mind," no. 1, *WJE* 6:338.

76. Cf. Augustine, *On the Holy Trinity* in *The Nicene and Post-Nicene Fathers*, 125, 143, 156. Jonathan Edwards was aware of Augustine's work through Chevalier Ramsey. See "Miscellanies," no. 1253, *WJE* 23:184ff.

worldview it facilitated was the only one that consistently brought together divine revelation, spiritual sensibilities, the power of reason, and scientific observations concerning the physical world, into one compelling interpretive framework of intelligible reality. Thus, in light of its internal and external, subjective and objective confirmation, Edwards began re-evaluating theology, conversion, history, creation, natural philosophy, and anthropology.

Despite his unconventional formulation of the Trinity and the panentheistic implications of his account of God's relation to the world, Edwards nonetheless was willing throughout his career to put his signature to the Westminster Standards. He was always willing to do so, not because he was a hypocrite or a latitudinarian freethinker in sheep's clothing (or Genevan gown, as the case may be), but because He did not think his speculative philosophical-theologizing was outside the creedal parameters of Reformed orthodoxy.[77] In fact, his hope, if not confidence, was that his intellectual efforts in the realm of metaphysics would set a bulwark against the prevailing modern theologies in Britain and, as he was learning, at Harvard and possibly in seminal form within his own alma mater.

True to his covenant faith and heritage, Edwards champions a doctrine of God-centeredness. For him, however, theocentrism is not a single doctrine, but a genus with many species. Characteristic of his thought is a theocentrism of ends. Above all things, what is important to Edwards is that God gets the glory worthy of His being and nature. When he considers Romans 11:28, "for of him, and through him, and to him, are all things,"[78] Edwards emphasizes the "*to* him" beyond the "for him and through him." The theological equivalence of his telic-theocentrism lies in the *pactum salutis*, through which God brings about His glorification in the work of redemption by way of an intra-trinitarian eternal confederation. All things exist for God's glorification and are part of this divine work. Consequently, all things are tied to and moving toward a programmatic "ultimate end." Not only is a static God utterly foreign to his thinking, so is a static creation, because, for him, reality itself is the matrix of God's beautiful being moving toward that "ultimate end." In fact, divine goal-orientation is so dominant a concept in his thinking apparatus that it remains doubtful he discusses any item in his corpus outside of its aegis. It is not surprising, therefore, to find all things—creation, providence, causality—affected, indeed, subjugated to its agenda. This is what makes Edwards both peculiar and uncongenial to the modern temper.

But Edwards goes even further, God is not only central to the believer's reality, but also the unbeliever's ontological reality; for God Himself *is* "real existence," which "comprehends all being"—even the existence of those outside of Christ. Thus, according to Edwards's new aesthetic and theocentric vision and the ontic, telic, and cosmic conclusions he draws from it, all created existences derive their being and value from God's "comprehension." This means that God's comprehensiveness holds both ontological and epistemological consequences for all created intelligence: whether regenerate or not, every man's metaphysical reality is directly related to, encompassed by, and derived from God.

---

77. Fiering, *Moral Thought*, 51.
78. See "The Nature of True Virtue" in *WJE* 8:551. There is no record of Edwards preaching this text.

In Edwards's way of thinking, if Reformed theology was to compete in the hostile marketplace of Enlightenment thought (such that was unsympathetic to and failed to have deference for Protestant symbolics regarding divine immanence and all that entailed in terms of Calvinist soteriology), it needed to articulate its worldview in terms that encompassed all aspects of a reality undergoing a paradigm shift in physics and philosophy.[79] On a sophisticated level, he learned that this could be done through metaphysical concepts of "Being in general," "being-as-manifest," and "all-comprehensive being." Sensibly, these abstractions become concrete or earthy through typological associations in connection with a theology of nature.

Whether philosophically or concretely, God's essential presence and purpose in the world are founded upon three fundamental concepts: excellency, idealism, and law-like relational-dispositions. Edwards's twofold doctrine of occasionalism serves the latter two. The world is an ideal one, but one manifest and comprehendible in terms of law-like dispositions. The relationality or plurality of the world articulates its beauty or excellence, which, to Edwards, is mental existence, an instance of "excellence" comprehended by God.

Edwards's theocentrism of ends or metaphysics of finality brings his thoughts on excellency, idealism, and relational-dispositions, under one heading to express and explain the single point that God indeed gets His glory. All things in their goal-oriented dispositional structures are therefore predestined, prescribed, and perfectly exercised according to the divine will to glorify God Himself in His *ad extra* manifestation in spatiotemporality. As we shall see in the next chapter, these ideas especially apply to human agents, because in the world according to Edwards human beings created in divine image are God's principle means for accomplishing His self-glorifying ends.

---

79. Fiering, *Moral Thought*, 60.

The Beauty of Being
An Aesthetic Ontology of Human Being

> Man, or intelligent beings, are the consciousness of creation, whereby the universe is conscious of its own being, of what is done in it of the actions of the Creator and Governor with respect to it.
>
> —"Miscellanies" no. 1

THE PRECEDING CHAPTER CONCLUDED WITH A BRIEF EXAMINATION OF EDWARDS'S depiction of a human being's dispositional essence as a nexus of laws tending to three relationships. Relations were understood to be internal to being, descriptive of the ontological structure within the dispositional constitution of human being: hence, Edwards's commitment to a doctrine of internal relations. The implications of the three categories of relations—to one's self, to others, and to the whole (i.e., the beauty of God)—were seen to have crucial meaning for the way in which Edwards regards and interprets the existence and purpose of man with relation to God's program of self-glorification/self-replication. For Edwards, the existence and purpose of any thing is never detached from God's teleological purposes. The same principle gained from his theocentric re-evaluation of creation is now applied to human beings. Indeed, whatever supposed independent purposes an individual may have for himself is altogether subservient to God's self-glorifying purposes in, through, and by his existence. Going directly to Edwards's point, God's teleological comprehensiveness is total—nothing is exempt from fulfilling His determinative ends.

Theologically, Edwards's doctrines of predestination, providence, and the divine decrees insure that whatever secondary purpose an individual may have for himself is ultimately linked to and terminates in God's glorification and the manifestation of one or more of His attributes, regardless of whether the individual is voluntarily consenting or conscious of it.[1]

According to Edwards, who happily subscribed to the Westminster Confession, the chief end of man is indeed to glorify God. Whether man enjoys God or not does not detract from the fact that God most definitely will glorify Himself in, by, and though man. Man's happiness or enjoyment of God is, nevertheless, the chief personal benefit of a consenting (loving) relation to God. As man consents to God, God is glorified through the dynamics of that *direct* relation of *mutual consent*. As God is glorified, spiritually cog-

---

1. "Miscellanies," nos. 29, 51 and 75, *WJE* 13:216–17, 228–29, 243; cf. *The Sole Consideration, that God is God, Sufficient to Still All Objections to His Sovereignty* (1735), Banner-Works 2:108–9.

nizant man rejoices in that glory and becomes, in Edwards's estimation, "happy above all things." The ontological benefit for man in this relation is the increased substantiality (realness, excellence, proportion) of his being. Epistemologically, it gives man access to a dimension of reality unobtainable in an unregenerate condition. In Edwards's mind, the fulfilled spiritual happiness of man—stemming from a spiritually restored state of mind—can be measured by "degrees" that directly correspond to the "excellency or proportion" of man's being.[2]

As explained in the Introduction, Michael McClymond demurs at this point. He remains unconvinced that man, especially the natural-man, could have any degree of "excellency or proportion." If, he argues, the conceptual link between Edwards's teleology and ethics is the crucial idea that might be termed the "principle of proportionate regard" (where in Edwards, "'tis fit that the regard of the Creator should be proportioned to the worthiness of objects, as well as the regard of creatures"), then God, no less than human beings, is ethically bound to "take into account and respect the inherent worth of each entity."[3] The question then is, what inherent "worth," "value," or "fitness"—designators which indicate that moral agency rests on inherent values—does man possess?

McClymond's proposal of a "principle of proportionate regard" permits Edwards to ground his ethics on ontology and evaluate God's intentions in creating (the treatise *Two Dissertations* develops this fully). Yet, as McClymond points out, basing a calculus of values on God's being does not easily translate over to finite beings. For instance, if the worthiness of any given object is reckoned as the mathematical product of its "degree of existence" multiplied by its "degree of excellence," and God—who is "infinitely excellent" *and* "infinite being" and is therefore "infinitely honorable and worthy"—has infinite and supreme regard for Himself, that is, He has perfect regard for the only infinitely worthy being, viz., Himself, then what value or excellence is left for the creature? It seems that God should only have regard for Himself. But Edwards does not stop there, he also says that *only* God has "real being" and excellence or (using alternative Edwardsean phraseology) that God is "the sum of all being and excellence."[4] It would follow, then, that only God is worthy to be regarded by Himself. Edwards says as much in *End of Creation*: "As the Creator is infinite, and has all possible existence, perfection and excellence, so *he must have all possible regard*."[5] But he says so with even more clarity, in "Miscellanies" no. 1077:

> 1077. GOD'S HOLINESS is his having a due, meet and proper regard to everything, and therefore consists mainly and summarily in his infinite regard or love to himself, he being infinitely the greatest and most excellent Being. And therefore a meet and proper regard to himself is infinitely greater than to all other beings; and as he is as

---

2. Such a conclusion may efficiently be deduced from not only "The Mind" nos. 1 and 45, but also "Miscellanies," nos. 662, 699, 701 and 702; *WJE* 18:200; 282; 283; 283–309, esp. 299, where Edwards summarizes this principle by saying, "Those that God is pleased to show most love to, we may well suppose he has set his love most upon. God communicates his love to enjoyment by manifestation. None can enjoy [but] only as God manifests; the enjoyment therefore will be proportionable to the manifestation."

3. "End of Creation" in *WJE* 8:424; McClymond, *Encounters with God*, 53–54.

4. "The Mind" no. 6, *WJE* 6:345; "The Nature of True Virtue" in *WJE* 8:551; "Miscellanies," no. 1077, *WJE* 20:460.

5. *WJE* 8:424. Emphasis mine.

it were the sum of all being, and all other positive existence is but a communication from him, hence it will follow that a proper regard to himself is the sum of his regard.[Vid.] TRINITY.[6]

Unable to reconcile the perplexities this principle engenders, McClymond concludes: "When all is said in *End of Creation*, it is hard to see how God's proportionate regard includes a concern for mere mortals. Moreover, there is a moral as well as a metaphysical issue, since humans are not only finite but sinful. The morally depraved are not obvious objects for God's proportionate regard."[7]

In short, not only do the presuppositions of Edwards's ethics seem inconsistent in light of the proportionate regard principle, but also his teaching on unmerited grace appears superfluous.

Although Edwards primarily employed proportionate regard to underscore the ontological uniqueness and incommensurability of God, not to analyze the possible relations between creatures of differing "degrees of excellence," which he rarely and only generally does between the regenerate and unregenerate portions of humankind.[8] Yet the point remains: Can God have regard to man within this scheme? If so, what (if anything) comprises man's excellence?

Stephen Holmes, looking at this problem through a theological lens, accentuates the crisis in Edwards's thought by focusing on the reprobate. He builds his case through an examination of Edwards's trinitarian creation-theology. We noted in the preceding chapter that Edwards subsumes the doctrine of divine perfections under the doctrine of the Trinity. Its relation to creation was in the following: just as God's internal (*ad intra*) glory consists of His trinitarian being, so too God's external (*ad extra*) glory is trinitarian. In Holmes's words: "The flowing out of God's glory is twofold, consisting in the communication of knowledge to the creature and the communication of love to the creature. These correspond to the internal begetting of the Son, or Logos, or Wisdom, of God, and proceeding of the Spirit, or Love, of God."[9] Creation, then, is an inner-trinitarian event, an *ad extra* communication of the inner-divine perfections, particularly the Son, but also the Spirit.[10]

When Holmes considers the church (the elect) in this respect, God's self-communication *as* the Son is internally coherent. The redeemed participate in God's perfect knowledge of Himself through their union with Christ, and they participate in God's perfect love of Himself through the indwelling presence of the Holy Spirit (who is the sum "purchase" of all of Christ's work).[11] Creation—*with respect to the church*—is eminently gospel-cen-

6. "Miscellanies," no. 1077, *WJE* 20:460.

7. McClymond, *Encounters with God*, 62.

8. Cf. Jinkins, "Being of Beings"; McClymond, *Encounter with God*, 31; and Miklos Vëto, *Le pensée de Jonathan Edwards*, 49. Jonathan Edwards also employed this principle to considerable effect in his theodicy and rationale for hell as a place of infinite punishment, as well as to explain certain elements in his doctrine of heaven (e.g., the delight of the saints proportionate to their ontological stature in Christ) and, as we shall see in chapters 12 and 13, the doctrine of justification.

9. Holmes, *God of Grace*, 55.

10. Ibid., 70, 98.

11. Holmes insightfully notes that Jonathan Edwards was not content to say with his tradition that the

tered and therefore valuable and meaningful to God: "The end of the creation of God was to provide a spouse for His Son Jesus Christ that might enjoy Him and on whom He might pour forth His love."[12] The fulfillment of this "end" is then threefold: (1) there is the ingathering of the elect, "Christ's bride," who from eternally past are divinely constituted as one with Him; (2) through the Church's participatory union with Christ or *ekstasis*, God is genuinely communicated and replicated *ad extra* in a christological-creation; and (3) all is accomplished within the framework of a gospel-centered narrative.

Here McClymond finds an answer to at least the elect portion of humanity: Edwards's Christ-centered doctrine of predestination constitutes all elect natural-men (past, present, and future) as *in* Christ. God elects His Son to mediatorial office through being joined to the man Jesus Christ and God elects this man to mediatorial office through union with His Son, and thus God elects the God-man, Jesus Christ to be the "head of election and the pattern of all other election."[13] On the basis of Edwards's metaphysic of divine constitution God's election is creative: "the glory of God's love, and the communication of his goodness . . . give both . . . being and happiness."[14] Consequently, the elect have divine worth and value because (*i*) they are ontologically united to Jesus Christ, a divine person with infinite excellencies, and therefore are capable of replicating the divine perfections; (*ii*) they are His bride (final eschatological fulfillment notwithstanding) and, therefore, (*iii*) the goal God aimed for in creating the world: "the elect creatures . . . must be looked upon as the end of all the rest of the creation";[15] and lastly, (*iv*) God metaphysically constitutes them as *in* Christ in the election from, as it were, eternity past. The elect, even while in their "natural condition," are understood to be in Christ "before the foundation of the world" (Eph 1:4). The graciousness of the gospel is retained in that they are non-meritorious recipients of God's mercy through Jesus Christ. God's creation and regard for the elect is therefore telic, theocentric, christocentric, and crucicentric.

Concerning the reprobates, Holmes holds that all those who die in an unredeemed, unregenerate state are by very definition "Christless" and "Spiritless," the status of not only their humanity but also their existence being uncertain. Election for the Bride of Christ, the so-called invisible church, is redemptively creative, but not so for the reprobate. Therefore, claims Holmes, Edwards proves inconsistent in his trinitarian and gospel-oriented account of creation and, consequently, predestination. If created being was mediated christologically and pneumatologically, and if, as Holmes has argued, the same is true of election and the salvation dependent upon it, then should not the determination of the non-elect be the same?

Spirit "merely applied the gifts of salvation that the Son had 'purchased' from the Father," but went further by arguing that "the Spirit must Himself be seen as what is purchased" in redemption (*God of Grace*, 182).

12. "Miscellanies," no. 710, *WJE* 18:339.

13. "Miscellanies," no. 769: "we [i.e., the elect church] are elected in Christ, as we are elected in his election" (*WJE* 18:418); Holmes, *God of Grace*, 132.

14. "Miscellanies," no. 704, *WJE* 18:316–17. It is for this reason that Jonathan Edwards subordinates both creation and providence to the decree of redemption. Here, Jenson (*America's Theologian*, 106) and Holmes (*God of Grace*, 164) see Jonathan Edwards anticipating the christological doctrine of election developed by Karl Barth.

15. "End of Creation" in *WJE* 8:443.

But Holmes argues that it is not: the reprobate live out their determination with no reference to Christ. And since Edwards clearly maintains that being human has *immediate* reference to Christ, Holmes has no alternative but to say that, "the [reprobate] are, and there is no other way of saying it—less human (or at least 'differently human') than the elect."[16] They appear neither to be properly human nor possess a God-glorifying function in the world (and afterlife) consistent with Edwards's doctrines of divine participation through the Son and creation through the Son. Holmes concludes that Edwards exhibits "a prior failure to let the gospel story inform his position sufficiently," which renders his position concerning the reprobate "finally indefensible."[17]

At the heart of both McClymond's and Holmes's criticisms is the problem of Edwards's Calvinistic particularism, a problem which seems to engender two essentially different kinds of human being.[18]

Jonathan Edwards sees a world in which God has always aimed to glorify and communicate Himself through the redemptive work of His Son and the outpouring of His Spirit: the encompassing work of the atonement and resurrection are the means by which this is achieved; they are the central narrative of the Christ-church relationship. Creation, history, and all divine providences are the necessary accompaniments of God's gospel design. The telic-orientation of the elect church is to cognitively and affectionally conform to Christ's image in cross-bearing and Spirit-living. He is their soteriological Redeemer, their ontological excellence, and their essential happiness. Thus, from God's primordial purposes of communicating and glorifying Himself in and through His perfections (the Son and the Spirit) the relationship between God, redemption, creation, providence, history, and the church is a consistent theological, teleological, eschatological unit. The reprobate, however, have no share in particular redemption and, by direct inference, no share in a christological-creation or Christ-confirmed humanness. Therefore, the reprobate cannot have any measure of "excellence" or "existence."

Yet, for Edwards, reprobates manifestly exist. The question is, how? Moreover, how are they connected with the "end of creation"? Holmes finds their existence an unanswered enigma in Edwards's system. However, he remains certain that their main purpose in existence serves what he calls a "vision across the chasm," by which he means "the saints rejoicing over the sight of sinners being punished and sinners suffering more from seeing saints in glory."[19] But, according to Holmes, this theodicy fails because Edwards's

---

16. Holmes, *God of Grace*, 165.

17. Ibid., 240.

18. Richard A. Muller (*Christ and the Decree*) indicates that the orthodox Reformed tradition, beginning with Calvin and continuing through Beza to Perkins (and, as Holmes suggests, Jonathan Edwards), spoke positively of the elect's association, in terms of predestination and identity, with Christ, while, in the words of Holmes, "the rejected live out their damnation with no reference to Christ . . . The shadow side of the decree proceeds with no influence from the Son and no work of the Spirit" (*God of Grace*, 165–67). The suggestion is that in Jonathan Edwards's analysis of God's primordial, gospel-oriented purpose in creation, he takes his tradition's teaching on predestination to its logical but unsatisfactory conclusion, viz., that *only* the elect are linked to a christological-creation and Christ-defined humanity.

19. *God of Grace*, 213. Both Jonathan L. Kvanvig (*The Problem of Hell*) and Holmes (*God of Grace*, chap 6) contest Jonathan Edwards's theodicy and find it theologically and metaphysically objectionable. But see sup-

christological-creation prevents consistency: for, although in Edwards sin and evil are part of God's act of self-glorification, yet God's primordial consideration is emphatically gospel-oriented, not creative.[20]

McClymond, on the other hand, speculates that since the reprobate are without "excellence," that Edwards probably follows Hutcheson in thinking "the Deity benevolent in the most universal impartial manner";[21] or in other words, that God maintains a posture of objectivity concerning them. How this is possible for beings without a measure of excellence and, therefore, existence is a mystery, if not a logical or ontological impossibility. Still, McClymond perceives the logic of Edwards's theocentric teleology and says: "Even the damned served to increase the good attained by God and the saints in heaven by giving God an opportunity for self-manifestation and to the saints a spectacle of God's justice and power."[22] But because his traditional doctrine of the reprobate did not fuse with the principle of proportionate regard, Edwards made no reference to them in *End of Creation*. According to McClymond, "The text in fact maintains an eerie silence regarding hell and damnation; its concluding section is written as though there were a single, eternal destiny for all humanity." He concludes that Edwards had no recourse in that treatise but to offer an apology on the misery of hell and comparative happiness of heaven. While this may have its place in Edwards's decidedly anti-universalistic worldview, yet how a being with no being helps facilitate God's self-beautification with no beauty remains to McClymond totally incoherent.

By McClymond's and Holmes's combined account, the reprobate are a disjointed portion of a non-christological-creation (if there can be such a thing), inappropriately designated "human," rendered wholly expendable for God to glorify Himself in "their destruction only."[23]

The final assessments given by both accounts, however, are premature. While it is true that Edwards gives us two avenues of investigation into his biblical anthropology: a metaphysical and theological approach; yet these are not exclusive options; they overlap; they are merely avenues of emphasis. Understood as emphases, McClymond finds the former insufficient, Holmes the latter. Nonetheless, a closer, internal examination of Edwards's writings reveals that he provides an internally consistent account of man, both metaphysically and theologically, by defining "human" not in terms of two essentially dif-

---

port for Jonathan Edwards's theory in Davidson, "Reasonable Damnation," 47–56, and Wainwright, "Original Sin" in Morris, *Philosophy and the Christian Faith*, 33ff.

20. "Miscellanies," no. 993, *Works* 20:323. Schafer and McClymond suggest that the elect serve in a representative relationship to the rest of creation (i.e., the reprobate). As McClymond explains it, the elect "fulfilled in actuality what God willed in principle for all creatures" (*Encounters with God*, 63; cf. Schafer, "Jonathan Edwards' Conception of the Church," 51–66). The purpose of the elect is then reduced to the aforementioned theodicy. Holmes seems to believe that Jonathan Edwards, following lockstep in the Calvinist doctrine of the reprobate, does not even try to reconcile this tension with his creation-theology, but rather concentrates on this theodicy of the "vision across the chasm."

21. Hutcheson, *Inquiry Into the Original of Our Ideas of Beauty and Virtue* cited in McClymond, *Encounters with God*, 63.

22. McClymond, *Encounters with God*, 63.

23. *Wicked Men Useful in their Destruction Only* (July 1744), *Banner-Works* 2:125.

ferent classifications—elect and reprobate—but through a single ontological characterization. The metaphysical emphasis within Edwards's system provides a sufficient account of man that addresses the theological, while the converse also holds true.

Here we shall concentrate on this metaphysical emphasis, while giving tangential reference to the theological. How the reprobate relates to Edwards's trinitarian/christological/gospel-oriented creation (Holmes's theological concerns) shall be discussed in chapters 10 and 11. For the present, we turn our attention to key metaphysical questions; questions that take into account the problems discussed above, as well as in the preceding chapters, concerning Edwards's panentheism and telic-cosmology. The following questions arise: How is God in man and man in God, in Edwards's panentheistic scheme? Or, alternatively, How does the Divine Being encompass created minds and in what way do they participate in God's *ad extra* replication? As a further complication we ask with McClymond, How do *sinful* creatures participate in God's beautiful being? That is, what is the ontological function of the natural-man and reprobate in God's grand program? We also ask whether or not there is only one kind of human being; and, if so, what makes a human being a human being? Is it the image of God? If it is, then, of what does Edwards's understanding of the image of God consist?

The answers emerge from a more in-depth examination of the nexus of laws tending to the three relations determinative of human being. The ontological structure that Edwards prescribes for intelligent perceiving beings itself substantiates the claim that the bare existence of any person, including the reprobate, is intrinsically God-glorifying and possesses inherent value. The consent of "being to its own being" (what I call "the relation to self") will receive the most attention, for it embodies key concepts within Edwards's ontology and serves in a foundational capacity for the other two relations— "being's consent to other beings" (other-relation) and "being's consent to being in general" (relation to God and the whole matrix of existences).[24] The catalyst and mine for this examination is Jonathan Edwards's "The Mind" notebook, particularly its first entry entitled "EXCELLENCY." There Edwards begins to explain that God embeds in each of these relations principles that glorify Him and function to facilitate further manifestations (replications) of His internal perfections and glory. The first and second of these relational principles are essential to all human beings, regenerate and unregenerate alike. They define "human being." The third relation, though in man as an original principle at his creation, is the one lost in the episode of the Edenic Fall and restored through supernatural regeneration.

Starting with concreated Adam and Eve and continuing through all their fallen and selectively restored posterity (the elect), and even those on the "shadow side" of double predestination, all human beings are teleologically crafted by God, in His image, and with inherent God-glorifying ontological principles: their mere existence glorifies God. In *End of Creation*, it is not accurate to say that Edwards took asylum in a beleaguered "vision across the chasm" theodicy because there was no place for the reprobate in his telic creation-theology or so-called "proportionate regard" thesis, as Holmes and McClymond

---

24. See "The Mind," no. 1, *WJE* 6:338.

respectively argue.²⁵ Quite the contrary: reprobates have a perfectly useful purpose in God's program of self-manifestation right here in this life, a purpose that, for Edwards, continues and intensifies in an afterlife of hell torments.

A central theme throughout this chapter concerns the prominence of Edwards's telic-theocentricity in his metaphysical thought. Repeatedly, we find him explaining a facet of the nature of being human or the created order as a corollary or application of some thought immediately related to God. If there is some new thought concerning the nature or being of man, it is held up to what may be called "the law of the whole," which is for Edwards "the beauty of God." But more times than not, the development of some anthropological point is simply an appropriation of a concept previously harmonized with his doctrine of God or, more precisely, his trinitarian ontology.²⁶

"Happiness" and Being

If McClymond and Holmes were to press their analyses a little further and unpack the aesthetic contents of Edwards's ontology, particularly in his formula from "The Mind" No. 1 on "Happiness," they would have found at least metaphysical answers to their questions.

"Happiness," Edwards explains, "strictly consists in the perception of these three things: of the consent of being to its own being; of its consent to being; and of being's consent to being [in general]."²⁷ Into this one word he condenses and combines the cores of his teleology, philosophical anthropology, moral theory, and ontology.

"Happiness" itself, as the end of creation, appears as an early, frequent, and enduring theme in his thought. This is because God's communicated happiness is an aesthetic and telic element woven into His creative purposes. Indeed, it is even woven into the very being of His sentient creatures. What the creature necessarily pursues for happiness, namely, existence, is programmatically linked to God's "ends" concerning Himself. Recalling that Edwards's theocentrism is driven by the vision of God pursuing and achieving His "ends in creation," it is no wonder he conceives of man's most fundamental and essential principle as one in which the creature's happiness and God's happiness are inextricably interconnected. Here we have the final application of Edwards's post-conversion agenda, namely, to redefine all existence (this time with man in view) in light of God's goal-oriented, comprehensive reality.

Redefining man in light of God's all-encompassing being arrives not as a late reflection, though it looms large in *End of Creation*, but one that follows hard on his reconcep-

---

25. Holmes suggests that this theodicy gradually disappeared after 1700 (due to deistic and universalistic challenges), but was renewed by Jonathan Edwards (*God of Grace*, 199ff).

26. "The Mind" and "Miscellanies" notebooks frequently show Jonathan Edwards applying his conclusions about the Deity to humanity and vice versa. "The Mind" nos. 1 and 45 are typical of how he finishes a philosophical thought with immediate implications for his understanding of the will and being of God, and then makes a corollary application to created intelligent beings.

27. *WJE* 6:338. Certainly the third of these relations ("being's consent to being [in general]") is indirectly indicated. God, as the "sum of all being," entails existence or being itself. Jonathan Edwards's use of "consent" remains unaltered from the specialized metaphysical sense discussed in chap 3.

tion of matter and causality. Hence, as early as "Miscellanies" no. 3 (May 1723), Edwards explains:

> Now what is glorifying God, but a rejoicing at that glory he has displayed? And understanding of the perfections of God, merely, cannot be the end of the creation; for he had as good not understand it, as see it and not be at all moved with joy at the sight. Neither can the highest end of the creation be the declaring God's glory to others . . . Wherefore, seeing happiness is the highest end of the creation of the universe, and intelligent beings are that consciousness of the creation that is to be the immediate subject of this happiness, how happy may we conclude will be those intelligent beings that are to be made eternally happy![28]

Even in this early entry we can see that the affectional aspects of human existence are distinguished and emphasized as a dimension of knowing more dynamic and complete than mere cognition. But Edwards wants to emphasize that the happiness of a human being lies in perceiving and delighting in the beauty of God. He obviously aims to turn "happiness" into an ontological principle by making it a key concept in his aesthetic theory. He accomplishes this by combining two fundamental ideas in his thought: (1) that the primary and essential element in "true religion" consists in the positive affectional cognition of God; and (2), religion, taken in this sense, is the very purpose of the entire creation. When the two are combined in conjunction with his idealism "happiness" emerges with ontological signification: "HAPPINESS IS THE END OF CREATION, as appears by this, because the creation had as good not be, as not rejoice in its being. For certainly it was the goodness of the Creator that moved him to create; and how can we conceive of another end proposed by goodness, than that he might delight in seeing the creatures he made rejoice in that being that he has given them?"[29]

Underlying this "Miscellanies" entry is the philosophical association of "happiness" or "pleasantness" with "excellence" and beauty. This is in keeping with the whole Platonic and Augustinian tradition into which Edwards was reared.[30] That tradition held a real and even a necessary connection between goodness and a human being's desire and pleasure.[31] In Edwards's case, the basis for proceeding rests on the assumption that real beauty and real good "are some one thing," namely, "*proportion*"; which in the end is fundamental to the nature of being; it is the happiness in the "consent to being." He further supposes that the explanation why this one thing *is* beauty and goodness will also show why it pleases and satisfies minds. The explanation he furnishes states that they are in fact basic to being; they too are principles of ontology.

Recalling the distinction he makes in his theory of beauty between primary and secondary beauty, we remember that the two kinds of beauty pertain to the difference between the spiritual (mental) and the natural (material) dimensions of reality. The kind of similarity or agreement that exists in primary beauty is the "consent" (or love) between

---

28. *WJE* 13:199–200.
29. "Miscellanies," no. 3, *WJE* 13:200.
30. See Plato, "Symposium" in *Plato: Collected Dialogues*, 201–12; Plotinus, *Enneads*, 1.6.1f; Augustine, *Confessions* in *The Nicene and Post-Nicene Fathers*, 1:46, 63f.
31. Anderson, "Editor's Introduction," *WJE* 6:81–82.

perceiving beings, while the agreement in secondary beauty is only an "image" of spiritual consent. In Edwards, "consent" or love is "the highest kind" of *spiritual excellence*; it is a beauty that is "higher and happier" than mere agreement among nonsentient things.[32] It follows that the consent that exists in God is the most beautiful, "infinitely excellent," as the Northampton minister would put it time and again. Likewise, Edwards reasons that the happiness of a human being—who is a *spiritual* being at the top of the "great chain" of created existences—lies in the perceiving of primary beauty: "The soul of man is spiritual and a spirit being requires a spiritual happiness."[33]

He starts now only a couple of steps away from explaining how God uses "happiness" as an ontological principle in man to fulfill telic purposes. All that remains is to connect "happiness" with the tendency toward being and include human being in God's being. So he writes in "The Mind," "being, if we examine narrowly, is nothing else but proportion." In Edwards's way of reasoning this means that there must be some kind of proportion or excellence basic to human being when "examined narrowly," i.e., in its specifics and most fundamental sense. Such "excellence" of being is nothing other than "the consent of being to its own being," or the love a perceiving being has for its own existence. This is to say, a human being's happiness must, at the very least, consist of "the consent of being to its own being," just as he says in his summary on "Happiness."[34] Thus, a human being necessarily consents to its own being because its happiness and beauty are internal to its being.

Edwards now easily and naturally turns the discussion toward God. God Himself is "the sum of all being" in which all excellence is resolved. God prescribes glory for Himself through "the consent of being to its own being" by designing inherent beauty and happiness in intelligent perceiving existence. Its happiness is a spiritual or mental happiness, and therefore of the highest order of excellence—being or proportion—by virtue of its "loving" its own existence and, by default, the "sum of all being."[35] Therefore (if we may conclude with Edwards), the happiness of human being is, at least in some respect, perceiving and rejoicing in bare existence ("Being in general" qua being). Such happiness is the first descriptive aesthetic/ontic relation of a being in his formula on "Happiness."

The upshot of this metaphysical arrangement is manifold, but here I mention but one implication to address McClymond's concern for man's worth. "Being's consent to being" is for Edwards an instance of "excellence" and, therefore, being-as-manifest, i.e., God *ad extra*.[36] As an instance of excellence, man, whether sinful or not, has "value" or "worth" on the "great scale of being," and may be regarded by God as an appropriate candidate for grace and mercy, benevolent or complacent love, or whatever. For in regarding the creature's excellence, God really regards His own happiness, His own manifest excellence.[37]

32. "The Mind," no. 1, *WJE* 6:336–38.
33. 303. [L. 3r] Sermon on Proverbs 27:22 (Nov. 1733), *WJE Online* 48.
34. "The Mind," no. 1, *WJE* 6:338. Cf. Augustine, *Confessions* in *The Nicene and Post-Nicene Fathers*, 1:45.
35. Ibid., 337, 338.
36. Or, in the language of "The Mind," it is the in-built beauty of "being consenting to its own being" that intrinsically contributes to the *ad extra* excellence of "being in general" (God).
37. Thomas reasons that, "Every being, as being, is good" and therefore may be considered of God's goodness (*Summa Theologia*, I, 5.3). Jonathan Edwards says essentially the same thing but in aesthetic terminology.

The modus operandi within *Two Dissertations* and the sermon *God Glorified in Man's Dependence* is precisely this premise: God is not only the cause of true virtue and being, but their substance and source.

If we shift the focus from man to God, we discover how Edwards metaphysically ensures God's glory with respect to human ontology. Bearing in mind that God's glory is not intermittent but manifest every moment in the creation (per "Miscellanies" nos. *gg*, 1, 3, and 87), the logic of Edwards's *End of Creation* teleology works out thus: All things have a God-glorifying purpose: there are some purposes ("subordinate ends") which lead to and terminate in other more significant and overarching purposes ("ultimate" and "supreme ends"). Yet there is one purpose that remains constant that all other ends presuppose and operate upon, namely the *perception of existence*. If each moment of time is a God-empowered movement toward the "ultimate end," then each moment existence is perceived must be an end itself, a God-glorifying/replicating end. In Edwards's philosophical-theology, human beings are purposely designed to do just that—perceive existence. In the perception of existence God is manifest; in His manifestation He is glorified. All human beings perceive existence; therefore all participate in God's replication.

The presumed "eerie silence" about the reprobate in *End of Creation* simply is not accurate. First, Edwards does not suppress his discussion about the "damned" but makes open reference in three sections. Second, many sections are applicable to the "reprobate" even if they are not explicitly mentioned. Third, the *basic* "end" of the present life of the reprobate is parallel to that of the elect church: just as the redeemed in Christ "manifest [God's] perfections," so too the spatiotemporal life which the so-called "heathen" live is "a manifesting or making known his divine greatness and excellency."[38] The perception of excellence or, synonymously, existence, is the perceiving and *ad extra* replicating of God. Edwards leaves no room for doubt about this when he equates divine excellence (or being itself) with divine glory, and divine glory with God "*existing ad extra*."[39] Thus, every intelligent thing that perceives existence participates in God's ultimate end. *This* is why the conclusion of *End of Creation* (to cite McClymond) "is written as though there were a single, eternal destiny for all humanity." There *is* only one destiny for humanity—replicating God's perfections. Eternal punishment secures that destiny for those perfections the reprobate will remanate, just as heaven secures it for the elect. In the end, McClymond's own analysis unwittingly satisfies his own queries.

Edwards does not launch into a lengthy discourse on the doctrine of reprobation because *End of Creation* was intended to serve as a catalyst to shift the Enlightenment conversation away from a false discussion about man affecting his own destiny onto the historical reality of theocentric, spatiotemporal existence.

One Kind of Human Being, Three Kinds of Dispositions

But before proceeding, we must note that, for Edwards, man can only be placed in one of three ontological categories: concreated, fallen or "natural" (in the sense of "natural-

---

38. *WJE* 8:522. Cf. Fiering, *Moral Thought*, 238–39 n. 107.
39. Ibid., 527f.

man"), and regenerate. According to Edwards, "our first parents," Adam and Eve, were the only humans to have the status of "concreation."[40] Postlapsarian Adam, all of his posterity (excluding Jesus Christ), and the reprobate comprise the second set. And lastly, the spiritually restored or "born-again" persons are the third. What is clear, however, is that, for Edwards, these are different *categories* for human beings, not different *kinds* of "humans."

Additionally, whenever he speaks about what is essential to human being as such, that is, what fundamentally constitutes the essential dispositions in man,[41] the reference will always and primarily be to the first relational disposition and, secondarily, but not necessarily, the second relational disposition. As to the third relational disposition, it was in Adam in his creation, not as something that defined human being as such, though, indeed, it functioned *as* "a principle of nature." The Fall nullified this relational principle, and only spiritual regeneration restores it, not to make a human being a human being, but to directly relate (unite) a person to God through the Holy Spirit through a relationship of mutual consent.[42] (More shall be said about this later.)

Thus, what all three ontological categories have in common (and this speaks directly to Holmes's concern about essentially different *kinds* of human beings) is *an essential disposition that tends toward its own existence*. This is what makes the one kind of human being a human being. It is man's most basic ontic principle, a principle that ascribes inherent value to every person and metaphysically (or panentheistically) locates his or her existence in God's being.

For Edwards, this first dispositional tendency functions as a human being's intellectual and inclinational relationship to one's self, a sort of immanent action, even the "happiness" of a being "consenting" to its own being (not unlike God's triunity). Self-relation, as the first and foremost ontic principle in man, possesses important implications for much of Edwards's thought, not the least of which are his moral, harmatological, and soteriological theories.

But as the formula on "happiness" indicates, human beings are also determined to relate to other beings through their knowledge and love of *them*.[43] In his dissertation, *The*

---

40. *WJE* 3:381. Concreation is the divine act of creating man's constitution with an original righteousness, a creation *with* (con) righteousness. According to the Augustinian/Reformed view, man is said to have possessed the divine image by the fact of his creation, and not by a subsequent bestowal of it. By contrast, Pelagianism denies that holiness is concreated. It asserts that the will of man by creation, and in its first condition, is characterless. Its first act is to originate either holiness or sin. Generally speaking, the Tridentine anthropology is a mixture of Pelagianism and Augustinianism: God created man "*in puris naturalibus*," without holiness or sin. This creative act, which left man characterless, God followed with another act by which he endowed man with holiness.

41. Usually in terms of "the soul's essence," "man's being," man's essential "nature" or "principles." See, *WJE* 2:188; *WJE* 3:399–402; 42. Sermon on Deut 32:4 (1728), *WJE Online* 42; and *Born Again* (1731), *WJE* 17:186–95.

42. The general resurrection does not affect Jonathan Edwards's appraisement of "human being" either. At the general resurrection, that which is essential to human beings is either governed more perfectly by God so as to be sufficiently sanctified for His presence (as the case will be with the saints) or becomes "exceedingly loathsome and hateful" (the damned). See 394. Sermons on Isa 33:17 (June 1736), *WJE Online* 51; and 69. Sermon on Matt 10:28 (1733), *WJE Online* 43.

43. Lee, *Philosophical Theology*, 86.

Nature of True Virtue, Edwards writes that by "a law of nature which God has fixed" human beings are capable of knowing and loving the "*secondary beauty*" that makes up the inner structure of all created beings. Such is the function of the second relational principle of human being—to "consent to [other] being[s]." The reason secondary beauty delights human beings lies in its correspondence with *primary beauty*, which is purely mental, moral, and spiritual; in a word, it is "Being in general," the Divine Being.[44] Secondary beauty images forth, shadows, and mirrors primary beauty as (and this is a key phrase) "being-as-manifest"; for it lacks the *direct mutual consent* between minds, which is the highest form of excellence or being. Like the disposition of self-love, the disposition of other relation is essential and determinative to human being, as well.

Originally, human beings were created with a third disposition to *directly* relate to the whole or God Himself, by knowing and loving His beauty, the *primary beauty*, that principle in harmony with which all finite beings are created.[45] A man, then, truly knows and loves himself and others only if he knows them through a relationship with God's beauty: "a natural [man] may love others, but 'tis some way or other as appendages and appurtenances to himself," writes Edwards, "but a spiritual man loves others as of God, or in God, or some way related to Him."[46] Regenerate persons have this disposition by supernatural restoration. No one since the Fall in Eden, however, is created with it.

In Edwards's ontology, the three principles of self-love (self-relation), other-relation, and God-relation are the basic orientations of the entire self, which operate in, as, and through, the intellectual and the inclinational activities. The first principle is foundational and definitive to human being; likewise, the second organically belongs to human being as such; but, while the third relation substantiates the existence of a human being, it does not define human being as such, nor does it necessarily belong to man's essential composition. The extent of a human being's intellectual and inclinational participation, or perhaps, "consent," in each of these internal relations reflect not only their "value" and place on the "scale of being," but also the kind of participation they have in God's self-glorifying scheme: for God is glorified in a different manner through each of these relational dimensions. As man's "happiness" increases, certain dynamics of God's perfections "enlarge" through replication, in accordance with Edwards's idealistic principles of perception and existence. Alternatively, a man with merely fractional consent, limited happiness, and, therefore, comparatively diminished substantiality, replicates other dynamics only remotely associated with consenting participation.

∽

The formula on happiness is a reductionistic statement about the existence of intelligent perceiving being. When unpacked, it discloses how God fashions the internal ontological dispositions of human beings to pursue that which is, according to Edwards's definition in

---

44 "Nature of True Virtue" in *WJE* 8:570–75.

45. Ibid.

46. "Miscellanies," no. 821, *WJE* 18:532–33.

Freedom of the Will, the most apparent good or, aesthetically, the most beautiful or agreeable to being and, simultaneously, the divine purposes of self-replication.

Behind all of his ruminations on excellence and happiness lies divine beauty or God's beautiful being. For Edwards, it is the ultimate reality that constitutes the aesthetic and ontological matrix of *all* perceivable realties. God's beauty also contextualizes the "simple equalities" of secondary beauty to give them reference and meaning. Furthermore, it facilitates an intelligent perceiving being's participation in primary beauty through a mental or spiritual relation/union (which, in turn, substantiates being). In short, it is what the aesthetics of happiness, relation, and excellence, are resolved into, namely proportion or being.

The Consent of Being to Its Own Being: Self-Love and the Relation to Self

Long before Edwards set out to write his major polemical treatises against deism and incipient Arminianism, indeed, even before he set down to defend the Great Awakening through an innovative articulation of the psychology of religious conversion, he had already settled upon a philosophical anthropology; the whole of which was based upon a dispositional theory of internal relations. His early-established philosophy of being gave him well-defined principles to differentiate between the marks of true and false conversions, determine how God achieves His "ends" through man's nature, contrast "common virtue" with "true virtue," defend the doctrines of original sin and progressive sanctification, and refute "prevailing notions of that freedom of the will." Because his ontology was already in place, all the hallmarks of his later treatises were standard fare within his preaching ministry before the first page of his writing went to press in July 1731.[47]

If the essay on "Excellency" is the mine from which Edwards extracts the philosophical and theological implications of his ontology, then the formula on "happiness" is its core. Of the three dispositional relations contained within that core, the relation of a given sentient entity to itself is the most important feature of his theory of human nature and the analysis of that nature.[48] It is what makes a human being a human being; it is the essence of man's *imago Dei*.

Yet the law of the whole regulates even this idea. For an entity's relation to itself is only a part within the whole, an instance of being within the network of interrelated existences. Edwards's theocentrism ensures that priority and emphasis will always be given to the whole, especially in matters of ontology, because the whole bespeaks of God. Thus, it is only when we step back and look at the part's place within the grand design of existence that we clearly see how God is active in that particular existence or group of existences

47. See (in order), 125. Sermon on Matt 15:26 (1729), *WJE Online* 44; *God Glorified in Man's Dependence* (1730), *WJE* 17:200–14; *Serving God in Heaven* (1731), *WJE* 17:253–61; 47. Sermon on Matthew 5:22 (1726), *WJE Online* 42; and 36. Two sermons on 1 Peter 1:15 (1726, 1727), *WJE Online* 42; and *The Threefold Work of the Holy Ghost* (1729), *WJE* 14:375–436. The "Miscellanies," entries written before the July 1731 publication of *God Glorified* (viz., nos. *aa*–497) also give ample evidence to this assertion.

48. Although angelic beings could be included in this statement and much of the foregoing discussion, yet my intension is to focus on human beings. Therefore angelic spirits will be commonly excluded.

for the glorification of Himself, as well as something of that being's (group's) specific telic function in creation.

With respect to human beings, the metaphysics behind Edwards's telic-theocentricity focuses on a principle of "*self-love*," a concept that emerges as the central component in his ontology. In fact, self-love is the ethical translation of the metaphysical expression "the consent of being to its own being," which makes it the most important feature of his philosophical anthropology.[49]

But the claim that Edwards identifies a human being's first and essential dispositional tendency with a concept of self-love raises several questions, and even revives the same ones answered in the preceding section. For instance, if Edwards's concept of self-love is tantamount to the *imago Dei* and, therefore, worthy of the divine benediction (Gen 1:31), then does that not put him at odds with Calvin, who called for the eradication of all self-love, as well as his own Calvinist heritage? Furthermore, how does self-love factor into the panentheism spoken of earlier; that is, how can creaturely self-love be something beautiful in the Creator's being? Furthermore, we ask: What is self-love's relation to the psychological constitution and personal identity of man? What place does it hold in his moral theory? We turn to a further examination of the three relational dispositions to answer these questions.

Solomon Stoddard, the Calvinist Tradition, and the Idea of Principle Self-Love

The "Miscellanies" and "The Mind" notebooks make it clear that, prior to December 1723, Edwards had already settled upon a relational conception of the Trinity. Yet, it should be recognized that it was not until his exposure to Solomon Stoddard's philosophy of the natural-man that he began to understand man's nature and being in conjunction with a self-loving *disposition*.[50]

This idea combined with the modeling of man's psychological constitution upon the trinity of divine knowledge, love, and joy (à la Cotton Mather)[51] constitutes Edwards's

---

49. In some respect "being's consent to its own being" could be subsumed under the third determinative relation of being, "the consent to being in general." For, as I show below, "the consent of being to its own being" is, in the final analysis, a consent to God, albeit indirectly and without *mutual consent*. Nonetheless, Jonathan Edwards allows for a self-conscious being (specifically, natural-man) to directly oppose ("dissent from") "Being in general" (as with the case of, say, a malignant atheist) and yet exist. Therefore it is appropriate for Jonathan Edwards to treat self-relation as a distinct (though not a totally separate) relation in the nexus.

50. Cf. Fiering, *Moral Thought*, 151–53, 159 n.23. Stoddard (1643–1729), renowned as the "Pope of the Connecticut Valley," was a native of Boston and a graduate of Harvard (1662), where he later served as College librarian. In Nov. 1669, Stoddard received the call to the Northampton Church and departed for the western frontier where he was ordained (Sept. 1672) and remained until his death. He exercised considerable influence within the region's congregational churches through the Hampshire Association, which he helped to form in 1714. The story of the intimate relationship between Jonathan Edwards and his maternal grandfather need not be rehearsed here. Stoddard's influence upon Jonathan Edwards's piety and, perhaps to a lesser degree, his thought is indisputable. Aside from the personal access to Stoddard, which Jonathan Edwards's associate position at Northampton afforded, Jonathan Edwards had from before his time at Yale ready access to all of Stoddard's writings, published and unpublished.

51. Cf. Mather's *Blessed Unions*, passim, or *Religio Philosophica*, 301.

basic ontological principles for man. Whether Edwards learnt Stoddard's "philosophy" indirectly from his father Timothy Edwards or Stoddard's published sermons is not certain, though the latter is most likely. However this may be, Edwards took the Stoddardean idea that "a spirit of self-love" accounts for the moral inclinations and volitions of humanity—good or evil—and made further application by maintaining that it also accounts for the first and most fundamental relational dimension of the nexus of laws comprising a human being's ontological structure. This is to say, Edwards believed that the relation to self, the idea of the activity of a lawlike disposition of self-love, accounts for the primary ontological *what*-ness of human being. However, this does not preclude a concept of *substance*, but constitutes it in nearly the same way that God's idea of Himself is His essence. For Edwards, it is this same what-ness of being for man that glorifies God in a basic aesthetic sense.

"The best philosophy I have ever met"

The context in which Edwards discloses his most fruitful resource for the analyzing of the natural-man surrounds a number of "Miscellanies" entries on the Fall of Adam, sin, and original sin. For this reason he writes, "The best philosophy that I have met with of original sin and all sinful inclinations, habits and principles, is undoubtedly that of Mr. Stoddard's."[52] Although Edwards makes this disclosure in a 1727 discussion on the Fall of Adam and sinful inclinations, yet his employment of Stoddard's "philosophy" in a variety of settings antedates this entry by at least three years, during which time it gains certain metaphysical attribution for a wider range of usages.[53]

An autumn 1723 sermon on 1 Corinthians 2:14, published as *A Spiritual Understanding of Divine Things Denied to the Unregenerate*, contains Edwards's first clear attempt to utilize Stoddard's philosophy in conjunction with his own aesthetic ruminations on excellency from "The Mind" notebook. The Corinthians sermon appears to be product of culminating thoughts from "The Mind," a series of "Miscellanies" exploring the ontology of the Trinity and principles of nature,[54] as well as reflections on Stoddard's philosophy of natural and infused principles. All of these items were written within the space of a few months, revealing that, at the time, Edwards was well occupied with testing the ontological soundness of his theory of excellence through applications in the spheres of theology, soteriology, and ethics. Stoddard's theory concerning the principles within man appeared to Edwards as a complementary way to explain how the significant aesthetic and moral elements of his ontology could be synthesized and harmonized with an "orthodox" biblical anthropology.[55] In the end, its contribution to Edwards's final theory provided a useful

---

52. "Miscellanies," no. 301, *WJE* 13:387; cf. 154. Two sermons on Romans 7:14 (1730), *WJE Online* 45.

53. Ramsey believes that Jonathan Edwards held Stoddard's philosophy on sinful inclinations from his mid-twenties (1727–28) ("Editor's Introduction," *WJE* 8:252–53 n.1). Such a late date, however, overlooks the fact that from late 1723 several of Jonathan Edwards's sermons and "Miscellanies," entries identify the natural and supernatural principles in man with self-love and divine love respectively.

54. Namely, "Miscellanies," nos. 73, 77, 87, 92, 93, 94, 96, 98 (*WJE* 13).

55. As codified in the subordinate standards that Jonathan Edwards would have deemed biblical, namely the Westminster Standards and Savoy Declaration.

explanation of man's role within the world and, secondly, how man's being could likewise be conceived in law-like dispositional terms. The importance of Stoddard's theory, then, lies in its contribution to extending Edwards's telic-oriented perspective on the world to human beings, which in turn gave it an internal coherence.

In his analysis of the Corinthians sermon, Kenneth Minkema suggests Edwards may have derived his well-known analogy of the "sweetness of honey," as well as the differentiation between the unregenerate and regenerate based upon natural verses "infused" principles, from Stoddard's *Three Sermons Lately Preach'd at Boston* (1717).[56] Corroborative evidence reinforces this suggestion. Prior to the composition of this sermon, Edwards's philosophical anthropology appears noticeably undeveloped. From the first of his extant sermons in the autumn 1720 up to the spring of 1723, he makes no significant advance concerning the essence and nature of man. Furthermore, what becomes in his later writings the familiar language of "natural" and "supernatural," "inferior" and "superior principles" is noticeably absent. The exception is the several entries on "RELIGION," which further Edwards's philosophical idealism and link the teleological purposes of man with human existence. Yet after Edwards discovers Stoddard's "philosophy" in the *Treatise Concerning Conversion* and particularly *Three Sermons* (which likely occurred during the end of his New York pastorate),[57] he explicitly begins to speak of man's nature and the influence of the Holy Spirit in terms of natural or infused *principles*.[58] These "principles" quickly become associated with the natural or essential being of man—a principle of self-love, and the nonessential "indwelling principle of holiness," that is, the Holy Spirit united to the soul, influencing it "as a real, spiritual, active and vital—yea, immortal [principle]."[59]

---

56. *WJE* 14:67, 76 n.9. The Corinthians sermon itself is the homiletical product of "Miscellanies," nos. 73 and 77. Jonathan Edwards may also (or instead) have had in mind Locke's "pineapple" illustration.

57. During the New York pastorate, as well as the interim before the Bolton, Connecticut, charge, Jonathan Edwards spent time preparing his M.A. dissertation, *Quaestio* (an essay on the nature of justification), and "reading religious books" and "sermons" (*WJE* 16:772–74). His close proximity to East Windsor (where he spent his time after the New York period) would have provided easy access to his father's library, which contained Stoddard's *Treatise* and *Three Sermons* (Minkema, "The Edwardses," 646–66).

58. The first sermon in which Jonathan Edwards speaks of the Holy Ghost "governing" man as "a vital principle of true holiness" is Luke 13:5 (*WJE* 10:515). Written close to the same time, the sermon on John 6:68 explicitly states that this principle of holiness is a "infused grace" (526). The sermon on Haggai 1:5 makes a distinction between inherent principles within man and a principle of love to God, which Jonathan Edwards identifies with the Holy Ghost. And finally, within the two unit sermon on Philippians 1:21, Jonathan Edwards clearly identifies the "natural self" with "that false, inordinate, irregular, mistaken self-love, whereby we seek to please ourselves and none else" (569). Still, it is within the 1 Corinthians 2:14 sermon that Jonathan Edwards begins to regularly and explicitly designate the essential disposition of self-love in man as the ontic "natural principle" and the holy and spiritual aspect of humanity as the "supernatural principle," i.e., the Spirit.

Although absent from "Miscellanies," no. 34 "ORIGINAL SIN" (July 1723?), yet the idea is implicitly found in nos. 89 and 117, written only months later (the principle subjects of these entries chiefly relate to the ontological Trinity). No. 123 continues the idea of an epistemological distinction between regenerates and unregenerates, with Jonathan Edwards now regularly explaining in terms of holiness, excellency of principles, and beauty, that their epistemic disparity results from different ontological statuses and organization.

59. *WJE* 10:569, 474.

Divergent Streams of Self-Love

The crux of Stoddard's moral philosophy was this: there are two types of self-love, holy or lawful self-love and sinful or inordinate self-love. His explication of a divergent pair of self-loves was a conscious reaffirmation of Augustine's eudemonism. While such an assertion departed from Calvin, who replaced the Augustinian emphasis on *true* self-love and well-being with a non-teleological abandonment to God's will, it nonetheless proved faithful to the authoritative Puritan thought of Perkins, Ames, and Watson, all of whom affirmed the basic theme of "proper" self-love and denounced "improper" self-love.[60]

Reiterating the general idea of this Augustinian-eudemonistic wing of Reformed thought, Stoddard stated that a holy or lawful self-love is a principle of grace and, therefore, not a collective or inherent characteristic of fallen human nature. Consequently natural-man lives incapable of virtuous love to God or others.[61] However, both principles were present in Adam while he maintained a moral and ontological integrity. Stoddard did not explain, however, the ontological significance of self-love in either Adam or his posterity; he simply states: "There is much of a spirit of self-love in man."[62]

Edwards, on the other hand, found a use for self-love that Stoddard and his Puritan forbearers never employed. Indeed, he applied variations of this "philosophy" well beyond the subject of lapsarian man: it found its way into his discussions on original righteousness, the *imago Dei*, the ontological and epistemological dissimilarity between regenerates and unregenerates, aesthetics, and, prominently, his ethical theory. However, its most important usage was to elucidate human nature. For Edwards, more than anything else it functioned as a unifying principle around which the teleological, moral, and aesthetic aspects of human existence were discussed and elucidated. Thus, where Stoddard was content to speak of self-love as a "course of life," Edwards went deeper to express the self-love in man as an essential *habitus*, or disposition. The disposition of self-love "is the nature of the soul to crave and thirst after well-being."[63] What Stoddard lent to Edwards, then, was not a modern dispositional philosophy, but a succinct and appropriate analysis—from within the Reformed tradition—of the active tendency in human beings that corresponded nicely with Calvinistic doctrines of total depravity, soteriology, and the nature of God, to name a few. What Edwards did with the Augustinian-Stoddardean philosophy of self-love was to make it more basic to man: the primary disposition for a human being is a lawlike disposition of self-love.

---

60. Calvin, *Institutes*, III.7.1. See, for instance, Thomas Watson, *Body of Divinity*, 13–24 and William Ames, *Medulla SS. Theologica*, 250f. Jonathan Edwards would have been well versed in Ames's *Medulla* (an autographed copy annotated by Jonathan Edwards in 1721 is part of the Beinecke collection), Perkins's *Works* (Edwards quotes and refers to Perkins as "The famous Mr. Perkins" in *Religious Affections*), and Watson's *Body* (cited in Yale catalog of 1715). All were standard New England fare. Cf. Thuesen, "Editor's Introduction," *WJE* 26:43–46.

61. Stoddard, "That Natural Men are under the Government of Self-Love" in *Three Sermons*, 34–64.

62. Ibid., 36.

63. *The Future Punishment of the Wicked Unavoidable and Intolerable* (Apr. 1741; repreached Feb. 1755), *Banner-Works*, 2:81.

Edwards's metaphysically charged notion of self-love is not what moral philosophers commonly call psychological egoism,[64] neither should it be equated with the altruistic virtue of which Bishop Butler spoke, nor should it be understood as an agent's predominant aim at individual, private satisfaction.[65] Certainly Edwards has a place in his thought for altruistic virtue motivated by disinterested self-love, as well as for what Gene Outka calls an "acquisitive" self-love, that wholly nefarious self-love of Reinhold Niebuhr, who historically linked self-love, pride, and sin to the core of human depravity.[66] But in this context, Edwards intends something much more fundamental than identifying self-love with some arbitration of conscience or a moral theory of psychological egoism in which "acquisitive" self-love constitutes *de facto* the sole spring of behavior, identical for every man. To be sure, when he deals with the depravity of the natural-man he will descriptively say that, at the deepest level, all moral aims and determinations are reducible to acquisitive self-love.[67] Instead, he is making an important *ontological* statement: the primary disposition and defining characteristic of human beingness is a self-loving/self-preserving disposition. That is, the soul's distinguishing nature *and* essence is an active lawlike disposition which tends in the first place toward self-preserving, or, in the abstruse metaphysical language of "The Mind" notebook, "being's being is the consent or inclining to being"; or again, "being consenting to its own being." Hence, Edwards's assertion: "The *nature* of the soul Endeavours to support itself."[68] This is to say, the essential *habitus* of the soul is in some sense self-promoting.

∽

Edwards reconfigures self-love in such a way that it can no longer be confined to an ethical theory. He requires its recognition as (primarily) a principle of human nature with derivative ethical implications. Self-love, therefore, certainly belongs to his ethical theory, but as a consequence of his philosophy of being. Like Augustine, whose use of self-love held an important if not central place in his theological and metaphysical convictions, so too Edwards's theory of self-love possesses salient metaphysical and theological signification.[69] It is to this twofold signification that we now turn.

---

64. Psychological egoism, as distinguished from *ethical egoism*, is not a normative ethical theory of the "right and good" so much as a theory about human motivation. Jonathan Edwards's ethical theory certainly embodies most of the major tenets of psychological egoism, but as I argue here, it is also, and in the first place, for Edwards, an essential ontic principle for man—the law-like activity of "being consenting to its own being."

65. Joseph Butler, *Fifteen Sermons*, sermons X, XI; Outka, *Agape*, 56–57.

66. Niebuhr, *Man's Nature and His Communities*. Jonathan Edwards discusses both types of self-love in *The Nature of True Virtue*.

67. Fiering, *Moral Thought*, 118. As an ethical phenomenon, self-love is an important, though complex concept in Jonathan Edwards's ethical theory. He offers three types of love (simple, compounded, holy) with further distinctions among these (benevolence, complacence), all of which bear on his ethical analysis of self-love, which itself is a pivotal concept in his distinction between common morality and *true* virtue.

68. 148. [L. 4r] Sermon on Isa 33:14 (1730), *WJE Online* 44.

69. Cf. O'Donovan, *The Problem of Self-love in St. Augustine*.

9

Reconceiving Human Being

> Many have wrong conceptions of the difference between the nature of the Deity and created spirits. The difference is no contrariety, but what naturally results from His greatness and nothing else... So that if we suppose the faculties of a created spirit to be enlarged infinitely, there would be the Deity to all intents and purposes.
>
> —"Miscellanies" no. 135

Theocentristic Influences

"Mr. Stoddard's philosophy" is not the sole contributing factor to Edwards's conception of human being. Setting aside biblical propositions, the Puritan tradition, and even John Locke's important concept of the self's reflexive or introspective experience of internal acts for the moment,[1] Edwards's own theocentricity plays a major role in his ontological considerations of man's essential being. This is where we shall concentrate our present attention.

Edwards's theocentricity influences his ontology in at least three respects. First, it dictates that the most fundamental and defining principle of human existence immediately relates to the glory of God (Edwards's characteristic theocentrism of ends). Second, God's being itself serves as the ontological archetype for man. Third, the relational structure of Edwards's ontological and psychological Trinity serves as the model for the internal dispositional and psychological structure of human beings. We shall consider each point in turn.

Instances of Excellence

In the first place, God designs human existence to glorify Himself through a telic prescription that grounds "human being" in divine "excellency." Grounding human being, within Edwards's vision of reality, in God's beautiful being serves four purposes:

I. it answers the question of how God encompasses created minds and concludes the question of how "God comprehends all being";

II. it provides a statement about what is shared by *all* human beings, whether concreated or fallen, elect or reprobate, regenerate or unregenerate;

---

1. See Locke, *Essay* II, i, 1–5.

III. it shows how every individual, regardless of salvific status, every moment fulfills a God-glorifying purpose by their bare existence; and

IV. it secures man's intrinsic "worth" on account of which God may have "regard" to him.

I

When Edwards applies his ontological axiom from "The Mind" notebook entry on "EXCELLENCY," "being is proportion or excellency" to "perceiving being" or "spirits," the conclusion which emerges is that the highest excellency and, therefore, the greatest "degree" of proportion, consists in the consent of spirits "one to another" or the mutual consent of "being to being."[2] The reason equality or the beauty of proportion pleases the mind and inequality displeases is because disproportion or inconsistency contradicts mental existence, i.e., proportionality. Proportionality may then be understood as the aesthetic equivalence of mental consent, which, for Edwards, *is* being. The upshot means that every intelligent existence is, to one degree or another, an entity of excellence or, synonymously, an instance of proportion or a consenting being.[3]

Having established his metaphysic, he makes the turn toward panentheistic inclusivity. If God is *Ens Entium* and "the sum of all being," then any and all human beings are comprehended by "Being in general."[4] Which is to say, at the most basic level of existence for "perceiving being" or "spirits," God is the sum; or, in other words, God's own existence envelopes their excellence or proportionality and, in fact, may be said to comprise it.[5] As Edwards states it, "consent to entity and consent to God are the same, because God is the general and only proper entity of all things."[6]

Edwards not only subsumes all things beneath the blanket of God's comprehensiveness, but in equating being with excellence he renders all intelligent perceiving minds

---

2. *WJE* 6:336, 338.

3. In "The Mind," no. 64, Jonathan Edwards explains: "Excellency may be distributed into greatness and beauty. The former is the degree of being the latter is being's consent to being" (*WJE* 6:382).

4. Clearly this is conclusion of "Miscellanies," no. 1077 (*WJE* 20:1077).

5. "The Mind," no. 15: "'Tis impossible that we should explain and resolve a perfectly abstract and mere idea of existence; only we always find this, by running of it up, that God and real existence are the same" (*WJE* 6:345). Cf. "Miscellanies," no. 1077, *WJE* 20:1077. Though it was explained earlier that the most important implication of Jonathan Edwards's definition of excellency is the claim that every real being must, as a condition of its reality, stand in some relation to other things, and even to all other things, yet a soul may exist even if it directly dissents from other entities and "Being in general." The possibility of the existence of an intelligent perceiving being, which consents only to its own being, is explained by the "natural agreeableness" of intelligent perceiving being consenting to be. (The same idea can be explained in terms of a constitutive and necessarily reflexive disposition of self-love.) To Jonathan Edwards, the contrary is an ontological inconsistency. A being that only consents directly to its own being must exist, for its dissent to other relations assumes their and God's existence. According to Jonathan Edwards, dissent is "not to nothing" but to something, namely another intelligent mind. Thus, the existence of an entity is determined positively (via consent to being), negatively (through dissent), and necessarily, by virtue of the interconnectedness of existence within the network or matrix of being (see "The Mind," no. 45, where Jonathan Edwards expounds upon the concepts of self-love and conscience [*WJE* 6:365–66]).

6. "Miscellanies," no. 117, *WJE* 13:283. Cf. *WJE* 6:337; and "Nature of True Virtue" in *WJE* 8:541.

aspects of God's beautiful being, the matrix of existence. Since human being is so inextricably bound up with "Being in general" (God *ad extra*), it is not difficult to see how, in Edwards's philosophical-theology, God wields sovereign control over creation. Matters of salvation, providence, and causality, are easily interpreted as God asserting His *ad extra* Self to move the matrix of existence closer to its "ultimate end."

II

In Edwards's eyes God is glorified not only by "comprehending universal existence," but also by created intelligent being's "consent to its own being." Though "Being in general" is not the *direct* object of *mutual consent*, nonetheless the Divine Being receives consent, strictly considered, as the "sum of all being." Why does created intelligent being "consent to its own being" and thereby consent to "Being in general"? The answer for Edwards is simple: God designed it that way, not out of necessity, but because it suited the divine prerogative.[7]

Here enters Edwards's telic-oriented dispositions once again. In this arrangement, the essential and law-like disposition of human being does not consent, but it *is* the consent. Men (i.e., *all* mankind) do not simply consent to being by accident, evolution, or autonomous choice; rather they are designed by God to do so through a law-like disposition directed toward a specific end, "consent to being." So, for any given man to exist is for him to inescapably consent to "Being in general" *qua* being; for without "being's consent to its own being," a human being would theoretically be contrary to its own being and cease to exist,[8] that is, it would not have the disposition that distinguishes human being as such. It is important to note that *Edwards does not restrict this disposition to the elect; it belongs to every human being* at every moment of their existence as an essential and defining feature of their humanity. God in-builds the plurality of excellence (relational consent) into all manifest being, and thereby secures the externalizing of His being. Man, therefore, whether regenerate or not, is inescapably related to God through a divinely contrived disposition of consent to being.

If we ask what distinctive ways self-love exercises a law-like disposition, Edwards surprisingly replies that, in addition to "perceiving and willing being," it functions in a manner similar to matter. The being of an atom, we recall, is the activity of "resistance," so that, solidity, indivisibility, and resisting annihilation are, for Edwards, the same thing. Being and persevering, then, is akin to an *activity of self-preservation*.[9] So, too, a human being's existence is promoted by a self-loving disposition exercised in self-preservation. Within Edwards's ontology for intelligent perceiving being, there is the linking of self-love with self-preservation. Quite simply, self-love includes a notion of self-preservation.[10] The self-love disposition not only (negatively) resists annihilation: "[Man's] soul abhors annihilation, wherein it must be discontinued"; but also (positively) inclines to be: "Man

---

7. "Miscellanies," no. 1263, *WJE* 13:202–7.

8. "The Mind," nos. 1 and 45, *WJE* 6:337, 362–63; "Miscellanies," no. 99, *WJE* 13:267.

9. "Of Atoms" in *WJE* 6:211.

10. Cf. Fiering, *Moral Thought*, 192. Where Richard Dawkins might attribute a propensity toward self-preservation to a gene (*Selfish Gene*, 36), Jonathan Edwards would attribute it to an essential disposition.

was created with a propensity, that is, a disposition and capacity proportionate to the happiness intended for him."[11] So while the ontological reality of the self-love disposition is ideal, yet Edwards treats it as an *activity*, consent—the consequence of a law-like disposition. In sum, this law-like active tendency consents and regards being: what it does characterizes what it is.

God, however, stands as the architect who ensures that dispositions function in accord with His purposes. According to Edwards, all the exercises of the power and activities of sentient beings (their active tendencies) are but God's continual and immediate influence. Whether atoms or events, all emerges from the immediate operation of God. So it must have seemed entirely reasonable to Edwards to say that the active tendency of moral agents "is nothing but God's influencing the soul according to a certain law of nature." The "law of nature" of which he speaks is nothing other than the divinely-established disposition of self-love/self-regard. Thus, God remains the sole causal agent and, inasmuch as a perceiving being is an idea, that is to say, excellent mental existence, He also comprehends it. God, therefore, is glorified "according to certain rules of proportion,"[12] which He Himself teleologically establishes in all human beings alike.

III

Edwards teaches that an entity's "consent to being" constitutes mental excellence and, therefore, it exhibits an instance of *ad extra* divine beauty. God is glorified through such instances of excellence; the whole of which comprises the matrix of created existence, the matrix of divine beauty. As long as a human being exists (which, according to the religious purpose of creation, they will forever), this instance of excellence is manifest.[13] And since it is the principal law-like disposition of "human being" *en bloc*, every perceivable moment some instance of God obtains an *ad extra* manifestation. This, Edwards believes, will continue into eternity or else God's manifest glory "be altogether in vain that it was," because the eternal purposes of God require conscious beings.[14] Therefore it follows that man must immortally and eternally perceive God. We must bear in mind that beauty is not an abstracted concept for Edwards; it is his word for what human beings consent to in existence—"Being in general."

In this, Edwards essentially combines nuanced elements of the Augustinian-Stoddardean position on self-love with aesthetic rudiments from Shaftesbury's moral philosophy to (*i*) produce a distinctly dispositional conception of man, and (*ii*) bring the whole under his operating principle of telic-theocentricity.

But here Edwards turns Shaftesbury's ideas inside-out, or rather, outside-in. In response to the theory of psychological egoism indicative of Thomas Hobbes and Bernard Mandeville, Shaftesbury proposed a phenomenological description of the human encounter with beauty to account for ethical behavior. He believed the "moral sense," a mental

---

11. "Miscellanies," no. 99, *WJE* 13:268.
12. Ibid., 267.
13. "Miscellanies," no. gg, *WJE* 13:185.
14. "Miscellanies," no. 1, *WJE* 13:197.

faculty unique to us that involves reflection and feeling and constitutes our ability to discern right from wrong, was analogous to a purported "aesthetic sense," a special capacity by which we perceive, through our emotions, the "proportions and harmonies" of which, on his Platonic view, beauty is composed. Additionally, Shaftesbury believed every creature has a "private good or interest," an end to which it is naturally disposed by its constitution. The "end" corresponds to empirical factors, namely, what is perceived to be beautiful, harmonious, and excellent. These ideas resonated with Edwards, but required reordering so as to make them agreeable with his understanding of Christian anthropology, not the optimism of humanism.

Edwards would say that moral distinctions do not issue from the natural world, nor does morality exist independently of theistic religion, as Shaftesbury and Hutcheson believed. As a non-naturalist, he maintains that moral distinctions are internal and spiritual, absolute and foundational. But what is more, he believes that it is the Divine Being that stands as the beauty of aesthetic. So, once Edwards naturalized Shaftesbury's external "proportions and harmonies" and made them ontological designations grounded in God's being, then he was only one step removed from his Augustinian-Stoddardean position on self-love. For him, "excellence" is not so much an idea produced in us when we experience pleasure upon thinking of certain natural objects or artifacts, nor is it analogous to Lockean secondary qualities. Instead, excellence is ontic. What Shaftesbury and Hutcheson denominate a "moral" or "aesthetic sense" is really an instance of excellence itself, viz., a law-like disposition given (internally) to consent to existence—"Being in general."[15] Morality is not determined by what flows into an agent and is perceived by a moral or aesthetic sense. Instead, it is a matter of what an agent's inner disposition manifests.

Imago Dei and the Analogia Entis

The major second influence of Edwards's theocentrism becomes apparent evident in the correlation he draws between "the deity subsisting in the prime, unoriginated, and most absolute manner" and the inner logic of man's essence.[16] Here Edwards imputes his conception of God's ideal essence to man, so that an analogy of being may be established and man's ontological "worth" may be grounded in the "excellence" of mental existence. That is, having achieved a satisfactory trinitarian ontology, Edwards moves outward from this absolute center of being (God) to explain the being of man in accord with the divine archetype.[17]

Holmes and McClymond fail to acknowledge that neither Edwards's theocentrism nor his understanding of the *imago Dei* allow for an alternative ontological model for man in the sense that there could be competing, unrelated structures of being. The possibility of there being two essentially separate kinds of human beings is never an option for Edwards. The upshot is that the basic, non-theological "worth" or "value" that God regards

---

15. See Holbrook, *Ethics of Jonathan Edwards*, chap 8.

16. "Discourse on the Trinity" in *WJE* 21:131.

17. Cf. Pauw, *Supreme Harmony of All*, chap 2. That moving from God to man in the sphere of ontology was Jonathan Edwards's expressed method, see *WJE* 6:388 and "Miscellanies," nos. 91, 94, 96 in *WJE* 13.

in every man, from Adam to Judas to Mother Theresa, is the same. The determination of man's "value" is metaphysically based on the "excellence" (which God comprehends) inbuilt to being. Thus, God's regard for *all* human life, from the greatest sinner to the most sanctified saint, is really a regard for His own beautiful being manifest *ad extra*.[18]

God's essence is the idea of Himself, while the content of that idea consists of "essential knowing" and "loving."[19] As Richard Weber explains, this forms the heart of Edwards's metaphysical formulation of the Trinity.[20] Correspondingly, when Edwards contemplates the essence of man, he has in mind (*i*) the metaphysical notion that mental "substance" consists in idea, and (*ii*) the idea that the first relation of the divine essence to itself—"knowing" (the Son) and "loving" (the Spirit) the primordial Divine Being (the Father), or divine self-love/self-regard—serves as the archetype of a human being's essential *habitus*.

According to Edwards, the Father's idea of Himself includes a necessary disposition toward knowing and loving Himself. This disposition is *of* and *in* that one idea God has of Himself: it is a kind of reflexivity built into the very nature of God's "self." The Father, however, is the irreducible and inexplicable source of that idea which consists of a disposition to know and love "the essence of the Godhead in its first subsistence."[21] Translated into the relational terms of excellency, the first relation of God is to His own being: there is no further reduction of being than God's idea of Himself; it is the Deity in its irreducible, direct existence.[22] Edwards carries this same rational pattern of *a priori* thought into his consideration of man: there is no more antecedent principle for a "human being" other than its *essential idea* of being *a self* that exists. How that idea is (*i*) manifest in the matrix of existence and (*ii*) becomes conscious of itself and (*iii*) even perpetuates, as it were, its own existence, is through the dispositional knowledge and love of its (derivative) being. This is what Edwards calls "essential" or "natural self-love."[23]

Conscious that such an account of God may engender improper perspectives on God's self-love (i.e., charges of selfishness), Edwards warns against conceiving of it as "common." By common self-love he means the "vulgar" and "inordinate" selfish self-love generally associated with fallen moral agents.[24] Distinct from this moral understanding of self-love is, of course, the ontological (from which the moral is derived). When Edwards speaks of God's self-love he invariably means the latter, though he never excludes its moral dimension. This self-love is consistent with "the deity subsisting in the prime." He de-

---

18. "Miscellanies," no. 1077, *WJE* 20:460.

19. "Discourse on the Trinity" in *WJE* 21:114–36; "Miscellanies," no. 679, *WJE* 18:237–39.

20. Weber, "Trinitarian Theology of Jonathan Edwards," 305.

21. "Discourse on the Trinity" in *WJE* 21:141. See Lee, *Philosophical Theology*, 78ff.

22. Ibid., 131, 135, 143.

23. "Substance" is discussed in below. Jonathan Edwards uses "natural self-love" to refer to the fundamental relation of the self to its own being in a neutral sense (meaning that it is essential or "natural" to human being). Sometimes, however, he incautiously uses it in a negative sense to refer to the source of "every kind of wickedness." This tends to make it synonymously with his more descriptive referents "inordinate self-love" and "common self-love." Jonathan Edwards's negative usage typically emphasizes self-love's moral connection, which without distinction has the effect of de-emphasizing its ontological significance.

24. "Charity and Its Fruits" in *WJE* 8:255, 257–59; cf. "The Mind," no. 1, *WJE* 6:337; "Miscellanies," no. 117, *WJE* 13:283.

scribes it as perfectly "excellent," trinitarian in nature, and inextricably woven together with the divine reality.[25]

Likewise for human beings: the first relational dimension or characteristic of being for human beings is the most fundamental. In Edwards's ontology dispositional self-regard is the "being" of "being-in-relation." This is to say, in the logical order of a being's relations, *self-relation* is logically prior. This does not mean that other-relation and God-relation are any less determinative of human being. It simply means that the disposition of self-relatedness is basic and primary, a *sine qua non* of human being.[26] Thus, self-love is part of the very essence of human being.[27] "Being's consent to its own being" is synonymous with being disposed to be, or being loving existence, or (which is the same thing) the self-love of a human being.

In the vision of Jonathan Edwards, then, created human being is an ideal self, which—*in the first instance*—exercises itself as a mental disposition toward "being," thereby instantiating "excellence." God not only fashions such an instance of excellence through a dispositional prescription but does so after His own image; for "Being, and disposition or Inclination ben't Different in God [as] in our selves."[28] "Excellence," in terms of intelligent existence, is in fact the truest sense in which man exists as the image of God. In turn, the *imago Dei* stands as the most certain form of the *analogia entis*. Thus, the inherent "value" or "worth" of human being that concerns McClymond is determined by an *ontology of kinds*. Kind of existence is divinely determined by an entity's basic mental structure. Human beings are a kind of mental existence like God: "DEITY. Many have wrong conceptions of the difference between the nature of the Deity and created spirits. The difference is no contrariety, but what naturally results from His greatness and nothing else . . . So that if we suppose the faculties of a created spirit to be enlarged infinitely, there would be the Deity to all intents and purposes, the same simplicity, immutability, etc."[29]

Edwards's "ontology of kinds" thesis explains two things: First, it tells us that mental existence determines the kind of entity on the "scale of being." Mental existence carries at least a *basic* "degree of excellence," which is determinative not only of kind, but also an entity's basic realness or *analogia entis*. Second, it gives us insight concerning Edwards's proportionate regard thesis. When the basic "degree of excellence" is arithmetically combined with the basic "degree of existence" or realness, then it results in an essential value. Appraising the value of kinds then becomes elementary. To use Edwards's own example: "*An archangel* must be supposed to have more [mental] existence . . . than a *worm* or a *flea*";[30] likewise, a flea more than a stone. Certainly the employment of mathematical com-

---

25. Ibid., 257–59. Cf. Lee, *Philosophical Theology*, 186–88.

26. 204. [L. 3v–L. 5v]. Sermon on Job 11:12 (c.1731/2; repreached Aug. 1753), *WJE Online* 46.

27. "The Mind," no. 1: "[T]his that they [i.e. moral sentimentalist philosophers] call self-love is no affection, but only the entity of the thing, or his being what he is" (*WJE* 6:337).

28. 42. [L. 2r]. Sermon on Deut 32:4 (1728), *WJE Online* 42. Cf. Aldridge, *Jonathan Edwards*, 138–39.

29. "Miscellanies," no. 135, *WJE* 13:295. It goes without arguing that Jonathan Edwards's analogy of being implies no matter how excellent a created being may be or become, its knowing and loving itself is never an essential knowing and loving in the same way that the Son is *suigeneris* and the Holy Spirit eternally spirates.

30. "Nature of True Virtue" in *WJE* 8:546 n. 6.

putations within the realm of eighteen-century moral philosophy was nothing new.[31] Yet Edwards's use of a calculus of value to ascertain an *ontological* denomination of beings was something novel.

We may now fully address McClymond's concern about the application of proportionate regard to all three categories of human being. How is it possible that God could regard man, even sinful, reprobate man? Answer: by regarding the basic degree of excellence every human being inherently possesses in the relation AdA.[32]

A Trinitarian Model of the Mind

The third and last influence of his theocentrism that we shall consider is really a further elucidation of the second influence discussed above. It concerns a parallel regard Edwards establishes between the *activity* of God's primordial disposition of loving and knowing Himself and the first relation of created intelligence to itself.

Edwards explains that the content of God's essential idea of Himself consists of actively knowing and loving His excellence.[33] When Edwards develops this idea, indicating that the Father's knowing and loving is an *essential* knowing and loving, he has his ontological Trinity. In due course, he draws a parallel with man: God's internal relations serve as the archetypal pattern of the inner constitution of man. In a typical passage he says, "There is . . . an image of the Trinity in the soul of man. There is the mind and its understanding or idea, and the will or affection, or love: answering to God, the idea of God, and the love of God."[34]

However, it is not enough simply to say that Edwards applies the *model* of the Trinity to the structure of the self as a willing and understanding agent (this much is evident in the psychological constitution of man), but that created spirit *itself* possesses the same kind of *self-union* that God does: man's essence consists of actively knowing and loving existence.

In Edwards, the understanding and the will are neither separate faculties nor conjoined. Rather, they are the activities or products of the mind or spirit, which is expressed in acts of law-like dispositions. Consequently, the existence as well as the direction and manner in which these two faculties function is determined in the first place by the underlying disposition or "principle of nature."[35] This dispositional activity gives a human being "self-*union*," and indeed *is* its "self-union."[36]

---

31. Newton, Hutcheson, and others, used a moral calculus in their determinations of "value," "worth," and "propriety." Later, Jeremy Bentham, J. S. Mill, and others, forged a movement where utilitarian ethics were largely determined by mathematical computation and scientific methods. But Jonathan Edwards aims for a determination of the ontological value of being, not a moral calculus per se.

32. *AdA* is a modal representation of a reflexive dispositional structure that yields self-relation.

33. "Discourse on the Trinity" in *WJE* 21:113–14, 121.

34. "Miscellanies," no. 362, *WJE* 13:435. When Jonathan Edwards speaks about the psychological constitution of man or anything referring to it, as a rule he uses the terms "will," "affections," "inclinations', and "love," interchangeably.

35. *WJE* 2:96–98, 206.

36. "The Nature of True Virtue" in *WJE* 8:589. Jonathan Edwards in fact uses "self-love" and "self-union" interchangeably (ibid.). Ramsey makes a similar observation, but stops short of the meaning intend here. In

Substance, Essence, and Personal Identity

A Note on the Idea of "Substance" or "Essence."

So far we have a self and an essential disposition that, from its inception and in accord with its telic prescription, engages in the knowing and loving of being. We also know that the exercise of this self-loving disposition is the property of an ideal substance, which itself is an instance of excellence and, therefore, an instance of divine beauty. Furthermore, we know a spirit's substance may possess other properties of dispositions that *directly* relate it to other beings and God. But according to Sang Lee, all there is to intelligent perceiving beings are dispositions; there is no *"substance"* in which dispositions inhere. While this may be true in Edwards's account of bodies, yet in the case of self-conscious existences it is not. The same reasons delineated in chapter 4 regarding God's substantial essence are applicable here. First, Edwards retains the language and meaning of "substance" for human beings.[37] Second, he speaks of the defining dispositions of a human being as having a *locus*: they are, for example, *in* or *of* the "substance of the soul."[38] Third, the soul cannot be a disposition given the centrality for Edwards of *self*-love and *self*-relation. This is to say (over-against Lee), Edwards holds to the conventional position that a substance is what is capable of having properties (in this case dispositions), but is not itself a property of anything else. Consequently, Edwards gives an account of the self in non-dispositional terms. Lastly, because he models man's being step for step after God's being, we know that the substance of a human being, of a self, is going to be (all things considered equal) the same—an idea. Thus, the essential dispositions of a human have their *locus* in an idea designated a "self." The question, then, is what constitutes the idea of a self?

A "self," for Edwards, must be excellent; that is, it must have proportion, because only excellence is being, and only "real being" may be considered (substantial) mental existence.[39] So, taking into account what he says about God comprehending all existence, we may infer that "the substance of the soul" or what constitutes the idea of a self is, quite simply, divinely communicated existence, but such that—*as a law*—perceives itself, i.e., that has self-awareness/self-consciousness.[40] The cart, however, has not been put before

---

his "Editor's Introduction," Ramsey rightly argues that Jonathan Edwards uses a reoccurring theme about the Trinity (viz., since any idea perfectly like a thing *is* that thing and "wants nothing that is in the thing") to make the case in *True Virtue* that man's conscience consists in "a disposition . . . to be uneasy in a consciousness of being inconsistent with himself and, as it were, against himself in his own actions." From this Ramsey concludes, "ease of conscience is consistency" with self-identity. Thus far Ramsey and I agree, but he proceeds no further. He sees no ontological significance in "self-love," even though he says that the reflex action of conscience is at least one element in what Jonathan Edwards "means by intelligent willing creatures being in the 'natural image' of God," and that for Jonathan Edwards, "conscience is, itself, a relation" (*WJE* 8:42, 43). Instead, self-love/self-union is subsumed under a discussion on conscience—a dynamic of the psychological trinitarian image in man.

37. See *Religious Affections*, *WJE* 2:188; *Original Sin*, *WJE* 3:399, 400, 401, 402; 42. Sermon on Deuteronomy 32:4 (1728), *WJE Online* 42.

38. *Religious Affections*, *WJE* 2:188. In the same place, Jonathan Edwards refers to the soul as "an active substance." Cf. *Original Sin*, *WJE* 3:399–402.

39. "Miscellanies," no. 41, *WJE* 13:223.

40. "The Mind," no. 16, *WJE* 6:345.

the horse simply because a "self" itself is an idea expressed through a disposition that perceives ideas, even the very idea of itself. For the essential and most basic disposition of a self is also a divinely communicated ("created") idea. In fact, it is a property of the ideal substance called "self." A "self" is, then, a particular substantial idea of existence or instance of excellence communicated by God that, through the essential dispositional properties of that idea, reflects upon itself in a law-like manner. Just how "the substance of the soul" is an idea of itself may be explained through Edwards's work on personal identity in *Original Sin*.

A Note on Personal Identity

Affixed to the end of his 1758 treatise *The Great Christian Doctrine of Original Sin Defended* are a series of "Answers to Arguments," one of which aims to further justify the doctrine of original sin by rendering personal identity *in* a time and *through* time totally dependent upon God's determination. The metaphysical thinking behind this attempt is ingenious but radical. Its ingenuity lies in its simplicity: God simply regards or constitutes all humanity in Adam and his fall, as He does all the elect in Christ's death and resurrection. To God, Adam and his posterity are ontologically one. It is that simple. So too, personal identity *in* a time (i.e., what constitutes personal identity for a "self" in a particular moment strictly considered: we may consider this the "actual self" in its constitutional objectivity) is simply a matter of God's determination. That is, God determines and communicates the particulars that attribute individuality and personal identity.[41] However, simplicity gives way to complexity when we scrutinize how God perpetuates *through* time the link between personal identity and a created being's ideal substance.

Edwards's account of personal identity through time, like modern accounts of the same, commences with Locke's thoughts on the topic. Locke, who holds that the identity of a person consists neither in the identity of an immaterial substance (*à la* Cartesian dualism) nor in the identity of a material substance, nor "physical body," states that personal or self-identity consists in "same consciousness."[42] His view appears to assert that the persistence of a person through time consist in the fact that certain actions, thoughts, experiences, etc., occurring at different times, are somehow united in memory. This theory is familiar to philosophical discussion as the memory criterion of personal identity.

David Hume, however, radically dissents from Locke's position by denying that we have any idea of a "self," either in a time or through time. He intends by this seemingly paradoxical repudiation of an idea of the self to push the question, "What is meant by the 'self'? From what impression could this idea be derived?" This beckons a further question: "Is there any continuous and identical reality that forms our ideas of the self?" Upon reflection, Hume retorts that no one impression can be invariably associated with the idea of self. Thus Hume denies the existence of a self-identity in a time, let alone a continuous

---

41. "Notes on Knowledge and Existence" in *WJE* 6:398.

42. Locke, *Essay* II, xxiii, 27, nos. 5, 9. See, Helm, "Locke's Theory of Personal Identity," 173–85. This is not to ignore the contributions of Descartes to whom Locke refers in his own discussion on personal identity (see "Meditation VI" in *Meditations*).

self-identity, and regards the rest of mankind as "nothing but a bundle or collection of different perceptions."[43]

His thorough denial of the existence of any form of substance leads Hume to deny the existence of a continuous self that in some way retains its identity through time. Locke retained the idea of substance, though he spoke of it as that "something, which we know not what."[44] And even though Berkeley denies the existence of substance underlying qualities, yet the Bishop retains the idea of *spiritual* substances.[45] Hume denies that substance in any form exists or has any coherent meaning. If what is meant by the *self* is some form of substance, Hume argues that no such substance can be derived from our impressions of sensation. He made clear that the question of personal identity through time was a three-step process: first one had to argue for a "self" and then establish personal identity in a time, then through a time.

Edwards first enters the discussion assuming a "self" and sympathizing with a Lockean notion of personal identity in a time. But before long he breaks with Locke and complains, "Identity of person is what seems never to have been explained. It is a mistake that it consists in sameness or identity of consciousness."[46] Later we find he sides not with Hume, as Lee might suspect, but with Berkeley's subjective idealism and thereby joins a tradition of reaction against Locke, through the denial of substance underlying qualities and in the retention of the idea of spiritual substances. But without the aid of Berkeley's works,[47] his conception of spiritual or mental substances differs from the Bishop's. Where Berkeley is content to think of mental substance as "mind," Edwards clearly identifies mind with "idea."[48]

From this position, Edwards explains (over-against Locke's notion that the continuity of the ideas, or the ideas' continuity, constitutes self-identity) that the divine communication of a person's *present* consciousness toward existence comprises personal identity *in* a time. This stands consistent with the notion considered earlier, that it is the idea (of existence) that constitutes the mental substance of human being.

Edwards's departure from Locke and, indeed, from some of his Calvinist predecessors stems from what lay beneath their notions of self-conscious intelligence, namely (1)

---

43. Hume, *Treatise of Human Nature*, 200–201; 252.

44. Locke's understanding of "substance" in connection with self-identity seems to be consistent with his usage of "substratum" or "substrata" elsewhere. That is, they probably mean the same thing. The important thing for Locke, however, is that whatever this substratum or substance may be, it upholds the continuity of mental organization, even through considerable changes in consciousness.

45. Berkeley, *Principles of Human Knowledge* in *Works of George Berkeley*, 2:55.

46. "The Mind," nos. 11 and 72, *WJE* 6:342–43, 385–86. See Locke, *Essay* II, xxvii, 9f. Anderson offers an insightful discussion as to why and how Jonathan Edwards rebuffed Locke's account of personal identity in "The Mind," no. 11, and more extensively in *Original Sin* (Part IV, chap 3). See "Editor's Introduction," *WJE* 6:116–17.

47. Though Berkeley's *Theory of Vision* (1709), *Principles of Human Knowledge* (1710), and *Alciphron* (1734) are listed on the "Catalogue" as nos. 319, 318, and 350 (Thuesen, "Editor's Introduction," *WJE* 26:76), Jonathan Edwards did not cross them off (as was his practice) to indicate that they had been read (Johnson, "Jonathan Edwards' Background Reading," 212). Whether Jonathan Edwards read Berkeley or not, he would have been familiar with his ideas via secondary sources (Fiering, *Moral Thought*, 14–16).

48. "The Mind," no. 16, *WJE* 6:345.

"certain real essences" that were not identified with *ideas* and, (2) along with the idea of essence, that of enduring through time as *that* identical essence.⁴⁹ In Edwards's view, substances that were not identified with ideas left the door open for a dualist account of reality. If this did not lend itself to skepticism or Hobbes's materialism, then it tended to separate a conception of a *single* ideal reality with multiple perceivable dimensions (e.g., spiritual-moral/spatial-empirical), such as Edwards proposed. Furthermore, non-ideal essences and Lockean substratum were untenable because there was no way to discover a substratum or essence. In Edwards's mind, since all existence is perception, we have no evidence of immaterial substance.⁵⁰

But, he asserts, we *do* perceive ideas; ideas that God communicates to a passive mind.⁵¹ In fact, and as we have seen above, God communicates an idea of a particular existence that reflects upon itself and constitutes "the substance of the soul."⁵² Moreover, it serves as a nexus or, synonymously, link, tie, or connection, between the essential dispositions that constitute man's consciousness.⁵³ So much for identity in a time, what about *through* time?

In Edwards, that which constitutes a continuous self, or the identity of a spirit through a time, is "a composition and series of perceptions, or an universe of coexisting and successive perceptions connected by such wonderful methods and laws" constituted by God.⁵⁴ The continuous identity of a spirit, then, is not some kind of non-ideal spiritual substance in which particular human qualities inhere, or whose moral temper governs human behavior. Rather, as Allen Guelzo states, "Just as the essence which 'upholds the properties of bodies' is really 'he by whom all things consist,' so all our ideas proceed in a relationship issuing not from ourselves but from God. The *nature* which the mind has, and which governs its temper and its liking or not liking of motives, resolves ultimately into the act of God himself."⁵⁵ Edwards does not deny that sameness of consciousness and memory are "one thing essential" to self-identity (i.e., that they are necessary to it but are not it). But when asked what constitutes self-identity and its continuance through time? he replies that it is God's conception or idea of a being's self-identity, as well as the activity of God in the communication of that divine ideal series. For instance, in *Original Sin* he writes, "'Tis evident, that the communication or continuance of the same consciousness and memory to any subject, through successive parts of duration, depend wholly on a divine establishment."⁵⁶

Here Edwards makes a sophisticated twist and calls for a radical change in perspective. He regards as essentially wrong the ordinary thought and language that people commonly employ about the objectivity of the world as well as their enduring personal identity and says—*against* a common sense position—that it is fundamentally wrong; it conflicts

49. Calvin, *Institutes*, I.15.2; Locke, *Essay* II, xxiii.
50. "The Mind," no. 40, *WJE* 6:356.
51. "The Mind," no. 3, *WJE* 6:339.
52. *WJE* 3:399–400.
53. Ibid., 126; "Miscellanies," no. 241, *WJE* 13:358.
54. "Notes on Knowledge and Existence" in *WJE* 6:398.
55. Guelzo, *Edwards on the Will*, 74–75. Cf. "The Mind," no. 61, *WJE* 6:380.
56. *WJE* 3:398.

with contingent reality. Instead, he favors an "error theory"[57] of personal identity through time and the existence of the world, and describes it in a way ordinary people simply do not talk. He wants to say that God determines the course and order of the successive ideas and states of consciousness that constitute the identity of a spirit through time; or, in other words, the establishing of a mental existence is nothing but a mental exercise of knowledge and perception *on the part of God*. Reality, as we know and experience it, is really re-created each moment—and us with it. Time itself has no intrinsic continuity, but is an idea communicated to us like frames in a movie.[58] Moreover, he wants to say that God's determination is nothing but an "arbitrary operation," according to "Miscellanies" no. 1263 and "The Mind" notebook. His purpose for doing this is fourfold: it dispossesses the deists of a distant God; it wrestles reality out of the hands of materialists and radical humanists and puts it back into God's control; it provides an opportunity to revisit the discussion on human nature and ethics; and it argues for a theocentric morality based on the revelation of God and "The Great Christian Doctrine of Original Sin."[59]

There is then no method or law prior to God's fashioning mental existences. It is a pure mental/spiritual/moral exercise, whereby "all union and all created identity is arbitrary," that is, it is determined by God's arbitration.[60] God determines, however, that He is the most "fitting" model and therefore "suitably" fashions man after His own mental and arbitrary likeness:

> 'Tis the glory of God that he is an arbitrary being, that originally he, in all things, acts as being limited and directed in nothing but his own wisdom, tied to no other rules and laws but the directions of his own infinite understanding. So in those that are the highest order of God's creatures, viz. intelligent creatures, that are distinguished from other creatures in their being made in God's image, 'tis one thing wherein consists their highest natural dignity, that they have an image of this. They have a secondary and dependent arbitrariness . . . These things being observed, I would take notice that the higher we ascend in the scale of created existence and the nearer we come to the Creator, the more and more arbitrary we should find the divine operations in the creature, or those communications and influences in which he maintains and intercourse with the creature. And it appears beautiful and every way fit and suitable that it should be so.[61]

But because man's arbitrariness is "dependent" and derivative, we may go on to speak of the effects of God's fashioning, for example, the mind's perception of the idea of phe-

---

57. Mackie (*Ethics*) coined the phrase "error theory" in his discussion of the status of ethics. He adopts a distinctive version of subjectivism, i.e., an "error theory" of the *apparent* objectivity of values.

58. In "Miscellanies," no. 1263, Jonathan Edwards explains that time emerges from God's "arbitrary operation," though time itself is a "mixing of arbitrary with natural operations" (*WJE* 23:203, 205). Cf. Fiering, *Moral Thought*, 100–101.

59. It should be noted that Jonathan Edwards originally contemplated producing a single major treatise which would have included *Original Sin* and *Two Dissertations*, and that these treatises would have undoubtedly held a central place in his projected *magnum opus*. See Holbrook, "Editor's Introduction," *WJE* 3:22–23 and Sang Hyun Lee's editor's notes on the "Book of Controversies" and this same notebook in *WJE* 21:291–327 (or, within the original "Book of Controversies" notebook, 97, 101–2, Jonathan Edwards Collection; published as *"Controversies" Notebook, WJE Online* 27). Cf. *Worcester-Works*, 5:440–47.

60. "Notes on Knowledge and Existence" in *WJE* 6:398.

61. "Miscellanies," no. 1263, *WJE* 23:202–3. Cf. "Miscellanies," no. tt, *WJE* 13:189–91.

nomena, or even its own being, as retaining the character of a Newtonian system in that God establishes the "coexisting and successive" perception of those ideas in invariable laws, or as Edwards chose to put it, in "wonderful methods and laws." Ultimately, God's arrangement grounds causal connections in "the infinitely exact and precise and perfectly stable idea in God's mind together with his stable will,"[62] which in turn gives the perception of "regularity" or "succession" to natural phenomena and even ideas.

But more must be said with regard to "the *nature* which the mind has," mentioned by Allen Guelzo. Although God's original motion to create intelligent perceiving consciousnesses and ideas may be considered "purely arbitrary," yet not only is the subsequent manner in which God communicates the ideas "connected by such wonderful methods and laws" but even *what* exist as "*a composition*" or "*an universe*" of coexisting and successive perceptions" are certain fixed and established laws.[63] In fact, they exist as the divine idea of law-like receptions or perceptions of divine communications: hence the place of dispositions in Edwards's system.

My point may be better explained through an examination of Edwards's choice of words in his explication of personal identity through time: "[self-identity consists in] a composition and series of perceptions, or an universe of coexisting and successive perceptions connected by such wonderful methods and laws." Present here is an equating or further elucidation of "a composition" with "an universe." He aims to explain that there is an ontological something—"a composition" or "an universe"—that exists and is composed of a *series* or succession of coexisting perceptions. In Edwards, the notion of "a composition" or "an universe" implies the idea of an established order or law. Thus, "an universe of coexisting and successive perceptions" is the same thing as a law or disposition of perceiving. This claim is further supported by its consisting in a "series of perceptions," in that "series" and "succession" also imply some order or regularity. Such order or regularity is governed by or established as a law, which in turn establishes its abiding nature in the divine mind.

The key word in his definition from "Miscellanies" no. 13 is "coexisting." By "coexisting" perceptions he means that "an universe" or "a composition" exists *with* and *in* the perception of ideas. And since the ideas that God communicates about intelligent perceiving being are of a particular sort (i.e., a law-like series of perceiving the idea of existence), its own existence is established as an idea in God's mind in a law-like way, that is, after a particular composition or series.

But the importance of "coexisting" is not yet exhausted. To exist with or in the perception of the idea of existence is to be related or somehow internally associated with that perception. That is, since all of intelligent perceiving being's perceived ideas are from God (which includes intelligent perceiving being's idea of itself or the idea of *that* intelligent perceiving being), then contained within those "fixed and regular" communications from God must also be the idea of *that* idea received or perceived. The which, when pursued further, is understood as the idea of being intellectually and inclinationally consenting to its own existence—that is, perceiving the idea of itself or the idea of existence. Self-

---

62. "The Mind," no. 13, *WJE* 6:344.
63. Ibid.

consciousness, in Edwards's worldview, is therefore a *sine qua non* feature of created intelligent being, in the same way that God's self-consciousness is a necessary feature of His own existence.

Edwards thought to understand self-identity in the idea of self-consciousness as an immediate and continuous creation of God, in which perceived ideas are connected to each other not because of something in them or in their surroundings but by God's initial arbitrary constitution that joins them in a series according to "fixed" laws established by God. The problem of self-consciousness with memory is treated accordingly: memory involves the repetition of an idea together with an act of judgment that it was perceived (or, better, communicated by God) before; "and that judgment not properly from proof," argues Edwards, "but from natural necessity arising from a law of nature which God hath fixed."[64] God's retention and communication of all such ideas are after His "natural operation." Contrary to Locke's *tabula rasa* thesis, personal identity in a time and through time is located in innate dispositions determined by God, according to Edwards.[65]

Edwards locates the difference between "real" minds and the intelligence he attributes to "brutes and beasts" in the reflexivity of self-consciousness. But the reflexivity is not merely contemplative: thought is distinguished from mere perception in that men have "voluntary actions about their own thoughts."[66] Thus, when he comes to define consciousness as such, he writes: "the mind's perceiving what is in itself—its ideas, actions, passions, and everything that is there perceivable. It is a sort of feeling within itself."[67]

Reflexivity of consciousness can also be explained as the "remanation" (a favorite term of Edwards) of the spiritual image of God in man. Intelligent perceiving being's remanation of the ideas that God "emanates" or communicates, specifically the idea of self-relatedness (and, secondarily, other-relatedness), is what Edwards would acknowledge to be *consciousness*—the intellectual and inclinational internalization of the idea of the relationship to the self, or self-existence, or relatedness, etc. In man's intellectual and inclinational relation to God's ideas (be what they may) we have, in the words of Edwards, "both an *emanation* and *remanation*. The refulgence shines upon and into the creature, and is reflected back to the luminary. The beams of glory come from God, are something of God, and are refunded back again to their original."[68] The divine idea of an intelligent perceiving being's reflexivity of consciousness is, thus, an act of remanation, or the mental imaging of divine ideas. As Edwards says in "Miscellanies" no. 260, "There is no other properly spiritual image but [an] idea."[69] This is to say, the law-like active tendency of the

---

64. "'The Mind,' no. 69, *WJE* 6:384.
65. Cf. Lee, *Philosophical Theology*, chap 5.
66. "The Mind," no. 59, *WJE* 373–74.
67. "The Mind," no. 16, *WJE* 6:345. Here, Jonathan Edwards's constructivist worldview (in which language or, more precisely, trinitarian communication, "constructs" the world) is evident: "self," for Jonathan Edwards, assumes self. Cf. Daniel, "Postmodern Concepts of God and Edwards's Trinitarian Ontology" in *Edwards in Our Time*, 45–64; and Daniel, *Philosophy of Jonathan Edwards*, 114–28. Kevin J. Vanhoozer's *First Theology*, 127–58, offers a lucid explanation of this theory.
68. "End of Creation" in *WJE* 8:531.
69. *WJE* 13:368.

dispositions constituting "human being" is, at the very least, the continual reception and remanation of the idea of existence.

Clearly Edwards was on the way to creating a doctrine that stated such consciousnesses are ultimately a set of dispositions by virtue of their (1) self-relatedness, (2) relative metaphysical independence as *self*-consciousnesses,[70] and (3) present disposition toward ideas (and not the ideas' continuity) which constitutes one's identity. All of this, of course, is founded upon his metaphysics of time and used in *Original Sin* to secure such traditional dogmas as the imputation of Adam's sin, inherent corruption, providence, and free grace.

God's determination of *which* particular series of ideas He intends to communicate in conjunction with the idea of "an universe" determines, for Edwards, perceptual existence and, consequently, personal identity.[71]

In Edwards's thinking, self-awareness or self-consciousness gives spirits a degree of substantiality or realness. Matter and animals, however, are not self-reflective mental existences and therefore not primary instances of proportion. The one is insensate, the other annihilated at death. But minds of a superior ontological kind are ideas that are composed of self-loving/self-conscious dispositions. According to "Miscellanies" no. 1263, this makes them more "arbitrary," i.e., less ordered by laws and therefore more mental, spiritual, and moral, or, in a word, "real," after God's idea of Himself.

Edwards's logic thus argues that those beings that have knowledge and consciousness are "the only proper and real and substantial beings, inasmuch as the being of other things is only by these."[72] "From hence," Edwards concludes in "Of Being," "we may see the gross mistake of those who think that material things the most substantial beings, and spirits more like a shadow; whereas spirits only are properly substance."[73]

Although he allots human beings a substance, yet he still can say (as he does in his 1757 "Notes on Knowledge and Existence") that God is "the only substance" because only God has being all at once.[74] Other existences have only *momentary existences* as events

---

70. By "independence" I do not mean an "autonomous self-perpetuation," but that man, unlike any other spatiotemporal existence, does not require another to actuate (substantiate) the idea of his being. That is, while Jonathan Edwards's idealism requires an intelligent perceiving mind for the spatiotemporal realization of all non-intelligent perceiving minds, yet the reflexivity of consciousness attains the end of self-realization for any given intelligent perceiving mind. Also intelligent perceiving beings, as continuing entities, have their substantiality only in God's mind, they exist only in that God forms and communicates a coherent law-like "series" of ideas about them. So while they are indeed images of God (as consciousnesses), yet they are dependent and "always behind His clarity. He communicates to them, and so they have being" (Jenson, *America's Theologian*, 33). This idea does not cloud God's existence, however, for God, according to Jonathan Edwards, is an independent mind of independent innertrinitarian relations. (Cf. Lee, "Editor's Introduction," *WJE* 21:20–27.) For more on "autonomous self-perpetuation" and its relation to consciousness and self-maintenance, see Shoemaker, "Functional Consciousness" in *Experimental and Theoretical Studies in Consciousness*.

71. See "Miscellanies," no. 267, *WJE* 13:373.

72. "Of Being" in *WJE* 6:206.

73. Ibid.

74. *WJE* 6:398.

in a temporal series. This is Edwards's "error theory" of existence in time, which comes out in his treatise *Original Sin*. There he sets forth his doctrine of divine conservation or continuous-creation, stating that the world is momentarily quenched and replaced by a similar world of new ontological realities.

Leon Chai's criticism that the immediacy of God's continuous-creation excludes the employment of laws "no matter how specific"[75] clearly does not apply. In Edwards's version of divine conservation, what God quenches and recreates each moment is something that possesses a prior ontological reality as the idea of an *ad extra* reality to God. Here, again, we have the answer to how law-like dispositions possess an ontological reality apart from temporal manifestation: they are present within "a series" in God's mind. Because the whole series of God's work and presence *ad extra* is complete and full in His mind, God considers them in His atemporal knowledge all at once—*in their series*—as an actuality. Each divinely communicated moment of the world is really part of a unified series to God. Likewise, each and every dispositional exercise is part of a network or matrix, not just in terms of structure (one entity or event standing in relation to another), but also in terms of sequence or chronology—past, present, and future. The matrix of existences, temporal progression, and emanation/remanation, constitute one permanent, interrelated and unbreakable series in God: hence the world's mode of abiding or prior reality.

Edwards's causality requires a cause to be equal to or greater than its corresponding effect. The idea of the world or any thought in the mind of perceiving beings does not possess causal power to sustain that idea, nor even the idea of themselves.[76] God, therefore, must literally re-create that idea for them, and even of themselves to themselves, each and every moment. This makes Edwards's doctrine both unique and uniquely counterintuitive from the perspective of the human agent. He does not reiterate the traditional doctrine of divine conservation, which purports that: given that x exists now at T^1 and also at T^2, can only be accounted for by God's will. Rather, he says that x at T^1 is not numerically the same x at T^2. Such a strong revisionist proposal claims that all other perceptions of reality are in error.

What then is re-created each and every moment is the idea of an external world, plus the idea that a remaining world is the one perceived. Anything less than a creative power will not cause the constant effect of a perceived reality.[77] Yet from the perspective of God it is not an entirely new ontological creation similar to a quenched preceding world. Rather, it is the next idea of the world in God's determined series. So, for example, an intelligent perceiving being's perception (reception) of divine ideas of its own existence follows after a reproduction of a divine series, communicated to that intelligent perceiving being one frame at a time, with the appearance of $T^1 \rightarrow T^2$, etc. The body and soul in T^2 are *not* numerically identical with the original (prior) body and soul in T^1. It is not that they have been reproduced in T^2, but that they are an entirely new mode of physicality and mental constitution of consciousness. Man's identity, then, does not lay in his "constituent parts," which are, at different moments in time, numerically distinct effects, but "in the *arbitrary*

---

75. Chai, *Limits of Enlightenment*, 144.
76. "Miscellanies," no. 267, *WJE* 13:373.
77. *WJE* 3:400–401.

constitution of the Creator; who by his wise sovereign establishment so unites these successive new effects, that he *treats them as one*, by communicating to them like properties, relations, and circumstances; and so leads us to regard and treat them as one."[78]

For all intents and purposes, then, the idea of the world and of the self in a preceding moment is "past, and what is gone is not";[79] unless, of course, that moment is connected in a series with the present and future, which, according to Edwards, it certainly is, just like stills in a move reel. This is what gives us the impression that the world and ourselves are (other things considered equal) the same through time.

Temporal series are nothing more than expressions of God's power, or pulses of divine power to the perceiver; to God it is all one and He is all one. Consequently, Edwards's talk of substance and personal identity continuing through time is really only by license, derivatively, and the predication of language, because finite spirits and, consequently, the world (unlike God) are dependent upon the communication of that series for existence: hence, Edwards's hierarchy of beauty and being and stress upon the vertical dimension of created order and being. He stresses the ethereal because it fully envelops the temporal. Both dimensions, however, are really perceptions of a single reality, the substance of which is ideal. The *locus* of *that* idea is another idea—God's idea of created minds modeled after Himself.

∼

Contrary to the Enlightenment announcement that man carries out his own destiny and is the forger of his own identity,[80] Edwards declares that man enters the world as the effect of God's determination and continues in existence and identity only by God. In *Original Sin*, he is not simply defending an outmoded doctrine. Instead, he calls for a complete abandonment in the way not only the self but also the world is conceived. So dependent is causation upon God, that not a single thing in the universe can continue one moment without *immediate* divine power to recreate it one frame of time after the other.

But Edwards leaves us with more questions than he answers in *Original Sin*. For instance, Rem B. Edwards questions how self-consciousness works with relation to his continuous-creation from the perspective of the human agent. If a human agent does not persist more than a moment, then how can that agent be morally responsible for his actions as *his own* actions? Philip Quinn also scrutinizes the causation issue in *Original Sin* and finds the point on the integrity of human actions defective without a contiguous temporal element.[81] Edwards simply does not provide an account thorough enough to answer these questions.

---

78. *WJE* 3:403. Cf. "Miscellanies, no. 1263, *WJE* 23:202–7.
79. "Miscellanies," no. 134, *WJE* 13:295.
80. Cassirer, *Philosophy of the Enlightenment*, 18.
81. Edwards, *Return to Moral and Religious Philosophy*, 68; Quinn, "Divine Conservation, Continuous-Creation, and Human Action" in Freddoso, *Existence and Nature of God*, 55–80.

Paul Helm also has pointed out that the problematic gap between Edwards's occasionalistic causality extends to the issue of personal identity in *Freedom of the Will*.[82] One may offer a speculation reconstruction based on Edwardsean principles to answer some of these questions (just as Quinn); but knowing Edwards's proclivity toward imbibing principles from other thinkers and creatively synthesizing them with his own inventive ideas, doubtful conclusions may be the only fruit of such an endeavor.

One can only suppose that Edwards, who was occupied with numerous projects and ecclesiastical (as well as personal) issues, simply did not have opportunity to complete his thoughts on these points, but intended to do so, perhaps in his projected *magnum opus*. Presumably someone as intellectually rigorous as Edwards would have pondered the additional burden divine conservation placed upon the incarnation before publishing his version of the doctrine in *Original Sin*. Whatever may be the case, he certainly was driven by the thought that God could not make the world and therefore man disorderly if He intended a telic movement for creation. For Edwards, nothing could be more orderly than laws in the mind of God. Unlike his freethinking Enlightenment counterparts, and especially the Arminians, he sees more order as a determinist than the indeterminists.

Edwards's world simply is not the same as the world according to the deist or Hobbes or even Locke. His vision of the existence of the world is really a perception of God communicating to intelligent minds the movement of Himself (the matrix of existences) to His consummate end. In the mind of God this supreme end is one and eternally complete, yet one in which He communicates in series form to other minds one frame at a time. Such is Edwards's treatment of the doctrine of divine preservation: he simply subsumes it under continuous-creation: God's retention of the series that He communicates preserves of the world. Charles Hodge, A. H. Strong, and others within the intellectual and theological heritage of Jonathan Edwards, were, of course, to vigorously disagree with their forefather Edwards on this point,[83] and so indicate that his "error theory" was too radical, too abstract, for those who followed in his brand of the Reformed tradition.

Psychological Constitution

Edwards deals with the psychological constitution of man in the same way as man's ontological constitution, by modeling it after the Trinity.

Not only does a trinitarian treatment remain consistent with Edwards's theocentrism, it also complements the applied dimensions of his dispositional ontology. Just as there is a trinity of sorts within the being of man, so too a psychological analysis of the human soul reveals an analogy of the Trinity: "There is a resemblance to this threefold distinction in God, a threefold distinction in a created spirit; namely, the spirit itself, and its understanding, and its will or inclination or love. And this indeed is all the real distinction there is in created spirits."[84] Elsewhere he says: "There is yet more of an image of the Trinity in the soul of man: there is the mind, and its understanding or idea, and the will or affection or

---

82. Helm, *Faith and Understanding*, 174–75.
83. Hodge, *Systematic Theology*, 1:577, 2:217f; Strong, *Systematic Theology*, 416.
84. "Miscellanies," no. 259, *Works* 13:367.

love—the heart, comprising inclination, affections, etc.—answering to God, the idea of God, and the love of God."[85]

In Edwards's trinitarian model, the Father is designated the position of "mind," the Son "understanding," and the Spirit "will or affection or love."[86] In a parallel way a human being is a "mind" (in the first way of conceiving) that possesses "understanding" and "will."[87]

What stands out in these "Miscellanies" passages and, indeed, Edwards's whole approach to the philosophy of mind is the way the dispositional-ontological concepts appear to have been modified into psychological concepts and the ontological vocabulary translated into psychological terminology. For instance, Edwards's ontology holds that the relation to self, or the self-love disposition, is the *sine qua non* of human being. The same concept can be explained in psychological terms by saying that consciousness (involving perception and knowledge of self) is necessary for the existence of any and all human beings.[88]

Similarities in concepts and terminology are no coincidence. The psychological approach to explaining the existence, state, and function of minds, not only was part of Edwards's theological tradition (one immediately thinks of Augustine), but the fashion of his day. Moreover, it was more accessible and familiar to his New England auditors than the onerous language of "being." Still, in order to plumb the depths of his ontological concepts, Edwards occasionally had no other alternative but to employ psychological categories and terms. For example, after concluding that the soul's essence "consists in powers and habits" or "dispositions," he explains that the relational structure of being is in or through the unified intellectual and inclinational "faculties" of the mind.[89] The perceiving and affectional cognition of man is, for Edwards, *consciousness* or mental existence itself.[90] Psychological terms and ideas are not only useful for Edwards to fully explain his ontological conceptions, but they offer a concreteness that his metaphysical abstractions do not.

Consciousness itself, however, emerges as the unifying principle to his thoughts concerning the integrity or unity of the soul. Both in his idealism and ontology, consciousness is synonymous with intelligent perceiving existence in the sense that it is impossible that anything intelligent should exist and "nothing know it," for "nothing has any existence anywhere else but in consciousness. No, certainly nowhere else, but either in created or

---

85. "Miscellanies," no. 362, *WJE* 13:435.

86. "Miscellanies," no. 308, *WJE* 13:393. See also Lee's "Editor's Introduction," *WJE* 23:11–18.

87. When Jonathan Edwards says that the mind, understanding, and will are the only "real distinctions there is in created spirits," he does not intend that there are in fact three particulate and concrete things that make up the psychological constitution of man. The unity of the soul persists in this theory also (*WJE* 1:163; *WJE* 2:96–97). The oneness of God's ideal being serves as the prime ontic source of Jonathan Edwards's unified integrity-of-the-soul thesis. This integrity of self or "self-union" supplies him with another instance of the divine image in man. For inasmuch as God is one, so too man is one in the divine mental image.

88. This point could be expanded further by directly referring to Jonathan Edwards's idealism, which requires a created consciousness to perceive and know, for the existence of anything whatsoever.

89. "Miscellanies," no. 94, *WJE* 13:256–63; Nature of True Virtue, *WEJ* 8:589–90.

90. See "The Mind" nos. 1, 3, 16, 34, 45 and 51 in *WJE* 6.

uncreated consciousness."[91] This includes the agent of consciousness itself. Thus man's essential being manifests itself in and through (to use the psychological designation) *consciousness*, an intellectual and inclinational engagement with its own existence ("the consent of being to its own being").

The "image" of the Trinity in a man can be represented and further elucidated (other than ontologically) through an analysis of psychological self-knowledge. Consider "Miscellanies" no. 94:

> Man is as if he were two, as some of the great wits of this age have observed. A sort of genius is with man that accompanies him and attends wherever he goes; so that a man has a conversation with himself, that is, he has a conversation with his own idea. So that if his idea be excellent, he will take great delight and happiness in conferring and communing with it; he takes complacency in himself, he applauds himself; and wicked men accuse themselves and fight with themselves, as if they were two. And man is truly happy then, and only then, when these two agree, and they delight in themselves, and in their own idea and image as God delights in his.[92]

Here several previously discussed facets of Edwards's thought are collected together, particularly the aesthetic, telic, and ontic dimensions of human existence. None of these, however, are thought of entirely independent of the others, but together they explain the "mind" of human being. Since Edwards presents mental existence as mind reflecting on itself, then there must be some instance of "proportion" effected, as well as "consent" and, therefore, self-fulfillment. In Edwards, the reflexive action of mind is aesthetic and teleological: an intelligent perceiving being's idea of its own being is "excellent" or "agreeable" and, therefore, an instance of aesthetic beauty (ontic proportion) in which telic fulfillment ("happiness") is achieved.

The image of the psychological trinity in man, then, is his mind (equal to the Father) "conversing" or intellectually (the Son, the divine Logos) and inclinationally (the Spirit) perceiving the idea of its state of existence at each and every moment. The "first" man is his mind; the "second" is the reflex action of the mind in self-consciousness through the faculties of understanding and will.[93]

When these thoughts are applied to the realm of virtue ethics, mental consciousness gains a moral dimension as a human being's natural conscience. For Edwards, "natural conscience" is an inherent "disposition in man to be uneasy in a consciousness of being inconsistent with himself and, as it were, against himself in his own actions."[94] In the relational terms of his ontology, a human being's dissent from Being in general or any mental

---

91. "Of Being" in *WJE* 6:204.

92. *WJE* 13:260.

93. Ibid. Fiering notes similarities between Jonathan Edwards's ontological and psychological theories and Aquinas, as well as Protestant Scholasticism and Platonism (*Moral Thought*, 325–26). Carse adds Augustine (*Jonathan Edwards and the Visibility of God*, 95–113). Here, too, I maintain that Jonathan Edwards used his dispositional analysis of the ontological Trinity to serve as the prime analogate for human beings. Although the language and concepts that he adopts are the standing psychological terms and ideas of his day, yet his understanding of Being-as-triune so shaped and influenced his thinking about man that man's ontic and psychological constitutions conform to his conception of God, not vice versa.

94. "Nature of True Virtue" in *WJE* 8:589.

instance of primary or even secondary beauty, results in the comparative diminution of that human being's existence (or, at least, the contracting of it). In other words, natural conscience is the mental perception of a human being's "disagreeableness" or "contradiction" with its own relational existence within the matrix of divine beauty. Conversely, true ease of conscience is a human being's "consistency" with self, proper "consent to its own being," and a harmonious relation of the beautified self.[95] In short, a "good conscience" is "some image" of the psychological (and ultimately, ontological) oneness of the triune Divine Being.[96]

∼

The theocentric influences in Edwards's thought display both his originality as a philosophical theologian and a desire to remain within the parameters of his tradition. We also see him one moment as a man of his age, borrowing from Stoddard, Shaftesbury, Locke, and perhaps Berkeley, while in the next moment departing from them with some novel application or theory. In all cases, however, what dominates his thought about man's basic ontic constitution are God and the world of ideas that God categorically determines for some telos ("Miscellanies," no. 94).

To empathize with his depiction of man means rethinking reality in light of God's programmatic purposes, sometimes in ways that run counter to common sense. Edwards is not afraid to employ and reinvent concepts that conflict with stalwarts in his tradition in order to hold fast to his vision of God's end. His innovative reconception of the self-love is a prime example. He does not merely empower self-love with dispositional status; he makes it the ontological axle upon which his moral theory and God's telic-orientation for man turn.

Neutral and "Inordinate" Self-Love

Though Edwards asserts that love of one's own happiness, or individual self-love is "universal" in all and "the same degree in all," he nevertheless has two distinct usages of self-love: essential or "natural" self-love (the topic of the foregoing discussion) and "inordinate" or nefarious self-love.[97] The former is an ontological disposition. As such, it is a natural

---

95. Ibid., 589–99; "The Mind," no. 1, *WJE* 6:336. Taken further, "natural conscience," Jonathan Edwards would argue, is never at ease until it reaches full union with Being in general, through Jesus Christ. Only then may one exercise himself in thought and action (and even then, only by degrees) in a manner agreeable with the law of the whole. Only then does one's existence begin to be "happy" and unified. Ramsey underscores the significance of Jonathan Edwards's idea of conscience with relation to his ethical theory when he adds, "The spontaneous reflex of ease or disease may be the reason Edwards is willing to have *his* understanding of conscience called the 'moral sense' . . . In any case, conscience is not an intuition. It is not Francis Hutcheson's 'moral sense' that registers approbation upon an apprehension of benevolence wherever it may be found." Ramsey insightfully concludes, "For Edwards, conscience is, itself, a relation," but then limits this thought to the spheres of psychological constitution and moral philosophy by adding, "It is golden rule morality writ small in the self's consciousness *to* self" ("Editor's Introduction," *WJE* 8:42–43).

96. "Miscellanies," nos. 94, 96, 98 (*WJE* 13:256, 263; 263–64; 265) and 1263 (*WJE* 23:206–8).

97. In this sense, "natural" is synonymous with inherent. "Common self-love" may be added to the list of negative usages. Augustine and Aquinas likewise distinguished between a "neutral," "universal" self-love and

instance of proportion. Morally speaking, in and of itself it is neutral; but if governed by "a superior supernatural principle" of divine love (the Holy Spirit) its active tendency may very well be truly virtuous.[98] The latter usage, however, is strictly negative. For example, in "Miscellanies" no. 530, the first mention of self-love is virtually synonymous with immoral selfishness; the second is descriptive of the ontic principle in man: "Self-love is either simple mere self-love, which is a man's love to his own proper single and separate good, [or it] is what arises simply and necessarily from the nature of a perceiving and willing being. It necessarily arises from that without the supposition of any other principle. I therefore call it simple self-love because it arises simply from that principle, viz. the nature of a perceiving willing being . . . [it is] the necessary nature of a perceiving and willing being."[99]

This entry illustrates the importance of discerning which use Edwards intends whenever the subject enters into one of his theological, ethical, or philosophical discussions, as it frequently does. If confusion arises, it usually stems from his use of the same phrase for both employments. What may add to the confusion is that self-love, as a principle or *habitus*, is the same in both cases. Man has only one disposition of self-love, but it may be morally neutral (as the case may be with newborn infants), negatively immoral (per natural-man), or positively virtuous (concreated Adam and the potential of regenerate persons).

Essential Self-Love

The neutral use, as the above quote indicates, is natural and intrinsic to man's being. Despite the idea of self-love being, from time to time in certain Protestant and Roman Catholic quarters, associated with επιθυμια or condemnable φιλαυτια or narrow selfishness, Edwards did not shy away from regularly employing the term with neutral or even distinctly positive theological-anthropological connotations. In this, he consciously aligns himself with those within the Reformed tradition that look to Augustine not Calvin on the issue of self-love.

"perverse" self-love. Cf. O'Donovan, *The Problem of Self-love in St. Augustine*, 93–111 and *Summa Theologia*, II–II, 27.7.

98. "Charity and Its Fruits" in *WJE* 8:253. See Fiering, *Moral Thought*, 171–72; and Ramsey, *WJE* 8:252–53 n.1.

99. *WJE* 18:134. Other Puritans make a similar distinction between "natural self-love" and corrupt self-love, deemed the "root" of sin. For example, Matthew Henry (1662–1714) says, "There is a self-love which is corrupt, the root of the greatest sins, and it must be put off and mortified: but there is a self-love which is natural, and the rule of greatest duty, and it must be preserved and sanctified" (note on Matt 22:34–40, *Exposition of All the Books of the Old and New Testaments*. Another Jonathan Edwards favorite, Matthew Poole (1624–79) explains self-love just as Henry (see his commentaries on Matt 22:39 and Gal 5:14 in *Synopsis Criticorum*). Neither, however, goes so far as to distinguish self-love as an essential ontic principle. Later, several thinkers come much closer to Jonathan Edwards's meaning, yet without the same ontological sophistication. For instance, Adam Clarke (1762–1832) would say seventy years later: "*Self-love* . . . has been grievously declaimed against, even by religious people, as a most pernicious and dreadful evil. But . . . If I am to love my neighbour as *myself* and this 'love worketh no ill to its neighbour,' then *self-love*, in the sense in which our Lord uses it, is something excellent. It is properly a disposition essential to our nature, and inseparable from our being, by which we *desire* to be happy, by which we seek the happiness we have not, and rejoice in it when we possess it. In a word, it is a uniform wish of the soul to avoid all evil, and to enjoy all good" (*Holy Bible . . . with Commentary and Critical Notes*, 5:375).

Augustine, showing his debt to Plotinus, formulated a theology of natural principles, the maxim of which was (to paraphrase the *Catechism of the Catholic Church*): "All men desire to live happily."[100] Thinking processes, motives, volitional acts, human behavior, and biblical anthropology were explicated upon this premise. "Happiness," then, is achieved when "that which is man's chief end is both loved and possessed."[101] The pursuit of happiness, specifically happiness found in God, was extolled as a principal Christian virtue. When the principal desire in man (*amor sui*) was directed toward God it was sanctified, when toward anything else it was sinful: There was no difference between Christian love for God and "proper" self-love. Augustine's eudemonistic conception of the moral law had no place either for a virtue of self-love independent of love for God or love of God without self-love. In man's telic quest for happiness, he manifests true love for himself by pursuing it in a relationship with God and "finds his repose."

The line from Perkins to Stoddard advances the Augustinian notion of self-love to Edwards, and underscores two points: (1) that God works with created aspirations of human nature to achieve His purposes; and (2) that true charity desires fulfillment in union, while selfishness epitomizes isolation and estrangement, in a word, sinfulness. Both themes are picked up in Edwards. The first became the cornerstone of his teaching on "preparation" or "seeking," among other things;[102] the second is important in his ontology of internal relations, upon which his evangelistic strategy of preparationism is based, as well as his hamartiology.

Luther, of course, branded the Augustinian notion of self-love "*amor concupiscentiae*."[103] Luther's commentary on Romans everywhere condemns human acquisitive desire.[104] The Wittenberg Reformer, therefore, joined a litany of clerics dating back to Theodore, Lombard, and Duns Scotus, in rejecting "the wicked filth which theologians call 'self-love,'" in favor of a system in which self-denial was the defining feature of true (Christian) love.[105]

Calvin agreed. In his *Institutes* he denounced self-love and strove to purge the Augustinian emphasis on it from the Christian ethic, and replace it with a non-teleological abandonment to God's sovereignty.[106] Hell was to be preferred rather than have God's glory dishonored. From the Reformers' collective position the doctrine of *resignatio ad infernum* was reintroduced.[107] Doctrines of total sovereignty and a self-denial theology of the cross de-emphasized concern for wellbeing. François Fénelon, Cotton Mather, and

---

100. 1718. *Catechism of the Catholic Church*, 478. Augustine, "The City of God" in *The Nicene and Post-Nicene Fathers*, 2:1. Plotinus pictured even an "ugly" soul pursuing beauty since its intellect (the soul's essence) was beautiful "like to God" (*Enneads*, 1.6.4–6).

101. Augustine, "City of God," *Nicene and Post-Nicene Fathers, First Series*, 2:1.

102. See chap 13.

103. Luther, *WA*, 56:391.

104. Ibid., 304f., 325, 391f.

105. Ibid., 391f.; 18:486. I am here indebted to Stephen G. Post's *Christian Self-Love and Self-Denial*, chap 2, for the substance of this and the following paragraph.

106. *Institutes*, II.1.2; II.7.6; III.7.1.

107. "Reintroduced," i.e., from the medieval mystical tradition. George, *Theology of the Reformers*, 78.

Edwards's disciple, Samuel Hopkins,[108] all critiqued the Augustinian position and rejected a theology of natural principles to advocate in its place a "pure love" of benevolent disinterestedness (Fénelon) or suffering (Mather) or self-negation vis-à-vis God's will (Hopkins), among other things.

Such thought not only ran counter to the most basic principle of Edwards's ethical theory, as the whole treatise *The Nature of True Virtue* shows, but also his theory of being. So opposed was he to this kind of thinking that he labors in *Charity and Its Fruits*, *The Nature of True Virtue*, and many sermons, to dispel strictly negative connotations of self-love through an explanation of it that did not necessarily involve sin—the anti-Augustinians' core accusation against self-love. His motive was not to align himself with his grandfather in the long-standing Mather-Stoddard feuds (he would oppose Stoddard as well as support him), but to articulate an ethic based upon an ontology that reflected internal metaphysical cogency and yet was empirically justifiable (answerable to the likes of John Taylor, George Turnbull, and Hutcheson) and manifested biblical integrity (answerable to competing Calvinists). His modus operandi was not to link self-love so close to human nature that its exercise was characteristic of its nature, as Augustine had done. Instead, he openly equates human nature with a self-love disposition. Consider his comments in *Charity and Its Fruits*:

> It is not a thing contrary to a Christian that a man should love himself; or what is the same thing, that he should love his own happiness. Christianity does not tend to destroy a man's love to his own happiness; [for if it did] it would therein tend to destroy the humanity . . . That a man should love his own happiness is necessary to his nature, as a faculty of the will is; and it is impossible that it should be destroyed in any other way than by destroying his being.[109]

The mere involuntarily possession of a principle of self-love is not sinful; it is necessary, natural, and reasonable. As an essential principle of intelligent perceiving existence, it is neither necessarily praiseworthy nor blameworthy, though without it there is no human being.

To declare a principle of self-love inherently sinful, then, was to impugn God as the designer and fashioner of an inherently sinful principle in man, from the genesis event itself.[110] Such a position fails to see the necessity of this principle for voluntary choosing.

Love of oneself, or the love of one's own happiness, is necessary for any preferring, choosing, or inclining of the will, as well as understanding and perceiving that which is "good" to/for the self: this is the ethical side of *Freedom of the Will*. Stoddard's eudemonistical statement, "It is lawful for [natural-men] to aim at themselves" in happiness, carries

---

108. The *resignatio* doctrine is especially associated with Hopkins's pamphlet *A Dialogue between A Calvinist and Semi-Calvinist* in *Sketches of the life of the late Rev. Samuel Hopkins*, where he sets forth his formula for a "willingness to be damned for the glory of God."

109. *WJE* 8:254. Cf. Stoddard's similar statements in *Three Sermons Lately Preach'd*, 36.

110. Here Jonathan Edwards differs from not only those following in Calvin's footsteps, but twentieth-century Lutheran ethicist Anders Nygren (*Agape and Eros*, chap 4), whose condemnation of self-love, as Outka demonstrates in *Agape: An Ethical Analysis*, is "applies exhaustively to all 'natural' possibilities" (ibid., 58–59).

over into Edwards's definition of natural self-love as love of one's own happiness. This principle, as the foremost orientation of the self, operates in, as, and through, the unified intellectual and the inclinational activities. In short, it is simply one's ability to value what he or she is inclined to value, namely one's own happiness.[111] To destroy this is tantamount to "destroying [man's] being" made in the image of God. So, for one to love himself, viewed *simpliciter*, is for one to love his own happiness just as God loves His own happiness.[112]

Passages from Scripture are given as authoritative crowning evidence in the validation of a natural, non-sinful self-love. The appeal to Holy Writ is meant to convince gainsayers, from within Edwards' tradition and without, that his is no speculative moral philosophy but a biblical anthropology rooted in revelation. "The Scripture," he avers, "from one end of the Bible to the other is full of things which are there held forth to work upon a principle of self-love." Essential self-love, "is no fruit of the Fall, but is necessary and what belongs to that nature of all intelligent beings which the Creator hath made, that it is alike in all."[113]

The effectiveness of Edwards's arguments and appeal to Scripture in *Charity and Its Fruits* and *The Nature of True Virtue* is difficult to measure. On the one hand, if we consider that his own pupil, Samuel Hopkins, advocated adherence to the *resignatio* doctrine and equated all self-love with sinfulness, then Edwards did not fare so well. On the other hand, it was Hopkins (along with Joseph Bellamy) who posthumously published *Two Dissertations* and saw the *resignatio* doctrine vilified and rejected as a stipulation for ordination. But it was also Hopkins and Bellamy who were the principal architects of the "New Divinity," which did little to reflect Edwards's teachings on natural, non-sinful self-love as an essential and defining principle of human beingness.[114] In the end, "New England Theology" found Edwards's analysis too deterministic (and perhaps too innovative and thus disturbing) and opted for a less constrained notion of individual freedom and human ability.

In his repudiation of the *resignatio* and leveling of essential human nature (for all mankind) to a self-loving disposition, Edwards, so far from "asserting God at the expense of humanity," as Alexander Allen charges, actually affirms the integrity of authentic human choice (as an expression of the strongest motive in a person's ontic nature) and offers a single definition of "human being" at a basic level.

111. "Miscellanies," no. 530, *WJE* 18:73–76. In his *Essay*, Locke also developed a theory of desire in which "happiness, and that alone" moves it.

112. Ramsey, "Editor's Introduction," *WJE* 8:15. Here Ramsey notes a radical difference between Jonathan Edwards and the Augustinian tradition. He writes, "In that tradition, a telling response to the account of the Augustinian 'synthesis'... would be to carve out a legitimate place for *creatures*' 'need-love' to God—as did C. S. Lewis in *The Four Loves*... Jonathan Edwards would not have limited himself to that rejoinder" (ibid., 15–16 n. 8). Ramsey's point is that, in correlating the nature of the will with love, and of love with happiness, Jonathan Edwards requires the inference that "happiness" cannot be other than "*one's own*" while it is willed and loved and enjoyed.

113. *WJE* 8:255: "'Saints and sinners' in this life love happiness alike, and have the same unalterable propensity to seek and desire happiness."

114. Dwight and Jonathan Edwards Jr. continued Hopkins and Bellamy's trend to view sin as an accumulation of actions rather than primarily a state of being based on a self-loving nature or disposition issuing in evil deeds.

Inordinate Self-Love and the Deformity of the Reprobate

The second way in which Edwards uses self-love is in his diagnosis of human depravity. Negative self-love, or what both he and Stoddard called "inordinate self-love," is the "cardinal principle of corruption" and "an inordinate disposition to self-exaltation" from which every sinful thought and action arise.[115] However, it is not a distinct disposition in man that competes with natural self-love. There is only one principle of self-love. The "inordinate self-love" of which Edwards speaks is a categorical designation of the *relational exercises* of the one disposition that are *limited to the self*. That is, the "inordinacy" is descriptive of the intellectual and inclinational regard for the self to the exclusion of others—the *selfishness* that is endemic to fallen man.[116]

Prior to the Fall, man was governed by a third relational disposition (love to God), a "superior principle" of holiness—the Holy Spirit. This was man's concreated original righteousness. Man's lapse, however, affected the loss of the "superior principles," which kept the inclination to one's own benefit in due subordination, reduced natural self-love to a mono-dimensional principle, not entirely dissimilar to Luther's *incurvatus in se* thesis, nor Outka's analysis of "acquisitive self-love."[117] As Edwards argues, "[the] self-love which is the selfishness to which a Christian spirit is contrary is only an inordinate self-love."[118] Consequently, since the removal of the superior principles:

> man's self-love governs alone; and having not this superior principle to regulate it, breaks out into all manner of exorbitances, and becomes in innumerable cases a vile and odious disposition, and causes thousands of unlovely and hateful actions. There is nothing new put in the nature that we call sin, but only the same self-love that necessarily belongs to the nature working and influencing, without regulation from that superior principle that primitively belongs to our nature and that is necessary in order to the harmonious existing of it. This natural and necessary inclination to ourselves, without that governor and guide, will certainly without anything else reproduce, or rather will become, all those sinful inclinations which are in the corrupted nature of man.[119]

In Edwards's analysis, self-love exclusively inclined to self has no regard or "disposedness" toward holiness or the excellence of relations beyond the self:

> Man naturally has no other principle to direct and govern him in his actions but only self-love. Man is born into the world ... with no other principle to direct and govern those [remaining] powers and their activity but self-love. Nothing else but this holds the reins. So that we may easily know what judgment to make as to man's disposition. Man as he comes into the world has no principle of love to God. Nor

---

115. "Miscellanies," no. 747, *WJE* 18:391.

116. "Miscellanies," no. 1032, *WJE* 20:370–71. Certainly Jonathan Edwards was aware of the fact that Augustine, the Schoolmen, and even Malebranche owned a similar principle within their respective ethical systems.

117. Luther, *WA*, 18:786; *Agape: An Ethical Analysis*, 56–63. See chapter 10 for Jonathan Edwards's dispositional account of man's creation and fall.

118. "Nature of True Virtue" in *WJE* 8:577, 255.

119. "Miscellanies," no. 301, *WJE* 13:387.

has he any principle of love to men but only so far as self-love may in some cases be a principle to love to others and no further . . . This being the only principle he has to govern him all that a man is prompted to pursue is his own private and separate interest then he will have no sincere regard at all to the glory of God or the good of others.[120]

This constitutes the heart of the Edwardsean moral inability, the strength of which rests on the ontological significance of self-love.[121] His doctrine of moral inability/natural ability only makes sense in this context. Though God has so ordered the self-love disposition to operate in, through, and as the intellectual and inclinational faculties, so that man is capable of approving and condemning all things whatsoever (that is, he has natural ability), yet he never loves excellence for the beauty and harmony of the whole. Man wills nothing other than what he selfishly deems his own good, for he possesses no other principle (i.e., the Holy Spirit) by which he may be inclined virtuously. For Edwards, "true virtue," as distinguished form "common" or non-spiritual virtue, is "general beauty," that is, "beautiful in a comprehensive view as it is in itself, and as related to everything that it stands in connection with." In short, true virtue is "love to Being in general."[122] The "inordinacy" of the self-love disposition, then, lies in the fact that it operates without an excellent governing principle, divine love, and is exclusive.

Thus, the chief moral consequence of the Fall is the result of an ontological deficiency. Sinfulness is the catastrophic consequence of ontological deprivation.

Man's sinfulness, however, does not merely lie in an ontological deprivation, which renders him totally unable to instance primary beauty in a mutually consenting relation; it is also something positive. Morally speaking, "inordinate self-love" is positively exercised as "a man's regard to his confined *private self*, or love to himself with respect to his *private interest*."[123] By "private" Edwards means that which most immediately consists in those pleasures, or pains, that are strictly *personal* and at the expense of others (or the whole). Religiously, inordinate self-love positively disposes the agent to "dissent" to "Being in gen-

---

120. 230. [L. 5r, L. 5v]. Sermon on Matthew 10:17 (1732), *WJE Online* 47; cf. "The Nature of True Virtue" in *WJE* 8:577–79.

121. The inability of the natural-man to do *any* act that *fundamentally* attains the divine standard (God's will and law); and the notion that unregenerate persons are unable to change their principle confined and exclusive preference for self (self-love) and sin, are called "total inability." Total inability does not mean that the natural-man is without ability to perform natural and civil good, and external religious acts. He simply cannot attain to the divine standard, which requires *true virtue* (the product of infused love and faith) to initiate, color, and effect all such motions. Jonathan Edwards and the New School of New England (e.g., Bellamy, Nathaniel Taylor, and Lyman Beecher) distinguished between moral and natural inability (see *Freedom of the Will*, *WJE* 1:159–62). The import of their teaching states that natural-man still possesses all the natural faculties that are required for doing spiritual good (intellect, will, etc.), but lacks moral ability, that is, the ability to give proper direction to those faculties. The distinction under consideration is advanced in order to stress the fact that man is willfully sinful. Jonathan Edwards's influential distinction was not new to Reformed theology: Turretin made a similar distinction in his *Institutes*, 1:681–83.

122. "Nature of True Virtue" in *WJE* 8:541.

123. "Miscellanies," no. 747, *WJE* 18:391–92.

eral," which in turn renders them a "deformity" or "irregularity" within God's beautiful matrix.[124]

~

Jonathan Edwards reasoned that, when all things are considered, the beauty of the relation to self *by itself*, such that the reprobate would and could only exhibit per the logic of his dispositionally determined ethics, is "so debased as to become little or less, as bad or worse, than nothing."[125] The almost non-being of the reprobate is the result of two things: the relative simplicity of their beauty and the deforming consequences of positively dissenting to "Being in general." The comparative non-complexity of their beauty is due to the fact that, though the relation to self, by itself, is indeed mental and therefore an instance of primary beauty (it may still be regarded by God), yet because of its near isolation from other beings, and positive dissent to "Being in general," its beauty is so diminished so as to become almost secondary.[126]

One wonders how this catastrophic alteration in the reprobate's being could possibly add to the beautification of God or represent His the *ad extra* manifestation of His beauty? That is, how is their deformity a part of maximal divine excellency? Edwards's answer is found in an analysis of the second relation determinative to being.

Being Consenting to Beings: The Relation to Others

Earlier we reaffirmed Sang Hyun Lee's contention that the most important implication of Edwards's definition of excellence is the claim that every being must, as a condition of its reality, stand in some relation to other things, and even to all other things.[127] When Lee began to explore this facet of Edwards's model for ontological structure through a presentation of the first of its three important elements, namely, "what an entity is, is inseparable from its relations,"[128] he had in mind to clarify how relations are internal to being. Though Lee neglects the ideal substance of man and sometimes fails to equate things with ideas, yet how his analysis of the internality of relations relates to "the consent of being to beings" is certainly correct: human beings are not merely constituted by a law-like disposition of self-relation, but also a disposition of *other*-relation.[129]

The disposition of other-relatedness is significantly more determinative to a human being's status, value, and position within the "scale of being," than mere self-relation. Therefore we may say that the disposition of other-relatedness is not merely the extension of the primary relation of self-love, though within the interpersonal relations of fallen

124. See "Miscellanies," nos. 950 and 1032, *WJE* 20:208–10; 369–70. Cf. Augustine, *Enchiridion*.

125. "Miscellanies" no. 41, *WJE* 13:223.

126. I say "near isolation" because the reprobate's basic ontic structure makes it neither a stark singularity nor an isolated existence. In Jonathan Edwards's philosophical system, there is no such thing as total aesthetic detachment or total ethical disinterestedness.

127. Lee, *Philosophical Theology*, 77.

128. Ibid.

129. "Miscellanies," no 864, *WJE* 18:95–106. See Fiering, *Moral Thought*, 193f.

man, it may be so considered. Instead, the disposition of other-relatedness brings with it a transformed notion of self-love. In fact, the primary exercise of the essential disposition of a human being is always and indissolubly in conjunction with the exercise of this second disposition. Ideally, then, self-love is exercised not as narrow, isolated self-consent, but as a consenting to man's existence in a manner harmonious with the law of the whole or the beauty of God.[130]

Self-relation introduces man's existence on the "scale of being" and designedly renders it more excellent than non-sentient entities by virtue of the arbitrary and mental kind of its existence: erstwhile, other-relation determines the particular quality of existence. By these two ontological factors Edwards establishes a hierarchy among sentient beings.

The Complex Beauty of Mental Existence

The second relation connects the first and most basic instance of "proportion" with other "minds" and thereby exhibits a more complex instance of proportion or excellence.[131] This *mutual consent between minds* is the greatest kind of beauty and/or love, and may be quantified in order to determine the specific excellence and "realness" of a human being.[132]

The complexity of relational or *inter*relational beauty has to do with superiority of mental or spiritual beauty juxtaposed to the inferiority of natural or material beauty.[133] The former is "primary beauty" and the latter "secondary." Natural beauty is a simple equality, or may be reduced to simple equalities. It is being-as-manifest. In a figure from "The Mind," no. 1, Edwards illustrates simple beauty thus:

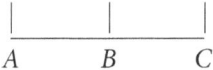

The equality between *AB* and *BC* structure a simple beauty, where *AB* is similar to *BC*, or the relation of *C* to *B* is the same as of *B* to *A*. This is the lowest or most simple kind of beauty "because by equality or likeness one part consents with but one part."[134]

---

130. "Charity and Its Fruits" in *WJE* 8:252–71.

131. "The Mind," no. 45, *WJE* 6:363–65.

132. "Miscellanies," no. 398: "There is no other way of different spirits being thus united, but by love" (*WJE* 13:463).

133. In "The Mind," no. 1, Edwards intimates a distinction between being consenting to other being(s) and the *mutual* consent of beings (*WJE* 6:335). Although Edwards there gives priority to the whole of universal harmony and beauty, yet we may conclude that the consent of being *A* to being *B*, while in itself is excellent and significant for *A*, yet without the mutual consent of *B* the exhibited beauty of relation *AB* is limited and of the harmony of the whole {*A*, *B*} comparatively diminished. See "The Nature of True Virtue" in *WJE* 8:561–62.

134. "The Mind," no. 62, *WJE* 6:380. Edwards is not saying that a particular object of natural beauty, such as a flower, tree, man's body, etc., does not embody a complicated harmony—quite the opposite. A flower, for example, is composed of "millions of equalities" and, therefore, when viewed as a whole, a complicated harmony. Yet, every particular (minute) examination of it may be reduced to a simple equality. Natural beauty, then, is really a complicated collection of simple equalities. When one draws back even further to view, say, the flower within its environmental context, then one is able to discern that all the natural motions and tendencies and figures of bodies in the universe are done according to proportion. Therein lays their general beauty or universal proportion—"shadows" of primary beauty.

Proportion, however, is *complex beauty*, and involves a complex nexus of relations, where even one part "may sweetly consent to ten thousand different parts, all the parts may consent with the rest, and not only so, but the parts taken singly may consent with the whole taken together."[135] Edwards provides the following example of complex beauty, again, from "The Mind" no. 1:

```
   .         .    .    .
   A         B    C    D
```

While *BCD* is "similar" to *ABC*, yet there now are three terms necessary in each of the parts between which is the relation, so that here simple beauties such as correspondency, symmetry, and regularity are omitted. Nonetheless, explains Edwards, there is a "general complex beauty." Viewed as particulars, there is no simple equality to be found. Viewed as a whole, however, and despite its irregularity, there is proportion—*a complex beauty*, where *BC* is not as *AB*, nor *CD* as *BC*, yet *BCD* is as *ABC*. It is this kind of proportion which is analogous to, or, to use Edwards's description, "shadows" primary beauty—*the mutual consent of minds*.

Primary beauty by definition is a *consciously perceived* beauty, rather than a standing equality.[136] The capable perceiving agent, however, does not merely apprehend this or that occasion of primary beauty; rather, in a monodimensional or mutual consenting relation it itself becomes an instance of primary beauty.

What remains unclear is Edwards's account of disagreeableness to being. One wonders what arrangement of dots on a page would not be complex beauty? Edwards has not been specific enough. His only criteria—"disagreeableness is pain"—is curiously elusive. Disproportion, he tells us, will be disagreeable with our being; it will grate us. But precisely how this happens is left unanswered by him and we begin to uncover the limitations of his philosophical system.

Unconcerned with these details, Edwards nonetheless bases the hierarchy of sentient beings upon a theory that values the extent of an agent's conscious perception of primary proportion; and correspondingly devalues an agent's relational dissent and inability to perceive primary proportion. The conscious perception of primary beauty intellectually and inclinationally relates the subject to the object, and therefore makes it an occasion of "excellency." Earlier we saw how Edwards equates perceiving primary beauty with spiritual "sight" or "sensibility," as well as how he equates the ability to perceive primary beauty with regeneration. Here, we have the ontological thinking behind it: while the perceiving

---

135. Ibid.

136. *WJE* 6:336. This is said recognizing that, for Jonathan Edwards, natural beauty also is an idea perceived by minds. Speaking of the beauty itself, natural beauty has simplicity as to its laws, whereas, according to Edwards, complex beauty requires a perceptual dynamic beyond the mere acknowledgment and appreciation of simple equalities. It has a mental complexity. So while there is no "unconscious" perception and all perception is by the unified consciousness, which means that all that is perceived each and every moment is mentally adjudicated as agreeable or disagreeable to an intelligent perceiving being, yet if an intelligent perceiving being were only to perceive the secondary beauty of *x* it would not be discerning the mind or mental/spiritual/moral aspect *in x* (i.e., God), and the "consent of minds" would not be achieved. Thus Fiering states that, "For Edwards all that is normally meant by 'beauty' was to be understood only as a *symbolic* counterpart to a higher correspondence, that of wills" (*Moral Thought*, 82).

agent does become an instance of primary beauty, it is only by way of *participating* in the larger schema of *divine beauty*.[137] Such are the metaphysics behind his doctrine of union with Christ.

The participation in primary (divine) beauty, then, is the quantifying factor for the value of being. Edwards's universal definition of "excellency" requires as much: "The consent of being to being, or being's consent to entity. The more the consent is, and the more extensive, the greater is the excellency."[138] A being's consent to an entity or another being produces a multiplication of relations, not in terms of secondary, but primary beauty: for the whole of existence is a network of relations. Natural-man is capable of perceiving the secondary beauty in all things. But an excellent relation, a relation of mutual consent is necessary to perceive primary beauty. With this in mind, one imagines that Edwards would calculate the value of being on his scale in the following manner:

> If being A consents to B, then the context of B may be included in that relation. Hence, $AB(x)$.

Additionally,

> Any AB relation implies the consent of A to "Being in general" or $B(x\infty)$.

He arrives at the second of these by an ultimate inclusion of entity into "Being in general":

> God is proper entity itself, and these two [i.e., being and entity] therefore in him become the same; for so far as a thing consents to being in general, so far it consents to him."[139]

The calculus of value, which determines the specific "degree of existence" and "degree of excellence" of each and every being, ultimately rests upon a paradigmatic relation to God, who (through Christ) connects any being A with another being B and the extent of B's relations (x). In other words, if A consents to B, then God—whose "*ad extra*" reality is His idea or image of Himself, that is, His Son—is present in, as, and through the consent, and is consented to by the network design of relations that extends A's consent to $B(x)$.[140] Thus, value, existence, and excellency increase proportionately as A consents to $\{x\}$ or $C(x)$, or $D(x)$, etc., or a combination of these relations. As A extends its relations or gives greater more pervasive consent, the more A internalizes proportion, and consequently, participates in and replicates divine beauty or excellency.[141] Theologically this is akin to *theosis*, the divinization of human beings via a participatory union with the Divine Being. It can also be explained through Edwards's aesthetic language of happiness, as found in *End of Creation*: "The creature is no further happy with this happiness which God makes his ultimate end than when he becomes one with God. The more happiness the greater the union: when the happiness is perfect, the union is perfect." Consequently, the nearer in

---

137. See "Miscellanies," nos. 210 and 211 where Jonathan Edwards makes this explicit (*WJE* 13:342).
138. "The Mind," no. 1, *WJE* 6:336.
139. Ibid., 337. Cf. "End of Creation" in *WJE* 8:461.
140. MS sermon on Job 11:12 (1732), Jonathan Edwards Collection.
141. "Miscellanies," no. 241, *WJE* 13:358.

nature beings are to God, "so much the more properly are they beings, and more substantial; and that spirits are much more properly beings, and more substantial, than bodies."[142] However, for Edwards, the dual experience of individuality in participation is the real basis for personal relationship and identity. The value of individuality is not diminished but enhanced by being's proximity to God.

The Place of Reprobate in the Matrix of Divine Beauty

The natural-man, as one who is governed by a self-loving disposition alone, may be understood to be a self-referential being who never engages in truly excellent mutual consent. Yet, natural-man possesses an ability to appreciate the secondary beauty of all being, even after the Fall: "The *cause* why secondary beauty is pleasing to *men* is only a *law of nature*, which God has fixed."[143] This law is an active, dispositional tendency of consent to secondary beauty. Thus man is, by his very ontological structure, *other*-related.

To explain why God designed intelligent beings to be disposed to secondary beauty, Edwards resorts to a calculus of values once again. He explains that this kind of beauty affects the minds more (other things being equal) when taken notice of in objects which have considerable more importance "than trivial matters." Thus, the symmetry of the parts of the body affects the mind more than the beauty of a flower; likewise, the beauty of the universe more than a tree.

But Edwards gives another reason why God made this kind of inferior consent and agreement of things secondarily beautiful: "there is in it some image of the true, spiritual original beauty . . . consisting in being's consent to being, or the union of minds or spiritual beings in a mutual propensity and affection of heart."[144] Secondary beauty, then, bespeaks, mirrors, shadows, or is an image of that beauty which is spiritual, and therefore, truly excellent. Through the uniformity of simple equalities diverse things become, as it were, one, as it is in the cordial union of primary beauty.

Ultimately, however, it is because God is pleased "to observe analogy in his works" that the universe of created existence is a matrix of divine beauty.[145] The analogy of secondary beauty is simply another dimension of the matrix that is the externalization of the divine beautifying disposition. This analogy then serves in a facilitating capacity for God's self-glorification, as various divine attributes are replicated via the perception of created minds. In turn, however, God's establishing inferior things in an analogy to superior things assists the minds of created beings in their apprehension of divine realities: hence the value of typological associations.[146]

The reality that the analogy represents is God's complex beauty. And here we find the ultimate aesthetic function and value of the reprobate. Edwards claims that God's being is

---

142. "Miscellanies," no. 135, *WJE* 13:295; cf. "The Nature of True Virtue" in *WJE* 8:533–34; "Natural Philosophy," no. 44, *WJE* 6:238; and "Miscellanies," no. 1263, *WJE* 23:203, 206–7.

143. "Nature of True Virtue" in *WJE* 8:561–62.

144. Ibid., 564.

145. Ibid.

146. See Fiering, *Moral Thought*, 112–17.

infinitely the most excellent being, which means it consists of the greatest complexity. Such a complexity would necessarily include "irregularities" or "deformities," as he calls them. The reprobate are, ontologically speaking, such deformities. Hence, the "irregularity" of reprobates (when considered in light of the whole matrix of beautiful being) is actually a significant contribution to the complexity of God's beautiful being. That is, reprobates positively contribute to the overall "*ad extra*" beauty of God, by replicating/remanating its *complexity* by way of their own "deformities."

Edwards is not afraid to follow consistently the logic of his aesthetic ontology, even to this surprising, even shocking conclusion, given his avowed Reformed allegiances: God's being includes, as it were, "irregularities" and "deformities." Following the logic of Saint Augustine and Thomas Aquinas, who both said in their consideration of the universe as a whole that, if you have a state of affairs that is good, it does not necessarily follow that every detail is good, Edwards makes a further, more daring panentheistic application to the being of God. However, the thinking for doing so is well established in his broader theological tradition.[147]

But would not this thinking violate the *Deus simplicitum* theory? Edwards does not think so. He acknowledges no distinction between God (a beautiful Being) and His ideal essence (of infinite excellency or proportion). Therefore, in his way of thinking, God is simple because His ideal essence of an infinitely complex beauty is perfectly and totally integrated in all that God is and does. For this reason Edwards admits no distress with God purposely orchestrating the Fall, decreeing sin and evil, and facilitating pain, suffering, and damnation.[148]

~

Edwards's philosophy of being holds that a being not only is defined or constituted through its relations but also exists as to itself and God's predetermined series only through its relations; that is, its existence is established, appraised, and determined through relations that God prescribes. The whole of reality is, as it were, a network of interrelated relationships.

The second relation of Edwards's model for ontological structure carries with it, then, the implication of the absolute comprehensive extent of the mutual relations of all entities. This may be seen through his categorization and appraisal of the existence and value in the larger context of the network of relations that is the matrix of divine beauty.

Thus, the beauty or excellence of God is the standard, point of reference, goal or "end," and defining reality for all beings. All value and substantiality of being is to be understood in terms of "nearness of relation" to God primarily and other beings derivatively. Being is not simply determined by being-in-relation, even to the whole of being, but being's quality and quantity of being-in-relation. Being-in-relation necessarily means being part of the network of relations, and to a "degree" related to all relations. The moral and teleological dimensions within Edwards's philosophy of being are simply interchangeable. The operative word for Edwards, however, is "degree." Regenerate persons have more being and

---

147. See Augustine, *Enchiridion*; and Aquinas, *Summa Theologia*, I, 6.3, 4.
148. See the opposing opinion of Crisp, "Jonathan Edwards on divine simplicity," 23–41.

therefore are more real, while the reprobate are, in Edwards's comparative rhetoric, "perfectly equivalent, or rather, less and worse than, no being."¹⁴⁹ Though stated in the form of a hyperbole, reprobates are the least "significant" category—*not kind*—of human being. Notwithstanding their sinfulness and relative ontological paucity (as well as the ambiguity of Edwards's theory of complex beauty), God created them with a purpose, which, by the telic-orientation of their ontic structure, they will attain. Their bare existence makes possible God's program to glorify Himself through them, and their continued existence gains it for Him. God's comprehensiveness is total in the sphere of ontology: it does not discriminate between the spiritual man and the natural-man, or the elect and the reprobate.

An Agent of Divine Glory

According to Edwards's understanding of God's self-manifesting purposes, reprobates are unalterably fixed in their predestined state. They will never be able to attain the excellence of a mutually consenting relation, but must settle for secondary beauties. The reason why secondary beauty does not attain to primary beauty in and of itself should now be obvious: the sensation of secondary beauty is devoid of that immediate spiritual union and agreement (mutual consent) requisite in the sensation of primary and spiritual beauty.¹⁵⁰ Here it becomes easy to see how Jonathan Edwards would make ethical or even theological use of this theory. One may not ascend from the "secondary beauty" of the created order to the "primary beauty" of God, unless there is a prior union (or participation) of being. Edwards does not allow for such a leap.¹⁵¹ The connection to excellent loving relations is an all or none deal. One is either in a primary relation (i.e., a divinely beautiful relation) or one is not.¹⁵² The movement is always from the superior to the inferior and back to the superior again, but never the superior terminating in the inferior, or from a state of inferiority to superiority. Hence the fundamental difference between "true virtue" and "common morality"; hence, the difference between spiritually perceptive regenerates and "blind" unregenerates.

Theologically and apologetically Edwards preserves the priority of regeneration, the integrity of spiritual realities, and the nature of the human experience of the beautiful, by insisting on an ontological union with a being who has comprehensive entitlements to primary beauty.¹⁵³ Discussions about the damned have their place, but in the end Edwards

---

149. "Miscellanies," no. 41, *WJE* 13:223.

150. Union in this sense is not to be understood in terms of absolute unification, but, as Jonathan Edwards explains, a "propensity of *minds* to mental or spiritual existence."

151. See, e.g., 552. [L. 3r]. Sermon on Romans 11:7(b): "Doc: Though a people that live under means [of grace] are wont in general to seek and hope for salvation, yet 'tis the election only that obtained and the rest are blinded" (May 1740), *WJE Online* 55; and *Seasons of Ingathering* (1741), *WJE* 22:479–89: "*Obs* I. The righteous and wicked are both the Lord's, as the produce of the husbandman's fields and vineyards . . . God has an use for both . . . *Obs* II. There are certain appointed and remarkable seasons for the ingathering of both elect and reprobates" (480, 481).

152. Or, soteriologically, one *becomes* through regeneration what one before was not.

153. 505a. MS sermon on Eph 1:10: Doctrine: "Jesus Christ is the great medium and head of union in whom all elect creatures in heaven and earth are united to God and to one another. The doctrine manifestly contains two distinct propositions: 1. [It is in Christ] in whom they are united to God, and 2 [it is in Christ]

admits that he can neither rightly identify them nor infallibly "sift the wheat from the chaff," all the while being perfectly convinced that there are in fact reprobates.[154] For this reason the emphasis in his sermons and treatises rests upon a third and distinctive relational principle—a *disposition of love to God*. *End of Creation* becomes a metaphysical gospel narrative in the same way *The Nature of True Virtue* is a meta-ethical gospel narrative. How a man can be right with God is translated into how a finite man (much less a sinful one) can have proportionate regard for an infinitely worthy being? The answer is that he cannot, unless he is united to an infinitely excellent being. For Edwards, this union or participation is in and with the Son, through the Spirit. It is by the Spirit—so united to the being of man and influencing his inclinational and intellectual activities in *direct mutual consent to God*—that man gains access to primary beauty.

The first two relational dimensions, Edwards insists, are to be governed by the third dimension. Only spiritual regeneration restores the "supernatural principle of divine love" to the heart and the Holy Spirit to the throne of man's governance. The Christian religion is the means by which that third relation is restored to the inner being of man, and it also provides the means by which the governing of the Spirit is increased and understood as progressive sanctification.

This disposition facilitates truly virtuous relations with others through direct relation to God. Consider Edwards's explanation in a 1731 sermon on Job 11:12: "Man before the fall saw so much of the excellency and glory of God . . . and it was then when love to God reigned in his heart. This [i.e., a principle of love to God] made man to love his fellow creatures for those that love God will love the image of God, [that is] their neighbor also."[155]

Several metaphysical principles stand behind this statement: the importance of relation to God, the interrelatedness of all being within the network of existence via the matrix of divine beauty, and the spiritual/moral dynamics of primary beauty. Significantly, the common feature in these things is a disposition of consent to Being in general.

Through an intelligent perceiving being's union with the Spirit the essential self-love disposition is "governed" or "regulated" by the superior "arbitrariness" of the disposition of love to God, and intellectually and affectionally values God as its beautiful object of true happiness. For, as Edwards affirms, the knowledge communicated is the knowledge of God and the love communicated is the love of God, and the happiness communicated is joy in God—all of which results in the expansive replication of God. In Edwards's words,

> In the creature's knowing, esteeming, loving, and rejoicing in, and praising God, the glory of God is both exhibited and acknowledged; his fullness is received and returned. Here is both an *emanation* and *remanation*. The refulgence shines upon and into the creature, and is reflected back to the luminary. The beams of glory come from God, are something of God, and are refunded back again to their original. So

---

in whom God unites them one to another" (Feb. 1739), Jonathan Edwards Collection. This MS is a fragment.

154. To be sure, Jonathan Edwards does assert and gives considerable attention in *Original Sin* that the self-love characteristics of reprobates, indeed, all men, are empirically discernible in their effects (*WJE* 3:105–219).

155. 204. [L. 6r]. Sermon on Job 11:12 (1731; repreached Aug. 1753), *WJE Online* 46.

that the whole is of God, and in God, and to God, and he is the beginning, and the middle, and the end.[156]

Thus, humanity functions in Edwards's idealism as both receiver and relay of not only the general laws which constitute the reality of created existences, but also God's self-communication toward self-enlargement in time and space.[157]

Whether Edwards discusses the disposition of love to God explicitly, or in the onerous metaphysical language of "being," or couches its ontological density in theological, ethical, or aesthetic discourse, there are three fundamental principles latent in this disposition. These principles emerge time and again as Edwards's discusses God's self-glorification through human beings. The first principle of the third relation is one shared by the others; it is internal to being. Second, and as an expanded explanation of the first, the difference between direct constitutive consent to God and indirect, non-constitutive consent exactly corresponds to the metaphysical differences between primary and secondary beauty. And third, although the law-like tendency of love to God inseparably concurs with the exercising of the "self-love disposition," yet it is not a sinful thing, for the former "governs" or "regulates" the activity of the latter by virtue of its superior nature and "arbitrariness."[158]

If we ask *why* Edwards make this an "arbitrary" feature of divine intercourse with His creation, then we find his theocentric impulse behind every answer, and that they all immediately suggest divine self-glorification. This is Edwards's way of looking at the big picture of existence. There is no simple or single etiological law for why God has fashioned man thus. In Edwards's provision of a number of "fitting" reasons (some logical, some ethical, others ontological), he keeps present before his mind the "chief end" of all created existences—the multidimensional expansion of divine beauty. Consider the following reasons:

a. The divine regulating of "the communication of . . . more or less of His Holy Spirit" is an exercise of divine sovereignty, and sovereign dispensations always are, for Edwards, "purely arbitrary."[159]

b. Thus, intelligent perceiving beings exist in a state of total dependency upon the divine will for the full achievement of their ontological potential (among other things).

c. God designs His own "chief end" to be their "chief end," and thereby establishes the potential (upon the consent of being to being in general) for the manifestation of the highest form of excellency to be effected, viz., the consent of minds.

d. In this way God temporalizes Himself in a way consistent with His various biblical attributes, e.g., goodness, generosity, power, wisdom, etc.

e. It accords with the "spiritual way of ideas" (i.e., Idealism).

---

156. "End of Creation" in *WJE* 8:531.
157. Anticipating chap 11, this principle entails the replication of God's redemptive attributes.
158. "Miscellanies," no. 1263, *WJE* 23:202, 207–11. See Lee, "Editor's Introduction," *WJE* 21:53–57.
159. "The Mind," no. 45, *WJE* 6:362; "Miscellanies," no. 1263, *WJE* 23:201–12.

f. It is religious or spiritual. And since man was created for the express purpose of spiritually and morally exercising his dispositional nature through the mind, the most spiritual and moral means ought to be utilized to obtain the end of "true religion."

Other reasons could be added that give greater attention to the moral "fitness" of the supernatural origin, dispensing, and exercise of the disposition of love to God, or to the primary beauty of such an arrangement, etc. One could even give a theological translation of each of the reasons listed, and so on.

~

The ontological structure of intelligent perceiving being is inseparably connected with the actualization of that desire in God to find Himself glorified and replicated in temporality.[160] In Edwards's idealism, the repetition or communication of God's internal fullness in the temporal realm requires sentient creatures who can repeat in time God's dynamic internal life. For this reason he says, "God has made intelligent creatures capable of being concerned in these effects, as being the willing active subjects, or means; and so they are capable of actively promoting God's glory."[161] Intelligent perceiving beings actuate the reality of God's self-glorifying communication of His beauty in time and space. According to Edwards, the ontological facilitates the aesthetic: there is a correspondence between the type of beauty and the dimension of its reality—secondary is shadow existence, primary is real.

Concluding Remarks

Self-love and True Virtue

While retaining positive and negative ethical connotations, Edwards makes self-love a universal, though not-necessarily-sinful, ontological principle. In doing so, he shows a strong affinity with the Thomist tradition. Within the Thomist tradition, love has been used in a wide metaphysical sense to mean a movement toward, or a force maintaining cohesion and unity, whether of the universe at one extreme or of the individual personality at the other.[162] This idea of cohesion and unity has tended to yield an idea of self-love as a kind of personal ontological integrity, where one identifies with one's self and adheres to one's self. Viewed in this respect, self-love, so far from being the reviled among loves, becomes the archetype of all, a presupposition for all further loving relationships, which will, given the interrelatedness of all agents, necessarily lead on to other loving relationships. It is not difficult to see several points of contact between Edwards's notion of self-love and our sketch of the Thomist tradition. To mention just two, Edwards espouses a principle of cohesion or unity grounded in aesthetic/ontological notion of beauty. Secondly, the Edwardsean notion of self-love has its archetype in God. Yet the created disposition of

---

160. Lee expounds this point at greater length in *Philosophical Theology*, 196–210.
161. "Miscellanies," no. 1218, *WJE* 23:153.
162. Bourke, *St. Thomas and the Greek Moralists*, 15–21; Barad, *Consent*.

self-love also function in the role of the archetype, as the "happiness" of created intelligent beings (even as found in and through other beings) ultimately terminates in a regard for self-being. In Edwards, the moral appraisal of all other creaturely loves is always determined by the moral perception of a human being.

It is also worth mentioning that Edwards's moral theory, like Thomas Aquinas's, is a second order or derivative philosophical inquiry, grounded on the development of a dispositional view of human existence. It is a second order inquiry because it follows upon an analysis of the ontological theory of human being—his philosophical anthropology.

The demands of his biblical paradigm for "true virtue," which should never be mistaken as a Christianized form of egoism or narcissism, can only be enforced if his ontology is in place. Ethical behavior is an evidence of something ontological. For Edwards, both normative ethical theory and the meta-ethics of true virtue depend upon a prior account of ontology.[163]

Edwards's work contributed little to nullifying the moral sense school (indeed, it has continued on through David Hume in the past to Roderick Firth and Richard Brandt in the present). It did, however, establish self-love on more metaphysically sure ground (ultimately looking back to the Trinity) for the faction of Reformed theologians who empathize with his position. But his main objective was not to repudiate Scottish moral sense philosophy but articulate to *God's* end in creation and how He obtains it.

The End for Which God Created the World

Jonathan Edwards circumnavigates a perennial problem in Reformed theology concerning the ontological question of the reprobate and their inherent worth by responding unapologetically about their nature and condition, even in the treatise *End of Creation*. Do reprobates have inherent ontological value? Are they properly human? Yes, of course, every soul is human, whether elect or not. But all of this is secondary for Edwards. The primary issue is God. Just as in *Two Dissertations* the *End for which God Created the World* precedes *The Nature of True Virtue*, so too we must understand that his total response to the Enlightenment is a restatement or redirection of the great question about reality (that is, about existence, purpose, and meaning), which is followed by the provision of a supposedly biblical answer to that question—an answer from one with a truly spiritual perspective (an "error theory" perspective) on reality. The question for Edwards concerns not so much man's destiny as God's gospel-oriented self-glorification grounded *in history*, the same history to which man is subject. Meta-ethics, metaphysics, and, above all, ontology are the underpinnings of such a response. What is more, its scope is all-inclusive, panentheistic, and availing: nothing is exempt from God's all-comprehensive being and telic purposes; not even the reprobate.

---

163. Fiering, *Moral Thought*, 11.

God Glorified in Man's Existence

> END OF CREATION. There are many of the divine attributes that, if God had not created the world, never would have had any exercise.
>
> —"Miscellanies" no. 553

THE PROPER FUNCTIONS OF THE THREE RELATIONAL DIMENSIONS OF A HUMAN BEING'S ontological structure are not merely theoretical propositions of the ideal human. According to Edwards's literal understanding of Scripture, the first man, Adam, not only was created with these dispositions but lived and performed his intended telic role in God's scheme.

Though hardly considered a credible position for most today, Jonathan Edwards unreservedly held the Genesis creation account to be literal. More accurately though, and somewhat as a departure from the early New England Puritan exegetical tradition ("the plain style"), he took the first eleven chapters of Genesis both literally and typologically.[1] The same could be said for much, if not all, of the Old Testament Scriptures. When he read, "God created man in his own image," he took it to mean that "God was Adam's father and the earth was his mother";[2] that is, God literally formed Adam from the dust of the earth.[3] So when Edwards speaks of "the first man," he aligns himself to a tradition which regarded the Genesis narrative to be abundantly more than religious folklore for allegorizing. Indeed, it was a non-fictional and trustworthy chronology of primitive humanity.[4]

Edwards sees in Scripture two men that have had incomparable roles in God's great plan of self-glorification: Adam and Jesus of Nazareth. Adam's role was to initiate the divine beauty in this realm like no other creature, angelic or otherwise. Insofar as Adam walked with God in a state of innocence and obedience, brief as that period may have been, God was glorified through His self-replication in the temporal realm. The idealist circuit was complete: God communicated Himself in, through, and to, an intelligent perceiving being who, through his spiritual perception of the reality of the excellency of God,

---

1. For more on Jonathan Edwards's principles of hermeneutic see Stein, "The Quest for the Spiritual Sense," 99–113; and "Editor's Introduction," *WJE* 15:1–34.

2. *The Nakedness of Job* (1722), *WJE* 10:405.

3. See for examples, "Notes on Scripture," nos. 110, 322, and 399 (*WJE* 15:81, 304–6, 396–99). In fact, the whole of Jonathan Edwards's hermeneutical, ideological, theological, and philosophical foundations rest, at one place or another, on the belief that the biblical record is indeed a supernaturally inspired chronicle of historical events, persons, and circumstances, as well as the only "infallible" source of divine revelation.

4. "Notes on Scripture," no. 416, *WJE* 15:423–69. Cf. Stein, "Editor's Introduction," *WJE* 15:14.

actuated the idea of the reality of the divine presence in the temporal world. God was, as it were, externalized and replicated. Actuating the idea of the reality of the divine presence, however, requires holiness (an intimate union with God). Holiness, for Edwards, is the distinguishing facet of humanity that perfects his nature theologically and morally. Adam possessed it as his original righteousness but was not "confirmed" in it, while regenerate persons possess it by virtue of their union with the divine person, Jesus Christ. How Adam was able to fulfill his telic role before the Fall, however, depended on the matter of his creation, not salvation. And therein lies Edwards's philosophical-theological angle on the necessity of the Fall.

God's idea of Himself is inextricably bound up in the images represented in the gospel narrative. The problem with Adam's "uprightness" is that it gives no place for the Divine Being to *fully* reveal Himself in His perfect idea of Himself—a Redeemer. Adam has to fall, according to Edwards, because the God Adam knows is not entirely compatible with God's idea of Himself. This does not mean that Adam is flawed, but only that an overarching and controlling narrative takes precedence to creation, namely, "the great work of redemption."

Adam, therefore, had a two-fold unparalleled role in God's creative purposes, subordinated to His redemptive purposes: to actuate the divine presence in temporality in an unrivaled and totally unique fashion; and to plunge humankind into a naturally irretrievable state of lostness in order to pave way for the Second Man, Jesus Christ, the consummate agent of God's self-communication and glorification.

With his ontology in place, as well as the working story of "God's electing love and the covenant of redemption," which Edwards thought was "but one work, one design . . . to accomplish the glory of the blessed Trinity in an exceeding degree,"[5] the conversation necessarily moves to epistemology: being is about perceiving being or, more precisely, existence is perceiving because existence is ideal, a mental construct. The conversation about God fashioning mental instances of excellence in order to form an ontological matrix of relational existences (the Divine Being *ad extra*) only goes so far. What God does in terms of ontology necessarily defaults into an epistemological description of the ontic. So, while it remains true that Edwards's ontology is the foundation of his epistemology, yet his ontology is inextricably epistemological. We cannot speak of man's existence without speaking of what he perceives and knows. Such is the nature of Edwards's theory of being.

Since Edwards's metaphysics of finality suggests that the "ends" appropriate to human nature are built into the very essence that determines human being, and those "ends" have to do with perception, then the reason *why* God created man, indeed, created anything at all, ultimately terminates in something epistemological—perceiving "Being in general." Edwards gives this assertion theological expression when he says: "Man was made for the reason of religion—this is why God gave this particular formation of dust the power of reason and reflection."[6]

God prescriptively made man's mind sensible to "Being in general" two ways: when the mind judges that anything is good or excellent; and when the individual is sensible of

5. *Sermon One*, WJE 9:118, 125.

6. 1004. MS sermon on Ps 119:60(b) (Sept. 1751), Jonathan Edwards Collection.

good in another sense, "when it is so sensible of the beauty and amiableness of the thing, that 'tis sensible of pleasure and delight in the presence of the idea of it."[7] This second sense of good or excellence carries in it an act of the will, or spirit of the mind, as well as the understanding. Thus, the discoveries of God's "excellencies" are two ways: by reflection and immediately by affectional intuition.

It is important to note that while the soul is one and the understanding never functions independent of the will nor the will from the understanding, yet there are key epistemological distinctions between them. In "Miscellanies" no. 540, Edwards reminds himself to underscore these distinctions in a future treatise:

> Remember when speaking of the creation of man and the state and nature with which he was created, to distinguish between mere speculative and rational understanding and that which it implies—a sense of heart—or [which] arises from it, wherein is exercised not merely the faculty of understanding, but the other faculty of will or inclination or the heart, and to make a distinction between the speculative faculty and the heart. And then to show how many principles of heart God created man with, viz. natural and supernatural principles.[8]

Two sets of things are distinguished. First, Edwards discriminates between "mere speculative and rational understanding" and the "sense of the heart"; and, secondly, between the "faculties" themselves. The first distinction is between "mere" propositionally connective or intuitive or *a priori* knowledge[9] and a unique affectional knowing that was not necessarily connected with empirical perception whatsoever. Edwards's epistemic distinctions, then, prove themselves an analysis of two categories of perception, speculative or notional and sensible or affectional. The latter type of knowledge is not merely confined to one particular kind of the objects of human knowledge, viz., those things that appertain or relate to the will and the affections. Instead, sensible knowledge extends to all the knowledge a person may have of all objects and ideas whatsoever: hence Edwards's qualifier, "and that which it implies . . . ," which supports his emphasis upon the integrity of the soul.

The perception of any thing (whether a notional idea or external object) relates to the sensibility of an agent (in terms of good or evil, agreeable or disagreeable, important or otherwise) as an ingredient to individual happiness or misery. All things therefore considered by an agent intuitively or by reflection, whether notional or sensible, are ultimately a factor in the relation to self, others, and God.[10]

All perceiving, then, is on a conscious level, whether progressively in reflection or continuously in perception-existence. But this process of perception-existence, warns

---

7. "Miscellanies," no. 489, *WJE* 13:533. Cf. "Miscellanies," nos. 428 (*WJE* 13:480) and 782 (*WJE* 18:452–66).

8. *WJE* 18:164. This distinction plays a critical role in the treatises *Original Sin* and *The Nature of True Virtue*. Interestingly, Jonathan Edwards originally wrote the last line thus: "love to God and self." And although the words were changed from what has been said in chapter 4 it is not difficult to see the ontological significance of his replacement.

9. For Jonathan Edwards, such "types" or means of knowledge fall under the category of "reason" or "understanding," where reason and understanding are at times used interchangeably. See "Miscellanies," no. 1340 (*WJE* 23:359–65).

10. "Miscellanies," no 782, *WJE* 18:452–66.

Edwards, happens so rapidly and continuously (as God communicates each "idea of existence" in the divine series), that one cannot be engaged in ratiocination each and every moment concerning each and every perception. Edwards wishes to emphasize that, although mental contemplation does not occur for each and every perception, yet the concerted mind consciously relates to all things perceived—*including the idea of existence and Being in general*—sometimes individually, sometimes as a whole, either approvingly or disapprovingly. This is how God, by a teleological ontic design of human being, guarantees the religious (i.e., epistemological) replication and glorification of Himself.

Edwards's epistemological distinctions have to do with the relational connection of the collective self *with* the object of its perception, whether "merely speculative" or "a sense of the heart." The key issue is what governs perception and consequent adjudications. If the "natural principles" govern, then the relation to a given object x may only be speculative. But if it is governed by "supernatural principles," then there is not only access to supernatural objects but also the potential for affectional disposedness toward object x. In this sense, "reflection" or a "speculative or notional" relation to an object may correspond with the self-love disposition's exercises: the aesthetic relation to the object is prescribed in terms of secondary beauty only. Likewise, the intuitive "sense of the heart" or "spiritual sense" corresponds with a disposition of love to God and, therefore, primary beauty. This distinction makes all the difference in the world between "*true religion*" and religion baldly considered. Edwards states it that way in *Freedom of the Will*: "As religion is the great business, for which we are created, and on which our happiness depends; and as religion consists in an intercourse between ourselves and our Maker; and so has its foundation in God's nature and ours, and in the relation that God and we stand into each other; therefore a true knowledge of both must be needful in order to *true religion*."[11]

Thus, while Adam was governed by the third relational disposition of love to God, i.e., the Holy Spirit, he found his "happiness" in a "Being in general" referential existence; all the while, God fulfilled His purposes in that "happiness."[12]

But it is not just Adam who is religious; *all* human beings are religious persons, regardless of their ontological constitution and self-loving nature. According to Edwards, "There are no neuters in religion."[13] When Adam fell, God's purposes were not suspended: Adam and all his fallen posterity, including the most obstinate reprobate, continue to fulfill religious or, better, ontologically grounded, epistemological functions. Edwards's philosophical anthropology and theocentric worldview may, therefore, be reproduced in the following system: "Three propositions . . . 1. God aims at his own glory in all his works. 2. God has specially made his reasonable creatures for this end. 3. He will obtain this end with respect to all his reasonable [creatures] whether they be his servants or his enemies."[14] Whether governed by the Holy Spirit or not, all human beings are religious persons who,

---

11. *WJE* 1:133.

12. 693p. Sermon on 1 Peter 3:10–11 (c.1739/1740), *WJE Online* 60; 930. Sermon on Proverbs 19:8(a) (May 1749; repreached July 1752): "DOC. Self-love duly regulated is a thing of great use in religion," [L.v1]. *WJE Online* 67.

13. 82. Sermon on Matthew 12:30 (June 1746; repreached 1756), *WJE Online* 64.

14. Sermon on Ezekiel 28:22–26 (1748) Quincer, *Jonathan Edwards' Sermon Outlines*, 80–84.

throughout their lives, fulfill epistemic roles by their being made to inescapably perceive something of "Being in general."

The distinction between "true religion" and "common religion" or, in ethical terms, "true virtue" and "common virtue," is, on the one hand, a mutually consenting relationship between God and man through a supernatural and holy principle of love to God and, on the other hand, non-Holy Spirit originated religious understanding, affections, and consequent practice. In other words, *true* spiritual knowledge is critically dependent upon spiritual union with the source of true virtue. According to Edwards, there can be no view or knowledge that one spiritual being can have of another, except it be immediate and intuitive, or mediate, or by some typological/figurative manifestation or signification. An immediate and intuitive view of any mind, if it is consequent and dependent on the prior existence of what is viewed in that mind, is the very same with consciousness. In Edwards, to have an immediate view of a mind is to have an immediate view of the thoughts, volitions, exercises, and motions of that mind (for this *is* mind). But to have an immediate view of the ideas and exercises of any mind consequent on their existence, is the same as to have an immediate perception or "sense or feeling" of them as they pass or exist in that mind.[15] Again, there is no difference between immediate "seeing ideas, and immediate having them." Neither is there any difference between a created mind's immediate view of the "sense or feeling" of a mind, "either of pleasure or pain, and feeling the same." "Therefore," Edwards concludes, "a spiritual, created being can't have an immediate view of another mind without some union of personality."[16] When God made Adam, the first man both possessed a disposition and perceived God immediately through the union that the Spirit's indwelling governance affords.

But what about the Fall that brought ruinous ontological and epistemological consequences to Adam and his posterity? If God's religious/epistemological purposes did not cease amidst the atrocity of sin and the dissolution of the spiritual union, then what does the natural-man and reprobate perceive in that connection?

Edwards's answer comes through this recognition of the mediating factors of reason, nature, society, and history. His is a realistic concept of immediacy in which God enters directly into the sanctified consciousness in, with, and under its total environment. So while perception of God is critically dependent upon spiritual union, nevertheless God has been pleased to mediate Himself to accommodate the creature's finitude and intellectual inferiority to His infinite and holy Being through time, reflection, communion (in community), and nature. Thus it was in the pristine conditions of Eden, thus it is with fallen humanity. Man, *regardless of his ontological structure,* is religious by virtue of his perception of mediated primary beauty in secondary beauty and divine attributes and perfections in reason, nature, society, and history. This synthesis of elements from the ontological and teleological spheres engages both the cognitive power of reflection and empirical perception. While it is Edwards's unique argument for genuine religious experi-

---

15. "Miscellanies," no. 777, *WJE* 18:427.
16. Ibid.

ence (and the existence of God), yet it also provides a rationalization for the purpose and value of non-elect persons.

Next we consider how, within Jonathan Edwards's vision of reality, the natural-man and reprobate continue to fulfill an epistemological function in God's program of self-replication and glorification. We will see that, ultimately, this is done within the framework of a *gospel-centered narrative*. In our investigation we will also find within the Northampton minister's vision of reality an explanation to Stephen Holmes's concern about Edwards's "prior failure to let the gospel story inform his position" regarding the creation and predestination of reprobates. According to Edwards, reprobates are a creation of the Trinity, predestined in Christ, and immediately related to the gospel narrative, not only in this life but in the afterlife as well.

When Edwards gives his chronological account of the history of the work of redemption his biblical anthropology starts with Adam and Eve. In doing so, he allows his dispositional ontology to inform his rendition of their "primitive state" which, in turn, advances a dispositional account of the Fall of Man. As we shall see in below and the following chapter, Edwards offers interesting, inventive, if not internally consistent accounts of both man's original status and ominous fall. How he accounts for man's transition from a state of concreation to fallenness, as well as what the epistemological purpose of "five-sixths' of the "heathenish" world might be, can be explained by tracing the logic of Edwardsean dispositions.

Man, Version 1.0

Characteristic of pre-Darwinian creationist accounts of the origin of humanity, the creation of man for Jonathan Edwards was in the strictest sense of the word an instantaneous act of God. He also subscribed to the immutability of species: evolutionary theory being neither a major force in thought, nor in possession of a champion, early in the eighteenth century. Edwards taught that the unity of the race stems from its being descended from a single pair, Adam and Eve. This "fact," he thought, was so well established that one need not appeal to divine revelation to ascertain its factuality: one could be convinced of its truthfulness merely through the evidences produced by history, philology, natural science or comparative physiology.[17]

In distinction from the inferior creatures of the earth, man was created after a divine type. Edwards immediately signals man's highly personal, that is to say, relational nature. Humanity is the act of a Personal Agent who fashions man after His own image and addresses them as covenant participants and agents, like Himself. Unlike any other generated existence, man is commissioned to effect spiritual and moral purposes for God within the created order. Man's origin, nature, and purpose of existence are all intertwined with the Divine Being. Reflecting on this original state, Edwards writes: "Man was at first

---

17. See, for example, "Notes on Scripture," nos. 199, 409, 415, 428, *WJE* 15. Jonathan Edwards's practice was to copy passages from borrowed books for later purposes. Many of these excerpts and citations concerned archeological or anthropological research that would lend credence to biblical themes, such as the unity of the race. The accuracy of their contents and effectiveness of his method are discussed in Sweeney, "Editor's Introduction," *WJE* 23:10–33.

created in an innocent, holy, pleasant, and happy state," and was in his primitive state, "a noble piece of divine workmanship," who enjoyed "a blessed communion with God and there was a free intercourse between God and him."[18] This was Edwards's conviction in the early years of his Northampton ministry and throughout his life.

In saying these things, Edwards reveals his partisan allegiance regarding the contentious issues of original sin and inherent corruption. These much disputed doctrines, along with original righteousness, total depravity, and irresistible grace, became the focal point of a series of calculated repudiations of established Calvinist orthodoxy from the pens of able eighteenth-century deists and upstart Unitarians.[19] Edwards quickly perceived that this was no inconsequential conversation among petty theologians on the periphery of the church; but rather a burgeoning consensus amongst Anglican and Presbyterian clerics (even non-conformist types) piloted by formidable "Christian humanist" thinkers. Early stages of this theological virus, in the form of Arminianism, had already become epidemic in the Old and New Worlds, or, at least, Edwards thought so. "The modern prevailing notions of free-will," however, were merely symptomatic of a deistic plague on the horizon. Those imbued with the ethos and pathos of Enlightenment religion, men such as John Taylor, George Turnbull, and Matthew Tindal, were forging what Edwards believed an unparalleled crisis in Christian history, namely a universal defection from established biblical divinity. Debates over "enthusiasm" became trifles to him when the foundations of the faith were being compromised. Consequently, around 1748–49, we notice a shift of priorities in Edwards. No longer would his published writings primarily reflect his views on conversion and the outworking of his own experience of affectional religion. To be sure, they would have a prominent and foundational place in his major treatises. But, now, the burden of the day was the encroachment of "deistical religion" upon orthodoxy in New England. His priority now was to rectify deism's exalted opinion of man and corresponding depreciation of God's work, presence, and purpose in the world. The situation had only intensified since his collegiate years at Yale.

However, complications arose in the preparations of his projected multi-volume response to "fashionable religion" when his church in a single vote opted to permanently relieve him of his ministerial duties. Inevitable delays followed as he moved his family to the frontier of Stockbridge and settled into missionary responsibilities among the Housatonic and Mohawk Indians. From this outpost, *Freedom of the Will*, *Original Sin*, and *Two Dissertations* were the first fruits of what promised to be a long polemical series against Enlightenment freethinking.[20] But the core issue in his published responses, as

---

18. "Notes on Scripture," no. 397; *WJE* 15:394–95; *Natural Men in a Dreadful Condition* (1734), *Dwight-Works*, 8:5–43.

19. Wilber, *A History of Unitarianism*, 2:212ff; Wright, *Beginnings of Unitarianism*, 5–15, 71–78.

20. Jonathan Edwards began compiling several notebooks designated "Book of Controversies" "A," "B," and "C," which target Taylor and others deists with polemical treatises on justification and predestination, faith, perseverance, and efficacious grace, in short, all of the distinguishing tenets of creedal Calvinism. The "Book of Controversies" (along with Lee's editorial comments) is reproduced in *WJE* 21:312–413. Lee's "Editor's Introduction" (*WJE* 21:1–106) provides an important analysis for understanding this collection of notes. See also Holbrook, "Editor's Introduction," *WJE* 3:22–23.

well as anticipated treatises, was the same—the articulation of a universally discernable biblical-anthropology within the framework of a theocentric depiction of reality.

Original Status, Original Righteousness, and Image of God

The biblical-anthropology debate, which dates back to the controversies between Pelagius, Coelestius, Julian, and Augustine, concerns itself with the issue of whether or not original righteousness (*iustita originalis*) was an essential property of man's original constitution. Simply put, the core issue is: In what consists the image of God in which man was created? Surrounding issues concern the circumstances in which man was placed and the mutability of his constitution, all which culminate in intensive discussions about the Fall and original sin and, pertinent to our study, larger issues of human worth and purpose within God's creation.

Pelagians and semi-Pelagians, along with post-Reformation Jesuits, Socinians, and select Remonstrants, deny the Augustinian doctrine of *iustita originalis* (where original righteousness and holiness are essential to man's *status integritatis*), asserting in its stead that the first man was created (and all of his posterity thereafter) in a state of pure nature,[21] and that any grace added to man was a post facto *donum superadditum*. The supernatural endowment, superadded to nature, was, of course, to become a peculiarity of Roman Catholic anthropology.[22] By denying a place for original righteousness in the natural or original constitution of man, those who held to a Pelagian or semi-Pelagian theological anthropology made it possible to also reject or modify the Augustinian (and later, Reformed) doctrine of original sin.

The Augustinian/Reformed tradition states that man (biblical Adam) possessed original, or more specifically, "native" righteousness. This state of original righteousness or perfect integrity is sometimes expressed by saying that man was created "in the image of God" or, in more technical language, that he was concreated. Calvin continued the Augustinian position by affirming the doctrine of the essential righteousness of original man,[23] as did Beza and Turretin. Reformed theology did not hesitate to say that the image of God in fact constitutes the *essence* of man. Edwards primarily links it to the self-love disposition. The Reformed continued to distinguish, however, between those elements in the image of God which man cannot lose without ceasing to be man, consisting in the essential qualities and powers of the human soul; and those elements which man can lose and still remain man, namely, the good ethical qualities of the soul and its powers. The "image of God" in this restricted sense is identical with what is called original or native righteousness. It is the moral perfection of the image that could be and was lost by sin according to Calvin and the majority of those who side with Calvinism.[24]

---

21. "In pure naturals" meaning that man consists of his own parts and essential properties without the gift of original righteousness and without any "superadded" qualities or habits: hence, it is called a state of pure nature (*status purae naturae*) by a negative and not a positive purity.

22. See Bellarmino, "De gratia primi hominis" in *Opera Bellarminus*, 4:23f; and Jedin, *A History of the Council of Trent*, 2: chaps 2 and 5.

23. *Institutes*, I.15.4.

24. Calvinist theologian R. L. Dabney (1820–98) dissents from the majority view in his *Systematic*

The Reformed position can be explained this way: Man's righteousness consisted in the perfect harmonious concurrence of all the habitual tendencies or inclinations of his soul, and, consequently, of all his volitions prompted thereby, with the decisions of his conscience, which in its turn was correctly directed by God's holy will. His righteousness was *a natural and entire conformity* in principle and volition with God's law. Adam was possessed of a free will in the sense that in all his responsible, moral acts, his soul was self-determined in its volitions (i.e., he chose according to his own understanding and dispositions, free from any coaction). Just as man's dispositions decisively incline his will in a state of fallen nature to ungodliness, so then they inclined it to holiness. This inclination was prevalent and complete for the time, yet not immutable, as the event proved. Consequently, the sense in which "image of God" was to be understood was not as an essential, formal and intrinsic participation in the divine nature, but as an analogical, accidental and extrinsic participation (by reason of the effects analogous to the divine perfections which are produced in man) by the Holy Spirit, in accordance with what is the spiritual and moral image of God.

Edwards's position is only slightly more nuanced. He does not construe anything *of* man's essential being as originally righteous or holy. What constitutes the entity "human being" does not, as a defining characteristic or element of its essence, necessarily include inherent holiness: "Man had not holiness necessarily, as an inseparable qualification of human nature."[25] A human being is a human being with or without concreated holiness.

This prompts the question: Was original righteousness natural or supernatural? The Reformed state that "natural" has respect to the entire state, necessary to the perfection of the entire nature and pertaining to the "native" gifts of the entire man. Though they allow that original righteousness can be called a "grace" or "a gracious gift," it is understood in descriptive terms of God's composing the nature of man. The "gift" itself they do not admit is supernatural, rather it is inherent in man because he was uniquely created like God, by God.

Similarly, Edwards agrees that man is not something less than man if one excludes the notions of the theological and moral soundness of man or, in other words, his holiness. But he does not agree with Turretin and other Calvinists from the same perspective. First, he cannot separate man's essential being from the teleological purpose of his existence—religion. Here, ontology is determined by teleology and aesthetic theory. Man is more substantially a spirit because his being is grounded in the extent of his dynamic relations with "Being in general" (man's theological soundness) and beings (man's moral soundness). Man's being may increase through greater consenting relations within the law of the whole. Holiness, in Edwards's way of thinking, would do just that. But the nature of the first man did not require essential holiness in his faculties to be a natural human being.[26] The same holds true for the fallen posterity of Adam. Natural-men and reprobates are still human beings, but ones whose dynamic potential is not achieved because the

---

Theology (295–96), as have many Neo-orthodox Reformed theologians, such as Karl Barth, who emphasized an infinite qualitative distinction between God and humanity.

25. *Born Again* (1730), *WJE* 17:205.
26. *Original Sin*, *WJE* 3:381–82.

expressly revealed purpose of their existence (not the ultimate end, i.e., that glorification of God accomplishes in the destruction of the reprobate) *seemingly* goes unfulfilled. Without the fulfillment of theological and moral consenting relations man has less being than otherwise, but is nonetheless man. Hence, Edwards's histrionic rhetoric: "[Man] is not himself—not answering the End of his Creation—but contradicting of it."[27]

As far as concreated original righteousness is concerned, Edwards systematically defends it in *Original Sin*, but its defense in based upon a crucial distinction between "natural" and "supernatural" principles. And it is in "supernatural principles" that he places holiness and original righteousness, thereby rendering it a quality "above nature."

A Diatribe on Human Nature

In Edwards's estimation, the maintenance of the orthodox doctrine of original sin (which rested in an important sense upon the doctrine of concreated righteousness) was part of the first line of defense against the encroachment of "unorthodox, rationalistic, and freethinking" sentiments of Arminians or worse still, deists, upon the established Calvinistic tradition within the British Isles and the Christian haven of the New World.[28] So central was the verity of Adam's Fall and its consequences of original sin and total depravity to the Christian religion in Edwards's mind that, when published contrary notions began to be countenanced in Britain and the Colonies, he immediately began compiling a mass of notes intended to counter their position, and in particular the views contained within Dr. John Taylor's controversial book, *Scripture-Doctrine of Original Sin*.[29]

Taylor intended to emancipate humanity from the two elements of original sin, original guilt and original pollution, by reasoning, "what is natural to us, as the Passions of Hunger and Thirst, or the Frailty of our Bodies, we can by no means help or hinder." The *Scripture-Doctrine* exemplified a polarized opinion to that of the Augustinians and Calvinists regarding natural-man's responsibility for the dispositions, habits and desires tending to moral judgments and volitions. Representing a Pelagian and semi-Pelagian position, Taylor said that since responsibility cannot be more extended than freedom of the will, no blame (or approbation) can be attached to dispositions, which were held to be involuntary. Thus he judged that nothing done under the auspices of compulsion could

---

27. 230. [L. 2v.]. Sermon on Matthew 10:17 (1732), *WJE Online* 47.

28. Jonathan Edwards believed that the heresies of Arminianism and Deism were already in New England, as his private correspondence, sermons, and notebooks reveal. In particular, he was concerned about the influence of John Taylor's *Scripture-Doctrine of Original Sin*. Tagged with the invective, "that author who has so corrupted multitudes in New England," Jonathan Edwards believed Taylor was responsible for attracting the English and New England communions (including his own former Northampton congregation!) to "new, fashionable, lax schemes of divinity" (*WJE* 16:483–84). New Englander, Experience Mayhew, confirmed Jonathan Edwards's angst by showing in his work, *Grace Defended*, how Taylor's work could be synthesized with New World orthodoxy. Later others, such as Charles Chauncy, approvingly appropriated portions of the *Scripture-Doctrine* their own treatises (e.g., Chauncy's *Mystery Hid from Ages & Generations* and *Salvation for All Men*) and thereby promulgated its content. This was precisely what Jonathan Edwards wished to address and prevent.

29. Taylor (1694–1761) was an English Nonconformist pastor and theologian. Later in life he made a dramatic move from his early professions of confessional Presbyterianism and doctrinal Calvinism to an anti-Trinitarian and Pelagian position, though he viewed himself more of a Christian humanist.

be labeled sin or carry the least degree of guilt. Taylor was obviously reacting against the Augustinian assertion that original sin (*peccatum originale*) was a moral punishment for the "root" sin of Adam. And although Taylor admitted the almost universal presence of sin through his empirical assessment of the world, as well as Scriptural authority, he nonetheless repudiated every notion of total depravity and inherited pollution.[30] Sin, for the rationalist who acknowledged such a thing, consisted of only right and wrong actions of the soul.

For Taylor, then, the equation of biblical-anthropology goes as follows: responsibility and duty must be proportionate to power and ability; and since God states the expectation of duties and also gives powers to men, duty cannot be greater than ability; therefore, the Christian religion consists of our making "a due use of the powers we already have before we receive and in on order to our receiving, further help."[31] For him, the issue over free will would be a moot point if the notion of moral necessity excluded the idea of total depravity. In essence, Taylor simply took what the Calvinist asserts as the moral inability of man, and characterized it as mere natural deficiency: God did not provide certain powers, capacities or abilities.[32] Taylor concludes that the naturally deficient agent is not a culpable agent, unless, of course, God is a "monster." Thus, what God requires of man must be within his power. To fulfill the requirements and duties proportionate to divinely allotted *natural* abilities, capacities and powers is the whole of religion, which presumably is rewarded with additional graces, what Taylor calls "further help." Thus, Taylor claims that the doctrine of original righteousness is entirely inconsistent with the nature of virtue and freedom. For if holiness were concreated it would disrupt the liberty, that is, the choice and consent of the moral agent to own it for himself; thereby nullifying the goodness of free-willing virtue.

Edwards believed, in the words of commentator Clyde Holbrook, "that to follow this line of reasoning was nothing less than disastrous for the gospel scheme." "It will follow on our author's principles, not only with respect to infants, but even *adult* persons," Edwards explains, "that redemption is needless, and Christ is dead in vain."[33] As he wrote in 1752 to his former congregation: "Taylor's scheme of religion . . . utterly explodes the doctrines you have been formerly taught concerning eternal election, conversion, justification; and so, of a natural state of death in sin; and the whole doctrine of original sin, and of the mighty change made in the soul by the redemption of Christ applied to it.[34] For if, as Taylor taught, men do have a duty to God that they can sufficiently fulfill of themselves

30. *Scripture-Doctrine*, 160, 167–68.

31. Ibid., 256.

32. Holbrook, "Editor's Introduction," *WJE* 3:35–36. William Cunningham describes moral inability, as that "which arises solely from want of will to do the thing required, from the opposition of will or want of inclination as the cause or source of the thing required not being done,—there not being in the way any external or natural obstacle of the kind just described" (*Historical Theology*, 1:600). There is an obvious distinction from external coaction, which the reason and conscience of man recognizes as a different state, which would supersede responsibility. Jonathan Edwards essentially forged the usage of the terms "moral inability" and "natural inability" for polemical purposes to express the distinction.

33. "Editor's Introduction," *WJE* 3:35, 356.

34. Letter to the First Church of Christ, Northampton," June 1752, *WJE* 16:483–84.

and wholly avoid sin, then, as Holbrook states it, "Christianity is thrown back into that works righteousness from which Paul and the Reformers had rescued it."[35]

In this way, Taylor's opinions were bringing "vital religion" to the brink of an unprecedented crisis, so says Edwards a few weeks later to John Erskine:

> I thank you for giving me an account of Mr. Taylor's writings and the things which he is doing to propagate his opinions. It now appears to be a remarkable time in the Christian world; perhaps such an one as never has been before. Things are going downhill so fast; truth and religion, both of heart and practice, are departing by such swift steps that I think it must needs be, that a crisis is not very far off. And what will then appear, I will not pretend to determine.[36]

Gone, here, is the optimism of *An Humble Attempt to Promote Explicit Agreement and Visible Union of God's People in Extraordinary Prayer, For the Revival of Religion and the Advancement of Christ's Kingdom on Earth* (1748). Gone, too, it seems are the preparatory postmillennial expectations for America.[37] It seems the lack of lasting fruit from the Awakenings,[38] the bitter pill of being turned out of his ministerial charge, negative reports about the state of "true religion" in Scotland, England, and the Netherlands, as well as the proliferation of heterodox, if not heretical, theology throughout former Calvinistic enclaves, left Edwards vexed about the future of Christianity. Instead of irenic appeals for prayer and the propagation of affectional religion, the turn now is to the fundamentals of the faith.[39] Dogma not discourse, polemics not prayers are his weapons in urgent times. The former enemy was skepticism, Arminianism, and to a lesser degree, Romanism: the chore, to discern the "distinguishing marks" of spiritual religion in the heart, as well as further the demise of the papacy through the reinforcement of Protestant *sola fide*.[40] Now the enemy is, in the words of John Wesley, "old deism in a new dress": the task for Edwards is expose it for what it is—"a great evil . . . and apostasy"—and eradicate its presence from the halls of faith.[41]

Edwards's first blow came in the form of the magisterial treatise *Freedom of the Will*. The second of his incursions, *Original Sin*, was specifically aimed at Taylor and his ilk. He argues in it, first, that the choosing of a thing is not the origin or source of true virtue, but the antecedent "good disposition or affection."[42] He then adds, for a moral agent to be pronounced "good" while subject to moral obligations to/from God, is the same thing as to be "perfectly *innocent* . . . perfectly *righteous*." Through an identification of

---

35. "Editor's Introduction," *WJE* 3:35.

36. Letter to the Reverend John Erskine," July 7, 1752, *WJE* 16:490–91.

37. Jonathan Edwards believed the Great Awakening revivals were precursors to, but not the start of, the Church's "latter-day glory," that is, the millennium itself. Gerald McDermott has appropriately designated them "premillennial revivals" (*One Holy and Happy Society*, 77). Cf. Withrow, "Future of Hope," 75–98.

38. See Jonathan Edwards's confessions in "Distinguishing Marks" in *WJE* 4:285; *Religious Affections*, *WJE* 2:460; "Miscellanies," no. 821, *WJE* 18:532.

39. Cf. Fiering, *Moral Thought*, 106, 131.

40. Goen, "Editor's Introduction," *WJE* 4:4–18.

41. Wesley, "Doctrine of Original Sin" in *The Works of John Wesley*, 9:211; *WJE* 3:298–99.

42. *WJE* 3:225.

the righteousness of Adam with original innocence rather than with the moral rectitude wrought by personal endeavors, Edwards recasts Taylor's principle point of contention. According to Holbrook, "Edwards argued that Adam was immediately capable of behaving as a moral agent under the rule and principle of right action."[43] Earlier in his *Scripture-Doctrine* Taylor charged that "Adam could not sin without a sinful inclination,"[44] which thing Edwards also granted, but in turn used the principle against Taylor by saying, "just for the same reason, he could not do right, without an inclination to right action."[45] In Genesis, Edwards would argue, God pronounced man not just "good" but "very good." "For in order to man's being happy in the blessing [i.e., life in Eden], two things were needful: first, that the enjoyments granted should be good; and second, that the subject should be good, or in a good capacity to receive and enjoy them."[46] Hence, from the first moment of his existence, Adam possessed an inclination to "right action, or, which is the same thing, a virtuous and holy disposition of heart."[47] By subjecting Taylor's moralism to the same logical scrutiny employed in *Freedom of the Will*, Edwards was not only able to established a credible defense of original righteousness, but rest his thesis upon a disposition within man, from the first moment of his existence. God, then, was to be exonerated from the charge of "author of sin," at least at this level, for creating a "very good" man with an upright disposition of heart (*iustitia habitualis*). That is, God created man with a right principle, toward obedience, to do his duty (*iustitia actualis*).

However, when the question then turns to the immutability of Adam's disposition and/or the mutability of his original grace against the background of the Fall, Edwards then seems to say two things. First, he maintains that the immutability of Adam's essential nature is not to be associated with his holiness or original righteous state.[48] This stays in line with his tradition, but creates an awkward tension in not allowing for a mutable notion of grace. Secondly, he makes certain that the original righteousness of Adam was *supernatural*.

Concerning the first point, Edwards says that Adam's *status integritatis* consisted of his being created with the *duty* or obligation, maintained by conscience and reason, to be inclined toward full obedience, and not in an immutable disposition itself; though, to be sure, he did possess a righteous disposition toward holiness, but that disposition was "above" his nature. Thus Edwards begins his argument against Taylor's denial of original righteousness and assertion that man was created *in puris naturalibus*, by contending that Adam was created in a state of moral rectitude and holiness: "There can be no *medium* between sin and righteousness, or between being right and being wrong, in a moral sense, than there can be a medium between straight and crooked, in a natural sense. Adam was brought into existence capable of acting immediately, as a moral agent; and therefore he

---

43. Ibid., 49.

44. Taylor, *Scripture-Doctrine*, 442. Jonathan Edwards's paraphrase in *WJE* 3:228.

45. *WJE* 3:228—29.

46. "Notes on Scripture," no. 398, *WJE* 15:395.

47. *WJE* 3:229.

48. Gerstner (*Rational Biblical*, 2:303–22), Crabtree (*Jonathan Edwards' View of Man*, 21–24), Pfisterer (*Prism of Scripture*, 20–30), and Storms (*Tragedy in Eden*, 222–23), erroneously interpret Jonathan Edwards's concept of original righteousness as one of fixed moral perfection.

was immediately under a rule of right action: he was obliged as soon as he existed, to act right. And if he was obliged to act right as soon as he existed, he was even then *inclined* to act right."[49]

The moral agent, Adam, created as a mature man and immediately capable of moral decisions and actions, was under an obligation to obey a two-fold "rule of right action": (*a*) the command in Genesis 2:15; and (*b*) the "positive precept" of 2:17.[50] However, Edwards does not disclose what it is *in* man that inclines him to right action; he simply says that man was thus inclined and that it rendered him perfectly innocent or righteous. The "what" is answered through the distinction between the natural and moral image of God, which serve as synonymous terms for *natural* and *supernatural* principles. Edwards explains that just as there are two kinds of attributes or, better, perfections in God—His moral attributes consisting of His holiness (the Spirit), and his natural attributes of knowledge, reason, understanding, strength, etc. (the Son)—so there is in man two kinds of principles. Thus, in a lecture on Genesis 3:24, Adam's "perfect innocence" and inclinations are identified with concreation in the traditional terms of *imago Dei*: "The natural image of God that consists in reason and understanding was then complete . . . His mind [also] shone with the perfect spiritual image of God, being without any defect in its holiness and righteousness, or any spot or wrinkle to mar its spiritual beauty. God had put his own beauty upon it; it shone with the communication of his glory."[51]

Not only did Adam possess those faculties of understanding and will whereby he resembles the Godhead (the natural image), but also his exercise of these faculties in humble love and obedience was a mirror of the divine glory (the spiritual image). This, of course, is simply a further expression of the structure of the soul corresponding to the Trinitarian model. The natural and spiritual images of God are not mere reflections, but "inferior" and "superior" principles. Of these two kinds of principles, Edwards says in *Original Sin* that, "There was an *inferior* kind, which may be called *natural*, being the principles of mere human nature; such as self-love, with those natural appetites and passions, which belong to the nature of man . . . these when alone, and left to themselves, are what the Scriptures sometimes call *flesh*. Besides these, there were *superior* principles that were spiritual, holy and divine, summarily comprehended in divine love; wherein consisted the spiritual image of God, and man's righteousness and true holiness; which are called in Scripture the *divine nature*."[52]

The spiritual image of God or the "superior principles," Edwards explains, may be called "*supernatural*" and, therefore, "above those principles that are essentially implied in, or necessarily resulting from, and inseparably connected with, *mere human nature*."[53]

---

49. *WJE* 3:228.

50. "Miscellanies," nos. 400, 401, *WJE* 13:465–66. This distinction was important in the prevention of being charged with failing to cover the lapse of Adam's active obedience. Not only did Adam positively sin a sin of commission (willfully eating the fruit), but also negatively through a sin of omission by failing to "keep the garden." Jonathan Edwards includes the latter with the former under the rubric of covenant stipulations.

51. *East of Eden* (1731), *WJE* 17:333–34. For Jonathan Edwards's definition of reason, see "Miscellanies," no. 1340, *WJE* 23:359.

52. *WJE* 3:381. Cf. Stoddard, *Treatise Concerning Conversion*, 39.

53. Ibid., 381–82. Cf. outline of "A Rational Account" in *WJE* 6:396.

The supernatural, superior principles immediately depend upon "man's union and communion with God, or divine communications and influences of God's Spirit."[54] One must not confuse Adam's essential human constitution with that which is "above" and nonessential to it when considering his inherent spiritual good.[55]

> To prevent all cavils . . . I here use the words, "natural" and "supernatural": not as epithets of distinction between that which is concreated or connate, and that which is extraordinarily introduced afterwards, besides the first state of things, or the order established originally, beginning when man's nature began; but as distinguishing between what belongs *to*, or flows *from*, that nature which man has, merely *as* man, but a truly *virtuous, holy,* and *spiritual* man; which, though they began in Adam, as soon as humanity began, yet are not essential to the constitution of it, or necessary to its being: inasmuch as one may have everything needful to his being *man* exclusively of them.[56]

Consequently, in terms of both concept and semantic constraints, what Edwards says about the original righteousness of man sounds surprisingly similar to the Tridentine Roman Catholic position. Just as Rome would say that the first man was made holy *ab initio*, so too Edwards says that Adam was "holy" in a comparable sense. And when Rome would say that original righteousness was not a natural *habitus* of his own will, that is, it did not belong to the nature of man in its integrity but was a supernatural grace, communicated to him temporarily by God, Edwards combines both Reformed and Roman Catholic positions by arguing that man from the first moment of his created existence was indeed inclined toward holiness (the Reformed position), not because it was essential to him, but because the supernatural principle in him inclined him toward holiness (similar to the Roman Catholic position). Edwards explains that this is due to the fact that, "God made man at first with two sorts of principles, viz. *natural principles of self-love* and *supernatural principles of love to God*." But only the "natural belonged to human nature. [It is] impossible that men should be without them."[57] In short, the natural principles are of the defining dispositions of human nature, while the supernatural principles are of divine grace.

Thus, when Edwards says of Adam, "from the beginning he had a supreme and perfect respect and love to God: and if, so, he was created with such a principle," we must understand that the twofold "rule of right action" or "duty to God" was a characteristic of the superior principles; and though they were with him from his inception, they were not essential to him. "Therefore, if any morally right act at all, reflection, consideration, or anything else, was required of Adam immediately, on his first existence, and was performed as required," reasoned Edwards, "then he must, the first moment of his existence, have his heart possessed of that principle of divine love; which implies the whole of moral rectitude in every part of it . . . which is the thing taught in the doctrine of original righteousness."[58]

---

54. *WJE* 3:382.
55. See "Notes on Scripture," no. 398, *WJE* 15:395–96; and Lee, *Philosophical Theology*, 143.
56. *WJE* 3:381 n.5.
57. 249. [L. 8v.]. Sermon on Rom 3:13–18 (1732), second unit, *WJE Online* 47.
58. *WJE* 3:230.

In his reply to Taylor, then, we find that the moral or spiritual image of God, the rule of right action *and* original righteousness all come together in the supernatural, superior principle of divine love. Edwards said as much ten years previous in his treatise on the nature of the affections and their importance in religion.[59] Although in *Religious Affections* he focuses on regenerate and unregenerate souls—a *post*-lapsus subject, nevertheless his statements concerning the principles of holiness, righteousness, love and grace, are completely applicable to the case with Adam: "There is no essential difference between that principle of grace which believers have and that original holiness which our first parents and the angels had." Adam, then, who was a "religious person," possessed that principle from which all "true religion" including "love of duty to God" arise, namely, "holy love." Elsewhere he says, "I certainly conclude, that virtue and holiness are given by way of immediate emanation from God."[60]

Significantly, the principle of divine love is not a "*what*" but a "*who*"—the Holy Spirit:[61] "righteousness, virtue and holiness [are] called grace, not only because 'tis entirely the free gift of God, but because *'tis the Holy Spirit in man*; which, as we have said, is grace or love."[62] Thus,

> Man's original righteousness consisted in his supernatural principles and in the entire subordination of natural principles to them. [It] did not consist in his natural principles of self-love . . . in themselves considered there is no virtue or goodness in them. Considered as subordinate to the supernatural, indeed they are good, but not in themselves. Rather, original righteousness consisted essentially in the other sort of principles. These were the only fount and spring of all man's righteousness before the Fall . . . *Those supernatural principles did not flow from the nature of man but altogether from the Spirit of God.*[63]

Because Edwards identifies the superior principles with the Holy Spirit he never explicitly uses the Scholastic and later Roman Catholic terminology of *donum superadditum* or, as John Gerstner points out, Augustine's *adiutorium*, but the implications of Edwards's meaning, nonetheless, are identical: God created man endowed with the Spirit of God, from the first moment of his being, as a vital principle of holiness and righteousness, governing the natural principles of man that summarily consist in a disposition of self-love: hence, Edwards's Calvinistic claim that righteousness is never really inherent to man.

Edwards's response to Taylor, then, is based upon the thesis that the Holy Spirit is that principle of divine love in man, which, from the beginning, produced or instigated within man a "supreme and perfect respect and love to God." This holy principle was not only in external duties, but internal duties, such as summarily consist in love. This is because a holy principle is nothing other than an ontological disposition of holiness, or again, God's essential disposition to love Himself reflexively, or again, the Person of the Holy Spirit. So, when Edwards speaks of the principle of divine love as a "vital" principle in Adam, he is

---

59. Cf. Smith, "Editor's Introduction," *WJE* 2:36.
60. "Miscellanies," no. 187, *WJE* 13:331.
61. Cf. Lee, "Editor's Introduction," *WJE* 21:46–53
62. "Miscellanies," no. 220, *WJE* 13:345. Emphasis added.
63. 249. [L. 9v.]. Sermon on Romans 3:13–18 (1732), second unit, *WJE Online* 4. Emphasis added.

in no way espousing a state of dispositional *equilibrio*. Adam was never in a state of moral limbo or equipoise. Rather, the disposition of holiness in man has its vitality from the first moment of Adam's existence. For, as Edwards writes in "Miscellanies" no. 289, "It's evident that the habit of grace is always begun by an act of grace."[64] Adam, therefore, could not be said to be in possession of a habit of grace without that grace being exercised immediately to incline him, through the principle's superior governance, in its God-loving tendencies.

Human nature itself, he argues, must be created with some dispositions; otherwise it must be without any such thing as inclination or will. Naturally, the defining disposition within humanity is the disposition of self-love, described earlier as the first determining relation of being. This essential disposition *from the first* was governed by the supernatural principle of divine love, thereby rendering the whole of man an image of God, correctly inclined to holiness. Holiness, Edwards explains, renders all harmonies in the soul, all the powers and relations of being, one consent; so that there is no opposition between one faculty and another.[65] The governance of the Holy Spirit acts through and upon man's natural disposition or consciousness, so that self-love continues in a natural capacity but is extended and rendered excellent through a spiritual and relational union with the Spirit, to the effect that the natural tendencies of self-love are not immediately self-referential, but motivated out of an ultimate and supreme love to God.[66]

By removing grace and righteousness beyond the boundaries of essential or inherent human constitution, Edwards proposed an account of man in his original state possessed of a holy disposition, able to choose with preference things that were most excellent, beautiful, and good, contrary to allegations of Taylor. Thus, if one is to speak of grace with reference to man and true virtue (/religion) in Edwards's system, then one must speak about *divine* grace, that is, one must make reference to the indwelling governance of the Spirit.

When the Calvinist answers that Adam's righteousness was native, that is, it was conferred upon him, as the original *habitus* of his will, by the creative act which made him an intelligent creature, and that the exercise of holy volitions was the natural effect of the principles which God gave him, Edwards demurs. Instead, he holds that God set Adam in motion toward righteous behavior and decision-making by the governing and influence of the supernatural principles.[67]

The disposition of love to God, however, is not an active, lawlike tendency in the same way *as* other dispositions. Created dispositions manifest their tendencies when certain conditions are present: on the occasion c disposition D yields manifestation m. The disposition is, as it were, always pressing to yield m when c because it is created as a lawlike tendency to m whenever c. But it does not work that way with the disposition of love to God. Why? Because the Holy Spirit is an arbitrary Being, not some impersonal force or prescriptive power, according to Edwards.[68]

---

64. *WJE* 13:381.
65. *The Pleasantness of Religion* (1723), *WJE* 14:107.
66. "Treatise on Grace" in *WJE* 21:175. Similar statements can be found in *Original Sin* (*WJE* 3:278, 279).
67. 230. Sermon on Matthew 10:17 (1732), *WJE Online* 47.
68. "Miscellanies," no. 1263, *WJE* 23:202–11. Cf. Lee, "Editor's Introduction," *WJE* 21:53–57 and Fiering's discussion on divine and human arbitrariness, where he likewise explains that "Divine operations are themselves 'more or less arbitrary'" in *Moral Thought*, 97–103.

When it comes to governing man's essential self-love disposition, the Spirit has relative liberty to function, not according to certain arrangements of circumstances and powers to yield a particular result, but (from a human standpoint) with virtual autonomy. We say "relative" and "virtual" because there are two senses in which the Spirit does act in a lawlike way. First, the Spirit, out of ontological necessity, always acts in accord with His nature—holy. Second, the Spirit has covenanted with the Father and Son in a "holy confederation" to effect certain divinely appointed ends in the "great work of redemption." Consequently, we may say that the Spirit functions within man as a governing principle with "weak arbitrariness" as opposed to the "strong arbitrariness" of God's essential mental nature. The Spirit directs the self-love disposition by presenting *His good* before the sensible mind, so that the self-love disposition, functioning in its natural capacity, capitulates in *that* good for its own good and thereby achieves some God ordained "end." Thus, the manner in which God influences man commits no violence to the will whatsoever. Certainly man is predestined, but God's causal operations do not "force" his will. Instead, God teleologically wields sovereign control over all of man's affairs by designing the mind to "will . . . as the greatest apparent good is."[69] When the Spirit internally governs a man, He determines what man actually does by becoming man's reason for it. In short, the governing of the Spirit is simply an override mechanism offering effective motives to a consciousness that is readily sensitive to such divine motions. The fact that the Spirit does not necessarily have to govern each and every instance (i.e., that He is weakly arbitrary in this exercise) becomes of crucial importance in Edwards's treatment of the Fall.

The Garden of Glorification

Creating man in the divine image is the nucleus of God's self-replicating scheme. Man was made to exhibit and reproduce the divine being, not as a replacement or substitute for God but as a divine agency or channel: a mental existence of/from God for/to God. In a word, man displays God's ideal of Himself in visible form. Consequently, the powers that God gives to man give him the dominion in this "lower world" and make him, as Edwards says, "to be God with respect to the rest of creation."[70]

In the Garden of Eden, then, Edwards's complex system of idealism and dispositional ontology become concrete and meaningful for both God and man. There, God's plan in creating the world with respect to redemption is initiated in its external actualization. The end of creation, we recall, is to replicate God's prior internal actuality *ad extra*. In time and space God's beautifying disposition "enlarges" through the perceptions of intelligent beings and thereby is "greatly glorified."[71] With respect to the inception of a perceivable world, this process of communicating the idea of a beautiful matrix of existences (God *ad extra*) is initiated with the world-perception of the angels. After all, "the end of all created existences," according to Edwards, is to mentally facilitate the external "repetition" of the

---

69. *WJE* 1:142.

70. 230. [L. 2v.]. Sermon on Matthew 10:17 (1732), *WJE Online* 47. Cf. "Miscellanies," no. 383, *WJE* 13:451–52.

71. "End of Creation" in *WJE* 8:435.

divine beautifying disposition.[72] But the angels were only capable of fulfilling this role in a limited sense, there were a number of things they were incapable of perceiving due to the inferior status of their mental arbitrariness[73] and their station in another dimension of created reality. By their conscious agency the network of existences may be actualized as to secondary beauties and therefore the physical world or the world of senses may be all present at once, but this does not argue that the primary beauty, the beauty between God's mind and other intelligent perceiving minds' perception of His excellency mediated through a beautiful matrix and their own divine image, would be manifest. Because God's beauty is such an arbitrary beauty its communication must be more direct, immediate, and complex: hence the need for the presence of the *imago Dei* in nature in order to actuate the full reality of God's primary beauty which is only represented in secondary beauties. So while the world may be said to exist upon the perception of a single angel at one point during the creation,[74] yet there would remain a need for intelligent perceiving minds fashioned in His image in *this* realm. This was Adam's initial epistemological purpose.

Not only is Adam's God-saturated-reality perception dependent which, of course, makes it subjectivistic in terms of human experience of time, environment, and society, but also it carries with it an in-built epistemological safeguard for objectivity and truth. The truth of reality (that is, "proper" knowledge of what is real in terms of spiritual, moral, and mental existence) depends upon a correspondence between the spiritual reality and a mental receptacle, explained elsewhere as the sharing in God's objective ideas. "Holiness," for Edwards, functions as the *conditio sine qua non* or link between spiritual reality and spiritual perception. His epistemology, then, is fundamentally theocentric in two ways: God is always the object of all proper knowledge; and all proper knowledge is Spirit-dependent.

The concept of holiness is important to Edwards, not only because it provides a key to the resolution of the puzzling issues of his own conversion experience and perception of the world, but also a philosophical-theological answer to his investigations into the end of creation and man's religious role therein. For this reason, we sometimes find holiness presented in his meditations as an abstract, *a priori* concept *and* experience— an *experienced idea*, in effect. As such, it is the dynamic mediator between the Divine Being and earthly being, or between truth and reality. Only that which is mentally holy conforms to the supreme Spirit of God to the end that its perceptions and knowledge of truth are finally consonant and accurate. Adam, then, was imbued with a principle that transfigured both nature and spiritual reality, revealing an ultimate harmony between the spheres of "religion" and experience. Even while venturing into the abstractions of teleologically loaded epistemology, Edwards does not neglect a more traditionally theological

---

72. Ibid., 436–39.

73. In "Miscellanies," no. 1263, Jonathan Edwards explains that "the higher we ascend in the scale of created existence and the nearer we come to the Creator, the more and more arbitrary we should find the divine operations in the creature" (*WJE* 23:203). Through this argument Jonathan Edwards leads his readers to the conclusion that the divine operations in/upon the creature are more arbitrary (less constrained by laws) proportionate to the creature's likeness to God in terms of arbitrariness.

74. "Miscellanies," no. 438, *WJE* 13:487.

description of this process of God actuating His temporal presence: the Holy Spirit and His epistemic operations are constantly emphasized in his subjective or experiential and thus psychological depiction of reality.

Holiness in man is man's ineffably profound fitness to image forth God's glorious being through everlasting knowledge, joy, and happiness in God. Edwards not only had a different idea as to how the image of God consisted in "gifts" bestowed upon man at creation, but also what the purpose of these gifts were for. Granted, Edwards and his Calvinist predecessors and counterparts employed the same phraseology when speaking about the means and manifestation of God's presence and glorification. But Edwards's vision of the communicative activities of God through that image was much more sophisticated and dynamic. What made Adam unique was the dispositional governance of the Holy Spirit that turned essential dispositions outward to nature, others, and, first and foremost, God. It was God or, better, the Holiness of God, who extended man's relations to all other things.[75]

The created order, then, also stands as a medium of accommodation for God to communicate Himself intelligibly to the mental capacities of man, to the end that the concreteness of the world conveys, by association, things spiritual, moral, and mental.[76]

By emphasizing the mind's "seeing" or perceiving a visionary present in terms of such intensity that things are not merely felt and known but experienced as mediatorial relevancies between perceptions in the mind and what exists in the phenomenal universe of God, Edwards clearly presents a world that is, above all, qualitative not quantitative.

Edwards highly values the mediating position of reason, nature, society, and history. As Elwood explains it, "His is a realistic concept of immediacy in which God enters directly into our consciousness 'in, with, and under' . . . our total environment."[77] In other words, God has been pleased to mediate Himself to accommodate the creature's inferiority to His infinite and Holy being through time (to slowly communicate to the creature's comprehension the ultimately incomprehensible), and reason (that the creature may begin to commune and understanding the Creator), and society (which is a model of the relationship between the dependent and serving creature and the Creator), and nature (preparing them to absorb the attributes of God).[78] Whereas earlier Reformed theologians tended to believe that the Bible speaks of man, as a rule, not in his relation to nature, but in his distinction from it, Edwards insisted that although man is conscious of his distinctiveness, he is nonetheless intimately and indispensably related to nature for the existence of both.

∼

Adam's knowledge and experience of God, nature, and self-discovery, was not static, but rather a continuous, progressive perception of the spiritual through what could be dubbed

---

75. *WJE* 3:231. In *Original Sin*, Jonathan Edwards explains that Adam, by virtue of the influential governing of the principle of holiness within him, "chose" and "regarded" excellence and beauty.

76. "Miscellanies," no. 42, *WJE* 13:224.

77. Elwood, *PTJE*, 24.

78. Ibid.

"ordinary experience." His conscious existence was an unbroken intuitive response to the reality of God's communicated presence. Consequently, "Adam's perfection in holiness did not render utterly impossible that he should love God more."[79]

As Adam's knowledge and experience of God progressed through perceiving primary beauty in himself and nature, so too God's excellencies were replicated in greater degrees.[80] The body was (is) instrumental in this process because through it man perceives certain divine perfections, thus providing a means by which rational reflection and passional affections may take place and be intensified. In Edwards, affections and passions are well expressed through the body. Thus, the body itself is "fittingly" capable of denoting those dispositions of mind, which, he says, "exceedingly readily will appear in their bodies, the bodies being more easily and naturally susceptive and manifestive of the affections and dispositions of the mind."[81]

So, while man's dispositional holiness provides an intellectual view by which God is seen, that is, the soul by virtue of its union has in itself those powers whereby it is capable of apprehending spiritual objects without looking through the windows of the outward senses, yet those outward senses are vital for providing a living encounter with the Eternal Presence that confronts man along the entire range of spatiotemporal living.

Thus, through the interrelatedness and connectedness of all things, to one degree or another, the self-communication/expansion/glorification of God extends to the whole of creation. Since the whole of the created order is an expression and replication of the inner actuality of God's fullness, God's relation is excellent. As a result, the idea of the interrelatedness of the whole of the cosmic order or network of existences links non-sentient entities, simple equalities, intelligent perceiving beings, and, of course, primary beauty, in the process of divine self-communication, expansion, and glorification.[82]

Man's individuality is experienced not in terms of actual independence of being, but in terms of self-consciousness in organic relatedness. Man alone, of all creation, is equipped to participate directly and consciously in his environment. Animals participate indirectly and impersonally, that is, without the conscious experience of self and relation to other selves; they are not "religious." Man, however, lives in conscious encounter with his environment aware that the world he perceives is a world replete with the spiritual and moral reality of God. This encounter must continue forever if it is to be meaningful to God and man. Edwards's doctrine of immortality is, therefore, principally associated with the *purpose* of existence, not the incorruptible substance of the soul. The soul is immortal for the simple reason that God's ideal purposes concerning the soul are eternal.[83] The way of

---

79. "Miscellanies," no. 894, *WJE* 20:153.
80. "Miscellanies," no. 662, *WJE* 18:200.
81. "Miscellanies," nos. 174 and 149, *WJE* 13:325, 301.
82. "Miscellanies," no. 547, *WJE* 18:93–95. Cf. *WJE* 8:532. Lee explores the possibilities of God's self-enlargement through the natural order in "Edwards on God and Nature" in *Edwards in Our Time*, 15–44.
83. "Miscellanies," no. 1006, *WJE* 20:334–35. Jonathan Edwards reminds his readers that God could, if He so pleased, extinguish all created existences. God is under "no obligations" to created beings, and created beings cannot persevere without the continued exercise of divine power (*Banner-Works* 2:4–5). This is to omit the intra-trinitarian covenantal obligations within the divine confederation concerning redemption.

telic-ontology to the knowledge of God is superior to the way of cosmology and etiology: hence Edwards's man-made-for-religion thesis. Adam was gifted with "the strength and comprehension of mind sufficient to have a clear idea of general and universal being, or, which is the same thing, of the infinite, eternal, most perfect divine Nature and Essence," for the express purpose of mentally replicating the "divine Nature and Essence."[84] Adam initiated this process at the highest level when he was the agent of divine glorification in the Garden of Eden; but just as the angels could not fulfill certain conditions to replicate God equivalent to His arbitrariness, so too Adam, in his concreated state, could not replicate God in His perfect image of Himself as Savior and Redeemer. Something redeemable was needed: a fall from grace was in order.

84. *WJE* 1:182.

The First Sin

> 'Tis easy to observe that wisdom of God, that seeing He designed [man] for such a height of glory, that it should be so ordered that he should be brought to it from the lowest depths of wretchedness and vileness.
>
> —"Miscellanies" no. 571

A Dispositional Account of the Fall

WITH THE ABOVE QUOTE FROM "MISCELLANIES" NO. 571,[1] WE HAVE ONE OF EDWARDS'S theodicies for the Fall and presence of evil in God's universe. It argues in terms of comparative appreciation for blessedness from the perspective of man. But this theodicy, like others that pertain to maximal good,[2] is "ordered" by two laws operating in Edwards's system.

1. The "principle of subordination and dependence" or "derivativeness" that runs through all nature and grace. This law is a necessary element in Edwards's conception of God's primordial and structured decision to "enlarge" Himself in an "orderly" way.

2. The "law of progression," in which there is a methodological movement to God's linear ordering and completion of the redemption scheme, and by which lower ends are typical of the higher, and introductory to them.

Principle "1" orders the theological hierarchy of God's thematic decrees. The eternal *pactum salutis* possesses, as its substance, a "confederation" among the members of the triune Godhead that the Father would "accomplish the glory of the blessed Trinity in an exceeding degree" by "repeating" the Divine Being's perfect image of Himself through

---

1. "Miscellanies," no. 571, *WJE* 18:110.

2. In several places Jonathan Edwards essentially repeats the central thesis of Leibniz' *Essays in Theodicy* (1710), namely that the existence of evil is a necessary condition of the existence of the greatest moral good. Jonathan Edwards also argued in his "Miscellanies" and sermons that Adam also had an imperfect knowledge of evil. According to Jonathan Edwards, experiential knowledge of evil prior to the encounter at the Tree of Knowledge of Good and Evil is ruled out by virtue of the account of the Fall. In this theodicy, the "lively perception of good" properly depends on the knowledge of its contrary evil, that "there was much attained of new knowledge of good, as there was knowledge of evil; and this was the end of it principally, the knowledge of good" ("Miscellanies," no. 172, *WJE* 13:324).

a scheme of redemption. All other regulative decrees, such as providence and creation, are subordinate and derivative of this "covenant of redemption [which] never had a beginning."[3] The redemption scheme "confederated upon" yields other subordinate thematic decrees, namely providence and, subordinate to providence, creation.[4]

Principle "2" chiefly pertains to the *ordo salutis* and *historia salutis* agreeable to the controlling *pactum*. The "law of progression" offers a logical and specific ordering of the details that subsist within the larger thematic decrees. If God is to get His glory through a redemption narrative, then something will be put into a redeemable position. That "something," of course, is man. The *ordo salutis* spells out the logical issue and execution of the divine decrees within the overarching scheme of redemption. The historical ordering and unfolding of the decrees are in themselves traceable revelatory items.

Edwards tempers what otherwise would be hyper-supralapsarianism (where the decrees of redemption and a fallen subject precede creation) by adopting early in his theological career Peter van Mastricht's mediating position on predestination. Stephen Holmes succinctly states Edwards's position: "God's decision that some creatures should share His love is dependent only on God's ultimate end ... described as "glorifying his love and communicating his goodness." The decree that this should happen through God being merciful to undeserving creatures, by contrast, is logically dependent on the Fall. The fact of election is decreed *supra lapsus*; the form of election *infra lapsus*."[5]

So, then, man is created for the glory of God, because man is a proper means of it. Edwards wants to say with his Dutch and Genevan counterparts that everything else that God decrees concerning man is in intention *after* this end, "because they are all a means of it."

The logic stands clear enough, but sin and evil are no less vital to God's act of self-glorification. In Edwards's aesthetic ontology, "irregularities" are necessary for an infinitely excellent being; complex beauty requires it. Theologically and morally this translates into the involvement of fallen intelligent beings. In Edwards's mind, God not only *wants* the fall, but also (in both an ontological and epistemological sense) *requires* it. He does not stop short of actually saying it either: a fall is necessary for a redemption scheme; it is necessary for *bona fide* replication of the divine perfections according to "Miscellanies" no. 553: "There are many of the divine attributes that, if God had not created the world, never would have had any exercise: the power of God, the wisdom and prudence and contrivance of God, and the goodness and mercy and grace of God, and the justice of God."[6] "Miscellanies" no.348 is even more specific, more explicit: "'Tis necessary that God's awful majesty, his authority and dreadful greatness, justice and holiness should be manifested. But this could not be unless sin and punishment had been decreed ... The shining forth of God's glory would be very imperfect ... without them.[7]

   3. *Sermon One*, *WJE* 9:119.
   4. "Miscellanies," no. 993, *WJE* 20:323.
   5. Holmes, *God of Grace*, 129. See "Miscellanies," no. 292 (*WJE* 13:383–84) where Jonathan Edwards admits his reliance upon Mastricht and Turretin on matters of predestination, and cites Mastricht, *Theoretico-Practica Theologia*, Lib. III, cap.2; and Turretin, *Institutio*, 2:376–86.
   6. "Miscellanies," no. 553, *WJE* 18:97.
   7. "Miscellanies," no. 348, *WJE* 13:419–20.

God desires and requires a fall because Adam neither needed nor could appreciate the full revelation of God. If no fall, then no redemptive nature meaningfully replicated, no divine exercise in effulgence, no spouse for Christ, and so on. Man, for Edwards, was intended to perceive the "excellencies" of God through Jesus Christ. This was the end of religion and therefore the end of the creation. It takes a redemption scheme that presupposes an object of redemption to perceive the attributes of mercy, grace, and justice, to name a few. Ultimately, then, Edwards is uncompromisingly supralapsarian. Holmes has it right where he says, "Regardless of the place of the decree of reprobation [or the Fall], God's first thought is emphatically that He will redeem, not that He will create."[8]

A New Approach to an Old Problem

Since fallenness indispensably serves God's glory and was eternally decreed, temporally orchestrated and unalterably brought about by Him, Edwards's typical theodicies, in which he states that God is "under no obligation in justice to determine that man surely shall not fall" because "'tis much better that the determination should be left to the good pleasure of an infinitely wise being, than to blind causes," become red herring defenses about arbitrariness.[9] The real issue for Edwards concerns the vindication of God from the usual charge of "the author of sin" from the likes of Taylor, by accounting for the "spontaneous" rise of a sinful inclination in Adam. Fully conscious that the plausibility of both his disputation with Taylor and aesthetic/telic-oriented vision of reality rests in no small part on an internally consistent and adequate account of the Fall, Edwards gives considerable attention to the issue.[10]

He typically begins his discussion, as he does in the following excerpt, with the announcement of human culpability: "The act of our first father in eating the forbidden fruit was a very heinous act";[11] which, in turn, either precedes or trails an intimation of God's exculpation through the doctrine of concreation. "Eating the fruit" encapsulates all that entails Adam's first sin, an act that rendered himself and all of his posterity "odious and abominable to God."[12] Whether the fruit was real or merely figurative is uncertain: Edwards speaks baldly of "the fruit of the tree." Either way it is irrelevant for Edwards: the *real* sin occurred before the action, specifically in Adam having "a mind to be like God" and "imagining" that "knowing good and evil . . . would be a great exaltation of [his] nature."[13] The volitional act was simply the outward product of an inward occurrence. The responsibility, guilt, and cause of the sin wholly lay in Adam. Of course, the problem with

---

8. Holmes, *God of Grace*, 131.

9. "Miscellanies," no. 490, *WJE* 13:534.

10. Dozens of sermons offer substantial discussions on the Fall, with no less than nine expounding it as the main doctrine. Jonathan Edwards also lists fifteen entries under the heading of the "Fall" in his "Table to the Miscellanies." At least as many entries intimately relate to the Fall or discuss it in corollaries, as do the "Book of Controversies," *Original Sin, Freedom of the Will*, and *Religious Affections*.

11. 504. [L. 3r] "Doc" for four Sermons on Gen 3:11 (Feb. 1738), *WJE Online* 54.

12. *East of Eden* (1731), *WJE* 17:336.

13. Ibid.

exonerating God from charges of creating an automaton or having any such causal influence on man invites the question: What occurred in Adam?

This question historically has been Augustinian theology's *onus probandi*: How could a being created with *originalis iustitiae* and inclined solely to holiness, will to do evil? Edwards himself invites the same scrutiny when he says in the midst of one sentence: "This is doubtless true: for although there was no natural sinful inclination in Adam, yet an inclination to that sin of eating the forbidden fruit, was begotten in him."[14] Clyde Holbrook reiterates the problem as it relates to Edwards: "Once having established Adam's original righteousness, how could he explain the take-over of the lower faculties? The withdrawal of the supernatural principles *followed and did not precede or cause* the fall itself. Whence then arose Adam's inclination to sin, since, by Edwards's own oft-repeated thesis, a cause must be found for every act?"[15] Holbrook goes on to describe Edwards's attempted solution to Adam's first sin as "nothing more than circular reasoning" and "inconsistent."[16] Is Edwards's defense of original sin in *Original Sin* just another exercise in the long list of failed attempts to reconcile this paradox?

Philosopher John Kearney does not think so. He examines Edwards's account of Adam's first sin and judges it "coherent and adequate."[17] Opposing Holbrook, Storms, Gerstner, Crabtree, Sam Logan, Jr., and an unnamed consensus of Edwards commentators, Kearney offers from Edwards a three-part solution to the problem of Adam's fall, consisting of: (1) a distinction between "sufficient" and "efficacious" grace; (2) the "perversion" of Adam's rational will; and (3) Adam's imperfection as a creature.[18] Kearney asserts that the combination of these three conditions not only supply a rational account of the fall, but vindicate God from the usual charge as the author of sin.[19]

Though Kearney's final conclusion may be correct, his approach nonetheless should be rejected. Kearney pursues a resolution of Edwards's position through a faulty analysis of "sufficient" and "efficacious" grace, which, in the end, contradicts his thesis.[20] The internal coherence of Edwards's account of the Fall results from following the logic of his dispositional ontology, not a distinction between "sufficient" and "efficacious" grace.

Confusion over Edwards's position begins with his statements in "Miscellanies" no. 290, where he says: "If it be inquired how man came to sin, seeing he had no sinful inclinations in him, except God took away his grace from him that he had been wont to give him and so let him fall, I answer there was no need of that; there was no need of taking away any that had been given him, but he sinned under that temptation because God did not give him more."[21] Although a sufficient *cause* for the Fall is not addressed in this quote, differentiated graces are spoken of by Edwards: the grace Adam possessed while he was

---

14. *WJE* 3:228–29 n.6.
15. Holbrook, "Editor's Introduction," *WJE* 3:51. Emphasis added.
16. Ibid.
17. Kearney, "Jonathan Edwards' Account of Adam's First Sin," 127–41.
18. Ibid., 128.
19. He defends the latter point in his article, "Jonathan Edwards and the 'Author of Sin' Charge," 10–16.
20. See to this thesis Appendix B: "Sufficient and Efficacious Grace."
21. *WJE* 13:382.

"perfectly innocent," which was his "original righteousness," and grace withheld from him, i.e., "confirming grace, that grace which is given now in heaven, such grace as shall fit the soul to surmount every temptation."[22] But the effectualness of grace applied—whether sufficient or efficacious—is a moot point; that is *not* the issue in the Fall; the government of the indwelling Spirit is the issue.

By distinguishing between applications of grace rather than kinds, two problems could be addressed: (1) the familiar charge by Arminians, Socinians, Taylor, etc., against the Calvinists' logic, which, they believed, led to "God as the author of sin"; and (2) introducing sin without retreating from the insistence on original righteousness. Edwards addresses these problems by first critiquing his tradition from within. He does not believe the question, "How could a being created with original righteousness and inclined solely to holiness, will to do evil?" really is the right question. "Original righteousness" is neither a sole inclination to righteousness nor God "pointing Adam in the right direction" (Kearney's claim). Rather, it is Adam's possession of a disposition of love to God and holiness.[23]

His sole natural inclination was toward himself: the essential exercising of the self-love disposition, per the specification of his telic-oriented essential constitution. The Holy Spirit governing the natural principle of self-love by a superior principle of God-relatedness made man originally righteous, holy, and perfect. Consequently, the questions for Edwards were: (1) In what fashion did the Holy Spirit govern Adam; and (2) What were the circumstances that attributed to the cause of the first sin?

Concerning the first question, Anri Morimoto wishes to say that a gracious disposition in man functions with nomological necessity when certain conditions are fulfilled. That is, the principle of grace (i.e., the Spirit) acts in an identifiable law-like fashion in accord with prescriptive rules and is, therefore, scrutable under cause and effect analysis. But Edwards nowhere says this. Instead, the Spirit acts with unpredictable arbitrariness; save upon the instance of infusion. So while the nature of a disposition effects its enactment upon initial possession, that is, "a habit [or disposition] of grace . . . is always begun with an act of grace that shall imply faith in it, because a habit can be of no manner of use till there is occasion to assert it,"[24] yet the Spirit may suspend His governing influence without

---

22. Ibid.

23. This is where Kearney's analysis falters: he equates original righteousness with what he understands to be Jonathan Edwards's two-fold definition or usage of sufficient grace: (1) that Adam was created with an inclination to "right action" (a bias toward good); and (2) that Adam was originally a free agent with respect to his "whole will" and his "rational will" ("Adam's First Sin," 128, 131). The issue of "actual grace" is, however, entirely omitted by Kearney, as if Jonathan Edwards were silent on the point. By not equating sufficient grace and original righteousness with actual grace or the indwelling governance of the Holy Spirit, Kearney completely misconstrues the crux of Jonathan Edwards's theodicy. So instead of adequately investigating Jonathan Edwards's statements on grace outside of *Original Sin*, Kearney forges ahead to subsume the superior principles (which Kearney inadequately defines as "a 'sense' of duty to God and love of duty to God") within his two-fold definition of sufficient grace (ibid., 136). The problem for Kearney remains the same as the Augustinian tradition—Adam's "'sense' of duty . . . and love of duty to God" are withdrawn *after* the fall: for how else could Adam be, as Jonathan Edwards would say, "wholly given to wickedness"? If Adam retained anything of the sufficient grace which Kearney has all but naturalized, then one could argue that Jonathan Edwards permitted a place for works righteousness—a thing totally repugnant to his soteriological thought.

24. "Miscellanies," No. 241, *WJE* 13:358. See also chapter 12.

rendering original righteousness void. Though this may seem unfair, for Edwards it is really a matter of perspective: the Spirit may justly withhold or remove His grace from the impeccable because the retention of man's original status is an inferior and subordinate "end" to God's principal ends in redemption. The standing and falling of man is simply a means to something more important to the will of God.[25]

A consequence of the supernatural operation of the superior principle is that it immediately depends upon "*man's union and communion with God, or divine communications and influences of God's Spirit.*"[26] Thus, in order to maintain a declaration of "perfect innocence or righteousness," Edwards must say that "from the beginning he [Adam] had a supreme and perfect respect and love to God: and if so, he was created with such a principle."[27] From the first, then, the Spirit governed Adam's conscious existence, that is, his self-love disposition. This governing was a gracious governing, sufficient to prevent the Fall when exercised by the Holy Spirit. But Edwards unequivocally asserts that God neither was obligated to constantly govern nor was it His intention to do so. God may suspend the governance of the Spirit without compromising Adam's *status integritatis* or abrogating His justice, which thing He did during or just prior to the provocation.

According to Edwards, God's purpose in suspending the governance of the Spirit was to test Adam during his probationary period: hence the meaningfulness of the divine injunction, promise, and cautionary. If God were not addressing Adam as on trial, the admonition of death would be an idle threat. God, however, tested man to see if Adam would under specific circumstances adjudicate rightly and exercise his self-love disposition in accord with Being in general. This is what Edwards means by "sufficient" grace—that "Adam had sufficient *assistance* of God *always present with him* to have enabled him to obey if he had used his natural abilities in endeavoring it."[28] Edwards chooses his words quite intentionally, "it was *present* with him." He does not say that it was actively and therefore efficaciously governing him at that precise moment. His sermon on Romans 5:6 makes this point explicit.[29]

When the Spirit withdraws or suspends His governing powers He disengages His dispositional influence over the "less noble principles." The superior principles are present, but not active. Under such circumstances the self-love disposition and the disposition of love to God are "entirely distinct and don't enter one into the nature of the other at all."[30] Adam, for all intents and purposes, was left on the occasion of the provocation to adjudicate the situation according to "the extraordinary freedom" that he possessed.[31]

The discussion on Adam's freedom in "Miscellanies" nos. 501 and 436 becomes crucially important now that the Spirit has been subtracted from the equation. In no. 501 Edwards writes: "Man might be deceived, so that he should not be disposed to use his

---

25. This idea is implicitly found throughout *A History of the Work of Redemption* and *End of Creation*.
26. *WJE* 3:381–82. Italics added.
27. Ibid., 230.
28. "Miscellanies," no. 501, *WJE* 18:51. Emphasis added.
29. *Our Weakness, Christ's Strength* (1735), *WJE* 19:382.
30. "Miscellanies," no. 530, *WJE* 18:134.
31. Ibid.

endeavors to persevere; but if he did use his endeavors, there was a sufficient assistance always with him to enable him to persevere. See No. 436."[32] Setting aside "sufficient grace," Edwards presents a man with natural abilities or "endeavors," which, if fully utilized, would preserve man through most, but not all, circumstances. Man's "endeavors" are explained in "Miscellanies" no. 436 in terms of the freedom he possessed prior to his lapse. There Edwards begins by saying that upright Adam possessed a freedom of will different than fallen Adam. Since the Fall man has, as it were, a bifurcated will, "a will against a will." He describes these "two wills" as the *rational will* and the *appetite*, together forming "the whole will." The rational will is man's "rational judgment of what is best for him." Its functioning falls within the boundaries of reasoning, the utilization of logic and judicious principles to discern what is best for him. The other will or inclination arises from the "liveliness and intenseness of the idea, or sensibleness of the good of the object presented to the mind, which we may call appetite."[33] This will of appetite is against or contrary to the "reason and judgment of the rational will" and "begets a contrary inclination." In fallen man and natural-men the appetite has overthrown the rational will and keeps it subjection. "So that although man with respect to his whole will, compounded of these two (either arising from the addition of them together when they concur, or the excess of one above the other when they are opposite), is always a free agent," write Edwards, "yet with respect to his rational will, or that part of his inclination which arises from a mere rational judgment of what is best for himself, he is not a free agent, but is enslaved; he is a servant of sin.[34]

The case with Adam's original state, however, was altogether different, at least up to the point of his first sin. His rational will was not subjugated to the inclination of appetite. Instead, the appetite worked in conjunction, harmony, and acquiescence to the rational will. The rational will was free in just the same manner as the "whole will." Sufficient grace simply *rendered* man a free agent, not only with respect to his whole will, but his rational will, or "the will that arose from a rational judgment of what was indeed best for himself."[35] It was not the freedom itself, merely the ordering of the appetite so that the rational will, whether governed by the third disposition or not, could will with strength above and beyond the appetite. He could arbitrate more dispassionately. He had a certain *enkrateia*—strength of will, continence, self-control; what Edwards calls "primitive strength."[36]

The pieces are now in place to give account of the *cause* of the sinful act that Holbrook seeks. Edwards knows that whatever the *causa efficiens* might be, it cannot be spontaneously generated: to argue for a spontaneous free choice would, of course, undermine his magisterial work *Freedom of the Will*, and play right into the hands of the Arminians. According to Edwards, the cause was always there: It is the self-love disposition. There are, however, several contributing factors, all of which pivot on the possibility of "the

---

32. "Miscellanies," no. 501, *WJE* 18:51. The reference is to "Miscellanies," no. 436: "ADAM'S FALL." (*WJE* 13:484–86).

33. *WJE* 13:484.

34. Ibid., 484–85.

35. Ibid.

36. *Our Weakness, Christ's Strength* (1735), *WJE* 19:382.

whole will" freely arbitrating. On this critical point, Edwards seems to have imbibed Malebranche's thesis from the 1680 *Treatise on Nature and Grace* concerning the suspension or subjugation of the appetite to rational arbitration.

In a discussion on whether sufficient grace and efficacious grace are intrinsically the same, Malebranche said that actual grace, like other motives, is *not* invincible or efficacious by itself with respect to consent to the inclination efficaciously induced in the will.[37] Though Edwards, of course, could not agree (because, for him, such grace, which is both united to the soul *and* assertive, actually exemplifies invincibility—the logic of superior dispositions, as well as the principle of subordination, control the outcome), yet he was attracted to the idea which supports it, namely, that whether, on a given occasion, specific actual grace will turn out to be efficacious with respect to a given agent's consent or merely sufficient (and, hence, not efficacious) depends upon free choices of the agent in question in the circumstances then current. Thus, while on the one hand, Malebranche held that God's total causal contribution to creation up to and including the instant at which a free creaturely choice occurs—a consent or non-consent to a volition—is metaphysically and physically consistent with the non-occurrence of that choice; Edwards, on the other hand, redefined Malebranche's "sufficient grace" as "suspended grace," thereby removing it from the equation, and then spoke of transient circumstantial causes as the *causa deficiens* contributing to the *causa efficiens* of the whole will, which is primarily moved by the rational will. It seems as if Malebranche may have supplied the basic ideas concerning "perfect freedom," the suspension of consent, and gracious motives, but Edwards recast the whole in a dispositional mold.

Thinking in terms of neatly defined dispositions, some natural, some supernatural, Edwards strictly links the possibility of passional willing "primary beauty'" with the *active* governing of the disposition of love to God: "I say, this must be meant by his having sufficient grace, viz. that he had grace sufficient to render him a free agent, not only with respect to [his] whole will, but with respect to his rational, or the will that arose from a rational judgment of what was indeed best for himself."[38] When Edwards says, "his judgment of what is best for himself," he does not mean Adam's judgment of what is best "absolutely." As he explains, the mind's sense of the "absolute loveliness" (or, in his aesthetic terminology—primary beauty) of a thing directly influences only the will of appetite. Only a disposition of love to God, then, may directly influence the will of appetite in cases of absolute loveliness or primary beauty. This is significant because only the primary beauty of a thing can draw the appetite. Thus, the self-love disposition does not and cannot be drawn to primary beauty unless actively governed by that which gives direct access to it. The agent, operating on the basis of a free rational will, may only have primary beauty *indirectly influence* it, as the judgment may be convinced that "what is most lovely in itself will be best for him and most for his happiness." Rationally judging that a thing is "lovely in itself," devoid of an affectional sensibleness of its primary beauty, according to Edwards, "signifies nothing towards influencing the will, except it be in this

---

37. Malebranche, *Oeuvres completes*, 7:353–56.
38. "Miscellanies," no. 436, *WJE* 13:485.

way, that he thinks it will therefore be best some way or other for himself." According to Edwards's logic of dispositions, if an agent (Adam) merely rationally adjudicates that a thing is "lovely," but does not have a sensibleness of its primary beauty, and simultaneously does not believe it absolutely best for himself (that is, the primary beauty of it is not invincible), then "he will never choose it"; though if he is sensible of the primary beauty of it "to a strong degree," he may will it, "though he thinks 'tis not [absolutely] best for himself." Perhaps consciously following the logic Malebranche offers in *Méditations chrétiennes et métaphysiques*, Edwards then concludes:

> Hence it follows that a person, with respect to his rational will, may be perfectly free and yet may refuse that which he at the same time rationally judges to be in itself most lovely and becoming, and will that which he rationally knows to be hateful. Therefore man, having that sufficient grace as to render him quite free with respect to his rational will (or his will arising from mere judgment of what was best for himself) could not fall without having that judgment deceived, and being made to think that to be best for himself which was not so, and so having his rational will perverted.[39]

The test implied that man was able to withstand certain temptations: Adam would have adjudicated rightly in most circumstances. However, by the "extraordinary manifestation of God's sovereignty," there was at least one circumstance in which Adam would not choose correctly, namely, circumstances in which his mind was deceived. The goal "to be as God" was deemed rationally good; the "whole will" was taken up in the natural movement of the self-love disposition; man did not employ his "endeavors" (i.e., appetite), leaving him to willfully but wrongfully choose that deemed best for himself under those unwieldy circumstances. "God," explains Edwards, "might so order [man's] circumstances, that from these circumstances, together with his withholding further assistance and divine influence, his sin would infallibly follow."[40]

So, on the one hand, man with the Spirit was *posse non peccare* and, on the other hand, under divinely orchestrated "infallible" circumstances, in which the Spirit's governance was temporarily suspended, he was only *posse peccare*. Man under those circumstances was only acting according to how God had made him, and when he sinned, Edwards insists, only he was culpable.

Does suspending sufficient grace, withholding confirming grace, giving man a relatively unstable constitution, and providentially fixing "coincidental circumstances" (which triggered the fall) make God culpable to the charge of "author of sin"? Edwards says, absolutely not. Man choosing out of the rational exercises of the self-love disposition is not a divinely implanted seminal principle of contrary inclination (Augustine's *rationes seminales*). Neither does Adam's mutability reflect upon the creator: it is simply a *condito sine qua non* of finite existence (per Augustine). Moreover, Adam's failing deliberation is an instance of deception, a "perversion" of the will, not incontinence. But, like the following excerpt from *Freedom of the Will*, Edwards is willing to indicate a "yes" to *causa deficiens*:

39. Ibid. Cf. Malebranche, *Oeuvres completes*, 10:66.
40. *WJE* 1:413.

> Therefore I sometimes use the word "cause," in this inquiry, to signify any antecedent, either natural or moral, positive or negative, on which an event, either a thing, or the manner and circumstances of a thing, so depends, that it is the ground and reason, either in whole or part, why it is, rather than not; or why it is, rather than otherwise; or, in other words, any antecedent with which a consequent event is so connected, that it truly belongs to the reason why the proposition which affirms that event, is true; whether it has any positive influence or not.[41]

One may question whether the comprehensiveness of this definition makes the deficient, as well as the efficient, true causality. In the end, Edwards's privative or negative cause with relation to God seems to fall into the categories of Leibniz's principle of sufficient reason, and, consequently, evokes the conclusion of necessity and, therefore, true and sufficient causality.[42] Certainly if Edwards was emphasizing anything, it was not Taylor's contention that our original parents sinned in the same manner that all men do, by errors of judgment made in ignorance of consequences and with free exercise of choice. Rather, he admitted and emphasized the more difficult conclusion that God created man—not sin—fully knowing that the telic-orientation of man, if left ungoverned under providentially orchestrated circumstances, would certainly result in a fall. Edwards would have his auditors keep in mind that, when it comes to the charge of "GOD THE AUTHOR of sin," that there is a "Difference between the SECRET AND REVEALED WILL OF GOD."[43] "'Tis evident that God may be the orderer of sin for a good and important end, and yet punish that sin severely."[44] That "good and important" end is God's self-manifestation and glorification itself. Although scandalous to moderate Calvinists, yet Edwards had no misgivings teaching this because it was part of his worldview, the logical outcome of his theocentric vision of reality.

~

After an undisclosed time of probationary trial in the garden of Eden, man, if he remained steadfast, was to be "confirmed," and would have been put beyond all possibility of lapsing through an endowment of efficacious or confirming grace.[45] Man's immutability, however, would not have been self-produced nor could it have been self-sustained. According to Edwards, sinning for man was "Not beyond a natural possibility—no creature ever was or ever will be naturally impeccable or naturally incapable of sinning." If man is prevented from sinning and dying, God would have to actively and continuously engage the soul,

---

41. Ibid., 180–81.

42. See Alexander, *Leibniz-Clarke Correspondence*, 16. Simply, the Principle of Sufficient Reason states that "nothing is without a reason" (or "cause" or "because"). In the words of Leibniz, "nothing happens without a reason why it should be so, rather than other wise." (ibid.) For Jonathan Edwards, the "because" is God's overarching plan of self-glorification via redemption. See also James Dana's criticism of Jonathan Edwards's necessitarian and deterministic conclusions in *Examination of the Late Reverend President Edwards's "Enquiry on Freedom of the Will,"* 59ff.

43. "Efficacious Grace, Book [of Controversies] II," *WJE* 21:225.

44. Ibid.

45. "Notes on Scripture," no. 51, *WJE* 15:65.

"as we have all reason now to conclude that it is with the [holy] angels."[46] For Edwards, God determines the ultimate standing or falling of man. The *pactum salutis* guarantees a redeemable subject; the decree and orchestration of the Fall provides necessary subject material.

While sin's origin may be privative in character, the cause of sin abides as a real dispositional principle in man. In a figure from the "Book of Controversies," Edwards encapsulates his whole dispositional theory on the fall and sin's derivation in a scale model: "If there be weight in opposite scales the balance may be kept even but if the weight of one scale be removed the other will have the entire government and will put the balance out of order without and addition."[47] As Holbrook points out, the important phrase here is "without any addition": sin is not a positive entity. However, the cause of sin *is* a positive entity. The law or principle that offsets the scale is the self-love disposition; it *causes* the other side of the scale to drop, and with it, Adam and all his posterity into a morass of sin. As unpleasant and repugnant as it may have appeared to Edwards's eighteenth-century audience, he nonetheless believed it truth from God that was logically demonstrable to all who would consider it in light of Scripture and reason.

The reception and evaluation of Edwards's defense were mixed in the eighteenth and nineteenth centuries. By the twentieth century, however, his efforts to reconcile the problems of the Fall had become anachronistic. Perry Miller, Reinhold Niebuhr, and Clyde Holbrook, for example, while commending instances of philosophical originality within *Original Sin*, either completely dismiss or denounce Edwards's account of the Fall as antiquated "circular reasoning." However, viewing Edwards's treatment in the dispositional terms he originally intended yields a surprisingly consistent, even conceivably adequate account (nothing short of a monumental achievement for his theological tradition). If the later eighteenth or early nineteenth century had produced a study substantiating the coherence and sufficiency of his dispositional treatment in detail, then perhaps the sophistication, innovativeness, and importance of *Original Sin* would have receive recognition comparable to *Freedom of the Will*. But it was not too be: neither New England's mood concerning its forlorn subject matter nor Edwards's weighty presentation offered much of a future for *Original Sin*.

The failure of his eighteenth-century audience and later commentators to pick up on the real issue of dispositions largely rendered his efforts against Taylor fruitless. Notwithstanding this historic failure, Edwards's treatment of the Fall was a central and foundational issue for his system and worldview: it provided a rationale for what God both desired and required for His proper self-glorification, viz., (fallen) agents with epistemic abilities to perceive and replicate attributes that, "never would have had any exercise" if it were not for them.[48]

---

46. *East of Eden* (1731), *WJE* 17:335.
47. Cited by Holbrook, "Editor's Introduction," *WJE* 3:50.
48. "Miscellanies," no. 553, *WJE* 18:97. Cf. "Miscellanies," nos. 348 and 407, *WJE* 13:419–20, 469.

A Species of Sinners

"Immediately upon our first parents eating the forbidden [fruit], God took away His Holy Spirit from him, which left him destitute of original righteousness and all that moral excellency of mind which before he was endowed with, and left him under the dominion of sin."[49] Man's ontological deprivation means that, aesthetically, he has become a comparative "deformity," an "irregularity." Fallen man is not only without superior principles to govern his natural principles, but the natural principles themselves are "injured." Man becomes the embodiment of depravity or "the greatest and only evil" by virtue of his exclusive disposedness toward self-being. Though a natural and defining disposition, the truncated scope of the exercise and sensitivity of a self-loving disposition renders it unharmonious, asymmetrical, and disagreeable with the law of the whole. Human depravity, then, is being exactly the opposite of a "Being in general" minded spirit.[50] It is the governing of the total self by inordinate self-love.

Edwards's dispositional ontology makes it easy for him to distinguish between the destruction of man's *essentia* and the loss of a non-essential disposition. Consequently, the death that sin brought was not so much dehumanizing as it was anti-relational. This is the legacy that Adam left to his posterity, since they not only were constituted in him and share in the first sin as their own, but also because he federally represented them.[51] The effect of the sin—of original sin and Adam's first sin—consists chiefly in their being born without the third relational disposition. The resulting implications are manifold: spiritual and physical death; bondage to sin; no access to primary beauty; etc. And since each soul is an immediate creation of God,[52] God cannot be faulted with creating a sinful being: He simply (and justly) creates a soul with only that which is essential to human being. This is why Edwards insists that infants are morally neutral, not corrupt. But without the superior governing principle to regulate their self-love disposition, they begin to sin "as soon as they are capable of it."[53] That is, with the first motion of their minds, they exercise a restrictively self-referential disposition. This natural but now inordinate (sinful) disposition is invincible and voluntary (since a movement of the will); persisting while the person persists.

So while Adam may have had strength of character and will, it is not the natural-man who is weak-willed; rather, he is in naturally irremediable bondage. The atrocity of sin, then, was not only that it vitiated Adam's entire being but that it was an inescapable self-

---

49. *East of Eden* (1731), *WJE* 17:333.
50. "The Mind," no. 1, *WJE* 6:338. Cf. Fiering, *Moral Thought*, 61–62.
51. *WJE* 3:404–12.
52. "Miscellanies," no. 541, *WJE* 18:89.
53. *WJE* 1:134. Catherine Brekus calls this state "'non-innocent' rather than inherently depraved." She continues by adding, "But because of Edwards' deep sense of human frailty, he insisted that children committed their first sin almost immediately after birth. Tragically, their 'non-innocence' as so brief that [it] was virtually meaningless. As he explained, the 'time of freedom from sin be so small' that it was 'not worthy of notice'" (Brekus, "Suffer the Little Children: Remembering Edwards's Ministry to Families," unpublished paper delivered at the conference: "Jonathan Edwards in Historical Memory," University of Miami, March 2000; *WJE* 1:134–35).

loving energy that could not be conquered by ordinary means. Herein is the tragedy of human existence apart from actual grace: natural-man suffers profound epistemological consequences on account of the fall and does not sensibly perceive his spiritual plight. Man simply continues to will and desire in a sinful manner irrespective of the fact that he can do nothing in his own strength to alter his condition.[54] For the elect, however, Edwards's soteriological answer to *The Modern Prevailing Notions of that Freedom of the Will* is *God Glorified in Man's Dependence*: God breaks through the epistemic darkness with "A Divine and Supernatural Light immediately imparted to the Soul by the Spirit of God."[55]

For the reprobate, however, there is no supernatural light, no glorious Redeemer to administer grace, no answer to their human condition. Reprobate natural-men remain in darkness because they have no knowledge or perception, experience or direct consciousness, of primary beauty or spiritual excellencies.[56]

Edwards articulates a scenario in which reprobates, with only two dispositions and no direct access to the spiritual dimension of reality, serve an ontological function in the replication of God's maximal complex beauty. Ever mindful of his idealist teleological axiom, that the *purpose* of being is to be perceived, Edwards offers a view of world reality in which the reprobate natural-man perceives things which pertain to God's attributes and being, as well as the matrix of existence, so that God gets His glory from their terrestrial existence.

The Reprobate's Window on the World

In "Miscellanies" no. 777, Edwards divides humanity into two classes of perceiving existence: those spiritual beings that have direct access to spiritual knowledge; and those natural beings who do not. What separates the two is an ontological union with the source of spiritual knowledge—"the Spirit of Christ." According to Edwards, when man sinned, "God the Father would have no more to do with man immediately . . . He would henceforth have no concern with man but only through a mediator, either in teaching men or in governing or bestowing any benefits on them."[57] The relational principle at work here says that a created being cannot have an immediate view of another mind without some union of personality. Therefore, no creature can thus have an immediate sight of God or true knowledge of spiritual realities, but only through the Spirit of Jesus Christ.

In saying this, Edwards opens the door for certain knowledge of God to be ever available for the natural-man and those left permanently in that condition, the reprobate. He calls the kind of knowledge they may have "common illumination," a general revelation of the internal sort, whereby one may be innately conscious of the deity through natural sensibilities and conscience. However, it operates in conjunction with general revelation of the external sort: the phenomenal world and history. The two forms of general revelation

---

54. For Jonathan Edwards, it is the born-again Christian who suffers from *akrasia*. Akratic action is a fact of life for the elect in this world, as they wrestle with the existing *semper iustus et peccator*. Their incontinence is exhibited primarily in intentional behavior that conflicts with their own divinely illumined values.

55. *God Glorified in Man's Dependence* (1734), *Banner-Works* 2:12.

56. "Miscellanies," no. 239, *WJE* 13:354–55. This is an idea everywhere present in *Religious Affections*.

57. *Sermon Two, WJE* 9:131.

emerge out of Edwards's single vision of a purposeful creation by the trinity: the world is a divine idea intended to communicate God's perfections (Son and Spirit); it is, as it were, a mechanism of interface between the Divine Ideal and man's perception-existence. This is to say, the world itself is a mediator of sorts, saturated with theological and moral meaning. To be sure, a soteriological chasm is fixed: "Natural-man may have convictions from the Spirit of God, but 'tis from the Spirit of God only as assisting natural principles, and not infusing any new and supernatural principle."[58] Yet, notwithstanding this qualification pertaining to special grace, the natural principles of the reprobate do perceive/receive knowledge in the same way as all other creatures in heaven and earth, namely, by means or manifestations or signifiers originating in God and mediated through Jesus Christ: "Jesus Christ, who alone sees immediately, [is] the grand medium of the knowledge of all other things; they know no otherwise than by the exhibitions held forth in and by him."[59] Thus, whatever reprobates *do* perceive is necessarily something God mediates by Jesus Christ through His Spirit in "manifestations" or "signs held forth."

Of these signs, Edwards identifies in "Miscellanies" no. 777 four sorts "by which anything that is another spiritual being can be manifested, or made known":

1. Images or resemblances;

2. Words or declarations, or voluntary significations, either inward or outward, equivalent to speaking;

3. Effects; and

4. A priori.[60]

In addition, there are two ways of understanding and thinking about the things received by reflection or consciousness: by mere cognition, an indirect view of the things themselves in signs, which is a "kind of mental reading, wherein we don't look on the things themselves (i.e., by the actual presence of their ideas or sensation of their resemblances)"; and, secondly, apprehension, "wherein the mind has a direct *ideal view* or *contemplation* of the thing thought of."[61] Translated into the accessible language of his treatises, the former is that understanding which consists in "mere SPECULATION or the understanding of the head', and the latter, the SENSE OF THE HEART."[62] The reprobate have full and unmitigated access to the former which, due to the interpenetrating nature of the faculties, generates a certain sense of the heart concomitant to perceived/received, indirect ideas about God.

If Edwards were asked what precisely do the reprobate perceive about God, he would reply, extraordinary and common perceptions. Extraordinary perceptions are always associated with gospel "seasons of grace";[63] they are religious and internal, intended either to

---

58. "Miscellanies," no. 626, *WJE* 18:155.
59. "Miscellanies," no. 777, *WJE* 18:428.
60. Ibid., 428–31.
61. Ibid., 428.
62. "Miscellanies," no. 782, *WJE* 18:458–59.
63. *Living Unconverted Under an Eminent Means of Grace* (1729), *WJE* 14:359–70.

divinely prepare a sinner for salvation or "harden his heart" and thereby confirm his just damnation and ultimate reprobation. This is a Spirit-induced "conviction of the truth, and what is called the knowledge of the truth, viz. the truth of the things of revealed religion"; the highest kind of inward motions "that ever the natural-man have."[64] However, when the Spirit "assists" the natural principles, He does not give glimpses into the excellency of Christ, for in Edwards's celebrated analysis of religious affections, whether in the treatise bearing that name or *Distinguishing Marks of a Work of the Sprit of God* or *A Faithful Narrative of the Surprising Work of God*, sensing the "excellency of Christ" functions as *the* distinguishing characteristic of those who have saving union with Christ; it is the encounter with God that converts the soul, whereby "The whole soul . . . doth in a lively manner accord and consent to it, and cleave to it."[65] Reprobates never experience this kind of affectional, faith initiating illumination. In Edwards, the reprobate's inability to sense the "reality" of divine things constitutes the damnable noetic gap between natural-men and spiritual men. Because spiritual excellencies (moral/mental union between minds) "don't seem real to 'em," their only knowledge of religious truth concerns a conviction of evil as the Holy Ghost acts upon them merely as "an external occasional agent."[66] This may be two ways: a conviction of the judgment by reason that evinces the truth of the things of religion, that respects natural good; and a sense of heart of natural good. God assists these principles in common illumination,[67] but always within the context of conviction of sin.

In distinction from the extraordinary, there are common perceptions: "the manifestations [God] makes of himself in the works of creation and providence, and in his providential dealings with them, preserving them, bestowing good things on them, and correcting them for their sins."[68] This is general revelation externally considered, and wherein the reprobate's primary contribution to the replication of God *in this world* commonly consists.

Recalling Edwards's maxim, "Man was made for the purpose of religion," common perceptions qualify as religious ends, though for the reprobate they have no salvific benefit, only enough general revelation to "render them inexcusable."[69] The natural-man "commonly perceives" in universal phenomena God's "power and wisdom." This is to say, the world communicates God's intellectual superiority and supreme power: "But the greatness of vast expanse, immense distance, prodigious bulk and rapid motion," Edwards declares, "is but a little, trivial and childish greatness in comparison of the noble, refined, exalted, divine, spiritual greatness. Yea, these are but the shadow of greatness and are worthless,

64. "Miscellanies," no. 782, *WJE* 18:458–59.

65. *The Threefold World of the Holy Ghost* (1729), *WJE* 14:409; cf. *The Excellencies of Jesus Christ* (1736), *Banner-Works* 1:680–89. *Distinguishing Marks* (1741) and *Faithful Narrative* (1738) are reproduced in *WJE* 4.

66. Ibid. "Natural men think they believe that Christ is savior, etc. They hear a great deal about it, and . . . they don't deny the force of the arguments. Yet for all that, it don't seem real to them." Cf. *Warnings of Future Punishment Don't Seem Real to the Wicked* (1727), *WJE* 14:200–212.

67. *True Grace Distinguished from the Experience of Devils* (1752), *Banner-WJE* 2:46–47.

68. "Miscellanies," no. 706, *WJE* 18:324.

69. *The Justice of God in the Damnation of Sinners* (1734–35), *Banner-Works* 1:668–79; 794. Sermon on Deut 29:4 (Sept. 1745): "DOC. Persons are not at all excused for any moral defect or corruption that is in them" [L. 1v.], *WJE Online* 63.

except as they conduce to true and real greatness and excellency, and manifest the power and wisdom of God.[70]

Spiritual man may perceive "true and real greatness and excellency" (primary beauty), while the natural-man perceives "the power and wisdom of God" that is intrinsic in the medium of creation. But the world of secondary beauties only conveys the moral, mental, and spiritual, even redemption-related (though not redeeming) qualities inherent in nature (per Edwards's panentheism) as "types," "shadows," and "images of divine things" because the world and all of its phenomenological occurrences (to which their epistemic abilities are limited) are not the deity in its most "direct existence." In virtue of this common perception, man voluntarily subdues it to itself *and* necessarily must submit himself in every circumstance of life. This is part of that relation to God-through-the-world (indirect consent to "Being in general") that expresses itself otherwise in the consciousness of existence and freedom and responsibility.[71] In other words, the consciousness of being susceptible, subject and dependent, not merely to natural, but to ethical and divine law, and, ultimately, the Divine Lawgiver.[72]

If the world is a communication from God about God, then Edwards's typological system is it's hermeneutic. Though Edwards expected "ridicule and contempt" for employing and extending typology beyond Scripture into literally every aspect of the human experience—relationships, nature, history, concepts—he knew that the sophistication of his worldview went beyond (in the words of Stephen Holmes) "just another pre-Enlightenment attempt to discover some form of general revelation"; it was thoroughly integrated within his philosophical-theology, his panentheism made types in history and nature inevitable.[73]

---

70. "Miscellanies," no. 42, *WJE* 13:224. Emphasis added.

71. See Fiering, *Moral Thought*, chap 2: "The Moral Achievements of 'Natural Understanding,'" esp. pp. 62–82, where Fiering treats the subjects of "Synteresis," "God's Retribution," "Conscience and Symmetry" and "Beauty," with regard to the natural-man.

72. For a detailed study on the connection between natural law/revelation and typology in Jonathan Edwards's thought see, Cooey-Nichols, *Jonathan Edwards on Nature and Destiny*.

73. *WJE* 11:152; Holmes, *God of Glory*, 105. Traditionally, typology involved the exercise of matching biblical types—prophetic figures, events, or circumstances—in the Old Testament with their antitypes of fulfilling figures, events, or circumstances in the New Testament. To be sure, New England Puritans had a typological tradition of their own. Their warrant for interpreting the Bible typologically did not so much come from Calvin, who approved of typological and allegorical interpretations (*Institutes*, II.11.4), as from the Apostle Paul in Romans 5:14. The dissenting Puritan tradition, however, regulated prophetic or typological interpretations as well as allegorical interpretations of certain texts, by giving prominence to a literal and historical interpretation of the whole of Scripture. Well-known New England advocates of "the plain style" were John Cotton, Thomas Shepard, and Thomas Hooker (see Davis, "The Traditions of Puritan Typology" in Bercovitch, *Typology and Early American Literature*, 37f). Their kind of typological prefiguration and fulfillment, though at times extraordinarily imaginative, never eclipsed the boundaries of the Bible's internal regulative hermeneutic. There was an accepted amount of latitude with regard to extracting types and depicting their antitypes. Dealing with the same text, several ministers could offer varying parallels between types and antitypes, depending on the proximity each would allow between the "typological" revelation and "allegorical" representation. This gave the practice of coupling types and antitypes more the impression of artistic expression than a theoretically objective hermeneutical discipline. And without question, Jonathan Edwards contributed a good deal of artistry to the received practice. But where Jonathan Edwards departed from their hermeneutical tradition and aligned himself with more innovative exegetes (such as Increase and

The world of types, then, is an inescapable part of God's pastoral conversation, a sometimes verbal and, in this case, sometimes non-verbal, communication between the Creator and minds created in His image. Likewise, the creature's understanding of God's pastoral conversation is verbal and non-verbal, Scriptural and phenomenological. For spiritually responsive persons moments of spiritual sensitivity/enlightenment are *given* by divine orchestration and communication through the Spirit. They cannot be artificially conjured up: God is glorified not by partial but total dependence, even with respect to saints.

The redeemed have the potential advantage of refining, as it were, their skills of perception. Mundane experiences, if coupled with the ordinary means by which God works—the Word of God—can (with the aid of the Holy Spirit) transform a routine occurrence into an encounter with God. The non-verbal language of God, if it is ever to be meaningful, must be deciphered by the verbal language of God, Jesus Christ inscripturated and incarnated.[74]

But since in Edwards's predestinarian soteriology God is neither the Father nor Shepherd of the reprobate, it would be better to speak of God's typological communication as "the language of God."[75] It is a language with which God never creases to communicate and man never ceases to perceive in terms of two things, secondary beauties and certain attributes.

Since the reprobates' diminished ontological structure and consequent epistemic restrictions mean that the perception of "true and real greatness and excellency" or primary beauty (as it thematically pertains to redemption-accomplished-and-applied replication) belong only to the regenerate elect, reprobates are left to perceive and replicate (1) secondary beauties, (2) those attributes which all "commonly perceive"—power, wisdom, and justice, and (3) those attributes that "never would have had any exercise," but which do not pertain to redemption-accomplished-and-applied replication, namely, perfect hatred and wrathful power.[76]

Natural-men approach very near to the spiritual consent of minds when they apply their remarkable natural abilities in works of art, philosophy, literature, architecture, mathematics, physical science, and other "noble pursuits," though primary beauty is never properly obtained. Moreover, Edwards would say that the natural-man himself and in

---

Cotton Mather) was in his application of biblical typological principles to nature and history. He continually pushed beyond conventional parameters and applied his philosophy of typology to contemporary historical events and natural phenomena. Such an unconventional practice of amplifying correspondence between the natural/historical world and themes thought to be reserve for special revelation, predictably invoked disparaging challenges from a number of critics, to whom Jonathan Edwards responded by justifying his apprehension of the signification of all reality through appeals to the spiritual sense, philosophical reasonableness, and biblical sanctioning of the practice. For an excellent analysis of Jonathan Edwards's typological writings, see Anderson, "Editor's Introduction," *WJE* 11:3-48.

74. "Miscellanies," no. 108, *WJE* 13:279.

75. Knight, "Learning the Language of God," 531-51.

76. "Charity and Its Fruits" in *WJE* 8: "In hell God manifests his being and perfections only in hatred and wrath" (ibid., 390).

his relations, family, society, and environment, is an analogy, type, shadow, and image of primary beauty.

Along with regenerate persons, natural-men also perceive God's power, wisdom, and justice in typologically associated "manifestations and signs," temporal relations and occurrences. But, unlike regenerate persons, natural-men alone replicate the punitive dimensions of God—those attributes which must receive full exercise and for which Christ's propitiatory and atoning work was designedly inoperative. So while it is true that Jesus Christ experienced punitive and retributive divine exercises, even to an infinite degree, yet it was only for His "elect church" and with an element of hope and promises of vindication and victory.[77] In a sense, Christ perfectly replicates the redemptive aspect of God's punishment/ abandonment of human beings—but *only for the elect*. For His act of replication entails crucifixion *and* resurrection, punishment-cum-justification: it is the good news of God's wrath placated for all who believe and are "born-again." But in Edwards's thinking, for God's attributes of hatred, righteous indignation, and wrathful power to have perfect exercise, they must be *perpetually perceived and infinite in duration and exercise*.[78] Christ's substitutionary suffering was neither eternal in duration nor representative of God's personal infinite hatred, according to Edwards. "Christ," he says, "had not to consider that God hated him . . . God withdrew his comfortable presence from Christ, and hid his face from him, and so poured out his wrath upon him . . . but yet he knew at the same time that God did not hate him, but infinitely loved him . . . Christ's sufferings lasted but a few hours, and there was an eternal end to them, and eternal glory succeeded."[79]

Universalism, therefore, is an impossibility: God must have some intelligent perceiving being(s) perpetuate the replication of His hatred, wrath, and retribution. If all were made born-again Christians by the effect of Christ's sacrifice, then certain attributes would cease to be ("Miscellanies," no. 662). It was "fitting," therefore, that God should not only let man fall and bring his fallen posterity into the world, but allow at least some of them (in Edwards's view, most) to continue thus throughout their terrestrial lives, even into eternity, that God may exercise and replicate Himself in their minds, to His eternal glory.[80]

An Eternity of Hell Torments

The sermon doctrine for 1 Corinthians 11:32, "'Tis a dreadful thing but yet a common thing for persons to go to hell," reveals both Edwards's personal conviction of the dreadfulness of the subject and his professional conviction that it is the pastor-scholar's duty to study and impart "the whole counsel of God," and human reality in light of it, as a manifestation of God's glory. The interpretative framework for Scripture and reality is, of course, the drama of redemption history. The drama, Edwards tells us, has two culminative points: the episode concerning the Messiah's birth through His ascension; and the

77. *Christ's Agony* (1739, 1757), *Banner-Works* 2:871.

78. *The Eternity of Hell Torments* (1739), *Banner-Works* 2:83–89. See also "Miscellanies," nos. 1348 and 1356, *WJE* 391–411, 575–99.

79. Ibid., 872. Cf. 175. Sermon on Zechariah 11:8 (1731): "DOC. There is a mutual loathing and abhorrence between God and wicked men" [L. 2r.], *WJE Online* 45.

80. "Charity and Its Fruits": "Hell is . . . a world prepared for the expressions of God's wrath" (*WJE* 8:390).

consummation of the age in the last judgment, etc. The first has been achieved, the world now moves toward the penultimate end. But it is not just the world that advances; heaven and hell mirror the progression on earth.

After the first rash of awakenings in 1734–45 (dutifully recounted in *A Faithful Narrative*), Edwards began contemplating the relation of the outbreaks within the larger scheme of God's great work of redemption. He figured that these revivals, indeed, even the Great Awakening of 1740–43, merely precipitated a glorious millennial era in the near future. God was noticeably advancing His kingdom, and Edwards, through a number of publications, would do what he could to underscore the moment's urgency and fragility, as well as notify, steady, and hasten ministers in their revival responsibilities. His thoughts are collected under the "Miscellanies" rubric "WORK OF REDEMPTION," which reaches its greatest concentration of entries in 1739, the year he preached the thirty-sermon series posthumously published as, *A History of the Work of Redemption* (1774).

But his interest in a chronology of redemption was neither romantic nor simply historical. Rather, it was fundamentally apologetic. True enough, Edwards began his theological career endeavoring to provide a systematic "Rational Account of Christianity, or The Perfect Harmony between the Doctrines of the Christian Religion and Human Reason." But on the eve of the Great Awakening he abandoned this project to take up based upon biblical prophecy and the history of the world "both sacred and profane."[81]

Casting theology in a historic mold harmonized well with his teleological methodology already in place. God's "ends" are "ends" because there is a linear development to His plans and activities, at least when considered *sub specie aeternitatis*. His principles of subordination and progression always said this, but now they, not rationalism, are the featured method. Thus, any advancement in redemption history refers to both the visible and invisible realms.

The driving force behind the alteration in his thinking is radical theocentrism; the mechanism that makes historical progression meaningful and coherent in both realms is idealism. "Miscellanies" no. 662 brings all things together in a revised recapitulation of his telic worldview:

> END OF CREATION. GLORY OF GOD. It may be inquired why God would have the exercises of his perfections and expressions of his glory known and published abroad. *Ans*. It was meet that his attributes and perfections should be expressed ... It was the will of God that they should be expressed and should shine forth. But if the expressions of his attributes ben't known, they are not; the very being of the expression depends on the perceptions of created understandings. And so much the more as the expression is known, so much more it is.[82]

Divine arbitrariness put aside, the "end" is one: if God's attributes are not expressed, known and consequently replicated, then "they are not"—whether on earth, in heaven or hell. And because the realms are created dimensions of a single reality, they share the same sequence of time; an effect in one has a corresponding effect in the other. As the last line of

---

81. Cf. Chamberlain, "Editor's Introduction," *WJE* 18:30.
82. *WJE* 18:200.

this entry reveals, the issue has become intensification. Advancements in redemption history, then, may be conceived as a device to measure the actualization of divine attributes in both realms, as well as the incremental knowledge perceiving agents may have of the Divine Being. For these reasons, Edwards speaks of the "progressive states" of the earth, heaven and hell.[83]

The earth is the center stage of the drama of redemption history. God's acts within it are, one way or another, revelatory: knowledge of God goes forth in His spatiotemporal movements, agents perceive these movements, gain knowledge, and facilitate the *ad extra* glorification of God. Likewise, Edwards writes of heaven: "'Tis certain that the inhabitants of heaven do increase in their knowledge." Saints and angelic hosts witness "new and glorious advancements" that "consists very much in BEHOLDING the manifestations that God makes of himself in the WORK OF REDEMPTION."[84] Their knowledge increases not simply because God unveils/communicates more of Himself, but also because in heaven the view of God is less mediated—so too in hell.[85]

In hell, the "MISERY OF DEVILS AND SEPARATE SOULS IS PROGRESSIVE, as well as the happiness of the separated souls of saints, and is advanced at the same time and by like degrees."[86] The "terribleness of God," which is "part of his glory," must be exercised upon some agent and perceived across *both* sides of the "chasm": "a sense of it should be kept up in the minds of creatures is needful in order to their right and just apprehensions of his greatness and gloriousness . . . in the spiritual sight and knowledge of him."[87] To be sure, God exercises sovereignty in the matter: "None can enjoy [or suffer] but only as God manifests; the enjoyment [or misery] therefore will be proportionable to the manifestation."[88] Yet, Edwards believes the Spirit of God makes the minds of separated souls in hell more acute, like "lightning," that they may experience unencumbered and precise sensations of mind. That is, damned souls have certain "spiritual sight and knowledge." In *The Future Punishment of the Wicked Unavoidable and Intolerable* (1741), he explains that although reprobates on earth cannot perceive divine and spiritual realities, nonetheless "God will hereafter make them seem real."[89] Edwards means that their existence in hell carries with it the full weight of apprehension by immediate intuition, reflection, and affectional encounter; the unified consciousness being acutely aware of all that God intends to communicates about Himself.

In their progressive perception, experience, and knowledge of God's terribleness, wrath, hatred, furious power, greatness, righteousness in judgment, and glory, the Divine Being perfects the exercise and therefore replication of "many of the divine attributes that . . . never would have had any exercise." This is how the reprobate's damnation posi-

---

83. "'Tis only God that is unchangeable. The whole universe, consisting in upper and lower worlds, is in a changing state," writes Jonathan Edwards in "Miscellanies," no. 796 (*WJE* 18:498).

84. "Miscellanies," nos. 701, 777, *WJE* 18:283; 427.

85. "Charity and Its Fruits" in *WJE* 8:390–92.

86. "Miscellanies," no. 805, *WJE* 18:507.

87. "Miscellanies," no. 407, *WJE* 13:469.

88. "Miscellanies," no. 702, *WJE* 18:299.

89. *Banner-Works* 2:79. Cf. "Miscellanies," no. 280, *WJE* 13:379.

tively contributes to God's program of self-glorification and, secondarily, the happiness of the saints in heaven.

The Sinking of the Soul

That Edwards establishes the immortality of the soul principally in teleology and secondarily in his dispositional ontology is also evident in what he says about the torment of wicked souls in hell. Though the future punishment of the wicked will be unavoidable, remediless, and intolerable, it will nonetheless continue forever for the reason that God intends to be *eternally* manifest *ad extra*. Subordinate to this are the theological reason (that God intends to be glorified in the vindication of His majesty and the execution of judgment) and the ontological reason (that souls are created with law-like dispositions which love self-being and "abhor annihilation"). Edwards, of course, typically employs a theorem of proportionate regards concerning the eternality of hell torments and the infinite honor, love, and duty owed to God, but ethics also are a subordinate issue to glorification.[90] It is the exercising of the idea of God's self-glorification that sustains the existence of beings in hell; for, as Edwards says, if it were not for the perfecting of God's attributes, the wicked would cease to exist. Hence, the eternal purpose of God explains why their essential ontological structure inclines in a law-like manner to being, even in the midst of eternal death:

> [I]n hell . . . [the soul's] torment and horror will be so great, so mighty, so vastly disproportionate to its strength, that having no strength in the least to support itself, although it be infinitely contrary to the nature and inclination of the soul to utterly sink; yet it will utterly and totally sink, without the least degree of remaining comfort, or strength, or courage, or hope. And though it will never be annihilated, its being and perception will never be abolished; yet such will be the infinite depth of gloominess into which it will sink, that it will be in a state of death, eternal death.[91]

So while wicked men in hell approach the status of "nothing,"[92] yet their existence never extinguishes: reprobates persist as long as they perceive.

Damned reprobates degenerate into almost "nothing" because their sins and hatred toward God grows: "[A]lthough the strength of their pain is very great . . . yet the strength of their malice is proportionably great; which puts them forward industriously to pursue their works of malice, even in the midst of pain."[93] Edwards dialectically proposes that while their knowledge increases their being decreases, and while being destroyed they perpetuate their existence; and, apologetically, he submits the thesis: the agent that eternally sins is an object of just, eternal punitive retribution.[94] But Edwards's aesthetic formula best explains wicked man's approximation to nothingness: "Excellency may be

---

90. Cf. Fiering, *Moral Thought*, 332–33.
91. Ibid., 81.
92. "Miscellanies," no. 237, *WJE* 13:353.
93. "Miscellanies," no. 282, *WJE* 13:380. It also could be argued that the despairing soul in hell desiring not to be, in turn, actually perpetuates its existence by desiring this good for itself, namely, non-existence. Cf. "Charity and Its Fruits" in *WJE* 8:390–92.
94. "Miscellanies," no. 545, *WJE* 18:90–92.

distributed into greatness and beauty. The former is the degree of being, the latter is being's consent to being [in general]."[95] "Nothing" corresponds with diminutive greatness or "degree of being," and because there lacks obvious consent to Being in general, wicked men have no obvious beauty, that is, their "excellency" amounts to almost "nothing." Thus, their progressive ontological "ugliness" offers an eternal aesthetic contribution to God's complex beauty.[96] This is the inevitable but inherent conclusion to Edwards's aesthetic philosophy of all "being" in God.

Damned reprobates also have comparatively less being because they have comparatively less arbitrariness of being: "And when they [i.e., saints] come to die, the positive effects of God's arbitrary influence is immensely greater in the souls of the saints in their glorification than in the souls of the wicked in their damnation."[97] Edwards's rationale for this pertains to the privation of good in death: "The soul of man and all other created minds . . . they stand in great necessity of good. The mere absence of good don't leave the soul in a state of indifferency without either good or evil; but it is itself an exceeding great evil; it's an evil necessarily accompanied by dismal, doleful, horrible darkness—it's death."[98]

In hell, therefore, though the beings of the wicked approaches "nothing," as they dissent from Being in general, and indeed have no "strength to be," yet they have a real and valuable existence to God, in terms of life, knowledge, and activity.

What is more, "the bodies of wicked men as well as their souls will be punished in hell."[99] The reason for this is twofold: (1) bodies are added in the resurrection to perfect the exactitude of their sensibilities; and (2) to fit wicked men with proper "sepulchers for their souls."[100] Since Edwards thinks "'Tis probable that this earth, after the conflagration, shall be the place of the damned,"[101] it is only "meet" that reprobates possess vehicles adapted to convey elemental torture. Thus, in a world turned into a lake of fire, God enlarges His being in the domain of hell through, in, and upon damned perceiving agents. And therein lays the startling functional value of reprobates in this world and the afterlife, according to the Puritan Jonathan Edwards.

Christ the Avenger

At several points in his book, Stephen Holmes suggests that Jonathan Edwards was "uneasy" with the doctrine of limited atonement. Edwards, Holmes says, was so impressed with the magnitude of Christ's death that it lead him to struggle "with the idea that anything could remain untouched by it." According to Holmes, Edwards's difficulties with particular redemption arose out of ontological questions: "[If] the whole of the being of

---

95. "The Mind" no. 64, *WJE* 6:382.
96. "The Mind" no. 62, *WJE* 6:380–81.
97. "Miscellanies," no. 1263, *WJE* 23:211.
98. "Miscellanies," no. 427, *WJE* 13:480.
99. 69. [L. 2.r]. Sermon on Matt 10:28 (1728), *WJE Online* 43.
100. 500. Sermon on Matt 23:15 (Jan. 1739): "DOC: Wicked men are the children of hell" [L. 5v.], *WJE Online* 54.
101. "Miscellanies," no. 275, *WJE* 13:376.

creation is defined by the gospel story, then the being of the reprobate must be so defined, or they become some special class separated from not just true humanity—the elect—but God's creation as well. Edwards was too sharp a thinker to miss this line, and so felt the need to speak of some universal component of the atonement."[102]

Holmes gives us an uncharacteristically taciturn and laconic Jonathan Edwards who experiments and equivocates in a slow movement toward "a genuinely universal sense to the work of redemption," but in the end fails to let the gospel story "sufficiently" inform his position on the ontology and creation of the reprobate.[103]

For Holmes, there must be some direct connection with the atonement: Christ is elected for the atonement; His elect are elected in Him; thus, the gospel story defines the elect's human existence. The same must apply to the reprobate or else they must be "some special class separated from not just true humanity . . . but God's creation."[104]

But Holmes defines Edwards's understanding of gospel story too narrowly, too much in the shadow of Karl Barth. To be sure, Holmes does not re-present the "inclusivist" if not "universalist" Edwards of either Morimoto or McDermott. He recognizes Edwards' doctrine of reprobation, but he finds it inconsistent with Edwards's philosophical-theology. Notwithstanding, he does not perceive that, for Edwards, the gospel of Jesus Christ is *two-sided*: in addition to understanding God through Christ's sufferings and death as Savior and Redeemer, God may be understood from the perspective of Christ's resurrection as Judge *and* Avenger. There are no less than eleven homilies in Edwards's sermon corpus that have for their principal doctrine Christ—Judge of the world, as a complementary item to His atoning sacrifice. This is to say, part of Edwards's theology of the cross (and God's perfections manifest through the Son) is not only the Son condescended, crucified and slain, but also resurrected, victorious, and executing judgment.

In an exegesis of Proverbs 16:4, particularly the words, "God made all things for Himself . . . even the wicked," Edwards considers why the latter clause was added and concludes: "This is added to obviate such a thought, as though God were frustrated, or his aims thwarted and frustrated by wicked men."[105] His point is that the wicked are continually useful and valuable to God for His "ends and purposes" in Christ: "we are to understand that that is said of Christ, Col 1:16, 'All things are made by him, and for him'; i.e. all things are made by him, and for *his* ends and purposes."[106] True enough, Christ's "ends and purposes" are all wrapped up in manifesting the perfections of God (i.e., God's perfect image of Himself) in and through a gospel story, but Edwards connects both the salvific and punitive sides to the work of redemption. Moreover, the creation and therefore the creatures subordinate to Christ's "ends and purposes" are also connected. Edwards reasons, "Because all things are subordinated to the work of redemption, therefore both the beginning and the end of the world is by the Redeemer; and he is appointed of the Father

---

102. Holmes, *God of Glory*, 158–59.
103. Ibid., 158, 240.
104. Ibid., 159.
105. "Miscellanies," no. 581, *WJE* 18:117.
106. "Miscellanies," no. 586, *WJE* 18:121–22. Emphasis added.

to be both the Creator and Judge of the world."[107] Consequently, reprobates are created by Christ and for Christ, and if so, then they are created through and in Christ. Just as the elect portion of mankind are predestined in Christ the Redeemer, so too reprobates are predestined in Christ the Judge and Avenger.[108] If all knowledge of God is through Jesus Christ, then the reprobate's knowledge of those attributes manifest in them is through Jesus Christ as the wrathful Judge.

The Holy Spirit is involved in their creation as well. This is evident from "The Mind" no. 45, where Edwards says that "all that is the perfections of spirits may be resolved into that which is God's perfection, which is love," or the Holy Spirit. The Spirit is represented in self-love and therefore in the being of the reprobate. Thus, reprobates are a trinitarian creation.

Likewise, reprobates suffer a trinitarian damnation. In hell, the Spirit increases the capacity of their sensibilities. Edwards adheres closely to a biblical understanding of the Spirit's role in the two-sided redemption story: the ministry of the Spirit is to reveal Jesus Christ, to convince men of sin, righteousness, and of judgment—the judgment of Jesus Christ and, in hell, the punishment He executes.[109] The Spirit acts not only upon the reprobate, but also in them. Edwards, in a number of places, especially in his writings analyzing the Great Awakening, repeatedly speaks of the non-covenantal, non-regenerative influence of the Spirit upon the "natural sensibilities" of natural-men and reprobates during times of revival.[110] The same idea carries over in hell, but with an intensification of sensibility for the damned, not sporadically, but for all eternity.[111]

Thus, with respect to Christ as Judge, reprobates have a very real human existence, as well as a valuable role (albeit grim) in God's two-sided, gospel-oriented program of self-glorification.

Concluding Remarks

When Edwards sets forth his understanding of the world there can be little doubt that a conviction of the absolute and arbitrary sovereignty of God serves as the cornerstone of his entire thought. Consequently, in his mind, there are not any insurmountable difficulties in theodicy, much less reprobation. Instead, the difficulties rest in one's willingness to believe the truths of sovereignty and arbitrariness, as well as one's perception of their reality in world history. For some it may seem incommensurable that God would decree and providentially orchestrate evil in order to judge it in the quest to manifest Himself as the Eternal Judge. But, for Edwards, God decrees what is best and most desirable to Himself.

---

107. "Miscellanies," no. 702, *WJE* 18:294.
108. 205. [L. 2v.]. Sermon on Job 18:15 (1732), *WJE Online* 46.
109. *True Grace Distinguished from the Experience of Devils* (1752), *Banner-Works* 2:46.
110. See, e.g., *WJE* 2:206–9, 215, 220.
111. "Miscellanies," no. 662, *WJE* 18:200.

God has *sufficient reason* for this world—His own maximal glory,[112] which, in the end, makes this the best world. But that is a matter of spiritual perception: a vision reprobates and homocentric freethinkers do not share.

God maximizes (for Himself) the moral and aesthetic dimensions of this best world. Questions of incommensurability tend to rest on things moral, but Edwards believes the importance of the aesthetic/ontic does not diminish the importance of the moral. In fact, he considers them so interconnected that they may be considered equivalent and only theoretically distinguishable. While this strengthens Edwards's overall theodicy and thoroughly integrates his worldview, yet it makes it an all or nothing system: one either has spiritual sensibilities and can appreciate divine sovereignty and arbitrariness or one does not and is left in an endless digression of argumentation to rationalize the biblical worldview. History, however, would remain a powerful apologetical point of contact for Edwards with an unregenerate and skeptical world of deists and philosophers, as we shall see in chapter 13.

History can be explained in terms of three episodes, creation, Christ, and consummation: Edwards's idealism and dispositional ontology factor large in all of them. In the creation man is fashioned in God's mental and moral likeness: dispositions ensure the inalienability of man's essential constitution, as well as the Fall itself. Man's mental dispositions give him the capacity to replicate the Divine in spatiotemporality. Similar things could be explained concerning Christ.[113]

In the consummation of the age, saints have a counterpart role to the dispositional and idealistic function of reprobates. God's "ultimate end" is all about intensified and climatic emanation and remanation, for, in Edwards, reciprocity is inherent in the notion of divine communication.[114] Because of their dispositional ontic constitution, reprobates continue to perceive in hell, as they did when natural-men prior to their death and judgment, but with greater intensity and sensibility, which, in turn, intensifies God's self-manifestation and ensures the full externalization of His aesthetic complexity:[115] hence Edwards's "sufficient reason" for their eternal existence.

During the Great Awakening period, where we find Edwards frequently explaining in graphic detail the torments of hell, we must not think that he was merely employing "sensational rhetoric" as part of some scare tactic to frighten souls into a state of conversion. There was a sophisticated and well-reasoned metaphysical and ethical system beneath it. Whether or not his imprecatory sermons issued in conversions, he nonetheless was satisfied with the uncomfortable thought that five-sixths of the world going to hell still had and always would have a very real, valuable, and integral place in God's scheme of glorification.[116] God gets His glory on the backs of humanity. Whether it was for good or for ill was a matter of spiritual perception and true religion. Though deists and "Christian humanists" were scandalized by such a thought, Edwards was not. When the Bible said

---

112. "Miscellanies," no. 348, *WJE* 13:419–21.
113. Sang Lee's "Editor's Introduction," *WJE* 21:31–38.
114. "The Nature of True Virtue" in *WJE* 8:551.
115. "Miscellanies," no. 662, *WJE* 18:200.
116. *End of the Wicked Contemplated by the Righteous* (1733), *Worcester-Works* 4:290–91.

that God did not desire that any should perish but is a God "who will have all men to be saved, and to come unto the knowledge of the truth" (1 Tim 2:4), it meant, of course, all men who are of God's eternal election. The reprobate segment of humanity was precluded from such platitudinous statements in Scripture. Edwards's aesthetic philosophy simply remained in keeping with the parameters of a theological tradition that touted a "particular redemption" (an atonement limited to the elect). In this sense the he merely extended the inevitable logic of an already existing Reformed predestinarian soteriology into the sphere of ontology. And despite the heavy outcome of the great majority of humanity being damned and, seemingly, God's being possessing a disconcertingly high degree of "irregularities," all was justified by a doctrine of divine sovereignty that he could see and, well, Enlightenment freethinkers could not.

Jonathan Edwards's Vision of Salvation

> None but those that do live under the calls of the Gospel shall be saved ... That is God's way and his only way of bringing men to salvation, viz. the Gospel.
>
> —Sermon on Matthew 22:14

JONATHAN EDWARDS'S WORLDVIEW CONSISTS OF A VISION OF GOD IN WHICH THE DEITY accomplishes His purposes through a metaphysic of finality. Human beings are the central means by which God's purposes come to fruition. Whether the saintly Paul, reprobate Judas, or the Messiah, Jesus of Nazareth, all human beings are valuable in themselves by virtue of their ontic composition and, especially, their functional role within God's bilateral redemption scheme.

Is Edwards a misanthropist? No, he recognizes the dreadfulness of the doctrine of hell and laments that "'tis a common thing for persons to go to hell." Yet, in unison, he perceives and appreciates the revealed truth and even the beauty of double particular election. So, in the "Sole Consideration, that God is God," Edwards resigns "All Objections to His Sovereignty," and in light of its arbitrary "excellence," he lovingly ascribes absolute sovereignty to God.[1]

Do men go to hell and suffer eternal torments? Not only does Edwards answer, Yes, but says that it is *necessarily* so. But he no more than any of his predestinarian predecessors had any knowledge of who—while in their natural state—were elect and who were reprobate. However, a few things were certain to him by way of special revelation: (1) no soul since Adam's lapse was, is, or will be, created with a holy disposition that unites them to God, save for the God-man Jesus Christ; (2) this same Jesus accomplished redemption through an atoning sacrifice of Himself; (3) the sum total of Christ's redemptive purchase was the Holy Spirit; and (4) God applies the reconciling and regenerative benefits of Christ's redemptive "purchase" (i.e., the Spirit) through divinely appointed gospel "means and ordinances."

In the last point we find that Edwards thoroughly subscribes to the Reformation theology of *theatrum salutis* (forum of salvation);[2] a theory which purports that the dis-

---

1. *Sole Consideration, that God is God Sufficient Silence All Objections to His Sovereignty* (1735), Banner-WJE 2:107; "Personal Narrative" in *WJE* 16:792.

2. See for instance, 1036. Sermon on Proverbs 8:34–36 (April 1752), Jonathan Edwards Collection; 417. Sermon on Cantecles 4:8 (Jan. 1737), *WJE Online* 52; *Stupid as Stones* (c.1731), *WJE* 17:173–83; 1135. Sermon on Matthew 10:14–15 (Mar. 1755), Jonathan Edwards Collection; 1122. Sermon on John 10:27 (July 1754),

semination of the gospel word creates a "forum" in which God communicates Christ's saving benefits by the Spirit through faith. Salvation or, synonymously, conversion, for Edwards, is a black or white issue: one is either savingly united to Christ the Redeemer or one is not. Although with his Reformed predecessors he says that God possesses the liberty to convert a soul without ordinary, gospel-conveying means,[3] yet salvation always contains the same objective elements of (a) regeneration—conversion through the "ingeneration" of a holy disposition; (b) humiliation; (c) faith; (d) repentance; (e) trust; (f) and (g) adoption and justification.

Nonetheless, the ordinary, regular, ordained and only means of salvation lies in heralding the gospel of Jesus Christ. Edwards repeatedly would assert a seemingly restrictivist position by insisting that special revelatory concepts of *sola gratia*, *sola fide*, and *solus Christus*, are absolutely necessary (and sufficient) for salvation. Nothing else can issue forth saving grace: hence Edwards's evangelistic zeal and pastoral concerns. Without saving grace men are "doomed." His responsibility as a called and ordained ambassador of Jesus Christ was to proclaim the good news within the construct of "the whole counsel of God," i.e., His revealed law and decrees.

By this account, Edwards seems no more adrift from Reformation orthodoxy in his evangelistic theology than Martin Luther with his *fides ex auditu* thesis, or William Perkins in his *Arte of Prophesying*, or the Westminster divines for that matter.[4] If salvation is about Christ, and Christ is the Word, and, as Luther put it, the nature of the word is to be heard,[5] then salvation is always logocentric, always a faith response to the living Word of God. Edwards, it would appear, could not agree more.

Yet recent revisionist accounts of Edwards's thought argue otherwise. Anri Morimoto, in particular, reinterprets Edwards's evangelistic concerns in light of his philosophy of dispositions, and asserts that Stoddard's successor was not concerned with salvation from damnation *per se*, but with justification, something totally different. According to Morimoto, initial salvation occurred at the cross: this work of Christ is universal in scope and application—all reap the saving benefit of an infused gracious disposition. The bare (i.e., unexercised) possession of it constitutes regeneration and, therefore, salvation. For Morimoto, Edwards's soteriology is primarily about ontological transformation; justification is a secondary issue.

So, in addition to this kind of universalism, Edwards also evinces a more prominent inclusivistic position, particularly when he publicly presses for a justified community. In Morimoto's reading, Edwards's evangelistic preaching was not about salvation from imminent damnation, but intended to "trigger" the gracious disposition to an exercise of faith, thereby "converting" the individual and allowing them the benefit of *affectionally* enjoying

---

Jonathan Edwards Collection; and *Profitable Hearers of the Word* (1728–1729), WJE 14:246–77; *A Divine and Supernatural Light* (1733), WJE 17:408–26; *The Blowing of the Great Trumpet* (1741), WJE 22:438–47; and "Some Thoughts Concerning the Present Revival of Religion" in *WJE* 4:484–88.

3. E.g., The Second Helvetic Confession (1566) states that "We know . . . that God can illuminate whom and when He will, even without the eternal ministry, for that is His power" (chap 1).

4. Title of Ernst Bizer's study of Luther's doctrine of justification: *Fides ex Auditu*; Perkins, *Arte of Prophesying* in *Perkins-Workes* 2:643–73; Westminster Confession of Faith, chaps VIII, X, XIV.

5. Luther, WA 4:9: "Natura verbi est audiri."

Christ's saving work. According to Morimoto, when an individual exercises their inherent gracious disposition in faith, God "rewards" them with a second salvation.[6] Since all are, for all intents and purposes, accounted believers because of the faith *virtually* contained within the disposition (hence, its law-like *tendency*), only those who exercise it attain this sort of "higher Christian life." Regeneration and conversion are utterly distinct phases or levels of salvation. The disposition, Morimoto maintains, is not unlike Edwardsean dispositions in causality: in a prescribed connection, a law-like disposition yields its manifestation. In this case, the gracious disposition yields faith amidst divinely ordained "means and ordinances": hence, the full title of Morimoto's book: *Jonathan Edwards and the Catholic Vision of Salvation.* "Means and ordinances" have an *ex opere operato* effect upon the disposition that Christ has made inherent in all. Still, not all religions have these "means and ordinances," and so it is in this sense that Edwards cannot be called a thoroughgoing Universalist.

Gerald R. McDermott advances Morimoto's revision as he considers Edwards's extensive interest in non-Christian religions. While convincingly arguing that deism, not Arminianism, was Christianity's most formidable opponent in Edwards's eyes, McDermott suggests that Edwards was preparing before his death a sophisticated theological response to Enlightenment religion that hinged on the relationship between reason and revelation. McDermott demonstrates, for example, that Edwards perpetuated the *prisca theologia*, a tradition dating back to the early church fathers that looked for elements of "true religion" in non-Christian systems of thought, such as Greek philosophy and Chinese I-Ching. He explains that Edwards's principal purpose in employing the *prisca theologia* was to show against the deists, "that nearly all humans have received revelation, and therefore all knowledge of true religion among the heathen is from revelation rather than the light of natural reason."[7] The upshot means that philosophical and theological reasoning about ethics and religion becomes the product of prior revelation and may be expanded by natural revelation. Taking his lead from Morimoto, McDermott argues that, in light of Edwards's dispositional philosophy, the combination of the powers of reasoning in the "heathen" and the plethora of natural revelation available to them allows for the possibility of those unreached by the gospel—the "five-sixths of the world" who not so much have heard of Christianity—to worship and even be "justified," i.e., converted, by the Christian God of special revelation, *without* having to explicitly trust in Jesus Christ for salvation.[8] Just as the disposition yields justifying faith in connection with Christian "means and ordinances" in Morimoto's "Catholic vision of salvation," so too, according to McDermott, God has provided the "heathen" with non-Christian "means and ordinances" to educe an exercise of "faith" for their justification. In this scheme, Edwards is not an inclusivist regarding "second salvation," but a hyper-inclusivist.

Why then Edwards's concern with justification? Answer: Eschatology. An expanded—worldwide—community of justified believers hastens the establishment of Christ' kingdom on earth and, consequently, His parousia and bodily reign. Edwards, therefore, is eschatology/apocalypse driven in his evangelism, not soteriology driven.

---

6. Morimoto, *Catholic Vision*, 100.

7. McDermott, *Confronts the Gods*, 94.

8. Ibid., 3, 12–13. Cf. Morimoto, *Catholic Vision*, 78–101.

My conclusions here differ decidedly from those of Morimoto and McDermott. The unconverted/unjustified glorify God on a metaphysical and aesthetic level, never in terms of "true religion," unless, of course, one calls bearing the punitive attributes of God "religious worship." To be sure, there is a sense in which the unconverted fulfill a doxological role in their associations with secondary beauties, but this is categorically different from the "true religion" and "virtue" of primary beauty. There are three main reasons for this. First, Edwards, in no uncertain terms, resolutely denies that non-Christians have gracious dispositions and therefore epistemological access to truly moral and spiritual dimensions of reality. In a word, no gracious disposition means no regeneration, no salvation, no bona fide spiritual data, and certainly no justification. Second, his soteriology does not permit a hard and fast distinction between regeneration and conversion; indeed, he often uses the terms interchangeably. Third, Edwards does not divorce regenerating grace from the divinely ordained means of special revelation—the word of God. There may be extraordinary cases, but on the whole Edwards remains skeptical and restrictivistic. To him, unregenerates cannot access regenerating grace in natural revelation because the oral tradition of the *prisca theologia* was (*a*) never intended to redeem, that is, it was not an "ends" but a "means"; (*b*) it was superseded by special revelation in a covenantal context and (*c*) contextualized within the history of redemption as being merely preparatory for that which does facilitate regenerative salvation—the gospel means of Christ alone.

This is to say, Morimoto and McDermott misinterpret Edwards's philosophy of dispositions and, consequently, his soteriology, evangelistic engagement with unbelievers, and vision of the history of the work of redemption. This chapter thus concentrates on providing a critical assessment of Anri Morimoto's recent monograph on these subjects, focusing particular attention on Morimoto's interpretation of Edwardsean dispositions. Offering a response to Morimoto destabilizes the work of McDermott and thereby facilitates a corrective re-evaluation of how Edwards's conception of the natural-man and reprobate manifests itself in particular aspects of his theology, as well as his ministerial perspective and practice.

The Fiction of Jonathan Edwards's Catholic Vision of Salvation

While Morimoto's thesis may be an inspired offshoot of Sang Hyun Lee's highly influential work on Edwards and dispositions, his motivation for casting Edwards as an inclusivist does not stem from Lee, but from an expressed aversion to the restrictivistic soteriological doctrines of confessional Calvinism and sympathetic collaboration with inclusivist if not universalist theologies of John Sanders, Clark Pinnock, and Hans Küng.[9] Consequently, when Morimoto says, "The implication of [Edwards's] dispositional view is not limited to the Christian community . . . Edwards's soteriology envisions a new and radical paradigm for understanding the salvation of people who are called 'non-Christian,'"[10] the Northampton minister usually described as a Calvinist metaphysician[11] comes off sounding as progressive as John Hick.

---

9. Morimoto, *Catholic Vision*, 2, 64–69.
10. Ibid., 2.
11. Bebbington, "Remembered Around the World," 178.

By extending the implication of Edwards's dispositional views "a little further," Morimoto believes we may with Edwards reconsider the destiny of those who stand outside the visible circle of Christian faith: "In Edwards's view of faith, the division between Christians and non-Christians is not simply a division between those who have faith and those who do not. Rather, the difference lies in whether or not the disposition into faith has been actualized."[12] This is to say, the mere possession of a disposition that embodies the tendency to exercise faith and not the actual exercise of faith itself provides common ground in which all may share "salvation." In order to ascertain the viability of this proposal Morimoto evaluates three presumably decisive questions: "Is this change of disposition really the work of the Holy Spirit? Does the Spirit work in any way other than infusing and indwelling in human nature? Can the new disposition remain dormant and unexercised?"[13]

Concerning the first question, Morimoto rightly affirms on Edwards's behalf that, indeed, the change of disposition is the supernatural work of the Holy Spirit. Likewise, the Spirit does work upon man other than through infusion and indwelling by assisting what man possesses as inherent principles. Lastly, Morimoto states that the new disposition can remain dormant and unexercised for not only extended periods, but also the whole life of an individual.

Having satisfied his criteria for plausibility, Morimoto articulates the significance of his answers in terms of soteriology. Christ's redemptive work achieves a universal restoration of a gracious disposition in every newly created soul. That is, all persons either sometime during their prenatal development or shortly after their birth are savingly infused (regenerated) with what amounts to "created grace." "Uncreated grace" (the Spirit) may assist in the exercising of the disposition, which, in turn, would result in "Christian conversion" and a "reward" of justification. The condition of the Spirit's presence (particularly during revivals) and certain external "means and ordinances" trigger a faith response and, as Morimoto describes it, "God Crowns His Own Gift" of regeneration with conversion and justification. But then again, if all these conditions are not present during a person's lifetime the disposition remains dormant. This lapse of time translates into the difference between regeneration and conversion. Thus, "one must conclude that non-Christians can be saved on the same grounds. They may not as yet manifest their saving disposition into a faith that is specifically Christian, but they might as well be given the disposition and counted as saved because of that disposition. They may even remain non-Christian for their whole lifetime, and still be saved ... The point is whether they *have* the saving disposition, not whether they *exercise* it or not."[14]

From Infants to Infidels

While Morimoto acknowledges that Edwards usually did not make fastidious distinctions between such terms as calling, regeneration, and conversion, but rather they all mean the same reality of grace infused at one instance, yet he asserts that, for Edwards, the

12. Morimoto, *Catholic Vision*, 3.
13. Ibid., 25.
14. Ibid., 66.

case with infants was different: "he had to admit that 'regeneration' is a better word than 'conversion.'"¹⁵ This is to say, infants are, by an ostensibly universal infusion of grace, regenerated but not converted. For the subject, the difference between them lies in the "sensibleness" of grace, for God the difference lies between initial salvation and secondary justification, between regeneration and conversion: the one is universal and instantaneous, the other occasional and gradual.

According to Morimoto, once Edwards made this distinction with infants the next step was to consider unconverted infidels. He appeals to "Miscellanies" no. 393 as evidence: "a person according to the gospel may be in a state of salvation," writes Edwards, "before a distinct and express act of faith." On Edwards's behalf, Morimoto concludes that no act of the disposition whatsoever "neither faith nor humiliation, is necessary at all for one to be in the state of salvation,"¹⁶ and cites Edwards to this effect from "Miscellanies" no. 27b: "The disposition is all that can be said to be absolutely necessary."¹⁷ Morimoto believes that Edwards, so impressed with the magnitude of Christ's redemptive work, could not conceive that the gracious disposition was procured for only a small fraction of the world's population. Thus, once Edwards began to affirm that infants who did not "sensibly" exercise the gracious disposition are saved (because their habit possessed its own mode of reality—a *virtual* exercise of faith—even before it exercised itself in faith or in other virtuous habits), he could not but affirm that many infants mature never exercising their converting dispositions but remained "saved" just the same. The principle held true for Edwards not just in the New World, but the whole world.

But in both "Miscellanies" entries (nos. 27b and 393), as well as no. 849, Morimoto completely neglects the context in which Edwards makes these and similar statements, and thereby misconstrues their intended meaning. The discussions in "Miscellanies" nos. 27b, 393, and 849, which produce the above quotes, entail the *appearance* of "a principle of faith" *to the agent* by its exercises, or, as Edwards writes, "a discovery of the of the mercy of God in Christ, whereby [a person] becomes justified *in his own conscience*, and *acquires a sense* of his own justification."¹⁸ Regeneration and conversion are simultaneous and instantaneous; *consciousness* of its effect is not necessarily so. The "Miscellanies" Morimoto cites categorically refer to the subjective apprehension of gracious exercises, not the objective exercises attendant with regeneration. Since "the graces are all the same in principle," humiliation, faith and trust all occur simultaneously *at the moment of infusion*.¹⁹ The agent, however, may only "see" them one at a time and consciously have corresponding affections on an occasion that may not always coincide with the time of infusion. An infant, of course, cannot properly discern its "sinful, doleful condition" so as to express *affectional* humiliation, repentance, and faith. Though humiliation, repentance, and faith are absolutely necessary for salvation, according to Edwards, yet the *conscious and affectional* exercising of them is not. Strictly speaking, *as to the agent*, "The disposition

15. Ibid., 31.
16. Ibid., 32.
17. *WJE* 13:213.
18. "Miscellanies," no. 393, *WJE* 13:458. Emphasis added.
19. Ibid., 457.

is all that can be said to be absolutely necessary." However, when the infant matures, he/she may have a subsequent exercise of the gracious disposition, which, again, *as to the agent*, may be considered a conversion.[20]

Edwards is not saying anything substantially different from what his Puritan forbearers said in their examinations of "cases of conscience"—protracted attempts to assure beleaguered parishioners of their justified status with special reference to the application of Christian ethics to specific cases.[21] The objective reality of Christ's work and covenant held true even when "distinguishing marks" lay dormant. Quite simply, "Miscellanies" nos. 27b, 393, and 849 are not about the order of saving activities, much less "God Crowning His Own Gift." To be sure, Edwards expresses a certain measure of anxiousness, not over particularity, but about how God gets His glory through the communication of Christ's salvific attributes ("Miscellanies," no. 849).

Moreover, Edwards is not optimistic and inclusivistic about infant salvation, but rather pessimistic and particularistic. "Miscellanies" no. 816 (1740) bears out his skepticism, along with the "Book of Controversies."[22] There he writes: "The following reasons seem to render it probable that FEW ARE CONVERTED IN INFANCY," and delineates items which emerge from and terminate in his teleological worldview. He states that humiliation, repentance, and faith are necessary for salvation because such responses are "fitting" to the Creator/creature relationship, especially in light of man's sinfulness and total dependence. In these divinely mediated responses God receives due honor and glory—the "ends" of creation. But in the hypothesis of infant salvation the *principal purposes* of creation seem to go unfulfilled. God infuses "the new creation [i.e., disposition]" into an agent "to be in him a vital principle," not to remain unexercised or dormant (which, incidentally, would contradict Edwards's teaching on ontic-mental dispositions). In other words, regeneration or conversion is purposeful; there is an idealist metaphysic of finality that controls the redemption narrative.[23] To Edwards, infant salvation does not make obvious the telic purpose of their regeneration/conversion. In his way of thinking, it is out of step with God's program of self-glorification in replication. Therefore, it is probable that "FEW ARE CONVERTED IN INFANCY."

Thus, Edwards remained unsure of the grounds of infant salvation and skeptical that more than a few *covenant children* might be saved from hell.[24] Morimoto, however, does

---

20. Ibid., 456–57.

21. See for example, Perkins, "Dialogue of the State of a Christian" in *Perkins-Workes*, 1:353–414; Ames, *De conscientia*; Sibbes, *The Bruised Reed*; Brookes, *Precious Remedies against Satan's Devices*.

22. "Controversies" Notebook Original Sin (esp. §13, but also §§4–8, 106, 11a and 15), *WJE Online* 27.

23. "Miscellanies," no. 702, *WJE*, 18:97.

24. See "Miscellanies," nos. 713, 771, 772, 816 (*WJE* 13:169–70; *WJE* 18:343–44; 419; 419–22; 526) and *WJE* 3:410. According to Jonathan Edwards, infants which came under "gracious influences" were likely to be the offspring of a believing parent or parents, who would have the word in and about them ("Miscellanies," no. 849, *WJE* 20:75–79; *Things That Belong To True Religion* (Jan. 1751), *WJE* 25:574. This is to say, in this "extraordinary" case he remains logocentric. Nonetheless, Jonathan Edwards's skepticism did not diminish in the 1750s but *grew*! In his *Humble Inquiry* (1749), *Farewell Sermon* (1750), and *Misrepresentations Corrected* (1752), two themes ring clear: that many New England parishioners (including those of his former Northampton Church) were deceived in thinking themselves saved—baptism notwithstanding (cf. *Things That Belong To True Religion* [Jan. 1751], *WJE* 25:571, 574); and, as David D. Hall explains it, "condemning as

not seem at all conscious of Edwards's all-pervading theocentrism and, consequently, interprets his position on infant salvation as non-teleological. Therefore, to make further application to "infidels," as Morimoto does, only moves oneself another step away from Edwards's thinking.

Lombard, Aquinas, and Edwards: Uncreated and Created Grace

"Grace in the heart," Edwards writes, "is no other than the Spirit of God dwelling in the heart and becoming there a principle of life and action."[25] Morimoto reads a statement like this and associates Edwards's idea of grace in the soul as the direct presence of the Holy Ghost with Peter Lombard's pneumatology, which identifies both the infused gift (*donum*) and the giver (*donator*) with *gratia increata* (uncreated grace) or the Spirit Himself.[26]

However, according to Morimoto, Edwards was not only strongly inclined toward the Lombardian motif, he also fully embraced the Thomistic habitual principle of *gratia creata* (created grace). Aquinas believed that without an intermediary habit for the Spirit to work through, the mind would function in a way contrary to the nature of a voluntary act. As Morimoto explains: "In order for the will to be itself . . . 'there should be in us some habitual form superadded to the natural power, inclining that power to the act of charity.'"[27] Thus, if we are to understand Edwards "correctly," we must view his notion of internal principle as "a close correlative of Thomas's notion of the 'intermediary habit,'" though without rejecting the Lombardian motif. The Spirit never "*becomes* created grace," but He does "issue in" the formation of a new habit through which He operates. Consequently, according to Morimoto, "while virtue is a product of God's supernatural and immediate work of infusion, it is nonetheless a virtue of one's own. It is so because the infused gift is really *in-fused*, namely, let *into* the depths of human nature and *fused* with it, establishing there an intrinsic principle of action. The grace infused from outside does not eradicate or supplant human freedom."[28] In other words, the virtue that issues from the supernaturally implanted disposition is *our* virtue, a created virtue or grace. Edwards, therefore, may be seen to depart from Calvin (who concurs with Lombard and rejects Thomas on this point) and prove himself more of a Tridentine theologian than a Reformation theologian with regards to the doctrine of regeneration. Or so it would seem, for these claims may be disproved on at least four points.

First, Morimoto's argument rests, in part, on an argument from silence: "Edwards may not have been aware of this controversy [i.e., the Reformation/counter-Reformation debate about the nature of the operation of grace in humanity] at all. He does not use

---

insincere the practice, crucial to the being of popular religion, of allowing parents readily to secure baptism for their children . . . What else did the townspeople [of New England] regard as a 'known and established principle' that Edwards now condemned as hypocrisy? Nothing less than the central motif of popular religion, the expectation of lay men and women that their children would benefit from the sacrament of baptism" ("Editor's Introduction," *WJE* 12:59).

25. "Blank Bible," note on Gal 5:17, *WJE* 24:1085.
26. Morimoto, *Catholic Vision*, 43. Cf. Petri Lombardi, *Sententiae In IV Libris Distinctae*, 1:2.142.
27. Ibid., 42. Cf. Thomas Aquinas, *Summa Theologia*, 2–2.23.2.
28. Ibid., 45.

the terms 'created grace' and 'uncreated grace' characteristic to the controversy."[29] So Morimoto takes the liberty to fill in the blanks. But he need not do so. Edwards has plenty to say about the nature of the operation of grace in humanity without having to open the *Canons and Decrees of the Council of Trent*. For instance, Edwards manifests, if not his knowledge of the debate, at least his understanding of the principal distinctions and use of nomenclature: "Yet the grace of God in men's hearts can hardly be called created. 'Tis God's own beauty and excellency that is uncreated and eternal, which is not properly made but communicated. It is as we said before the Spirit of Christ itself; it is God himself. Therefore, they that are full of grace are full of Christ; [that is] they are full of God."[30] Clearly, for Edwards, the habit *is* and *remains* the Spirit, not something created. Likewise, the acts of the Spirit are not *gratia creata* but the very fruit of the Spirit, *gratia increate*. Edwards writes: "The saints as saints act only by the Spirit in all their transactions wherein they act by a mediator; i.e. in all their transactions with God, they act by the Spirit, *or rather it is the Spirit of God that acts in them* . . . The Holy Spirit dwelling in them is their principle of life and action."[31] Thus, neither the origin nor function of the principle indicates that anything new is created in man in terms of a spontaneously generated disposition through which the Spirit works.

Second, the same applies to holy virtues and actions—they are manifestations of the Spirit, just as the above quote indicates. For Edwards, there is no distinction: the Spirit *is* a personal disposition of holiness given immediately by God and grace can only be grace if God is the only and immediate source, medium, and result of grace. "There is no gift or benefit that is so much of himself, of his nature, that is so much a communication of the Deity as grace is." Edwards concluded, "'Tis therefore fit that when it is bestowed, it should be so much the more immediately given, from himself and by himself."[32] Or consider the following excerpt from *God Glorified in Man's Dependence* (1731):

> The several ways wherein the dependence of one being may be upon another for its good, and wherein the redeemed of Jesus Christ depend on God for all their good are these, viz. That they have their good of him, and that they have all through him, and that they have all in him: That he is the *cause* and original whence all their good comes, therein it is *of* him; and that he is the *medium* by which it is obtained and conveyed, therein they have it *through* him; and that he is the *good itself* given and conveyed, therein it is *in* him.[33]

So, while it remains true that the virtues of the Spirit are a gift, yet they are not separable from the divine nature. In short, the "principle of life and action," which Morimoto

---

29. Ibid., 43.

30. 72. [L. 6r.]. Sermon on 2 Corinthians 3:18(a) (after July 1727), *WJE Online* 43. My transcription. Jonathan Edwards preached this sermon under Stoddard's tenure. If Jonathan Edwards came to Northampton without knowing the controversy and/or relevant concepts (which is doubtful), he soon found instruction under his grandfather's tutelage.

31. "Miscellanies," no. 614, *WJE* 18:146. Emphasis added.

32. "Miscellanies," no. 537, *WJE* 18:83. Cf. *A Divine and Supernatural Light* (1733), *WJE* 17:422; "Miscellanies," nos. 107, 220, and 341, *WJE* 13:277–78; 345; and 415.

33. *Banner-Works* 2:3–7.

believes to be in some sense created, is simply another way for Edwards to talk about the *manner* of the Spirit's indwelling and operation; that is, to talk about uncreated grace.

Third, Morimoto misses the point that the occasional advances in sanctification, or sporadic manifestations of "the fruit of the Spirit," are not due to Edwards's causal theory of dispositions, but the weakly-arbitrary operation of the indwelling Spirit. This is to say, the progressive state of sanctification (Calvin's "secondary sanctification") is no less dependent upon the full and immediate operation and will of God than in regeneration. Though Edwards links the disposition of holiness to "means of grace," yet the arrangement perpetually remains non-causal. The blessings of salvation in this life, namely, sanctifying graces, depend "wholly and entirely on God's immediate and arbitrary bestowment."[34] "Means" merely provide a "proper and fit" opportunity for the exercise of grace, but in no way do they trigger an exercise. Nothing does, for there are no "laws" which govern the operation of the Spirit, other than a covenantal agreement between the members of the Godhead concerning the advancement of Christ's kingdom—the vehicle by which God moves toward His consummate goal. Hence,

> The Word and ordinances and works of God are means of grace, as they give opportunity for the *proper and fit* exercise of grace, and are in a sort of means of that exercise; though not in the same manner as things are the means of the exercise of natural principles, because *not only the principle of grace, but every exercise of it, is the immediate effect of the sovereign acting of the Spirit of God*. Indeed, in natural things, means of effects, in metaphysical strictness, are not proper causes of the effects, but only occasions. God produces all effects; but yet he ties natural events to the operation of such means, or causes them to be consequent on such means according to fixed, determinate and unchangeable rules, which are called the laws of nature . . . *But means of grace are not means of the exercises of grace in such a manner, for the actings of the Spirit in the heart are more arbitrary and are not tied to such and such means by such laws or rules*, as shall particularly and precisely determine in a stated method every particular exercise and the degree of it.[35]

The upshot of this important quote is fourfold: (i) though means are "necessary" for both regeneration and progressive sanctification, yet they are not sufficient; (ii) Morimoto's notion that, "The act of faith must naturally and necessarily arise out of the disposition on specific occasions," that is, "When certain conditions are met, the disposition as an active and purposive tendency . . . come[s] into exertion," proves false;[36] (iii) Edwards's explanation of the Spirit infused into the hearts of men "only after this general law, viz. that it shall

---

34. 104. Sermon on 1 Peter 1:3 (1729). See n. 4 in "Notes on Scripture," no. 1902, *WJE* 15:104, concerning the content of this, now, non-extant MS sermon once cited in "Miscellanies," no. 409.

35. "Miscellanies," no. 629, *WJE* 18:157. Emphasis added. Cf. "Miscellanies," no. 481: "SPIRIT'S OPERATION. In grace not only consists the highest perfection and excellency, but the happiness of the creature: and therefore, although other things are bestowed upon men by ordinary providence, that is, according to the fixed laws of the succession of events from preceding events or preceding human voluntary acts; yet this has God reserved to be bestowed by himself, according to his arbitrary will and pleasure, without any stated connection, according to fixed laws, with previous voluntary acts of men, or events in the series of natural things" (*WJE* 13:523); and *WJE* 2:259–60. See also Fiering, *Moral Thought*, 123.

36. Morimoto, *Catholic Vision*, 32, 62. Although Jonathan Edwards, like Malebranche, maintained that general laws governed the grace of universal providence, yet both insisted that saving graces were particular providences.

remain there and produce acts *after the manner of* an abiding, natural, vital, principle of action," simply underscores his emphasis on resemblance not exact equivalence;[37] and (iv) Morimoto's thesis that conversion and justification are consequent upon a latter encounter with means, in which a previously infused, regenerative, but dormant disposition becomes active, is rendered foundationless: there are no laws, rules, constant conjunctions, occasionalistic connections, or any other causal relation between the exercising of the disposition of holiness and means that "trigger" faith, save for the weakly-arbitrary operation of the Spirit.[38] "Means" have more of an aesthetic and mediatorial function: "they give opportunity for the *proper and fit* exercise of grace."

Fourth and lastly, Edwards says in no uncertain terms that the disposition is not *infused* in the same sense that Morimoto indicates. Rather, the disposition of holiness and all the gifts and virtues associated with it could leave man's heart at any time just as the Spirit left Adam, because they are *not* essential to human nature, to that which necessarily constitutes "human being." The Spirit stays, however, because of a covenantal agreement: the believer belongs to Christ and Christ has "purchased" the Spirit for them—forever.[39] Man does not become intrinsically or essentially holy. Instead, he is always a sinner, but also a justified sinner, i.e., a saint, because of Christ's imputed righteousness, his being divinely constituted in Christ, and his ontological union with Christ that communicates all of His "excellencies."[40] Edwards maintains that even in heaven it is theoretically possible for God to withdraw this gracious disposition, since the redeemed are not and never become "gods," unition and participation notwithstanding.[41] In sum, the disposition of which Edwards speaks simply is not the same as that of Aquinas, and it is even further removed from anthropology and soteriology of the Greek Fathers.

∼

Edwards shows his familiarity with the Scholastic and Tridentine division between "created" and "uncreated" grace and expressly distances himself from the former type. Morimoto therefore errs in his appraisal of Edwardsean dispositions and doctrine of regeneration. Edwards is neither a prototypical Karl Rahner, grounding justification in the disposition of the human person and further attempting to urge the notion that created grace demands, as its proper correlative, uncreated grace, nor is he a forerunner to Paul Tillich or Sir Francis Younghusband who succumb to the logic of universalism.[42] Morimoto ar-

---

37. "Miscellanies," no. 629, *WJE* 18:157. Emphasis added. In "Miscellanies," no. 709 and other entries, as well as the "Treatise on Grace" (*WJE* 21:153–97), Jonathan Edwards repeatedly stresses the point that the Spirit simply "acts *as* a principle" in the redeemed (ibid., 334–35).

38. "Miscellanies," no.689, *WJE* 18:253. Cf. Fiering, *Moral Thought*, 93–103.

39. "Miscellanies," no. 402: "The sum of all that Christ purchased is the Holy Ghost. God is he of whom the purchase is made, God is the purchase and the price, and God is the thing purchased: God is the Alpha and Omega in this work. The great thing purchased by Jesus Christ for us is communion with God, which is only in having the Spirit" (*WJE* 13:466). Cf. Holmes, *God of Grace*, 142–47.

40. *Christ, the Light of the World* (1721), *WJE* 10:543; "Miscellanies," no. 571, *WJE* 18:111.

41. "Miscellanies," no. 957, *WJE* 20:231–34; 919. Sermon on Col 1:12(a) (Jan. 1749; repreached Jan. 1756), *WJE Online* 67.

42. See Rahner, *Theological Investigations*, 1:319–46. Here I refer to the well-known words of Tillich that particular religions are only provisional and inevitably must discard their particularity: "In the depths of

rives at his conclusions because he asks the wrong questions about dispositions and the nature of regenerating grace. His second question should not be, "Does the Spirit work in any other way than infusing and indwelling in human nature?," but rather, Does the Spirit work in any other way *within the regenerate* to produce spiritual manifestations? For he takes a principle which Edwards reserves for the Spirit's influence upon natural-men, namely *assisting* their natural, inherent principles, and unacceptably applies it to those indwelt by the Spirit, thereby creating an intermediary element between the Spirit and His virtuous expressions.

As a result of his misappropriation of dispositions, Morimoto's third question, "Can a new disposition remain dormant and unexercised?" suggests a Thomistic soteriology of ontological transformation and subsequent conversion and justification which Edwards hardly would have countenanced, let alone acknowledged as his own.

"As soon as ever divine grace enters, the man is willing"

In order to separate the instantaneousness of justification from regeneration, Morimoto proposes: (a) that the infused disposition (Holy Spirit) can remain dormant subsequent to ingeneration; (b) that conversion (and resulting justification) "takes a long and gradual process before it is fully realized";[43] and (c) that faith becomes an inherent quality in man consequent upon the infused disposition.

We have already dealt with (c) by showing that any fruit of the disposition is the very fruit of the Spirit Himself, or the virtues of Christ communicated through the regenerate's participatory union by the Holy Spirit. According to Edwards, the communion of saints with Christ consists, at the very least, in receiving of His fullness and partaking of His grace: "And in partaking of that Spirit which God gives not by measure unto him, partaking of Christ's holiness and grace, his nature, inclinations, tendencies, affection, love, desires, must be a part of communion with him."[44] If no communion, then none of these graces issue; for they are not merely *of* Christ, but are *through* Him and *to* Him, and *are* Him. In Edwards, whatever Christ assumes into union to Himself must be by the Holy Spirit that acts as the principle of union.[45]

What of (a) and (b) then? First (a). While it holds true that, for Edwards, some dispositions D, particularly those that relate to phenomenological occurrences, can remain inactive for nearly the whole duration of D, yet he proposes an entirely different set of rules for mental dispositions to accommodate their arbitrariness.

According to Edwards, an agent cannot be said to possess a given *ontological* disposition D, where D may be counted as constitutive of an agent's ontic structure either by necessity or participatory union, unless D is exercised. That is, such dispositions must manifest

---

every living religion there is a point at which the religion itself loses its importance, and that to which it points breaks through its particularity to a vision of spiritual freedom and to a vision of the spiritual presence in other expressions of the ultimate meaning of man's existence" (*Christianity and the Encounter with World Religions*, 97; Seaver, *Francis Younghusband*).

43. Morimoto, *Catholic Vision*, 32.
44. "Miscellanies," no. 683, *WJE* 18:247.
45. "Miscellanies," no. 709, *WJE* 18:335.

at least an initiatory exercise or else it is "of no manner of use." In other words, they are not constitutive of that agent's ontic structure without consciousness of it as the agent's own ideal-existence. Which is to say, an ontic-mental disposition without an initiatory exercise must be classified not as one with a virtual mode of reality, but as non-existent. Without the exercise of such a disposition, it cannot be assumed to persist or exist. Consequently, in Edwards, there is a difference between constitutive ontological dispositions that define human being and nature as such and dispositional properties exemplifying personal propensities, characteristics, and traits. One could be dispositionally courageous without ever having the opportunity to express it, but one could not possess an ontic disposition of holy consent to God without an initiatory exercise of it.

In the network of phenomenological occurrences, dispositions without perceivable or actual applications may be assumed, but within mental structures they cannot, for their express mode of reality constitutes the "ideal-existence" of the agent who possesses them. It is the difference between *actually* being a certain category of human being and not being so. In Edwards's soteriology, real dispositional union is crucial for justification, for "What is real in the union between Christ and his people, is the foundation of what is legal,"[46] says Edwards. By equating the two distinct kinds of dispositions within Edwards's philosophical-theology, Morimoto builds his thesis not upon dormant dispositions but defunct dispositions.

In "Miscellanies" no. 241 titled, "REGENERATION," Edwards writes: "It may be in the new birth as it is in the first birth." While he notes that the vivification of a prenatal infant "is exceedingly gradual," "Yet," he quickly points out, "there is a certain moment that an immortal spirit begins to exist in it by God's appointment." Recalling Edwards's point about infant regeneration and the gradual, subjective apprehension of converting graces, he continues by saying, "there is doubtless a remarkable and very *sensible change made at once* when the soul is newborn . . . yet the *sensible change is very gradual.*" Here we have neither an equivocation nor a separation between regeneration and conversion. Instead, Edwards means that at the moment of regeneration the "sensible" elements necessarily bound up in conversion (viz., humiliation, repentance, and faith) are exercised in a "reflex act" of the Holy Spirit, and that, subsequently or gradually, the agent becomes sensible to the "great change made in the soul." A "habit of grace" is, then, "always begun with an act of grace that shall imply faith in it, because a habit can be of no manner of use till there is occasion to exert it . . . [Therefore] the first new thing that there can be in the creature must be some *actual alteration*.[47] In the new birth the infusion of the new disposition is "always with an *act of grace*," i.e., an exercise of faith, though a period of inactivity may follow this necessary initial act, depending on the sanctifying purposes and activities of God.

In Edwards's soteriology, the faith producing act of the Holy Spirit in regeneration brings together (a) and (b), so that conversion is instantaneous and occurs instantaneously with infusion. Such ideas are often repeated in his sermons and "Miscellanies." For instance in "Miscellanies" no. 673, Edwards teaches that, "conversion is a work that is done at once, and not gradually" by the Spirit. In the same entry he underscores the instanta-

---

46. "Miscellanies," no. 364, *WJE* 18:105.
47. *WJE* 13:357–58. All italics added. See also "First Sign" in *Religious Affections*, *WJE* 2:197–239.

neousness of conversion as he equates it with effectual calling and regeneration: "There is something immediately put into their hearts at that call that is new, that there was nothing of before... And that the work of conversion is wrought at once, is further evident by its being compared to a work of creation." Later he alludes to the Spirit's faith producing act, as he plainly articulates his particularist position:

> [C]onversion [is] an immediate and instantaneous work... by which we must understand that [natural-men] have none of that kind of grace, or disposition... Natural men, or those that are not savingly converted, have no degree of that principle from whence all gracious actings flow, viz. the Spirit of God, or of Christ... because having *of the Spirit* is given as a sure sign of being in Christ... Hereby 'tis evident that they have none of that holy principle that the godly have; and if they have nothing of the Spirit, they have nothing of those things that are the fruits of the Spirit.[48]

The substance of this "Miscellanies" is further expanded in Edwards's magisterial treatise on the nature and substance of "true religion," *A Treatise Concerning Religious Affections* (1746), particularly the "Seventh Sign":

> Another thing, wherein gracious affections are distinguished from others, is, that they are attended with a change of nature. All gracious affections do arise from a spiritual understanding, in which the soul has the excellency and glory of divine things discovered to it, as was shown before. But all spiritual discoveries are transforming; and not only make an alteration of the present exercise, sensation and frame of the soul; but such power and efficacy have they, that they make an alteration in the very nature of the soul; "But we all, with open face. Beholding as in a glass, the glory of the Lord, are changed into the same image, from glory to glory, even as by the Spirit of the Lord" (2 Cor 3:18). Such power as this is properly divine power, and is peculiar to the Spirit of the Lord: other power may make a great alteration in men's present frames and feelings; but 'tis the power of the Creator only that can change the nature, or give a new nature. And no discoveries or illuminations, but those that are divine and supernatural, will have this supernatural effect.[49]

Edwards's whole point, whether in the formulative "Miscellanies" or the polemical *Religious Affections*, is to safeguard the doctrine of *soli Deo gloria* by insisting on an absolutely monergistic, irresistible, and supernatural conversion within a sinful subject. For Edwards, the Spirit's faith-producing act within a non-cooperative subject alleviates the aesthetic/relational tension that there should be the mutual act of each party (Christ/sinner) for a union. In his own words, there must be "consent on the part of both, each should receive the other, and actively join themselves to each other."[50] Since "'tis an utter impossibility that ever man should do what is necessary in order to salvation, nor do the least towards it," the Spirit Himself "takes up" the faculties of man and irresistibly implants consenting faith.[51] As he says elsewhere, faith "receives and accepts the gift, or is the person's active uniting with the gift, with its qualities and relations, viz. as a free gift,

---

48. *WJE* 18:230, 231, 232, 233.
49. *WJE* 2:340.
50. "Miscellanies," no. 568, *WJE* 18:105.
51. "Miscellanies," no. 71, *WJE* 13:238.

the gift of God, the fruit of his power, etc."[52] Or, in other words, to say that regeneration has occurred is to say that there is a union, and if a union, then consent or love must be mutually expressed.[53] Contrary to Morimoto's design, "The Spirit," Edwards says, "[does] not do His work to the halves."[54]

~

By postponing the converting disposition's exercise of faith, Morimoto runs counter to the most fundamental element of Edwards's doctrine of regeneration, namely, "'Tis not only principles, *but especially acts*, that are the condition of salvation, for acts are the end of principles, and principles are in vain without 'em."[55] Stoddard's successor had a number of ways of expressing it; Morimoto seems to have missed them all. Consider the following examples from the "Miscellanies":

- 637. "The Jews put circumcision instead of regeneration, instead of *that faith that is wrought in regeneration*, or instead of that righteousness of Christ that faith has or that is virtually in faith."
- 665. "The very first effect of saving grace that touches the will is to abolish its resistance and incline the will . . . *As soon as ever divine grace enters*, the man is willing."
- 675. "The Spirit of God . . . ingenerated the human nature of Christ; which is *a work to which conversion is compared*, which is an ingenerating Christ into the heart, as that was an ingenerating Christ in the womb [of Mary]."
- 772. "The Holy Spirit brings God to dwell with their souls on earth *in their conversion*."[56]

It is, therefore, certain in Edwards's soteriology that a sinner undergoes regeneration, union, conversion, and therefore justification on the first and necessary act of faith wrought by the Spirit at the point of infusion. (Again, the whole "Seventh Sign" in *Religious Affections* is devoted to conversion as regeneration.)[57] On this point, the difference between Edwards and his tradition cannot be more than marginal. Calvinism was inclined to portray converting grace through faith as irresistible with the result that conversion became a virtually spontaneous turning of the one who was elected-called-regenerated to receive grace. The teaching in Northampton was the same as in Westminster, or Geneva for that matter.

Edwards's problems with infant salvation are always teleological. That God may regenerate an infant soul with all the affectional elements concomitant with converting graces is no difficulty at all—it is all the work of the Spirit of Christ. But how God gets His glory perceived and acknowledged (replicated) in spatiotemporality through infants

---

52. "Miscellanies," no. 632, *WJE*, 18:159.

53. See *The Distinguishing Marks of a Work of the Spirit of God*, *WJE* 4:255–59; and *Some Thoughts Concerning the Present Revival of Religion*, Part I in *WJE* 4:293–347; and *Religious Affections*, *WJE* 2:240–53.

54. "Miscellanies," no. 600, *WJE* 18:200.

55. "Miscellanies," no. 800, *WJE* 18:500. Emphasis added.

56. *WJE* 18:167, 211, 236, 422. All italics added.

57. *WJE* 2:340–44. See also the "First Sign," 2:197–239.

Edwards finds altogether perplexing. Thus, he maintains a willingness to discuss conversion as *both an event and a process*—just as his Reformed theological mentors had taught for generations.[58]

What Is Real, the Basis of What Is Legal

When it comes to the doctrine of justification, Edwards allows no room for synergism or neonomianism. He even disapproves of calling faith "the instrument wherewith we receive justification" for fear of making it man's contribution to salvation.[59] Not that he repudiates Calvin's definition of faith, it is just that he, like other Reformed theologians, thought it wise to neutralize the suggestion of causality in faith's instrumentality.

Morimoto, however, while arguing that Edwards retains a "Protestant character" to his doctrine of justification, makes the author of the anti-Arminian lectures *Justification by Faith Alone* (1738)[60] not only Arminian but semi-Pelagian in his treatment of conversion and justification. In a section labeled "Human Goodness Prior to Justification," Morimoto argues that in Edwards's soteriology unconverted persons possess "inherent goodness" which "becomes 'acceptable' and 'rewardable' only after justification."[61] His point is that unconverted persons may be regenerate and yet have no union with Christ. For Morimoto, it is by the inherent gracious disposition men now possess, that they put their "rewardable" faith in Christ and "play their own part in this mutual act of 'unition.'"[62] In brief, the regenerate soul that encounters certain disposition activating means exercises faith, the result of which establishes a union, a Spirit assisted conversion, and the pronouncement of justification. For this reason Morimoto says with Thomas Schafer, "there is nothing that keeps Edwards from becoming a Roman Catholic except for his rejection of the concept of merit."[63]

"Miscellanies" no. 364 or, alternatively, no. 568, factors largely in Morimoto's anomalous account. The key passage he employs is one that many commentators have thought compromising to Edwards's confessional position. The passage, repeated verbatim in both entries, is as follows: "What is real in the union between Christ and his people, is the foundation of what is legal; that is, it is something that is really in them and between them, uniting [them], that is the ground of the suitableness of their being accounted as one by the Judge."[64] Morimoto starts off well by identifying "what is real" or what it is that

---

58. E.g., Perkins, *Armilla Aurea*, reproduced in *Perkins-Workes* as "A Golden Chaine," 1:9–116; Turretin, *Institutes*, 2:15–17, 501–724.

59. *Justification by Faith Alone* (1734), *Banner-Works* 1:624.

60. In 1734 Jonathan Edwards preached a two-unit lecture on justification (Rom 4:5) that was published in 1738 as *Justification by Faith Alone*. The published version was significantly revised and expanded from the original lectures. Prompted by the famous "Robert Breck Controversy" and William Rand's (minister at Sunderland) reportedly aberrant doctrine of justification, Jonathan Edwards endeavors to oppose "the Arminian scheme of justification by our own virtue" (*Banner-Works* 1:621).

61. Morimoto, *Catholic Vision*, 93.

62. Ibid., 92.

63. Ibid., 130; Schafer, "Jonathan Edwards and Justification by Faith," 61.

64. *WJE* 18:105.

constitutes the "fitness" or "suitableness" of the union between "Christ and his people" as *consent*. No compromise here. But there he stops in his analysis and turns the discussion to the active role human beings provide in mutual consent for their justification: "[Edwards] defines faith as that which constitutes a union with Christ, providing the faithful with an ontological foundation for 'their being accounted as one [with Christ] by the judge.'"[65]

Noticeably absent from Morimoto's account, however, is any mention of the Holy Spirit or whether the framework from which Edwards speaks is a temporal or eternal recognition of ontological union. As a matter of fact, in his thirty-page chapter on "Justification: God's Crowning of His Own Gift" the only reference to the Holy Spirit belongs to a quote from W. G. T. Shedd on secondary sanctification, and not a single sentence is provided to substantiate Morimoto's claim that the union God recognizes as justifying occurs within time. To exclude the Spirit and the *eternal context* in this matter could not deviate further from Edwards's thinking. For him, the ontological basis for forensic imputation, i.e., the transaction of Christ's faith and righteousness to the believer, fundamentally concerns the Spirit in an eternal arrangement. Indeed, in Edwards's soteriology, if the topic is faith, love or consent, *especially mutual consent*, then these ideas must be understood in terms of the Spirit; and the forensic arrangement for justification must be understood against the background of its eternal context, namely, the eternal "confederation," the *pactum salutis*.[66]

What is real in the union between Christ and his people, which is the foundation of what is legal qua imputation and justification? Answer: mutual consent—or love, the "greatest" and "highest excellency," which, when between two spirits, *is* the Holy Spirit.[67] Thus, it is "suitable" that God should account that which He constitutes to be "united" to His triune Self, through the Spirit, just as it were the Son; or, which is to say the same thing, to reckon that "Christ's satisfaction and righteousness should be theirs, because Christ and they are so united that they may be well looked upon as one."[68] One could emphasize the "*as one*," for in his forensic thinking the ontological union that provides "the foundation" of justification does *not* take place in the temporal sphere—that is, there is no infusion of grace—logically prior to a declaration of righteous. Instead, in the eternal confederation, God constituting the union with Christ and His church provides the basis for an antecedent declaration of righteous, which, in turn, provides the efficient cause of the temporal union via regeneration. For this reason Edwards says that, in a certain sense, even the unregenerate elect have a legal right to Christ's benefits as a wife is entitled to that which belongs to her husband; for the Spirit Himself, who, in God's constituting a union between the sinner and the Son, is the "unition"—the Spirit belongs to them legally because He does really. God, as it were, regards the Spirit "purchased" by the Son *as the mutual consent or actual unition* between the sinner and the Son, and therefore imputes righteousness to the sinner on account of what Son has procured for them—the Spirit:[69] for when the Son "purchased" the Spirit for His bride, He also "purchased faith and con-

---

65. Morimoto, *Catholic Vision*, 85–86.

66. *Sermon One*, *WJE*, 9:117, 119; 456. [L. 4v.ff]. Sermon on 1 Peter 1:19 (Jan. 1738; repreached Mar. 1753, Mar. 1756), *WJE Online* 53.

67. "The Mind," nos. 1 and 45, *WJE*, 6:336–38, 362–66.

68. "Miscellanies," no. 568, *WJE* 18:105.

69. "Miscellanies," no. 755, *WJE* 18:403–4. See also "Miscellanies," no. 507, 568, 627 and 712 in *WJE* 18.

version" for them in the Spirit.⁷⁰ In Edwards, then, the *ordo salutis* may be discussed in terms of eternal arrangement and constitution, as well as the logical ordering of temporal applications. This, too, was in keeping with his tradition.⁷¹

What, then, is the faith that unites man to Christ in the *actual moment* of salvation? Answer: A communication or manifestation of the Spirit of Christ. Understood in a way conscious of the contexts within which Edwards considers the legal and ontological dimensions of salvation, faith no more becomes a synergistic exercise than infusion, though, to be sure, the faculties of man are "taken up" in temporal "union." Discussions about "the ground of *suitableness*" (Edwards's aesthetic substitute for "*condition*") and "acts of faith" in justification, therefore, immediately pertain to the Person of the Spirit, not "Human Goodness Prior to Justification."

Virtual Faith/Real Savior

In numerous places Edwards explains that there is a twofold fitness to the human state, one moral the other natural. An agent is morally fit for a state, when by his "excellency or odiousness his excellency or odiousness commends him to it." The aesthetic arbiter "suitable" coordinates an agent's excellency with a "good state" or, conversely, odiousness with an "ill state." Once again, the theme of Spirit "haves" and "have-nots" is repeated.⁷² He accepts the former as belonging to the believer but rejects the latter. This is because a "moral suitableness" always includes a "natural," but the natural "by no means necessarily includes a moral."⁷³ Union with Christ establishes a "natural suitableness," i.e., it fulfills the "condition," so that justification need not flow out of a "moral suitableness." This is to say, human acts never have by nature a virtue or merit that God respects. Herein lays the difference between the Calvinist and the Arminian, between Jonathan Edwards and, say, Charles Finney.

Where "moral fitness" serves the basis of justification for Arminians, "natural fitness" is for Edwards. The means to justification by "natural fitness" is faith: that is, faith alone; faith as consent; faith as the "condition" between the believer and Christ; faith as the Spirit of Christ.

"Natural fitness" also is the vehicle of imputation—another doctrine rejected by the Arminians as "legal fiction." How could Christ's righteousness, in the moment of justifica-

---

70. "Miscellanies," no. 1159, *WJE* 23:72–74. Also, "Table to the Miscellanies," *WJE* 13:127.

71. Advancing Calvin's work, Reformed soteriology sought to take for its point of origin the eternal union established in the *pactum salutis* between the Son and those whom the Father has given Him, in virtue of which there is an eternal imputation of the righteousness of Christ to those who are covenantally His. Though the notion of an eternal imputation was hotly debated amongst Calvinist theologians and ministers from the sixteenth through the nineteenth centuries, in the main, Reformed theologians of the period (while focusing on the more scriptural-based idea of the application of redemption accomplished by Jesus Christ to the elect) would move from the sphere of the eternal *pactum* (covenant of redemption) to the temporal realm and continue the *ordo* with justification, regeneration or "effectual" calling, and thus accentuate the fact that, from its incipiency to fruition, the application of Christ's redemptive benefits was a sovereign work of God. See, Ferguson, "Ordo Salutis" in *New Dictionary of Theology* and Barth, *Church Dogmatics*, 4:2.

72. Jonathan Edwards articulates essentially the same principles in volitional terms within *Freedom of the Will*.

73. "Miscellanies," no. 712, *WJE* 18:341.

tion, be transferred to an agent by nature unworthy to receive it? "Natural fitness" places the orthodox response on more sure grounds than the traditional forensic explanation. As Ava Chamberlain explains, "The concept of natural fitness emphasizes that imputation is preceded by a preexisting union with Christ . . . Because the union with Christ, which occurs by faith, creates the ontological foundation necessary for imputation, it is fitting that the faithful are justified."[74] Thus Edwards says, "God sees it fit that they only that are one with Christ by their own act, should be looked upon as one in law."[75]

By virtue of the believer's union with Christ by the Spirit (in faith/consent)—something real in the eternal sphere and realized in temporality—he/she becomes the possessor of all the righteousness, holiness, faith and love of Christ.[76] Justification by faith/union with Christ is immediate, perfect, and inalienable—as long as the union holds which, according to God's eternal covenantal purposes and promises, it will forever. To be sure, what is real in the union is the basis of what is legal. Again, this is a basic difference between Edwards and Rome.

But how does the union hold in a temporal context when there is no express consent? That is, if the believer ceases to believe at any point in time, what would be the ground of his/her justification? As John H. Gerstner asks, "Would it not be better to say that he will be justified if he continues as he now is?"[77]

Keenly aware of these questions—especially in lieu of their relevance to the Connecticut Valley revival and its aftermath, when many, even in his own Northampton congregation, "cooled" in their religious affections and exercises—Edwards sought for a way to articulate the importance of a faith that *perseveres*, even when parishioners did not. But this created a dilemma for him: a persevering faith, according to his reading of the Scriptures, is not dormant but active. His tradition reconciled Luther's difficulty with The Epistle of James by asserting that St. James and St. Paul were in complete agreement: faith alone justifies, but it is an *active* faith. Not only is *True Grace Distinguished from the Experience of Devils* in terms of "true" religious affections but also accompanying performance.[78] Hence, Edwards reasoned that, if conversion brings a "very great change to the soul," then along with persevering faith there ought to be persevering Christian practice in the religious life. In other words, a persevering faith leaves "distinguishing marks." As his critical analysis of the awakenings and so-called "communion controversy" make certain, Edwards found mere "profession" highly suspect. Whether in a four-year-old child like Phoebe Bartlett or a seasoned ecclesiastic like Solomon Stoddard, conversion *really* alters a person. So the tension was this: on the one hand, Edwards reasoned that hypocrites have no claim to either congregational privileges or eternal life; while on the other hand, he was fully conscious of the frailty of the human condition and that justification in no way depends on the individual but on Christ. Faith, then, if it is the faith Christ grants, must overcome; it must endure. But how, since the evidence of its presence in the believer, as the Great Awakening proved, wildly fluxes and quickly wanes?

74. Chamberlain, "Editor's Introduction," *WJE* 18:17.
75. "Miscellanies," no. 568, *WJE* 18:105. Cf. "Miscellanies," no. 709, *WJE* 18:333–35.
76. *Banner-Works* 1:627. Cf. "Miscellanies," nos. 1250 and 1354, *WJE* 23:183; 506–43.
77. Gerstner, *Rational Biblical*, 3:202.
78. *True Grace Distinguished from the Experience of Devils* (1752), *Banner-Works* 2:41.

The difficulty of striking a balance is remarkable: antinomianism, neonomianism, nominalism, and legalism are all to be avoided, while at the same time there is the reality of *simil iustius et peccator* with which to contend. Edwards finds an innovative solution by proposing a theological doctrine that did not rest upon an evaluation of one's own "works," but Christ's: he (1) grounds initial justification in the conditional "first act of faith"; and (2) also makes the status of "justified" conditional upon perseverance; but then (3) declares that Christ has actually persevered in faith and practice for the believer. "Miscellanies" no. 729 sums up Edwards thoughts: "For though a sinner is justified on his first act of faith, yet even then, in that act of justification, God has respect to perseverance, as being virtually in that first act; and 'tis looked upon as if it were a property of the faith, and the sinner is justified by that, as though it already were, because by divine establishment it shall follow."[79]

According to Edwards, the first act of faith gives a "title" to salvation, because it does, virtually at least, "trust in God and Christ for perseverance among other benefits, and gives a title to this benefit with others, and so virtually contains perseverance."[80] Interestingly, this is nothing more than what nineteen-year-old Jonathan Edwards wrote in "Miscellanies" no. *y*: "Christ has already acted on the part of those that believe, and those merits are sure and certain that he has purchased. So that although Adam could fall, [it] is no argument that we may. For what Adam was to be made happy for was not yet performed; but ours is, and that fully."[81] Salvation is, therefore, in itself sure and certain after the first faith-act of consent, not because justification's futurition is certain *in itself*, for, as Edwards writes, "that is as certain in itself by the divine decree," but because the faith-act establishes a congruity between salvation and the subject. Ava Chamberlain describes the implications of Edwards's reconditioning the doctrine of justification:

> By insisting that the "sinner is justified on his first act of faith," Edwards avoids the Arminian view "that the act of justification should be suspended, till the sinner had persevered in faith." But he elevates the status of perseverance by asserting that faith "virtually contains" perseverance, which "God has respect to" and looks "upon as if it were a property of faith, by which the sinner is then justified" (["Miscellanies"] No. 729). This concept of "virtual perseverance" clearly exposes the limits of the orthodox doctrine of justification.[82]

Actual perseverance on the part of the believer does not justify, indeed, it is impossible for those who are *simil peccator*. But because Christ "has *actually persevered* through the greatest imaginable trials," and the believer stands in "actual union of the soul with Christ," then "we shall stand and persevere in him" for He "persevered not only for himself, but for us."[83] Thus, when Edwards speaks of "virtual" faith or righteousness or perseverance, he does not mean dormant, but complete in Christ, complete in our union with Him by the Holy Spirit: which things, due to the "fittingness" of God's ordering of

---

79. "Miscellanies," no. 729, *WJE* 18:354.
80. Ibid., 355.
81. *WJE* 13:176.
82. Chamberlain, "Editor's Introduction," *WJE* 18:38.
83. "Miscellanies," no. 695, *WJE* 18:276–81.

redemption, as well as His plan for self-glorification, outwardly manifest themselves via the "new spiritual sense." The Holy Spirit, as that new spiritual sense or disposition of love to God, is given by Christ not just to regenerate, but to rule and reign. Consequently, we find that time and again Edwards both comforts his auditors with words of assurance, "Christ has accomplished all," and warns that "Persons ought not to rest ignorant and unresolved about their own state, whether they be real Christians or no."[84] "Justified" is not only the *real* legal status of absolved and righteous, but the *reality* of a vital union with Christ through a Divine Person (the Holy Spirit) who is "pure act."[85]

~

Without question, Edwards's soteriology is a complex labyrinth fraught with a variety of theological innovations, of which we have here considered only a few. But these innovations, as well as his whole theory of salvation, clearly show affinity with Geneva and Westminster's emphasis on "union with Christ," rather than the emphases characteristic of Roman theology and, in particular, Trent. So while Morimoto may be right to say that Edwards espouses a Lombardian soteriology of ontological transformation, yet he wrongly superimposes a Thomist and Tridentine template onto it; the result of which leaves much of Edwards's telic-theocentrism neglected and his philosophy of dispositions misappropriated.

In Edwards, neither a prior infusion of grace or holiness is the basis of justification, nor, as John Henry Newman taught, is the declaration itself renewing/creative. Rather, the divinely constituted union—*that which is real in God's estimation*—is the foundation of what is legal.

Within New England Theology, it was not Jonathan Edwards but Samuel Hopkins's "New Divinity" that separated conversion and regeneration. Hopkins, unlike Edwards, carefully distinguished in salvation between "regeneration," which he saw as totally the work of the Spirit, and "conversion," the active, volitional exercise of the human will which leads to holiness. Thus, within the "New Divinity" system, one could be chosen by God and still play the major role in one's conversion.[86] In contrast to the impression one gets from Morimoto, this was a departure from Edwards's theology not an expression of it.

---

84. 368. [L. 2v.]. Sermon on 2 Corinthians 13:5 (1735), *WJE Online* 50.

85. "An Essay on the Trinity" in *Treatise on Grace*, 108. Cf. "Discourse on the Trinity" in *WJE* 21:121, 131.

86. Hopkins's blend of Calvinism with revivalism became known as "Hopkinsianism," his chief contribution to the "New Divinity." See his lecture on John 1:13 "Regeneration and Conversion."

13

Dispositional Peculiarity, History, and Edwards's Evangelistic Appeal to Self-Love

> None but those that do live under the calls of the Gospel shall be saved... That is God's way and his only way of bringing men to salvation, viz. the Gospel.
>
> —Sermon on Matthew 22:14

A Strange, New Edwards?

JONATHAN EDWARDS CATEGORIZED HIMSELF IN RATHER UNAMBIGUOUS TERMS. HIS EXpressed theological allegiances were so lucid that for well over two centuries after his untimely death one would have been hard pressed to find any notable debate over Edwards's theological classification. Instead, the contentious issue among schools and scholars regularly fell along lines of "claiming rights": who more rightly could claim Edwards as their theological patriarch—Princeton or Yale, Old School or New School?[1]

Edwards unapologetically profiled himself as Christian, confessional, Calvinist. For instance, in a 1750 letter to the Reverend John Erskine (1721–1803) of Kirkintilloch, Scotland, Edwards (recently dismissed from his Northampton ministerial charge and contemplating opportunities on the other side of the Atlantic) disclosed the following admission:

> You are pleased, dear Sir, very kindly to ask me whether I could sign the Westminster Confession of Faith, and submit to the Presbyterian form of church government; and to offer to use your influence to procure a call for me to some congregation in Scotland... As to my subscribing to the substance of the Westminster Confession, there would be no difficulty: and as to the Presbyterian government, I have long been perfectly out of conceit with our unsettled, independent, confused way of church government in this land.[2]

---

1. See Noll, "Jonathan Edwards and Nineteenth-Century Theology," in *American Experience*, 260–87.

2. Letter to the Reverend John Erskine, July 5, 1750, *WJE* 16:355. See Jonathan Edwards's enthusiastic approval of the tenets of the Massachusetts "Association Covenant," a society of both clergy and laity who bound themselves to "see to it that we be sound and clear in the great doctrines of the gospel, which are the life of our holy religion (we here intend those doctrines which are exhibited in our excellent Westminster Catechism and Confession of Faith); and that we all boldly and impartially appear in the defense thereof... That we manifest our approbation of the Westminster Assembly's Catechism, as containing an excellent system of divinity: and we purpose to preach agreeable to the doctrines of the Bible exhibited therein" (Letter to the Reverend James Robe, May 23, 1749, *WJE* 16:277, 279).

Four years later and within the "Preface" to his magisterial *A careful and strict Enquiry into The modern prevailing Notions of that Freedom of the Will* (1754), Edwards, while disavowing "a dependence on Calvin" for the substance of that treatise, writes: "I should not take it at all amiss, to be called a Calvinist."[3]

Christian, confessional, Calvinist: this is Jonathan Edwards on Jonathan Edwards.

By his own words, works, and reputation, from the time he implicitly endorsed the Saybrook Platform through his attendance at Yale College to the time he affirmed the divinity of Savoy and Westminster as a requirement for ordination through to his expressed ownership of the doctrinal standards required by the Presbyterian and Reformed trustees of the College of New Jersey in the final year of his life, Jonathan Edwards stood as a stalwart, though creative and resourceful, proponent of Christian particularism in the Calvinist tradition. Or so it would seem.

Some contemporary commentators on Edwards argue that there is a difference, a striking and surprising difference, between the *public* Jonathan Edwards and the *private* Jonathan Edwards. True enough, commentators such as Anri Morimoto and Gerald R. McDermott would say, in Edwards's published treatises he ably articulates and defends confessional Calvinism. But these writings, like his preached sermons and personal correspondence, were open to *public* perusal and thus, in his mature years, were skillfully crafted so as to render his theology orthodox to the scrutinizing eye of Reformed Protestantism.

Meanwhile, behind closed doors, contend Morimoto and McDermott, Edwards surreptitiously experimented with heterodoxical thoughts, compromised his confessional affiliation, and pursued the logic of strange new doctrines in genuinely private notebooks and short theological essays, the most important of which are his famed ten "Miscellanies" notebooks, especially the last few notebooks. Things simply were not what they appeared to the public eye. The sage of Stockbridge may have been rethinking his commitment to confessional Calvinism and his private notebooks evidence this phenomenon.

Of course, the idea of "private Edwards" verses "public Edwards" should ring familiar to Edwards commentators and enthusiasts. Oliver Wendell Holmes floated such a thesis in 1880, when he set forth accusations concerning Edwards's supposedly suspect trinitarianism. Holmes wrote that, "Edwards' views appear to have undergone a great change in the direction of Arianism, or of Sabellianism, which is an old-fashioned Unitarianism, or at any rate show a defection from his former standard of orthodoxy."[4] Holmes refers to the then unpublished *Observations Concerning the Scripture Oeconomy of the Trinity and Covenant of Redemption*, a short treatise comprising a number of "Miscellanies" but mainly consisting of the floating essay "Miscellanies" no. 1062.[5] The issue *then* was the doctrine of God. According to Oliver Wendell Holmes, Edwards's trinitarianism was two-faced: orthodox in public, unorthodox in private.[6] It was his private notebooks that revealed the "great change" and "defection."

---

3. *WJE* 1:131.

4. Holmes, "Jonathan Edwards," 125.

5. "Miscellanies," no. 1062 reproduced in *WJE* 20:430–43. Compare the contemporaneous "Discourse on the Trinity," *WJE* 21:109–44.

6. For further discussion see, Park, "Remarks of Jonathan Edwards on the Trinity," 367ff; Stephens, *God's Last Metaphor*; and Lee, "Editor's Introduction," *WJE* 21:10–38, 109–11.

Today, however, the issue is soteriological: Edwards is particularistic in public, but sympathetically pluralistic, if not inclusivistic or (if one maintains the course of Edwards's logic) hypothetically universalistic, in private. So writes celebrated commentator Gerald McDermott: "On the question of salvation, [Edwards] usually only conceded the possibility that heathen could be saved..."[7] Later McDermott speaks even more confidently: "But for Edwards there was indeed a possibility... Edwards is not dogmatic about the heathen being saved through truth they receive in the *prisca theologia*, but here [in "Miscellanies," no. 1338] and elsewhere he opens the door to that possibility..."[8]

McDermott (and elsewhere Anri Morimoto) argue that Edwards was exploring in his private notebooks the possibilities of a new soteriological paradigm; one built upon a dispositional ontology—a logic of being in terms of lawlike powers and forces, in which dispositions are conceived as active and real tendencies that have ontological reality even when unexercised.

Where, on the one hand, Morimoto says that, for Edwards, a gracious "disposition" in human beings was "all that was necessary for salvation," but maintains in his interpretation of Edwards a distinction between those justified Christians who had their gracious disposition activated through contact with converting *Christian* "means and ordinances," McDermott, on the other hand, proposes that Christian "means and ordinances" (i.e., the gospel of Jesus Christ and its accompaniments) are *not* necessary for the conversion of the "heathen" soul. McDermott thus opposes Morimoto, yet at the same time stands in fundamental agreement with him that "The inner disposition, not any particular acts and exercises, is the only essential prerequisite to salvation."[9] For both McDermott and Morimoto, an inner disposition has been granted to all persons as a universal benefit of Jesus Christ's work on the cross (pace: Roman Catholicism's notion of infused prevenient grace concomitant with sacramentarianism: hence the title of Morimoto's book).[10] The difference between them has to do with what triggers the disposition and, indeed, if triggering the disposition is necessary for salvation.

McDermott suggests that, in Edwards's metamorphic, clandestine theology, theoretically there is enough non-Christian revelation in the world to mechanistically "trigger" the disposition and justify the religiously or philosophically inclined. But McDermott goes even further; for in his reading of Edwards's interest in non-Christian religions none of this soteriologizing need be christocentric. Dispositions, such that are saving, have been possessed by man since his creation: "Edwards defined a saving disposition, which is common to Christians, Old Testament Jews, and all other religionists '*from the beginning of the world*': 'a sense of the dangerousness of sin, and of the dreadfulness of God's anger... [such a conviction of] their wickedness, that they trusted to nothing but the mere mercy of God, and then bitterly lamented for their sins' ('Miscellanies,' no. 39)... No particular act, even the act of receiving Christ, is necessary [for salvation]."[11]

7. McDermott, *Confronts the Gods*, 144.
8. McDermott, "Response to Gilbert," 79–80.
9. McDermott, *Confronts the Gods*, 134.
10. Morimoto, *Jonathan Edwards and the Catholic Vision of Salvation*.
11. McDermott, "Jonathan Edwards" in *Jonathan Edwards: Philosophical Theologian*, 129–30.

This abandonment of christocentrism and particularism, according to McDermott, was all part of Edwards's progressive philosophy of history, a history that envisioned the world moving toward a millennial era of "true religion"—the kingdom of God on earth, in which all with a gracious disposition would be converted. "True religion," *but not necessarily the Christian faith*, would reign on earth universally.[12]

Despite the problematic interpretations of Jonathan Edwards's philosophy of dispositions[13] and its soteriological implications (or non-implications, as the case may be) within Anri Morimoto's book on the subject, McDermott nonetheless adopts the Morimoto thesis that Edwards indeed separated regeneration and conversion, and did so because his theology was stealthfully becoming ever more inclusivistic as a result of the logical trajectory of his dispositional ontology. In *Jonathan Edwards Confronts the Gods*, Professor McDermott advances Morimoto's work through a presentation of "A Strange, New Edwards";[14] one that was (secretly?) exercised by the "scandal" of traditional Christian particularism and set out to show the deists of his day that non-Christian religions of the world also encased "the most important truths of Christianity,"[15] such that were potentially, if not *de jure*, salvific.

A pluralistic, if not universalistic, inclined Edwards would indeed be "A Strange, New Edwards." Yet, as we have seen in previous chapters, Edwards's soteriology hardly suits an inclusivistic Edwards, let alone a pluralistic or universalistic one.[16] Indeed, neither his vision of God, nor his conception of redemptive history, nor even his philosophy of dispositions—as innovative as they may be—lend themselves to the proposals of Morimoto and McDermott. Edwards remained consistent to his theological profession, both publicly and privately.

---

12. John F. Wilson states that Jonathan Edwards displayed "an incipient universalism" in the outworking of his theory of redemptive history ("Editor's Introduction," *WJE* 9:89). Wilson's suggestion legitimated by Schafer's article, "Jonathan Edwards and Justification by Faith," 55–67, which suggested that Jonathan Edwards's soteriology facilitated inclusivism, initiates the contemporary discussion of Jonathan Edwards's supposed inclusivistic/universalistic propensities and theologizing.

13. In addition to the critique of earlier chapters, see also Holmes, "Does Jonathan Edwards Use a Dispositional Ontology?" in *Jonathan Edwards: Philosophical Theologian*, 99–114.

14. McDermott, *Confronts the Gods*, 3. See also McDermott, "Jonathan Edwards" in *Jonathan Edwards: Philosophical Theologian*, 129–30.

15. McDermott, *Confronts the Gods*, 92.

16. See also Gilbert, "The Nations Will Worship," 53–76. To be sure, McDermott acknowledges that Jonathan Edwards "never reached this explicit conclusion [of inclusivism], at least in his published writings or private notebooks." This is to say, Jonathan Edwards never consciously professed or espoused inclusivism as such. However, McDermott unmistakably concludes that Jonathan Edwards's private notebooks reveal a distinct movement toward inclusivism: "Edwards' soteriology resembles Roman Catholic theology in ways that makes it easier for him to consider the salvation of the heathen . . . his own theology lays the groundwork for such an interpretation" (*Confronts the Gods*, 137); "While he made some cryptic remarks in the Miscellanies about how the heathen might use religious truth for the good of 'their own souls' (*Misc.* 1162), these concessions were largely limited to his private notebooks; in his published treatise and sermons, 'heathen' was usually a synonym for 'damned.' Yet the extensive use he made of the *prisca theologia*, the advances he made in typology, and his development of a dispositional soteriology prepared the theological way—for whatever use he or others might later have used them—for more expansive views of truth in the religions and salvation for religious others" ("Jonathan Edwards," in *Jonathan Edwards: Philosophical Theologian*), 130.

What then are we to make of Edwards's sixty or more "Miscellanies" entries on "heathen religions" and pagan sages to which McDermott draws our attention and marshals as evidence of Edwards's later theological reconfiguration toward inclusivism?[17] What role did non-Christian religions play within his philosophy of history? Further, what was the climate or context within which Edwards wrote these entries? Were they penned in connection to some on-going controversy or (as the case frequently was with Edwards) genre items germane to a future project or polemical treatise? The answer to this last question is "Yes": Edwards was busy collating materials not for a reassessment of Christian particularism or a pluralistic eschatology that would recapitulate a universalistic protology, but rather a body of divinity in an entire new method, being thrown into the form of an history," which he called "*A History of the Work of Redemption*,"[18] that would have been (among other things) a resolute defense of Judeo-Christian particularism and the necessity of the revealed gospel for salvation within that, and only that, covenant community.

In order to follow the logic of Edwards's preparations for his unfinished *magnum opus* we first investigate the climate or context that prompted Edwards to the project, namely the challenge deistic Enlightenment thinkers marshaled against historic Christianity particularity.

The Context: Enlightenment Religion

McDermott's *Jonathan Edwards Confronts the Gods* exhibits considerable erudition in its account of the deist challenge to the limitations of Christian peculiarity. John Toland, Matthew Tindal, Thomas Chubb, and other deists, with some of whom Edwards was well acquainted,[19] concentrated on issues of goodness and justice and, consequently, the nature of God and His relation to rational beings in their critical reassessment of historic Christian theology and soteriology. As McDermott aptly states it, "For it was finally a debate about the relationship between 'natural religion' based on abstract principles and 'revealed religion,' said to be rooted in the religious experience recorded in Scripture."[20] For Enlightenment freethinkers, the widely celebrated Newtonian paradigm offered a new, efficient world emancipated from the divine panopticon. This coupled with avant-

---

17. See McDermott, *Confronts the Gods*, passim; and "Response to Gilbert," 77–80. Seven (of ten) MS "Miscellanies" notebooks (nos. 4, 5, 7, 8, 9[A], 9[b], and 9[c]) from Jonathan Edwards's corpus contain literally hundreds of folio pages of notes on non-Christian religions and "HEATHEN PHILOSOPHERS." Perhaps the first entry specifically designated to this genre is "Miscellanies," no. 953 (1742), while the last ("Miscellanies," no. 1359) was composed shortly before the commencement of his presidency at Princeton (Jan. 1758) and death (Mar. 1758). All are reproduced in *WJE* 23.

18. Letter to the Trustees of the College of New Jersey, October 19, 1757, *WJE* 16:727. This unfinished treatise is not to be confused with the thirty-sermon series posthumously published in 1774 with the same name reproduced in *WJE* 9.

19. Jonathan Edwards refers to Tindal in "Miscellanies," no. 1337 (*WJE* 23:342–45) and cites Tindal's *Christianity as Old as Creation* (London, 1730) in "Miscellanies," no. 1340 (*WJE* 23:359–61), and Jonathan Edwards certainly alludes to him whenever on the issue of "deistical religion." Chubb, of course, is a key polemical target in Jonathan Edwards's magisterial treatise, *A Careful and Strict Enquiry into The modern prevailing Notions of that Freedom of Will* (Boston, 1754).

20. McDermott, *Confronts the Gods*, 18–19.

garde Lockean philosophy, in which Locke established the maxim that "Nothing that is contrary to, and inconsistent with the clear and self-evident Dictates of Reason, has a right to be urged, or assented to, as a Matter of Faith,"[21] only served to embolden deists toward the consideration that even the restrictivist parameters of salvation dogma could be radically reassessed, and reassessed in its entirety. This, of course, would have only been in keeping with the Cambridge Platonists, who fortified the Pelagian/semi-Pelagian belief that unaccompanied human reason was sufficient to recognize and appropriate divine truths to its own eternal benefit.[22]

For deists like Lord Herbert of Cherbury, Toland, and Tindal, the traditional Christian notions of revelation and salvation through Jesus Christ *alone* were unjust to the vast portion of humanity. Consequently, time-honored doctrines surrounding Jesus Christ's substitutionary atonement and propitiatory sacrifice, and especially the distinguishing tenets of Calvinism, were repudiated *in toto*. Likewise, the Judeo-Christian monopoly on revelation was not contested and evenly distributed among the world's religions, but made redundant in its entirety. "*Natural religion*" supplanted revealed religion for Enlightenment thinkers: God spoke to all peoples through nature and reason. As reports from merchants, explorers, adventurers, and scholars poured forth details, controversialists told of scores of non-Christianized civilizations whose morality eclipsed their "sophisticated" Western counterparts. By arguing that Greco-Roman mythology and philosophy, as well as highly ethical non-Christian religions, were *self-contrived*, *self-defined*, and *successful*, or, in other words, that pagan perspicacity and "heathen" religious systems developed civilized ethical worldviews independent from biblical revelation, the deists not only naturalized religion but negated the Christian necessity for divine revelation—along, of course, with its particularist message.

In short, according to the deist and their ilk, God *had* provided a mediator for all mankind when He created man with reason to direct his behavior and beliefs. Therefore an incarnate Redeemer was superfluous at best, repugnant at worst. To quote McDermott, "for the deists, particularity and goodness were mutually exclusive terms."[23] If God was good, He was fair; and nothing was fairer than living by the light of reason and nature, no matter where on earth one dwelt, nor when one did so. The "true religion" of the world was, therefore, *a*historical (not bound to redemptive history but perpetual from creation) and *a*cultural (not confined to Semites or Christianized Gentiles). Instead, it was natural—the product of the moral character of the heart directed by universal reason.

Edwards's Rejoinder

Enlightenment religion found revelation the epistemological chink in Christianity's armor, and history, the deists believed, substantiated their position. Edwards himself

---

21. Locke, *Essay* IV, 18, 6. In *Reasonableness of Christianity As Delivered in the Scriptures* (London, 1695), Locke furthers the thesis that revealed religion must be subjected to the judgment of reason. Moreover, in his *Letters Concerning Toleration* (London, 1689/92), Locke attempted to embed historical revelation and the proof of its reasonableness in the general system of rationality.

22. Whichcote, *Moral and Religious Aphorisms*, 74–77. See also McDermott, *Confronts the Gods*, 22.

23. McDermott, *Confronts the Gods*, 51.

quickly perceived that the issue with "the more considerable Deists" was not so much ontological and etiological, as it had been with Hobbes and Mandeville, but epistemological and moral—recurring themes in the philosophy of history.[24] The burning issue over the will, of course, was foundational to the deist scheme: self-determination empowered humanity to attain to "true religion" without revelation or supernatural grace. A chief reason why Edwards attacked the basis of Arminian thought was that it accommodated deistic principles and provided, as Paul Ramsey put it, "the breach through which deism poured, [to] the abandonment of Christianity."[25] In essence, Arminian theology put the power of salvation in the hands of the individual; it personalized salvation and made it readily available by de-emphasizing localized Christian "means and ordinances," i.e., the gospel revealed through word, sacrament, and sacred community. As the deists saw it, self-determination was "divinity's greatest gift to humanity";[26] their doctrines helped to vindicate, before the eyes of Europeans, the religious practices of the heathen, who, though historically and culturally isolated from institutionalized Christian means, nevertheless possessed that universal religious ability of self-determination and, comparatively speaking, moral virtue. Indeed, the heathen appeared to live more righteously than the gospel saturated Europeans. Special revelation held no advantage. Spiritual regeneration availed no more than moral reformation.

Edwards determined that deism's infiltration into Christian orthodoxy or, rather, orthodoxy's mutation into deism occurred by three subtle steps, culminating in a decisive fourth: (1) an aberrant opinion of man's mental (i.e. reasoning and volitional) abilities; (2) an extra-biblical appraisement of man's moral propensities and constitution; (3) an anthropocentric worldview leading to a naturalistic moral philosophy; and (4) open and unforgivable apostasy.

Having determined the priority of the issues to be addressed, he began his calculated counterattack with *Freedom of the Will*, a treatise aimed to demolish the "idol of free will" and destabilize the mechanism by which deistic principles were propagated within the Church, viz., Arminian theology.[27] Next came *The Great Christian Doctrine of Original Sin* (1758), which at its heart proposed to show, by reason, empirical observation, and Scripture, that man is not by nature innately good (another pillar of Enlightenment religion) but inherently sinful. This was a clarion call in support of an authentically Christian anthropology (and corresponding soteriology), as well as elenctic exposé of John Taylor's heretical model of Christianity-as-deism.

Two Dissertations (posthumously published 1765) was the adroit polemic against the third phase of deist ideology. And here is where Edwards intends to reclaim world history from the deist camp, namely through an opposing theocentric worldview that proposed the two-pronged thesis: "[*God*] *makes himself his end*" in creation; and, God is a

---

24. "The Nature of True Virtue" in *WJE* 8:541.
25. Ramsey, "Editor's Introduction," *WJE* 1:69.
26. McDermott, *Confronts the Gods*, 33.
27. *Freedom of the Will* also had the aim to buttress the Calvinist theory of reprobation, as the conclusion suggests.

communicating being.²⁸ Thus, "While deists condemned God to silence outside the secret dictates of the inner mind," explains McDermott, "Edwards proclaimed that God was ever communicating, and through many and diverse media—not only through Scripture but also through nature, history, and the history of religions."²⁹

God's ultimate end in creation includes innumerable subordinate ends that envelop every thing, person, and moment in world history, a history in which the vestiges of revelation remains with every culture and time, to greater or lesser degrees. Of course, neither *A Dissertation Concerning the End for which God Created the World* nor *The Nature of True Virtue* explicitly bears this out, but his unwritten *magnum opus*, which he in fact named "*A History of the Work of Redemption*," would have done so.³⁰

There were four central points to make in the appeal to history. First, contrary to the deist claim that pagan wisdom and non-Christian religious systems largely developed independent of revelation, Edwards's counterarguments were intended to show that both Greco-Roman philosophies and heathen religions were in fact dependent upon revelation.³¹ Secondly, he intended to provide opposing evidence from the same historical theatre as the freethinkers concerning the sufficiency of human reason (and will) to uncover the true God. Thirdly, he meant to show that the deists were asking the wrong questions: "true religion" was not *primarily* about morality but doxology: true virtue was a consequence of true doxology; both of which were revelatory items. And fourthly, overagainst the Enlightenment accusation that Christianity—specially Christian dogma—was static thinking from antiquity, Jonathan Edwards asserted that Christian eschatology was fused with history, which was not static but rather moving toward a teleological goal. The history of the deists was neither outside nor above the linear progression of redemptive history. The movement of history belongs to Yahweh and the fate of the deists and those who sympathized with their worldview is tethered to the Christ's bilateral redemptive and apocalyptic reed. We consider each point in turn.

The "Trickle-Down" Effect

McDermott's research to substantiate Edwards's first point remains unprecedented and comprehensive. Quotes are furnished from dozens of "Miscellanies" entries, as he evidences Edwards's contentions: "Contrary to what freethinkers say, [Edwards] charges, philosophy has given little or no knowledge of the true God, and what true knowledge

---

28. *WJE* 8:437; "Miscellanies," no. 332, *WJE* 13:410.

29. McDermott, *Confronts the Gods*, 43.

30. See McClymond's intriguing essay "A Different Legacy?" in *Jonathan Edwards at Home and Abroad*, 16–39. In it McClymond suggests that the evidence in Jonathan Edwards's letters links the unwritten project to such works as *A History of the Work of Redemption* (1774), *A Dissertation Concerning the End for which God Created the World*, and the "Miscellanies." Though the proposed treatise bears the same name as the published 1739 sermon series, it was not to be the same sort of "history," but a body of divinity "thrown into the form of an history . . . in an entire [sic] new method," i.e., the traditional content of Protestant theology chronologically developed in conjunction with sacred and profane history (*WJE* 16:727). See Minkema, "The Other Unfinished 'Great Work'" in Stein, *Jonathan Edwards's Writings*, 52–65; and Ahlstrom, *A Religious History*, 310.

31. McDermott, *Confronts the Gods*, 38–39.

existed among the heathen had come from revelation (*Misc.* 986). The history of religion is a history of degradation, decline, and the corruption of an original pure deposit of revelation (*Misc.* 986)."[32]

The heathen, according to Edwards, received their wisdom and knowledge of God not through "natural religion," reason and nature alone, "but by tradition from revelation given to the fathers of their nations."[33] Thus, in addition to the conventional Calvinistic appeal to divine general revelation, Edwards also appropriated the so-called *prisca theologia* ("ancient theology"), a theory propounded for example by Theophilus Gale in his multi-volume *Court of the Gentiles* (1669-1677) and Hugo Grotius' influential *De Jure Belli et Pacis* (1625), which in principle taught that God's special revelation as it pertained to the "HISTORY OF THE OLD TESTAMENT FROM MOSES' TIME" was "CONFIRMED FROM HEATHEN TRADITIONS."[34] Edwards was concerned to substantiate the two-pronged point that "HEATHENS had what they had of truth in divine things by TRADITION from the first fathers of nations, or from the Jews"[35] and that this divine "truth" or revelation trickled-down through non-Jewish cultures to ancient Greece and Rome, India and Africa, and even to China and the Americas. The idea was to demonstrate that every major thinker from Socrates and Plato to every leading religion from Islam and Confucianism to the animism of the Iroquois and Delaware Indians were indebted to God's special oral (and sometimes transcribed) revelation to Adam, the line of Seth, the Patriarchs, and, particularly, Moses's Pentateuch.

In his refusal to concede the point that five-sixths of the world has been left without revelation (that is, to grant that God is unfair), Edwards, as McDermott explains, "insisted that human beings before the advent of Christ and outside the borders of Christian nations were not and are not deprived of revelation, as the deists claimed, but have been fairly inundated with the voice of God."[36] If the divine revelation filtered down through ancient sources—which provided true knowledge of God and sundry other items of divinity—were not enough, the heathens also possess ever-present typological forms in nature, history, and circumstances, as well as their consciences, to educate them beyond the light of reason.[37]

His strategy to portray the history of the work of redemption as "a series of revelations by God to the heathen"[38] proved its point against the deists, even if many of his sources were unverifiable or simply erroneous.[39] God did not "lock out" the heathen, but

32. Ibid., 44.
33. Ibid., 41.
34. "Miscellanies," no. 1020, *WJE* 20:351.
35. "Miscellanies," no. 959, *WJE* 20:239.
36. McDermott, *Confronts the Gods*, 43.
37. See Fiering, *Moral Philosophy at Seventeenth-Century Harvard*.
38. McDermott, *Confronts the Gods*, 103.
39. On the whole, Edwards was without recourse to verify the historical accuracy of his sources concerning non-Christian religions, many which were flawed. And, so, he took them as practically reliable. More accessible, however, were the ancient classics texts at Harvard and Yale. But it seems Edwards was little interested in devoting time to confirm the (at times, incorrect) claims of Gale, Grotius, Cudworth, Chevalier Ramsey, Samuel Bochart, and others, whom he cited regarding pagan wisdom and mythology. His motives

blessed them with enough light to glorify and thank Him, in addition to providing them with wisdom for societal living. Therefore, says McDermott, "In Edwards' new history God was still good, in the context of the new knowledge of pluralism, because knowledge of God the Redeemer had been available from the beginning."[40]

Because of Reason, Revelation is Necessary

According to Edwards, the deists had it backwards: history did not show the sufficiency but the deficiency and futility of human reason (and will) to provide true knowledge of God. Certainly there were qualitative similarities between Judeo-Christianity and Plato's "The One" or Plotinus' "The Good"[41] or even the conceptual and moral thought of non-Christian religions—such was the inevitable residual result of prior revelation; but the dogmatic expression and praxis of pagan philosophers and heathen religions were, in the words of McDermott, "just so many manifestations of the human proclivity to deny and distort the original revelations given to the fathers of the nations."[42]

Edwards's theory of reason argues in "Miscellanies" no. 1338 that its sufficiency in religion lies only in the ability to "confirm" the reasonableness of an idea *p* already discovered but is generally incapable of ascertaining *p* to start with. The reason heathens were/are not Jews or have become Christians is because they have largely perverted, suppressed and ignored God's progressive revelation to them. So far from advancing mankind in terms of true religious knowledge, natural-man's reason and will have been the foremost impediments.

The issue again becomes one of dispositions—the "haves" and the "have-nots." Only this time, conscious of the Enlightenment—à la Lockean—challenge to allow "Nothing that is contrary to . . . clear and self-evident Dictates of Reason . . . as a Matter of Faith" (i.e., the validity of revealed truths must be confirmed by reason), Edwards sets forth his powerful apology concerning the epistemic access *regenerate* as opposed to *unregenerate* reason possesses, the thesis concerning the "new spiritual sense." He makes the issue not one of hardware (his doctrine of natural ability stipulates that the rational mind is fully capable of speculative knowledge of God), but software: the unregenerate can "agree" with the notional reasoning of believers, but they can never sense, feel, or appreciate its truth or reality, "for the disposition . . . must necessarily be changed first."[43] For the unregenerate a disposition of "holy consent"—spiritual sensibilities to the aesthetic dimension of reality—remains entirely lacking. Consequently, the heathen abide in "darkness in religious

---

were not those of a historiographer but of a theologian. Thus, he was source-sensitive only in terms of the didactic potential of a historical text's content.

40. McDermott, *Confronts the Gods*, 103.

41. For Jonathan Edwards's comparisons between the Triune God and ideas of the divine as found in Plato, Aristotle, the Pythagoreans, Neo-Platonism, and Plotinus, see "Miscellanies," nos. 955, 970 and 992, *WJE* 20:227–29, 253–54, 321–23.

42. McDermott, *Confronts the Gods*, 88. See 95. Sermon on Amos 8:11 (Mar. 1729; repreached Sept 1756), Jonathan Edwards Collection.

43. "Miscellanies," no. 23, *WJE* 13:287.

things."[44] The difference between unregenerate and regenerate reason leveled the epistemic playing field: reason has warped boundaries; revelation is necessary. McDermott summates the situation thus: "So heathen all over the world were given enough light to enjoy true religion—if they would only take advantage of it ... The heathen usually did not have the right disposition to 'improve their advantages,' but Edwards had proven his point. Despite the postponement of the Messiah's coming until thousands of years after the Creation, knowledge of true religion was nevertheless available during those years, and not only to the Jews. So Edwards's fairly traditional chronology could still stand against deist charges of injustice and cruelty. His God was vindicated."[45]

A New Historical Agenda: The Wrong Answer to the Right Question

It is only when we get to the third point of Edwards's alternative representation of history that McDermott's otherwise valuable and scholarly study disappoints by suggesting a soteriological agenda for Edwards that is essentially irreconcilable with the whole character of his Calvinistic thought and corpus. However remarkable it may be that Edwards, on the outskirts of the New World frontier, privately amassed data on every religious item from the activities of the Pope to the writings of Muhammad in order to developed an elaborate scheme for the roles other religions had and were playing in the drama of redemption, he was not pursuing an alternative salvation scheme for the heathen nor did he "open the door to that possibility," as McDermott proposes.[46] Such a door would have to dragged from some other written corpus into Edwards's theological vision and be tacked on to the exterior of his own writings.

When Edwards sets worship as the focal point of "true religion" he offers an opinion opposite to the deists' worldview. Not man's morality, but God's glorification is at center. Although he conceives that both devotees of the Living God and those who pay homage to idols offer worship as a response to revelation, yet there are strict parameters as to what constitutes "true" (i.e., acceptable) worship.[47] Here McDermott is ambivalent. On the one hand, he reproduces Edwards's qualifications for "true worship"—a new disposition and participation in the divine;[48] while, on the other hand, he nullifies their significance *as* qualifications: dispositions become universal and participation in the divine is only a matter of coming into contact with elements of primary special revelation apparently residually present in nearly every socio-religious community.

According to McDermott, Edwards's "new approach to soteriology" simply holds that an inner religious consciousness—a new disposition—is "the only prerequisite to salvation ... faith is subsumed by the category of disposition."[49] Repeating Morimoto, McDermott says that disposition functions as the ontological ground of forensic imputa-

---

44. *Sermon Twenty-One*, WJE 9:400.
45. McDermott, *Confronts the Gods*, 104–5.
46. McDermott, "Response to Gilbert," 80.
47. "Miscellanies," no. 986, WJE 20:309–11.
48. McDermott, *Confronts the Gods*, 89, 133–34.
49. Ibid., 89, 133–34.

tion. As McDermott himself puts it: "Martin Luther's salvation by faith *alone* becomes for Edwards salvation by faith *primarily*. While Luther emphasizes that in justification sinners are *counted* as righteous, Edwards insists that sinners are actually *made* holy in the act of regeneration."[50]

Under this account, Edwards's emphasis on disposition as primary and faith as secondary undermines not only his Reformed but also the Reformation contention that salvation is the justification of the *ungodly* and, therefore, the *unholy*. Instead, salvation is the bare possession of a saving disposition, which, *de facto*, renders one holy. Justification is subsequently grounded in the holy disposition of the human person.[51]

Following this line of thought, McDermott suggests a new perspective on Edwards's interest in the heathen and history. He portrays an Edwards who, while in the process of not only attempting to circumvent the deists attack on orthodoxy's epistemology, but also in his collative studies on non-Christian religions, observed in the heathen the same exercises of disposition peculiar to Christian contexts and concluded that they, too, can obtain justification but through non-Christian means. All evidence begged this conclusion: Isaac Barrow, Samuel Clarke, Ralph Cudworth, Daniel DeFoe, and others, provided seemingly incontrovertible evidence that some heathens worshipped, perhaps without knowing it, the true God.[52] There also was evidence of revealed religion in everything ranging from trinitarian elements in Dao-de-jing and messianic foreshadows in I-Ching to incarnational theology in Greco-Roman "pagan" philosophers and propitiatory doctrines in Native American animism and, so, a seminal gospel nearly everywhere. Of course, the potential efficacy of Jesus Christ's redemptive work could easily infuse a saving disposition in every person born into the world. Indeed, the dynamics of heathen moral behavior and religious systems tended to confirm it. If all these things were the case, according to McDermott, then Edwards could not but draw the conclusion that the revelatory items, which were not entirely despoiled over the years and present in a variety of forms throughout the world, could induce a generic faith-act for justification. Thus the history of God's special revelation should not be interpreted in narrow, restrictivistic terms, but more broadly: God desires the conversion of the heathen for their happiness, which, in turn, makes Him happy. Yet they are never "lost" in an absolute sense: they have salvation in a disposition and, bear in mind, justification is only an encounter away.

According to McDermott, the scope of the historical redemption drama did not narrow prior to the millennial age. Rather, due to the "progressive nature of revelation," it could only widen; for "In Edwards' view a saving disposition was nearly always a disposition to receive Christ."[53] Consequently, the progress of revelatory-redemption history

---

50. Ibid., 136.

51. McDermott, *Confronts the Gods*, 136, 138.

52. Jonathan Edwards collated materials about non-Christian religions and pagan philosophers from a variety of sources including dictionaries, encyclopedias, travelogues, monographs, newspaper articles and tangentially referential sources (such as sermons). The *Catalogues of Books* (*WJE* 26) and the individual "Miscellanies" entries, in which various passages from the aforementioned sources were copied, cite both references and the sources Jonathan Edwards desired to procure.

53. McDermott, *Confronts the Gods*, 139, 140.

neither served to render non-Christians all the more "inexcusable" for their idolatry and religious "darkness," nor did it hold a preparatory function (either to facilitate pedagogical intercourse with the Jews or prepare the Gentiles for a future encounter with the gospel), per traditional Calvinism. Instead, in keeping with McDermott's reading of Edwards, advancing revelation effects a greater, even global, conversion-cum-justification of the masses. Jesus Christ would reign on earth, but not necessarily over Christians: the kingdom of God is more generous than that.

Aside from the misunderstanding and misappropriation of Edwardsean dispositions, the difficulty with this reading lies in the fact that Edwards's corpus does not accurately support it. To start with, instead of opposing Luther, Edwards can be seen joining the Wittenberg Reformer's "Disputation Against Scholastic Theology" through his conviction that that which preceded conversion was not a disposition, but an indisposition and active rebellious and unbridled selfishness.[54] As a result, Edwards sustained throughout his public preaching ministry a restrictivist soteriology that required regeneration and forensic imputation for "true religious worship." For example, just as his Northampton congregation heard him preach in 1733 that "those that die heathen [God] will prey upon and Exert his Cruelty Upon forever," so too, in 1751, his Housatonnuk and Mohawk auditors in Stockbridge heard (through an interpreter) that, all those who "don't worship the true God that made the world and Jesus Christ his Son" go to hell.[55] Scores of sermons could be cited that (a) insist on the necessity of regeneration, (b) equate the heathen with the "lost," and (c) speak of the inevitability of judgment, eternal torments, and salvation through faith in Christ alone. Consider, however, a small sample of sermon "doctrines" from 1746 through the end of his tenure at Stockbridge in January 1758:

- Matthew 13:47–50 (1746): "Wicked men will hereafter be cast into a furnace of fire."

- Exodus 9:12–16 (1747): "They that will not yield to the power of God's word shall be broken by the power of his hand."

- Ezekiel 22:14 (1741, 1755): "Since God has undertaken to deal with impenitent sinners, they shall neither shun the threatened misery, nor deliver themselves out of it, nor can they bear it."[56]

- Revelation 6:15–16 (1732, 1755): "That wicked men will hereafter earnestly wish to be turned to nothing and forever cease to be that they may escape the wrath of God."

- 1 John 3:10 (1756): "All mankind through the whole world are one of these two sorts, either God's people or the devil's people."

- Revelation 6:16 (1747, 1757): "The weight of rocks and mountains is light in comparison of that wrath of God that shall hereafter come on ungodly men."

---

54. Luther, *WA*, 1:225.

55. Sermons on 105. Revelation 3:15 (1729) and 973. Matthew 7:13–14 (Jan. 1751), Jonathan Edwards Collection.

56. Published as *Future Punishment of the Wicked Unavoidable and Intolerable* in *Banner-Works* 2:78f.

- Mark 10:17–27 (1743, 1757): "Obs[ervation]. 1. There are many persons that have a great desire to have eternal life and seek it with some earnestness, that yet never obtain it."

From 1750 through to his departure for Princeton, Edwards frequently re-preached sermons from the 1730s and 40s, retaining in almost every case their doctrinal content that repeatedly articulated an unmistakable particularist theology requiring the new birth, God-given holiness and Jesus Christ's righteousness, and defensive treatments of hell.[57] Which is to say, Edwards was hardly dissatisfied, embarrassed, or "scandalized" with his theological development in the 1730s. Indeed, it would be extremely difficult to show any deviation whatsoever in his restrictivist soteriology from the mid-1730s through 1758, the year of his death.[58]

Likewise, his (semi-private, not private) "Miscellanies" notebooks[59] reveal a particularist account of history and redemption and purport the same prerequisites for "true worship." Here we need only consider "Miscellanies" no. 1357, one of Edwards's last, in which he records from John Brine (1703–65) the "defects" of "heathen morality" and "pagan philosophers['] morality" for the express purpose of indicating their categorical lack of "true virtue."[60] Without "true virtue" religious worship is blind worship.[61] God does not receive it for the same reason that "common morality" and "inordinate self-love" are not truly virtuous—no dispositional union with the Mediator through the Spirit; that is, no holiness. As he previously said in "Miscellanies" no. 1153: "Other kinds of sincerity of desires and endeavours" are "good for nothing in God's sight [and are] not accepted with him as of any weight or value to recommend, satisfy, excuse, or counter-balance." He continues in the same entry to make his repudiation of the principal doctrine of Enlightenment religion complete:

---

57. Of the approximately 345 sermons preached between 1751 and Jan. 1758, more than half (approximately 54 percent, or 183) were repreached sermons with an original composition prior to 1750. Moreover, the majority of these repreached sermons are from 1741 and earlier.

58. See Fiering, *Moral Thought*, 105, 203, 208–9 and 238–39.

59. Ava Chamberlain rightly argues that not only did Jonathan Edwards lend volumes of his "Miscellanies," to his protégées and colleagues (e.g., Samuel Hopkins and Joseph Bellamy) but also "various features of the 'Miscellanies' manuscripts lend them a public character." Chamberlain points out that Jonathan Edwards composed the "Miscellanies" in complete sentences, "first writing rough drafts that he would later carefully edit and transcribe—using his 'public' hand—into the notebooks . . . He even elaborately structured the longer entries" ("Editor's Introduction," *WJE* 18:9). Both Chamberlain and Schafer conclude that Jonathan Edwards employed his "faire" hand in the "Miscellanies" precisely because he had an eye to their eventual publication. What is more, scores of "Miscellanies" reappear, many with little to no alteration whatsoever, in a host of his published treatises.

60. Brine, "Of the Defects which attended the Doctrine of Morality" in *A Treatise on Various Subjects*, chap 3. See also "Miscellanies," no. 1162, where Jonathan Edwards contemplates, "It may be worthy of consideration whether or no some of the HEATHEN PHILOSOPHERS had not, with regard to some things, some degree of INSPIRATION of the Spirit of God, which led 'em to say such wonderful things concerning the Trinity, the Messiah, etc. Inspiration is not so high an honor and privilege as some are ready to think. Many bad men have been the subjects of it, yea, some that were idolaters . . . Yea, the devils themselves seem sometimes to have been immediately actuated by God and forced to speak the truth in honor to Christ and his religion . . . Why might not Socrates and Plato and some of the wise men of Greece have some degree of inspiration, as well as the wise men from the East who came to see Christ when an infant?" (*WJE* 23:84).

61. "*Miscellanies*," No. 1334 *WJE* 23:325–34.

> Hence we learn that nothing appears in the reason and nature of things—from the consideration of any moral weight or validity of that former kind of sincerity that has been spoken of[62]—at all obligating us to believe or leading us to suppose, that God has made any positive promises of salvation or grace, or any saving assistance, or any spiritual benefit whatsoever to any endeavors, strivings, prayers, or obedience of those that hitherto have no true virtue or holiness in their hearts though we should suppose all the sincerity, and the utmost degree of endeavor which it is possible to be in a person without holiness.[63]

In a second corollary headed, "SALVATION OF THE HEATHEN," Edwards is more specific as he flatly rejects the possibility of non-christocentric, non-biblical logocentric salvation in any form: "Hence we learn that nothing appears in the reason and nature of things . . . that can justly lead us to determine that God will reveal Christ and give the necessary means of grace, or some way or other bestow true holiness and saving grace, and so eternal salvation, to those heathen that are sincere."[64] The point is that they *neither have a gracious disposition nor any ability to exercise true virtue and, consequently, to offer true worship.*[65] Nor, in fact, do they have any recourse outside "the necessary means of grace," that is, the gospel of salvation by grace through faith in the covenant-keeping God, which, in Edwards, is not simply a post-Advent phenomenon.

Thus it would be a mistake to say that the second treatise in *Two Dissertations* (or even the first treatise!), *The Nature of True Virtue*, was exclusively or essentially concerned with Scottish moral sentimentalists; it had the foundering of deists more immediately in view.[66] In Edwards's carefully calculated rejoinder, the treatise *The End for which God Created the World* lays the foundation of a theocentric worldview, while *The Nature of True Virtue* tears up the moorings of the deistic worldview. There can be little doubt that their collective thesis would have been the centerpiece of his unfinished *magnum opus*.

---

62. I.e., in p.455 of "Miscellanies" notebook no. 6 (Trask Library, Andover Newton Theological Seminary).

63. *WJE* 23:56. See Jonathan Edwards's discussion in *Freedom of the Will*, Pt. III: "Freedom and Responsibility," §5: "Sincerity, No Excuse": "Hence it follows, there is nothing that appears in the reason and nature of things, which can justly lead us to determine, that God will certainly give the necessary means of salvation, or some way or other bestow true holiness and eternal life on those heathen, who are sincere . . . in their endeavors to find out the will of the deity, and to please him, according to their light, that they may escape his future displeasure and wrath, and obtain happiness in their future state, through his favor" (*WJE* 1:319).

64. Ibid.

65. See Fiering, "Hell and the Humanitarians," in *Jonathan Edwards' Moral Thought*, 200–260.

66. To be sure, Jonathan Edwards acknowledges that his "discourse on virtue is principally designed against that notion of virtue maintained by My Lord Shaftesbury, [Francis] Hutcheson, and [George] Turnbull," but he gives this statement in conjunction with his purposes for writing a defense of the doctrine of original sin against John Taylor's *The Scripture-Doctrine of Original Sin*, as well as *Freedom of the Will*. Edwards linked both the treatise on *Original Sin* and *Two Dissertations*, along with *Freedom of the Will*, as I have argued above, with "the modern opinions which prevail concerning these two things [viz., "*God's End in Creating the World* and *The Nature of True Virtue*], [which] stand very much as foundations of that fashionable scheme of divinity, which seems to have become almost universal," namely the naturalized religion of deism (Letter to the Reverend Thomas Foxcroft, February 11, 1757, *WJE* 16:696).

There is no indication in either Edwards's private or public records that he favored or was developing a non-particularistic salvation scheme. In fact, the evidence holds the opposite patently true. To be sure, he believed that pre-Israelite characters such as Melchizedek enjoyed salvation, as well as the "Old Testament church"—God effectually working through the Word-based protoevangelium revelation first given to their antediluvian fathers and then to them.[67] Nevertheless, the same could *not* be said about Greco-Roman thinkers, Chinese philosophers, or (prior to the New Testament dispensation) non-Jewish religions and (subsequent to the First Advent) non-Christian religions. Though Edwards held that the sages of Athens and Rome were "eminent for many moral virtues" derived from ancient revelation, yet without "true virtue" obtained from the God of the Hebrew religion and the "means" pertaining thereto, their morality was but *splendida peccata* and their theological insights "almost" and only "seemingly" divine truths.[68] But nobody according to Edwards is *almost* saved: "heathens" and "infidels" who "die in unbelief" and "don't worship the true God . . . and Jesus Christ his Son," quite plainly, are "destroyed."[69] Edwards's dispositional soteriology, so far from offering (in the words of McDermott) "A Possibility of Reconciliation" for the heathen, actually accentuates the particularistic dimensions of his philosophical-theology.

So while the Cambridge Platonists may have argued that the most important truths of Christianity had been propagated universally from the beginning, and that those truths chiefly pertained to worship and happiness, and so we may have Jonathan Edwards echoing John Smith, yet in Edwards *true* worship and happiness have their contexts *exclusively in light of God revealed as Redeemer*. McDermott makes the heart of this gospel message, perhaps inadvertently, peripheral for Edwards, which it certainly was not.

The manuscript evidence in Edwards's corpus tells a different story to that of McDermott. The "Miscellanies," sermons, letters and treatises, present a God who safeguards the aesthetic and moral quality of the worship He receives by:

1. Having it mediated through Jesus Christ;

2. *Emanating* it from Himself, receiving it to Himself (the indwelling Spirit), and *remanating* it back again and thereby replicating Himself, by Himself (the Son); and

3. Employing means—*very specific means*—so as to control and precisely determine every component of the closed, not open, process.

4. And all within a covenantal context.

Consequently, the heathen are subject to what is called in Reformed theology, "circumstantial unbelief"—an apology of theologians dating back to Augustine's *On the City*

---

67. "Notes on Scripture," nos. 138a, 232, 236, *WJE* 15; *The Blowing of the Great Trumpet* (1741), *WJE* 22:438–47.

68. "Charity and Its Fruits" in *WJE* 8:310; "Miscellanies," nos. 965 and 979, *WJE*, 20:249, 291–96.

69. 973. Sermon on Matthew 7:13–14 (1751), Jonathan Edwards Collection. In fact, Jonathan Edwards's most sustained defense of hell was written in 1755 in the virtual mini-treatises of "Miscellanies" nos. 1348 and 1356 (*WJE* 23:391–411; 575–603); a point that alone renders McDermott's thesis almost altogether unfounded.

of God, which taught that God exercises judgment on particular individuals or (especially) people groups and nations by sovereignly and justly withholding the means to the external call of salvation. Edwards owned this doctrine in its entirety. As a matter of fact, it is a regulative principle in his philosophy of history. His theocentric worldview holds that God unfolds a program of redemption for His *ad extra* glorification, but that that process is historical and, significantly, means centered and means identifiable.

The Redemption Discourse, Phasing, and the Moorings of Preparationism

Aside from the polemical appeal to history, Edwards also found the concept of chronological development constructive for systematics. This comes out in his 1739 thirty-sermon series, *A History of the Work of Redemption*, where he provides for himself an objective model and methodological foundation for his theological perspective, which he had been striving toward since his teenage conversion.[70] Ultimately, the strategy of the "Redemption Discourse" discloses (in John F. Wilson's phraseology) the culmination of Edwards's "technical soteriological achievement," the great effort toward "a final synthesis" of his theological, exegetical, and philosophical thought in a persuasive "historical or mythic narrative."[71]

To avoid wrongly construing Edwards's purpose in *Work of Redemption*, it must be understood that it is not primarily a historical work, but rather a theological treatise within a historical framework.[72] As Stephen R. Holmes and Amy Plantinga Pauw have shown how the interrelationships within the Trinity function as the theological fulcrum for Edwards's understanding of soteriology (and, indeed, of all theology),[73] so it is within a historical framework that God's work of redemption is best made intelligible and communicable. For Edwards, the theoretical infrastructure and foundation of theology is a Trinity-effected redemption, which is best explained and understood within the biblically disclosed time-boundaries given to the subject.

By the "Redemption Discourse" Edwards intends to (re)align what was initially his auditor's perspective and appraisal of time/history *and* space to an inherently valuable *biblical* account of spatiotemporality. Beyond his growing anxieties about deism and New England's incipient Arminianism, the impetus behind these intentions emerged from certain sociological developments that occurred in Northampton, which also provided occasion for the original publicizing of his historically integrated redemption-theology. Space does not permit a proper examination of these events, but suffice it to say that, with the anticlimactic denouement of the 1734–35 awakening, spiritual declension began to settle in amongst Edwards's parishioners. "Backsliding" in all of its ugly forms required

---

70. The ministerial setting of the Redemption Discourse is presented by Ola E. Winslow, *Jonathan Edwards, 1703-1758*, chap 8; and Patricia J. Tracy, *Jonathan Edwards, Pastor*. Jonathan Edwards also refers to this work and the future project of its expansion into his *magnum opus* as the "Redemption Discourse" and the "Work of Redemption." In the following discussion I shall do likewise.

71. See Wilson, "Editor's Introduction," *WJE* 9:1–14.

72. Ibid., 9:2–5.

73. See Holmes, *God of Grace*, and Pauw, *The Supreme Harmony of All*.

addressing.[74] The mood Edwards perceived from his congregations communicated to him that not only was Christianity's role being marginalized in the spheres of business, politics and society, but his role too. Christianity's pervasiveness was, little by little, vanishing from all aspects of everyday life. As his personal letters and sermons show, he could not help but wonder if the evils of Arminian antinomianism or, worse, deistic secularism, were infiltrating his Puritan enclave.

Despite adjustments to his homiletical technique, Edwards's early attempts to stabilize and navigate his congregation through these low points were only met with continued stolidity and regression. He therefore altered his rhetorical strategy further. Wilson H. Kimnach comments, that in the closing years of the 1730s, Edwards exhibits a distinct tendency to "write more complex sermons and, finally, sermon series."[75] By taking one doctrine or principle and attempting to exploit all its potential in an extended series, Edwards was able to string together several intimately and tangentially related theological, philosophical, biblical and ethical themes, issues, and concepts and present them with a sense of continuity and pervasive relevance. In other words, the sermon series became the most efficient way, short of a treatise, to communicate the depth and scope of the Christian worldview.

The "Redemption Discourse" was his most ambitious "worldview" series. As a theological work, it systematically expanded the ultimate unity of the spiritual and material, the local and global, the divine and the human spheres: the God of Northampton was no deistic conception. By casting the project in an elementary historical framework, Edwards places the urgent and the mundane affairs of mankind in the context of eternity and, in so doing, critically evaluates the projects and dealings of his colonial auditors and even "Old Light" antagonists and Enlightenment opponents within the eternal plan of the Trinity.

Thus Edwards strategically used the "Redemption Discourse" as a pastoral tool to adjust community and personal perspectives by instilling sacredness to all time and space. "The work of God," he taught, "is but one. 'Tis . . . but . . . one scheme, one contrivance."[76] We have already noted the one goal by which the scheme becomes one, namely, "God created the world to provide a spouse and kingdom for his Son"; now Edwards builds on this premise to emphasizes God's and therefore true religion's continued importance by connecting all time, all nations, and all personal history and futures, with redemption history.

Three Major Divisions

There are three sources which Edwards consults for a holistic view of redemption history: Scripture history; biblical prophetic history; and the secular history of philosophers, historians, and rhetoricians. From these literary sources, he discerns three major divisions in God's work of redemption. These are distinct segments or periods that mark out different stages in its constitutive "history."

---

74. See Tracy, *Jonathan Edwards, Pastor*, 125–30.
75. Kimnach, "General Introduction," *WJE* 10:103.
76. "Miscellanies," No. 702, *WJE* 18:296. See also "Sermon One," *WJE* 9:113–26.

1. *Preparation*—"The first reaching from the fall of man to Christ's incarnation"
2. *Accomplishment/Achievement*—"The second from Christ's incarnation till his resurrection, or the whole time of his humiliation"
3. *Application/Realization*—"The third from thence to the end of the world"[77]

The inference is that preparation leads to salvation "purchased" by the life and death of Jesus Christ, which is then applied to the church, until the consummation of the age: "So that the whole dispensation as it includes the preparation and the imputation and application and success of Christ's redemption is here called the Work of Redemption."[78] The three periods are subdivisions, therefore, of one organic process, "the Work of Redemption." Nevertheless, each period possesses distinctive characteristics.

The first of the three is discussed in sermons "Two" through "Twelve." It is defined by his conventional Christian interpretation of the Old Testament. The Jewish Scriptures not only point to the coming of Messiah, but also define him and explain his anticipated work, albeit in figural and typological schemes.

The second "great period" is the center of history, "the fullness of time" when the Son of God was incarnate. Referring back to the first period from christological "Sermon Eighteen," Edwards teaches that "all that success of Christ's redemption that was before [the incarnation] was only preparatory and was by way of anticipation, as some few fruits are gathered before the harvest. There was no more success before Christ came than God saw needful to prepare the way for his coming."[79] This is to say, the few who were redeemed in the world prior to the First Advent were necessarily associated with the preparatory means, i.e., the Hebrew nation with the Hebrew Scriptures. As we shall see, for Edwards, *means availability* is what determines the salvific status of the nations.

We now focus, however, on the "preparation" period, the first great periodization of the "Work of Redemption," because it is here in which Edwards gives so much attention to the positive aspects of pagan thinkers and "heathen" religions. In the "Redemption Discourse," preparatory periods and activities contextualize their proximity to and agency within the divine work, but only in accordance with the two technical uses Edwards reserves for the term "preparation."

First, he means it temporally. By the linear unfolding of the work of redemption where one event leads into or precedes another, God, as it were, sets the stage or *prepares* for the next episode or period, building to the great christic event.[80] In this way, Edwards establishes a connection between two events and/or persons in such a way that the preceding event (the preparation) is not only reflected in the next event but the next event involves and develops its *prooemium*. However, Edwards insists that the *essential* linkage between them has nothing to do with temporal or causal considerations. Rather, both events are constitutively linked to divine providence. God decrees one thing to the next

---

77. *Sermon Two*, WJE 9:127.
78. *Sermon One*, WJE 9:117.
79. *Sermon Eighteen*, WJE 9:344.
80. *Sermon Five*, WJE 9:177.

in the *historia salutis* according to "his good pleasure," agreeable to the *pactum salutis*—the eternal compact by which the Triune God unfolds His covenant promises, plans and purposes in spatiotemporality to achieve an ultimate end, the incarnation, and a supreme *telos*, the consummation of the age.[81]

Looking back, then, one of the first great movements of progression in the work of redemption was the separating and preparing of a people and nation from which the Messiah would come.[82] Another example was the "final dispensation," from the Diaspora to the first Advent, which marked the preparation of the Gentile world through the Jewish religion and messianic expectation. In pagan world events, Cyrus prepared the way for the Jews to return to Canaan; the destruction of the Persian Empire, which preceded the emergence of the Greek, led to a universal language by means of which the Hebrew Scriptures could be disseminated in script and discussion. Consequently, the proliferation of learning and philosophy, Semitic and Hellenistic, paved the way for the future propagation of the gospel message. And lastly, the *pax Romana* settled world events but also emphasized the bondage nature of the world, both of which were important for the stage in which the Messiah would enter: "The great works of God in the world during this whole space of time were all preparatories to this."[83] Thus, the heathens had their positive roles in the temporal preparation for the Christ.

The second technical usage of "preparation" relates to the inner-structure of redemption theology itself. Again, not by any inherent causal connection, but according to the aesthetic "fitness" of the divine will, there is present in the work of redemption a pattern by way of ordering and identifying the process. Whether at the cosmic, logical, temporal, or personal level, the process is "ordinarily" distinguishable through its triadic pattern: preparation, achievement, realization.[84] And although this pattern resembles the programmatic series of the old Puritan preparationist model of contiguity, where each standardized step is predictably followed by another, yet it possesses a depth dimension beyond the personal level, rendering it paradigmatic by virtue of the universal elements within and interrelatedness of all redemptive activity, whether in time or humanity, heaven or earth.

The common elements of the work of redemption (preparation, achievement, realization) obtain "objective" status as properties of the *historia salutis* and by a necessary antecedent relation, the *pactum salutis*. Consequently, while the "Redemption Discourse" makes use of a branching structure, or the pattern of subordination of parts within the logical framework, it is, nevertheless, theologically governed by the threefold division of preparation/achievement/ realization. Equally important for Edwards is their relatedness to Scripture. Since the work of redemption is itself a matter of divine revelation, the theoretical objectivity of the common elements can only be authenticated if they are inherently biblical. This, however, is not a problem. For Edwards, not only are the patterns and concepts implicitly and explicitly present in the Bible, but also the terminology: hence, the

---

81. See "End of Creation" in *WJE* 8:405ff.
82. *Sermon Five*, *WJE* 9:177–80.
83. *Sermon Two*, *WJE* 9:128.
84. Jonathan Edwards's analytic reasoning bears little resemblance to the triadic movement of Hegel's dialectic process.

employment of the biblical language of "promise," "performance," and "preservation" as interchangeable terminology for his triadic pattern of "preparation," "achievement," and "realization."[85]

At the level or perspective of the divine, preparation corresponds with the Triune "confederation" decreeing the work of redemption, providence and creation. Achievement means the incarnation, while realization happens though the salvific work of Jesus Christ in His sin bearing, crucifixion, and resurrection. The final judgment and Jesus Christ's surrendering all things to the Father is the consummation. At the historical level, where Edwards divides "this whole space of time into three periods," preparation compares with the fall of man to the incarnation; achievement to "Christ's incarnation till his resurrection, or the whole time of his humiliation"; and realization concurs "from thence to the end of the world."[86] Finally, at the personal, corporate or national level, preparation relates to *the providences and means of grace associated to the "external calling" of the gospel*, which effectually culminate in salvation, the achievement. Realization is identified with divine preservation through to heavenly glorification. Thus, the personal, subjective or interior level, which may be spoken of in terms of a larger scale—a religion, a nation, is isomorphic of the historical. The historical, in turn, mirrors the divine. It is noteworthy that, at the personal, corporate, or national level, preparation may take one of two courses: either preparation for salvation or preparation for damnation.

Contrary to the inclusivistic redemptive agendas of Morimoto and McDermott, Edwards pursues an interpretation of redemption history with two distinct paths for two distinct categories of people. Both paths, however, are determined by their moment-to-moment access to the progressive revelatory means of salvation.[87]

The Mediator of Means

In *Work of Redemption*, Edwards sets forth the one axiomatic requirement for reconciliatory possibilities between God and man—a mediator. When man sinned, "God the Father would have no more to do with man immediately . . . He would henceforth have no concern with man but only through a mediator [i.e., the Christ], either in teaching men or in governing or bestowing any benefits on them."[88] The Mediator Himself would be the means of instruction, the substance of the communication, and salvation itself. All divine revelation to the world, then, is to be understood in terms of the Word of God (the Son) as the *w*ord of God (the Son inscripturated), the special revelation of God, originally conveyed through oral tradition, enduringly by Scripture, ultimately in Jesus of Nazareth, and always through history and natural types.

---

85. See *WJE* 9:160–65, 169, 215, 525.
86. *Sermon Two*, *WJE* 9:127.
87. "Miscellanies," nos. 1162 and 1357, 84–85; 604–7. See also Fiering, *Moral Thought*, 108.
88. *WJE* 9:131. The late 1730s saw a flurry of "Miscellanies" entries on "MEDIATION OF CHRIST" and "MEDIATOR, why the second person of the Trinity" ("Table to the "Miscellanies" in *WJE* 13:140). See, e.g., "Miscellanies," nos. 539, 594, 622, 733, 737, 764a, 772, 773, and 781 in *WJE* 18.

The Mediator is, therefore, the means, such as have been necessary for salvation since the tragedy in Eden. Thus, according to Edwards, "The Word of God," *as* mediatorial revelation, "was not given for any particular age, but for all ages."[89]

Edwards delineates several reasons why God uses logocentric, word-invested means, all which revolve around the idea that "'Tis suitable and becoming" that God should do so, since the Christ is the divine Word. This is to say, the raison d'être of God's logocentric means of grace is both aesthetic and didactic. Since "means" are associated with the Christ in terms of His nature, that is, in terms of specially revealing God, Edwards believes that "We can't find them out by the light of nature, for they are such as depend on God's arbitrary constitution."[90] "Means which God designs" are, then, an "immensely more excellent and glorious way [of religion] than by the light of nature" because they too reflect the mental/relational excellence inherent to God's arbitrariness.[91] Therefore, "'Tis only because 'tis God's pleasure to annex his blessing to the means of his own appointing . . . for seeing God is the sovereign bestower of salvation he will bestow it in his own way."[92] The particular way God has chosen to "annex his blessing" to means involves the Holy Spirit, who illuminates and impassions recipients of God's logocentric revelatory means with religious affections engendered from a vision of Christ's excellencies.[93] Moreover, since "the sum" of what Christ "purchased" for the elect is the Holy Spirit, "means and ordinances" themselves may be seen as "conveyancers of the Spirit."[94] A trinitarian principle governs Edwards's theology of "means and ordinances." God's dealings with man are always to be understood in terms of the Son and the Spirit, and always within covenantal frameworks and strictures.

Edwards cautions, however, that though "we know that God's manner is to bestow his grace on men by outward means . . . And, therefore, if persons are out of the way of those means, there is no likelihood of their receiving grace," yet in and of themselves, "they have no influence to produce grace, either as causes or instruments, or any other way," though they are "necessary in order to it." Divine means, therefore, are necessary but not sufficient for grace, for in order to their effectiveness each Person of the Trinity must be involved, but "we know not when the Spirit's time is."[95]

In lieu of the centrality of special revelation in God's self-glorifying scheme, Edwards's history of the salvific status and function of the nations can be determined by

---

89. "Miscellanies," no. 583, *WJE* 18:119.

90. 379. [L. 7v.]. Sermon on Ezekiel 33:4–5 (Feb. 1736), *WJE Online* 51.

91. 316. [L. 7r.]. Sermon on Isaiah 5:4 (Mar. 1734; repreached Aug. 1757), *WJE Online* 49.

92. 379. [L. 7v.]. Sermon on Ezekiel 33:4–5 (Feb. 1736), *WJE Online* 51. Italics added.

93. Cf. *A Divine and Supernatural Light* (1733), *WJE* 17:408–26.

94. "Miscellanies," no. 689, *WJE* 18:253.

95. "Miscellanies," nos. 538, 539, *WJE* 18:83–84, 84, 86–87. Here Jonathan Edwards emphasizes the arbitrariness of the operation of the Holy Spirit, as Sang Lee, rightly explains in his "Editor's Introduction" (*WJE* 21:57–62). However, Lee is unclear about the role of means of grace to facilitate the *infusion* of the Holy Spirit (as a disposition of holiness) when he writes: "The means of grace are need and useful only if 'infused'—if grace is 'in the heart'" (ibid., 58). Jonathan Edwards clearly states that the word of the gospel is indispensable for facilitating the infusion of the Holy Spirit—not out of causal necessity, but because the Divine Will finds it "fitting" and because Christ is present *in* the gospel itself.

the special revelation made available to them. The history of redemption unfolds a narrative with juxtaposing storylines, just like the two sides of predestination or the bilateral effects of the gospel: the one of promise, blessing and salvation, the other of forswearing, cursing and damnation. Both storylines, however, are developed by the theme of *means availability*—a sort of hermeneutic for reading history. God gives and advances special revelation in one nation to their potential benefit, while He denies or withholds further revelation from another. The key is when the substance of a nation's revelatory content fails to keep pace with the historical progress of redemption, the "old" revelation, for all intents and purposes, becomes redundant in terms of salvific potential and (as we shall see in the following section) only serves to condemn. Conversely, reception of fresh revelation elevates one's status in the preparatory state (exposure or invitation into the covenant community), to the threshold of achievement—salvation itself.

Spiritual Judgments

Preaching on the text of Amos 8:11, Edwards assert the doctrine: "Spiritual judgments are the most terrible that can befall a people."[96] Special revelation is the topic at hand within this "Fast-day" sermon. According to Edwards all temporal spiritual judgments may be reduced to these two heads: "1. A being deprived of the outward hearing of God's word; 2. a being deprived of the inward hearing of it." In this context "Spiritual judgment" number "1" is synonymous with the more sanitized "circumstantial unbelief." Destitute of the means to the external call, the prospect of an effectual internal call is, according to Edwards, quite doubtful: "the circumstances of the great part of the world be such that their reconciliation [to God] be very improbable."[97] Again, if their reconciliation has any hope of being "not utterly impossible," then they have to "come to an acquaintance with divine revelation," i.e., the gospel of God's reconciliation through Jesus Christ alone.[98]

When he applies the doctrine of spiritual judgments in his work on the history of redemption, number "1" is prominent in the discussion on pre-Christian, non-Jewish nations.

The first apostasy from the revelation given to Adam and proliferated through his posterity to the "fathers of the nations" resulted in mankind's near complete annihilation. Noah, however, preserved the former and also furthered the special revelatory knowledge of God in the next age: he receives a covenant in which Yahweh swears never to destroy the earth and all life within it because of the wickedness of man. But again declension immediately follows. So while all heathen nations came originally from those that were acquainted with the "true God and the true religion," yet "they all by little and little degenerated into gross idolatry and ignorance of the true and became wholly destitute of the word of God *excepting* [sic] *only the posterity of Abraham*."[99] The Semites, like the Sethites,

96. 95. Sermon on Amos 8:11 (Mar. 1729; repreached Sept. 1756), Jonathan Edwards Collection.

97. "Miscellanies," no. 1299, *WJE* 23:246–48.

98. Ibid., 247.

99. 95. Sermon on Amos 8:11 (Mar. 1729; repreached Sept. 1756), Jonathan Edwards Collection. Emphasis added.

amalgamate with the Hamites: humanity unites in a rebellion at Babel; Yahweh scatters the nations and, yet, mercifully commits His purposes and plan for man and the world to Abraham in a new and gracious covenant. The work of redemption moves forward: humanity (i.e., the Gentile nations) is exiled from the covenant which only Abraham and his descendants inherit.

Overlooked by McDermott, this last clause is pivotal to understanding Edwards's pre-Advent, "preparatory period" approach to the heathen nations. At the time of the call to Abram, "true religion" was, for all intents and purposes, extinct on the earth—there was not so much as a Noah figure left once Terah died.[100] But instead of judging the earth (which Yahweh vowed not do in His oath to Noah, et. al. [Gen 9:8f.]), God reveals His redemptive plan to Abram. The terms had simply changed: the oral tradition had become a covenant tradition; special covenant revelation displaced so-called "natural" religion.[101] The "exiled nations" outside of the Abrahamic Covenant would have to wait to have it brought to them through Abraham's descendants.

Thus, the history of redemption narrows dramatically at Abram: positively, a covenant of grace is announced, negatively, head "1" stipulates that only one particular nation will possess the means by which God would administer redeeming grace. Revelation progressed and the history of redemption leapt forward. God had trumped His own oral tradition of the "protoevangelium" and transformed the Adamic promise (Gen 3:15) and Noahic oath (Gen 9:9–11) into a covenant with Abraham. Now Abraham/Israel had become a type of ark until the time of Christ—the climatic antitype.[102] *The nations of the world were being judged*. But instead of drowning them, God excludes them from the "ark" of the Abrahamic covenant in the same way He "shut the door of mercy" to Noah's ark on the world's inhabitants.[103]

The cultic system in the Hebrew nation trained them to look to God to provide a sacrifice, that is, to look to God as a merciful Savior and redeemer, to acknowledge His holiness, majesty, and jealousy, "which," Edwards thought, "is the exercise of the same disposition of mind as is exercised in actually believing on Christ crucified, and is the same sort of act."[104] The Jews, therefore, could have a gracious disposition infused within them because they were the possessors of the means by which God fittingly covenanted to bring salvation (both among the members of the Trinity and, subsequently, with key figures in redemption history), first to them and then to the wider world, the exiled nations. The Israelites could be justified in the same way as the future Christian church: not by obedience (which was impossible because of standing consequences and binding power of the Adamic covenant), but in trusting God to provide and accept a sacrifice for sin and having faith that He would be a Savior to humanity and grant righteousness or, in other word, through faith in God to be faithful to His covenant promises. Thus Edwards reasoned that

---

100. *Sermon Four, WJE* 9:158 59, 165–66.

101. "Miscellanies," no. 598, *WJE* 18:140.

102. *Sermon Three, WJE* 9:152.

103. 687. Sermon on Matthew 25:10 (Nov. 1742; repreached Jan. 1756): "DOC": "The shutting of the door of mercy" [L. 2v.], Jonathan Edwards Collection.

104. "Miscellanies," no. 326, *WJE* 13:406.

the two covenants were really different versions of the same covenant of grace initiated with Abraham, but having its roots in the protoevangelium.[105] Salvation then was the same as today: by grace through faith in the covenant-keeping God. (All but standard fare for covenant theology.)

The Mosaic/Sinaitic Covenant provided a "trial" not only for the Jews but the whole world as to whether they could be obedient to the revelation thus far. It too was preparatory, yet with a revelation so much more refined and lucid than the ambiguous protoevangelium that was surpassed by the Abrahamic covenant.

In the covenant of grace, however, God reserves the prerogative to implement the second head of spiritual judgments. In the sermon on Amos 8:11, Edwards warns: "The second sort of spiritual judgment upon a people is with respect to the inward hearing of the word of God, when there is a famine or scarcity of the good influence of the word of God upon men's minds it is a withholding of the Spirit of God."[106]

With greater privileges and clarity come greater responsibilities and expectations. Neglect God's means at either individual or corporate levels and spiritual judgments follow, bringing in their wake a host of tribulations. So reads Edwards' history of national Israel. Saul slights covenant privileges and the word falls on stony ground; likewise, with Israel. As a nation it was the bearer of God's word, but though that "word be quick and powerful, yet it is nothing; it is a dead letter without the application of the Holy Spirit."[107] Consequently, when the next advancement in redemption history came at hand, God rendered a judgment on the Jews: their revelation became law to condemn them, and the Spirit was given to illumine the Gentiles.

The residual revelation preserved amongst infidel nations rendered them "inexcusable" for neglecting original revelation and what they currently possessed.[108] Yet, it could still serve in a preparatory sense to lead them to the Jews' religion and the future hope for a mediatorial Messiah.[109]

The pattern continues into the First Advent and Christian period; this time, however, the second spiritual judgment receives equal emphasis with the first.

The deists inveighed against the Calvinists because only one-sixth of the world had means to the gospel, which meant that particularist theology left hell brimming with souls. They simply failed to appreciate that spiritual judgment number "1" remained in full effect. Unlike his deistic contemporaries, Edwards saw the Christian era of circumstantial unbelief both positively and negatively. Positively, their circumstantial unbelief was part and parcel of the preparatory movement of the divine drama: knowledge of new lands and peoples, though devoid of salvific means and therefore damned, only heightened mil-

---

105. "Miscellanies," no. 1354, *WJE* 23:506–43; *Sermon Twenty-Five*, *WJE* 9:449–50, 525.

106. 95. Sermon on Amos 8:11 (Mar. 1729; repreached Sept. 1756), Jonathan Edwards Collection.

107. *WJE* 10:543.

108. Although Puritans such as Richard Baxter, Philip Doddridge, Cotton Mather, and Isaac Watts (all of whom McDermott cites) acknowledged that a scant few among the "heathen" were saved, Jonathan Edwards never explicitly or implicitly agrees. Rather, even in his most sanguine moments, he refuses to offer more hope for them than, "there is no likelihood in their receiving grace" ("Miscellanies," no. 538, *WJE* 18:84).

109. *Sermon Two*, *WJE* 9:137.

lennial expectations; for Western knowledge of them soon meant their knowledge of the West's religion, Christianity. God, in the meantime, providentially preserves and cultivates ancient residual revelation in preparation for "their more readily receiving the great doctrine of the gospel of Christ."[110]

Hence Edwards's optimism about the Native Americans stemmed not from their supposed possession of "saving disposition,"[111] but because the gospel was being brought to them. It was all very eschatological: they were emerging out of circumstantial unbelief, the day of grace was at hand for the barbarians, exile from the Abrahamic covenant was ending, and Christ's millennial reign was dawning—at least from the perspective of the Housatonic River.[112]

Negatively, circumstantial unbelief could also be preparation of a more ominous sort. For example, in a MS sermon on Revelation 14:15 (1743) Edwards writes, "Let what has been said on this subject lead sinners to consider what *they* are ripening for. There are two kinds of persons that are here in this world in a preparatory state, elect and reprobates. Both are continued here in a state of preparation for an eternal state. Elect are here to be prepared [for heaven]. Reprobates are preparing [for hell]. They are ripening. And there are none [who] stand still, neither saints nor sinners."[113] Thus, the progress of redemption (and damnation) moves on, not only at the individual level, but also with collective people groups and nations. God getting His glory all the way.

Just as with Israel in the Old Testament dispensation, so, too, the second spiritual judgment takes place amongst those with immediate access to the gospel. Edwards preaches it this way: "The word of God let it be enjoyed in never so great plenty with never so great purity and dispensed with never so much faithfulness signifies nothing as to the designed effect and benefit of it without the Spirit of God. It is no purpose that the word is heard outwardly unless it be heard inwardly."[114]

To Edwards, it is a judgment proportionate to the "excellency" and availability of the light, therefore, it is the more severe: "the wrath of God is especially increased against unbelievers by that sin of unbelief. Because . . . they do in effect give God the lie."[115] For

---

110. *Sermon Two, WJE* 9:137.

111. McDermott, in his chapter "American Indians" (11), repeatedly emphasizes Jonathan Edwards's rather innocuous use of "inclination" and "disposition" in connection with Native Americans to suggest something ontological, and therefore makes a rather artificial connection with the soteriology articulated in *Religious Affections* (*WJE* 2). He ignores the fact that, on some occasions (such as with Indian interests "to be instructed in the Christian religion" [*WJE* 9:434]), these words may not have any dispositional soteriological connection. See McDermott, *Confronts the Gods*, 198–99.

112. Jonathan Edwards believed that at least two thousand years would elapse before the parousia ("Miscellanies," nos. 1198 and 1199, *WJE* 23:119–23). His enthusiasm about the Indians relates to a sense of confirmation: he understood the ingathering of barbarous nations a precursor to the Second Advent.

113. 712. Sermon on Revelation 14:15 (Jan. 1744), Jonathan Edwards Collection. Cf. 1106. Sermon on Revelation 14:15 (Jan. 1754); and 973. Sermon on Matthew 7:13–14 (Jan. 1751): "Doctrine": "All mankind of all nations . . . are going in one or the other of these paths, either in the way that leads to life or the way that leads to destruction," Jonathan Edwards Collection. Reproduced as *All Mankind* in McMullen, *The Blessing of God*, 225–30.

114. 95. Sermon on Amos 8:11 (Mar. 1729; repreached Sept. 1756), Jonathan Edwards Collection.

115. 347. [L. 5r.]. Sermon on John 3:36(b) (Dec. 1734; repreached May 1755), *WJE Online* 49. See also *Sermon Twenty-Eight, WJE* 9:489–90.

this reason, God continues to exercise this judgment upon Islam, which, according to Edwards, with accurate knowledge of the Christian message, rejects it and "perverts" it into the religion of Satan.[116] Likewise, Roman Catholicism's day of grace has come and gone. In Edwards' history, Rome sold her birthright during the Reformation and fused the "Apostles' gospel" with "superstition." Consequently, God has withheld inward illumination from the minions of "popery," to the end that it has become "Antichristian Rome . . . spiritual Babylon."[117] And Judaism, for failing to amalgamate with its Christian successor, also has been "given over to blindness of mind and hardness of heart."[118]

∽

So while McDermott is correct to bring attention to the eschatological dimension of Edwards's thought concerning "other" religions and nations, yet he departs from the substance of his sources and the spirit of Edwards' theology by diminishing the role of logocentric means and the punitive elements allied with them, in order to play up the possibility of an Edwardsean inclusivist-soteriology. But contrary to the analysis of McDermott and Morimoto, Edwards, in his evangelistic outreach to the unconverted, does not appeal to "*gracious* dispositions" for an exercise of faith, but rather he appeals to their *self-loving* disposition. His motivation for doing so lies in the second head of spiritual judgments; his optimism lies in their abiding within the compass of gospel means.

The Usefulness of Self-love

Edwards, of course, was not only a philosopher-theologian, but also a Puritan minister. His whole professional career, save for two short months as the president of the College of New Jersey, was spent as a parish pastor or gospel missionary. In that capacity he saw the dissemination of the gospel as the necessary and indispensable means of supernatural redeeming grace: "We have [no] notice given us of any restoration, any other way than by the gospel."[119] Consequently, he held that inclusivistic and pluralistic theories were apostate theologies: "if unbelievers have anything forgiven them, then there is forgiveness out of Christ, and contrary to God's everlasting and unalterable constitution of grace."[120] The Mediator and His means are absolutely necessary, for all other systems of salvific hope, particularly the sentimental deistic theories, are ultimately built upon semi-Pelagian or Pelagian foundations: "What some call trusting in the ABSOLUTE MERCY OF GOD, i.e. trusting in his merciful nature without any consideration of a mediator to make way for and obtain the exercises of that mercy, is not much different from trusting in our own righteousness."[121] Therefore, Edwards declares in the strongest particularist language: "None but those that do live under the calls of the Gospel shall be saved . . . So there are

---

116. "Miscellanies," no. 613, *WJE* 18:145–46; *Banner-Works* 2:488.
117. *Sermon Twenty*, *WJE* 9:374.
118. "Types of the Messiah" in *WJE* 11:322 n.5.
119. "Miscellanies," no. 596, *WJE* 18:130.
120. "Miscellanies," no. 648, *WJE* 18:186.
121. Ibid., 188.

none saved but only those that hear the calls of the Gospel. That is God's way and his only way of bringing men to salvation, viz. by the Gospel . . . So that all those that never have heard the joyful sound of the Gospel are excluded, as they are not chosen."[122]

But in light of the second spiritual judgment, Edwards couples this doctrine with an additional proposition: "Even of them that are called by the external call of the Gospel but few are saved."[123] Hence Edwards found it his duty to admonish the unregenerate to "seek" and "strive," that is, to "prepare" for salvation in the hope that they might become non-meritorious recipients of mercy. Their only hope lies in "living under the calls of the Gospel," that is, exposure to the gospel community and, more immediately, faithful and true preaching (*theatrum salutis*).[124] This had been the primary gospel strategy of the Reformation, which in Edwards's Puritan tradition became codified through the works of William Perkins.

Contrary to Perry Miller's proposal, the *theatrum salutis* is not an external environment where beliefs are formed on the basis of "sense perception" or "rhetoric of sensation."[125] Rather, it is the means-laden "forum" in which God sovereignly dispenses saving grace in an identifiable and meaningful fashion. The minister's objective was to lead sinners to the place where God gathers and waters His flock.

Consequently, and in spite of his doctrine of double particular predestination, Edwards refines a strategy of sermon rhetoric for the "Application" portion of his sermons,[126] which presses the unregenerate to autonomously "prepare" for salvation, not by advancing from one "step" to another, but through exposure to God's forum of grace. Such thinking underscores an important distinction between Edwards's dispositional theory of autonomous preparation and other forms of "preparation for salvation" consisting of

---

122. 235. [L. 1v.]. Sermon on Matthew 22:14 (1732), *WJE Online* 47.

123. Ibid, [L. 2v.].

124. When Jonathan Edwards explains in "Miscellanies" no. 629, that the "means of grace" consist of "the word and ordinances and works of God" (*WJE* 18:157), Lee aptly explains that these things are to be understood as "Scripture, sacraments, and providence" ("Editor's Introduction," *WJE* 21:58). However, Lee's next statement is incautious: "Thus, the proclamation of the gospel through preaching, the sacraments, teaching, and all of God's works in history and nature are the means of grace that can move a habit of grace into exercise" (ibid.). This is not true for Jonathan Edwards. For, then if Lee is correct, there is nothing that does not qualify as a gospel means of grace and the gospel becomes indistinct from, say, Law or reprobation or evil, etc., thus leaving Jonathan Edwards with a sort of pan-gospelism view of reality, which certainly is not the case. Rather, Jonathan Edwards's "the works of God" (what Lee perceives as "providence") should be understood as the works of God in redemption history to accomplish the great Christic events, typology notwithstanding.

125. See Miller, "Jonathan Edwards on the Sense of the Heart," 127–28.

126. Here the influence of Timothy Edwards and Solomon Stoddard is noteworthy. Both provided homiletical models for Jonathan Edwards to follow, and in that respect he offers nothing new, though his compositional artistry was of a superior nature. "In effect, then, the Application is a period of experience for Jonathan Edwards's auditory, a time of living imaginatively, through a 'willing suspension of disbelief,' a series of fictive experiences created and controlled by the artist-preacher" (Kimnach, "The Literary Techniques of Jonathan Edwards," *WJE* 10:50). "Application" is synonymous with "Exhortation" or "Use of Instr[uction]." In the midst of and subsequent to the periods of revival in 1734–35 and 1740–42, it was not uncommon for "Applications" to find their way into the "Doctrine" segment. "Doctrine" and "Improvement" became mixed modes when "seeking" and "trusting God" were explicated.

either (i) the ability of the sinner to independently prepare him/herself by gradual and definite advancements toward the threshold of conversion,[127] or (ii) the Roman Catholic expressions of cooperative preparation for grace,[128] or, especially, (iii) the sinner being "prepared" from first to last by God—a heteronomous preparation—which itself is an "if/then" scenario: *if* God prepares, *then* it proves effectual.[129] In contrast to this latter scenario, Edwards's autonomous preparation by the sinner should not be considered divine preparation at all. In Edwards's scheme, the sinner merely "seeks" divine help, and sinfully at that. Hence it would be better to call Edwards's scheme a doctrine of "seeking" rather than "preparing for salvation": "seeking" is done by the sinner, whom one presupposes "seeks" and "strives" without the soul-transforming assistance of the Spirit. Though, to be sure, the Spirit may "in an extraordinary manner" heighten the *natural* sensibilities of the unregenerate to previously unattained levels.[130] *Divine* (or heteronomous or compositional) preparation, however, is only truly verified in retrospect, i.e., after the sinner experiences salvation—when the seeking or striving activities may then be credited to the availing monergistic work of the Spirit. This Edwards analyzes into minutiae, tracing the "distinguishing marks" of those under divine convictions, humiliation, etc., in *Religious Affections* and *Distinguishing Marks*.[131] Of this doctrine of heteronomous preparation, Edwards finds objectivity or verification for articulating this idea *as* a biblical doctrine in his philosophy of history. Only God's preparing could result in salvation: sinful seeking is in no way a personal turning to God. To espouse anything other only blurs the line between a synergistic salvation model and a monergistic model, between Arminian evangelism and Calvinistic effectual calling.

The call for the unregenerate to "seek salvation" in their own strength and out of selfish motives could be found not only in Stoddard's *Treatise Concerning Conversion* (1719) and *The Efficacy of the Fear of Hell* (1713), but also Thomas Shepard's famous *Parable of the Ten Virgins* (1660), and Thomas Hooker's disputed *The Soul's Preparation for Christ* (1632), to name but few.[132] In this respect Edwards may be seen to simply follow in the steps of Perkins-Sibbes-Shepard-Stoddard. Yet Edwards did have something innovative to offer when he ensured the method by founding it, in large part, upon principles stemming from his dispositional ontology. And this is where Morimoto and McDermott entirely misunderstand Edwards. Edwards did not optimistically exhort

127. One might term this "Arminian" preparationism (see Norman Pettit, *The Heart Prepared*, 125–29).

128. Schaff, "The Canons and Decrees of the Council of Trent," in *The Creeds of Christendom*, 2:92–94.

129. William Perkins, for example, underscores the difference between what I am calling "autonomous" preparation and "heteronomous" preparation when he distinguished the beginnings of preparation and the beginnings of composition: "Beginnings of preparation arise from the work of the Law and are not necessarily works of God's Spirit" which are "the effect of regeneration begun" (Perkins, *Perkins-Workes* 1:638–41; 2:13). Heteronomous preparation is equivalent to irresistible grace and, therefore, rejected by Arminian theology, which asserted individual "free assent."

130. See *Religious Affections*, Part II, *WJE* 2:127–90.

131. See Mark Valeri's analysis: "Evangelical Humiliation as Preparation for Conversion" in "Editor's Introduction," *WJE* 17:36–40; and Smith, "Editor's Introduction," *WJE* 2:8–43.

132. Their collective position, which made provision for natural-man's affective nature, stands opposite to John Cotton's extreme negation of such a notion (see Pettit, *The Heart Prepared*, 129–57).

Dispositional Peculiarity, History, and Edwards's Evangelistic Appeal to Self-Love

the unconverted to engage means because their disposition *would* issue in a faith-act. Instead, true to his philosophical-anthropology, he appeals to their inordinate self-love precisely because it *would not* issue in a faith-act, but it might move them out of fear and self-loving self-preservation to "live under the calls of the Gospel," where haply regenerating grace could supernaturally work a saving faith-act, according to God's (covenant bound) arbitrary will.[133]

Edwards proposes in *Religious Affections* that, in addition to reasonably engaging the rational mind through the word of God, the Christian minister must also appeal to natural-man's innate operating principles, to the very structure of his being, that is, to man's "inordinate" self-love and its "less noble" principles of fear, self-preservation, and self-interest. For, according to Edwards, only two things will move the whole will (rational will and appetites) of man, namely, fear and love: "There are no other principles, which human nature is under the influence of, that will ever make men conscientious, but one of these two, fear and love . . ."[134]

His answer to the problem of exposing unregenerates to God's forum of salvation is to appeal to natural-man's love for himself, to his dispositional nature. What will move the *will* of the unregenerate man is his inordinate, sinfully selfish concern for himself. Fear of pain, punishment and the plague of guilt and death, will move a man. Natural-man's interest in preserving his own life will motivate him to hear the gospel, not because he loves either it or its Author, but because he inordinately loves himself above all things, and needs it to preserve himself. This shallow self-loving concern to preserve oneself and serve one's interest, Edwards explains, is enough to at least move the sinner into the forum of salvation in which hope and (ideally) salvation may be found.[135] The logic of disposition was applicable to evangelism too.

This type of "seeking" of itself never issues in salvation; neither is it traceable nor meritorious. In this sense, preparation should not be thought of in terms of moving from one *step* or *stage* to another, but rather as a *status*. If one mentally engages the logocentric means (which, almost certainly effect some sort of non-meritorious moral reformation, while eliciting natural "affections"), then one is in a state of preparedness. Again, there is no gradual movement toward conversion, there is only the possibility of being converted by the Spirit if one retains "the seed of the word"—the Christ-"material" used by the Spirit to effect conversion. The matter finds rhetorical expression in terms of probability quotients: the more "material" one imbibes and the more consistent the engagement within the *theatrum salutis*, the greater the "possibility" of conversion: "The oftener these notions or ideas [of God's grace in the gospel] are revived, and the more they are upheld in the soul, the greater the opportunity for the Spirit of God to infuse grace, because he hath more opportunity, hath opportunity more constantly. The more constantly the matter for

---

133. *WJE* 2:108. See also Fiering, *Moral Thought*, 171. Hence the basic argument of *Freedom of the Will*: the "will" does not constitute a real entity but is an expression of the strongest motive in a person's character.

134. *WJE* 2:179.

135. See 474. Sermon on Proverbs 9:12 (May 1738; repreached 1751), Jonathan Edwards Collection; and 260. Sermon on 1 Peter 1:13 (1732), *WJE Online* 47.

grace to work upon is upheld, the more likely are persons to receive grace of the Spirit. 'Tis the wisest way to maintain the opportunity, for we know not when the Spirit's time is."[136]

Content and consistency are, therefore, the key to preparatory seeking, not stages. And even then all that Edwards can offer is the "possibility" of salvation: preparatory seeking comes with no promises. Consequently, in his promotion of the "possibility" of gospel benefits to selfish natural-man exposed to the Word, Edwards sometimes fashions his "Exhortations" similar to Pascal's "Wager."[137]

Spiritual judgment number "2" was, for Edwards, commonplace in revival scorning, religiously declining England and, to an increasing degree, New England. So he would preach, "Some men, whatsoever means and advantages they have, and how much soever the work of conversion is carried on, will never be converted."[138] The reasons for this are not just theological but dispositional: "I. I would shew what men cannot do in order to their salvation and in general men can do no part of the work of salvation. Whatsoever is properly any part of salvation is beyond their power—whether it be the imputation of their salvation by satisfaction for sin or purchasing salvation or whether it be the application of salvation in conversion, sanctification, and glorification."[139] The salvation of a sinner from the foundation to the top stone is the work of God. Every part of it is altogether beyond the power of a natural man. Men can do nothing towards saving themselves:

1. Men can't make any atonement for their sins . . .

2. They can't purchase heaven . . .

3. They can't convert themselves . . . And *they can't work a gracious disposition into themselves; so they can't put forth any gracious act. The least act of grace* is infinitely beyond their reach and out of their power.

4. They can't oblige or dispose God to give them conversion . . .

5. They can't do anything to fit themselves for Christ's acceptance . . .

6. They have no power to do any thing to entitle themselves to any promise . . .[140]

Hence, "owning to their want of disposition," the only hope for individuals, as well as their communities (which, if declension continued, then they could suffer the harsher spiritual judgment of apostasy), is to maintain "the diligent and constant attendance" on all means.

According to Edwards's ontology, natural-man can at least "abide" as an auditor of God's word out of self-preservation, fear, and self-regard—active manifestations of the self-love disposition. Corresponding with God's communication to them "according to

---

136. "Miscellanies," no. 539, *WJE* 18:86–87.

137. See, for example, the three sermons (78, 307, 311) on Ecclesiastes 9:10 (n.d.; Dec. 1733; Jan. 1734), *WJE Online* 63, 48, 49; and 379. Sermon on Ezekiel 33:4–5 (Feb. 1736), *WJE Online* 51.

138. 356. [L. 3r.]. Sermon on Ezekiel 47:11 (1735), *WJE Online* 50.

139. 379. [L. 3r.]. Sermon on Ezekiel 33:4–5 (Feb. 1735–36), *WJE Online* 51.

140. Ibid, [L. 3v.–5v.].

their *nature* and *capacity*," Edwards advocates unregenerate seeking from "an aversion to pain and desire of pleasure," though, to be sure, "it is in no wise from a good principle."[141]

∼

Edwards's appeal to the "less noble" principles of self-love, namely, fear, self-preservation, and self-interest in his evangelistic approach to the unregenerate serves his Calvinist scheme well. First, it preserves the sovereignty of God in the dispensing of salvation. Second, it retains the use and priority of the ordained means of salvation, namely, the word of God and preaching. And third, it approaches natural-man in accordance with the denunciatory pronouncements of Calvinism's anthropological assessment: man is spiritually dead in his sins and therefore morally and meritoriously unable to do anything cooperative toward salvation and, least of all, true worship.

Edwards's thoughts on preparation, like so many things, were affected by the way he attempted to convey the idea of God's direct interaction with the world. As he rehearses God's work of redemption "from the fall of man to the end of the world," we find that the natural-man and reprobate function, both at individual and collective levels, in a way that parallels repetitive stages in the work of redemption's constitutive history.[142] Just as the *historia salutis* develops along the lines of preparation, achievement, and application, so too the individual life is a microcosm of this work.

The heathen nations also take part collectively in the grand scheme of redemption history. Their knowledge of certain religious truths serves to prepare former reprobate nations for the application of regenerating grace. Conversely, their present rejection of the Messiah accounts for Edwards's negative theological assessment, as he holds the natural-man fully culpable for failing in his moral and epistemic responsibilities. Their place in redemption history is then twofold: to further the work of redemption for future generations and to replicate the punitive aspects of God's inner actuality (which also serves as a warning to others and exhibits the justice of God in the process). Edwards's interest in non-Christian religions was, therefore, part of his spiritual mapping or tracing of God's movements toward redemption history's consummate end in Christ.

Concluding Remarks

The Revealed God

By constructing a science of history as an apologetic device, where universal history is used as an attempt "to relate the sum of all God's works in providence," Edwards engages in the new production of a standardized and universally accessible type of religious knowledge. He purposely applies abstract theological and philosophical principles to every conceivable concrete, historical situation, in order to make the ethereal—spiritual realities—conceptually tangible for all, in all time. That is, by means of a redemption *narrative*, Edwards

---

141. "Miscellanies," no. 631, *WJE* 18:158–59.
142. *Sermon One*, *WJE* 9:116.

translates his theocentric vision of reality and makes it concrete, assessable, and meaningful. The God of Edwards is, therefore, no *deus absconditus*.

Because all participate in history and are subject to time, all have some point of contact with God's orchestration of the progress of redemption (some to their eternal benefit, others not), "to accomplish the glory of the blessed Trinity in an exceeding degree."[143] Consequently, all possess inherent value. The history of redemption is then the laboratory for examining true religion's interactions with surrounding peoples and cultures. Whether believer or unbeliever, the friend of the Christian religion or antagonist, all may read God's intentions in the mundane and remarkable accounts of history up to the present and, with the aid of scriptural prophecies, beyond the present.

In accord with his teaching in other places, elements of God's revealed glory may be known to the unregenerate, even the most deluded deist, simply by surveying history. But to know the truth of it, one must interpret it through the filter of redemption theology, which Edwards eagerly supplies. The full, spiritual glory, however, remains known and sensible to the regenerate only.

Edwards's evangelistic strategy of contextualizing the individual's existence historically rests heavily upon the time-honored principle that the acquisition of knowledge is indissociable from the training of minds. The effects of the Awakenings and other social and religious changes prompted Edwards's teaching the minds of Northampton and New England, Calvinists and deists, believer and unbeliever alike, to view all time as pregnant with eternal implications and spiritual significance. This point is pressed upon his auditors and readers, to view time and history as Edwards specifies, lest they perish through the delusion of a merely ethical, that is to say, deistic view of time and space.

In the Redemption Discourse, Edwards shows us where his theological investigations for a methodology have climaxed. It was to be upon the foundation of the Trinitarian *pactum salutis* for self-glorification, identifiable by the triadic preparation-achievement-realization pattern, that Edwards would refine his theology for the remaining years of his life. "Miscellanies" no. 1062 and the "Essay on the Trinity" exemplify the continuance of this method, which was to have found complete expression in the *magnum opus*, prevented only by his death.[144]

---

143. Ibid., 125.

144. William J. Scheick, however, does not read Jonathan Edwards's *History* in this way. In his article, "The Grand Design: Jonathan Edwards' *History of the Work of Redemption*," 300–314), instead of viewing Jonathan Edwards's methodology in the series from the whole (*pactum salutis*) to the particular (the redemption of individual saints), Scheick believes Jonathan Edwards, captive to the Puritan psychologized morphology of conversion model, projects the subjective dimension of conversion's application onto the collective Work of Redemption (300–314). The scheme works in reverse, from the minute to the grand, and is supposedly what Jonathan Edwards intended by "a body of divinity in an entire new method" (*WJE* 16:727). Contrary to Scheick's opinion, Jonathan Edwards employs the analogy opposite to many of his Puritan fathers, precisely because he *was* acutely aware of the distinction between the subjective side of redemption and the objective side (see Wilson, "Editor's Introduction," *WJE* 9:100). Jonathan Edwards worked toward the realization of this project by drafting an outline, compiling notes, collecting materials, and revising portions of the Redemption Discourse in his private notebooks. The threefold categorization of the *historia salutis* was to be retained and expanded. As sermon notebook "45" (e.g., pp. 9, 14, 41) and "Notebook 10" (e.g., proposed chapter four within "Notebook 10" [as part of a three notebook series, *10*, *25*, and *2*, devoted to the *History* project] was

The decisive significance of his interpretation of redemption from the whole to the particular shows his appreciation of the nature of human existence as inevitably historical, subjacent, and dependent upon sovereign divine dispensations. Immediately after his atypical conversion and early into his ministerial career he struggled with traditional Puritan preparationism as an element only being interpreted *within* the whole.[145] This raised long-term pastoral concerns for Edwards. Preparation was confined to the subjective appropriation of redemption. Certainly pastoral psychology was a significant factor in understanding the process, but the outworkings of redemption could not be founded upon such theologically and philosophically inept premises. Preparation was not an objective principle beyond its inclusion within the individual morphological pattern of conversion, which was taught from the Scriptures by his Puritan forefathers—ssomething Edwards seriously questioned for a time. Now, however, he finds the reality and authenticity for the conversion model not only in Scripture, but also in the necessity and pattern of redemption history (from the perspective of the present), and the reasonableness (according to the "fitness") of divine ordering. Consequently, he does not believe he is artificially employing or superimposing the preparation/achievement/realization model onto the individual conversion scheme. Rather, he is convinced that he has found the objective foundation of the preparationist scheme that legitimizes and requires its usage through his analysis of the eternal Trinitarian confederation, the revelation of Scripture, and the patterns and continuity of redemption history.

A Kinder, Gentler Jonathan Edwards

McDermott and Morimoto repeatedly attempt to convince their readers that Edwards—supposedly so troubled by deistic complaints that the supralapsarian God is capricious and cruel—followed Turretin and Mastricht in an infralapsarian approach to soteriology, so that he might soften the harsh realities of determinism, or at least explore the possibilities of inclusivism.[146] Unfounded as this may be, both scholars fail to note the larger point that the *ordo salutis* within Edwards's theocentric system is itself a product of the *pactum*

---

to address the issue of "preparation" in the Work of Redemption) show "preparation," again, was to hold a prominent place, with ascending movements to "achievement" and "realization," analogous to the *History of the Work of Redemption*. Scheick's thesis is simply counter to all extent evidence, as well as the theocentric impetus in Jonathan Edwards's thought.

145. Jonathan Edwards mentions the problem of his conversion in the *Personal Narrative*, where he notes the conspicuous absence of the more axiomatic elements of the preparationist pattern of subjective phenomena, particularly, conviction by "legal fear," terrors leading to contrition, and humiliation. The spiritual troubles relating to his own conversion experience are further recorded in the "Diary": "The reason why I, in the least question my interest in God's love and favor, is—1. Because I cannot speak so fully to my experience of that preparatory work, of which divines speak:—2. I do not remember that I experienced regeneration, exactly in those steps, in which divines say it is generally wrought" (*WJE* 16:773–74). A year later, Jonathan Edwards intimates a skeptical conclusion to his self-evaluation over-against the parameters of Puritan preparationism. Assured of the instantaneousness of conversion, he now resolves to critically uncover the foundations of why "the people of New England, and anciently the Dissenters of Old England . . . used to be converted in those steps" in order to establish a more objective foundation for the nature of conversion (ibid., 779).

146. See Holmes's excellent rehearsal of the "lapsarian debate" in this connection (*God of Grace*, 126–28).

salutis and its "hyper-supralapsarian" proposals. God gets His glory: salvation/damnation are His methods; election/reprobation are His means; the Son and Spirit is its sum.[147]

Despite their scholarly efforts "The Edwards of the Possible" proposed by Morimoto and McDermott bears little resemblance to the eighteenth-century figure displaced from his pastoral charge for, among other things, restricting access to the sacraments and publicly upbraiding children of prominent churchwardens for their unregenerate behavior. Instead of conducting himself like John McLeod Campbell, who, for the accommodating benefit of his parishioners, began to reassess confessional substitutionary soteriology in terms of a universalistic work of supererogation by Jesus Christ, Edwards underwent the rejection of his ministerial charge partly because of his increasingly restrictivistic opinions concerning the scope of the covenant and its associated privileges. Plainly, Edwards neither desired nor was in need of an inclusivist or Universalist scheme. Indeed, he was convinced that the resolute defense and espousal of particularism was in fact the defense and espousal of unalterable divine truth.[148]

For Jonathan Edwards, adherence to true biblical theology and an authentic Christian worldview included submitting one's self to the fact that God promotes that glory in two ways: redemption *and* damnation.

Over a century later, W. G. T. Shedd and other Northern Presbyterians gained fame for their articulation of a virtual, saving faith, but not Edwards. While Shedd and others believed in a "larger hope" outside of gospel proclamation, Edwards did not.[149] For Edwards, the heathen world beyond the compass of gospel means "is like a sinking ship."[150] He was part of an earlier orthodox tradition not embarrassed about the confessional doctrines that say that those who die unevangelized or unconverted are destined to eternal damnation.[151] He did not attempt to lay out a new paradigm to suggest anything otherwise. Instead, he attempted to theoretically buttress his own restrictivist tradition—amidst an Enlightenment assault on his own confessional tradition—through philosophical considerations of the aesthetic dimension/potential of double particular predestination and eternal damnation.

---

147. *The End of the Wicked Contemplated by the Righteous* (1733), *Banner-Works* 2:207–12.

148. Hence, statements like: "The glory of God [is] . . . of greater consequence than the welfare of thousands and millions of souls" (*Banner-Works* 2:209).

149. Shedd, *Calvinism Pure and Mixed*, 116–31.

150. "Miscellanies," no. 520, *WJE* 18:66.

151. See his most protracted meditation in defense of hell and reprobation in the 1755 essay, "The Endless Punishment of Those Who Die Impenitent," in Austin, *The Works of President Edwards*, 6:20–42. Fiering notes: "It is significant that these definitive statements on hell were written at approximately the same time that Jonathan Edwards was working on *Original Sin* and *Two Dissertations*. All four problems were closely related in Jonathan Edwards's system" (*Moral Thought*, 238–39 n.107).

Conclusion: Peculiar Particularism in Edwards

THROUGHOUT THESE CHAPTERS I HAVE CONDUCTED A PRESENTATION OF JONATHAN Edwards's philosophical anthropology, etiology, and approach to history, operating on his premise that God designs and orders all things for the ultimate end for which He aims, specifically, the glorification through manifestation-and-perception of His own perfections. In Edwards's vision, this was reality as spiritually envisioned and metaphysically articulated from a Holy Spirit-conferred, biblically-informed, theocentric perspective.

We have seen that in "Miscellanies" no. 581, as one of many examples, Edwards explicitly states that all things are telic-oriented to function according to God's design and plan to the end He wills to obtain and that "Even sin and wickedness itself, it comes to pass because God has a use for it, a design and purpose to be accomplished by it."[1] Natural-men and reprobates were found to be vital and necessary elements to the self-replication of God's complexly beautiful being both in this life and in an afterlife of eternal torments. God Himself encompasses imperfections and irregularities, not just with respect to justified sinner-saints united to Christ and possessing an ontological disposition of holiness—the Holy Spirit, but also those reprobates and apostates bound for hell.

These, as I have argued, are Edwards's ideas, internal to his written corpus, published from his pen, and proclaimed from his pulpits. This is God according to Edwards, the world according to Edwards.

But such ideas warrant comment from outside the intriguing world according to Edwards. This is what I intend in these closing pages, under the following three headings: "The Attractiveness of Jonathan Edwards as a Philosophical-Theologian"; "The Unattractiveness of Jonathan Edwards as a Philosophical-Theologian"; and "Edwards and the Rationalistic Method of the Enlightenment."

The Attractiveness of Jonathan Edwards as a Philosophical-Theologian

What may make this eighteenth-century Puritan thinker attractive to twenty-first-century philosophical-theologians and systematicians beyond the curiosity of his legendary ministry and famed works such as *Freedom of the Will* and the infamous Enfield sermon, are simply these three words: order, purpose, and meaning. Edwards's system is all about God ordering the world with a specific purpose in mind that in turn, invests it with significance and value. So where Bertrand Russell unapologetically announces that, (*q.d.*) "the world is just there, and that is all there is to say,"[2] Edwards hastens adds one more word—"*because.*"

---

1. *WJE* 18:117.

2. See Russell's argument on infinity and existence in *The Principles of Mathematics*, 358–59, as well as his argument against theistic teleology/cosmology in "A Free Man's Worship" in *Mysticism and Logic*.

Post-Enlightenment critics might very well upbraid Calvinism's particularism, but they cannot say that Edwards, inasmuch as he stood as a representative of Reformed theology, repudiated the inherent value of human beings as such. Edwards has an answer for the existence of both categories of human being—one that causes many minds to recoil—but an answer nonetheless. This speaks to another dimension of his thinking that may resonate with contemporary minds: the suggested comprehensiveness of his system of order and meaning.

In the same way that Edwards's God is "all-encompassing," so too the theoretical scope of his vision of reality incorporates all existences and occurrences within its purview. There is no such thing as a renegade molecule in Edwards's theistic universe; in fact, there is no such thing as a single atom without God willing it to be so, and for some "suitable" reason by which God will get His glory.

This translates over into the intelligibility and collective unity of every aspect of reality since the world exists to communicate something about God and His relation to man. With that said, it would not be inappropriate to speak of a principal metaphor for Edwards's typological universe in a way that juxtaposed Jorge Luis Borges' description of the universe as the "Library of Babylon" (an informative world of numerous bits of data that has no center, cannot be navigated, and possesses no unifying principle).[3] For Edwards, the "Book[s] of Nature"[4]—the created natural order in its minutiae and general assemblages—do not fill the "Library of Babylon" but the "Library of Zion," God's universe. Extending the metaphor further, the "Library of Zion" may be said to envision the universe as a repository of information, of revelation; and, in turn, represent life as an activity of retrieving (receiving) and interpreting information about God and, secondarily, man, and responding (remanating) with the appropriate affections. The fact that time and space are not barriers to this information but rather vehicles of accommodation, lend the world and existence an internal coherence and rhythm, despite its complexity and apparent cacophony. Experience has its place, but so does propositional objectivity. In a world of uncertainty, fragmentation, and flux, Edwards's system may indeed appear confident, unified, and stable.

From the beginning of his ministerial and literary career Edwards grounded his metaphysical ruminations upon primary doctrines such as the being and will of God, the Trinity, and a christocentric scheme of redemption. These were the *terminus a quo* and *terminus ad quem* of his thinking processes. These doctrines were essential to his desire to find *unity*, a fundamental unity for all existence. Topics such as infused grace, true virtue, original sin, human nature, Christian ethic, love, faith, existence, and holiness (all of which were articulated and philosophically buttressed by Edwards through the principles and logic of disposition—though not disposition only) therefore have an antecedent theological basis. Indeed, these topics were so interrelated that Edwards planned to unfold them within "the affair of Christian theology, as the whole of it, in each part, stands in

---

3. Borges, *Labyrinths*, 51–58.
4. MS title page of "Images of Divine Things" in *WJE* 11:50.

reference to the great work of redemption by Jesus Christ," not as philosophical appendages, but as "divine doctrines" of a single "body of divinity in an entirely new method."[5]

And while Edwards does not speak to every objection or state his position on every doctrine or apologetical issue in his written corpus, yet in light of how he viewed his own work,[6] to think that his projected *magnum opus* would have separated his speculative philosophy from his theology, or his ethics from his aesthetic and dispositional theory of being, or omitted a doctrine of reprobation or even preparation, would be to argue that he was planning a non-Edwardsean body of divinity, devoid of the unity and comprehensiveness characteristic of his philosophical-theology. It was the sheer fascination of the proposed unity and comprehensiveness of that never-to-be-completed treatise that attracted myself, and no doubt will continue to attract others, to the genius of one who not merely exercised himself as a metaphysician, but as a Calvinist metaphysician.[7]

Thus, as Elwood, Smith, McClymond, Fiering, and others have suggested, it may really be with an eighteenth-century New England Puritan and not Friedrich Schleiermacher (1768–1834), Samuel Taylor Coleridge (1772–1834) or Søren Kierkegaard (1813–55),[8] that we find the first modern attempt to write a theology, even a major systematic treatment of theology, from a particularly philosophical perspective. And even though that attempt never materialized, yet Edwards's efforts are exemplified throughout his surviving notebooks and published treatises to ensure, as they have for me, future interest in Jonathan Edwards as a resource for philosophical-theology, and not merely as an antiquarian novelty.

Edwards's philosophical-theology should not only be engaging, but also potentially useful for not only moral theorists interested in "virtue ethics," but especially contemporary evangelical and confessional theologians defending "classical" pronouncements of the doctrine of God over-against "open theists" and soteriological inclusivists. Edwards's strong determinist and particularist position speaks to contemporary advocates of divine passibility and openness, in that he makes an interesting, if not internally coherent, case for the planned and purposed expression of God's various attributes by the concept of remanation through human agents. Dispositions offer an explanation of the relative freedom and individualized uniqueness of human responses, struggles, knowledge, and existence, but also the mechanism by which God programmatically prescribes the kind of decisions humans make. Such thinking supplies elemental materials for contemporary efforts at theodicy, speculative theologizing, and articulation of divine immanence.

Following the logic of Edwards's dispositional ontology will not take one down the Morimoto-McDermott path of inclusivity or universalism (tempting as that path may be),

---

5. *WJE* 16:727–28. For Edwards's "new method" see McClymond, "A Different Legacy?," in *Jonathan Edwards at Home and Abroad*, 17–39.

6. The interrelatedness of topics is particularly evident within the treatises written at Stockbridge, the "Book of Controversies" notebooks, and *A History of the Work of Redemption*.

7. Cf. Bebbington, "Remembering Around the World," 178.

8. Hegel (1770–1831) has been omitted for two reasons. First, although he studied theology at Tübingen, one cannot really describe him as a theologian. His writings, even when on religion, are essentially philosophical. Second, though he did exercise considerable influence on theology in the nineteenth century, it is really in the twentieth century that one finds major writers in systematics utilizing Hegel.

but a path leading to the same restrictivist position as the Westminster divines or the formulators of the Canons of Dortrecht. Edwards, like Calvin and the tradition called by his name, championed the essential arbitrariness (omnisapiency) of God's power, His inalienable, incontestable right to save or condemn whosoever He pleases. If for nothing else, the possibilities of Edwards's dispositional philosophical-theology may have intellectual value for the maintenance of evangelical particularism as championed by the likes of, say, William Lane Craig and R. C. Sproul.

The Unattractiveness of Jonathan Edwards as a Philosophical-Theologian

But the same things that might make Edwards attractive to some contemporary thinkers are precisely what may render him an anachronism to others. His self-contained metaphysical system—in which he must have a rational answer or explanation for everything—fits awkwardly in today's postmodern climate. Indeed, welcomed, it sits almost entirely outside of mainstream intellectual and academic conversations. Contemporary philosophers do not readily resort to Edwards as a viable dialogue partner, save for gallant attempts by a few trend-buckers. Consequently, Jonathan Edwards continues to be omitted from both textbooks and curriculum on Enlightenment philosophy.

Likewise, his passion for systematic unity and comprehensiveness, to have a reasonable solution for every doctrine of Christianity, including the incarnation, the internal relations of the triune Godhead, and even God as God is in Himself, tend to strip all notions of mystery and inscrutability from things sacred for creedal Christianity, too. Neither heterodoxy nor orthodoxy is comfortable with an Edwardsean paradigm.

Such postures conjure up images of Jonathan Edwards as somewhat presumptuous, impervious, and egotistical. These are character and intellectual assessments that have appeared in contemporary biographical accounts, and not without justification.[9] Aside from clashes with parishioners, Robert Breck and his associates, the William's family in Stockbridge, and Old Light Calvinists, which in every case Edwards thought himself not only in the right but also generally above reproach, there was the whole epistemological issue: Edwards claimed to "see" things as they really were—spiritual and moral—and offer on behalf of confessional Protestantism an objective response to the Enlightenment worldview in both England and New England. Edwards was one of the "haves"; his opponents were of the "have nots." And while notable philosophers such as William J. Wainwright have powerfully argued for the warrant and plausibility of Edwards's epistemic perspective, yet the spiritual sense was still something Edwards intimates that he grasped and experienced well beyond others, thereby making himself the authority on the matter. Hence, he took the responsibility upon himself to discriminate what did and what did not qualify as authentic religious experience and affections in *The Distinguishing Marks of a Work of the Spirit of God* (1741), *Some Thoughts concerning the present Revival of Religion in New-England, and the Way in which it ought to be acknowledged and promoted* (1742),

---

9. See, for example, Levin, "Edwards, Franklin, and Cotton Mather," in *American Experience*, 34–49; Stout, "The Puritans and Edwards," in *American Experience*, 142–59; Jones, "The Impolitic Mr. Edwards," 64–79; and Marsden, *Jonathan Edwards*, chaps 18, 21–22.

A Treatise concerning Religious Affections (1746), and "Directions for Judging of Persons's Experiences" (n.d.). Without coming out and saying it, he seems to suggest and adjudicate that if one did not subscribe to the "world according to Edwards," then one remained outside the "world according to God." Then again, it appears that he did say it to his congregation perhaps a few too many times, netting him a one-way ticket to Stockbridge. It turned out that Jonathan Edwards's conception of reality and reality as understood by the good people of Northampton were incompatible visions.

Not least of all, Edwards's radical theocentricity, for all the value and significance it may ascribe to the natural-man and reprobate, still does present an attractive portrait of God in many respects. Thinking of the New Testament emphasis not on causal determination and divine arbitrariness but rather divine love and condescension, Thomas Chalmers once remarked: "I should like to be so inspired over again [as I was when I read *Freedom of the Will*], but with such a view of the Deity as coalesced and was in harmony with the doctrine of the New Testament."[10] Some might see Chalmers's criticism of causality and theodicy spilling over into the sphere of soteriology: Edwards's rigidly defined parameters for what constitutes dispositional regeneration simply not allowing for the possibility of inclusivity. As we have seen, he does not divorce regeneration from conversion, nor conversion from God's ordained means, and even then he is pessimistic about covenantal inclusivity and therefore baptism, in good keeping with his Half-Way Covenant inheritance. Consequently, there is little hope for infants (or children) who die in infancy, and none for those who hope for salvation by proxy or by the hypothetical retention of an unexercised gracious disposition.

Then there is Edwards's aesthetic vision of God as complexly beautiful. Setting aside the difficult issue of divine simplicity, there is something profoundly unsettling about ontological "irregularities" in God's beautiful being. One thinks of the ongoing and more recent profusion of global conflicts and violence, as well as natural disasters, and wonders how one would even attempt to explain avowed genocidal hatred, entrenched bigotry, acts of terrorist murder, the "collateral damage" of thousands in the crossfire of armed combatants, and countless bodies strewn ashore in the aftermath of killer tsunamis, in terms of God's complex beauty? Moreover, such a concept leaves one altogether perplexed over what the pastoral value of such a theory could be, since Edwards offers no explanation or practical use for the teaching outside of promoting the glorification of God.

Concerning the more common atrocities of the death of non-Christian children in non-Christian cultures and religions, Edwards's aesthetic analysis of reality and existence comes off both as insensitive and insulting when it denominates and interprets the lives of such children in terms of ontological "deformities." The discomfort of such thoughts are only reinforced when one considers that their eternal destiny consists of the intensification of perceptions and sensibilities of divine wrath for the express purpose of intensifying the full manifestation/replication of the Divine Being in glorious splendor.[11] Indeed, some

---

10. Quoted in Hanna, *Memoirs of the Life and Writings of Thomas Chalmers*, 1:17.

11. "Miscellanies," no. 662: "It was meet that [God's] attributes and perfections should be expressed. It was the will of God that they should be expressed and shine forth. But if the expressions of his attributes [like wrath] ben't known, they are not; the very being of the expression depends on the perception of created understandings. And so much the more as the expression is known, so much the more it is" (*WJE* 16:200).

would find the aesthetic philosophical augmentation of Edwards's Calvinistic particularism better left unsaid. From this perspective, God's relationship to the world, redemption history, and the reprobate, itself is in need of salvation.

Edwards and the Rationalistic Method of the Enlightenment

Prominent in our consideration of both the attractiveness and unattractiveness of Jonathan Edwards as a philosophical-theologian is his commitment to the Reformed tradition. Which brings us to this: for all of his commitment to confessional Calvinism, was Edwards after all tarred with the Enlightenment rationalism of his age, and if so, in what way?

The fact that Edwards was not indifferent to philosophical concerns, but imbibed Neoplatonic elements from Henry More, occasionalistic concepts from Malebranche, Scottish aestheticism from Hutcheson and Shaftesbury, metaphysical peculiarities from Smith and Norris, as well as a host of epistemological principles from Locke, and adapted them all within his Berkeley-like idealism to address the burning issues of his day concerning the mind, the will, causality, and universal order, points us in the direction of an affirmative answer.[12] Couple this statement with his first idea and methodological approach toward a *magnum opus*, "A Rational Account of Christianity, or, The Perfect Harmony between the Doctrines of the Christian Religion and Human Reason,"[13] and we have for all intents and purposes an Enlightenment rationalist who just so happens to be a devout Congregationalist minister. Or so it would seem.

For although early on Edwards subscribed to the Cambridge Platonist and Lockean notion that religion must conform to the principles of reason in order to be viable and valid, and thought that since God's program of self-glorification was so lucid and reasonable in his own mind, that such things could be conveyed through a systematic "Rational Account of Christianity," and that he himself should be the first in New England to compose such a treatise to prove "that the present fashionable divinity is wrong,"[14] yet one must bear in mind that just prior to the Great Awakening of 1740 Edwards abandoned this methodological project to take up another. This change in tactics signaled an important shift in his apologetical engagement with Enlightenment religion, as well as his opinion of the best method for doing theology.

The "Rational Account" itself is an enduring testimony to the influence the Enlightenment's high view of reason had upon Edwards. The fact that he clung to this vision of a "Rational Account" for nearly twenty years indicates that he considered the rationalistic method the cornerstone of his mental powers. One might add that Edwards himself may have been overly confident in his own intellectual abilities to accomplish such a monumental task, indeed, if such a task were possible through mere ratiocination.

In 1739, Edwards must have been asking himself this same question as he prepared and preached the sermons series that was to become *The History of the Work of Redemption*,

---

12. Cf. Oberdiek, "Jonathan Edwards," in Smith, *The Spirit of American Philosophy*, 194.
13. MS "Catalogue Letter," JE Collection. Cf. "Outline of 'A Rational Account,'" *WJE* 6:396.
14. "Miscellanies," no. 832, *WJE* 18:546. Chamberlain, "Editor's Introduction," *WJE* 18:27; cf. Aldridge, "Natural Religion and Deism in America," 835–48.

and while he continued to refine his thoughts on "divine and supernatural light"—the spiritual perception of "divine excellency."[15] Throughout the 1730s, Edwards was moving more and more toward the final conviction that the truth of Christianity was ultimately grounded not in human reason but in the perception of divine "excellency" conveyed by the "new spiritual sense." The first series of awakening that took place in the mid-1730s turned his attention to analyzing what took place in conversion. His conclusions, in large measure (and not surprisingly), confirmed the instantaneousness of regeneration/justification and the accent on the beautiful and affections, which he himself experienced fifteen years earlier. Certainly there was room for a variety of different experiences. Indeed, no two conversion experiences may be alike, though almost all share the same imprint of heteronomous preparations.[16] Notwithstanding, "divine and supernatural light" must be "immediately imparted to the soul, by the Spirit of God," according to Edwards.[17] The excellency that the light convey was itself regenerative. The aesthetic vision was a mental state, a consequence of union with Jesus Christ through the Holy Spirit. It afforded to the redeemed a "view" of the reality of spiritual things, which unregenerates have no access. Consequently, as Ava Chamberlain explains, "This higher form of conviction was ultimately unavailable for public discussion, for to the unredeemed who lack the perception of excellency, talk about it is 'foolishness' and 'words without a meaning' ["Miscellanies," no. 683]. A purely rational defense of Christian doctrine would have required Edwards to use, as did the latitudinarians in their anti-deist polemic, the standard of rationality advocated by his opponents."[18] To avoid this "tactical mistake" he moved away from a systematic defense based upon rationality to a historical defense based upon biblical prophecy and the testimony of redemption history, that is, the history of the world "both sacred and profane."

The diminished status of ratiocination and the corresponding rise of a historical method suggest that Edwards was not the thoroughgoing Enlightenment rationalist one might suspect, at least not in the last two decades of his life. To be sure, his historical method was altogether bound to rational arguments, but the *reason* he became attracted to a historical method was not due to its coherent organization and logic, but because it was "the most beautiful" and "fitting" method.[19] Thus, Edwards had finally surrendered his intellectual prowess to the logic of divine arbitrariness. Indeed, as "Miscellanies" no. 1263 makes certain, the doctrine of divine arbitrariness completely supplanted ratiocination as the operating principle of his theocentric perspective, and no doubt it would have been the regulating principle of his *magnum opus*. The process of surrendering to God's sovereignty may have begun some time during the spring of 1721, but it took almost another twenty years for Edwards to realize that human reason itself was an arbitrary convention of God, and that human reason itself must yield to God's arbitrary will.

15. "Miscellanies," no. 782, *WJE* 18:452–66.
16. See Goen, "Editor's Introduction," *WJE* 4:25–32; and Valeri, "Editor's Introduction," *WJE* 17:7–13.
17. *A Divine and Supernatural Light* (1733), *WJE* 17:408–26.
18. Chamberlain, "Editor's Introduction," *WJE* 18:30.
19. Letter to the Trustees of the College of New Jersey, October 19, 1757, *WJE* 16:728.

Appendix A

Panentheistic, But Not Process Thought

IN SOME WAYS IT MAY APPEAR THAT JONATHAN EDWARDS'S PROPOSAL OF A SELF-enlarging Being mirrors process thought. Douglas J. Elwood, for one, not only found Edwards's philosophical theology panentheistic (as do I), but also showing affinities with process thought. According to Elwood, Edwards's Neoplatonism relates "God and the world in a relationship of mutual immanence," as God "comprehended his own creation" without the use of "secondary causes." To which he concludes that Edwards really anticipates the panentheism of Charles Hartshorne and others.[1]

Elwood can hardly be blamed thinking thus (even though he strangely couples panentheism instead of pantheism with Neoplatonism), for there are a number of similarities between Edwards and process thought. For one thing, process theology attempts to portray God's being as at once complete or eternal. So does Edwards. But, unlike Edwards, process theologians have God engaged in becoming by promoting a dipolar nature of the divine being.[2] On the one hand, the process perspective presents God's primordial or conceptual side as changelessly complete (not unlike what Edwards would say), while on the other hand it characterizes God's consequent or concrete nature as an ongoing process of becoming—something distinctly foreign to Edwards. To him, God's being or existence cannot be viewed as the end of creation. The reason for this, according to Edwards, is that the Divine Being should be conceived as prior to any of God's acts or designs. God's being and existence must be presupposed as the ground of God's acts or design. Therefore, Edwards writes of God, "He can't create the world to the end that he may have existence; or may have such attributes and perfections, and such an essence."[3]

Edwards makes it clear that God's essence, attributes, perfections, or existence cannot be viewed as the "end of creation." Since God's being and attributes are already perfect and actual, the Divine Being cannot be seen as the result of or constituted by an ongoing world process: God is not "becoming" in any essential sense. Rather, the creation is a mode of divine *expression* and *perspectival expansion*.

---

1. Elwood, *PTJE*, 22, 53; 24–29.

2. Most process theology is grounded in the process theism derived from Alfred N. Whitehead's (1861–1947) notion that God is the primary example of metaphysical truths as well as the one who supplies the initial direction to every event. The primacy of events is the central element to his original metaphysical system. See his, *Process and Reality*. Charles Hartshorne was the first to develop a complete process philosophical theology, detailing a full concept of God "in process." See his, *The Divine Relativity*; cf. Pittenger, *"The Last Things" in a Process Perspective*.

3. "End of Creation" in *WJE* 8:469.

APPENDIX A

An apparent second likeness between Edwards and process thought lies in their metaphysical foundations. Just as process theology receives shape from process philosophy's conception of reality, so too Edwards's theology is largely shaped by his philosophical conception of reality. However, the principal difference is that process theology's philosophical conception of reality as inherently processive compromises the completeness and transcendence of God's own perfect actuality (especially with regards to divine knowledge and timelessness[4]), thereby rendering God's actuality a part or instance of the general process of reality, while Edwards, on the other hand, maintains the classical theistic position of God's unchangeability and self-sufficiency, yet with this improvement: God, as an essentially perfect actuality, exercises a disposition to repeat that actuality "*ad extra*," or, which is the same thing for Edwards, *in* the minds of created intelligences. For him, the movement of God's glorification in the temporal realm and human history is never God's self-realization, as in Hegel's philosophy of the "Absolute Spirit" or process theology.[5] Again, in process theology, God is not only given to movement but also is "in process" toward his own self-realization, while for Edwards, God's self-enlargement *is* God's self-replication, that is, the replication and manifestation in the historical process of what is already fully actual within the inner Trinity: for God's innertrinitarian life is completely exercised through the innertrinitarian relationships,[6] the divine disposition is already apart from and prior to the creation *and* consummation of the world.

In an interesting "Miscellanies" entry, Edwards contemplates why some philosophers and theologians struggle with or reject the doctrine of God's aseity and prior actuality and, rather, are given over to anthropocentric conceptions of God's existence:

> 'Tis from the exceeding imperfect notion that we have of the nature or essence of God, and because we can't think of it but we must think of it far otherwise than it

---

4. See, William Hasker, *God, Time, and Knowledge*, who limits foreknowledge to avoid fatalism; Richard M. Gale, *On the Nature and Existence of God*, chap 3: "The Omniscience-Immutability Argument," who forcefully argues against timelessness in the interests of a "religiously available" God; and Ward, *Rational Theology and the Creativity of God*, 142ff. Ward also limits divine omniscience for the reason that God cannot foreknow events as *actual* events prior to their occurrence. In citing these three, however, I am not categorically identifying them as process theologians. Although it has not been indicated thus far, I am sensitive to the significant and numerous differences between various strands of process thought among process theologians, open theists and philosophers, such as Gregory Boyd, John Cobb, Lewis Ford, David R. Griffin, R. E. James, Schubert Ogden, John Sanders, H. P. Owen, S. Sia, D. D. Williams, and others. My description of process/open theology and philosophy has been limited to the general themes characteristic to both. For responses opposing shared premises of "process" thought see, Bruce M. Ware, *God's Lesser Glory*; Royce G. Gruenler, *The Inexhaustible God*; Helm, *Eternal God*; and Alvin Plantinga's essay, "On Ockham's Way Out" (235–69), where he attempts to reconcile unlimited divine knowledge with human freedom; and, lastly, Stump and Kretzmann's essay, "Eternity" in Morris, *The Concept of God* (219–52), where they defend a Boethian concept of a timeless, eternal God.

5. Hegel, for instance, through the employment of his dialectic method of logic arrives at the concept of Absolute Idea, which he describes as Becoming, as a process of self-development. The *Idea* of which Hegel speaks is deduced in his logic by the same method that yielded Becoming out of Being. The Idea, however, contains its own dialectic, namely, life, cognition, and the Absolute Idea. Thus, Idea is the category of self-consciousness; it knows itself in its objects. The whole drift of Hegel's logic, therefore, has been to move from the initial concept of Being finally to the notion of the Idea. But this Idea must also be understood as being in a *dynamic process*, so that the Idea is itself in a continuous process of self-development toward self-perfection.

6. See Lee, *Philosophical Theology*, chap 7.

> is, that arises the difficulty in our mind of conceiving of God's existence without a cause. 'Tis repugnant to the nature of our souls and what our faculties utterly refuse to admit that anything that is capable of being one part of a proper disjunction should exist and be as it is, rather than not exist or exist otherwise, without causes. Our notions we have of the divine nature are so imperfect that our imperfect idea admits of a disjunction, for whatsoever is not absolutely perfect doth so.[7]

Edwards goes on to say that even as we explore creation and God, in that order, we must operate on the supposition of divine "absolute perfection."

A further distinction between Edwards and process thought is that nearly the whole of Edwards's foundationalist, compatibilist, and deterministic (Calvinist) theological content—from his doctrines concerning the *pactum salutis* and eternally decreed *ordo salutis*, to the predetermined *historia salutis*—runs counter to process theology, where God is conceived to be, in one degree or other, processive and response oriented. Thus, Edwards himself, by virtue of three things, namely, (i) his position regarding the classical incommunicable attributes of God; (ii) his understanding of God's "ad extra" replication being an ideal one; and, (iii) his inclusion of active dispositions in the being of God, prevents one from either reading him as a process theologian, or reading process thought back onto his theology or philosophy.

Yet, with that said, his statements concerning all in God and God in all cannot be taken any other way but panentheistically. Edwards wants the logical conclusions that follow from his analysis of God's relation to the creation, but he does not want to commit to pantheism. Panentheism, however, appears to be a whole other viable alternative for him, though throughout his career he struggles to curtail, in terms of language and conception, its consequence of temporalizing and spatializing God.

---

7. "Miscellanies," no. 650, *WJE* 18:190–91.

Appendix B

Sufficient and Efficacious Grace

IN EDWARDS'S SCHEME, THE DISPOSITION OF LOVE TO GOD IS A GRACE SOMETIMES CALLED "sufficient." Predictably, "sufficient grace" is distinguished from "efficacious grace," which also may be identified with the disposition of love to God. The designation "sufficient," however, does not indicate anything about its efficacy: sufficient grace is actual grace and, therefore, always efficacious in its application or exercise, in that its sufficiency flows from the infinite power and goodness of God. In this sense, it, like efficacious grace, comes under the traditional heading of "special grace."[8] Nevertheless, Edwards denominates it "sufficient" to specially qualify or distinguish it from "efficacious grace," not in terms of a *type* or *kind* of grace, but *purposeful application* of the one source of actual grace, the Holy Spirit.

Sufficient grace, then, ought to be equated with the temporary and occasional grace of original righteousness, while efficacious grace is identical with the "confirming grace" of "Miscellanies" no. 290, in terms of an eternally unfaltering grace designated for a different divine purpose, namely, confirmation and glorification.[9] On the one hand, sufficient grace is an internally present, actual grace effectually applied, *as God deems appropriate*, for a particular purpose in particular circumstances; while on the other hand, efficacious grace is a grace persistently applied for an enduring purpose. The former is intermittent and provisional, the latter unremitting and permanent. This is in perfect keeping with Edwards's concept of the weakly arbitrary, governing operation and influence of the Holy Spirit.

---

8. Special grace is distinguished from common grace. Special grace, traditionally speaking, is the grace by which God redeems, sanctifies, and glorifies His people. Unlike common grace, which is universally given and not necessarily or intimately associated with the Person of the Holy Spirit, special grace is personal and personally bestowed only on those whom God elects.

9. The "efficacious grace" referred to here is quite similar to that in chap XXXII of the Westminster Confession: "The souls of the righteous, being made perfect in holiness, are received into the highest heavens . . ." What *makes* them "perfect in holiness" is "confirming" or "efficacious grace." Elsewhere within the Westminster Confession, "efficacious grace" is distinguished from anything in fallen or regenerate humanity. Such efficacious grace which perseveres, preserves and translates the saints "depends not upon their own free will, but upon the immutability of the decree of election," and, in heaven, God conferring efficacious grace to his saints (chap XVII). On this point, the Westminster divines appear to be in accord with Augustine ("*De Correptione et Gratia*" in Schaff, *St. Augustine, Anti-Pelagian Writings, The Nicean Fathers*, 5:26) and Calvin (*Institutes*, I.15.8), and Edwards in accord with all three. Initially it would appear that the similarity between the Augustine and Jonathan Edwards is uncanny; but while their notions of "efficacious grace" or confirming grace (for Augustine, the grace of perseverance) were for all intents and purposes identical, their concepts of original righteousness differ.

To be sure, this distinction between the two purposeful applications of the one source of grace immediately bears on Edwards's doctrine of concreation, which, in turn, makes it decisive in his attempt to reconcile the problem of Adam's first sin.

Some scholars, however, fail to appreciate Edwards's differentiation. John H. Gerstner and Charles S. Storms, for example, believe Edwards fails to make a real distinction between confirming and sufficient grace. Gerstner, in particular, asserts that, "If grace is truly sufficient it must be efficacious; if it is not efficacious it is not sufficient."[10] Gerstner's case is built upon evidence from a MS sermon on Romans 5:6, where Edwards writes, "Adam had sufficient assistance of God always present with him to have enabled him to have obeyed if he had used his natural abilities in endeavoring it."[11] Gerstner objects and says that man's problem is always with his inclination and never with his natural ability. "Miscellanies" no. 501 adds to his case, where Edwards continues: "though the assistance was not such as it would have been after his confirmation to render it impossible for him to sin."[12] Gerstner reads this and exclaims: "Edwards has a distinction here without a difference. He distinguishes between sufficient and efficacious or confirming grace, but there is no difference in his own psychology . . . According to Edwards it was sufficient if the natural abilities were used; but it was not sufficient in itself at all. In other words it was not actually sufficient but conditionally or hypothetically sufficient; a very different thing."[13] According to Gerstner, sufficient grace could not even be conditionally sufficient unless the grace was "actual" which, he states, "it was not, it could never be sufficient, for unless a man had efficacious grace he would not utilize his natural ability, to call on his 'sufficient' grace." To be sure, Adam did have the inclination to obey before he succumbed to the temptation but at the time of his evil capitulation he obviously did not, for only the inclination to the good would have been sufficient. Gerstner concludes by saying sufficient grace is a contradiction in terms; sufficient grace is insufficient; "Only efficacious grace can be sufficient."[14]

But Gerstner, Storms, and others, completely miss Edwards's meaning. Edwards knows that, by definition, *posse peccare* excludes efficacious, confirmatory grace, but gives place for some concept of sufficient grace. The question then is, "What is sufficient about sufficient grace?" For Edwards, the sufficiency of sufficient grace to (i) prevent man from sinning and (ii) to empower him to lovingly obey God lies in its infused and *irresistible* character. It is infused because it does not belong to the nature of man. For Adam, this infusion of the Spirit took place at his inception: hence, Edwards's doctrine of concreation precludes any notion of created grace whatsoever.[15] So, while he writes at length of the "habit of grace," Edwards recognizes with Francis Turretin that speaking "physically"

---

10. Gerstner, *Rational Biblical*, 2:306.
11. Cited in Gerstner, *Rational Biblical*, 2:306.
12. *WJE* 18:51.
13. Gerstner, *Rational Biblical*, 2:306.
14. Ibid., 306–7.

15. While Edwards uses the Scholastic notion of "infused grace," he is careful to distinguish it from Thomistic created grace. For a discussion on this point see chapter 12, where I refute Anri Morimoto's claim that created grace is the disposition of love to God. Cf. Cherry, *A Reappraisal*, 34–39.

of grace as an infused disposition tends toward a naturalizing of the supernatural.[16] He therefore warns that when one describes grace as a disposition in Adam (or the saint for that matter), one must be careful not to turn the principle into "a natural disposition to act grace."[17] He argues that grace, as a disposition, though it is vitally united to man's faculties, does not become man's own natural principle, but rather the "perfection and excellency" of the soul is connected with "the will of God, and is dependent on nothing else."[18] Which is to say, the Spirit is (weakly) arbitrary in the manner of His ingenerated governance. Man does not govern the Spirit, but the Spirit man. The superior principle of holiness, righteousness, and virtue, are the foundation that the soul has *beyond* itself though internally related to itself through participation. Consequently, as Conrad Cherry states it: "the habit of grace remains grace: it is not given over to human control."[19]

Sufficient grace, therefore, is no weak grace; it is every bit as much actual grace as "efficacious grace." The only different is in the divine application of grace: when God the Holy Spirit exercises His gracious influence and operation, it is sufficient to its ends. This is a question of *if* and *when*. When the Spirit exercises Himself constantly, per His covenantal obligations, it is continuously efficacious. Either way, infused grace, when applied, assists "the natural powers" as "they work together" ("Miscellanies," no. *p*) to *irresistibly* obtain a divinely desired purpose: for, in the words of Edwards, "what God's Spirit doth, he doth; he doth so much as he doth, or he causeth in the soul so much as he causeth, let that be how little soever."[20] Divine assistance, therefore, is always efficacious to do that which He intends to assist; that is, "[if and] when God assists, he assists to all that he intends to assist to."[21]

Edwards could have averted the later confusion of Gerstner, Storms, and others, if only he had employed a more descriptive designation for sufficient grace. But Edwards has never been known for original terminology, only reinventing the meaning of established terms. As a result, commentators must be conscious of which preexisting kind of "sufficient grace" Edwards is taking the liberty to nuance in his definition of original righteousness. In a division of internal actual grace, sufficient grace is used either to mean (1) grace that gives sufficient ability to perform a salutary act, prescinding from the result (grace efficacious with the efficacy of power); or (2) purely sufficient grace, which does not obtain a good, free act, but gives power to produce one – grace inefficacious in the production of a good, free act.

Obviously Edwards does not precisely mean "sufficient" in the first sense because it falls right into the unresolved Roman Catholic distinction between graces "proximately" and "remotely" sufficient for a good act;[22] and by definition it is ultimately efficacious. The

---

16. Turretin, *Institutes*, 2:510–17.
17. Helm, *Treatise on Grace*, 55.
18. "Miscellanies," no. 481, *WJE* 13:523–24.
19. Cherry, *A Reappraisal*, 37.
20. "Miscellanies," no. 15, *WJE* 13:208.
21. Ibid.
22. Grace is proximately sufficient if it gives sufficient power to perform the act without addition aid, or, in other words, it is efficacious in and of itself; while grace is said to be remotely sufficient if for such and such a thing if further aid is needed, whereupon it is again efficacious.

second option, purely sufficient grace (inefficacious), is such grace which gives full power to perform a good, free act, even in the presence of contrary difficulties, but which lacks the effect due to the will's resistance. If Edwards meant this, he would have to respond to the following issues:

1. Would not "the will's resistance" be considered a "contrary difficulty" to which "full power" is sufficiently given to the agent for overcoming?
2. Would not this grace fundamentally be given for the empowerment of the agent's "whole will"?
3. The problem of answering Gerstner's criticism that sufficient grace "could not even be conditionally sufficient, for unless the grace was actual . . . it never could be sufficient, for unless a man had efficacious grace he would not utilize his natural ability, to call on his 'sufficient grace.'" So that in the end, it is always insufficient and really not actual grace at all.
4. Purely sufficient grace was not recognized by the Reformers or the Jansenists. Both acknowledged no other grace but efficacious grace only. For both the Reformers and the Jansenists even grace relatively sufficient was efficacious.[23]
5. The definition of "purely sufficient grace" is juxtaposed to sufficient grace as actual, infused and irresistible.

But Edwards does not deal with these issues because he fundamentally alters what "sufficient grace" historically means, as well as how it is used. He could say that the grace Adam possessed was sufficient for *all* temptations—because in terms of efficacy, it was. Instead, he says that it would have been sufficient *if* exercised. It really has nothing to do with man's natural ability in the sense Gerstner intends. Certainly man had the ability, *even* the moral ability. But the crux, for Edwards, concerns the *governing* of the mind's essential disposition and natural inclination: *that* is the issue. In each and every moment of his existence, Adam's self-love disposition functioned in accord with its telic prescription—not in a sinful way, but naturally. It required the governing disposition of love to God to make any motion of the mind truly virtuous. Sufficient grace is not really conditional upon the cooperation of Adam. Thus, man's dependence on the power of God is not only for the announcement of his original status and righteousness, but also for the disposing of the soul

---

23. Sufficient grace in Roman Catholic (RC) theology of grace is grace that, in contrast to efficacious grace, does not meet with adequate cooperation on the part of the recipient and hence fails to achieve the result for which it was bestowed. The Reformers found this notion not only inconsistent but reprehensible. In the Dominican view (represented by the Thomist theologian of Slamanca, Domingo Banez (1528–1604)), it required further divine motion (efficacious grace) to produce its intended result. On the other hand, the Jesuit view, Molinism (represented by the Spanish theologian, Luis de Molina [1535–1600]), held that "sufficient grace" was really adequate to produce such an intended result, needing only the consent of human free will to become efficacious. Within RC theology, both sufficient and efficacious graces are different forms of "actual grace." Molina's system was published in his *Concordia liberi arbitrii cum gratiae donis*, and was widely adopted by the Jesuits. However, conservative RC theologians, especially the Dominicans led by Banez, immediately assailed it. The result was one of the most extensive theological controversies in RC theology, culminating in the *Congregatio de Auxiliis*. The *Congregatio*, which met for 120 sessions from 1598–1607, was unable to harmonize party differences, and Pope Paul V dismissed the gathering undecided.

APPENDIX B

toward holiness and the performance of it: "Man was dependent on the power of God in his first estate . . . It was an effect of the power of God to make men holy at the first . . . and it was an effect of God's power to continue 'em in holiness." Continuing in holiness and righteousness or the exercising of the principle of divine love, then, was also the effect of the power of God; and if the effect of the power of God in man, then there must have been a sort of coaction. Because Edwards identifies the supernatural principles with the Holy Spirit, the denial of coaction does not resonate with him. For, according to Edwards, God is not glorified through man's *independent* obedience, but in and through his relational *dependence* upon God, and specifically, the indwelling Spirit "both to will and to do of His good pleasure."[24] In Edwards, all the good and virtue that humanity may have is through God: "That he is the *cause* and original when all their good comes, therein it is *of* him; and that he is the *medium* by which it is obtained and conveyed, therein they have it *through* him; and that however is the *good itself* given and conveyed, therein they are *in* him."[25]

By calling for a degree of coaction in the first man, indeed, in regenerate persons as well, Edwards safeguards the glory of God, reserving all the motions of true virtue—even original and continual righteousness and innocence—to the arbitrary operations of God Himself.

---

24. See 927. Sermon on Philippians 2:1 (Mar. 1749; repreached June 1754), "DOC. Divine love is a . . . inward principle and spring of religion in the soul" [col. 2], *WJE Online* 67.

25. *God Glorified in Man's Dependence* (1731), WJE 17:204.

Bibliography

Jonathan Edwards

Unpublished works (inclusive of all MS sermons) are from the Jonathan Edwards Collection, General Collection, Beinecke Rare Book and Manuscript Library, Yale University.

Cited Collected Works

Edwards, Jonathan. *The Works of Jonathan Edwards*. 73 vols. New Haven: Yale University Press, 1957–2008.
———. *Vol. 1, Freedom of the Will*. Edited by Paul Ramsey, 1957.
———. *Vol. 2, Religious Affections*. Edited by John E. Smith, 1959.
———. *Vol. 3, Original Sin*. Edited by Clyde A. Holbrook, 1970.
———. *Vol. 4, The Great Awakening*. Edited by C. C. Goen, 1972.
———. *Vol. 5, Apocalyptic Writings*. Edited by Stephen J. Stein, 1977.
———. *Vol. 6, Scientific and Philosophical Writings*. Edited by Wallace E. Anderson, 1980.
———. *Vol. 7, The Life of David Brainerd*. Edited by Norman Pettit, 1985.
———. *Vol. 8, Ethical Writings*. Edited by Paul Ramsey, 1989.
———. *Vol. 9, A History of the Work of Redemption*. Edited by John F. Wilson, 1989.
———. *Vol. 10, Sermons and Discourses, 1720–1723*. Edited by Wilson H. Kimnach, 1992.
———. *Vol. 11, Typological Writings*, eds. Wallace E. Anderson, Mason I. Lowance, and David H. Watters, 1993.
———. *Vol. 12, Ecclesiastical Writings*. Edited by David D. Hall, 1994.
———. *Vol. 13, The "Miscellanies" (Entry Nos. a–z, aa–zz, 1–500)*. Edited by Thomas A. Schafer, 1994.
———. *Vol. 14, Sermons and Discourses, 1723–1729*. Edited by Kenneth P. Minkema, 1997.
———. *Vol. 15, Notes on Scripture*. Edited by Stephen J. Stein, 1998.
———. *Vol. 16, Letters and Personal Writings*. Edited by George S. Claghorn, 1998.
———. *Vol. 17, Sermons and Discourses, 1730–1733*. Edited by Mark Valeri, 1999.
———. *Vol. 18, The "Miscellanies" (Entry Nos. 501–832)*. Edited by Ava Chamberlain, 2000.
———. *Vol. 19, Sermons and Discourses, 1734–1738*. Edited by M. X. Lesser, 2001.
———. *Vol. 20, The "Miscellanies" (Entry Nos. 833–1152)*. Edited by Amy Plantinga Pauw, 2002.
———. *Vol. 21, Writings on the Trinity, Grace, and Faith*. Edited by Sang Hyun Lee, 2003.
———. *Vol. 22, Sermons and Discourses, 1739–1742*, eds. Harry S. Stout and Nathan O. Hatch, with Kyle P. Farley, 2003.
———. *Vol. 23, The "Miscellanies" (Entry Nos. 1153–1360)*. Edited by Douglas A. Sweeney, 2004.
———. *Vol. 24, The Blank Bible*. Edited by Stephen J. Stein, 2006.
———. *Vol. 25, Sermons and Discourses, 1743–1758*. Edited by Wilson H. Kimnach, 2006.
———. *Vol. 26, Catalogues of Books*. Edited by Peter J. Theusen, 2008.
———. *The Works of Jonathan Edwards Online, Volumes 27–73*. The Jonathan Edwards Center. Yale University, 2008.
———. *The Works of President Edwards*. 8 vols. Edited by Samuel Austin. Worcester, MA: Thomas, 1808–9.
———. *The Works of President Edwards with a Memoir of His Life*. Edited by Sereno E. Dwight. 10 vols. New York: Converse, 1829–30.
———. *The Works of Jonathan Edwards*. Revised and edited by Edward Hickman. 2 vols. [London, 1834]. Reprint. Edinburgh: Banner of Truth, 1974.

Cited Separate Works

Edwards, Jonathan. *The Blessing of God: Previously Unpublished Sermons of Jonathan Edwards*. Edited by Michael McMullen. Nashville: Broadman and Holman, 2003.

———. *A Divine and Supernatural Light, Immediately Imparted to the Soul by the Spirit of God, Shown to Be Both a Scriptural and Rational Doctrine*. Boston, 1734.

———. *God Glorified in the Work of Redemption, by the Greatness of Man's Dependence upon Him*. Boston, 1731.

———. *Jonathan Edwards: Containing 16 Sermons Unpublished in Edwards' Lifetime. The Puritan Pulpit, The American Puritans*. Edited by Donald Kistler. Morgan, PA: Soli Deo Gloria, 2004.

———. *Jonathan Edwards' Sermon Outlines*. Edited by Sheldon B. Quincer. London: Pickering & Inglis, 1958.

———. *Miscellaneous Observations On Important Theological Subjects, Original and Collected*. Edinburgh: Gray, 1793.

———. *Observations Concerning the Scripture Oeconomy of the Trinity and Covenant of Redemption*. Edited by E. C. Smyth. New York: Scribner's sons, 1880.

———. *Selections from the Unpublished Writings of Jonathan Edwards of America*. Edited by Alexander B. Grossart. Printed for private circulation, 1865.

———. *Treatise on Grace and other Posthumously Published Writings*. Edited by Paul Helm. Cambridge: Clarke, 1971.

———. *True Grace Distinguished from the Experience of Devils*. New York, 1753.

Other Primary Works

Ames, William. *Conscience with the Power and Cases Thereof*. London, 1639.

———. *De conscientia et eius iure vel casibus*. Amsterdam, 1631.

———. *Medulla SS. Theologial*. Amsterdam, 1626.

———. *Theses logicae*. Leyden, 1633.

Anselm. *Basic Writings*. Edited by Charles Hartshorne. Translated by S. W. Deane. La Salle, IL: Open Court, 1962.

Aquinas, Thomas. *Summa Theologia* and *Contra Gentiles*. General Editor, Thomas Gilby. 61 vols. London: Blackfriars, 1964–66.

Aristotle. *Ethica Nicomachea*. In *The Works of Aristotle Translated into English*, translated by W. D. Ross. Vol. X. Oxford: Oxford University Press, 1915.

———. *Metaphysics*. In *The Works of Aristotle Translated into English*, translated by W. D. Ross. Vol. IX. Oxford: Oxford University Press, 1915.

Augustine, Aurillius. Works Works collected in *The Nicene and Post-Nicene Fathers, First Series*. General Editor, Philip Schaff. Vols. 1–14. [1886]. Reprint. Peabody, MA: Hendrickson, 1994.

Baxter, Andrew. *An Enquiry into the Nature of the Human Soul*. 3rd ed. 8 Vols. London: A. Millar, 1745.

Bellarmino, Roberto F. R. *Opera Omnia Roberti Bellarmini*. 4 vols. Naples: Josephum Giuliano, 1856–62.

Bentley, Richard. *The Folly of Atheism, and (What Is Now Called) Deism, Even with Respect to the Present Life*. Boyle Lectures. London, 1692.

———. *Remarks Upon a Late Discourse of Free-Thinking: in a Letter to F. H. D. D., by Phileleutherus Lipsiensis*. 5th ed. Cambridge: J. Morphew, 1716.

Berkeley, George. *The Works of Bishop George Berkeley, Bishop of Cloyne*. Edited by A. A. Luce and T. E. Jessop. 9 vols. London: Nelson, 1948–57.

Brine, John. *A Treatise on Various Subjects*. London, 1750.

Burgersdicius, Franciscus. *Monitic Logica*. London, 1697.

Butler, Joseph. *Fifteen Sermons Preached at the Rolls Chapel* [1726]. Edited by T. A. Roberts. London: SPCK, 1970.

Calvin, John. *Calvin: Institutes of the Christian Religion*. The Library of Christian Classics XX–XXI. Edited by John T. McNeill. London: SCM, 1961.

Chauncy, Charles. *Mystery Hid from Ages & Generations*. London, 1784.

Chubb, Thomas. *A Collection of Tracts on Various Subjects*. London, 1730.

Clarke, Adam. *The Holy Bible . . . with Commentary and Critical Notes; Designed as a Help to a better Understanding of the Sacred Writing*. 8 vols. London: Sargeant, 1810–26.
Clarke, Samuel. *Discourse Concerning the Being and Attributes of God*. 4th ed. London, 1716.
———. *The Leibniz-Clarke Correspondence*. Edited by H. G. Alexander. Manchester, UK: University of Manchester Press, 1956.
———. *Scripture Doctrine of the Trinity*. London, 1712.
Cudworth, Ralph. *The True Intellectual System of the Universe*. London, 1678.
Dana, James. *An Examination of the Late Reverend President Edwards's "Enquiry on Freedom of the Will."* Boston, 1770.
Descartes, René. *Meditations on First Philosophy*. Translated and edited by John Cottingham. Cambridge: Cambridge University Press, 1996.
Edwards, John. *A Free Discourse Concerning Truth and Error, Especially in Matters of Religion . . . Also a Preface Containing Some Brief Remarks on the Late Reflections on Humane Learning*. London, 1701.
Edwards, Timothy. *All the Living Must Surely Die: Election Sermon*. New London, 1732.
Emmons, Nathaniel. *The Works of Nathaniel Emmons*. Edited by Jacob Ide. 6 vols. Boston: Crocker & Brewster, 1842.
Gale, Theophilus. *The Court of the Gentiles: Or A Discourse Touching on the Original of Human Literature, both Philologie and Philosophie, From the Scripture & Jewish Church*. 2nd ed. 4 vols. Oxford: Gilbert, 1627–28.
Greenham, Richard. *The Works of Richard Greenham*. Rev. ed. London, 1612.
Grotius, Hugo. *De Jure Belli et Pacis*. Paris, 1625.
Heereboord, Adrian. *Ermhneia Logica, seu, Synopseos logicae Burgersdicanae*. London, 1658.
Henry, Matthew. *An Exposition of All the Books of the Old and New Testaments; Wherein Each Paragraph, or Verse, Reduc'd to its Proper Heads; the Sense Given, and Largely Illustrated with Practical Remarks and Observations*. 6 vols. London, 1708–10.
Hobbes, Thomas. *Leviathan, Parts I and II* [1651]. Edited by A. R. Waller. Cambridge: Cambridge University Press, 1904.
Hopkins, Samuel. *Life and Character of the Late Reverend Mr. Jonathan Edwards*. Boston, 1765.
———. *The Works of Samuel Hopkins*. Edited by Edwards Amasa Park. 3 vols. Boston: Doctrinal Tract and Book Society, 1852.
Hume, David. *A Treatise of Human Nature: Being and Attempt to Introduce the Experimental Method of Reasoning into Moral Subjects*. 2 vols. London, 1739.
Hutchenson, Francis. *An Inquiry Into the Original of Our Ideas of Beauty and Virtue* [1725] in *British Moralists, Being Selections from Writers Principally of the Eighteenth Century, Vol. 1*, edited by L. A. Selby-Bigge. New York: Dover, 1965.
Leibniz, Gottfried Wilhem Freiherr. *The Leibniz-Clarke Correspondence*. Edited by H. G. Alexander. Manchester: University of Manchester Press, 1956.
———. *Théodicée* ("Essays in Theodicy on the Goodness of God, the Liberty of Man, and the Origin of Evil"). In *The Philosophical Works of Leibniz*. Translated by George M. Duncan. New Haven, CT: Tuttle, Morehouse, & Taylor, 1890.
Leland, John. *A supplement to the first and second volumes of the deistical writers . . . etc*. London, 1756.
———. *A View of the Principal Deistical Writers That Have Appeared in England in the Last and Present Century*. 2 vols. London, 1754–55.
Leslie, Charles. *A Short and Easy Method with the Deists*. London, 1694.
Locke, John. *An Essay Concerning Human Understanding*. Edited by Peter H. Nidditch. Oxford: Clarendon, 1975.
———. *The Reasonableness of Christianity, As Delivered in the Scriptures*. London, 1695.
Lombardi, Magistri Petri. *Sententiae In IV Libris Distinctae*. Collegii S. Bonaventurae ad Claras Aquas. Rome: Grottaferrata, 1971.
Luther, D. Martin. *D. Martin Luthers Werke. Kritische Gesamtausgabe (WA)*. 58 vols. Weimar: Bohlau, 1833–1993.
Mastricht, Peter Von. *Theoretico-practica theologia*. [1680]. Utrecht, 1699.

Malebranche, Nicolas. *Father Malebranche's Treatise Concerning the Search after Truth. The Whole Work Complete. To Which Is Added the Author's Treatise of Nature and Grace: Being a Consequence of the Principles Contained in the Search.* Translated by T. Taylor. 2 vols. 2nd ed. London, 1700.

———. *Oeuvres Completes.* Edited by André Robinet. Paris: Ingold, 1886.

Mather, Cotton. *Blessed Unions.* Boston, 1692.

———. *Religio Philosophica or the Christian Philosopher.* London, 1721.

Mayhew, Experience. *Grace Defended in a Modest Plea for an Important Truth.* Boston, 1743.

More, Henry. *An Antidote Against Atheism: An Appeal to the Naturall Faculties of the Minde of Man, Whether There Be Not a God.* 2nd ed. London, 1655.

———. *A Collection of Several Philosophical Writings.* London, 1662.

———. *Divine Dialogue: Containing Sundry Disquisitions and Instructions Concerning the Attributes of God and His Providence in the World.* London, 1668.

Newton, Isaac. *Four Letters to Dr. Bentley, Containing Some Arguments in Proof of a Deity.* London, 1756.

———. *Optics.* Translated by Samuel Clark. [1704]. London, 1706.

———. *Philosophiae Naturalis Principia Mathematica.* London, 1689.

Owen, John. *The Works of John Owen.* Edited by William H. Goold. 16 vols. London: Johnson and Hunter, 1850–53.

Perkins, William. *The Workes of that Famovs and VVorthy Minister of Christ in the Vniversitie of Cambridge, M. William Perkins. . . .* 3 vols. London, 1612, 1613, 1631.

Plato. *Plato: Collected Dialogues.* Bollingen Series 71. Princeton: Princeton University Press, 1961.

Plotinus. *Enneads.* Translated by A. H. Armstrong. Loeb Classical Library. Cambridge: Harvard University Press, 1966–88.

Poole, Matthew. *Synopsis Criticorum aliorumque Sacrae Scripturae Interpretum.* 5 vols. London: Francofurti ad Moenum, 1669–76.

Richardson, Alexander. *Providence and Precept.* London, 1691.

Shaftesbury, Third Earl of (Anthony Ashley Cooper). *Characteristicks of Men, Manners, Opinions, Times.* 3 vols. London, 1711.

Smith, John. *Select Discourses.* Edited by J. Worthington. London: 1660. 2nd ed. Cambridge, 1673.

Stoddard, Solomon. *The Defects of Preachers Reproved.* New London, 1724.

———. *The Efficacy of the Fear of Hell, to Restrain Men from Sin.* Boston, 1713.

———. *Three Sermons Lately Preach'd at Boston.* Boston, 1717.

———. *A Treatise Concerning Conversion.* Boston, 1719.

Taylor, John. *The Scripture-Doctrine of Original Sin, Proposed to Free and Candid Examination.* London, 1738.

Tindal, Matthew. *Christianity as Old as the Creation.* London, 1730.

Toland, John. *Christianity not Mysterious.* London, 1696.

Turretin, Francois. *Institutio Theologiae Elencticae.* Translated by G. M. Giger. Edited by J. T. Dennison. 3 vols. [1679–82]. Phillipsburg: Presbyterian & Reformed, 1992–97.

Watson, Thomas. *A Body of Practical Divinity.* London, 1692.

Wesley, John. *The Works of John Wesley.* Edited by Thomas Jackson. 14 vols. [1831]. Reprint. Grand Rapids: Eerdmans, 1975.

Westminster Assembly, The. *The Confession of Faith; the Larger and Shorter Catechisms . . . etc.* Edinburgh: Blair and Bruce, 1841.

Whichcote, Benjamin. *Moral and Religious Aphorisms: Wherein Are Contained Many Doctrines of Truth; and Rules of Practice . . .* Norwich and London, 1703.

Whitby, Daniel. *A Discourse Concerning I. The True Import of the Words Election and Reprobation; and the Things Signified by Them in the Holy Scripture. II. The Extent of Christ's Redemption. III. The Grace of God; Where It Is Enquired, Whether It Be Vouchsafed Sufficiently to Those Who Improve It Not, and Irresistibly to Those Who Do Not Improve It; and Whether Men Be Wholly Passive in the Work of Their Regeneration? IV. The Liberty of the Will in a State of Trial and Probation. V. The Perseverance or Defectibility of the Saints; with Some Reflections on the State of Heathens, the Providence and Presence of God.* London, 1710.

Wollebius. *Compendium theologiae Christanae.* Basil, 1618.

Secondary Works

Catechism of the Catholic Church. New York: Doubleday, 1995.

Ahlstrom, Sydney E. *A Religious History of the American People*. New Haven, CT: Yale University Press, 1972.

Aldridge, Alfred O. *Jonathan Edwards*. New York: Washington Square, 1964.

———. "Natural Religion and Deism in America before Ethan Allen and Thomas Paine." *The William and Mary Quarterly* LIV (1997) 835–48.

Alexander, H. G., ed. *The Leibniz-Clarke Correspondence*. Manchester: University of Manchester Press, 1956.

Allen, Alexander V. G. *Jonathan Edwards*. American Religious Leaders Series. Boston: Houghton & Mifflin, 1889.

———. *Life and Writings of Jonathan Edwards*. Edinburgh: T. & T. Clark, 1889.

Audi, Robert, gen. ed. *The Cambridge Dictionary of Philosophy*. Cambridge: Cambridge University Press, 1995.

Barad, Judith. *Consent: The Means to an Active Faith According to St. Thomas Aquinas*. American Universities Studies, series 5, Vol. 126. New York: Lang, 1992.

Barth, Karl. *Church Dogmatics*. Translated and Edited by G. W. Bromiley and T. F. Torrance. Edinburgh: T. & T. Clark, 1956–77.

Bassinger, David. *The Case for Freewill Theism: A Philosophical Assessment*. Downers Grove, IL: InterVarsity, 1996.

Bebbington, David. "Remembered Around the World: The International Scope of Edwards's Legacy." In *Jonathan Edwards at Home and Abroad: Historical Memories, Cultural Movements, Global Horizons*, edited by David W. Kling and Douglas A. Sweeney, 177–200. Columbia: University of South Carolina Press, 2003.

Bennett Ramsey. "The Ineluctable Impulse: 'Consent' in the Thought of Edwards, James, and Royce." *Union Seminary Quarterly Review* 37 (1983) 302–22.

Biéler, Andre. *The Social Humanism of Calvin*. Translated by P. T. Furhmann. Louisville: Westminster/John Knox, 1964.

Bizer, Ernst. *Fides ex Auditu: Eine Untersuchung über die Entwicklung der Gerechtigkeit Gottes durch Martin Luther*. Neukirchen: Moers, 1958.

Blackwell, Albert, et. al., eds. *Faithful Imagining: Essays in Honor of Richard R. Niebuhr*. Atlanta: Scholars, 1995.

Bobik, Joseph. *Aquinas on Being and Essence*. Notre Dame, IN: University of Notre Dame Press, 1965.

Borges, Jorge Luis. *Labyrinths: Selected Stories and Other Writings*. New York: New Directions, 1964.

Bourke, Vernon. *St. Thomas and the Greek Moralists*. Milwaukee, WI: Marquette University Press, 1947.

Boyd, Gregory. *God of the Possible: A Biblical Introduction to the Open View of God*. Grand Rapids: Baker, 2000.

Brekus, Catherine A. "Jonathan Edwards's Ministry to Families." In *Jonathan Edwards at Home and Abroad: Historical Memories, Cultural Movements, Global Horizons*, edited by David W. Kling and Douglas A. Sweeney, 40–60. Columbia: University of South Carolina Press, 2003.

Bremond, A. "Le theocentrisme de Malebranche." *Archives de philosophie* 6 (1928) 281–303.

Bryant, Louise May and Mary Patterson, eds. "The List of Books Sent From England by Jeremiah Dummer. . . ." In *Papers in Honor of Andrew Keogh, Librarian of Yale University*, edited by the Staff of the Yale University Library, 423–92. New Haven, CT: Yale University Press for private circulation, 1938.

Carse, James P. *Jonathan Edwards and the Visibility of God*. New York: Scribner's sons, 1967.

Cassirer, Ernst. *The Philosophy of the Enlightenment*. Princeton: Princeton University Press, 1951.

Chai, Leon. *Jonathan Edwards and the Limits of Enlightenment Philosophy*. New York: Oxford University Press, 1987.

Channing, William Ellery. "Remarks on National Literature." *Christian Examiner* 7 (1830) 269–95.

Cherry, Conrad. *The Theology of Jonathan Edwards: A Reappraisal*. Garden City, NY: Anchor, 1966.

Chevreau, Guy. *Catch the Fire: The Toronto Blessing: An Experience of Renewal and Revival*. London: Marshall Pickering, 1994.

Cohen, Charles Lloyd. *God's Caress: The Psychology of Puritan Religious Experience*. New York: Oxford University Press, 1986.

Cooey-Nichols, Paula M. *Jonathan Edwards on Nature and Destiny: A Systematic Analysis.* Studies in American Religion, Vol. 16. Lewiston, NY: Mellen, 1985.

Colwell, John E. "Jonathan Edwards." In *The Dictionary of Historical Theology*, edited by Trevor A. Hart, 174–75. Carlisle, UK: Paternoster, 2000.

Cook, Monte. "The Ontological Status of Malebranchean Ideas." *The Journal of the History of Philosophy* 4 (1998) 525–44.

Copan, Paul. "Jonathan Edwards's Philosophical Influences: Lockean or Malebranchean?" *Journal of the Evangelical Theological Society* 44.1 (2001) 107–24.

Crabtree, Arthur Branford. *Jonathan Edwards' View of Man: A Study in Eighteenth-Century Calvinism.* Wallington, UK: Religious Education, 1948.

Cragg, Gerald R., ed. *The Cambridge Platonists.* New York: Oxford University Press, 1968.

———. *The Church in the Age of Reason, 1648–1789.* New York: Penguin, 1960.

———. *From Puritanism to the Age of Reason.* Cambridge: Harvard University Press, 1950.

———. *Reason and Authority in the Eighteenth Century.* Cambridge: Cambridge University Press, 1964.

Crisp, Oliver C. "Augustinian Universalism." *International Journal for Philosophy of Religion* 53 (2003) 127–45.

———. "Jonathan Edwards on Divine Simplicity." *Religious Studies* 39 (2003) 23–41.

———. and Paul Helm, eds. *Jonathan Edwards: Philosophical Theologian.* Aldershot, UK: Ashgate, 2004.

Crooker, Joseph. "Jonathan Edwards: A Psychological Study." *New England Magazine* 2 (1890) 159–72.

Cunningham, William. *Historical Theology.* 2 vols. [1862]. Edinburgh: Banner of Truth, 1960.

Dabney, Robert Louis. *Systematic Theology.* St. Louis: Presbyterian Publishing Co. of St. Louis, 1878.

Daniel, Stephen H. *The Philosophy of Jonathan Edwards: A Study in Divine Semiotics.* Bloomington: University of Indiana Press, 1994.

———. "Postmodern Concepts of God and Edwards's Trinitarian Ontology Theology." In *Edwards in Our Time: Jonathan Edwards and the Shaping of American Religion*, edited by Sang Hyun Lee and Allen C. Guelzo, 45–64. Grand Rapids: Eerdmans, 1999.

Davidson, Bruce W. "Reasonable Damnation: How Jonathan Edwards Argued for the Rationality of Hell." *Journal of the Evangelical Theology Society* 38.1 (1995) 47–56.

Davidson, Edward H. *Jonathan Edwards: The Narrative of a Puritan Mind.* Boston: Houghton-Mifflin, 1966.

Davis, T. H. "The Traditions of Puritan Typology." In *Typology and Early American Literature*, edited by S. Bercovitch, 11–45. Amherst: University of Massachusetts, 1972.

Dawkins, Richard. *The Selfish Gene.* New York: Oxford University Press, 1989.

Delattre, Roland Andre. *Beauty and Sensibility in the Thought of Jonathan Edwards: An Essay in Aesthetics and Theological Ethics.* New Haven: Yale University Press, 1968.

———. "Beauty and Theology: A Reappraisal of Jonathan Edwards." *Soundings* 51 (1969) 60–79.

De Prospo, R. C. *Theism in the Discourse of Jonathan Edwards.* Newark: University of Delaware Press, 1985.

Dexter, F. B. "The Manuscripts of Jonathan Edwards." *Proceedings of the Massachusetts Historical Society.* 2nd series, XV (1902) 2–16.

Edwards, Rem B. *A Return to Moral and Religious Philosophy in Early America.* Washington DC: University Press of America, 1982.

Ellis, Joseph. *The New England Mind in Transition: Samuel Johnson of Connecticut, 1696–1772.* New Haven, CT: Yale University Press, 1973.

Elwood, Douglas J. *The Philosophical Theology of Jonathan Edwards.* New York: Columbia University Press, 1960.

Faust, Clarence F. "Jonathan Edwards as a Scientist." *American Literature* 1 (1930) 393–404.

Ferguson, Sinclair B. "Ordo Salutis." In *New Dictionary of Theology*, edited by Sinclair B. Ferguson and David F. Wright, 480–81. Downers Grove, IL: InterVarsity, 1988.

Fiering, Norman. *Jonathan Edwards' Moral Thought in Its British Context.* Chapel Hill, NC: University of North Carolina Press, 1981.

———. *Moral Philosophy at Seventeenth-Century Harvard: A Discipline in Transition.* The Institute of Early American History and Culture. Williamsburg, VA: University of North Carolina Press, 1981.

———. "The Rationalist Foundations of Jonathan Edwards." In *Jonathan Edwards and the American Experience*, edited by Nathan Hatch and Harry S. Stout, 73–101. Oxford and New York: Oxford University Press, 1988.

———. "Solomon Stoddard's Library at Harvard." *Harvard Library Bulletin* 20 (1972) 262–69.

Foster, Frank H. *A Genetic History of New England Theology*. Chicago: University of Chicago Press, 1907.
Freddoso, Alfred, ed. *The Existence and Nature of God*. Notre Dame, IN: University of Notre Dame Press, 1983.
Gale, Richard M. *On the Nature and Existence of God*. Cambridge: Cambridge University Press, 1991.
Gay, Peter. *A Loss of Mastery: Puritan Historians in Colonial America*. Berkeley, CA: University of California Press, 1966.
George, Timothy. *Theology of the Reformers*. Nashville: Boardman, 1988.
Gerstner, John H. and Jonathan Neil Gerstner. "Edwardsean Preparation for Salvation." *Westminster Theological Journal* 42 (1979) 5–71.
———. *The Rational Biblical Theology of Jonathan Edwards*, 3 vols. Powhatan, VA: Berea, 1991–93.
Grasso, Christopher. "The Early Idealism of Jonathan Edwards." *Philosophical Review* 9 (1900) 573–96.
Greven, Philip. *Spare the Child: The Religious Roots of Punishment and the Psychological Impact of Physical Abuse*. New York: Knopf, 1991.
Gruenler, Royce G. *The Inexhaustible God: Biblical Faith and the Challenge of Process Theism*. Grand Rapids: Baker, 1983.
Guelzo, Allen C. *Edwards on the Will: A Century of American Theological Debate*. Middletown, CT: Wesleyan University Press, 1989.
———, and Sang Hyun Lee, eds. *Edwards in Our Time: Jonathan Edwards and the Shaping of American Religion*. Grand Rapids: Eerdmans, 1999.
Hall, David D. "Did Berkeley Influence Edwards? Their Critique of the Moral Sense Theory." In *Jonathan Edwards's Writings: Text, Context, Interpretation*, edited by Stephen J. Stein, 100–21. Bloomington, IN: Indiana University Press, 1996.
Haller, William. *The Rise of Puritanism*. New York: Columbia University Press, 1938.
Hanna, William. *The Memoirs of the Life and Writings of Thomas Chalmers*. Edinburgh: T. Constable and Co., 1851.
Hart, Trevor A., gen. ed. *The Dictionary of Historical Theology*. Carlisle, UK: Paternoster, 2000.
Hartshorne, Charles. *The Divine Relativity: A Social Conception of God*. New Haven, CT: Yale University Press, 1948.
Hasker, William. *God, Time, and Knowledge*. Ithaca, NY: Cornell University Press, 1989.
Hatch, Nathan, and Harry S. Stout, eds. *Jonathan Edwards and the American Experience*. New York: Oxford University Press, 1988.
Heimann, P. M., and J. E. McGuire. "Newtonian Forces and Lockean Powers: Concepts of Matter in Eighteenth-Century Thought." *Historical Studies in Physical Science* 3 (1971) 233–306.
Heimert, Alan. *Religion and the American Mind from the Great Awakening to the Revolution*. Cambridge: Harvard University Press, 1966.
Helm, Paul. *Eternal God: A Study of God without Time*. Oxford: Clarendon, 1988.
———. *Faith and Understanding*. Edinburgh: Edinburgh University Press, 1997.
———. "John Locke and Jonathan Edwards: A Reconsideration." *Journal of the History of Philosophy* 7 (1969) 51–61.
———. "Locke's Theory of Personal Identity." *Philosophy* (1979) 173–85.
———, and Oliver C. Crisp, eds. *Jonathan Edwards: Philosophical Theologian*. Aldershot, UK: Ashgate, 2003.
Hick, John. "The Non-Absoluteness of Christianity." In *The Myth of Christian Uniqueness*, edited by John Hick and Paul F. Knitter, 16–36. London, SCM, 1988.
Hindson, Edward, ed. *Introduction to Puritan Theology*. Grand Rapids: Baker, 1976.
Hodge, Charles. *Systematic Theology*. 3 vols. [1871–72]. Grand Rapids: Eerdmans, 1947.
Holbrook, Clyde, A. *The Ethics of Jonathan Edwards*. Ann Arbor, MI: University of Michigan Press, 1973.
Holmes, Oliver Wendell. *Over the Teacups*. Boston: Houghton, Mifflin, & Co., 1890.
———. *Pages from an Old Volume of Life: A Collection of Essays: The Writings of Oliver Wendell Holmes*. 8 vols. Cambridge, MA: Riverside, 1891.
Holmes, Stephen R. "Does Edwards Use a Dispositional Ontology?." In *Jonathan Edwards: Philosophical Theologian*, edited by Paul Helm and Oliver D. Crisp, 107–10. Aldershot, UK: Ashgate, 2003.
———. *God of Grace and God of Glory: An Account of the Theology of Jonathan Edwards*. Edinburgh: T. & T. Clark, 2000.

Hoopes, James. *Consciousness in New England: From Puritanism and Ideas to Psychoanalysis and Semiotic.* Baltimore: John Hopkins University Press, 1989.

———. "Jonathan Edwards's Religious Psychology." *Journal of American History* 69 (1983) 849–65.

Hornberger, Theodore. "The Effect of the New Science upon the Thought of Jonathan Edwards." *American Literature* 9 (1937) 196–207.

Hunter, Michael. "The Problem of 'Atheism' in Early Modern England." *Transactions of the Royal Historical Society.* 5th Series. 35 (1985) 135–57.

Jang, Kyoung-Chul. "The Logic of Glorification: The Destiny of the Saints in the Eschatology of Jonathan Edwards." PhD diss., Princeton Theological Seminary, 1994.

Jedin, Hubert. *A History of the Council of Trent.* Translated by Dom E. Graf. 2 vols. London: Nelson, 1957, 1961.

Jenson, Robert W. *America's Theologian: A Recommendation of Jonathan Edwards.* New York: Oxford University Press, 1988.

Jinkins, Michael. "'The Being of Beings' Jonathan Edwards' Understanding of God as Reflected in His Final Treatises." *Scottish Journal of Theology* 46 (1993) 161–90.

Johnson Paul D. "Jonathan Edwards's 'Sweet Conjunction.'" *Early American Literature* 16 (1981) 270–81.

Johnson, Thomas H. "Jonathan Edwards' Background Reading." *Publications of the Colonial Society of Massachusetts* 28 (1931) 193–222.

———. *The Printed Writings of Jonathan Edwards, 1703–1758.* Princeton: Princeton University Press, 1940.

Jones, Charles Edwin. "The Impolitic Mr. Edwards: The Personal Dimensions of the Robert Breck Affair." *New England Quarterly* 51 (1978) 64–79.

Kaakonssen, Knud. *Enlightenment and Religion: Rational Dissent in Eighteenth-Century Britain.* Cambridge: Cambridge University Press, 1996.

Kearney, John. "Jonathan Edwards and the 'Author of Sin' Charge." *The Princeton Theological Review* (April 1998) 10–16.

———. "Jonathan Edwards' Account of Adam's First Sin." *Scottish Bulletin of Evangelical Theology* (1997) 127–41.

Kistler, Donald, ed. *Jonathan Edwards: Containing 16 Sermons Unpublished in Edwards' Lifetime.* The Puritan Pulpit, The American Puritans. Morgan, PA: Soli Deo Gloria, 2004.

Knight, Janice L. "Learning the Language of God: Jonathan Edwards and the Typology of Nature." *William & Mary Quarterly* 48 (1991) 531–51.

Knitter, Paul F. and John Hick, eds. *The Myth of Christian Uniqueness.* London: SCM, 1988.

Kretzmann, Norman, and Eleonore Stump. "Eternity." In *The Concept of God*, edited by Thomas V. Morris, 219–52. Oxford Readings in Philosophy. Oxford: Oxford University Press, 1987.

Kvanvig, Jonathan L. *The Problem of Hell.* New York: Oxford University Press, 1993.

Laurence, David. "Jonathan Edwards, Solomon Stoddard, and the Preparationist Model of Conversion." *Harvard Theological Review* 72 (1979) 267–83.

Lee, Sang Hyun, and Allen C. Guelzo, eds. *Edwards in Our Time: Jonathan Edwards and the Shaping of American Religion.* Grand Rapids: Eerdmans, 1999.

———. "Edwards on God and Nature: Resources for Contemporary Theology." In *Edwards in Our Time: Jonathan Edwards and the Shaping of American Religion*, edited by Sang Hyun Lee and Allen C. Guelzo, 14–44. Grand Rapids: Eerdmans, 1999.

———. *The Philosophical Theology of Jonathan Edwards: The Idea of Habit and Edwards' Dynamic Vision of Reality.* Princeton: Princeton University Press, 1988.

———. "Jonathan Edwards on Nature." In *Faithful Imagining: Essays in Honor of Richard R. Niebuhr*, edited by Sand Hyun Lee et. al., 39–59. Atlanta: Scholars, 1995.

———. "Mental Activity and the Perception of Beauty in Jonathan Edwards." *Harvard Theological Review* 69 (1976) 369–96.

———, ed. *The Princeton Companion to Jonathan Edwards.* Princeton: Princeton University Press, 2005.

Levin, David. "Edwards, Franklin, and Cotton Mather: A Meditation on Character and Reputation." In *Jonathan Edwards and the American Experience*, edited by Nathan Hatch and Harry S. Stout, 34–49. New York: Oxford University Press, 1988.

Lesser, M. X. *Jonathan Edwards: An Annotated Bibliography, 1979–1993.* Westport, CT: Greenwood, 1994.

———. *Jonathan Edwards: A Reference Guide.* Boston: Hall, 1981.

Lisska, Anthony J. *Aquinas' Theory of Natural Law: An Analytical Reconstruction*. Oxford: Clarendon, 1996.

Lloyd-Jones, D. Martin. "Jonathan Edwards and the Crucial Importance of Revivals." In *The Puritans: Their Origins and Their Successors*, 348–71. Edinburgh: Banner of Truth, 1987.

Lyttle, David J. "The Sixth Sense of Jonathan Edwards." *Church Quarterly Review* 167 (1966) 50–59.

McClymond, Michael J. "A Different Legacy? The Cultural Turn in Edwards's Later Notebooks and the Unwritten *History of the Work of Redemption*." In *Jonathan Edwards at Home and Abroad: Historical Memories, Cultural Movements, Global Horizons*, edited by David W. Kling and Douglas A. Sweeney, 13–39. Columbia, SC: University of South Carolina Press, 2003.

———. *Encounters with God: An Approach to the Theology of Jonathan Edwards*. New York: Oxford University Press, 1998.

———. "God the Measure: Towards an Understanding of Jonathan Edwards' Theocentric Metaphysics." *Scottish Journal of Theology* 47 (1994) 43–59.

McCracken, Charles J. *Malebranche and British Philosophy*. Oxford: Clarendon, 1983.

McDermott, Gerald R. "Edwards, Missions, and Native Americans." Unpublished paper delivered at the conference "Jonathan Edwards the Theologian," Princeton Theological Seminary, April 2003.

———. *Jonathan Edwards Confronts the Gods: Christian Theology, Enlightenment Religion, and Non-Christian Faiths*. New York: Oxford University Press, 2000.

———. "Jonathan Edwards, John Henry Newman, and non-Christian Religions." In *Jonathan Edwards: Philosophical Theologian*, edited by Paul Helm and Oliver D. Crisp, 129–30. Aldershot, UK: Ashgate, 2003.

———. "Missions and Native Americans." In *The Princeton Companion to Jonathan Edwards*, edited by Sang Hyun Lee, 258–73. Princeton: Princeton University Press, 2005.

———. *One Holy and Happy Society: The Public Theology of Jonathan Edwards*. University Park: Pennsylvania State University Press, 1992.

———. "A Possibility of Reconciliation: Jonathan Edwards and the Salvation of Non-Christians." In *Edwards in Our Time: Jonathan Edwards and the Shaping of American Religion*, edited by Sang Hyun Lee and Allen C. Guelzo, 173–202. Grand Rapids: Eerdmans, 1999.

———. "Response to Gilbert: 'The Nations Will Worship: Jonathan Edwards and the Salvation of the Heathen.'" *Trinity Journal* 23 (2002) 77–80.

MacDonald, Scott C. *Being and Goodness: The Concept of Good in Metaphysics and Philosophical Theology*. Ithaca, NY: Cornell University Press, 1990.

Mackie, J. L. *Ethics: Inventing Right and Wrong*. New York: Penguin, 1977.

Manspeaker, Nancy. *Jonathan Edwards: Bibliographical Synopses*. New York: Mellen, 1981.

Marsden, George. *Jonathan Edwards: A Life*. New Haven, CT: Yale University Press, 2003.

Martin, C. B. "Dispositions and Conditionals." *The Philosophical Quarterly* 44 (1993) 1–8.

Miller, Perry. *Errand into the Wilderness*. Cambridge: Belknap Press of Harvard University Press, 1956.

———. *Jonathan Edwards*. Men of American Letters Series. New York: Sloane, 1949.

———. "Jonathan Edwards on the Sense of the Heart." *Harvard Theological Review* 41 (1948) 123–45.

———. *The New England Mind: From Colony to Province*. Cambridge: Belknap Press of Harvard University Press, 1953.

———. *The New England Mind: The Seventeenth Century*. Cambridge: Belknap Press of Harvard University Press, 1939.

———. "'Preparation for Salvation' in Seventeenth-Century New England." In *Nature's Nation*, 50–77. Cambridge: Harvard University Press, 1967.

Minkema, Kenneth P. "The Edwardses: A Ministerial Family in Eighteenth-Century New England." PhD diss., University of Connecticut, 1988.

———. "The Other Unfinished 'Great Work': Jonathan Edwards, Messianic Prophecy, and 'The Harmony of the Old and New Testaments.'" In *Jonathan Edwards's Writings: Text, Context, Interpretation*, edited by Stephen J. Stein, 52–65. Bloomington, IN: Indiana University Press, 1996.

Moody, Joshua. *Jonathan Edwards and the Enlightenment: Knowing the Presence of God*. Lanham, MD: University Press of America, 2005.

Morimoto, Anri. *Jonathan Edwards and the Catholic Vision of Salvation*. University Park: Pennsylvania State University Press, 1995.

Morris, Thomas V., ed. *The Concept of God*. Oxford Readings in Philosophy. New York: Oxford University Press, 1987.

Morris, William Sparks. *The Young Jonathan Edwards; A Reconstruction*. Chicago Studies in the History of American Religion, Vol. 14. Brooklyn, NY: Carlson, 1991.

Morison, Samuel E. *Harvard College in the Seventeenth Century*. Cambridge: Harvard University Press, 1936.

Muller, Richard A. *Christ and the Decree: Christology and Predestination in Reformed Theology from Calvin to Perkins*. Grand Rapids: Baker, 1988.

Mumford, Stephen. *Dispositions*. Oxford: Oxford University Press, 1998.

Murray, Iain H. *Jonathan Edwards: A New Biography*. Edinburgh: Banner of Truth, 1987.

Nadler, Stephen, ed. *The Cambridge Companion to Malebranche*. Cambridge: Cambridge University Press, 2000.

———. *Malebranche and Ideas*. Oxford: Oxford University Press, 1992.

Nelson, J. D. "The Rise of Princeton Theology." PhD diss., Yale University, 1935.

Niebuhr, Reinhold. *Man's Nature and His Communities*. New York: Scribner, 1965.

Niebuhr, Richard H. *The Kingdom of God in America*. New York: Harper Torch, 1959.

Noll, Mark. "God at the Center: Jonathan Edwards on True Virtue." *Christian Century* (Sept. 8–15, 1993) 857–72.

———. "Jonathan Edwards and Nineteenth-Century Theology." In *Jonathan Edwards and the American Experience*, edited by Nathan Hatch and Harry S. Stout, 260–87. New York: Oxford University Press, 1988.

Nygren, Anders. *Agape and Eros*. Translated by Philip S. Watson. London: SPCK, 1953.

O'Donovan, Oliver. *The Problem of Self-Love in St. Augustine*. New Haven, CT: Yale University Press, 1980.

O'Meara, Dominic J., ed. *Studies in Aristotle*. Washington DC: Catholic University of America, 1981.

Oberdiek, Hans. "Jonathan Edwards." In *The Spirit of American Philosophy*, edited by John E. Smith, 193–208. Albany, NY: State University of New York Press, 1983.

Opie, John, ed. *Jonathan Edwards and Enlightenment*. Lexington, MA: Heath, 1969.

Outka, Gene. *Agape: An Ethical Analysis*. New Haven, CT: Yale University Press, 1972.

———. *The Love Commandments: Essays in Christian Ethics and Moral Philosophy*. Washington DC: Georgetown University Press, 1992.

Parks, Henry B. *Jonathan Edwards: The Fiery Puritan*. New York: Minton, 1930.

Parrington, V. L. "The Anachronism of Jonathan Edwards." In *Main Currents in American Thought, Vol. 1, 1620–1800*, edited by V. L. Parrington, 1:148–63. New York: Harcourt, 1927.

———. *Main Currents in American Thought, Vol. 1, 1620–1800*. 3 vols. New York: Harcourt, 1927.

Patterson, Mary and Louise May Bryant. "The List of Books Sent from England by Jeremiah Dummer." In *Papers in Honor of Andrew Keogh, Librarian of Yale University*, edited by the Staff of the [Yale University] Library, 423–92. New Haven, CT: Yale University Press for private circulation, 1938.

Pauw, Amy Plantiga. "One Alone Cannot be Excellent: Jonathan Edwards on Divine Simplicity." In *Jonathan Edwards: Philosophical Theologian*, edited by Paul Helm and Oliver D. Crisp, 115–26. Aldershot, UK: Ashgate, 2004.

———. *The Supreme Harmony of All: The Trinitarian Theology of Jonathan Edwards*. Grand Rapids: Eerdmans, 2002.

Pettit, Norman. *The Heart Prepared: Grace and Conversion in Puritan Spiritual Life*. New Haven, CT: Yale University Press, 1966.

Pfisterer, Karl Dieterich. *The Prism of Scripture: Studies on History and Historicity in the Work of Jonathan Edwards*. Bern: Language, 1975.

Pinnock, Clark. *A Wideness in God's Mercy: The Finality of Jesus Christ in a World of Religions*. Grand Rapids: Zondervan, 1992.

Piper, John. *God's Passion for His Glory*. Wheaton, IL: Crossway, 1998.

Pittenger, Norman. *"The Last Things" in a Process Perspective*. London: Epworth, 1970.

Plantinga, Alvin. "On Ockham's Way Out." *Faith and Philosophy*, 3 (1986) 235–69.

Post, Stephen G. *Christian Love and Self-Denial: An Historical and Normative Study of Jonathan Edwards, Samuel Hopkins, and American Theological Ethics*. Langham, MD: University Press of America, 1987.

Pratt, Anne Stokely. "The Books Sent from England by Jeremiah Dummer to Yale College." In *Papers in Honor of Andrew Keogh, Librarian of Yale University*, edited by Staff of the [Yale University] Library, 7–44. New Haven, CT: Yale University Press for private circulation, 1938.

Quinn, Philip. "Divine Conservation, Continuous-Creation, and Human Action." In *The Existence and Nature of God*, edited by Alfred Freddoso, 55–80. Notre Dame, IN: University of Notre Dame Press, 1983.

Rahner, Karl. *Theological Investigations*. 23 vols. London: Darton, Longman & Todd, 1961–92.

Ramsey, Bennett. "The Ineluctable Impulse: 'Consent' in the Thought of Edwards, James, and Royce." *Union Seminary Quarterly Review* 37 (1983) 302–22.

Rupp, George. "The 'Idealism' of Jonathan Edwards." *Harvard Theological Review* 62 (1969) 209–26.

Russell, Bertrand. *Mysticism and Logic*. [1918]. Garden City, NY: Doubleday, 1957.

———. *The Principles of Mathematics*. 2nd ed. [1903]. London: Allen & Unwin, 1937.

Ryle, Gilbert. *The Concept of Mind*. Chicago: University of Chicago Press, 1949.

Sanders, John. *The God Who Risks: A Theology of Providence*. Downers Grove, IL: InterVarsity, 1998.

———. *No Other Name: An Investigation into the Destiny of the Unevangelized*. Grand Rapids: Eerdmans, 1992.

Schafer, Thomas A. "The Concept of Being in the Thought of Jonathan Edwards." PhD diss., Duke University, 1951.

———. "Jonathan Edwards." In *Encyclopedia Britannica*. 15th ed. London: Encyclopedia Britannica, 1986, 4:381–82.

———. "Jonathan Edwards and Justification by Faith." *Church History* 20 (1951) 55–67.

Schaff, Philip. *The Creeds of Christendom*. 3 vols. New York: Harper, 1878.

Scheick, William J., ed. *Critical Essays on Jonathan Edwards*. Boston: Hall, 1980.

———. "The Grand Design: Jonathan Edwards' *History of the Work of Redemption*." *Eighteenth Century Studies* 8 (1975) 300–14.

Schneider, Herbert and Carol Schneider, eds. *Samuel Johnson, President of King's College: His Career and Writings*. 4 vols. New York: Columbia University Press, 1929.

Seaver, George. *Francis Younghusband, Explorer and Mystic*. London: Murray, 1952.

Shea, Daniel B. Jr. "The Art and Instruction of Jonathan Edwards's *Personal Narrative*." In *New England: Essays on Religion, Society, and Culture*, edited by Alden T. Vaughan and Francis J. Bremer, 299–311. New York, St. Martin's, 1977.

Shedd, W. G. T. *Calvinism, Pure and Mixed*. [1893]. Reprint. Edinburgh: Banner of Truth, 1986.

Shoemaker, Sydney. *Experimental and Theoretical Studies in Consciousness*. Chichester, UK: Wiley & Sons, 1993.

Simonson, Harold, P. *Jonathan Edwards: Theologian of the Heart*. Grand Rapids: Eerdmans, 1974.

Smith, Claude A. "Jonathan Edwards and 'The Way of Ideas.'" *Harvard Theological Review* 59 (1966) 153–73.

Smith, John E. "Jonathan Edwards as Philosophical Theologian." *Review of Metaphysics* 30 (1976) 306–24.

———. *Jonathan Edwards: Puritan, Preacher, Philosopher*. Outstanding Christian Thinkers. Notre Dame: University of Notre Dame Press, 1992.

———, ed. *The Spirit of American Philosophy*. Albany: State University of New York Press, 1983.

Smyth, Egbert C. "Jonathan Edwards' Idealism." *American Journal of Theology* 1 (1897) 950–64.

———. "The 'New Philosophy' against which Students at Yale College Were Warned in 1714." *Proceedings of the American Antiquarian Society* XI (1896) 242–60.

Stein, Stephen J., ed. *Jonathan Edwards's Writings: Text Context, Interpretation*. Bloomington, IN: Indiana University Press, 1996.

———. "The Quest for the Spiritual Sense: the Biblical Hermeneutics of Jonathan Edwards." *Harvard Theological Review* 70 (1977) 99–113.

———. "The Spirit and the Word: Jonathan Edwards and Scriptural Exegesis." In *Jonathan Edwards and the American Experience*, edited by Nathan Hatch and Harry S. Stout, 118–30. New York: Oxford University Press, 1988.

Stephen, Leslie. *Hours in a Library*. 4 vols. London: Smith, 1907.

———. "Jonathan Edwards." In *Hours in a Library*. 1:300–44. London: Smith, 1907.

Stevenson, Sally Ann. "The Ministerial and Theological Purposes of Jonathan Edwards's Thought: A Study in Source and Context." PhD diss., University of Pennsylvania, 1983.

Stoever, William K. B. *"A Faire and Easie Way to Heaven": Covenant Theology and Antinomianism in Early Massachusetts*. Middletown, CT: Wesleyan University Press, 1978.

Storms, Samuel C. *Tragedy in Eden: Original Sin in the Theology of Jonathan Edwards*. Lanham, MD: University Press of America, 1985.

Stout, Harry S. "The Puritans and Edwards." In *Jonathan Edwards and the American Experience*, edited by Nathan Hatch and Harry S. Stout, 142–59. New York: Oxford University Press, 1988.

Stowe, Harriet-Beecher. *The Minister's Wooing*. Hartford, CT: Stowe-Day, 1978.

Strong, A. H. *Systematic Theology*. Philadelphia: Judson, 1907.

Stump, Eleonore, and Norman Kretzmann. "Eternity." In *The Concept of God*, edited by Thomas V. Morris, 219–52. Oxford Readings in Philosophy. Oxford: Oxford University Press, 1987.

Sullivan, Robert E. *John Toland and the Deist Controversy*. Cambridge: Harvard University Press, 1982.

Suter, Rufus. "A Note on Platonism in the Philosophy of Jonathan Edwards." *Harvard Theological Review* 52 (1959) 283–84.

Tarbox, I. N. "Timothy Edwards and His Parishioners." *The Congregational Quarterly* (1871) 256–74.

Tillich, Paul. *Christianity and the Encounter with World Religions*. New York: Columbia University Press, 1965.

Tracy, Patricia J. *Jonathan Edwards, Pastor: Religion and Society in Eighteenth-Century Northampton*. New York: Hill and Wang, 1980.

Tufts, James H. "Edwards and Newton." *Philosophical Review* 49 (1940) 609–22.

Vanhoozer, Kevin J. *First Theology: God, Scripture & Hermeneutics*. Downers Grove, IL: InterVarsity, 2002.

Veatch, Henry. "Telos and Teleology in Aristotle's Ethics." In *Studies in Aristotle*, edited by Dominic J. O'Meara, 279–86. Washington DC: Catholic University of America, 1981.

Vëto, Miklos. *Le pensée de Jonathan Edwards*. Paris: Cerf, 1987.

———. "Spiritual Knowledge according to Jonathan Edwards." Translated by Michael J. McClymond. *Scottish Journal of Theology* 31.1 (1996) 161–81.

Wainwright, William J. "Jonathan Edwards and the Sense of the Heart." *Faith and Philosophy* 7 (1990) 43–62.

———. "Jonathan Edwards, Atoms, and Immaterialism." *Idealistic Studies* 12 (1982) 79–89.

———. "Original Sin." In *Philosophy and the Christian Faith*, edited by Thomas V. Morris, 33–48. Notre Dame, IN: University of Notre Dame Press, 1988.

———. *Reason and the Heart: A Prolegomena to a Critique of Passional Reason*. Ithaca, NY: Cornell University Press, 1995.

Wallace, Dewey D. Jr. *Puritans and Predestination: Grace in English Protestant Theology, 1525–1695*. Chapel Hill, NC: University of North Carolina Press, 1982.

Walton, Craig. "Malebranche's Ontology." *Journal of the History of Philosophy* 7 (1969) 143–61.

Warch, Richard. *The School of the Prophets: Yale College, 1702–1724*. New Haven: Yale University Press, 1973.

Ward, Keith. *Rational Theology and the Creativity of God*. Oxford: Blackwell, 1982.

Ware, Bruce A. *God's Lesser Glory: A Critique of Open Theism*. Leicester: Apollos, 2000.

Watts, Emily. "Jonathan Edwards and the Cambridge Platonists." PhD diss., University of Illinois, 1963.

Weissman, David. *Dispositional Properties*. Carbondale, IL: Southern Illinois University Press, 1965.

Weber, Otto. *Foundations of Dogmatics*. Translated by Darrel L. Guder. 2 vols. Grand Rapids: Eerdmans, 1981.

Weber, Richard. "The Trinitarian Theology of Jonathan Edwards: An Investigation of Charges against Its Orthodoxy." *Journal of the Evangelical Theological Society* 44 (2001) 297–318.

Expectations." *Trinity Journal* 22 (2001) 75–98.

Westfall, Richard. *Science and Religion in Seventeenth-Century England*. New Haven, CT: Yale University Press, 1958.

Weyer, Stefan. *Die Cambridge Platonists: Religion und Freiheitin England im 17 Jarhhundert*. Frankfurt am Main: Lang, 1993.

White, Morton. *Science and Sentiment in America: Philosophical Thought from Jonathan Edwards to John Dewey*. New York: Oxford University Press, 1972.

Whitehead, Alfred North. *Process and Reality: An Essay in Cosmology.* New York: Macmillan, 1929.

Whittemore, Robert C. "Jonathan Edwards and the Theology of the Sixth Way." *Church History* 35 (1966) 60–75.

———. *The Transformation of New England Theology.* New York: Lang, 1987.

Winslow, Ola E. *Jonathan Edwards, 1703–1758.* New York: Collier, 1961.

Withrow, Brandon C. "A Future of Hope: Jonathan Edwards and Millennial Wilber, E. M. *A History of Unitarianism.* 2 vols. Cambridge: Harvard University Press, 1952.

Wright, Conrad. *The Beginnings of Unitarianism in America.* Boston: Beacon, 1955.

Wright, R. K. McGregor. *No Place for Sovereignty: What's Wrong with Freewill Theism.* Downers Grove, IL: InterVarsity, 1996.

Zakai, Avihu. "The Conversion of Jonathan Edwards." *Journal of Presbyterian History* 76 (1998) 127–38.

———. *Jonathan Edwards's Philosophy of History: The Reenchantment of the World in the Age of Enlightenment.* Princeton: Princeton University Press, 2005.

Name Index

Ahlstrom, Sydney E., 1, 261n30, 309
Aldridge, Alfred O., 40n19, 152n128, 294n14, 309
Alexander, H. G., 216n14, 307, 309
Allen, Alexander V. G., 5, 5n22, 171, 309
Ames, William, 30, 30n10, 33, 107, 144, 144n60, 239n21, 306
Anselm, 75n17, 76n27, 306
Aquinas, Thomas, 17, 18n66, 25, 40, 61n29, 62n41, 79, 84n23, 92n54, 95–98, 98n17, 100, 103, 103n40, 108, 166n93, 167n97, 179, 179n147, 184, 240, 240n27, 243, 306, 309, 313
Aristotle, 103n39, 263n41, 306, 314, 316
Audi, Robert, 309
Augustine, Aurillius, xi, 17, 124n76, 135n30, 136n34, 144–45, 145n69, 165, 166n93, 167n97, 168, 168n97, 169n100, 169n101, 170, 172n116, 174n124, 179, 179n147, 192, 200, 215, 269, 300n9, 306, 314

Barad, Judith, 183n162, 309
Barth, Karl, ii, 1n2, 7, 130n14, 193n24, 229, 250n71, 309
Basinger, David, 76n21, 309
Baxter, Andrew, 75n18, 278n108, 306
Bebbington, David, 236n11, 291n7, 309
Bellarmino, Roberto F. R., 192n22, 306
Bennett Ramsey. *See* Ramsey, Bennett
Bentley, Richard, 33, 33n22, 306
Berkeley, George, 16n59, 156, 156n45, 156n47, 167, 294, 306
Biéler, Andre, 30n8, 309
Bizer, Ernst, 234n4, 309
Blackwell, Albert, 309, 316
Bobik, Joseph, 309
Borges, Jorge Luis, 290, 290n3, 309
Bourke, Vernon, 183n162, 309
Boyd, Gregory, 76n21, 298n4, 309
Brekus, Catherine A., xi, 4, 4n16, 218n53, 309

Bremond, A., 309
Brine, John, 267, 267n60, 306
Bryant, Louise May, 31n13, 309, 314
Burgerdicius, Francisus, 33, 306
Butler, Joseph, 145, 145n65, 306

Calvin, John, ix, xvii, 2n4, 11n41, 17, 28–29, 30n8, 39, 39n16, 40, 92, 107n6, 131n18, 141, 144, 144n60, 157n49, 168–69, 170n110, 192, 222n73, 240, 242, 48, 250n71, 255, 292, 300n9, 306
Carse, James P., 166n93, 309
Cassirer, Ernst, 163n80, 309
Chai, Leon, 17n60, 98n20, 162, 162n75, 309
Channing, William Ellery, 4, 4n17, 309
Chauncy, Charles, 46, 194n28, 306
Cherry, Conrad, 1n2, 40, 40n20, 41n24, 41n25, 301n15, 302, 302n19, 309
Chevreau, Guy, 1n2, 309
Chubb, Thomas, 32n19, 258, 258n19, 306
Clarke, Adam, 168n99, 307
Clarke, Samuel, 74, 90n46, 216n42, 265, 307, 309
Cohen, Charles Lloyd, 309
Cooey-Nichols, Paula M., 222n72, 310
Colwell, John E., 7, 7n27, 11n40, 310
Cook, Monte, 116n45, 310
Copan, Paul, 21n74, 310
Crabtree, Arthur Branford, 80, 80n7, 197n48, 210, 310
Cragg, Gerald R., 4n15, 34n27, 310
Crisp, Oliver C., xi, 10n36, 82n14, 179n148, 310, 311, 313–14
Crooker, Joseph, 1n2, 310
Cudworth, Ralph, 33, 33n25, 262n39, 265, 307

Dabney, Robert Louis, 192n24, 310
Dana, James, 216n42, 307
Daniel, Stephen H., 160n27, 310
Davidson, Bruce W., 132n19, 310
Davidson, Edward H., 1n2, 310

Name Index

Davis, T. H., 222n73, 310
Dawkins, Richard, 148n10, 310
Delattre, Roland Andre, 60n28, 61n30, 62n37, 62n42, 86n27, 95, 95n3, 95n4, 120n61, 121n65, 310
De Prospo, R. C., 21n74, 47n49, 310
Descartes, René, xvii, 25–26, 31, 103, 155n42, 307
Dexter, F. B., 310

Edwards, John, 31, 307
Edwards, Jonathan, vi, ix–xvii, 1n1, 1n2, 2n4, 2n5, 4n15, 4n16, 4n18, 5nn19–22, 6n25, 6n26, 7n27, 8n29, 8n30, 11n39, 11n40, 12n43, 12n44, 13nn45–47, 14n51, 15n55, 16n58, 16n59, 17nn60–62, 18n64, 18n65, 19n67, 19n68, 21nn71–74, 23n75, 24n77, 27n3, 29n5, 29n6, 30n10, 30n11, 31n12, 31n13, 32n19, 33n21, 33n25, 35n33, 36n36, 37nn1–3, 38n4, 38n5, 38n10, 39n13, 40nn17–19, 41n21, 42n27, 43nn30–32, 46n44, 46n45, 46n48, 47n49, 48n52, 48n53, 56n9, 57n11, 57n12, 58n18, 60n25, 60n28, 61n32, 62n36, 62n40, 63n44, 63n45, 64n48, 64n51, 64n53, 67n59, 67n61, 69n66, 72n4, 75n14, 75n18, 76n27, 77n30, 77n32, 77n34, 80n6, 80n7, 81n8, 82n14, 83n19, 83n22, 84n23, 84n24, 85n25, 86n27, 86n30, 87n31, 88n38, 89nn43–45, 91n51, 92n54, 95n3, 96n13, 98n17, 98n20, 99n22, 100n26, 100n27, 100n31, 102n35, 103n38, 103n41, 104n42, 107n6, 108n10, 108n11, 109n15, 110n20, 113n28, 113n31, 113n33, 115n37, 116n45, 117nn47–50, 118n54, 118n55, 118n57, 120n61, 120n62, 124n76, 125n78, 128n2, 129n8, 129n11, 130n14, 131n18, 131n19, 132n20, 134n25, 134n27, 136n37, 138n42, 141n49, 141n50, 142n53, 142n55, 143nn56–58, 144n60, 145n64, 145n66, 145n67, 147n3, 147n5, 148n10, 150n15, 150n17, 151n20, 151n23, 152n28, 152n29, 153n31, 153n34, 153n36, 154n38, 156n46, 156n47, 157n55, 158n58, 158n59, 160n67, 161n70, 163n81, 165n87, 165n88, 166n93, 167n95, 168n99, 170n110, 171n112, 172n116, 172n117, 173n121, 174n126, 175n133, 175n134, 176n136, 177n137, 177n140, 179n148, 180n150, 181n153, 181n154, 185n1, 185n3, 186n6, 187n8, 187n9, 188n14, 190n17, 191n20, 194n28, 195n32, 196n37, 196n38, 197n44, 197n48, 198n50, 198n51, 203n73, 204n75, 205n82, 205n83, 207n2, 208n5, 209n10, 210n17, 210n19, 211n23, 216n42, 218n53, 218n54, 222n72, 222n73, 226n83, 233n2, 239n24, 241n30, 242n36, 243n37, 248n60, 248n63, 250n72, 254n1, 254n2, 255n4, 255n6, 256n10, 256n11, 257nn12–14, 257n16, 258n17, 258n19, 261n30, 262n39, 263n41, 263n42, 265n52, 266n55, 267n59, 267n60, 268n63, 268n65, 268n66, 269n69, 270n70, 271n74, 273n84, 275n95, 276n96, 276n99, 277n103, 278n106, 278n108, 279nn111–14, 281nn124–26, 283n135, 286n144, 287n145, 288n151, 291n5, 292n9, 294n12, 294n9, 294n12, 300n9, 301n15
Edwards, Rem B., 163, 310
Edwards, Timothy, 29, 29n7, 38n4, 98n17, 142, 281n126, 307, 316
Ellis, Joseph, 31n14, 310
Elwood, Douglas J., 11n40, 68n65, 77n30, 80, 80n5, 81, 81n8, 113n30, 204, 204n77, 291, 297, 297n1, 310
Emmons, Nathaniel, 307

Faust, Clarence F., 27n3, 310
Ferguson, Sinclair B., 250n71, 310
Fiering, Norman, 6n26, 18n65, 21n71, 21n72, 21n74, 61n33, 69n67, 98n17, 125n77, 126n79, 156n47, 158n58, 174n129, 176n136, 178n146, 196n39, 201n69, 218n50, 222n71, 262n37, 267n58, 274n87, 291, 310
  Disposition, 50n59, 108n13, 141n50, 243n38, 268n65
  Excellency, 69n66, 137n38
  Grace, 242n35, 243n38, 283n133
  Hell, 19n68, 227n90, 288n151
  Holy Spirit, 50n59, 168n98, 243n38
  Ontology, 62n41, 64n51, 76n27, 116n45, 145n67, 148n10, 166n93, 184n163
  Original sin, 19n68, 288n151

Foster, Frank H., 17n63, 311
Freddoso, Alfred, 163n81, 311, 315

Gale, Richard M., 298n4, 311
Gale, Theophilus, 262, 262n39, 307
Gay, Peter, 17, 18n64, 311
George, Timothy, 169n107, 311
Gerstner, John H., and Jonathan Neil Gerstner, 1n2, 17, 17n60, 197n48, 200, 210, 251, 251n77, 301–3, 301n10, 301n11, 301n13, 311
Grasso, Christopher, 311
Greenham, Richard, 39n13, 307
Greven, Philip, 1n2, 311
Grotius, Hugo, 262, 262n39, 307
Gruenler, Royce G., 298n4, 311
Guelzo, Allen C., 21n74, 157, 157n55, 159, 310, 313

Hall, David D., xiii, 239n24, 305, 311
Haller, William, 30n10, 311
Hanna, William, 293n10, 311
Hart, Trevor A., 310, 311
Hartshorne, Charles, 297, 297n2, 306, 311
Hasker, William, 298n4, 311
Hatch, Nathan, xiv, 305, 310–12, 314–16
Heereboord, Adrian, 33, 33n22, 107n7, 307
Heimann, P. M., 311
Heimert, Alan, 117n47, 311
Helm, Paul, xi–xii, 46n48, 48n53, 155n42, 164, 164n82, 298n4, 302n17, 306, 310–11, 313–14
Henry, Matthew, 168n99, 307
Hick, John, 43n32, 236, 311–12
Hindson, Edward, 311
Hobbes, Thomas, 32–33, 103, 103n41, 118, 118n54, 149, 157, 164, 260, 307
Hodge, Charles, 164, 164n83, 311
Holbrook, Clyde, xii, 5n22, 11n40, 77n31, 120n61, 150n15, 158n59, 191n20, 195n32, 195–97, 210, 210n15, 213, 217, 217n47, 305, 311
Holmes, Oliver Wendell, 4, 4n16, 255, 255n4, 311
Holmes, Stephen R., xi, 11n40, 81n8, 84n24, 287n146, 311
  Calvinism, 131, 132n20
  Disposition, 91n51, 138, 257n13
  Elect, 129–31, 129n11, 130n13, 130n14, 131n16, 131n18, 132n20, 229, 229n102
  Election, 208, 208n5
  Holy Spirit, 6, 6n24, 15n53, 88, 88n38, 88n39, 129–30, 129n9, 129n11, 131n18, 243n39
  Human being, 6, 6n24, 130–32, 138, 150, 229
  Jesus, 6, 6n24, 15n53, 88, 88n38, 88n39, 129–32, 129n9, 129n11, 190, 228–29, 243n39
  Justification, 131n16, 131n18
  Metaphysics, 131n19, 132–34
  Ontology, 22, 134, 138, 150, 228–29
  Pantheism, 222, 222n73
  Reprobate, 6n25, 9, 22, 129–33, 132n20, 134n25, 190, 209, 209n8, 229
  Trinity, 6, 15n53, 22, 77n32, 88, 88n38, 88n39, 129–30, 129n9, 133, 190, 270, 270n73
Hoopes, James, 21n74, 46n48, 312
Hopkins, Samuel, 27n2, 63n44, 170–171, 170n108, 171n114, 253, 253n 86, 267n59, 307, 315
Hornberger, Theodore, 27n3, 80n6, 312
Hume, David, 85, 116, 155–56, 156n43, 184, 307
Hutchenson, Francis, 34, 307
Hunter, Michael, 4n15, 308, 312

Jang, Kyoung-Chul, 15n55, 312
Jedin, Hubert, 192n22, 312
Jenson, Robert W., 199n59, 130n14, 161n70, 312
Jinkins, Michael, 62n41, 75n15, 129n8, 312
Johnson Paul D., 37n2, 312
Johnson, Thomas H., 21n71, 156n47, 312
Jones, Charles Edwin, 292n9, 312

Kaakonssen, Knud, 4n15, 312
Kearney, John, xi, 210–11, 210n17, 211n23, 312
Kistler, Donald, 12n44, 306, 312
Knight, Janice L., 68n64, 223n75, 312
Knitter, Paul F., 311–12
Kretzmann, Norman, 298n4, 312, 316
Kvanvig, Jonathan L., 131n19, 312

Laurence, David, 312
Lee, Sang Hyun, ix, xi, xiv, 9n34, 12n43, 13, 13n45, 95, 95n2, 95n5, 113n33, 116n46, 117n50, 118–19, 118n51,

Name Index

Lee, Sang Hyun (*cont.*)
  119n58, 120n62, 121n67, 122n71, 138n43, 151n21, 152n25, 156, 158n59, 160n65, 161n70, 182n158, 191n20, 199n55, 201n68, 205n82, 231n113, 298n6, 305, 310-13
  Causality, 8, 11, 22, 73, 91n51, 109, 109n16
  Disposition, ix, 8-11, 8n29, 8n30, 9n35, 13, 13n48, 22, 48n53, 58n17, 62n36, 73, 91n51, 94, 94n1, 96-99, 96n10, 96n13, 98n20, 104n42, 107-110, 107n6, 108n11, 112, 112n27, 120, 120n60, 122, 154, 174, 236
  Excellency, 58n17, 62n40, 96, 174, 174n127
  Grace, means of 275n95, 281n124
  Holy Spirit, 50n60, 200n61, 275n95
  Human being, 5n21, 8, 174
  Metaphysics, 8, 8n29, 105, 108, 108n14, 110
  Ontology, 8-11, 8n30, 13, 13n48, 94, 96-97, 96n10, 108, 109n15, 110, 112, 112n27, 122, 174, 183n160
  Trinity, 13, 50n60, 255n6

Leibniz, Gottfried Wilhem Freiherr, 18n65, 25, 89n45, 90n46, 207n2, 216n42, 307, 309
Leland, John, 4n15, 307
Levin, David, 292n9, 312
Leslie, Charles, 31n15, 33, 307
Lesser, M. X., xiv, 1n1, 305, 312
Lisska, Anthony J., 62n41, 84n23, 103, 103n40, 313
Lloyd-Jones, D., Martin, 1n2, 313
Lombardi, Magistri Petri, 240n26, 307
Locke, John, 16, 16n59, 21n72, 26-27, 31-32, 39-40, 39n16, 42-44, 43n32, 46, 46n44, 46n48, 55, 60n25, 72, 75, 82n16, 107-8, 107n8, 108n10, 108n11, 118, 118n55, 143n56, 146, 146n1, 150, 155-57, 155n42, 156n44, 156n46, 157n49, 160, 164, 167, 171n111, 259, 259n21, 263, 294, 307, 310-11
Luther, D., Martin, ii, xi, xvii, 28, 169, 169n103, 170n110, 172, 172n117, 234, 234n4, 234n5, 251, 265-66, 266n54, 307, 309
Lyttle, David J., 46n48, 313

McClymond, Michael J., xi, 4n18, 5n22, 10n38, 45-46, 44n34, 45n38, 45n41, 56n9 , 95n2, 129n8, 261n30, 291, 291n5, 313
  Excellency, 5, 44, 64, 128, 132
  Human being, 5, 128-29, 128n3, 129n7, 131-33, 136, 152-53
  Metaphysics, 5, 129, 129n7, 132, 134
  Ontology, 22, 47n49, 64, 128, 133-34, 150, 152
  Pantheism, 82-83, 83n19
  Reprobate, 6, 9, 22, 132-133, 132n20, 132n21, 137, 153
  Teleology, 128, 132-33, 132n22
  Theocentric, 6, 11n40, 132, 132n22, 150

McCracken, Charles J., 116n45, 313

McDermott, Gerald R., 3, 3n14, 5n21, 7n28, 10n36, 21n74, 32n17, 196n37, 229, 235n7, 257n14, 257n15, 258n17, 259n22, ,261, 263, 261n29, 261n31, 262n38, 263n40, 263n42, 269n69, 277, 278n108, 287, 313
  Calvinism, 11, 255, 264
  Disposition, ix, 8-11, 48n53, 235-26, 256-57, 56n9, 264-65, 264n45, 264n48, 264n49, 265n51, 265n53, 269, 279n111, 280, 282, 291
  Enlightenment, 4n15, 21, 26n1, 235, 258-59, 258n20, 259n23, 260n26
  Jesus, 235, 256, 256n11, 262, 262n36, 265-66, 265n53
  Justification, 10-11, 11n39, 235, 265-66, 265n50, 265n51
  Ontology, 8-11, 23, 256-257, 264, 279n111, 282, 291
  Salvation, 10, 54n5, 235, 256, 256n7, 256n8, 256n9, 256n11, 257n16, 264-65, 264n46, 265n50, 274, 288
MacDonald, Scott C., 92n54, 313
Malebranche, Nicolas, 18n65, 21n72, 31, 72, 72n4, 74, 76, 76n27, 79, 116, 116n45, 172n116, 214-15, 214n37, 215n39, 242n36, 294, 308-10, 313-14, 316
Manspeaker, Nancy, 1n1, 313
Marsden, George, 1n1, 292n9, 313
Martin, C. B., 313
Mastricht, Peter Von, xvii, 208, 208n5, 287, 307

Name Index

Mather, Cotton, 26, 33, 33n23, 141, 141n51, 169–70, 223n73, 278n108, 292n9, 308, 312
Mayhew, Experience, 194n28, 308
Milkos, Vëto, 313. *See* Vëto, Miklos
Miller, Perry, 1, 1n1, 21n71, 31n13, 40n19, 42–44, 42n27, 43n31, 43n32, 50, 54, 55n7, 117n47, 217, 281, 281n125, 313
Minkema, Kenneth P., xi, xiii, 29n7, 38n4, 97n14, 143, 143n57, 261n30, 305, 313
Moody, Joshua, 21n74, 46, 46n45, 313
More, Henry, 16, 31–35, 33n25, 34n29, 35n33, 35n34, 55–56, 56n10, 72–73, 294, 308
Morimoto, Anri, 7n28, 9n33, 109–10, 229, 314
    Calvinism, 11, 236, 236n9, 255
    Causality, 10–11, 211, 235, 242–243
    Disposition, ix, 8–11, 9n35, 10n37, 211, 234–38, 237n12, 237n13, 237n14, 242–45, 242n36, 247–48, 253, 256–57, 264, 280, 282, 291
    Grace, 211, 237–38, 240–41, 240n26, 240n28, 256, 256n10, 301n15
    Holy Spirit, 211, 237, 240–44, 237n13, 240n26, 240n27, 247, 249
    Jesus, 235, 237–38, 235n8, 248–49, 248n62, 249n65, 256
    Justification, 10, 234–35, 237–38, 243–44, 244n43, 248–49, 248n61, 256
    Ontology, 5n21, 8–11, 23, 234, 249, 253, 256–57, 264, 291
    Regeneration, 10, 234–35, 237–38, 243–44, 238n15, 247–48, 257
    Salvation, 10, 54n5, 234–40, 235n6, 235n8, 236n10, 238n16, 247, 256, 274, 288
    Teleology, 11, 239–40, 253
    Theocentric, 11, 239–40, 253, 287
Morison, Samuel E. 21.n71, 314
Morris, Thomas V. 132n19, 298n4, 312, 314, 316

Morris, William Sparks, 21n71, 69n66, 314
Muller, Richard A., 131n18, 314
Mumford, Stephen, 314
Murray, Iain H., 1n2, 31n12, 314

Nadler, Stephen, 116n45, 314
Nelson, J. D., 4n18, 314
Newton, Isaac, 16, 25, 27, 31, 39n13, 55, 72n5, 75, 82n16, 113n33, 118, 118n55, 153n31, 308, 316
Niebuhr, Reinhold, 145, 145n66, 217, 314
Niebuhr, Richard H., 1, 30n8, 309, 312, 314
Noll, Mark, 4n18, 254n1, 314
Nygren, Anders, 170n110, 314

O'Donovan, Oliver, 145n69, 168n97, 314
O'Meara, Dominic J., 314, 316
Oberdiek, Hans, 294n12, 314
Opie, John, 18n64, 21n74, 314
Outka, Gene, 145, 145n65, 170n110, 172, 314
Owen, John, 107, 308

Parks, Henry B., 4n18, 314
Parrington, V. L., 4n18, 314
Patterson, Mary, 31n13, 309, 314
Pauw, Amy Plantinga, xiv, 82n14, 150n17, 270, 270n73, 305, 314
Perkins, William, xvii, 29–30, 30n10, 39n13, 131n18, 144, 144n60, 169, 234, 234n4, 239n21, 248n58, 281–82, 282n129, 308, 314
Pettit, Norman, xiii, 38n4, 282n127, 282n132, 305, 314
Pfisterer, Karl Dieterich, 197n48, 314
Pinnock, Clark, 5n22, 236, 314
Piper, John, 314
Pittenger, Norman, 297n2, 314
Plantinga, Alvin, 298n4, 314
Plato, 65, 135n30, 262–63, 263n41, 267n60, 308
Plotinus, 61n32, 64n53, 135n30, 169, 169n100, 263, 263n41, 308
Poole, Matthew, 168n99, 308
Post, Stephen G., 169n105, 315
Pratt, Anne Stokely, 315

Quinn, Philip, 163–64, 163n81, 315

Rahner, Karl, 243, 243n42, 315
Ramsey, Bennett, 61n34, 309, 315
Ramsey, Paul, xii–xiii, 20, 20n69, 77n32, 89, 90n47, 101n31, 116n44, 117n48, 142n53, 153n36, 167n95, 168n98, 171n112, 260, 260n25, 305
Ramsey, Chevalier, 124n76, 262n39
Richardson, Alexander, 33, 33n22, 308
Rupp, George, 12n43, 16n58, 315

Name Index

Russell, Bertrand, 289, 289n2, 315
Ryle, Gilbert, 17, 42n28, 315

Sanders, John, 5n22, 76n21, 236, 298n4, 315
Schafer, Thomas A., xiii, 11n40, 16n59, 46, 46n43, 47n50, 56n11, 74n10, 77–78, 77n29, 77n33, 80, 80n2, 82, 83n21, 85n25, 132n20, 248, 248n63, 257n12, 267n59, 305, 315
Schaff, Philip, 282n128, 300n9, 306, 315
Scheick, William J., 60n28, 286n144, 315
Schneider, Herbert and Carol, 32n20, 315
Seaver, George, 244n42, 315
Shaftesbury, Third Earl of (Anthony Ashley Cooper), 16, 32–33, 59, 59n19, 61n32, 64n53, 72, 149–50, 167, 268n66, 294, 308
Shea, Daniel B., Jr., 37n2, 315
Shedd, W. G. T., 5n20, 249, 288, 288n149, 315
Shoemaker, Sydney, 161n70, 315
Simonson, Harold, P., 315
Smith, Claude A., 315
Smith, John, 13n47, 31, 33n25, 39n13, 55, 72, 269, 294, 308
Smith, John E., xii, 17n61, 40n17, 40n18, 95n3, 200n59, 282n131, 291, 294n12, 305, 314–15
Smyth, Egbert C., 31n14, 306, 315
Stein, Stephen J., xii–xiv, 185n1, 185n4, 261n30, 305, 311, 313, 315
Stephen, Leslie, 4n18, 17n61, 315
Stevenson, Sally Ann, 21n74, 316
Stoddard, Solomon, xvii, 9, 23n75, 38n4, 97, 98n17, 141–44, 141n50, 142n53, 143n57, 144n61, 146, 149–50, 167, 169–70, 170n109, 172, 198n52, 234, 241n30, 247, 251, 281n126, 282, 308, 310, 312
Stoever, William K. B., 38n4, 316
Storms, Samuel C., 197n48, 210, 301–2, 316
Stout, Harry S., xiv, 292n9, 305, 310–12, 314–16
Stowe, Harriet-Beecher, 4, 4n17, 316
Strong, A. H., 164, 164n83, 316
Stump, Eleonore, 298n4, 312, 316
Sullivan, Robert E., 32n17, 316
Suter, Rufus, 99n23, 316

Tarbox, I. N., 29n7, 316
Taylor, John, 170, 181, 191n20, 194–97, 194n28, 194n29, 197n44, 200–201, 209, 211, 216–17, 260, 268n66, 308
Tillich, Paul, 243, 243n42, 316
Tindal, Matthew, 3, 191, 258–59, 258n19, 308
Toland, John, 3, 32, 32n17, 258–59, 308, 316
Tracy, Patricia J., 270n70, 271n74, 316
Tufts, James H., 316
Turretin, Francois, xvii, 173n121, 192–93, 208n5, 248n58, 287, 301, 302n16, 308

Veatch, Henry, 103, 103n39, 316
Věto, Miklos, 129n8, 313, 316

Wainwright, William J., 45n39, 45n42, 55n7, 119n57, 132n19, 292, 316
Wallace, Dewey D., Jr., 30n10, 316
Walton, Craig, 316
Warch, Richard, 21n71, 316
Ward, Keith, 102n35, 298n4, 316
Ware, Bruce A., 76n21, 298n4, 316
Watson, Thomas, 144, 144n60, 308
Watts, Emily, 21n74, 316
Weissman, David, 316
Weber, Otto, 28n4, 316
Weber, Richard, 151, 151n20, 316
Wesley, John, 196, 196n41, 308
Westfall, Richard, 316
Westminster Assembly, The, 254n2, 308
Weyer, Stefan, 33n25, 316
Whichcote, Benjamin, 33, 33n24, 33n25, 34n27, 259n22, 308
Whitby, Daniel, 32, 32n19, 308
White, Morton, 316
Whitehead, Alfred North, 297n2, 316
Whittemore, Robert C., 17n60, 80, 81n8, 317
Winslow, Ola E., 270n70, 317
Withrow, Brandon C., 196n37, 317
Wollebius, Johannes, 30, 30n10, 308
Wright, Conrad, 191n19, 317
Wright, R. K. McGregor, 76n21, 317

Zakai, Avihu, 21n74, 29n6, 317

Subject Index

Adam, 2n5, 22, 133, 138, 142, 144, 151, 155, 161, 168, 185–86, 188–90, 192–95, 197–210, 198n50, 203–6, 204n75, 207n2, 209–15, 211n23, 217–18, 233, 243, 252, 262, 276–77, 301–3

aesthetic, vii, ix, 3, 8, 12, 27, 29, 34–35, 41, 44–45, 49, 53, 56–63, 56n9, 62n41, 64n51, 75n14, 78–79, 84n23, 86, 86n27, 121, 125, 127, 134–36, 136n37, 140, 142, 144, 147, 149–50, 166, 174n126, 177–79, 182–83, 188, 193, 208–9, 214, 218, 227–28, 231–32, 236, 243, 246, 250, 263, 269, 273, 275, 288, 291, 293–95

apostate, 32, 280, 289

Calvinism, 1, 2n3, 2n5, 3–4, 5n20, 17, 26, 29, 33–34, 40, 74, 191n20, 192, 194n29, 236, 247, 253n86, 255, 259, 266, 285, 288n149, 290, 294

Calvinist, 1n2, 4–5, 5n22, 11–12, 20, 33, 33n25, 37, 41, 56n9, 79, 108, 126, 132n20, 141, 156, 170, 170n108, 191, 192n24, 193, 285–86, 299

Calvinistic, 4, 7–8, 12, 20–21, 28–31, 29n5, 34, 80, 100, 131, 144, 194, 196, 200, 262, 264, 282, 294

causality, causal, cause and effect, etiology, 9–11, 17–18, 20, 22, 25, 30–31, 35, 42, 48, 53, 56n9, 72–73, 75–76, 81, 83, 85n25, 91–93, 100, 104, 106–19, 116n45, 117n47, 125, 135, 137, 148–49, 159, 162–64, 178, 195n32, 202, 206, 209–11, 213–17, 216n42, 235, 241–43, 248–49, 297, 299, 302, 304

disposition, dispositional, ix, xi, 3, 8–25, 8n29, 13n45, 14n51, 15n55, 18n66, 19n67, 28, 36, 44, 46–52, 48n53, 54–55, 58, 60, 62, 62n36, 65, 72–73, 86–87, 86n30, 91–94, 91n51, 92n54, 96–99, 98n20, 101–4, 102n35, 104n42, 106–24, 107n6, 108n11, 109n17, 120n62, 126–27, 137–46, 143n58, 147n5, 148–55, 148n10, 153n32, 154n36, 157, 159–62, 164–68, 166n93, 168n99, 170–75, 171n114, 172n117, 178, 181–85, 188–90, 192–94, 196–97, 199–205, 207, 210–15, 217–19, 227, 231, 233–48, 253, 256–57, 257n16, 263–69, 275n95, 298–300, 301n15, 302–3

elect, 2, 2n5, 6, 8, 23–24, 129–31, 130n13, 131n18, 132n20, 133, 137, 146, 148, 155, 180, 180n151, 180n153, 184, 219, 219n54, 223–24, 229–30, 232–33, 249, 250n71, 275, 279, 300n8

election, 2, 2n5, 23, 130, 130n13, 130n14, 180n151, 195, 208, 232–33, 288, 300n9

Enlightenment, 3–4, 4n15, 7, 11–12, 17–18, 17n60, 21, 25–28, 26n1, 31–36, 55, 69–70, 72, 75, 85, 85n25, 95, 107, 117, 124, 126, 137, 163–64, 184, 191, 222–32, 235, 258–61, 263, 267, 271, 288–90, 292, 294–95

Excellency, 5–6, 28, 35, 44–46, 49, 51–54, 57–60, 57n14, 60n25, 62–65, 63n44, 63n45, 64n48, 67, 69–70, 74–79, 81, 83n20, 84, 87–88, 92, 96, 112, 120–24, 126, 128, 133, 137, 140, 142, 143n58, 146–47, 147n3, 147n5, 174, 176–77, 179, 181–82, 185, 203, 218, 221–23, 227–28, 241, 242n35, 246, 249–50, 279, 295, 302

first sin, vii, 207, 209–11, 213, 218, 301

grace, 2, 2n5, 7–8, 23–24, 43, 51, 53–54, 56, 90, 129, 129, 136, 144, 161, 191–93, 195, 197, 199–201, 207–12, 211n23, 214–16, 219–20, 234, 236–38, 240–47, 242n35, 242n36, 251, 260, 268, 275, 277–85, 278n108, 281n124, 282n129,

325

Subject Index

grace (*cont.*)
    300–303, 300n8, 300n9, 301n15, 303n23
  efficacious, vii, 191n20, 210–11, 214, 216, 300–303, 300n9, 302n22, 303n23
  fall from, 6n26, 7, 206
  infused, 5n21, 65, 143n58, 237–38, 240, 253, 256, 275n95, 290, 301, 301n15, 302
  means of, 10, 66, 180n151, 242, 268, 274–75, 275n95, 281n124
  sufficient, vii, 210–15, 211n23, 300–303, 302n22, 303n23

hell, 2–3, 6–7, 6n26, 19, 19n68, 24, 34–35, 129n8, 132, 134, 169, 223n76, 224–28, 224n80, 227n93, 228n100, 230–31, 233, 239, 266–67, 269n69, 278–79, 288n151, 289
Holy Spirit, 6, 15, 30, 38, 41, 43–44, 46, 48–51, 53–54, 57, 63–68, 67n59, 71, 82, 86, 88–89, 93–94, 122, 124, 129–31, 130n11, 131n18, 138, 143, 143n58, 151, 152n29, 165–66, 168, 172–73, 181–82, 188–89, 193, 198–204, 211–12, 211n23, 215, 218–23, 226, 230, 233–34, 237, 240–53, 243n37, 243n39, 267, 267n60, 269, 275, 275n95, 278–79, 282–284, 282n129, 288–89, 295, 300–302, 300n8, 304
human being, vii, 2n5, 3–5, 7–8, 14–15, 14n50, 14n51, 17–19, 21–22, 24, 48n52, 63, 71, 83n22, 102, 107, 123–24, 126–28, 131, 133, 135–54, 138n42, 140n48, 151n23, 156, 161, 165–67, 166n93, 170–71, 174–75, 177, 180, 182, 184–86, 188, 193, 218, 224, 233, 243, 245, 249, 256, 262, 290

Idealism, 15–16, 16n59, 19n67, 45–48, 46n44, 47n49, 55, 58, 62n40, 63, 65, 73, 81, 83n22, 85n25, 87, 94, 99, 108–9, 112, 118, 126, 135, 143, 156, 161n70, 165, 165n88, 182–83, 202, 225, 231, 294

Jesus, Christ, Son, ix, 2, 6–7, 10, 15–16, 23–24, 30, 39, 41, 46, 48–50, 53–54, 57, 63, 65–66, 71, 82, 88–90, 88n40, 93–94, 125, 129–31, 129n8, 130n11, 130n13, 131n18, 137–38, 151, 152n29, 155, 165–66, 167n95, 177, 180n53, 181, 185–86, 190, 195, 198, 202, 209, 219–21, 221n66, 223–24, 228–31, 233–39, 241–53, 243n39, 250n71, 256, 259, 261–62, 265–69, 267n60, 271–72, 274–77, 275n95, 279–80, 281n124, 283–85, 288–89, 291, 295
Justification, 10–11, 38, 50, 129n8, 143n57, 191n20, 195, 224, 234–38, 234n4, 243–45, 247–53, 248n60, 250n71, 265–66, 292, 295

metaphysics, 8, 10–12, 14, 18, 18n65, 20, 22, 25–26, 28, 34, 42, 49, 54, 60n25, 73, 83, 89–90, 93–94, 104–5, 107, 112, 117, 125–26, 141, 161, 177, 184, 186

New York, 23n75, 38n4, 56–58, 56n11, 57n12, 143, 143n57
Northampton, ix, 1, 8, 10, 23n75, 57n11, 79, 136, 141n50, 190–91, 194n28, 195n34, 236, 239n24, 241n30, 247, 251, 254, 266, 270–71, 286, 293, 316

Occasionalism, 31, 88, 109, 112, 114, 116, 126
ontology, ontological, vii, ix, 5n21, 6, 8–11, 12n43, 13–14, 14n51, 16–19, 16n58, 19n67, 22–24, 28, 34, 46, 47n49, 48–52, 55–56, 58–64, 62n41, 64n51, 69, 72, 74, 75n14, 75n18, 76, 76n27, 78–79, 81, 83–87, 84n23, 85n25, 89, 94, 96–97, 99–100, 102n35, 103–4, 107–8, 108n11, 110–14, 113n31, 116, 119–25, 127–42, 129n8, 143n58, 144–55, 147n5, 150n17, 151n23, 153n31, 154n36, 159, 161–62, 164–67, 166n93, 168n99, 169–70, 173–76, 178–80, 182–86, 187n8, 188–90, 193, 200, 202, 206, 208, 210, 218–19, 223, 227–29, 231–32, 234, 243–45, 249–51, 253, 256–57, 260, 264, 279n111, 282, 284, 289, 291, 293
original sin, 6n26, 7, 19, 19n68, 140, 142, 155, 158, 191–92, 194–95, 210, 218, 268n66, 290

pantheism, 27, 69, 77, 80–83, 83n19, 89n43, 297, 299

Platonic, 30, 107–8, 135, 150
Platonic, Neo, 16, 77, 77n32, 85n25, 96–96, 263n41, 294, 297
Platonism, 99n23, 166n93, 316
Platonist, 13n47, 21n74, 31, 33–35, 33n25, 34n27, 39n13, 75, 259, 269, 294
Princeton, xi, 4n18, 8n29, 23n75, 254, 258n17, 267
Puritan, 1, 1n2, 4, 17–18, 20, 23, 25, 30, 37, 37n2, 39, 107, 144, 146, 168n99, 185, 222n73, 228, 239, 271, 273, 278n108, 280–281, 286n144, 287, 287n145, 289, 291

Reformed, 1n2, 5n21, 5n22, 8, 11, 17–18, 17n60, 21, 28–30, 29n5, 33, 92, 96, 98, 100, 107, 124–26, 131n18, 138n40, 144, 164, 168, 173n121, 179, 184, 192–93, 193n24, 199, 204, 232, 234, 248, 250n71, 255, 265, 269, 290, 294
Reformation, 26, 36, 192, 233–34, 240, 265, 280–81
regeneration, 2n5, 3, 10, 37–38, 43n30, 46, 50–51, 54, 68, 133, 138, 176, 180–81, 180n152, 234–40, 242–47, 249, 250n71, 253, 253n86, 257, 260, 265–66, 282n129, 287n145, 293, 295
reprobate, ix, 2, 2n5, 6–9, 6n25, 14–16, 18–19, 22–24, 119, 121, 129–34, 132n20, 137–38, 146, 153, 172, 174, 174n126, 178–81, 180n151, 181n154, 184, 188–90, 193–94, 219–21, 223, 226–33, 236, 279, 285, 289, 293–94

salvation, ix, 2–3, 5n20, 6–8, 10, 14, 19, 23, 26, 38n10, 39, 43, 53–54, 65, 130, 130n11, 148, 180n151, 186, 194, 221, 233–40, 242, 246–48, 250, 252–54, 256, 257n16, 258–60, 264–66, 268–70, 268n63, 272, 274–78, 281–85, 288, 293–94
Stockbridge, 23n75, 67n61, 191, 255, 266, 291n6, 292–93

teleology, 71, 76, 85n25, 93, 104, 128, 132, 134, 137, 193, 227, 289n2
Theocentric, theocentricity, 3–4, 6–8, 11–12, 11n40, 14–15, 17–20, 18n65, 24, 27–29, 35–36, 51, 53–56, 63, 68, 71–73, 75–79, 84, 89, 92, 94, 104–5, 107, 112, 120, 125, 127, 130, 132, 134, 137, 141, 146, 149, 158, 167, 182, 188, 192, 203, 216, 260, 268, 270, 286–87, 287n144, 289, 293, 295, 313
Trinity, Trinitarian, triune, 6–7, 12–15, 12n43, 22, 24, 39, 41, 46, 50–51, 62, 62n42, 66, 73–74, 77n32, 82, 84, 87–88, 88n38, 90, 92–94, 120–22, 124–25, 129–30, 133–34, 141–42, 143n58, 146, 150–53, 154n36, 160n67, 161n70, 164–67, 166n93, 184, 186, 190, 198, 205n83, 207, 220, 230, 249, 255, 263n41, 265, 267n60, 270–71, 273–75, 274n88, 277, 286–87, 290, 292, 298

Yale, x–xi, 1, 1n1, 13, 16, 23n75, 25–26, 28–31, 30n10, 31n12, 35, 36n36, 38n4, 39n13, 57n11, 59, 72, 98n17, 107, 107n6, 141n50, 144n60, 191, 254–55, 262n39

www.ingramcontent.com/pod-product-compliance
Lightning Source LLC
Chambersburg PA
CBHW082029300426
44117CB00015B/2409